I0814052

DAY BY DAY THROUGH THE CIVIL WAR IN GEORGIA

MERCER UNIVERSITY PRESS

Endowed by

TOM WATSON BROWN

and

THE WATSON-BROWN FOUNDATION, INC.

DAY BY DAY THROUGH THE CIVIL WAR IN GEORGIA

Michael K. Shaffer

MERCER UNIVERSITY PRESS
Macon, Georgia

MUP/ H1019

Published by Mercer University Press
1501 Mercer University Drive
Macon, Georgia 31207

25 24 23 22 21 5 4 3 2 1

Books published by Mercer University Press are printed on acid-free paper that meets the requirements of the American National Standard for Information Sciences—Permanence of Paper for Printed Library Materials.

Printed and bound in CANADA.

This book is set in Adobe Garamond Pro.

Cover/jacket design by Burt&Burt.

ISBN 978-0-88146-824-3
Cataloging-in-Publication Data is available from the Library of Congress

To my loving, supportive, and precious wife, Karen.

I sincerely treasure our thirty-five years of marriage

and your tolerance, patience, and understanding

of my passion for history.

All my love!

Contents

GEORGIA IN THE CIVIL WAR
1861–1863

Map Key

1. January 19, 1861: Georgia Secedes
2. June 11, 1861: Camp McDonald opens in Big Shanty; the largest training site in the state
3. April 11, 1862: Fort Pulaski falls to Federals
4. April 12, 1862: Andrews and his raiders steal the *General* in Big Shanty
5. July 1, 1862: First of several Federal naval attacks on Fort McAllister
6. May 3, 1863: Streight's Raid ends in Rome
7. September 19-21, 1863: Battle of Chickamauga
8. November 27, 1863: engagement at Ringgold Gap

George Skoch

GEORGIA IN THE CIVIL WAR
1864–1865

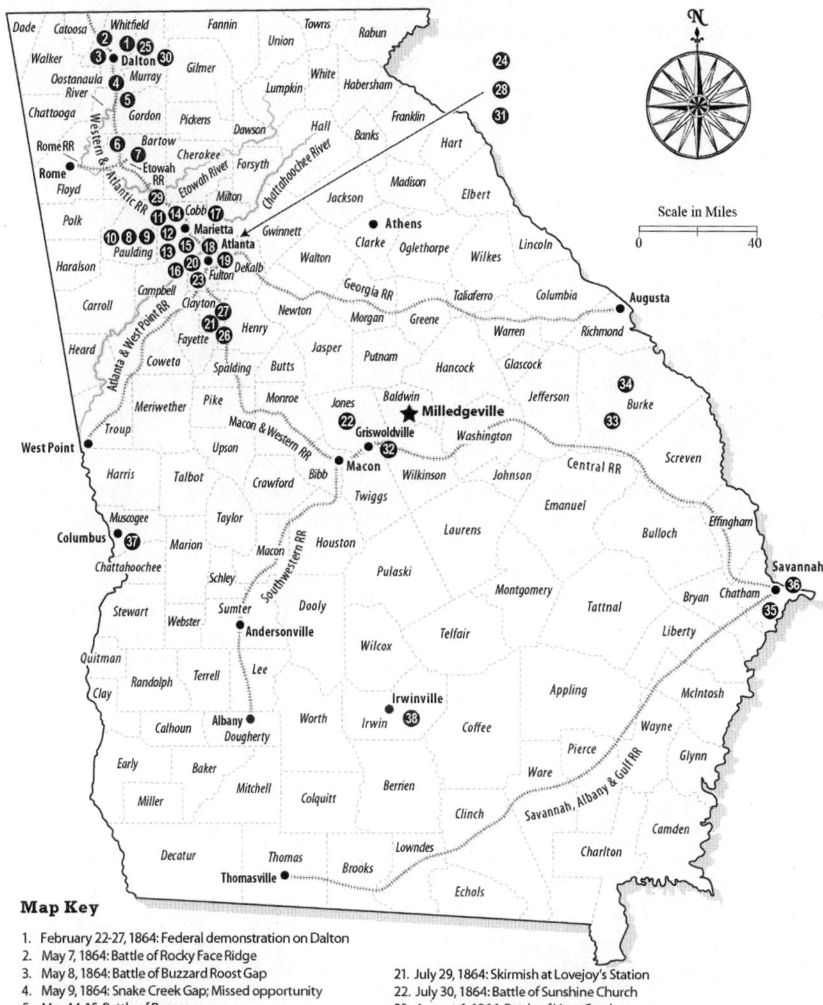

Map Key

1. February 22-27, 1864: Federal demonstration on Dalton
2. May 7, 1864: Battle of Rocky Face Ridge
3. May 8, 1864: Battle of Buzzard Roost Gap
4. May 9, 1864: Snake Creek Gap; Missed opportunity
5. May 14-15: Battle of Resaca
6. May 17, 1864: Adairsville affair
7. May 19, 1864: Johnston cancels attack at Cassville
8. May 25, 1864: Battle of New Hope Church
9. May 27, 1864: Battle of Pickett's Mill
10. May 28, 1864: Battle of Dallas
11. June 14, 1864: Lt. Gen. Polk killed on Pine Mountain
12. June 16, 1864: Lost Mountain and Gilgal Church skirmishing
13. June 22, 1864: Battle of Kolb's Farm
14. June 27, 1864: Battle of Kennesaw Mountain
15. July 4, 1864: Battle of Smyrna/Ruff's Mill
16. July 5-9, 1864: Actions on the Chattahoochee River Line
17. July 7, 1864: Roswell Mill workers arrested
18. July 20, 1864: Battle of Peachtree Creek
19. July 22: 1864: Battle of Atlanta
20. July 28, 1864: Battle of Ezra Church
21. July 29, 1864: Skirmish at Lovejoy's Station
22. July 30, 1864: Battle of Sunshine Church
23. August 6, 1864: Battle of Utoy Creek
24. August 9, 1864: Federal bombardment of Atlanta begins
25. August 14, 1864: engagement at Dalton
26. August 20, 1864: Battle of Lovejoy's Station
27. August 31 - September 1, 1864: Battle of Jonesboro
28. September 2, 1864: Federals occupy Atlanta
29. October 5, 1864: Battle of Allatoona Pass
30. October 13, 1864: Dalton garrison surrenders to Confederate cavalry
31. November 15, 1864: Savannah Campaign (*March to the Sea*) begins
32. November 22, 1864: Engagement at Griswoldville
33. November 28, 1864: Engagement at Buck Head Creek
34. December 4, 1864: Engagement in Waynesboro
35. December 13, 1864: Federals capture Fort McAllister
36. December 21, 1864: Federals occupy Savannah
37. April 16, 1865: Battle of Columbus
38. May 10, 1865: Jefferson Davis captured at Irwinville

George Skoch

Preface

When one conducts a review of the American Civil War historiography in Georgia, a void in the literature comes to the surface. During the 160 years since the conflict's termination, many fine accounts of wartime Georgia have rolled off various presses. Until now, a daily account (1,630 days) of Georgia's social, political, economic, and military events during the war did not exist. I concentrated on using only primary source quotations. Each daily entry derives from a quill scrolling the parchment or a press imprinting type on the day the activity occurred. Constraint proved a continuing challenge. The unearthing of a few dramatic quotes, without a date associated, negated their use in this resource. Historians will, hopefully, benefit from using this book in future research endeavors.

Most historians and students of the war keep a copy of E. B. and Barbara Long's *The Civil War Day by Day* near their keyboard. Students of Georgia events frequently consult A. A. Hoehling's *Last Train from Atlanta*, Franklin Garrett's *Atlanta and Environs*, Robert Myers's *The Children of Pride*, and Sydney Kerksis's *The Atlanta Papers*. The titles mentioned above (and many others) hold great value, but some sidle blue and others don the gray. With this effort, I strove to strike a balance between the combatants while remembering enslaved persons' struggles, folks on the home front, and merchants and clergy attempting to maintain some sense of normalcy. For those researching specific projects, each entry contains a footnoted citation.

Writing during the COVID-19 pandemic presented a few challenges but also ushered in welcomed surprises. In a time of uncertainty, one needs to stay busy. As I studied digitized newspaper pages, diaries, letters, and other period sources, voices from the past resurfaced. The struggles our nation faces during the pandemic mirrored events from the 1860s.

No project such as this can happen without a great press team. With Mercer University Press a repository of gold exists in Macon! Dr. Marc A. Jolley, director of MUP, thank you for the reformatting request, which produced a much better book! Absent your advice, I would have found myself on a picket line amid thick underbrush. Kudos to Marsha Luttrell and Mary Beth Kosowski! Your fine work does not go undetected. The generous efforts from each member of the Mercer University Press team have my lasting gratitude.

While all reserves went into action to ensure accuracy within these pages, any misfires remain the fault of this writer.

Introduction

Georgia, the "Empire State of the South," was home during the Civil War era to some of the country's most brilliant political minds, yet as a crisis loomed, Governor Joseph E. Brown, Howell Cobb, Alexander Stephens, Robert Toombs, and others could not avert secession and war. The Census of 1860 indicated 1,023,801 people resided in the state, including 447,082 African Americans, most of whom were held in bondage.[1] Georgia led the South in the textile industry. Her 1,400 miles of rail provided ample movement of goods during the early years of the war.[2] As the conflict continued, the condition of the railroads deteriorated, the blockade of the coast tightened, and folks on the home front and those on the front lines started to feel the squeeze.

When Georgia left the Union on January 19, 1861, various units eagerly volunteered, and Governor Brown took quick action to secure vital positions and ensure Georgia possessed the needed matériel. During the war, Georgia provided an estimated 120,000 troops to support the Confederate war effort; 40,000 never returned or came home with a permanent scars.[3]

With a few noted exceptions, especially along the coast, the hard hand of war avoided Georgia until 1864. Today, there exist many narratives that allow readers to study any of the various battles and campaigns in detail. (The bibliography of this book includes some of those works.) This account takes a different approach. From the Federal Navy's early attempts to secure strongholds along the coast, to the final action in Columbus, as Major General James Wilson's troopers destroyed the city's military capacity, readers can follow the troops and their various engagements within the state.

In chronological order, readers will get a glimpse of life from just before secession until after the termination of the American Civil War. Daily entries exist for the months of January through June from 1861, 1862, 1863, 1864, and 1865. After June 1865, one will find only the pivotal events from 1865 and select years beyond as war-related activity ebbed and daily references to the war subsided. I used material only from the actual day the cited event occurred. While one can read this book cover-to-cover, others may wish to consult as a daily read, following the current calendar through the book.

---

[1] Avery, *History of the State of Georgia*, 184.

[2] Coleman, *History of Georgia*, 188.

[3] Ibid., 161; Inscoe, *Civil War in Georgia*, 185.

Writing during a pandemic offered me the occasion to reflect again on the preciousness of life. Folks during our nineteenth-century conflict faced daily the unknown, much as we do today. Breaking news reports offer grim statistics on the increasing number of COVID-19 cases, hospitalizations, and deaths; our ancestors received bleak reports of the growing tally of dead from the battlefront while worrying about how they could provide the next meal.

No individual today can claim perfection. Neither could our ancestors. When evaluating all Georgians' actions in the mid-nineteenth century, one chronicler of the state's history offered the following assessment: "They miscalculated the method, and they staggered under the incubus of slavery, which closed to them the practical sympathy of the world, as well as that higher and more valuable support, the aid of the Divine Providence."[4] Let us learn from our past and pray for spiritual guidance as we navigate an uncertain future.

---

[4] Avery, *History of the State of Georgia*, 185.

DAY BY DAY THROUGH THE CIVIL WAR IN GEORGIA

Brigadier General William R. Boggs.
Courtesy https://web.archive.org/web/20071108021535/http://www.generalsandbrevets.com/sgb/boggs.htm

Howell Cobb.
Courtesy I.W. Avery, The History of the State of Georgia, 1850–1881

Davis & Stephens, provisional president and
vice-president of the Confederate States of America.

Courtesy Harper's Weekly, February 23, 1861

Alexander Stephens.

Courtesy I.W. Avery, The History of the State of Georgia 1850–1881

Dahlonega Mint.

Courtesy U.S. Coin Values

https://www.us-coin-values-advisor.com/dahlonega-georgia.html#Photograph

Charles McDonald, former governor and namesake of Camp McDonald.

Courtesy I.W. Avery, The History of the State of Georgia 1850–1881

Special Notices.

WANTED,

FOR

THE NAVY

OF THE

CONFEDERATE STATES.

200

Able Bodied Seamen, Ordinary Seamen and Landsmen.

RATES OF PAY.

SEAMEN, (per month)..........................$18 00
ORDINARY SEAMEN, (per month).............. 14 00
LANDSMEN, (per month)........................ 12 00

Four cents per day allowed in addition for grog ration.

C. MANIGAULT MORRIS,
C. S. Navy.

"Wanted for the Navy," a recruitment ad for the Confederate States Navy.
Courtesy Savannah Daily Morning News, June 20, 1861

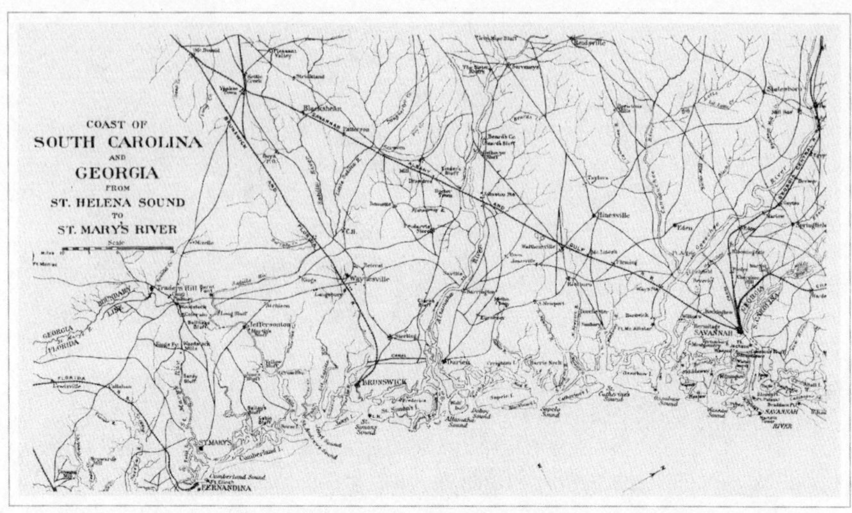

1861 Federal Navy map of the coasts of Georgia and South Carolina.

Courtesy O.R.N., 12: foldout

USS *Alabama* engages CSS *Admiral*.

Courtesy Harper's Weekly, February 1, 1862

Georgia's wartime Governor, Joseph E. Brown.
Courtesy I. W. Avery, The History of the State of Georgia 1850–1881

Brigadier General Thomas W. Sherman.
Courtesy Library of Congress

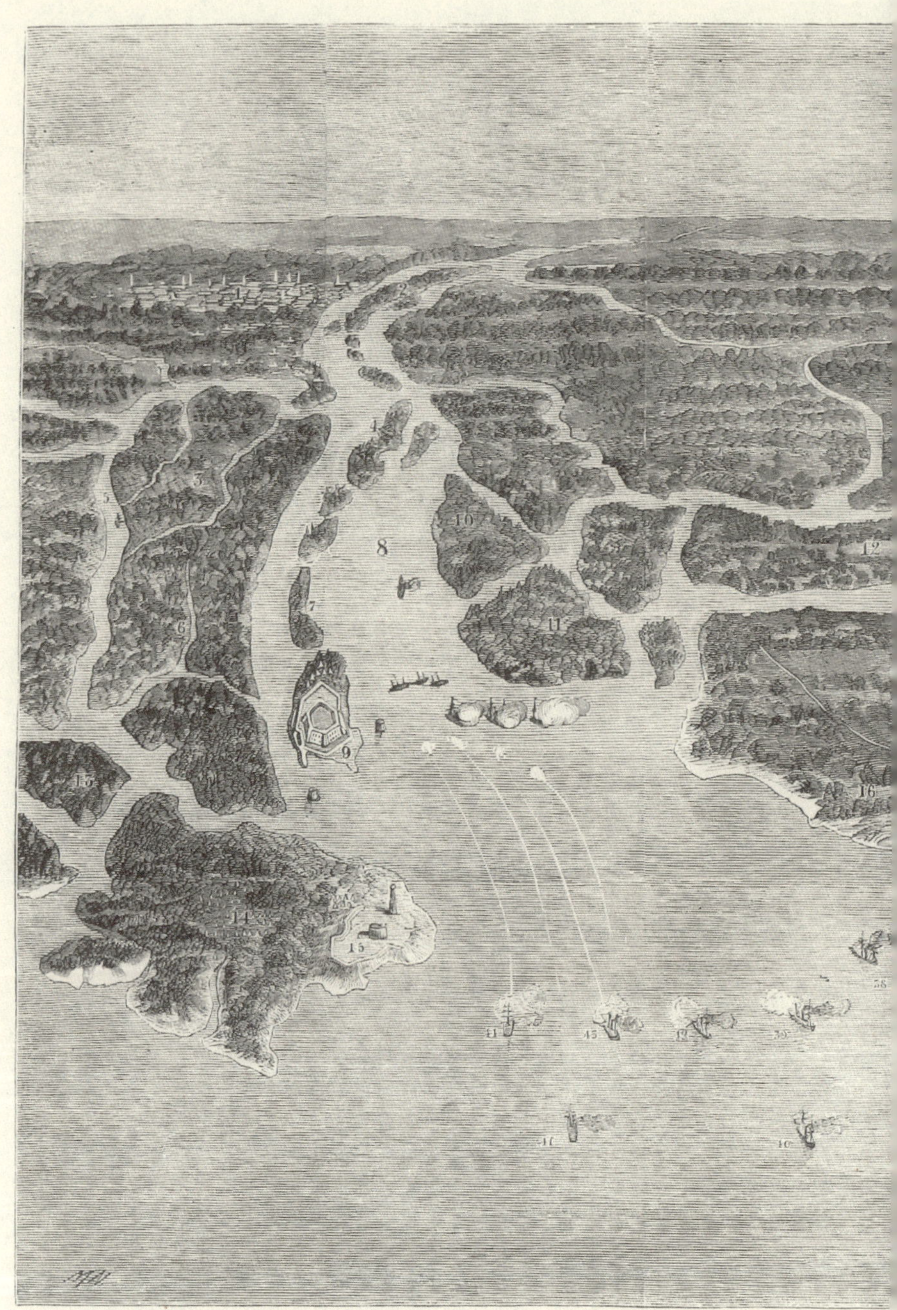

Map of Georgia coast.

Courtesy Harper's Weekly, January 4, 1862

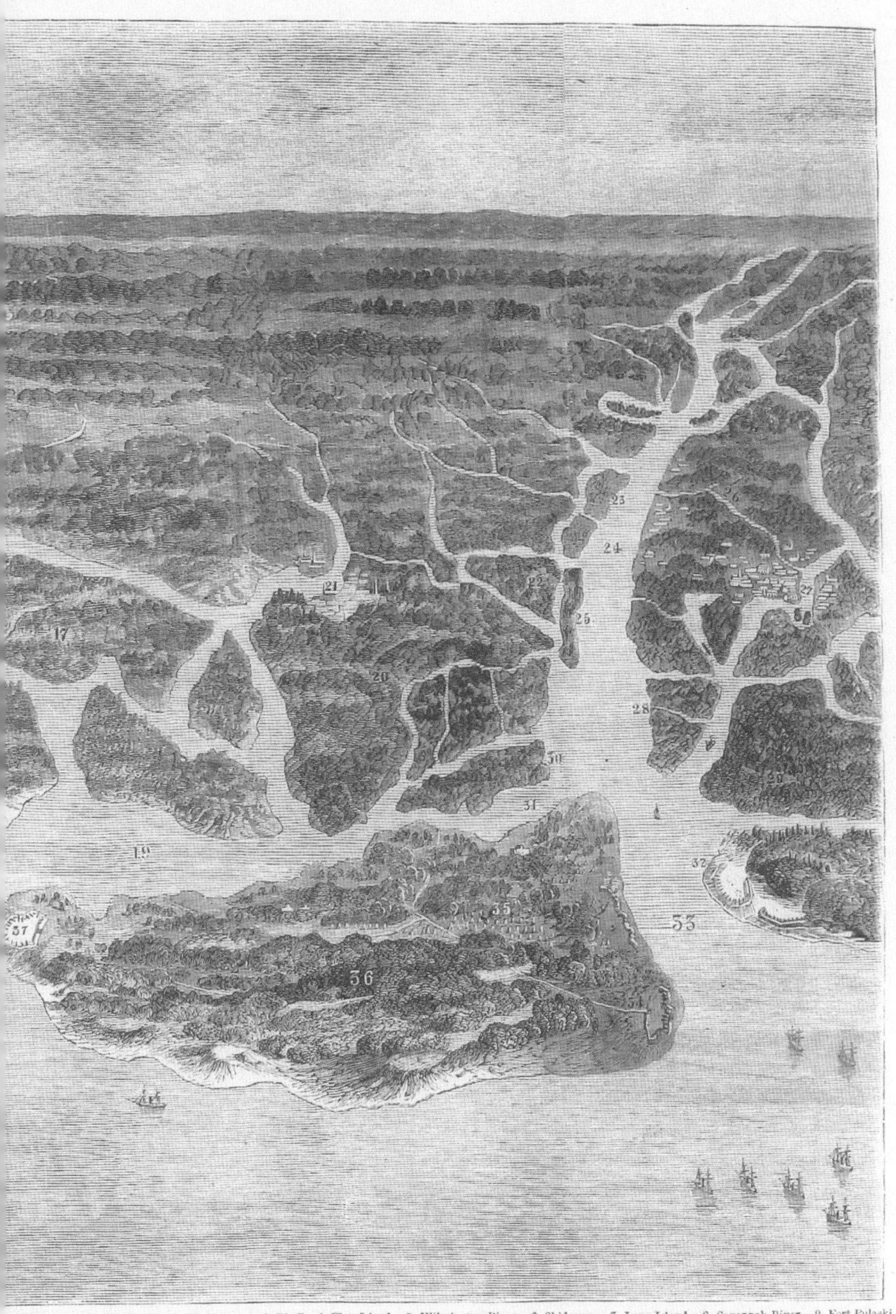

—References.—1. Savannah.—2. Hutchinson.—3. Bluff.—4. Flag Island.—5. Wilmington River.—6. Skidaway.—7. Long Island.—8. Savannah River.—9. Fort Pulaski.
and.—19. Calibogue Sound.—20. Colleton Neck.—21. Bluffton.—22. Rose Island.—23. Lemon Island.—24. Broad River.—25. Daws Island.—26. Port Royal Island.—
d Island.—37. Braddock's Point.—38. The Savannah.—39. The Flag.—40. The Augusta.—41. The Seneca.—42. The Pocahontas.—43. The Florida.—44. The M'Clellan.

Admiral Samuel Du Pont.

Courtesy Library of Congress

Flag of the Savannah Volunteer Guards.

Courtesy Savannah Daily Morning News, May 3, 1862

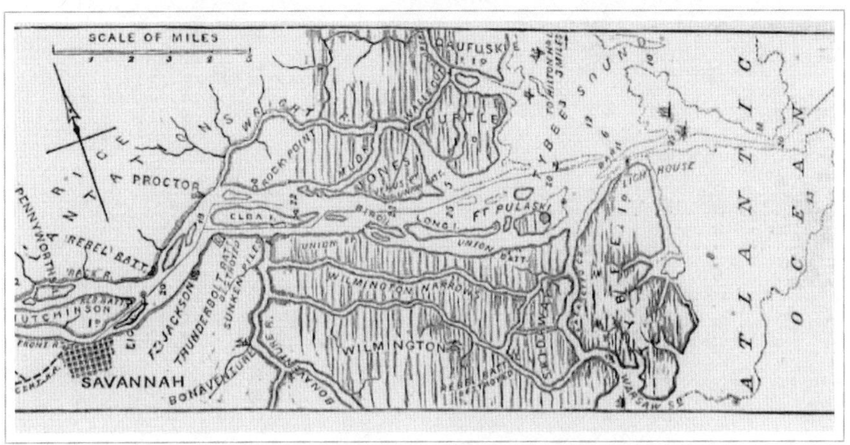

Map of approaches to Fort Pulaski.

Courtesy Harper's Weekly, April 19, 1862

Federal guards playing baseball inside Fort Pulaski.
Courtesy National Baseball Hall of Fame

Painting of CSS *Chattahoochee.*
Courtesy National Civil War Naval Museum

CSS *Nashville.*
Courtesy O.R.N., 13: between 696-97

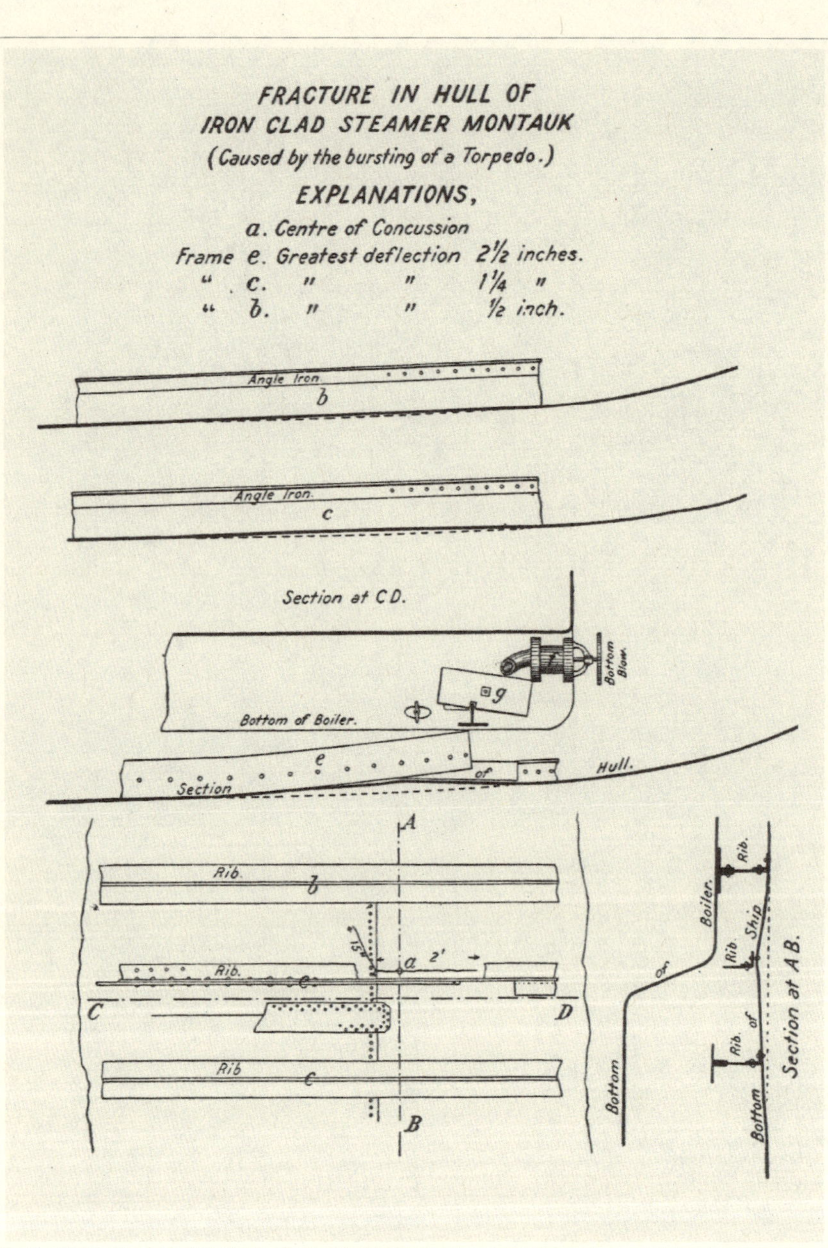

Damaged hull of the USS *Montauk.*

Courtesy O.R.N, 13:703

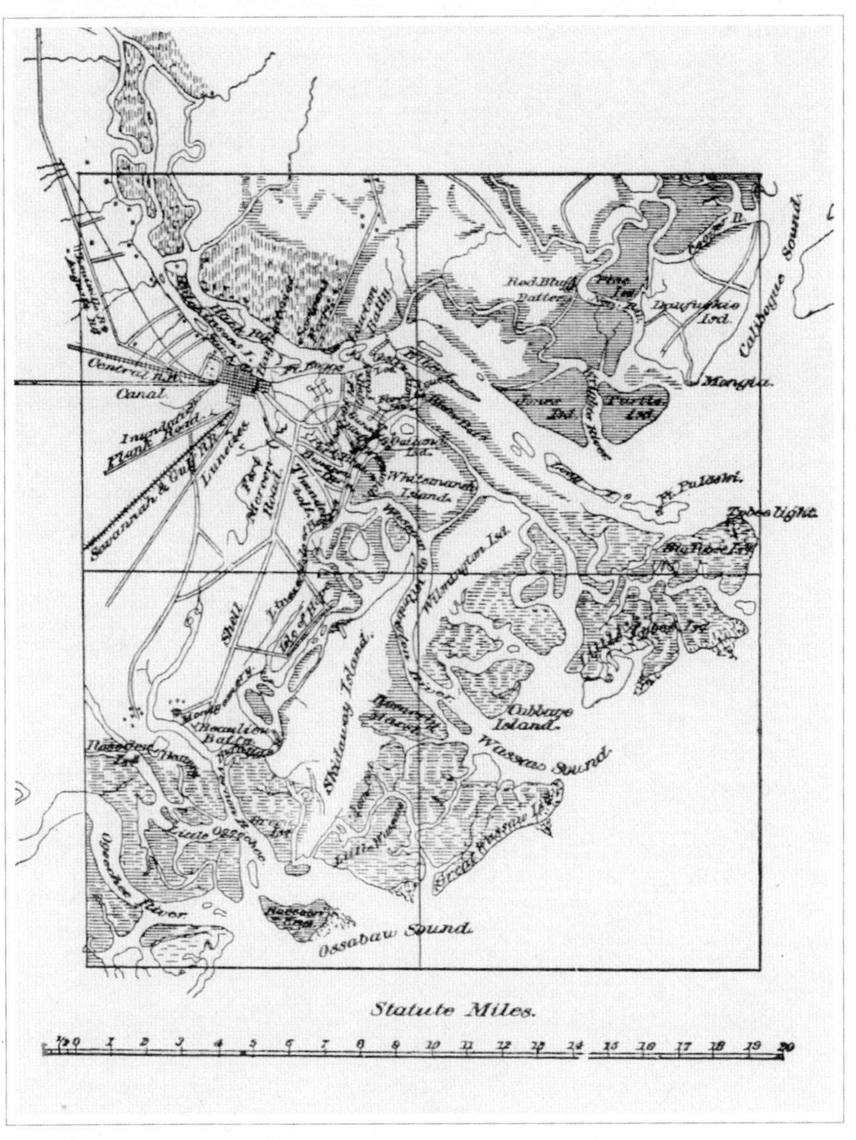

Major General Benjamin Huger's sketch of the approaches to Savannah.

Courtesy O.R., 14:855

USS *Weehawken.*
Courtesy O.R.N, 14: between 266-67

CSS *Atlanta.*
Courtesy Civil War Naval Chronology, 1861–1865, 3:94

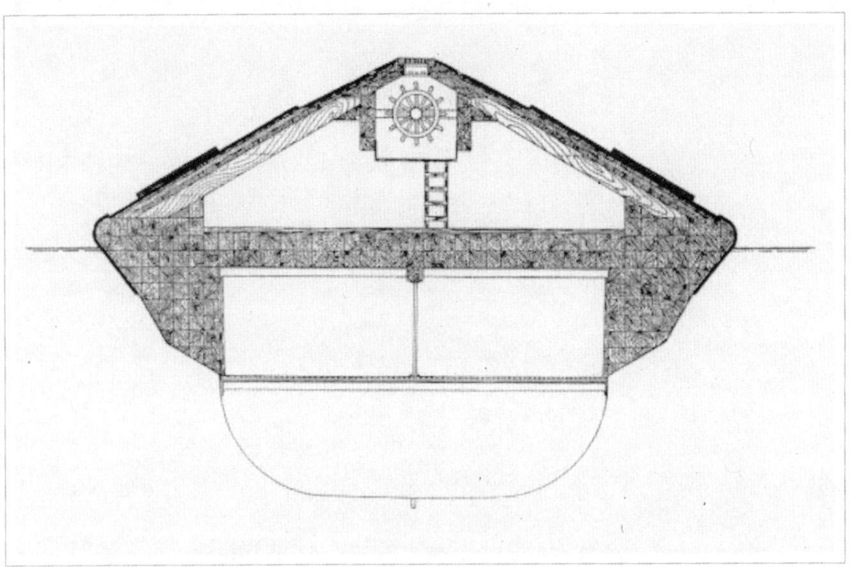

Transverse drawing of the CSS *Atlanta*.
Courtesy O.R.N., 14: between 290-91

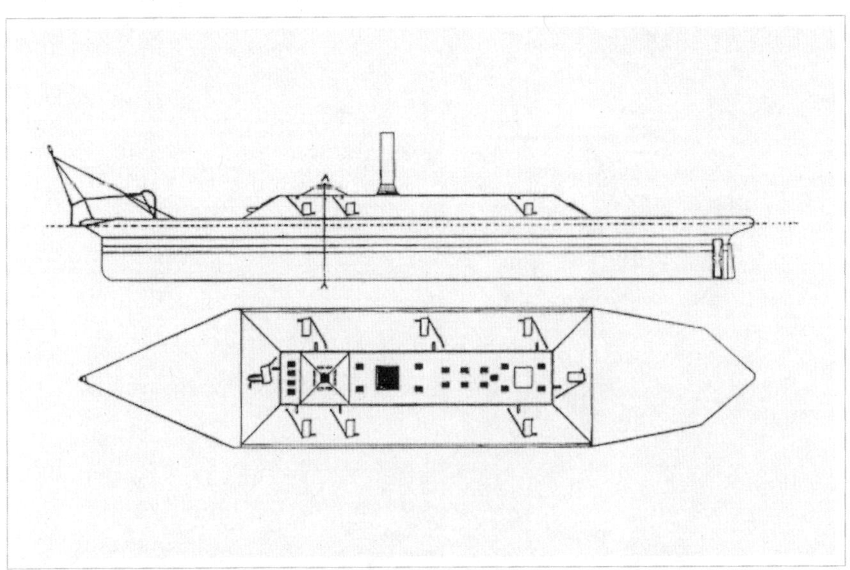

Outline drawing and deck plan of the CSS *Atlanta*.
Courtesy O.R.N., 14: between 290-91

Brigadier General Paul J. Semmes.
Courtesy Georgia Studies https://georgiainfo.galileo.usg.edu/gastudiesimages/Paul%20Jones%20Semmes.htm

Henry R. Jackson.
Courtesy I. W. Avery, The History of the State of Georgia 1850–1881

Lee & Gordon's Mills.

Courtesy National Archives

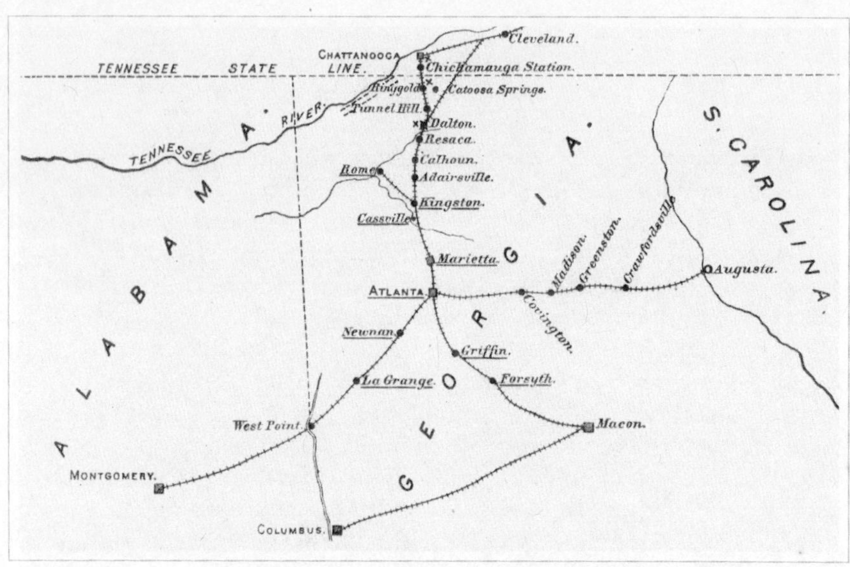

Surgeon Samuel Stout map Confederate hospital locations.

Courtesy O.R., 38, pt. 4:737

1861 Georgia Seal.

Courtesy Georgia Studies

https://georgiainfo.galileo.usg.edu/gastudiesimages/Georgia%20Seal%201861-1865.htm

Major General William T. Sherman.

Courtesy Michael K. Shaffer

General Joseph E. Johnston.

Courtesy Library of Congress

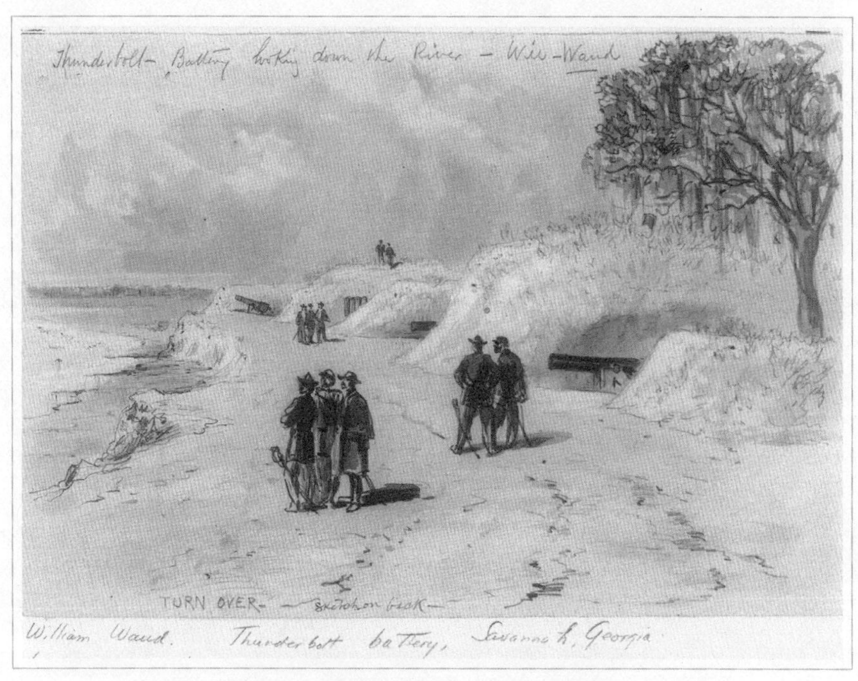

William Waud's 1864 sketch of Thunderbolt Battery.

Courtesy Library of Congress

Quartermaster General A.R. Lawton.

Courtesy I.W. Avery, The History of the State of Georgia 1850–1881

Illustration of Ringgold.

Courtesy Harper's Weekly, April 30, 1864

Illustration of Sherman's view of Buzzard Roost.

Courtesy Harper's Weekly, May 21, 1864

Illustration of Battle of Resaca.
Courtesy The Soldier in Our Civil War, Vol. 2

Federal troops enter Big Shanty.

Courtesy Harper's Weekly, July 9, 1864

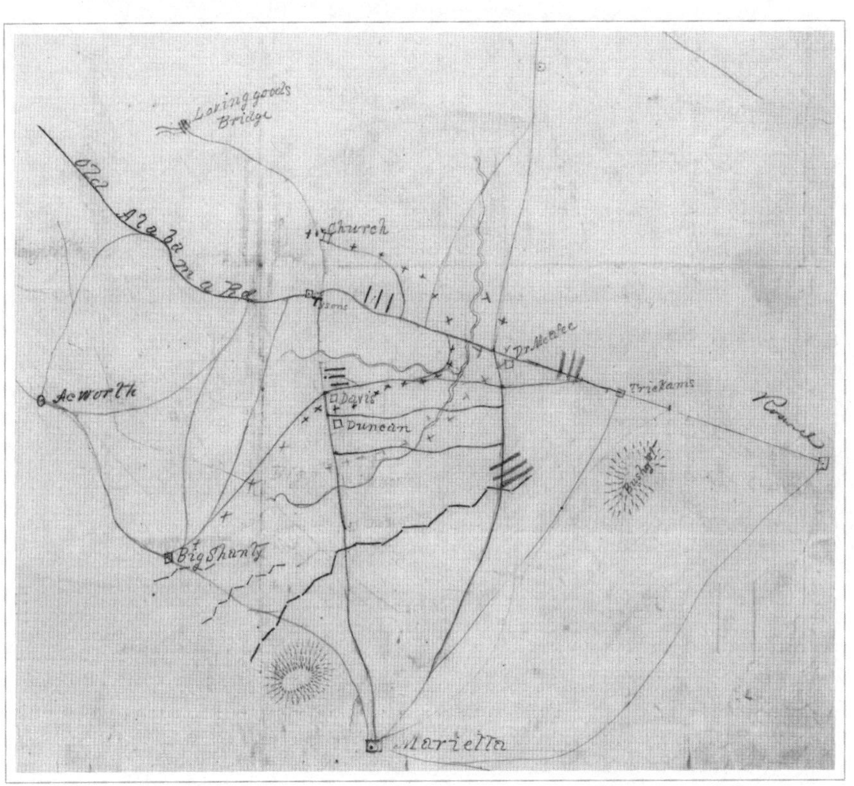

Map of NW Cobb County.

Courtesy Library of Congress

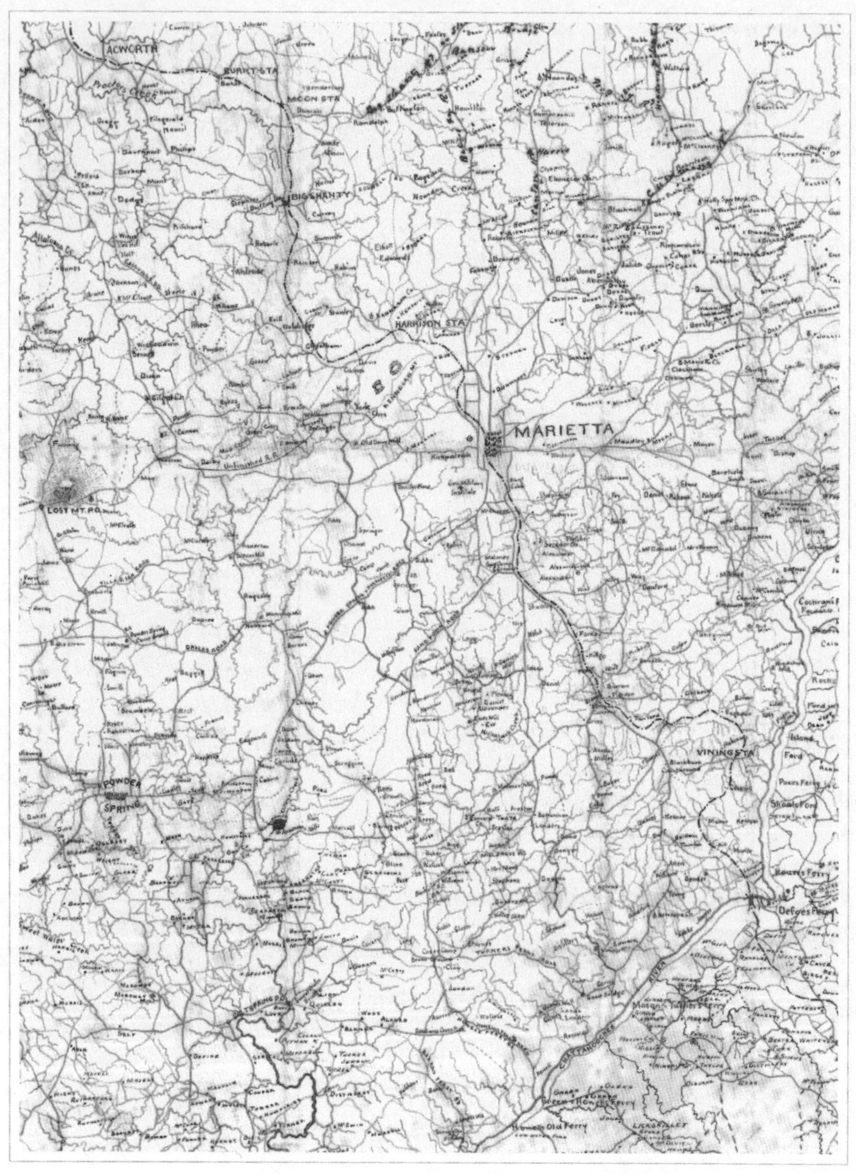

Henry D. Clayton's 1864 map of Marietta and vicinity.

Courtesy Alabama Department of Archives and History

The death of Lieutenant General Polk atop Pine Mountain.

Courtesy Library of Congress

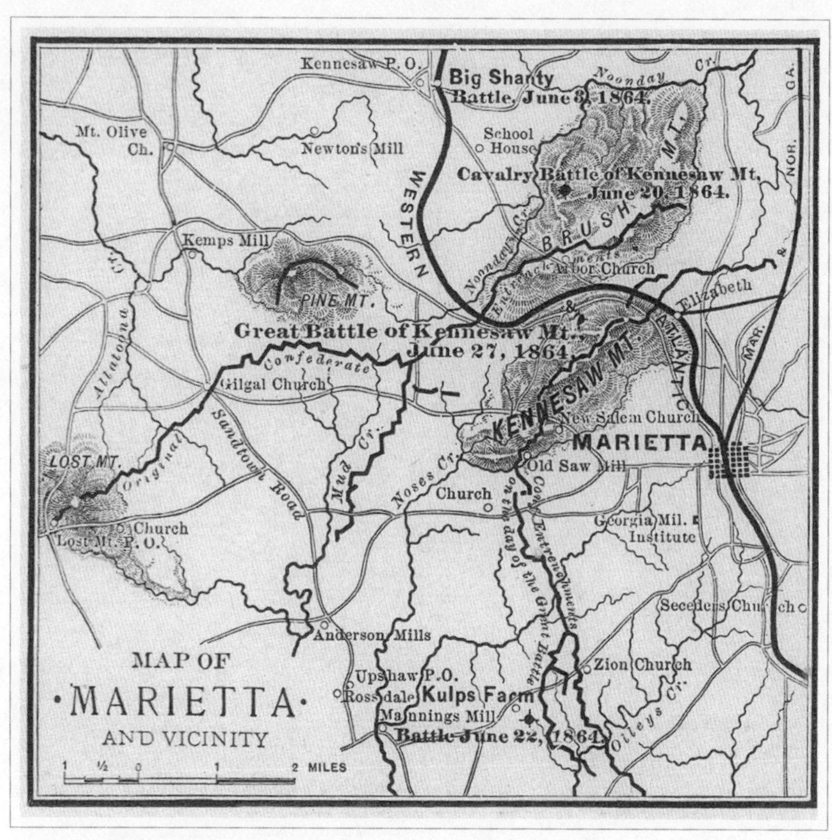

Map of Kennesaw Mountain and vicinity.

Courtesy Library of Congress

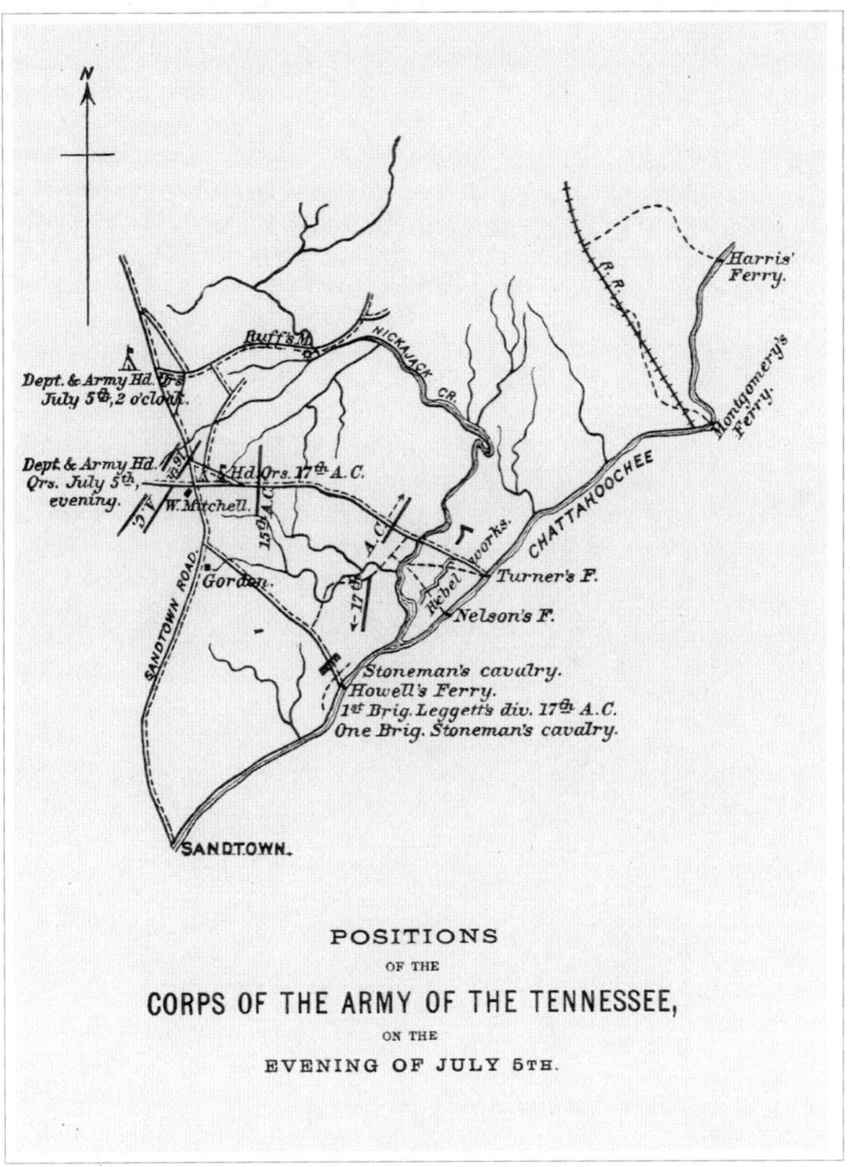

Map showing location of the Army of the Tennessee on July 5, 1864.

Courtesy O.R., 38, pt. V:57

General John Bell Hood.
Courtesy Library of Congress

George Barnard photo of a bomb proof in Atlanta.

Courtesy Library of Congress

George Barnard photo of ruins in Atlanta.

Courtesy Library of Congress

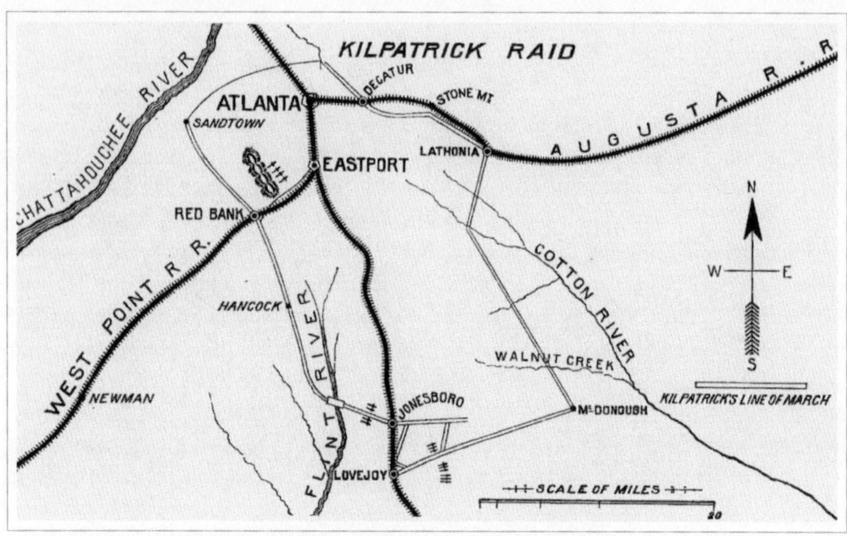

Kilpatrick Raid Map.
Courtesy Joseph G. Vale, Minty and the Cavalry

T.R. Davis sketch of Sherman's Advance
on Turner's Mill, Nickajack Creek, Georgia.
Courtesy Harper's Weekly, August 13, 1864

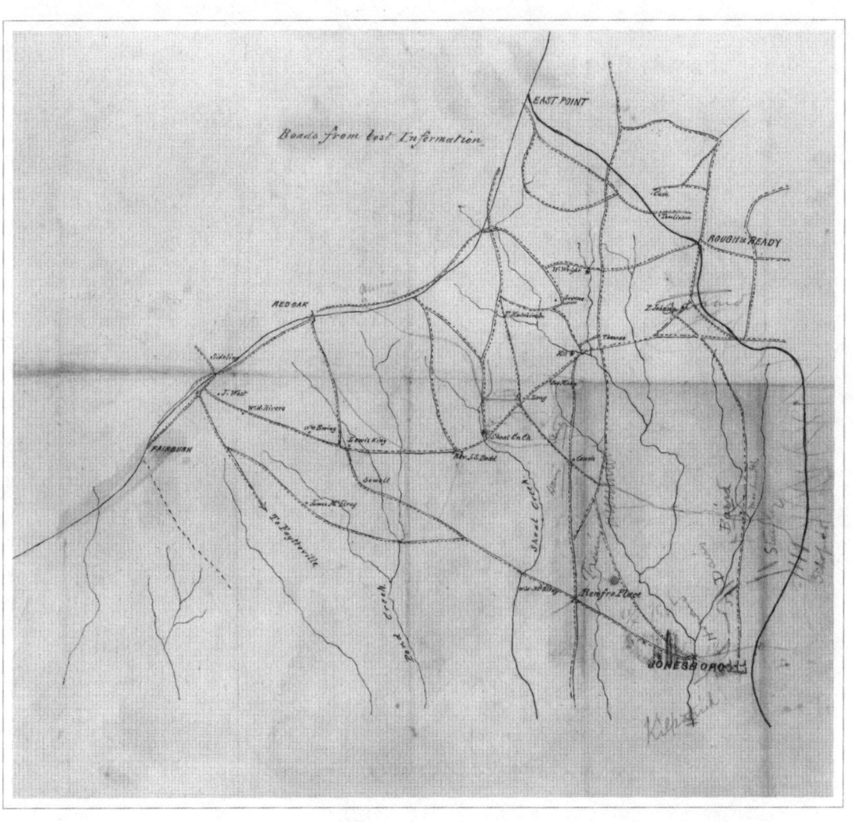

Map of troop positions near Jonesborough.

Courtesy Library of Congress

Barnard photo of destruction of ordnance trains in Atlanta.
Courtesy Library of Congress

Civilians leaving Atlanta.
Courtesy Harper's Weekly, October 15, 1864

Illustration of Lost Mountain.

Courtesy Harper's Weekly, July 16, 1864

Illustration of the fighting at Allatoona Pass.

Courtesy Georgia Studies

https://georgiainfo.galileo.usg.edu/gastudiesimages/Battle%20of%20Allatoona%201.htm

Atlanta Train Depot Ruins.

Courtesy Library of Congress

Illustration of Sherman's troops communicating via signal flag with Federal ships.

Courtesy The Soldier in Our Civil War, Vol. 2

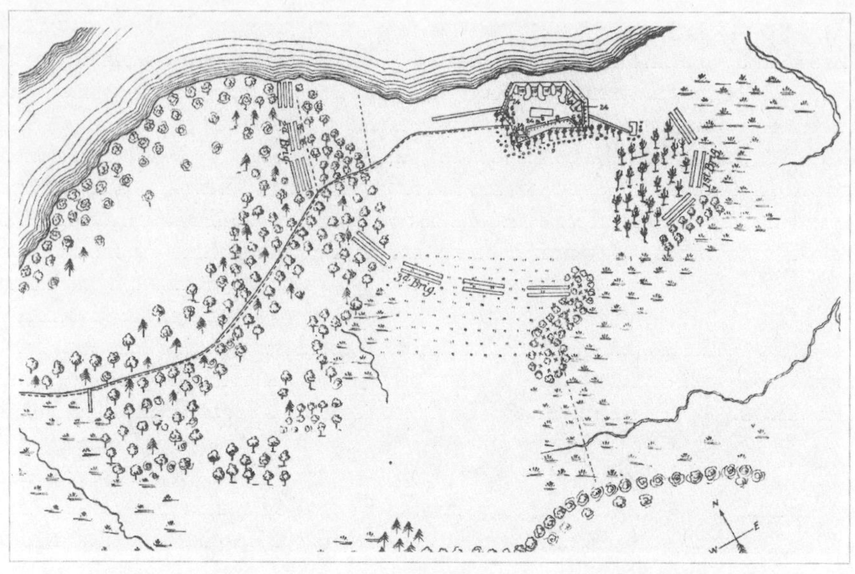

Brigadier General Hazen's map of approaches to Fort McAllister.

Courtesy O.R., 44:112

Hazen's troops attack Fort McAllister.

Courtesy Harper's Weekly, January 14, 1865

Sherman enters Savannah.
Courtesy Harper's Weekly, January 14, 1865

Portrait of Provisional Governor James Johnson.
Courtesy Georgia Capitol Museum

Governor Charles Jenkins.
Courtesy I. W. Avery, The History of the State of Georgia 1850–1881

Chapter 1

1860–1861

November 21, 1860 (Wednesday)
Governor Brown issued a proclamation calling for a convention to address the "crisis in our national affairs." Brown ordered the "elections for delegates in the several counties...all delegates elected...meet at the Capitol...on the sixteenth day of Jaunary [*sic*] 1861, to consider of the mode, measure and time of *resistance*."[1]

December 7, 1860 (Friday)
Prior to the delegates assembling in Milledgeville for the convention to deliberate secession, Governor Brown issued a letter to the public. Espousing the institution of slavery, and outlining the various difficulties in working with a federal government diminishing in respect across the South, Brown reminded citizens of the condition at hand.

> The President in his late message, while he denies our Constitutional right to secede, admits that the General Government has no Constitutional right to coerce us back into the Union, if we do secede. Secession is not likely, therefore, to involve us in war. Submission may. When the other States around us secede, if we remain in the Union, thousands of our people will leave our State, and it is feared that the standard of revolution and rebellion may be raised among us, which would at once involve us in civil war among ourselves. If we must fight, in the name of all that is sacred, let us fight our common enemy, and not fight each other.[2]

Moon Stage Legend: ◐ first quarter; ○ full, ◑ last quarter, ● new[3]

January 1, 1861 (Tuesday)
Governor Brown visited Fort Pulaski, and after consulting with state military officers, Brown commanded, "I take the responsibility and I direct the immediate occupation of the fort."[4]

January 2, 1861 (Wednesday)
Governor Brown wrote to Colonel A. R. Lawton regarding Fort Pulaski. Brown ordered the colonel to "detail one hundred and twenty-five men, or more if necessary, from your command, with the suitable number of officers, including one or more Medical Officers, to occupy immediately until further orders, Fort Pulaski at the mouth of the Savannah River."[5]

---

[1] Candler, *Confederate Records of the State of Georgia*, 1:209, 211. I have maintained the original spelling, punctuation, and capitalization of all cited sources.

[2] Freehling and Simpson, *Secession Debated*, 158.

[3] Ashmore, *Grier's Almanac*; I consulted editions 1862–1865.

[4] Candler, *Confederate Records of the State of Georgia*, 2:12.

[5] Ibid., 2:13.

January 3, 1861 (Thursday)
Colonel Lawton, acting under orders from Governor Brown, sent 134 Georgia militia forces to take possession of Fort Pulaski.[6]
January 4, 1861 (Friday)
Governor Brown wrote to his counterpart in Louisiana, Governor Thomas Moore, informing him of the decision to seize Fort Pulaski. "It being understood that the coercive policy is adopted by the Federal Government, I, as a precautionary measure, have occupied with troops, the Fort at the mouth of Savannah River till our Convention meets and decides the question. Have asked Governors of Alabama and Florida to do same in their state. What say you to the movement?"[7]
January 5, 1861 (Saturday)
Governor Brown, in a letter to John Shorter—a commissioner sent to Georgia from Alabama to encourage secession—posited strong feelings about the future of Georgia. "Longer continuation in a union with those who use the Government only as an engine of oppression and injustice cannot, it seems to me, be desired by any party in the Southern States."[8]
January 6, 1861 (Sunday)
Diarist Sam Richards was optimistic war could be avoided despite the ominous clouds forming on the horizon. "Nothing cheering as regards the state of our—Nation—there really appears to be some prospect of War but I hope wiser counsels will prevail."[9]
January 7, 1861 (Monday)
Senator Robert Toombs of Georgia offered a farewell address to the Senate. "The success of the Abolitionists and their allies, under the name of the Republican party, has produced its logical results already. They have for long years been sowing dragons' teeth and have finally got a crop of armed men. The Union, sir, is dissolved."[10]
January 8, 1861 (Tuesday)
The editor of the *Tri-Weekly Courier* in Rome pondered the issues facing the elected delegates to Georgia's Secession Convention: "The great question in which the people of Georgia, are now most deeply and vitally interested, is, what ought the Convention to do?" In offering his opinion of the pros and cons in Georgia's leaving the Union, the editor issued a cautious reminder for readers and for the delegates: "If we cannot agree, before we divide (allow me to use the word divide, instead of '*secession*')—there cannot, be any reasonable hope that we can agree afterwards; when the discordant and excitable elements, will be increased tenfold....[11]
January 9, 1861 (Wednesday)

---

[6] Irvine, *Military Operations of the Civil War*, 4:8.

[7] *OR*, ser. I, vol. 53:114.

[8] Ibid., 3:14.

[9] Richards, *Civil War Diary*, 41.

[10] W. Bryan, ed., *World's Famous Orations.*

[11] "What Ought the Convention to Do?," *Rome Tri-Weekly Courier*, January 8, 1861, sec. 2, https://gahistoricnewspapers.galileo.usg.edu/lccn/sn85034102/1861-01-08/ed-1/seq-2/.

Noticing the frenzy of activity in Savannah, editors for Augusta's *Weekly Chronicle & Sentinel* carried the following account: "Crowds were collected at every corner, and pressing around the bulletin boards with eagerness to read the latest news." The reporter speculated part of the excitement came because of recent pronouncements from Senator Robert Toombs, whom the reporter considered "a sentinel upon the tower, for this State at least…."[12]

January 10, 1861 (Thursday)

Residents along the coast learned, "A schooner arrived here yesterday, from the north, with 2000 barrels common powder, 75 kegs rifle powder, and a large quantity of musket powder, the property of the State."[13]

January 11, 1861 (Friday)

Reporting with news on the seizure of Fort Pulaski, the *Savannah Republican* carried the following story. "The first detachment of the Chatham Artillery, which went down to occupy Fort Pulaski, returned last night in good condition and spirits. We learn that, as they were leaving, some of the guns of the fort (32-pounders) were fired at a target, and gave evidence of the efficiency of these pieces."[14]

January 12, 1861 (Saturday)

Various military units in Savannah worked in rotation to garrison Fort Pulaski, as the *Savannah Republican* reported. "A detachment of seventy-five men from the *Republican Blues* went down to Fort Pulaski yesterday, to relive the infantry now on service there. They were equipped in marching order, with knapsacks, canteen, &c., and clothed with woolen shirts, instead of coats, which are just the thing for comfort while doing hard work, and there is no scarcity of the latter—a fact of which they will be sufficiently aware of before returning."[15]

January 13, 1861 (Sunday)

The Augusta arsenal presented a position of concern among many Georgians. An editorial in the day's newspaper detailed the mood in the state. "The fact of such a number of arms being so near, under the control of the United States, has caused considerable discussion as to the propriety of taking the property by force prior to the secession of Georgia—the affair at Fort Sumter having demonstrated the folly of trusting the Federal Government to take care of our interests."[16]

---

12 "Affairs in Savannah," *Augusta Weekly Chronicle & Sentinel*, January 9, 1861, https://gahistoricnewspapers.galileo.usg.edu/lccn/sn82014777/1861-01-09/ed-1/seq-1/.

13 "Large Arrival of Powder," *Savannah Republican*, January 10, 1861, https://gahistoricnewspapers.galileo.usg.edu/lccn/sn87062330/1861-01-10/ed-1/seq-2/.

14 "Savannah," *Savannah Republican*, January 11, 1861, https://gahistoricnewspapers.galileo.usg.edu/lccn/sn87062330/1861-01-11/ed-1/seq-2/.

15 *Savannah Republican*, January 12, 1861, https://gahistoricnewspapers.galileo.usg.edu/lccn/sn87062330/1861-01-12/ed-1/seq-1/. Italics in original.

16 "The United States Arsenal," *Augusta Daily Constitutionalist*, January 13, 1861, Genealogybank.com.

January 14, 1861 (Monday)
As the elected delegates prepared to meet for Georgia's Secession Convention, a newspaper editor painted, with his words, the importance of the moment. "On Wednesday next, the delegates will convene at the capitol and enter upon the labors before them. Never did a deliberative body assemble in our State charged with such grave responsibilities. The destiny of the State of Georgia, and perhaps of the Nation, is in their hands. It is a momentous work, and it is hoped that each delegate will go up with a solemn impression of the mighty trust."[17]

January 15, 1861 (Tuesday)
Espousing the weighty issues facing the delegates on the day before they assembled in Milledgeville, the editors of the *Columbus Enquirer* suggested Georgia would prove "the most influential State represented in the Convention [of seceded states]." The editorial continued to detail the importance of the gathering in the state capital. "Standing between the States that have seceded and the border States—evincing by her delay her solicitude for a union of all the States that have common wrongs to redress and common rights to preserve—her voice will be respectfully regarded by both, and her suggestions will be most likely to obtain general favor."[18]

January 16, 1861 (Wednesday)
The Secession Convention began in Milledgeville; the convention journal captured the opening. "In accordance with a proclamation issued by his Excellency, Joseph E. Brown, Governor of Georgia…delegates from the several counties of this State, duly elected by the people thereof, assembled this day in the Capitol."[19]

January 17, 1861 (Thursday)
A newspaper editor commented on the quality of the delegates elected to attend the Secession Convention. "The men selected by the people from this section of the State are all men of the highest position and integrity; they are men of sterling worth and capacity—the very best that could have been selected—far better than the selections generally are for the Legislature. We feel assured, if the people in other portions of the State have evinced the same judgement and prudence in the selection of their delegates to represent them…nothing will be done without mature deliberation."[20]

January 18, 1861 (Friday) ◑
Delegate Eugenius Nisbet introduced the following resolution in the Secession Convention taking place in Milledgeville: "That in the opinion of this Convention, it is the right and duty of Georgia to secede from the present Union, and to co-operate with such of the other

---

[17] "Georgia Convention," *Savannah Daily Republican*, January 14, 1861, https:// gahistoricnewspapers.galileo.usg.edu/lccn/sn87062330/1861-01-14/ed-1/seq-1/.

[18] "The Important Position of Georgia," *Columbus Enquirer*, January 15, 1861, https://gahistoricnewspapers.galileo.usg.edu/lccn/sn82014931/1861-01-15/ed-1/seq-1/.

[19] Candler, *Confederate Records of the State of Georgia*, 1:212.

[20] "The Convention," *Albany Patriot*, January 17, 1861, sec. 2, https://gahistoricnewspapers.galileo.usg.edu/lccn/sn82014211/1861-01-17/ed-1/seq-2/.

States as have or shall do the same, for the purpose of forming a Southern Confederacy upon the basis of the Constitution of the United States."[21]

January 19, 1861 (Saturday)

In a vote of 208 yeas and 89 nays, the delegates in Milledgeville approved a vote to "dissolve the Union between the State of Georgia and other States united with her under a compact of government entitled 'The Constitution of the United States of America.'"[22]

January 20, 1861 (Sunday)

Severing ties with the Union dominated the news of the day as evidenced in a report from the *Augusta Chronicle*. "Far and wide, throughout all the land, the telegraphic wires have flashed the news that Georgia is no longer one of the United States of America. Georgia, one of the old thirteen, one of the noblest and proudest (ah, we think the greatest and best) of the late Confederacy, has, by the Sovereign act of her people through the delegates duly chosen...declared herself, as of right she is entitled to be, a Free and Independent State."[23]

January 21, 1861 (Monday)

The delegates in Milledgeville prepared for an important event, as "The President, at 12 o'clock M., announced to the Convention, that the hour had arrived for signing the Ordinance of Secession, and having first placed his signature thereto, the Secretary was directed to 'call the counties,' when the delegates proceeded to affix their signatures to the same." Once each delegate present had placed their endorsement on the document, Delegate E. W. Chastain of Fannin County made a motion for adjournment until "ten o'clock tomorrow morning."[24] Motion passed.

January 22, 1861 (Tuesday)

The delegates continued to meet in Milledgeville, and each day they discussed various procedural components needed for Georgia to operate apart from the Union. But today, another issue arose.

> We, the undersigned delegates to the Convention of the State of Georgia, now in session, while we most solemnly protest against the action of the majority in adopting the Ordinance for the immediate and separate secession of this State, and would have preferred the policy of co-operation with our Southern sister States, yet as good citizens, we yield to the will of a majority of her people as expressed by their representatives and we hereby pledge "our lives, our fortunes, and our sacred honor," to the defense of Georgia, if necessary, against. hostile invasions from any source whatever.

The following names appeared with this dissension: James P. Simmons, of Gwinnett; Thomas M. McRae, of Montgomery; F. H. Latimer, of Montgomery; Davis Whelchel, of

---

[21] Candler, *Confederate Records of the State of Georgia*, 1:229.

[22] Ibid., 1:251; T. Bryan, *Confederate Georgia*, 248n31.

[23] "The Republic of Georgia," *Augusta Chronicle*, January 20, 1861, sec. 2, Genealogybank.com.

[24] Candler, *Confederate Records of the State of Georgia*, 1:271, 275.

Hall; P. M. Byrd, of Hall; and James Simmons, of Pickens.[25]

January 23, 1861 (Wednesday)

Responding to a notification of a gathering of the seceded states in Montgomery, Alabama, on February 4, delegates in Milledgeville passed another resolution. "Resolved: That this Convention will tomorrow at 12 o'clock elect ten delegates, to represent the State of Georgia in said Congress, with such powers as the Convention may hereafter confer upon them, and that a majority of all the votes cast shall be necessary to a choice…."[26]

January 24, 1861 (Thursday)

Governor Brown ordered State troops to seize the United States Arsenal in Augusta. The position fell on this day, and Captain Arnold Elzey sent the following telegraph to Colonel Samuel Cooper in Washington: "I have the honor to report that the arsenal was surrendered this morning to the governor of Georgia upon honorable terms, herewith inclosed. I am, sir, very respectfully, your obedient servant."[27]

January 25, 1861 (Friday)

The delegates in Milledgeville moved, "That a committee of five be appointed by the President of this Convention, to examine the Great Seal of the State of Georgia, and report whether any, and what, changes in the same have been rendered necessary by the withdrawal of this State from the late Federal Union."[28]

January 26, 1861 (Saturday) ●

Georgia militia, operating under orders from Governor Brown, took possession of Fort Jackson and the Oglethorpe Barracks in Savannah.[29]

January 27, 1861 (Sunday)

After the Georgia militia took possession of Camp Oglethorpe on January 26, the Federal ordnance sergeant at the post issued a report to officials in Washington. "I refused to recognize Colonel [Alexander] Lawton's authority, or to allow Lieutenant [W. S.] Bassinger to interfere with the barracks or public property. I do not think the State authorities design taking the stores from here at present, or that they will molest me so long as I allow them to keep my storeroom fastened."[30]

January 28, 1861 (Monday)

Alexander Stephens reported to the delegates in Milledgeville a resolution concerning those members selected to represent Georgia in Montgomery, Alabama. Stephens suggested they "be fully authorized and empowered, upon free conference and consultation with delegates that may be sent from other seceding States, to said Congress, to unite with them in

---

[25] Ibid., 1:277.

[26] Ibid., 1:283.

[27] United States War Department, *War of the Rebellion: A Compilation of the Official Records of the Union and Confederate Armies* (hereafter cited as *OR*), ser. I, vol. 1:321.

[28] Candler, *Confederate Records of the State of Georgia*, 1:293.

[29] Mosocco, *Chronological Tracking*, 6.

[30] *OR*, ser. I, vol. 1:324.

forming and putting into immediate operation, a temporary or Provisional Government, for the common safety and defense of all the States represented in said Congress."[31] The resolution passed.

January 29, 1861 (Tuesday)

Wrapping up affairs in Milledgeville, and contemplating a change of venue for the future, the delegates contemplated Savannah, Macon, or meeting again in Milledgeville. In a vote of 137 yeas to 100 nays, they selected Savannah.[32] On this day, the delegates approved the declaration of secession. (See Appendix 1.)

January 30, 1861 (Wednesday)

Governor Brown tapped T. Butler King "as commissioner to the Government of Queen VICTORIA, to the Emperor NAPOLEON III, and to the Government of the King of BELGIUM, with all the powers, and charged with all the duties, mentioned in the instructions accompanying this commission."[33]

January 31, 1861 (Thursday)

"Nothing could have been better devised than the order Gov. Brown has given to protect our interests on the coast. For Georgia has seceded from the 'Wreck,' as the *Montgomery Mail* [newspaper] calls the old Union, and whatever is Georgia's must be looked after immediately."[34]

February 1, 1861 (Friday)

With war looming on the horizon, menacing words on the printed page urged prompt action. "The present state of suspense and apprehension in which the country is held by the vassilating course of Mr. Buchanan is both perplexing and dangerous. If the revolution which has been inaugurated is to be cemented in blood, the sooner the battle begins the better...."[35]

February 2, 1861 (Saturday) ◐

Residents of Savannah viewed the new state flag, which flew above the Customs House. "Five red stars, with the blue star of Georgia at the top of the temple, and surrounded with a glory form the curve of an arch extending from the two lower corners of the flag. Over all is the All-seeing eye." The design of the flag would accommodate additional Southern states: "But this arrangement, while the coat of arms of our own State is the prominent feature of the banner, the seceding States, as they come into the constellation of our Southern Confederacy, will find their appropriate places in the arch of strength or the bow of

[31] Candler, *Confederate Records of the State of Georgia*, 1:331.

[32] Ibid., 1:371.

[33] Ibid., 1:20.

[34] "Military Moving Seaward," *Macon Weekly Georgia Telegraph*, January 31, 1861, sec. 2, https://gahistoricnewspapers.galileo.usg.edu/lccn/sn86077235/1861-01-31/ed-1/seq-2/.

[35] "Should Not the Issue Be Made at Once?," *Savannah Daily Morning News*, February 1, 1861, sec. 2, https://gahistoricnewspapers.galileo.usg.edu/lccn/sn82015886/1861-02-01/ed-1/seq-2/.

promise that spans our glorious banner of free and independent Georgia."[36]

February 3, 1861 (Sunday)

Commenting on political issues swirling about Savannah, an editorial shared the following concerns: "Our city, for some days past, has been the theatre of great and continuous excitement. The military movements of Major [Robert] Anderson in the forts near Charleston, the changes and rumors of changes in the Cabinet at Washington consequent thereon…all have furnished topics of very serious discussion, and have created impulses to action in the bosoms of our people, almost irresistible."[37]

February 4, 1861 (Monday)

Assembling in Montgomery, Alabama, the Provisional Congress of the Confederate States held their first session. After reviewing the secession documents of the six states already out of the Union, the delegates set about electing a chair. "Mr. [Robert, of South Carolina] Rhett moved that the Congress now proceed to the election of a president of the same, and put in nomination the name of Mr. Howell Cobb, of Georgia, and further moved that he be declared president by acclamation. The motion prevailed, and Mr. Cobb was chosen permanent President by acclamation."[38]

February 5, 1861 (Tuesday)

Governor Brown notified the governor of New York of his planned reprisal for the seizure of the Georgia-bound *Monticello*. Seems Governor Brown wanted his boat, and more importantly, the weapons onboard. He notified Colonel H. R. Jackson of action needed in Savannah. "I feel it my duty in this case to order reprisal. You will therefore, direct Col. Lawton to order out sufficient Military force, and seize and hold, subject to my order, every ship now in the harbor at Savannah, belonging to citizens of the State of New York." The governor closed, "I am determined to protect the persons and property of the citizens of this State against all such lawless violence, at all hazards. In doing so, I will, if necessary, meet force by force."[39]

February 6, 1861 (Wednesday)

"There are battles to be fought sooner or later upon the division of the Territories…the position of the Black Republican party, that which has driven us from the Union, is *hostility* to the South. Whenever, therefore, the Southern States demand a division of the Territories, for slavery extension, the probability of war between the two sections…will

---

[36] "The State Flag Hoisted on the Custom House," *Savannah Daily Morning News*, February 2, 1861, sec. 2, https://gahistoricnewspapers.galileo.usg.edu/lccn/sn82015886/ 1861-02-02/ed-1/seq-2/.

[37] "Occupation of Fort Pulaski," *Savannah Daily Republican*, February 3, 1861, sec. 1, https://gahistoricnewspapers.galileo.usg.edu/lccn/sn87062330/1861-01-03/ed-1/seq-1/.

[38] Confederate States of America, "Provisional Congress of the Confederate States, First Session, February 4, 1861, to March 16, 1861," *Journal of the Congress of the Confederate States of America, 1861–1865* (see memory.loc.gov/ammem/amlaw/lwcc.html; hereafter cited as *Journal of the Confederate Congress*) February 4, 1861, 1:16.

[39] Candler, *Confederate Records of the State of Georgia*, 2:24.

immediately resolve itself into a certainty." In closing his foretelling, the editor cautioned, "Georgia has declared that she will demand her share of the public property—let her see to it that she be able, at the time to support the demand with a military power equal to her necessity."[40]

February 7, 1861 (Thursday)

Rain dampened civilian transportation, especially those planning a trip from Atlanta to Chattanooga. "The trains on this road [Western & Atlantic Railroad]…have been interrupted for the last two or three days. They have not made their regular trips for the time above mentioned. It is reported that several bridges between this place [Atlanta] and Chattanooga have been washed away, and the track seriously damaged in many places. The telegraph line is also down, so that no definite information can be obtained of the damage done."[41]

February 8, 1861 (Friday)

Newspaper readers in Rome learned of a story from Augusta that urged a cautious approach in establishing a new nation. "Now that a Southern Confederacy is a fixed fact, and the secession of all, or nearly all, the slave States is a foregone conclusion, it is of the very first importance that the South pursue such a moderate, and even forbearing course as to avert any possible excuse for war."[42]

February 9, 1861 (Saturday)

The delegates meeting in Montgomery selected Jefferson Davis as provisional president. Filling the next executive seat, "the Hon. Alexander Hamilton Stephens, of Georgia, received all the votes cast, being 6, and he was duly declared unanimously elected Vice-President of the Provisional Government."[43]

February 10, 1861 (Sunday)

Updating readers of Governor Brown's continuing dispute with the governor of New York, a newspaper editor suggested citizens of the Northern state should proceed with caution. "The New Yorkers will find out, some of these days, if they undertake such infringements upon the rights of Georgia, that Gov. Brown is a 'big thing,' and in case he is selected Supreme Ruler of the Southern Confederacy, as is altogether probable, he will keep the accounts between the two sections balanced 'to a quarter of a cent.'"[44]

February 11, 1861 (Monday)

---

[40] "Let the South Prepare for War," *Thomasville Southern Enterprise*, February 6, 1861, sec. 2, https://gahistoricnewspapers.galileo.usg.edu/lccn/sn88054090/1861-02-06/ed-1/seq-2/. Italics original.

[41] "The State Road," *Columbus Daily Sun*, February 7, 1861, sec. 2, https://gahistoricnewspapers.galileo.usg.edu/lccn/sn82014939/1861-02-07/ed-1/seq-2/.

[42] "Let Moderation Prevail," *Rome Weekly Courier*, February 8, 1861, sec. 1, https://gahistoricnewspapers.galileo.usg.edu/lccn/sn82014071/1861-02-08/ed-1/seq-1/.

[43] *Journal of the Confederate Congress*, February 9, 1861, 1:40.

[44] "The Seizure of New York Vessels," *Augusta Chronicle & Sentinel*, February 10, 1861, sec. 2, Genealogybank.com.

In Montgomery, Alexander Stephens formally accepted his nomination as provisional vice president. Taking center stage, Stephens took the opportunity of the occasion "to return my most profound acknowledgments for this expression of confidence on the part of Congress. There are special reasons why I place an unusually high estimate on it. The considerations that induced me to accept it I need not state. Suffice it to say that it may be deemed questionable whether any good citizen can refuse to discharge any duty that may be assigned him by his country in an hour of need."[45]

February 12, 1861 (Tuesday)

Two Georgians received notice in Montgomery, Alabama, as the convention focused on symbols for the new nation. "Mr. Thomas R. R. Cobb presented a design for a flag, seal, and coat of arms for the Confederate States of America, forwarded by Edwin V. Sharp, of Augusta, Ga.; which, on motion of Mr. Cobb, were referred to the Select Committee on the Flag."[46]

February 13, 1861 (Wednesday)

Various Georgians resigned their commissions in the United States Army once their native state seceded. "Lieut. Boggs, of Augusta, Ga., having resigned his position as ordinance officer in the U.S. service, has been appointed by Gov. Brown Chief of the Ordinance for the Republic of the State of Georgia. Lieut. B. is every way qualified for the important position."[47]

February 14, 1861 (Thursday) (Valentine's Day)

Howell Cobb introduced to the Convention—and obtained passage of—a resolution concerning the forthcoming Constitution. Cobb resolved, "That the Secretary of Congress be allowed to have engrossed and arranged in proper form for publication the Provisional Constitution for the Government of the Confederate States of America, with the autograph signatures of the members of Congress, and the flag and seal of the Confederacy whenever adopted."[48]

February 15, 1861 (Friday)

Francis Bartow, the Savannah native representing Georgia in Montgomery, obtained passage of the following resolution: "That it is the sense of this Congress that immediate steps should be taken to obtain possession of Forts Sumter and Pickens by the authority of this Government, either by negotiation, or force, as early as practicable, and the President is hereby authorized to make all necessary military preparations for carrying this resolution into effect."[49]

---

[45] *Journal of the Confederate Congress*, February 11, 1861, 1:43.

[46] Ibid., February 12, 1861, 1:45.

[47] "Appointment," *Weekly Augusta Chronicle & Sentinel*, February 13, 1861, sec. 2, https://gahistoricnewspapers.galileo.usg.edu/lccn/sn82014777/1861-02-13/ed-1/seq-2/. William Robertson Boggs rose to the rank of brigadier general in the Confederate army (Eicher and Eicher, *Civil War High Commands*, 136).

[48] *Journal of the Confederate Congress*, February 14, 1861, 1:51.

[49] Ibid., February 15, 1861, 1:51.

February 16, 1861 (Saturday)
Across the state, regiments continued to form, and Governor Brown acted to name the officers of "two regiments for regular service." Two colonels received appointment, William J. Hardee, and W. H. T. Walker; both officers would rise through the ranks of the Confederate army as the war progressed.[50]

February 17, 1861 (Sunday)
The approaching birthday of our nation's first president prompted the editor of the *Daily Constitutionalist* in Augusta to call for a gala with a military flair. "We have already suggested to our military friends the propriety of celebrating Washington's birthday. We might venture a little farther, to suggest that the Sand Hills Home Guards, Richmond Mounted Riflemen, Walker Light Infantry, and the two companies of Minute Men, join with the Augusta Independent Volunteer Battalion on that day, and so let the display be grand and imposing."[51]

February 18, 1861 (Monday)
Governor Brown continued work in filling new regiments and dealing with the appointment of officers. "The full appointments for the two Regiments for regular service, which are to be organized under the late Ordinance of the Convention of this State, have been made by the Governor. All officers late of the U.S. Army are ranked according to their relative rank when they left the Army. When promotions have been made, it has been done according to their relative ranks."[52]

February 19, 1861 (Tuesday)
Updating readers on the continuing friction between the governors of Georgia and New York, one newspaper noted a resolution produced joyous results. "There is a broad grin over everybody's face at the lightening like rapidity with which the New York police *let go the guns* as soon as Georgia *seized the New York vessels*. We don't believe that, since guns were invented, muskets ever went off before as quickly as these Georgia guns."[53]

February 20, 1861 (Wednesday)
Passing a resolution that would later impact Georgia's coastal region, the delegates meeting in Montgomery established the Confederate Navy Department.[54]

February 21, 1861 (Thursday)
President Jefferson Davis wrote to the convention in Montgomery, submitting, "Robert

---

[50] "Georgia Regiments," *Savannah Daily Morning News*, February 16, 1861, sec. 1, https://gahistoricnewspapers.galileo.usg.edu/lccn/sn82015886/1861-02-16/ed-1/seq-1/.

[51] "Military Matters," *Augusta Daily Constitutionalist*, February 17, 1861, sec. 3, Genealogybank.com.

[52] "Army Appointments by the Governor," *Columbus Daily Sun*, February 18, 1861, sec. 2, https://gahistoricnewspapers.galileo.usg.edu/lccn/sn82014939/1861-02-18/ed-1/seq-2/.

[53] "Georgia and the Guns," *Milledgeville Southern Federal Union*, February 19, 1861, sec. 3, https://gahistoricnewspapers.galileo.usg.edu/lccn/sn87062317/1861-02-19/ed-1/seq-3/. Italics original.

[54] *Journal of the Confederate Congress*, February 20, 1861, 1:70.

Toombs, of Georgia, to be Secretary of State of the Confederate States of America." The president's motion "was unanimously decided in the affirmative."[55]

February 22, 1861 (Friday)

The promise of excitement in the army prompted several college students to form militia groups. "The students of Oglethorpe University have organized a volunteer corps, fifty strong, called the 'University Guards,' and have already been furnished with muskets by the Governor."[56]

February 23, 1861 (Saturday)

Working toward the establishment of a Confederate army and navy, the delegates in Montgomery passed a resolution that called for a favorable acceptance into Confederate service those who had functioned in the United States Army or Navy. "We suggest that all officers who have resigned or may resign their places in the Army and Navy of the United States...to file their applications where they desire service in the Army and Navy of the Confederate States as early as convenient with the Secretaries of War and Navy...we recommend all such applications to the favorable consideration of the Secretaries of War and Navy and of the President."[57]

February 24, 1861 (Sunday) ●

Delegates from Georgia's Secession Convention "from the several counties in this State," received a report to prepare for reassembling, albeit in a different locale. On Thursday, March 7, they "are...to meet in the city of Savannah."[58]

February 25, 1861 (Monday)

Most officials continued to focus their attention on the coast, Savannah in particular, and worked to steer weapons and other supplies to the area. One account reported Governor Brown "has ordered the three beautiful heavy brass cannon, which has just arrived in that city [Atlanta] for the Atlanta Grays, to be shipped immediately to Savannah, as there is a strong probability they will be needed for immediate use. The *Chronicle* says the guns at the Arsenal, near Augusta have also been ordered to Savannah."[59]

February 26, 1861 (Tuesday)

Reporting on the appointed members of Jefferson Davis's cabinet, a newspaper editor defended—against an editorial in the *Columbus Enquirer*—the various men tapped to lead the new Confederate government. After espousing on various selections, he closed with reference to a Georgian. "Why was the exalted office of Vice President conferred on Mr. Stephens? The truth is, the President has appointed men, whose ability, integrity, and

---

[55] Ibid., February 21, 1861, 1:73.

[56] "By Telegraph," *Savannah Daily Morning News*, February 22, 1861, sec. 2, https://gahistoricnewspapers.galileo.usg.edu/lccn/sn82015886/1861-02-22/ed-1/seq-2/.

[57] *Journal of the Confederate Congress*, February 23, 1861, 1:79.

[58] "Georgia State Convention," *Augusta Daily Constitutionalist*, February 24, 1861, sec. 3, Genealogybank.com.

[59] "Ordered to Savannah," *Columbus Daily Sun*, February 25, 1861, sec. 2, https://gahistoricnewspapers.galileo.usg.edu/lccn/sn82014939/1861-02-25/ed-1/seq-2/.

distinction entitled them to position."[60]

February 27, 1861 (Wednesday)

Unbeknownst to a newspaper editor, the Peace Conference, meeting in Washington City, ended on this day with no resolution toward saving the Union. The writer offered the question of "Peace or War! That is now the absorbing question. There is undoubtedly, both at the North and the South a class of persons, composed of sensation editors, desperate adventurers, and a few ardent spirits who are panting lor military fame, who would like to see the country involved in war." In closing, he opined, "In spite of the wishes and efforts of these reckless and mischievous men we believe there will be no war between the North and the South. Every true Christian and philanthropist should frown down all attempts to involve the country in the horrors of a civil war, and labor to promote the cause of peace."[61]

February 28, 1861 (Thursday)

Drilling occupied the time of militia groups across the state, and the City Light Guards of Columbus joined other units in learning the art of war. A notice in the newspaper called for the Guards to "turn out for target excursion in fatigue uniform on Monday, the 4th, at 2 P.M. The corps will contend for several prizes—a handsome fruit cake, presented by a lady; an elegant gold watch, &c."[62]

March 1, 1861 (Friday)

Weapons arrived in Savannah, and preparations commenced for distribution to militia units. The *Savannah Daily Morning News* reported, "The steamer *Swan*, from Augusta...brought six cases of arms for the use of the State troops now at the Barracks in this city."[63]

March 2, 1861 (Saturday)

Southrons turned their attention on Fort Sumter, and the efforts of Major Robert Anderson to continue garrisoning the position. One newspaper suggested Anderson "is a brave man and a Southerner [a Kentucky native], and the husband of a Georgia wife [Eliza Bayard Clinch of Camden County], and we cannot believe that he will hold Fort Sumter against his own section under a Black Republican President."[64]

March 3, 1861 (Sunday) ◐

---

[60] "The Enquirer and the Cabinet," *Columbus Daily Times*, February 26, 1861, sec. 2, https://gahistoricnewspapers.galileo.usg.edu/lccn/sn82015388/1861-02-26/ed-1/seq-2/.

[61] "Peace or War!," *Macon Georgia Journal and Messenger*, February 27, 1861, sec. 2, https://gahistoricnewspapers.galileo.usg.edu/lccn/sn85038491/1861-02-27/ed-1/seq-2/.

[62] "Target Exercise," *Columbus Daily Times*, February 28, 1861, sec. 2, https://gahistoricnewspapers.galileo.usg.edu/lccn/sn82015388/1861-02-28/ed-1/seq-2/.

[63] "Arrival of Arms," *Savannah Daily Morning News*, March 1, 1861, sec. 2, https://gahistoricnewspapers.galileo.usg.edu/lccn/sn82015886/1861-03-01/ed-1/seq-2/.

[64] "Probable Resignation of Major Anderson," *Savannah Daily Morning News*, March 2, 1861, sec. 1, https://gahistoricnewspapers.galileo.usg.edu/lccn/sn82015886/1861-03-02/ed-1/seq-1/; "Eliza Bayard Clinch Anderson."

An appointment in the Confederate War Department brought an officer to South Carolina who would soon have an impact on operations in Georgia. An incorrect first name in the orders soon resolved, as military personnel grew accustomed to ignoring Peter to obey Pierre! "Peter [*sic*] G. T. Beauregard having been appointed brigadier-general of the Confederate States of America, and having been ordered to assume command of the troops in and near Charleston Harbor, will be obeyed and respected accordingly, and all State officers of the volunteers, enlisted men, and militia, on duty, are commanded to obey all orders emanating from him."[65]

March 4, 1861 (Monday)

The Provisional Congress continued deliberations in Montgomery including specie. The body resolved, "the mints at New Orleans and Dahlonega shall be continued, and the proper arrangements made as soon as possible to procure suitable dies for the coin of the Confederate States."[66]

March 5, 1861 (Tuesday)

Years before Atlanta bid to host the 1996 Olympic Games, the city offered another proposition. "The establishment of a Southern Confederacy is no longer a dream, a fancy, but a fact; and, for *three reasons*, if not more, we suggest that the city of Atlanta is, *par excellence*, the most suitable point within the limits of the Southern Confederacy, for the location of the Capitol and other public buildings."[67] The article detailed the three reasons: accessibility, centrality, and healthfulness. The first national flag of the Confederacy, raised for the initial time in the state, as Lee's Volunteers mustered into Confederate service.

March 6, 1861 (Wednesday)

President Abraham Lincoln's inauguration speech on March 4 provided newspaper editors across Georgia with ample fodder for rebuttal. "If we have entertained doubts as to whether the fanatical usurpers, now in possession of the United States government, would enter upon the mad expedient of coercion, the character of this manifesto of Abe Lincoln has entirely removed these doubts."[68]

March 7, 1861 (Thursday)

The Georgia Secession Convention reconvened in Savannah and unanimously passed the following resolution: "That the people of Georgia in Convention assembled, most heartily approve the election by the Congress at Montgomery, of the Hon. Jefferson Davis to the Presidency, and the Hon. A. H. Stephens to the Vice-presidency of the Provisional Government of the Confederate States of America, the duties of which position their

---

[65] *OR*, ser. I, vol. 1:261.

[66] *Journal of the Confederate Congress*, March 4, 1861, 1:100.

[67] "The Capital City," *Atlanta Southern Confederacy*, March 5, 1861, sec. 3, https://gahistoricnewspapers.galileo.usg.edu/lccn/sn82014677/1861-03-05/ed-1/seq-3/; Avery, *History of the State of Georgia*, 184.

[68] "The Black Republican Declaration of War," *Savannah Daily Morning News*, March 6, 1861, sec. 2, https://gahistoricnewspapers.galileo.usg.edu/lccn/sn82015886/1861-03-06/ed-1/seq-2/.

distinguished public services, and acknowledged abilities eminently qualify them to discharge."[69]

March 8, 1861 (Friday)

The Convention continued meeting in Montgomery, and Francis Bartow proposed "A bill to admit certain materials for the construction of a telegraphic line from Savannah, in the State of Georgia, to Fort Pulaski free of duty; which was read the first and second times."[70] The bill passed.

March 9, 1861 (Saturday)

The Convention delegates in Savannah took measure to ensure two former officers from Georgia, serving in the United States Army, did not have suffer ramifications over their resignations from service. "Resolved: That neither General [David] Twiggs, nor Colonel [William] Hardee, requires any vindication among their old friends and neighbors in Georgia. Their defence may be found written by the point of the sword upon the battle-fields of their country, and upon the scarred forms of her enemies...."[71]

March 10, 1861 (Sunday)

A newspaper in Augusta carried a story praising a native son. "As Georgians, we feel a just pride in the reputation of our public men, and especially in regard to the influence of Mr. Stephens, whose triumphs in the Congress of the United States are often acknowledged in debate by his brother statesmen...."[72]

March 11, 1861 (Monday)

A Confederate general gained an experienced staff officer, one with ties to Augusta. "Capt. Wm. R. Boggs, of Georgia, 1st Lieutenant of the Ordinance Department U.S. Army, has been appointed Aide-de-Camp to Gen. Beauregard, at Charleston."[73]

March 12, 1861 (Tuesday)

Secretary of War Leroy Pope Walker requested 2,000 troops from Georgia, via a March 9 letter to Governor Brown. The governor responded on this day, "I am disposed to do all in my power to facilitate the action of the Government of the Confederate States in its preparation for the common defense. As the Georgia Convention instructed me to raise two regiments of regulars for the service which were expected to be turned over to the common Government, I have desired to know their status before taking further action to raise troops." Brown elaborated, "I have appointed the officers for the two regiments and they are now actively engaged enlisting soldiers. I desire to know whether you will accept these regiments with all the officers appointed by me and receive the men

---

[69] Candler, *Confederate Records of the State of Georgia*, 1:386.

[70] *Journal of the Confederate Congress*, March 8, 1861, 1:118.

[71] Candler, *Confederate Records of the State of Georgia*, 1:394. "Defenses" was commonly spelled as "defences" during this part of the nineteenth century.

[72] "The Southern Executive," *Augusta Daily Constitutionalist*, March 10, 1861, Genealogybank.com.

[73] "Capt. Wm. R. Boggs," *Columbus Daily Sun*, March 11, 1861, sec. 1, https://gahistoricnewspapers.galileo.usg.edu/lccn/sn82014939/1861-03-11/ed-1/seq-1/.

now enlisted as part of the 2,000 required…I cannot, in justice to the privates who have enlisted, tender the regiments unless they are received with the officers which I have appointed…."[74]

March 13, 1861 (Wednesday)

The delegates in Savannah referred an ordinance to the Committee on Military Affairs: "To transfer to the Government of the Confederate States of America the occupancy and use of the Forts and Arsenals in this State, and also to turn over to said Government the arms and munitions of war found in said Forts and Arsenals at the time of their occupancy by the authorities of this State…."[75]

March 14, 1861 (Thursday)

General Braxton Bragg received news of reinforcements on the way to Pensacola. "Requisitions upon the States of Alabama, Mississippi, Louisiana, Georgia, and Florida have been made for troops to the number of five thousand, to be placed under your command, and it may be expected that a large proportion of this force will be reported to you in the course of the next ten days."[76]

March 15, 1861 (Friday)

The Georgia Convention, meeting in Savannah, received a copy of the Constitution of the Confederate States of America, and ordered the document "to be placed in the appendix of the journal of this Convention."[77]

March 16, 1861 (Saturday)

Delegates in the Georgia Convention considered "the Constitution adopted by the Congress at Montgomery, in the State of Alabama, on the eleventh day of March, in the year of our Lord one thousand eight hundred and sixty-one, for the 'permanent federal government' of the Confederate States of America, be…adopted and ratified by the State of Georgia, 'acting in its sovereign and independent character.'" Alexander Stephens made a motion to "take up and agree to the report."[78] Passage occurred with 276 yeas and no nay votes cast.

March 17, 1861 (Sunday) (St. Patrick's Day)

Colonel Henry Jackson made a decision that altered his military path and positioned another officer to rise through the ranks. Jackson announced his "resigning the position of Major-General of the First Division of Georgia Volunteers. He resigns not because he is unwilling to serve Georgia in the high position assigned him by Gov. Brown, but acting from that lofty spirit of patriotism, and what he conceives a sense of right and justice to

---

[74] Candler, *Confederate Records of the State of Georgia*, 3:23.

[75] Ibid., 1:412.

[76] *OR*, ser. I, vol. 1:449.

[77] *Journal of the Public and Secret Proceedings of the Convention of the People of Georgia*, March 15, 1861, 161.

[78] Ibid., March 16, 1861, 188.

that distinguished Georgian and soldier, Col. Wm. H. T. Walker."[79]

March 18, 1861 (Monday)

A resolution regarding a new and improved Georgia government received approval of the Convention in Savannah. "Governments are instituted to secure the rights of the people, and protect them in the enjoyment of those rights. And Whereas, rigid economy in the public expenditures is an element of strength in Republican Governments, while recklessness and prodigality in such expenditures are detrimental to the public virtue." The act further stipulated, "That in the inauguration of the new government, the multiplication of unnecessary officers to provide positions for favorites, is condemned by the people of Georgia."[80]

March 19, 1861 (Tuesday)

The Provisional Confederate Congress, after adjourning, received accolades. "We verily believe that this Congress has accomplished more than any other Legislative body, in the same time, in the history of the world. They surely have worked like *statesmen* and *patriots* and every where on their return home they will be greeted by an appreciative people with the unanimous acclaim of 'Well done good and faithful servants.'"[81]

March 20, 1861 (Wednesday)

Secretary of War Walker wrote Governor Brown twice today. The first, "In reply to your enquiry I state that all tents, accoutrements, etc., which may be transferred to this Government and received by it would be paid for. Should your State make such transfer an officer will be appointed to inspect the articles, and if suitable receive them." Walker's second note was a follow-up to the first because Confederate officials expected prompt responses to requests for soldiers, and Brown did not always operate within their timeframe. "No reply to my requisition for troops. Will they be furnished, and when? Circumstances require immediate answer."[82]

March 21, 1861 (Thursday)

In Savannah, Vice President Alexander Stephens delivered his "Cornerstone Speech." (See Appendix 2.)

March 22, 1861 (Friday)

The Confederate War Department continued to mass troops at Fort Pulaski and in Pensacola, and Secretary Walker reminded Governor Brown of the urgency the situation demanded. "You will remember that in my requisition for 2,000 troops from your State I informed you that 1,000 were intended for Pulaski. So soon as I am advised that these

---

79 "Major-General of the First Division of the Georgia Volunteers," *Augusta Chronicle*, March 17, 1861, sec. 3, Genealogybank.com.

80 *Journal of the Public and Secret Proceedings of the Convention of the People of Georgia*, March 18, 1861, 197.

81 "The Confederate Congress," *Rome Tri-Weekly Courier*, March 19, 1861, sec. 3, https://gahistoricnewspapers.galileo.usg.edu/lccn/sn85034102/1861-03-19/ed-1/seq-3/. Italics in original.

82 Candler, *Confederate Records of the State of Georgia*, 3:30–31.

troops are ready to be mustered into service an officer will be assigned to the command of that fort." Walker also addressed the governor's concern for the coast of Georgia. "In regard to the company ordered by you to occupy Saint Simon's Island, I can only say that either it or some other company should continue to perform that duty, if there is any possible occasion to justify it, until such time as the Confederate Government is in condition to do so."[83]

March 23, 1861 (Saturday)

The delegates in Savannah approved the Confederate Constitution: "On motion of Mr. [Howell] Cobb, the Constitution, as amended, was then adopted as a whole." Cobb then made a motion, which was approved, "That ten thousand copies of the Constitution of the Confederate States, and of the State of Georgia, as adopted by this Convention, shall be printed and distributed to the several members of this Convention, for the purpose of general distribution."[84] (See Appendix 3.)

March 24, 1861 (Sunday)

Residents of Augusta received word of the new Confederate States Postal rates, "as the Postmaster General may, by proclamation, announce. Single letters not exceeding a half ounce in weight…distance under five hundred miles, five cents…over five hundred miles, ten cents…an additional single rate for each additional half ounce, or less."[85]

March 25, 1861 (Monday)

Writing on the closing session of the Convention in Savannah, a newspaper editor in the same city observed the gravity of the occasion. "The ordeal through which we have just passed, while it must convince the people of the free States that there is conservatism, statesmanship and public virtue at the South, to which they cannot lay claim, should, at the same time, strengthen our confidence in and attachment for the God-ordained institution upon which the Southern society and government are based."[86] The editor referred to the "peculiar institution"—slavery.

March 26, 1861 (Tuesday) ●

"In the midst of the 'rumors of wars,' which agitate the public mind, it seems to escape attention that the most pregnant source of trouble between the slave-holding and non-slaveholding states, must inevitably grow out of the foreign commercial relations of the two sections."[87] This newspaper article, titled "The Impending Commercial Issue between the

---

[83] Ibid., 3:33.

[84] *Journal of the Public and Secret Proceedings of the Convention of the People of Georgia*, March 23, 1861, 273.

[85] "Rates of Postage in the Confederate States of America," *Augusta Daily Constitutionalist*, March 24, 1861, sec. 4, Genealogybank.com.

[86] "The Convention," *Savannah Daily Morning News*, March 25, 1861, sec. 2, https://gahistoricnewspapers.galileo.usg.edu/lccn/sn82015886/1861-03-25/ed-1/seq-2/.

[87] "The Impending Commercial Issue between the North and the South," *Milledgeville Southern Federal Union*, March 26, 1861, sec. 2, https://gahistoricnewspapers.galileo.usg.edu/lccn/sn87062317/1861-03-26/ed-1/seq-2/.

North and the South," offered tariffs as yet another issue causing strife in Georgia and elsewhere.

March 27, 1861 (Wednesday)

Governor Brown and Secretary Walker spent the day working to get additional troops sent to Georgia. Walker to Brown: "Transportation from Columbus for 1,000 troops will be ready on Wednesday next, presuming they will rendezvous at that point." Brown's response to Walker: "Have already sent out the orders for the rendezvous at Macon on Tuesday. Send officers to muster them into service."[88]

March 28, 1861 (Thursday)

Secretary Walker continued to work with Governor Brown to provide reinforcements to Georgia. "Rendezvous your troops at Macon at time appointed. Transportation provided from there. Three hundred will leave daily until all are transported. This will prevent any detention here. Arrangements according to this programme have been perfected."[89]

March 29, 1861 (Good Friday)

The *Southern Confederacy* newspaper in Atlanta offered a commentary on the current state of affairs in the nation: "The time for mincing matters is past, things must now be called by their right names. Union men have been transmuted into Secessionists, or have *sunk* into abject Submissionists. Ask any man and he will tell you he is for the Union—this one for union with his brethren of the South—the other for the present union with Lincoln and Seward."[90]

March 30, 1861 (Saturday)

Folks across the South continued to prepare for war, and the state stood proud of her initial locally produced artillery piece. "The first gun made in Georgia, a 24 pounder, has been tried and found satisfactory and received by the State. That is one gun Georgia didn't go to New York for!"[91]

March 31, 1861 (Easter Sunday)

"For the first time in modern history, a civilized nation is called upon to travel an untrodden track. We are told that 'History is philosophy teaching by example,' but among all the nations of the earth which have risen and fallen before ours, we find no example to guide us in the future."[92] This newspaper editorial perhaps left many readers spending an uneasy

April 1, 1861 (Monday) (April Fools' Day)

Comprising a unit eventually named the 12th Georgia Heavy Artillery Battalion, one company arrived in Atlanta. "At 12 o'clock to-day, an extra train by the Atlanta & West Point Rail Road, brought to our city the 'Newnan Guards'—Capt. [George M.] Hanvey—

---

[88] Candler, *Confederate Records of the State of Georgia*, 3:35.

[89] Ibid., 3:36.

[90] "The True Issue," *Atlanta Southern Confederacy*, March 29, 1861, sec. 2, https://gahistoricnewspapers.galileo.usg.edu/lccn/sn82014677/1861-03-29/ed-1/seq-2/.

[91] "Columbus, Saturday, March 30, 1861," *Columbus Daily Times*, March 30, 1861, sec. 2, https://gahistoricnewspapers.galileo.usg.edu/lccn/sn82015388/1861-03-30/ed-1/seq-2/.

[92] "Recognition," *Augusta Chronicle*, March 31, 1861, sec. 2, Genealogybank.com.

composed of 80 men. This fine company arrived amidst stirring martial music and firing of cannon."[93]

April 2, 1861 (Tuesday)

Disagreeing over the official capacity of Georgia troops once mustered into Confederate service, Governor Brown and Secretary Walker exchanged messages. Brown wrote, "When the troops leave Georgia they under no law till they are mustered into the service. The officers object to leave the State till it is done. If you desire the troops please designate at once some one to muster them in here." Walker's response: "The troops will be mustered into service at Pensacola, but transportation has been provided from Macon, as I wrote you."[94]

April 3, 1861 (Wednesday)

Governor Brown received a response from Secretary Walker regarding the mustering of Georgia troops. "I cannot make an exceptional case of the Georgia troops, although anxious to oblige you as far as possible. The troops of the other States intended for service at Pensacola are mustered into service at that point. I desire to know without delay whether that arrangement will suffice?"[95]

April 4, 1861 (Thursday)

After finally compromising with the Confederate War Department, Governor Brown sent troops to Pensacola; Brown attached strings. "I tender these troops for the shortest time for which they can be received into the service of the Confederate States, which I believe is twelve months, unless sooner discharged, under the provisions of the Act of Congress upon that subject. An account of expense of equipping and preparing the regiment and battalion for service will be made out and forwarded to you."[96]

April 5, 1861 (Friday)

A newspaper editor harbored thoughts of disunion and Christmas in the same article: "When a wash begins on an embankment there is no arresting its progress in any way except by the removal of the cause, and the damage is perpetual until such arrest is effected. So with the work of secession. We want no Northern missletoe [*sic*] engrated on our Southern tree."[97]

April 6, 1861 (Saturday)

Residents of Savannah read of a regiment of Georgians assembling in Macon. "It is the subject of general remark that no regment [*sic*] of Volunteers was ever raised in Georgia, or any where else, that had more of the genuine characteristics and personal esprit de corps of

---

[93] "Arrival of Up-Country Volunteers—The Departure," *Atlanta Southern Confederacy*, April 1, 1861, sec. 2, https://gahistoricnewspapers.galileo.usg.edu/lccn/sn82014677/1861-04-01/ed-1/seq-2/; Sifakis, *Compendium of the Confederate Armies*, 121.

[94] Candler, *Confederate Records of the State of Georgia*, 3:37–38.

[95] Ibid., 3:38.

[96] Ibid., 3:39.

[97] "Secession," *Columbus Daily Times*, April 5, 1861, sec. 2, https://gahistoricnewspapers.galileo.usg.edu/lccn/sn82015388/1861-04-05/ed-1/seq-2/.

the soldier, than the body of men now rendeavoused [*sic*] in this city." The listing of the various companies under review included the Oglethorpe Infantry, Newnan Guards, Washington Rifles, Etowah Infantry, and the Ringgold Infantry."[98]

April 7, 1861 (Friday)

Troops in Augusta prepared to depart the city. "A number of our citizens, including about 60 of the Clinch Rifles, were to leave in the 12½ train of last night, for Macon, whither they go to take leave of their friends of the Oglethorpe Infantry. We hope the time is not far distant when we shall see all the 'old familiar faces' again at home."[99]

April 8, 1861 (Monday)

Days before the firing on Fort Sumter, Secretary Walker notified Governor Brown of the need to call for troops in Georgia. Walker suggested "to Your Excellency the necessity of calling at once for 3,000 volunteers, to be drilled, equipped, and held in instant readiness to meet any requisition from this Department. These troops will, of course, not be receiving pay until they shall be mustered into service, but the emergency is so pressing that Your Excellency will fully appreciate the great importance of thorough preparation, especially in regard to instant capacity to move."[100] Georgia troops seized the U.S. Mint in Dahlonega.

April 9, 1861 (Tuesday)

Secretary Walker wrote the governor regarding the use of Georgia surgeons. "I must request Your Excellency to transmit me a list of the surgeons and assistants for your troops; and with reference to the possibility that the Department may be unable to make acting assistant surgeons of all your appointees, you will oblige me by indicating the names you prefer to be retained and in the order of your preference."[101]

April 10, 1861 (Wednesday)

News of Governor Brown's various initiatives reached Montgomery, Alabama, and Secretary Walker took quick action, after learning of a transfer "of the forts, arsenals, ordnance stores, etc., within your State, I take the liberty of addressing you on the subject, for the purpose of being officially assured of the fact, if it be so…that it will be really promotive of the public interests if your Excellency can…advise this Department as to the time when the authorities of Georgia will be prepared to turn over the property mentioned to the Confederate States…."[102]

April 11, 1861 (Thursday)

Responding to a call on Georgia to provide 3,000 troops to the Confederate service, Governor Brown detailed guidelines to Secretary Walker. "I have every wish to accommodate,

---

[98] "The Georgia Regiment at Camp Oglethorpe," *Savannah Daily Morning News*, April 6, 1861, sec. 1, https://gahistoricnewspapers.galileo.usg.edu/lccn/sn82015886/1861-04-06/ed-1/seq-1/.

[99] "Gone to Macon," *Augusta Chronicle*, April 7, 1861, sec. 3, Genealogybank.com.

[100] Candler, *Confederate Records of the State of Georgia*, 3:40; Winter, "Gold Coins of the Dahlonega Mint: 1838–1861."

[101] Candler, *Confederate Records of the State of Georgia*, 3:43.

[102] Ibid., 3:44.

and Georgia will at all times be ready to do her part, but she will insist on having her rights and wishes respected when she is claiming the recognition of a principle of justice to her troops, as well as of obvious propriety."[103]

April 12, 1861 (Friday)

As the bombardment of Fort Sumter began, news from Savannah indicated Colonel Charles Williams, Fort Pulaski commander, had issued a special notice. "In consequence of hostile rumors...no vessel will be allowed to pass Fort Pulaski without previous information as to her pacific [*sic*] character."[104]

April 13, 1861 (Saturday)

A promotion in the Confederate ranks, as Secretary Walker notified the governor of a new leader at Fort Pulaski. "The President has appointed A. R. Lawton to command...staff and ordnance officers will be sent to him at once. I must beg you at once and without more delay to furnish my requisition of troops of March 9. If you still refuse to transfer the enlisted men except upon the terms heretofore suggested by you, I must earnestly insist that you issue a call for 1,000 volunteers for the defense of Fort Pulaski."[105]

April 14, 1861 (Sunday)

A front-page advertisement symbolized social conditions in much of the South. Beneath the headline "Negroes for Sale," potential customers learned "The subscriber offers for sale Six Likely Negroes—a Woman, 37 years old, a good cook, washer and ironer, and nurse; a Boy, 12 years old; a Boy, 10 years old; a Girl, 8 years old; a Girl, 5 years old, and a Man about 27 years old, a good hand in a Tannery."[106]

April 15, 1861 (Monday)

Secretary Walker notified Governor Brown, "Thirteen hundred men will be received for Pulaski and Tybee Island, and orders for their disposition will be forwarded to General Lawton. The news today indicates general war."[107]

April 16, 1861 (Tuesday)

The Confederate War Department notified Governor Brown of the need to raise additional soldiers. "I now beg leave to request Your Excellency to hold in readiness for instant movement 5,000 volunteer troops....The importance of holding the entire force...in absolute readiness Your Excellency will fully appreciate, in view of the hostile purpose of the Washington Government, as indicated in the recent proclamation of the President of the United States, which has just reached this Department...."[108]

---

[103] Ibid., 3:47.

[104] "Vigilance at Fort Pulaski," *Columbus Daily Sun*, April 12, 1861, sec. 2, https://gahistoricnewspapers.galileo.usg.edu/lccn/sn82014939/1861-04-12/ed-1/seq-2/.

[105] Candler, *Confederate Records of the State of Georgia*, 3:48.

[106] "Negroes for Sale," *Atlanta Southern Confederacy*, April 14, 1861, sec. 1, https://gahistoricnewspapers.galileo.usg.edu/lccn/sn82014677/1861-04-14/ed-1/seq-1/.

[107] Candler, *Confederate Records of the State of Georgia*, 3:50.

[108] Ibid., 3:50–51.

April 17, 1861 (Wednesday)
Secretary Walker notified Governor Brown that the pending government contracts for munitions "made by Your Excellency with the Tredegar Works...will probably be advantageous to this Government to have transferred to it [the contract]...as this Government has...a contract with that establishment...for thirty 10-inch guns, to be delivered at the rate of two per week...I must ask Your Excellency to furnish me copies, that the Department may be able to ascertain precisely times of delivery and the like...."[109]

April 18, 1861 (Thursday) ◑
A growing concern over the safety of Georgia's coast prompted Governor Brown to request reinforcements from the Confederate War Department. "I am informed by a telegram received from H. C. Wayne, adjutant-general, now in Savannah, that he has reliable information from Washington that a plan for retaking Fort Pulaski has been matured." Brown conjectured, "Taking this in connection with the declaration of Mr. Lincoln that he intends to retake all the Southern forts, I anticipate an attack on Fort Pulaski at no distant day. I therefore respectfully ask that you at once order 5,000 troops to Fort Pulaski and for defense of Savannah with its approaches."[110]

April 19, 1861 (Friday)
President Lincoln issued a blockade of all Southern ports, an act that certainly affected Georgia. In his proclamation, the president "deemed it advisable to set on foot a blockade of the ports within the States aforesaid [seceded states], in pursuance of the laws of the United States, and of the law of Nations, in such case provided." If any vessel attempted to run the blockade, "she will be duly warned...and if the same vessel shall again attempt to enter or leave the blockaded port, she will be captured and sent to the nearest convenient port, for such proceedings against her and her cargo as prize, as may be deemed advisable."[111]

April 20, 1861 (Saturday)
"*Cano Arma*, ('the words of Virgil') are now on the lips of every man, woman and child throughout our vast confederacy, the 'irrepressible conflict' is no longer a rhetorical flourish, but a stubborn fact. '*Grim visaged war*' no longer capers nimbly to the lascivious numbers of a lute, but stamps his red foot of battle and impresses its hideous, bloody deformity upon our native soil."[112] An editorial from Thomaston sought to evoke a spirit of patriotism among the region's population.

April 21, 1861 (Sunday)
"Neither States nor individuals can be neutral in this contest between Abolitionism and Southern rights. The war has begun. Argument has been exhausted. It is now man to man, and steel to steel. Let no man talk of neutrality. Either he must support Lincoln in his

---

[109] Ibid., 3:52.

[110] Ibid., 3:53–54.

[111] Basler, ed., *Collected Works of Abraham Lincoln*, 4:339.

[112] "Cano Arma!," *Thomaston Upson Pilot*, April 20, 1861, sec. 2, https://gahistoricnewspapers.galileo.usg.edu/lccn/sn85034395/1861-04-20/ed-1/seq-2/. Italics in original.

usurpation and war upon the South, or he must resist him with arms."[113] Frank and to the point, a newspaper editor took a no-nonsense approach to the conflict.

April 22, 1861 (Monday)

Secretary Walker looked to Georgia with a request for additional soldiers. "I make requisition on you for two regiments of infantry, to rendezvous without delay at Richmond, Va. Conform the organization as far as possible to the law providing for the public defense. They will be mustered into service at such place as you may designate, and transportation and subsistence provided accordingly. Answer."[114]

April 23, 1861 (Tuesday)

Responding to the call for additional volunteers, Governor Brown dispatched the Confederate War Department, noting he would send "two regiments of infantry. Can only tender them organized according to the laws of Georgia. Could send forth some companies very soon. If this is agreeable I will direct railroad companies in Georgia to send bills to you for transportation of companies, and you will please make arrangements beyond Augusta. Answer immediately, as I wish to know how to shape my orders."[115]

April 24, 1861 (Wednesday) ●

Fort Pulaski needed additional armaments, so Governor Brown worked with Secretary Walker in hopes of securing the needed matériel. "Again, I have been doing all in my power to get heavy guns and other munitions of war to the fort. I am getting on hand a considerable supply, but I am informed that the guns are being mounted very slowly indeed, for the reason that we lack scientific officers who understand the business."[116]

April 25, 1861 (Thursday)

Governor Brown questioned Secretary Walker: "Who appoints surgeons to volunteer regiments, and how many to each?" Walker quickly responded, "The law allows one surgeon and one assistant surgeon to each regiment. I appoint them."[117]

April 26, 1861 (Friday)

Governor Brown issued a proclamation detailing steps Georgians would take in lieu of the federal blockade. The preamble to Brown's edict indicated his actions were necessary due to recent events. "The oppressive and wicked conduct of the Government…of the late United States of America known as the anti-slavery States, war actually exists between them and the people of the Southern States…the President of the United States has issued his proclamation declaring his determination to blockade the ports…and is now collecting federal troops upon southern soil for the purpose of subjugating and enslaving us."[118] (See Appendix 4.)

---

[113] "No Neutrality," *Atlanta Southern Confederacy*, April 21, 1861, sec. 2, https://gahistoricnewspapers.galileo.usg.edu/lccn/sn82014677/1861-04-21/ed-1/seq-2/.

[114] Candler, *Confederate Records of the State of Georgia*, 3:57–58.

[115] Ibid., 3:58.

[116] Ibid., 3:60.

[117] Ibid., 3:61–62.

[118] Ibid., 3:33.

April 27, 1861 (Saturday)

On this day, the Virginia State Convention delegates accepted an earlier offer from Vice President Stephens. Little Alec addressed the representatives four days prior. After speaking on the closeness of Federal forces to Richmond, he suggested meeting the enemy could "best be done by having your military operations under the common head at Montgomery or it may be at Richmond. For, while I have no authority to speak on that subject, I feel at perfect liberty to say, that it is quite within the range of probability that, if such an alliance is made as seems to me ought to be made, the seat of our Government will, within a few weeks, be moved to this place."[119] Stephens proved correct regarding the move.

April 28, 1861 (Sunday)

Young men continued their eagerness to volunteer for military service. Communities across the state served as departure points for soldiers heading to the front lines. One such example describes a unit from Madison. "Of course they are everything they should be in the way of good soldiers. Among them are several personal friends—Knights of the quill, &c.—who can transfix an enemy with a sword as well as a pointed paragraph. They number 81 men. Their uniform is Georgia gray."[120]

April 29, 1861 (Monday)

Secretary Walker wrote to Governor Brown with another request for soldiers from Georgia. "I wish you to furnish immediately one regiment of infantry of picked men for Pensacola. Private—Bragg needs them for lodgment on Santa Rosa Island preparatory to opening upon Fort Pickens. Dispatch is necessary. One regiment goes from here in a day or two. Would like to have it consist of drilled companies, if possible."[121]

April 30, 1861 (Tuesday)

In Marietta, Governor Brown sent a message to Secretary Walker regarding troops needed in Pensacola. "I have sent most of my best drilled companies to Virginia. Will do the best I can for you. Do not believe it possible to have them ready with tents, knapsacks, and accoutrements immediately. Can you furnish any? The calls come so fast one cannot get enough made."[122]

May 1, 1861 (Wednesday) ◐

A celebration officially marking the arrival of spring offered an occasion for folks to enjoy special festivities. Savannah provides but one example. "Our volunteer companies will, as usual, celebrate their May-Day anniversary to-day.—We invite attention to the programme of the 'Ancient and Honorable Artillery,' who celebrate their 75th anniversary."[123]

May 2, 1861 (Thursday)

---

[119] Virginia State Convention, *Proceedings of the Virginia State Convention of 1861*, 4:388.

[120] "Home Guards," *Augusta Chronicle*, April 28, 1861, sec. 2, Genealogybank.com.

[121] Candler, *Confederate Records of the State of Georgia*, 3:65.

[122] Ibid.

[123] "War News," *Savannah Daily Morning News*, May 1, 1861, sec. 2, https://gahistoric-newspapers.galileo.usg.edu/lccn/sn82015886/1861-05-01/ed-1/seq-2/.

"Our people have been more than liberal in responding to the call made upon them to raise a fund for equipping the Albany Guards and preparing them for the field. But the whole work is not done; the wives, daughters and mothers of these brave men must be cared for; they have given up their dependence for a living to help on the cause of their country, and that country must provide for them."[124] Residents of Albany, and other localities in Georgia, began preparations to care for the state's soldiers, as well as those left behind.

May 3, 1861 (Friday)

Georgia males—Caucasian, able-bodied, and of military age—responded to the early call for volunteers. Across the state, these men assembled and readied for transportation to Virginia and other points. "The Brooks Rifles, a volunteer company formed in Quitman, Brooks county, Georgia, in November last, is now impatiently awaiting an order from His Excellency, Governor Brown, to whom the company has tendered their services for the support of the State Confederation."[125]

May 4, 1861 (Saturday)

Governor Brown continued work with the Confederate War Department, especially focusing on the environ about Savannah. "I have received…petitions from our fellow-citizens along the coast, which show that the state of alarm is so great…many of them are sending away their most valuable property and preparing to leave their homes because of the sense of insecurity which they feel. Almost all business is suspended and the excitement and alarm are very great."[126]

May 5, 1861 (Sunday)

Most cities and towns across the state continued to contribute young men to serve as soldiers. In Warrenton, "The McDuffie Rifles, Capt. [Edward] Pottle, is to be mustered into the Fifth Regiment. As soon as notice was given that the company was under marching orders, 90 men were at once enrolled."[127]

May 6, 1861 (Monday)

Confusion reigned between Governor Brown and Secretary Walker regarding when and where Georgia troops should deploy. "Several companies of the Fifth Regiment are now on their way to Macon. All are under orders and will be there to-morrow. Do you wish me to disband them and send them back home till you again require them, or will you receive them now? I have not funds to maintain them long in camp."[128]

May 7, 1861 (Tuesday)

Secretary Walker notified Governor Brown on the mustering of present and future soldiers. "I do not wish you to understand me as making it absolutely peremptory that the regiment

---

[124] "Meeting of Citizens," *Albany Patriot*, May 2, 1861, sec. 2, https://gahistoricnewspapers.galileo.usg.edu/lccn/sn82014211/1861-05-02/ed-1/seq-2/.

[125] "The Brooks Rifles," *Savannah Daily Morning News*, May 3, 1861, sec. 1, https://gahistoricnewspapers.galileo.usg.edu/lccn/sn82015886/1861-05-03/ed-1/seq-1/.

[126] Candler, *Confederate Records of the State of Georgia*, 68.

[127] "The McDuffie Rifles," *Augusta Chronicle*, May 5, 1861, sec. 1, Genealogybank.com.

[128] Candler, *Confederate Records of the State of Georgia*, 3:70–71.

to rendezvous at Macon to-morrow must be mustered in for war. Requisition having been made for this regiment some time ago, it might be unjust to so insist. I hope, however, they will consent. Hereafter all troops must so agree, as Congress has passed a law to that effect."[129]

May 8, 1861 (Wednesday)

Secretary Walker and the governor continued to exchange letters regarding the use of Georgia troops. Walker cited Confederate law to make his point. "Your Excellency will thus perceive that, however profound my sympathies may be with our gallant volunteers, I have no discretionary power by which I can supply clothing to the Georgia troops. The law, in fact, was intended, in view of the pressing exigencies demanding a large force in the field, without an organized quartermaster establishment, to supply the very deficiency you bring as a charge against the service."[130]

May 9, 1861 (Thursday)

Taking a more positive note, Secretary Walker notified Brown of plans for Georgia's coast. "I assure Your Excellency I profoundly appreciate the solicitude you feel in regard to the coast defenses of Georgia, but they have not escaped my attention...General Lawton's command was extended to embrace the coast, and he was ordered to report all necessary defenses." Walker assured the governor, "So soon as this report is received here no time will be lost in executing the measures recommended for the security of your citizens. Should it be required to make special requisition upon Your Excellency for troops in this connection it will be done."[131]

May 10, 1861 (Friday)

The editorial of the day in Savannah: "The Lincoln papers at the North are greatly annoyed at the silence of the Southern press in regard to the war plans of our government. While they are blustering and blowing about what they are going to do, making threats disgraceful to humanity, and developing a malignity of spirit only worthy of fiends, they cannot comprehend the quiet composure of the Southern journals, which they attribute to the military despotism under which they say we live."[132]

May 11, 1861 (Saturday)

Work continued along the coast, and the governor tapped "Genl. Ira A. Foster Special Agent of the State." Foster's task was to "proceed to Savannah and examine into the condition, quantity, quality, number, etc., of the Arms and Munitions of War in the State Arsenal there, and to report to me concerning the same. To cause to be transferred to the Arsenal in this city [Milledgeville], such of the State Arms and munitions of war now in said Arsenal at Savannah, or in said city of Savannah, as he may deem expedient as per

---

[129] Ibid., 3:71.

[130] Ibid., 3:73–74.

[131] Ibid., 3:74.

[132] "War News," *Savannah Daily Morning News*, May 10, 1861, https://gahistoricnewspapers.galileo.usg.edu/lccn/sn82015886/1861-05-10/ed-1/seq-2/.

instructions given him."[133]

May 12, 1861 (Sunday)

Wishing to cultivate additional loyalty, an editor printed excerpts from a speech, which signaled Georgia's early contribution to the war effort. "Georgia has done her part nobly. When she seceded, all sagacious men saw that the old Union was lost and gone forever—to us at least. Some of her best sons tried to stay the tide of revolution for a little time—till one more effort could be made to save the Union on principles that would be just to the South; but the people differed with these patriotic men."[134]

May 13, 1861 (Monday)

In brokering a deal with Secretary Walker, Governor Brown offered salt and saltpeter, provided "the Confederate Government will at the same time and on the same terms accept the transfer of all the ordnance, shot and shell which have been procured by this State from…Tredegar…since the beginning of our present troubles, and also the steamer *Huntress*…with the necessary attending expenses incurred in bringing her to Savannah."[135]

May 14, 1861 (Tuesday)

An editor in Milledgeville contrasted the differences between North and South. "The last few days have sufficed, we presume, to open the eyes of all the people of the South, the border States included, to the inconceivable malignity of those who have heretofore been in nominal alliance and union with us in the North. Surely with such facts as these the real spirit which actuates our citizens ought to be better understood."[136]

May 15, 1861 (Wednesday)

Governor Brown continued to clear confusion between his office and the Confederate War Department. To Secretary Walker, Brown stated, "although the term of service may be restricted to during the war, our volunteers will with alacrity respond to whatever calls the Confederate Government shall make, through the Executive, upon Georgia for troops, provided twelve months' volunteers are not accepted also—if this be the case it is apprehended that no companies will volunteer for the war if others are allowed to enter the service for one year only."[137]

May 16, 1861 (Thursday)

Some things just take time. Working through the details of raising Georgia regiments for Confederate service proved one of those things. Governor Brown to Secretary Walker: "In your telegram of the 6th instant you instruct me to make arrangements somewhere for two regiments instead of one, meaning the one then rendezvousing at Macon and one other. I have complied with your requisition, and now have the companies for the other regiment

---

[133] Candler, *Confederate Records of the State of Georgia*, 2:37.

[134] "Hon. Henry W. Hillard's Eloquent Speech," *Atlanta Southern Confederacy*, May 12, 1861, sec. 2, https://gahistoricnewspapers.galileo.usg.edu/lccn/sn82014677/1861-05-12/ed-1/seq-2/.

[135] Candler, *Confederate Records of the State of Georgia*, 3:75.

[136] "The South and the North," *Milledgeville Southern Recorder*, May 14, 1861, sec. 2, 2https://gahistoricnewspapers.galileo.usg.edu/lccn/sn82016415/1861-05-14/ed-1/seq-2/.

[137] Candler, *Confederate Records of the State of Georgia*, 3:78.

in camp ready to rendezvous on the shortest notice."[138]

May 17, 1861 (Friday)

Governor Brown's patience in dealing with Secretary Walker grew thin, as evidenced in yet another communique.

> I have responded very promptly to every call made on me for troops. The late act of Congress, to which you refer, authorizing tenders of troops to the President independent of State authority, I regard as a very dangerous infringement of State rights. I can in no degree increase dispatch in organizing regiments, as you have ordered from the Augusta Arsenal to Virginia all the new guns in the arsenal, with which, I think, Georgia troops should have been armed. I cannot consent to exchange what few guns still in the possession of the State, purchased by her, for the altered muskets now in the arsenal.[139]

May 18, 1861 (Saturday)

Communication between the governor and the Confederate secretary of war continued. Brown wrote, "Do you make requisition on me for Colonel [Lucius] Gartrell's regiment and for the Savannah volunteer regiment in addition to the Sixth Regiment which is to rendezvous in Atlanta 25th instant? If so please state where you wish the two regiments mustered into service." In Walker's response, he clarified his intentions. "I make no requisition for Gartrell's regiment. My letter to him will disclose the circumstances under which it was agreed to be received. Beyond this the matter rests with Colonel Gartrell and yourself. Nor do I make any requisition for the troops for Savannah. General Lawton can explain."[140]

May 19, 1861 (Sunday)

Georgians considered their officers selected thus far, equal to the task ahead. "We confidently believe that we have in our government the best military officers in the world, and a sufficient number of them to command our forces without placing inexperienced and untaught men at the head of our armies."[141]

May 20, 1861 (Monday)

An "Important Military Order" greeted readers of the *Daily Sun* in Columbus. "By authority of Gov. Brown, Adjutant General Wayne prohibits the Companies of the State from carrying out of the State without consent of the Commander in-Chief, any arms or accoutrements of any kind furnished them by the State, or which belong to the State, or have been procured by the companies at the expense of the State."[142]

May 21, 1861 (Tuesday)

---

[138] Ibid., 3:79.

[139] Ibid., 3:81.

[140] Ibid., 3:82–83.

[141] "Competent Commanders," *Atlanta Southern Confederacy*, May 19, 1861, sec. 1, https://gahistoricnewspapers.galileo.usg.edu/lccn/sn82014677/1861-05-19/ed-1/seq-1/.

[142] "Important Military Order," *Columbus Daily Sun*, May 20, 1861, sec. 1, https://gahistoricnewspapers.galileo.usg.edu/lccn/sn82014939/1861-05-20/ed-1/seq-1/.

Governor Brown had delivered; now he expected payment from the Confederate War Department. "The saltpeter and sulphur now worth in market twice what the State paid. You must take it and the ordnance and ammunition and boat together at the price the State paid for all. Will accept C.S. bonds for price of boat, balance in cash."[143]

May 22, 1861 (Wednesday)

Secretary Walker wrote to the governor detailing the focus of the Confederate War Department in mustering troops and the rationale behind their policy. "It is evident the Government at Washington is preparing for a prolonged and bloody war, the proclamation of Mr. Lincoln calling for enrollments for three years and enlistments for the war clearly shows a resolution to convert all their forces from the character of raw militia and volunteers into trained and disciplined regulars."[144]

May 23, 1861 (Thursday)

Folks in Albany received a call to take special precautions during a time of war, since little uncertainty remained "of the existence of *spies* and *Abolitionists*...there are no doubt of persons tampering with negroes...to entice them off from their owners or employers, we...suggest...the propriety of offering a suitable reward to any negro or negroes who will detect any white man or set of men, so as to afford legal evidence of the fact of any person who may be found violating the laws of Georgia in this respect."[145]

May 24, 1861 (Friday) ●

The war barely underway, yet greedy merchants could taste ways to make money. A reader wrote to the *Daily Morning News* in Savannah with a complaint regarding the developing economic squeeze...a big squeeze! "Allow me, through your columns, to draw the attention of our city authorities towards an evil which has attained such proportion as to call a speedy redress. It is the forestalling of our market by a band of unprincipled dealers, [who] not only will charge famine prices, but resort to any means to keep control of our markets, and oblige us to submit to their extortion."[146]

May 25, 1861 (Saturday)

Governor Brown issued a proclamation calling for a statewide election for ratification of the Confederate Constitution.

> Whereas, it is provided in Section Seventh of Article Fifth of the Constitution of this State, as adopted by the late Convention of the people thereof, on the 23rd day of March last, that there shall be an election held at all the places of public election in this State, on the first Tuesday in July, 1861, when all the citizens of this State entitled to vote for Governor, shall cast their ballots either for "Ratification" or "No

---

[143] Candler, *Confederate Records of the State of Georgia*, 3:83.

[144] Ibid., 3:86.

[145] "In Times of War Be Vigilant," *Albany Patriot*, May 23, 1861, sec. 2, https://gahistoricnewspapers.galileo.usg.edu/lccn/sn82014211/1861-05-23/ed-1/seq-2/. Italics in original.

[146] "Market Pirates," *Savannah Daily Morning News*, May 24, 1861, sec. 2, https://gahistoricnewspapers.galileo.usg.edu/lccn/sn82015886/1861-05-24/ed-1/seq-2/.

Ratification." The election "shall be conducted in the same manner as general elections; and the returns shall be made to the Governor."[147]

May 26, 1861 (Sunday)

General R. E. Lee reminded Governor Brown of the importance in letting Georgia soldiers leave the state with their weapons. "I deem it proper to call your attention to the fact…many of the volunteer companies from your State have arrived at Richmond without arms. The demand upon Virginia has been so great that all arms have been exhausted, except the old flint-lock muskets. I thought it probable that you would like to provide the men of your State with such better arms as may be at your disposal, and therefore take the liberty of bringing this matter to your notice."[148]

May 27, 1861 (Monday)

Georgians prepare for war; residents of Savannah readied to learn how they could assist the soldiers on the front lines. "It is scarcely necessary for us to direct the attention of our readers to the meeting called today, by the proclamation of the Mayor, for the purpose of organizing a Committee to receive donations for the aid of the families of the volunteers, and to take into consideration the propriety of levying a tax for that purpose."[149]

May 28, 1861 (Tuesday)

The first blockade vessels arrived off the coast of Savannah. Flag officer Silas Stringham reported to naval command. "I acknowledge receipt of your last esteemed favor under date of May 28, 1861, which reached me also off Charleston, with the arrival of the *Wabash*, *Flag*, and *Union*. I availed myself of the presence of the two former at Charleston to go off Savannah."[150]

May 29, 1861 (Wednesday)

President Davis notified Governor Brown, "Troops, armed and equipped, ammunition included, are much needed. Please urge such forward with all practicable dispatch." Brown swiftly responded. "Will hasten through the two regiments on hand, armed with muskets of 1842, with all possible dispatch. Will order to you, by express from Milledgeville, 10,000 ball and 10,000 buck-and-ball cartridges. Will continue to do all I possibly can to aid you."[151]

May 30, 1861 (Thursday)

Hostilities remained in the initial stages, and boys North and South feared the "great battle" would take place, and they would miss the affair. Eager volunteers, of many ages, joined the ranks. "Mr. John Minton, of Cobb county, as we learn from the *Rome Southerner*, came to that place and joined the Miller Rifles, as a private. He served in the Seminole war and

---

[147] Candler, *Confederate Records of the State of Georgia*, 2:38.

[148] Ibid., 3:89.

[149] "The Public Meeting To-Day," *Savannah Daily Morning News*, May 27, 1861, sec. 2, https://gahistoricnewspapers.galileo.usg.edu/lccn/sn82015886/1861-05-27/ed-1/seq-2/.

[150] United States Naval War Records Office, *Official Records of the Union and Confederate Navies in the War of the Rebellion* (hereafter cited as *ORN*), ser. I, vol. 5:726.

[151] Candler, *Confederate Records of the State of Georgia*, 3:90.

was in the Texan Revolution. Mr. Minton is over sixty-five years of age."[152]

May 31, 1861 (Friday)

Governor Brown continued correspondence with President Davis concerning officers for soldiers sent from Georgia. In this dispatch, he sought a brigadier generalship for Henry Rootes Jackson, a native of Athens. "If I can furnish the troops above proposed, Georgia will have six or seven regiments in Virginia and no general. A dispatch to me at Milledgeville by Monday saying that my request for Jackson will be granted would greatly oblige, and would give increased energy to all our movements."[153]

June 1, 1861 (Saturday)

Governor Brown's response to President Davis's complaint of Georgia soldiers arriving in Virginia without weapons: "I am doing all I can to put every gun at my command into the service, and am sending in the State regiments fully equipped. This I will continue to do with all possible promptness. I impose no restraint, only that they leave the State's arms. You shall have no cause to complain of my promptness in responding to every call while I have a gun."[154]

June 2, 1861 (Sunday)

A newspaper editor suggested "the Governor and President are right in taking men for the war in preference to twelve months—especially while so many hundreds of thousands of our brave men all over the land are eager to go for the war—determined to hear the crack of the last gun before they come back, or stay till the crack of doom. This patriotic impulse...seems to throb in the heart of nine-tenths of those who volunteer...."[155]

June 3, 1861 (Monday)

A physician in Atlanta reported on the intentions of his medical colleagues. "I understand 1,000 Georgia doctors have applied for Surgeons' places in the army. I now propose we form a regiment of doctors. All those to whom I have spoken are eager for it, all who are willing to serve their country in this way will write to me immediately, (giving name and post office plain)...we will rendezvous in Atlanta to form and tender our services to the President."[156]

June 4, 1861 (Tuesday)

Governor Brown exercised executive action to announce a proposed change in bond interest rates to help fund the war effort. "Whereas, in order to raise a sufficient amount of money to provide for the public defence, by the sale, at par, of Georgia six per cent. bonds,

---

[152] "Mr. John Minton," *Columbus Daily Sun*, May 30, 1861, sec. 1, https://gahistoricnewspapers.galileo.usg.edu/lccn/sn82014939/1861-05-30/ed-1/seq-1/.

[153] Candler, *Confederate Records of the State of Georgia*, 3:92.

[154] Ibid., 3:92.

[155] "For Twelve Months—For during the War," *Atlanta Southern Confederacy*, June 2, 1861, sec. 2, https://gahistoricnewspapers.galileo.usg.edu/lccn/sn82014677/1861-06-02/ed-1/seq-2/.

[156] "Doctors of Georgia," *Columbus Daily Times*, June 3, 1861, sec. 2, https://gahistoricnewspapers.galileo.usg.edu/lccn/sn82015388/1861-06-03/ed-1/seq-2/.

which were authorized to be issued and sold by Act of 16th November, 1860; I have found it necessary to assure parties proposing to take the bonds that I will, in my message to the next General Assembly, earnestly recommend the substitution of Seven per cent. bonds for the Six per cent."[157]

June 5, 1861 (Wednesday)

Working to get gunpowder, which belonged to the state, back from Confederate officials in Augusta, the governor penned a request to Secretary Walker. "The balance of the powder purchased by me (100,000 pounds in all) was left in Savannah and at Fort Pulaski for the use of the Confederacy, and will be charged to that Government. That now in Augusta I want, that it may be converted into cartridges at the penitentiary in this place [Milledgeville]."[158]

June 6, 1861 (Thursday)

Displaying a rarity in the newspaper business, the editor of the *Albany Patriot* offered honest testimony. "For the past week we have searched in vain for dispatches from the scenes of war. Nothing yet has reached us of a reliable character. Rumors to day are contradicted tomorrow. We are therefore unwilling to excite the public mind by false statements. So soon as we receive anything worthy of notice, our readers shall have it."[159]

June 7, 1861 (Friday)

Confederate officials grappled with the process of printing currency and striking specie. "Dies for the new coin of the Confederate States have been received at Dahlonega at the branch mint, and the superintendent has received orders from headquarters not to strike off any more United States coin, but to reserve the bullion."[160]

June 8, 1861 (Saturday)

Another Georgia regiment formed, and the governor notified General Cooper of their readiness. "At Colonel [Zephaniah T.] Conner's request I state that I make no objections to the reception of his regiment into service if they do not carry out of the State their arms or equipments."[161] Conner eventually served in the 12th Georgia Infantry.

June 9, 1861 (Sunday)

A newspaper editor offered early kudos to folks in the Gate City. "Atlanta has done nobly in her contribution of men to the State and Confederate Armies. Besides a large number of her citizens who have enlisted in the State Army, she has already in the field, in Virginia,

---

157 Candler, *Confederate Records of the State of Georgia*, 2:39–40.

158 Ibid., 3:94.

159 "War News," *Albany Patriot*, June 6, 1861, sec. 3, https://gahistoricnewspapers.galileo.usg.edu/lccn/sn82014211/1861-06-06/ed-1/seq-3/.

160 "Southern Coin," *Savannah Daily Morning News*, June 7, 1861, sec. 2, https://gahistoricnewspapers.galileo.usg.edu/lccn/sn82015886/1861-06-07/ed-1/seq-2/.

161 Candler, *Confederate Records of the State of Georgia*, 3:94; Sifakis, *Compendium of the Confederate Armies*, 208.

and elsewhere, five as gallant Companies as ever marched to the tap of the drum."[162]

June 10, 1861 (Monday)

An army marches on its stomach, and Cherokee County could provide the sustenance. "A correspondent…says Cherokee Georgia can bread the Confederate Army, and adduces the following figures to prove it: Floyd county will make a surplus of 200,000 bushels of wheat. Cass, Gordon, Whitfield and Murray will average a like amount, making 1,200,000 bushels. One bushel of wheat will make 40 pounds of flour, which will feed one soldier one month, twelve bushels will feed him twelve months…1,200,000 bushels will feed 100,000 troops for one year."[163]

June 11, 1861 (Tuesday)

The raising of troops across the state highlighted the need for training sites, places for young men to learn the art of war. Governor Brown worked to establish three primary sites: Camp Davis outside Savannah; Camp Stephens near Griffin; and opening on this day, the largest Georgia training location—more than sixty acres—Camp McDonald in Big Shanty.[164]

June 12, 1861 (Wednesday)

Folks in Thomas County took pride in one of their local units. "A *third* military company has made its appearance in Thomasville, under the command of Capt. [possibly I. D.] Dodd, who, by his usual energy and perseverance has succeeded in disciplining the boys of his school to an admirable degree.—For the want of a better name for the present we call them *Rebel Cadets*."[165]

June 13, 1861 (Thursday)

Across the South, folks paused to observe a day of fasting. A Columbus newspaper reminded readers of the day and opined on thoughts of the people of the North. "This recognition of our entire dependence upon the 'God of battles' and the necessity and duty of seeking His interposition in behalf of the cause of the Confederate States, is in striking contrast with the course of the vandals and infidels who blasphemously override the precepts and teachings of the Bible and appeal alone to the 'higher law' as the rule of their guidance and…causeless war of invasion…."[166]

June 14, 1861 (Friday)

The Confederate War Department, through General Samuel Cooper, continued their struggles with Governor Brown and equipping Georgia soldiers when leaving the state.

---

162 "To the Patriotic and Aspiring," *Atlanta Southern Confederacy*, June 9, 1861, sec. 3, https://gahistoricnewspapers.galileo.usg.edu/lccn/sn82014677/1861-06-09/ed-1/seq-3/.

163 "Can Bread the Army," *Columbus Daily Sun*, June 10, 1861, sec. 1, https://gahistoricnewspapers.galileo.usg.edu/lccn/sn82014939/1861-06-10/ed-1/seq-1/.

164 Smedlund, *Camp Fires of Georgia's Troops*, 201; Also see Shaffer, "History of Camp McDonald Park," http://www.campmcdonaldpark.org/history.html.

165 "Rebel Cadets," *Thomasville Southern Enterprise*, June 12, 1861, sec. 2, https://gahistoricnewspapers.galileo.usg.edu/lccn/sn88054090/1861-06-12/ed-1/seq-2/. Italics in original.

166 "Day of Fasting and Prayer," *Columbus Daily Sun*, June 13, 1861, sec. 3, https://gahistoricnewspapers.galileo.usg.edu/lccn/sn82014939/1861-06-13/ed-1/seq-3/.

"On the 10th instant Col. Z. T. Conner was telegraphed at Macon from this office, in answer to a tender of his regiment, that his regiment could not be accepted unless it was armed and equipped, and that the Governor of his State had declined to arm and equip it. On the 11th he telegraphed that he had everything but arms; that two companies arrived at Richmond and four on the way."[167]

June 15, 1861 (Saturday)

Governor Brown prepared to send another Georgia unit to Virginia, after receiving official acceptance from Secretary Walker. Walker wrote, "The Ninth Regiment of Georgia Volunteers will proceed to Richmond, where it will be mustered into service."[168] These soldiers would participate, for the duration of the war, in various eastern theater battles.

June 16, 1861 (Sunday)

The *Southern Confederacy* reported on Atlanta's contributions of soldiers in the early days of the war.

> We think this is a very fair showing for our city, and one which we have a right to be proud of; and when we consider the class of men of whom our companies are composed, we have additional reason to be proud. Many of them are wealthy. Many of them are married, and almost every one of them are our best and most substantial citizens. These men have gone into the ranks to serve their country from patriotic, and not from selfish or sordid motives. They are no hireling soldiery. It requires no Seer to foretell the result of a conflict, with such men in the field and such a cause as we have to fight for.[169]

June 17, 1861 (Monday)

Thomas Thomas sought to form a Georgia regiment and wrote to Alexander Stephens seeking his assistance. "If I can form my regiment…I can get them called into service and armed by the Gov. the third regiment from this time. The Gov. will do it if he has arms to arm three more…I understand him if three more are called mine shall be third. Will you do me the favour to see your company and ascertain if they wish to go with us for the war."[170] Thomas's unit did join the war, and later served as the 15th Georgia Infantry.

June 18, 1861 (Tuesday)

Camp McDonald buzzed with the influx of new volunteers, as Governor Brown, who took great pride in the training site, updated President Davis on Georgia's preparations for turning young men into soldiers. "I have General Phillips' brigade in camp of instruction. Will organize the mountain regiment next week. Will arm and equip both. They go for the war. My quartermasters have all they can do at present supplying brigade and preparing for next

---

[167] Candler, *Confederate Records of the State of Georgia*, 3:95.

[168] Ibid.

[169] "Atlanta and the War," *Atlanta Southern Confederacy*, June 16, 1861, sec. 2, https://gahistoricnewspapers.galileo.usg.edu/lccn/sn82014677/1861-06-16/ed-1/seq-2/.

[170] Toombs, Stephens, and Cobb, *Correspondence*, 570; Sifakis, *Compendium of the Confederate Armies*, 213.

regiment."[171]

June 19, 1861 (Wednesday)

A newspaper in Macon ran a story from the *Southern Episcopalian*, one reminding the soldiers of their Christian duties.

> You go forth at your country's call, to uphold your country's honor and preserve her institutions. Cherish a deep feeling of dependence on Almighty God, who alone can shield you in the hour of danger, and crown your mission with success. Remember the Sabbath day, and endeavor to keep it holy unto the Lord. Be sure to carry your Bible with you, and use it as a book given to men to be a lamp to their feet and a light unto their path. Seek to make your camp a Christian camp, where daily prayer shall be offered to Cod. Allow no vindictive or revengeful passion to have a place in your heart.[172]

June 20, 1861 (Thursday)

Citizens in Savannah received notification, via the *Daily Morning News*, of two opportunities to serve. The Confederate States Navy provided one option, but for those inclined to seasickness, boots on the ground offered another option. "Wanted. Two Thousand able bodied men, for the service of the State of Georgia, to serve for three years, unless sooner discharged by Competent authority. Said recruits are needed for such defensive service as the public security in this or neighboring States may demand."[173]

June 21, 1861 (Friday)

Five Native American Nations supported the Confederacy during the war: the Cherokee, Chickasaw, Choctaw, Creek, and Seminole peoples. Georgians learned today that "C. [Cyrus] Harris, Governor of the Chickasaw nation…proclaims the independence of the nation of the Federal Government, and calls upon all the warriors over eighteen and under forty-five years of age to organize at once into companies, battalions and regiments for the war, to be ready for service at a minute's warning. All over forty-five are advised to organize in a Home Guard."[174]

June 22, 1861 (Saturday) ●

The *Upson Pilot* in Thomaston shared an account from the *Chronicle and Sentinel* in Augusta, one posing thoughts on the early disagreements between Governor Brown and President Davis. "So far as we know, the Governor of Georgia is the only State Executive that has yet come in conflict with the President, as to the powers of each in relation to the war, or that has chosen to set up his authority as Supreme over the President's, in a State or that

---

[171] Candler, *Confederate Records of the State of Georgia*, 3:96.

[172] "To Our Volunteers," *Macon Georgia Journal and Messenger*, June 19, 1861, sec. 1, https://gahistoricnewspapers.galileo.usg.edu/lccn/sn85038491/1861-06-19/ed-1/seq-1/.

[173] "Wanted," *Savannah Daily Morning News*, June 20, 1861, sec. 2, https://gahistoricnewspapers.galileo.usg.edu/lccn/sn82015886/1861-06-20/ed-1/seq-2/.

[174] "Chickasaw Secession," *Columbus Daily Sun*, June 21, 1861, sec. 1, https://gahistoricnewspapers.galileo.usg.edu/lccn/sn82014939/1861-06-21/ed-1/seq-1/.

has assumed to declare an act of the Confederate Congress, sanctioned by the President, as unconstitutional and an invasion of State rights.[175]

June 23, 1861 (Sunday)

Words from the editor of the *Savannah Republican*: "Georgia commenced the work of reform in the Constitution adopted by her late Convention; let the people ratify, and our legislators persevere in the good work. We need no monarchy, constitutional or any other sort. We are competent to govern ourselves."[176]

June 24, 1861 (Monday)

"Some of our citizens—yea, many of them—have acted nobly and generously in *contributing* a fund for the support of the families of our soldiers who have gone to fight our battles; but, sorry to say it, in *distributing* that fund, they do not seem to be governed in every instance by those principles of generosity that we have a right to expect at their hands."[177] Alas, while most folks performed honest deeds, the deceitful among them sought personal gain.

June 25, 1861 (Tuesday)

Governor Brown wrote Vice President Stephens regarding the state's emphasis on training and arming men for battle. "I. . .have to equip Genl. Phillips's brigade and another regiment which is to rendezvous here next Monday, it will be impossible for me to supply the coast regiment till probably some time in August. The regiment to rendezvous on Monday will be the 10th [number of regiments from Georgia thus far]. These have all been fully armed accoutred [*sic*] and equipped *by the state*. I send them into the field with full outfit."[178]

June 26, 1861 (Wednesday)

Captain William G. Gill, an artillery officer, wrote Major Josiah Gorgas, Chief of Ordnance for the Confederacy, regarding a decision from the governor. "Governor Brown just ordered the arsenal-keeper not to issue anything to the order of a Confederate officer for the present. This locks up half a million caps and stops cartridge-making. I should like to see you and explain matters about the State ordnance."[179]

June 27, 1861 (Thursday)

In a letter containing a civil tone, which proved infrequent in discourse between the governor and the president, Brown wrote to Davis, "I am greatly obliged by the assurances received from you that my course in reference to the arms belonging to the State of Georgia meets your approval. I am sending into the Confederate service as fast as possible Georgia Regiments fully armed and equipped. This I shall continue to do as long as I have men

---

[175] "Col Bartow and Gov. Brown," *Thomaston Upson Pilot*, June 22, 1861, sec. 2, https://gahistoricnewspapers.galileo.usg.edu/lccn/sn85034395/1861-06-22/ed-1/seq-2/.

[176] "Monarchical Tendencies in the South," *Savannah Republican*, June 23, 1861, sec. 1, https://gahistoricnewspapers.galileo.usg.edu/lccn/sn87062330/1861-06-23/ed-1/seq-1/.

[177] "Give Us This Day Our Daily Bread," *Columbus Daily Sun*, June 24, 1861, sec. 3, https://gahistoricnewspapers.galileo.usg.edu/lccn/sn82014939/1861-06-24/ed-1/seq-3/.

[178] Toombs, Stephens, and Cobb, *Correspondence*, 571. Italics in original.

[179] Candler, *Confederate Records of the State of Georgia*, 3:98.

with guns, but I can only consent that the arms belonging to the State leave the State under my direction."[180]

June 28, 1861 (Thursday)

Big Shanty received a visitor, as Governor Brown inspected Camp McDonald. He notified Secretary Walker on conditions at the site.

> I have a fine brigade of State troops now in camp at this place. The brigade is organized under an act of our State Legislature for the defense of the State. It is a fine body of men, consisting of two regiments, armed with muskets, model of 1842; one battalion of rifles, armed with new Harper's Ferry rifles; one battalion (four companies) of artillery, armed with muskets of model of 1842, and now being practiced in the school of the piece, with a half battery of artillery; also a battalion of cavalry (four companies), well armed and on good horses.[181]

June 29, 1861 (Saturday) ◐

Secretary Walker notified Major Gorgas to allow the governor his portion of ordnance supplies. "I think the facts show that Governor Brown is entitled to 29,000 pounds of powder in the arsenal [in Augusta], and you will, therefore, direct it to be delivered to him."[182]

June 30, 1861 (Sunday)

Governor Brown received a call for troops from Secretary Walker. "The President deems it prudent, if not essential to the public safety, to form and organize a reserved arms corps of 30,000 men, and to apportion to Georgia the quota of 3,000." Brown also learned of the need to raise cavalry units. "In addition to the above requisition the Confederate States will need from Georgia two companies of cavalry, numbering from 60 to 100 men each, in order to complete the army corps contemplated by the President."[183] Many of the things suggested in Walker's letter, like the establishment of training camps, Brown had already completed.

July 1, 1861 (Monday)

Governor Brown received a follow-up letter from Secretary Walker regarding the raising of Georgia regiments. Walker wrote, "it has been deemed essential by the President, under all the circumstances at present surrounding the Government, that several other regiments from the States should be speedily gotten into the field. Georgia has never yet hesitated to give a patriotic response to calls made upon her by this Government for troops, and the President has no fears that she will hesitate or falter now."[184]

July 2, 1861 (Tuesday)

---

[180] Ibid.

[181] Ibid., 3:101–102.

[182] Ibid., 3:103.

[183] Ibid., 3:104–105.

[184] Ibid., 3:106.

Governor Brown responded to Secretary Walker's inquiry of drawing arms from Georgia. "In reply to your dispatch asking explanation about the arsenal at Savannah, I state that the arsenal and its contents are the property of the State. I can only permit supplies to be issued from it by a State officer under State authority, for which receipts must be given by a Confederate officer if he receives the supplies."[185] Georgia voters went to the polls and ratified the state's new Constitution.

July 3, 1861 (Wednesday)

Voters in Columbus received early local returns on the statewide vote on the new Constitution. "Ratification; 139; No Ratification, 102, being a majority of 37 for the former. The excitement created by the war overshadows everything, and comparatively little interest was manifested in the election."[186]

July 4, 1861 (Thursday) (Independence Day)

President Davis spent part of his day penning a message to Governor Brown. "Can you furnish a volunteer regiment five companies mounted and five on foot? The mounted companies to be armed with breech-loading carbines, the foot companies to be armed with rifles. If agreeable and consistent, I wish you to give this regiment priority in the issue of arms and equipments."[187]

July 5, 1861 (Friday)

Georgians continued to prepare at the various sites in the state in anticipation of the word to board the trains for Virginia. Governor Brown focused a great deal of effort on Camp McDonald in Big Shanty. Often, the governor would camp amongst the soldiers and conduct inspections. Just a few weeks after training began in earnest in the state, on this day, Brown wrote President Davis, "Shall I send General Phillips' brigade to Bristol?"[188] Phillips commanded Camp McDonald, and Bristol served as a stop on the route from Georgia to Virginia.

July 6, 1861 (Saturday)

The reply of Governor Brown to Secretary Walker regarding the previous call on Georgia to supply 3,000 soldiers to the Confederate army: "I will, if in my power, furnish the two companies of cavalry, armed and equipped. Having loaned the President 500 Sharps carbines for cavalry in Virginia, and having armed the battalion of cavalry now in the service of the State at Camp McDonald, I fear I may find it difficult to arm and equip the companies now required."[189]

July 7, 1861 (Sunday)

Prior to the American Civil War, William Hardee published a military manual that gained

[185] Ibid., 3:107.

[186] "Vote on the New Constitution," *Columbus Daily Sun*, July 3, 1861, sec. 3, https://gahistoricnewspapers.galileo.usg.edu/lccn/sn82014939/1861-07-03/ed-1/seq-3/. Final tally 11,499 for; 10,704 against (T. Bryan, *Confederate Georgia*, 14).

[187] Candler, *Confederate Records of the State of Georgia*, 3:107.

[188] Ibid., 3:108.

[189] Ibid., 3:109.

widespread use during the war, as officers blue and gray studied the work. Popularity turned to piracy as counterfeit copies of *Hardee's Tactics* surfaced. A newspaper editor in Atlanta wrote Hardee's manual proved "one of the most valuable military works on Infantry and Rifle tactics that ever was published in this or any other country." He then announced, "We are informed that attorneys in this State have been employed to prosecute all persons who shall hereafter sell any copies of the spurious editions."[190]

July 8, 1861 (Monday)

Governor Brown wrote to Vice President Stephens with an update on happenings in Georgia. "I am spending most of my time in the camp of Genl. Phillips's brigade seven miles above Marietta on the State Road. I am trying to recruit my health a little by camp life, and feel some benefit by it. I now have at the camp two regiments and three battalions fully armed and equipped. The organization is in strict conformity to the statute of the state." Brown further stated of Camp McDonald, "Genl. [Henry] Wayne and Maj. [Francis] Capers are both at the camp assisting in the training of the troops, and Wayne says he has never seen a body of troops improve so fast."[191]

July 9, 1861 (Tuesday)

Sermons from pulpits across the nation evoked patriotic spirit and encouraged volunteers to enlist. Milledgeville proved no different. "The Pastors of the several Churches in this city have, during the last week, been holding, and desire to continue on alternate mornings at 8 o'clock, special Prayer meetings of one hour for the country. The interest manifested has been quite encouraging."[192]

July 10, 1861 (Wednesday)

Responding to calls for more soldiers, Governor Brown "has ordered two more regiments of Georgia Volunteers to rendezvous at Atlanta, on Monday, the 15th instant.—Each regiment will contain ten companies."[193]

July 11, 1861 (Thursday)

The Confederate War Department and President Davis continued to disagree with Governor Brown on military matters. Secretary Walker wrote to Brown, "No right is claimed by the President to require the Governors of the States to aid in this mode of raising an army, but it was supposed a request would be followed by co-operation. If, therefore, instead of companies you prefer to tender regiments, organized by yourself, so be it, and I hope your preference will cause no delay or loss of efficiency from pursuing that plan."[194]

July 12, 1861 (Friday)

---

[190] "Hardee's Tactics," *Southern Confederacy*, July 7, 1861, sec. 2, https://gahistoricnewspapers.galileo.usg.edu/lccn/sn82014677/1861-07-07/ed-1/seq-2/.

[191] Toombs, Stephens, and Cobb, *Correspondence*, 572.

[192] "Prayer for the Country," *Milledgeville Southern Recorder*, July 9, 1861, sec. 2, https://gahistoricnewspapers.galileo.usg.edu/lccn/sn82016415/1861-07-09/ed-1/seq-2/.

[193] "More Troops," *Columbus Daily Sun*, July 10, 1861, sec. 2, https://gahistoricnewspapers.galileo.usg.edu/lccn/sn82014939/1861-07-10/ed-1/seq-2/.

[194] Candler, *Confederate Records of the State of Georgia*, 3:113.

Tensions heightened between the governor and Secretary Walker. Walker's terse words to Brown: "The crisis of our fate may depend upon your action. The two regiments you have organized are indispensable to success. For the sake of our cause and the country I beseech you to send them, without standing upon the point of the brigade organization. The President has no power to accept brigade. If you refuse you will regret it."[195]

July 13, 1861 (Saturday)

Seeking to make amends with the governor over a newspaper article, which appeared in Richmond regarding the continuing disagreements between Brown and the Confederate War Department, Walker avowed, "I may frankly say to you, in this unofficial manner, that there is no difference that I am aware of between the President and myself in regard to yourself. We both entertain, I am sure, the most cordial feelings of respect for your character, patriotism and public services…."[196]

July 14, 1861 (Sunday) ◑

Offering a rare Sunday dispatch, Governor Brown continued to struggle with President Davis's refusal to accept Brigadier General William Phillips into Confederate service as a general. So, to Davis, he declared, "I do not feel authorized by our statute to disband the brigade. If the act of Congress is in the way you can accept it as a whole by commissioning the general now in command."[197]

July 15, 1861 (Monday)

Holding his ground with the war department, Brown fired a return salvo in the direction of Richmond. "No truthful statement…will show that Georgia suffers by a comparison of the part she has performed in the contest with that of any one of her Confederate sisters. While she has a man and a gun she will continue to do more than her equal part. If the threat of consequences to me for disobedience to your behests…is intended, rest assured it fails to intimidate."[198]

July 16, 1861 (Tuesday)

Trying to make amends, Secretary Walker offered an olive branch: "You wholly misapprehend the purpose and spirit of my telegram…it not only did not contain a threat, but was not intended to convey one. My sole object was to make an appeal to your well-known patriotism, based upon facts known to the Department, but which it would be highly impolitic to make public."[199]

July 17, 1861 (Wednesday)

Newspapers fanned patriotic flames; some held fast during the earlier portion of the war while others remained resolute until the end. "Georgia…is likely to become the Empire State in war as well as in peace, and will, if her sons now in the field but respond to the high expectation of her people. Besides the many thousands of volunteer troops now under

---

[195] Ibid., 3:114.
[196] Ibid., 3:115.
[197] Ibid., 3:116.
[198] Ibid., 3:117.
[199] Ibid., 3:118.

drill in every part of the State, we have in Virginia and on the way, nearly double the number of any other State, excepting of course Virginia herself." The editor suggested, "The great difficulty is in restraining our people, not in getting them to leave their homes for the hardships of war."[200]

July 18, 1861 (Thursday)

Georgia needed weapons, so the governor issued a statewide proclamation.

> Whereas, it is believed that there are many old military guns of one kind and another scattered over the State, and not in the possession of organized volunteer companies, which, by being collected and altered from flint and steel to percussion, or otherwise repaired if necessary, could be made serviceable in the present crisis. I, therefore, issue this my proclamation calling upon all good and loyal citizens of the State to make diligent enquiry and search for such guns, being the property of the State, and to collect them up wherever found and deliver them to the Clerk of the Superior Court of each county; and as a compensation therefor, I will cause to be paid to said Clerks the sum of two dollars for each gun (which can be repaired and made fit for use) so delivered to him and forwarded to the Military Storekeeper, at Milledgeville.[201]

July 19, 1861 (Friday)

A Rome newspaper editor suggested readers seek the "bright side" of war: "There are times and circumstances in the development and history of all nations when wars are beneficial, if not absolutely necessary. This may appear strange and paradoxical to many, yet war has had its advocates in all ages of the world. So far as the South is concerned, there is reason to believe that the present war will be specially useful."[202]

July 20, 1861 (Saturday)

On occasion, Governor Brown's generosity showed. "I have offered all the saltpeter and sulphur and the steamer *Huntress* to the Secretary of War, together, at original cost to the State in cash. If he accepts my proposition I will order it shipped to you direct."[203]

July 21, 1861 (Sunday) ●

Communities worked to fill the ranks of the Confederate armies, and adjacent counties and even states often afforded more opportunities for young men to volunteer. "Troup county has sent five companies to the field, the last being the Ben Hill Infantry. And now Troups and her neighbor across the river, (Chambers county, Alabama) are making up another company to be called the Ben Hill Guard."[204]

---

[200] "The Banner State," *Sandersville Central Georgian*, July 17, 1861, https://gahistoricnewspapers.galileo.usg.edu/lccn/sn85034105/1861-07-17/ed-1/seq-2/.

[201] Candler, *Confederate Records of the State of Georgia*, 2:45–46.

[202] "The Bright Side of the Question," *Rome Tri-Weekly Courier*, July 19, 1861, sec. 2, https://gahistoricnewspapers.galileo.usg.edu/lccn/sn82014071/1861-07-19/ed-1/seq-2/.

[203] Candler, *Confederate Records of the State of Georgia*, **[vol?]**:118–19.

[204] "July 21, 1861," *Daily Augusta Chronicle & Sentinel*, July 21, 1861, sec. 1, Genealogybank.com.

July 22, 1861 (Monday)
Governor Brown could not spend all his days at Camp McDonald in Big Shanty, so he tapped a local man to serve as an assistant. "William H. Hunt of Cobb County be, and he is hereby appointed Aide-de-Camp to the Commander-in Chief, and that a commission issue to him accordingly. By Order of the Governor and Commander-in-Chief."[205]

July 23, 1861 (Tuesday)
A newspaper editor's message urged support of President Davis's call for steadfastness after the Battle of First Manassas/Bull Run: "Let the people everywhere, make ready to respond to the calls that must soon be made for more troops. Georgia has already sent to the field over twenty regiments, and is able to send twenty more. Let us be ready to respond at once to the additional call, which the President says will be made to meet the half million of thieving vandals which Lincoln's Congress has called out."[206]

July 24, 1861 (Wednesday)
An Atlanta military unit struggled financially, prompting a local man to dig into his coffers. "Mr. John S. Wright of this city, when apprised of the destitute condition of the Gate City Guards, procured, and sent to them…eighty, one dollar gold pieces—being one dollar for each man of the company. If this is not genuine whole souled Southern patriotism, we don't know the meaning of the term."[207] Robert Toombs resigned from President Davis's cabinet and joined the Army of Northern Virginia.

July 25, 1861 (Thursday)
In the immediate aftermath of the Battle of First Manassas/Bull Run, Georgians attended special church services to pause, offer praise, and pray. "Remember that this afternoon at 5 o'clock we meet at the Baptist Church, to pray for our Country and Soldiers. Let us all attend who can, to thank God for what he has done for us, and to pray for the distressed soldiers and friends of soldiers."[208]

July 26, 1861 (Friday)
Governor Brown called on Georgians, appealing "to the people in each county of this State having one Representative in the Legislature to form one volunteer company of eight rank and file, and to each having two Representatives to form two companies, and to arm said companies with country rifles of good substance and heavy barrel, and to notify me in each case, as soon as the guns are collected, that I may have them repaired at the expense of the State…."[209]

---

[205] Candler, *Confederate Records of the State of Georgia*, 2:47.

[206] "The President's Message," *Atlanta Southern Confederacy*, July 23, 1861, https://gahistoricnewspapers.galileo.usg.edu/lccn/sn82014677/1861-07-23/ed-1/seq-2/.

[207] "80 Gold Dollars," *Southern Confederacy*, July 24, 1861, sec. 3, https://gahistoricnewspapers.galileo.usg.edu/lccn/sn82014677/1861-07-24/ed-1/seq-3/; Phillips, *Life of Robert Toombs*, 237.

[208] "Union Prayer Meeting," *Columbus Daily Sun*, July 25, 1861, sec. 3, https://gahistoricnewspapers.galileo.usg.edu/lccn/sn82014939/1861-07-25/ed-1/seq-3/.

[209] Candler, *Confederate Records of the State of Georgia*, 2:49.

July 27, 1861 (Saturday)
Residents of Rome read of a new military unit forming in the city. "A Regiment is now being organized.... It will consist of ten companies of Light Infantry...Colonel, Hon. J. W. H. Underwood...to be selected with reference to military education. Companies desiring to go will report at once...at Rome...we have the authority of the Secretary of War for stating, that the Regiment will he ordered into immediate service, as soon as armed and organized."[210]

July 28, 1861 (Sunday)
The *Southern Confederacy* in Atlanta reported Governor Brown planned a trip to Camp McDonald and encouraged folks to turn out and "witness a grand brigade."[211]

July 29, 1861 (Monday) ◐
Georgians continued to answer the call to arms, as newspapers carried recruiting messages in prominent style. "Ten Dollars Bounty will be paid to every private enlisting in the ranks of the Georgia Guards, upon being mustered into the service of the State. Arms (Minie Muskets) and a handsome and serviceable uniform, being furnished with comfortable quarters on application to...[Dexter] D. B. Thompson."[212]

July 30, 1861 (Tuesday)
During the war, citizens at home would read daily newspapers to learn, sometimes in horror, of casualties from recent battles. Learning of the loss of a loved one must have proven exceedingly difficult. Soon after the Battle of First Manassas/Bull Run, names of the killed, wounded, and missing started to appear. On this day, folks in Columbus took the *Daily Sun*, and with a white-knuckled grip, scanned the front page for casualties from the following Georgia companies: the Coweta 2d District Guards, Atlanta Confederate Guards, Paulding Volunteers, Cobb Confederate Guards, Dekalb Light Infantry, Iverson Invincibles, Franklin Volunteers, Roswell Guards, Cobb Mountaineers, and the Davis Infantry.[213]

July 31, 1861 (Wednesday)
Gabriel Toombs, brother of Robert, sought assistance from Vice President Stephens. Gabriel asked Stephens for "your cooperation with me in trying to induce my brother to resign the office of General in the army. He has never been educated in the science of war and has no experience in the business, and besides is physically unfit for camp life. Since his last severe attack of rheumatism he has but little use of one of his arms, and his throat and lungs have been so much affected this winter and spring as to give his friends great solicitude for

---

[210] "Companies Wanted Immediately," *Rome Tri-Weekly Courier*, July 27, 1861, sec. 3, https://gahistoricnewspapers.galileo.usg.edu/lccn/sn85034102/1861-07-27/ed-1/seq-3/.

[211] "A Brigade Review," *Atlanta Southern Confederacy*, July 28, 1861, sec. 3, https://gahistoricnewspapers.galileo.usg.edu/lccn/sn82014677/1861-07-28/ed-1/seq-3/.

[212] "Attention Georgia Guards!," *Columbus Daily Sun*, July 29, 1861, sec. 3, https://gahistoricnewspapers.galileo.usg.edu/lccn/sn82014939/1861-07-29/ed-1/seq-3/.

[213] "A Correct List of the Killed and Wounded of the Seventh Georgia Regiment," *Columbus Daily Sun*, July 30, 1861, sec. 1, https://gahistoricnewspapers.galileo.usg.edu/lccn/sn82014939/1861-07-30/ed-1/seq-1/.

him."[214]

August 1, 1861 (Thursday)

In a move not repeated often, Governor Brown ceded to President Davis's prerogative of naming generals. "In view of the emergency I am obliged to yield the brigade organization, as I am determined to send the troops to the field. I consolidate the rifle battalion and cavalry and form a legion, which General Phillips will command as colonel. You consent that the artillery battalion of five companies, all armed with muskets, and half a battery of brass pieces, be attached to the legion, and would you give three more guns to complete the battery?"[215]

August 2, 1861 (Friday)

Adopting an uncharacteristic tone of appreciation, especially in communications with Governor Brown, President Davis responded to Brown's bending to the wishes of the president. "Thanks for decision as to the troops. The riflemen and calvary [*sic*]—say ten companies—can be well organized as a voltigeur [light infantry] regiment, but if there be five companies of each it is not well to organize artillery with infantry...we have need of all the armed troops you can send. Let the troops now offered proceed to Lynchburg...."[216]

August 3, 1861 (Saturday)

Action—or lack thereof—in the Confederate Congress impacted the coastal region of Georgia. "Committee on Military Affairs...[reported] a resolution inquiring into the expediency of authorizing the President to instruct the military officers in command of the several departments to prevent the accumulation of cotton at the various ports of the Confederacy during the blockade, reported that the committee deemed the proposed legislation as unnecessary...."[217]

August 4, 1861 (Sunday)

Financial matters proved challenging during the war, but occasional efforts sought to ease mounting problems. "The banks in Richmond and those in Savannah, including the branches of each, have made arrangements by which their notes will be received by each other at par. Volunteers and others may now go directly to the banks of the two cities and [receive] full value of their money. Cannot a similar arrangement be made between the banks in other cities?"[218]

August 5, 1861 (Monday)

Institutions of higher learning, along with other entities, participated in financing the war. "The Board of Trustees of Mercer University have resolved by an unanimous vote to invest $5,000 in the Confederate Loan. This is patriotic and praise-worthy. All hail to the noble

---

[214] Toombs, Stephens, and Cobb, *Correspondence*, 573.

[215] Candler, *Confederate Records of the State of Georgia*, 3:119–20.

[216] Ibid., 3:120.

[217] *Journal of the Confederate Congress*, August 3, 1861, 1:311–312.

[218] "Important Arrangement," *Augusta Chronicle*, August 4, 1861, sec. 3, Genealogybank.com.

University."[219]

August 6, 1861 (Tuesday)

The U.S. Congress passed the First Confiscation Act. From this point forward, as Federal troops progressed deeper into Southern territory, former slaves—those who safely made their way to federal lines—remained with the army and did not face a return to bondage.

> Be it enacted by the Senate and House of Representatives of the United States of America in Congress assembled, That if, during the present or any future insurrection against the Government of the United States, after the President of the United States shall have declared, by proclamation, that the laws of the United States are opposed, and the execution thereof obstructed, by combinations too powerful to be suppressed by the ordinary course of judicial proceedings, or by the power vested in the marshals by law, any person or persons, his, her, or their agent, attorney, or employé, shall purchase or acquire, sell or give, any property of whatsoever kind or description, with intent to use or employ the same, or suffer the same to be used or employed, in aiding, abetting, or promoting such insurrection or resistance to the laws, or any person or persons engaged therein; or if any person or persons, being the owner or owners of any such property, shall knowingly use or employ, or consent to the use or employment of the same as aforesaid, all such property is hereby declared to be lawful subject of prize and capture wherever found; and it shall be the duty of the President of the United States to cause the same to be seized, confiscated, and condemned.[220]

August 7, 1861 (Wednesday)

Annoyed with Secretary Walker, Governor Brown sought intervention from President Davis. "I can get no response from the Secretary of War to my letters or telegrams about the two new camps of instruction which he requires. I have recommended commissaries, quartermasters and surgeons as he requested. All ready to order out the troops at once if officers are appointed to take charge of them. Will the appointments be made? When do you wish the 3,000 men ordered into camp? Please answer."[221]

August 8, 1861 (Thursday)

Certainly, the governor expected a response on his letter of the previous day to the president; he received one. "You dispatched the President I do not answer your telegrams or letters," Walker responded. "I have answered both."[222] Brown, among all Southern governors, proved the biggest thorn in the side of the Confederate government for the duration of the conflict. Brown believed the citizens had elected him to look out for Georgia's interests. He concerned himself little with happenings in other states.

August 9, 1861 (Friday)

---

219 "Mercer University," *Savannah Daily Morning News*, August 5, 1861, sec. 1, https://gahistoricnewspapers.galileo.usg.edu/lccn/sn82015886/1861-08-05/ed-1/seq-1/.

220 "The First Confiscation Act," http://www.freedmen.umd.edu/conact1.htm.

221 Candler, *Confederate Records of the State of Georgia*, 3:122.

222 Ibid.

Realizing he had struck a nerve with Secretary Walker, Brown telegraphed him. "Your letter I have not received; only got your telegram yesterday evening. It was dated, however, then, the 5th—the fault of the line, it seems, not your fault."[223]

August 10, 1861 (Saturday)

During the early days of the war, volunteers from across the South hurriedly made their way to Virginia. Occasionally visits from these regiments made local news. An editor in Columbus wrote of one such stopover. "We learn that about two hundred recruits for the various companies of the 11th Alabama Regiment, commanded by Col. [James] Cantey, will arrive here to-day, *en route* for Virginia to join the Regiment. They are mostly or entirely from Alabama. Edward Croft, Esq., acting as Quartermaster for the Regiment here, will receive them and provide for their trip."[224]

August 11, 1861 (Sunday)

Politics and partisanship served as the themes in an Atlanta editorial.

> The "neutral" Yankees of Georgia are about arranging matters so that, in the absence of Southern Rights men in Virginia, the aforesaid Puritans can hold the balance of power and elect the Governor. If the Yankees had displayed half as much generalship at Manassas as their "neutral" brethren are developing in Georgia, the result of that great engagement might have been different. Every Southern man who leaves for the wars is practically another vote gained to the Yankees. In the absence of our brave Southern boys, the Puritans will have the election all their own way. We therefore suggest, in order to counteract this "neutral" Yankee element, that the wife, mother and sister of each absent volunteer be allowed to vote for Governor.[225]

August 12, 1861 (Monday)

Everyone could find a way to contribute to the war effort, even young artisans. "We learn that a number of the youth of the city, of both sexes, animated with the desire to contribute something to the relief of indigent families of absent soldiers, will give a dramatic exhibition at Temperance Hall…the plays selected for the occasion are 'Toodles' and 'The Young Scamp.' They have been engaged for a considerable length of time in preparation, and will, no doubt, entertain all who may attend."[226]

August 13, 1861 (Tuesday) ◑

The *Southern Recorder* in Milledgeville carried a story titled "The Bitter Cup," which read in part, "Thus it will ever be in this unjustified war upon the South. Wretched Lincoln,

---

[223] Ibid.

[224] "Recruits for Col. Cantey," *Columbus Daily Sun*, August 10, 1861, sec. 3, https://gahistoricnewspapers.galileo.usg.edu/lccn/sn82014939/1861-08-10/ed-1/seq-3/.

[225] "A Cute Yankee Trick—Georgia Women versus Submissionists," *Atlanta Southern Confederacy*, August 11, 1861, https://gahistoricnewspapers.galileo.usg.edu/lccn/sn82014677/1861-08-11/ed-1/seq-2/.

[226] "Exhibition of the Young Folks," *Columbus Daily Sun*, August 12, 1861, sec. 3, https://gahistoricnewspapers.galileo.usg.edu/lccn/sn82014939/1861-08-12/ed-1/seq-3/.

miserable [Winfield] Scott, faithless Seward, and all the deluded Cabinet at Washington, will most assuredly have a bitter experience with which to daub the pages of history. Lincoln is the cause, by attempting to chain the South to his victorious Presidential carriage wheels."[227]

August 14, 1861 (Wednesday)

Early work on producing matériel started in Georgia. "We have been shown an officer's sword made by S. C. Talmadge & Bros., of Monticello. The blade is well tempered, and the scabbard and other fixtures well finished."[228]

August 15, 1861 (Thursday)

Despite the patriotic spirit of early volunteers, some deserted. A newspaper noted that a "list of names has been handed to our Capt. [A. C.] Jones of the 'Miller Grays,' for publication. It embraces a list of men who have joined the company, and while members were kindly treated and cared for, on taking up the line of march they refused to follow. The good men of the county would do well to keep an eye on such men."[229]

August 16, 1861 (Friday)

The Georgia Military Institute in Marietta could rest easy; their commandant would remain. "Col. F. W. Capers, Superintendent of the Georgia Military Institute, having accepted the command of a regiment organized at Atlanta, has declined…in accordance with the request of the Board of Inspectors and Gov. Brown and the impression of his colleagues, that the Institute would go down, if he left…has concluded to retain his position at the…Institute."[230]

August 17, 1861 (Saturday)

During the early stages of the conflict, units volunteered and prepared for war carrying diverse types of shoulder-arms. "Mr. George W. Lamar, of this city, is now raising a company, to be armed with shot guns, with bayonets attached, with an assurance that they will be received immediately into the service in Virginia. Such a company well armed, will do a vast amount of mischief in a close engagement. By the way, we were shown…a shot gun bayonet, invented by Dr. Nunn, of this city, that works to a charm and seems perfect in all respects."[231]

August 18, 1861 (Sunday)

A unit in Augusta received notice akin to other 1861 calls going to other companies in the

---

[227] "The Bitter Cup," *Milledgeville Southern Recorder*, August 13, 1861, sec. 3, https://gahistoricnewspapers.galileo.usg.edu/lccn/sn82016415/1861-08-13/ed-1/seq-3/.

[228] "Georgia Made Sword," *Athens Southern Banner*, August 14, 1861, sec. 2, https://gahistoricnewspapers.galileo.usg.edu/lccn/sn82014069/1861-08-14/ed-1/seq-2/.

[229] "Deserters!," *Albany Patriot*, August 15, 1861, sec. 3, https://gahistoricnewspapers.galileo.usg.edu/lccn/sn82014211/1861-08-15/ed-1/seq-3/.

[230] "Col. F. W. Capers," *Columbus Daily Sun*, August 16, 1861, sec. 2, https://gahistoricnewspapers.galileo.usg.edu/lccn/sn82014939/1861-08-16/ed-1/seq-2/.

[231] "A Shot Gun Company," *Savannah Republican*, August 17, 1861, sec. 2, https://gahistoricnewspapers.galileo.usg.edu/lccn/sn87062330/1861-08-17/ed-1/seq-2/.

state. "The members of the Baker Volunteers are hereby ordered to be at their quarters on MONDAY MORNING, 20th inst., prepared to go into camp."[232] This notice, from Captain Anthony F. Rudler, provided the first step for a company, which eventually mustered in as the 3rd Georgia Infantry Battalion.

August 19, 1861 (Monday)

The governor responded to a call for more soldiers from Georgia, and updated President Davis on his plans. "Under the requisition of the Secretary of War for 3,000 men to be thrown into camp of instruction at two different points in this State as Georgia's quota of 30,000 to be thrown into camp of instruction, I have ordered two regiments of 800 men each into camp at Camp McDonald, near Marietta. On Tuesday, the 27th instant, they will rendezvous. I have also ordered two regiments into camp at Camp Stephens, near Griffin, to rendezvous at the same time."[233]

August 20, 1861 (Tuesday) ●

"Now, therefore, I, Joseph E. Brown, Governor and Commander-in-Chief of the State of Georgia, do issue this, my Proclamation, declaring that the Constitution adopted by the Convention as Savannah, on the twenty-third day of March, in the year of our Lord one thousand eight hundred and sixty-one, is adopted and ratified by the people of the State of Georgia, and is now the Constitution of said State." The governor, via proclamation, made the new document official.[234]

August 21, 1861 (Wednesday)

Expressing his opinion on a gubernatorial election in a time of war, Governor Brown stated he "repudiates a Convention to nominate a candidate for Governor...that 'under existing circumstances' there is no necessity for such a Convention." He went on to "[denounce] Conventions because they are gotten up by 'cliques of village politicians, wire workers, and office seekers, meeting together in small numbers without the knowledge of the honest, laboring masses of the people' etc."[235]

August 22, 1861 (Thursday)

Governor Brown wrote to Vice President Stephens on wartime preparations in Georgia.

> I have sent 20½ regiments of Georgia state troops to the field fully armed, accoutred and equipped...add to this the six or seven independent regiments of which I have no record, and Georgia now has fully 25,000 troops in active service. On Tuesday next I am to throw two other regiments into camp of instruction at Camp McDonald, and two at Camp Stephens near Griffin, which I had called in honor of yourself.

---

[232] "Attention, Baker Volunteers!," *Augusta Chronicle*, August 18, 1861, sec. 2, Genealogybank.com. Caps in original.

[233] Candler, *Confederate Records of the State of Georgia*, 3:123.

[234] Ibid., 2:51.

[235] "Governor Brown's Letter," *Columbus Daily Times*, August 21, 1861, sec. 2, https://gahistoricnewspapers.galileo.usg.edu/lccn/sn82015388/1861-08-21/ed-1/seq-2/.

They will add 3,000 to the number now in the field. I feel that Georgia has not been backward in doing her full share and I trust she never will be.[236]

August 23, 1861 (Friday)

Enrollment efforts continued in Savannah, and other locales, as Georgia contributed her share of soldiers to the Confederate war effort. "Washington Volunteers: We are requested to state that this fine company, Capt. Jno. McMahon, now in camp on the parade ground, will receive a few more recruits."[237] The unit eventually mustered into the 1st Georgia Infantry Regiment.

August 24, 1861 (Saturday)

The editor of the *Rome Tri-Weekly Courier* offered a perspective on the election of a new governor: "Although there is a great deal of well founded objection to the Convention plan, of putting a candidate before the people, yet we do not at present see a better plan, by which to concentrate public opinion upon one man—which if it is not done, Gov. Brown will, in all probability, be again elected—from which we most earnestly pray to be delivered."[238]

August 25, 1861 (Sunday)

Folks in Augusta received notice of an opportunity to listen to a series of public talks regarding efforts to care for wounded Georgia soldiers. "Mr. [Rev. J. S.] Lamar will address the citizens of a portion of the counties of the fifth Congressional District...the object of these address...to present information on the condition and wants of our sick and wounded soldiers.... Let every body be present.... Whatever concerns the well being of our suffering soldiers, should and will be promptly attended to."[239]

August 26, 1861 (Monday)

Georgian Thomas R. R. Cobb gained approval of an amendment in the Confederate Congress. "The commander of every volunteer company shall have the privilege of receiving commutation for clothing at the rate of twenty-five dollars per man for every six months, when they shall have furnished their own clothing."[240] Cobb worked to strengthen recruiting efforts in Georgia and elsewhere across the Confederacy.

August 27, 1861 (Tuesday)

Things appeared headed the governor's way, as Secretary Walker's letter regarding the acceptance of military units suggests. "The regiment of Colonel [Elijah W.] Chastain may be added to the four you report under the requisitions recently made upon Georgia for 3,000 men, provided it be partially armed, as suggested by you. Your Excellency will oblige this Department by having these regiments equipped at the charge of this Government. The

---

[236] Toombs, Stephens, and Cobb, *Correspondence*, 574.

[237] "Washington Volunteers," *Savannah Daily Morning News*, August 23, 1861, sec. 2, https://gahistoricnewspapers.galileo.usg.edu/lccn/sn82015886/1861-08-23/ed-1/seq-2/.

[238] "Gubernatorial Convention," *Rome Tri-Weekly Courier*, August 24, 1861, sec. 2, https://gahistoricnewspapers.galileo.usg.edu/lccn/sn85034102/1861-08-24/ed-1/seq-2/.

[239] "Rev. J. S. Lamar's Appointments," *Augusta Chronicle*, August 25, 1861, sec. 3, Genealogybank.com.

[240] *Journal of the Confederate Congress*, August 26, 1861, 1:411.

quartermasters and commissaries nominated by you have been appointed."[241]

August 28, 1861 (Wednesday)

On a busy day in the Confederate Congress, one act recognized various regiments from across the South. "The Chair presented to Congress a communication from the President, transmitting the following nominations for appointments in the Provisional Army of the Confederate States."[242] The Georgia regiments listed were the 1st, 8th, 10th, 12th, 16th, 20th, 4th Battalion, and T. R. R. Cobb's Georgia Legion.

August 29, 1861 (Thursday)

"100,000 MEN WANTED: Now is the time to enlist. A determined resistance at this critical juncture, will do more to opn [*sic*] the eyes of the Lincoln government to the impossibility of subduing the South and the utter folly of these aggressions, than any plan we can adopt. They are blind to facts and deaf to arguments." The call on patriotism continued, "Let each man feel his individual responsibility, to join in a solid phalanx and force them from our soil, and if necessary invade their own, and by fire and sword, show them that the South is fully aroused."[243]

August 30, 1861 (Friday)

Railroads proved instrumental in carrying men and matériel during the war. Georgians learned of the completion of a new line. Of the Brunswick & Florida Railroad, readers discovered that "iron is now laid, and the cars running from Brunswick to Tebeauville...on the Atlantic & Gulf Railroad. The completion of this road will prove a great convenience to the coast travel, besides adding no little to the military facilities in lower Georgia. In case of invasion we can now transport troops from any portion of the State to every important point on the coast, in...twenty-four hours."[244]

August 31, 1861 (Saturday)

Secretary Walker received an update from the governor regarding uniforms for troops. Brown's secretary, H. H. Waters, wrote, "His Excellency now directs me to state that, while doubtful of his ability to procure any large quantity of the clothing needed for the soldiers during the coming winter, he will, nevertheless, do all in his power to carry out the views of your Department relative thereto, and will at once give the directions to the quartermaster-general's department of this State suggested in your letter."[245]

September 1, 1861 (Sunday)

Facing a run for another term as Georgia's governor, Joe Brown received criticism from several newspapers across the state. Augusta proved no exception. "Evidently the plot

[241] Candler, *Confederate Records of the State of Georgia*, 3:124–25.

[242] *Journal of the Confederate Congress*, August 28, 1861, 1:433.

[243] "100,000 Men Wanted," *Rome Tri-Weekly Courier*, August 29, 1861, sec. 2, https://gahistoricnewspapers.galileo.usg.edu/lccn/sn85034102/1861-08-29/ed-1/seq-2/.

[244] "The Brunswick & Florida Railroad," *Columbus Daily Times*, August 30, 1861, sec. 1, https://gahistoricnewspapers.galileo.usg.edu/lccn/sn82015388/1861-08-30/ed-1/seq-1/.

[245] Candler, *Confederate Records of the State of Georgia*, 3:125.

thickens as we come near the election day. Gov. Brown is a declared candidate for re election, though possibly he may reconsider the matter, and gracefully withdraw from the contest, as he ought to do, if for no other consideration, simply for this one—that he is now the almost sole obstacle to harmony and unity in Georgia."[246]

September 2, 1861 (Monday)

Dr. Julian J. Chisolm's *Manual of Medical Surgery* would provide helpful information to surgeons in the field. "We are indebted to the publisher, W. S. Jones, of Augusta, for a copy of this work. The publication was prompted by the desire to place it within the reach of young physicians, many of whom have entered our volunteer service. It treats of matters not generally discussed, except in large and ponderous volumes, inaccessible in the camp and on the battle field."[247]

September 3, 1861 (Tuesday)

Young men across the state, like Robert Wade in Rome, left their homes to join one of many new military companies. The local newspaper reported Wade "will leave here this evening by the 8 o'clock train, as a recruit to the Miller Rifles. Any one wishing to send letters to any of their friends by him, can do so by leaving them at the store of Perry & Lamkin."[248] Wade eventually mustered into the 8th Georgia Infantry.

September 4, 1861 (Wednesday)

Commander Charles Green of the USS *Jamestown* reported events surrounding the capture of a blockade runner off the coast of Savannah. "I overhauled the rebel schooner *Colonel Long*, of 14 tons burden, belonging to Charleston, S.C., this day, and after taking her cargo out, Scuttled her. After the order had been given to destroy her, one of her crew…informed me that her papers were concealed under the ceiling of the cabin…they were found. They consist of a Confederate coasting license…and a Confederate States' flag, which…is in my possession."[249]

September 5, 1861 (Thursday)

Thoughts from a member of the 13th Regiment, writing from his post on the coast: "A Georgian abroad will face death, and is a terror to his enemies—a Georgian at home knows no fear, and will give no quarters. Let the vassals of Lincoln remember this. A commission to fight under their tyrant north of the Potomac is equivalent to a death warrant on the soil of Georgia."[250]

September 6, 1861 (Friday)

---

[246] "The Election," *Augusta Chronicle*, September 1, 1861, sec. 2, Genealogybank.com.

[247] "Manual of Medical Surgery," *Columbus Daily Sun*, September 2, 1861, sec. 2, https://gahistoricnewspapers.galileo.usg.edu/lccn/sn82014939/1861-09-02/ed-1/seq-2/.

[248] "Robert Wade," *Rome Tri-Weekly Courier*, September 3, 1861, sec. 3, https://gahistoricnewspapers.galileo.usg.edu/lccn/sn85034102/1861-09-03/ed-1/seq-3/.

[249] *ORN*, ser. I, vol. 6:166–67.

[250] "Georgia Coast Defense—Thirteenth Regiment," *Savannah Daily Morning News*, September 5, 1861, sec. 1, https://gahistoricnewspapers.galileo.usg.edu/lccn/sn82015886/1861-09-05/ed-1/seq-1/.

Governor Brown ordered "That the sum of Five Thousand Dollars be forwarded to Doctors Henry F. Campbell and Joseph P. Logan, for the benefit of the Georgia Hospital for the sick and wounded in Virginia."[251] Known as General Hospital #16, the First Georgia Hospital in Richmond carried a rent of $300 a year, and Dr. Campbell managed the facility.

September 7, 1861 (Saturday)

"Capt. T. W. Alexander's company have orders to rendezvous at Griffin, and will leave this place [Rome] on Tuesday, 17th inst., at 11 o'clock. A few more recruits will be taken."[252] The officer and his soldiers mustered into the 29th Georgia Infantry.

September 8, 1861 (Sunday)

Governor Brown telegraphed Secretary Walker with a request for reinforcements. "There is much alarm here about the coast. Stronger force and vigorous action absolutely necessary. Will you increase the force and quicken the energy, or will you furnish funds to support troops and approbate prompt State action for that purpose? I wish to avoid all conflict of authority, but prompt action is indispensable. Please answer immediately."[253]

September 9, 1861 (Monday)

Governor Brown issued a proclamation addressing various military issues. "While I desire to act in perfect harmony with the Confederate authorities, I feel that the period will very soon have arrived when action on my part, as the Executive of the State, by the use of the military force of the State, acting as State Troops, for the defence of the coast, will be justified both by the language and spirit of the Constitution. It will then be my duty to act, and to act with promptness and vigor."[254]

September 10, 1861 (Tuesday)

Commenting on the governor's proclamation the previous day, the editor of the Daily Morning News in Savannah took a confident view of matters. "With our extensive fortifications and the force which can be speedily brought into the field, we will be able successfully to repulse any attack that the Lincoln vandals may be emboldened to make upon our State."[255]

September 11, 1861 (Wednesday) ◐

Assembling in Milledgeville, delegates from fifty-eight counties nominated Eugenius Nisbet during the gubernatorial convention.[256]

September 12, 1861 (Thursday)

---

[251] Candler, *Confederate Records of the State of Georgia*, 2:51–52; Calcutt, *Richmond's Wartime Hospitals*, 131.

[252] "Capt. T. W. Anderson," *Rome Tri-Weekly Courier*, September 7, 1861, sec. 3, https://gahistoricnewspapers.galileo.usg.edu/lccn/sn85034102/1861-09-07/ed-1/seq-3/.

[253] Candler, *Confederate Records of the State of Georgia*, 3:126.

[254] Ibid., 2:53–54.

[255] "Proclamation of Gov. Brown—Defense of the Coast," *Savannah Daily Morning News*, September 10, 1861, sec. 2, https://gahistoricnewspapers.galileo.usg.edu/lccn/sn82015886/1861-09-10/ed-1/seq-2/.

[256] T. Bryan, *Confederate Georgia*, 34.

Another company, this time the Georgia Foresters, answered the call. The troops of "Capt. W. W. [William] Billopp, from Doctortown, arrived in Savannah, and are located for the present at Camp Lawton, on the Parade Ground. This company is made up of citizens of Wayne and Appling counties, on the Altamaha river, and has been uniformed principally by a few patriotic citizens of Savannah."[257] This company would muster into the 29th Georgia Infantry.

September 13, 1861 (Friday)

"Company A, *Georgia Hussars*, Capt. J. F. Waring, mustering some seventy-five men, leave this morning for Virginia by a special train via Charleston."[258] This unit eventually mustered into the 20th Georgia Cavalry Battalion.

September 14, 1861 (Saturday)

"We have been asked whether our absent soldiers will be entitled to vote in the coming election for Governor, Legislators and Congressmen. We have no hesitation in saying they cannot. The statutes of the State prescribe a certain way in which ballots are to be received, and there can be no other without positive legislation."[259] Not until the presidential election of 1864 did some Northern states develop ways for federal soldiers to vote in the field.

September 15, 1861 (Sunday)

"Mr. H. W. Blake, of Hall county, has requested us to say that he will be one of ten men to give one thousand dollars...towards purchasing land in Hall county, with agricultural implements, provisions, &c., for the use of the families of all soldiers going to war from that county, who may need assistance. The property to remain in possession of such families during the war...in the event of any soldier being killed, his wife to remain in possession of it during her lifetime."[260] Generous Georgians!

September 16, 1861 (Monday)

"I hereby accept the tender of the Oconee Grays, with not less than fifty, nor more than eighty men, rank and file, armed with guns which they have collected in the county; and order them to report to Brigadier General Geo P. Harrison, at Savannah, who will receive and muster them into the service of the State, and place them in Camp of Instruction at some point near the Central Railroad...so soon as he can make the necessary arrangements...."[261] These soldiers eventually mustered into the 57th Georgia Infantry.

September 17, 1861 (Tuesday)

"Our community will not forget that on to-night the ladies of Savannah will give a

---

[257] "Georgia Foresters," *Savannah Daily Morning News*, September 12, 1861, sec. 2, https://gahistoricnewspapers.galileo.usg.edu/lccn/sn82015886/1861-09-12/ed-1/seq-2/.

[258] "Georgia Hussars," *Savannah Daily Morning News*, September 13, 1861, sec. 2, https://gahistoricnewspapers.galileo.usg.edu/lccn/sn82015886/1861-09-13/ed-1/seq-2/. Italics in original.

[259] "Voting of Absent Soldiers," *Savannah Daily Republican*, September 14, 1861, sec. 1, https://gahistoricnewspapers.galileo.usg.edu/lccn/sn87062330/1861-09-14/ed-1/seq-1/.

[260] "A Liberal Offer," *Augusta Chronicle*, September 15, 1861, sec. 2, Genealogybank.com.

[261] Candler, *Confederate Records of the State of Georgia*, 2:55–56.

representation of various tableaux [artistic presentation], at the Athenæum, for the benefit of our brave and gallant soldiers now in arms for the defence of our common country.... In the language of Vice President Stephens, '*remember the soldier!*'"[262] Many across Georgia responded early, and enthusiastically on behalf of the boys in gray.

September 18, 1861 (Wednesday) ●

Governor Brown responded to a request of General Albert Sidney Johnston, in Nashville, for additional arms from Georgia. "There are no arms belonging to the State at my disposal; all have been exhausted in arming the volunteers of the State now in the Confederate service in Virginia, at Pensacola, and on our own coast, in all, some twenty-three regiments. Georgia has now to look to the shot-guns and rifles in the hands of her people for coast defense and to guns which her gunsmiths are slowly manufacturing."[263] Flag Officer Samuel Francis Du Pont received command of a new naval squadron, the South Atlantic, and gained responsibility for patrolling the coast of Georgia.

September 19, 1861 (Thursday)

Delegates in the gubernatorial convention had nominated Judge Eugenius Nisbet to run against incumbent Brown. The editor of a Rome newspaper (which supported Nisbet) wrote of Brown,

> As to the many little skirmishes Gov. Brown has had with Generals, Colonels, Captains, &c., of late, the writer has nothing to say, being quite willing to admit that as it is very common in these contests, "nobody is hurt." Men very frequently "draw on their fancy for the facts" even in larger fights, and Gov. Brown evidently did so when he attacked by insinuation, Jeff. Davis, a man of Calhoun views, as being un-mindful of State Sovereignty. Governor, you were in a big fight then, and hurt nobody as bad as yourself. Let us all admit Gov. Brown to be a clever man—Judge Nesbit [*sic*] a greater, and President Davis greater than either.[264]

September 20, 1861 (Friday)

Governor Brown issued a proclamation exempting from service "all persons engaged as operatives in the manufacture, by machinery, of woolen or cotton goods and other articles used for military purposes, and all persons employed at furnaces in making of iron, or in rolling mills...."[265]

September 21, 1861 (Saturday)

The *Savannah Daily News* ran a story from the *Augusta Constitutionalist* on the initial stages of various shortages developing in Georgia.

---

[262] "The Tableaux To-Night," *Savannah Daily Morning News*, September 17, 1861, sec. 2, https://gahistoricnewspapers.galileo.usg.edu/lccn/sn82015886/1861-09-17/ed-1/seq-2/.

[263] Candler, *Confederate Records of the State of Georgia*, 3:127; U.S. Naval History Division, *Civil War Naval Chronology*, 1:27.

[264] "For Governor—Hon. Eugenius A. Nesbit of Bibb—The Reasons for Voting for Judge Nesbit," *Rome Tri-Weekly Courier*, September 19, 1861, sec. 2, https://gahistoricnewspapers.galileo.usg.edu/lccn/sn85034102/1861-09-19/ed-1/seq-2/.

[265] Candler, *Confederate Records of the State of Georgia*, 2:56.

> Armies can be raised, money can be obtained, supplies can be furnished, to aid in the effort to crush and subjugate the free and independent people of the South; but when the starving women and children are thrown out into the "wide, wide world," with no shelter from the mid-day sun, or from the dews of evening—with not even a morsel of food to sustain life—"no steps can be taken for their relief"—no friendly hand is stretched forth to comfort and to succor them—no effort is made to give them even the means of obtaining a livelihood! What a commentary upon an American community! But what can be expected of a Government and a people that make war upon innocent women and children? They have crushed out freedom of opinion, freedom of speech, and freedom of the press—in a word, everything but freedom to starve.[266]

September 22, 1861 (Sunday)

Newspapers continued to throw their support behind a choice for Georgia's next governor. "The Governor of Georgia should cooperate and harmoniously with the Confederate Government in all the war movements with which the State may be connected. Judge Nisbet has been so intimately associated with the Government, that he can readily do this. He should then, by all means, be the next Governor of Georgia."[267]

September 23, 1861 (Monday)

A local unit formed near Savannah made front-page news. "This corps, from Effingham county…are now stationed at Camp Harrison, near Whitesville, on the Central Railroad. They number sixty-eight men, rank and file, and are as fine looking a body of men as we have seen."[268] The "Georgia Rangers," mustered into the 54th Georgia Infantry.

September 24, 1861 (Tuesday)

A recruiting officer advertised in the pages of the Rome newspaper. "I want some thirty or thirty-five recruits, for the 'Berry Infantry,' and wish to return with them in a few days. No company is blessed with a better set of officers."[269] These soldiers eventually mustered into the 29th Georgia Infantry.

September 25, 1861 (Wednesday)

Governor Brown and Secretary Benjamin exchanged messages regarding Georgia soldiers needed in their home state. Brown wrote,

> Colonel [Marcellus] Stovall, whose battalion is at Lynchburg, is here. Cannot send another gun out of the State. I ask that you order his battalion back to Brunswick on the coast, and I will fill it up to a regiment in the State. I also request that five other armed companies of Georgia troops be ordered back to the coast without delay, as an

---

[266] "Freedom to Starve," *Savannah Daily Morning News*, September 21, 1861, sec. 1, https://gahistoricnewspapers.galileo.usg.edu/lccn/sn82015886/1861-09-21/ed-1/seq-1/.

[267] "Harmony of Action," *Augusta Daily Constitutionalist*, September 22, 1861, sec. 2, Genealogybank.com.

[268] "Georgia Rangers," *Savannah Daily Morning News*, September 23, 1861, https://gahistoricnewspapers.galileo.usg.edu/lccn/sn82015886/1861-09-23/ed-1/seq-1/.

[269] "Soldiers Wanted," *Rome Tri-Weekly Courier*, September 24, 1861, sec. 3, https://gahistoricnewspapers.galileo.usg.edu/lccn/sn85034102/1861-09-24/ed-1/seq-3/.

> invasion of the coast is looked for daily and you have nearly all the State guns in the Confederate service

Benjamin responded, "Have sent orders to Maj. [James] Shackelford, as requested. Have ordered Bartow Artillery Company to Savannah to report to [Brigadier] General [Alexander] Lawton. Am reliably informed that the enemy will attack Brunswick. Be prepared."[270]

September 26, 1861 (Thursday)

Shareholders of the Brunswick & Florida Railroad in southeast Georgia lacked the funds to keep the line running. The war had hindered their ability to access financing from Northern banks, so they turned to the governor and asked the state to take temporary control of the railroad. Brown accepted their request and responded,

> Therefore...considering that it is a military necessity that the said railroad should be taken possession of and controlled by State authority as a means of public defense, I have, as Governor of Georgia and Commander-in-Chief of the army and navy of this State, and of the Militia thereof, taken charge of said railroad, to hold and manage the same, and to repair, run and place upon it in addition to what the company already has, such motive power, rolling stock and machinery, as the business of the road may from time to time require, and the exigencies of the public service may, in my opinion, demand, until such time as I may think proper to again leave the management of said road to said company, and to hold and conduct the same in such way as I deem compatible with the public service.[271]

September 27, 1861 (Friday) ◐

Governor Brown ordered, "That the German Artillery, a Volunteer Corps in Macon, Ga., Capt. Frederick H. Burghard, prepare and hold themselves in readiness to march on the twenty fourth day of October next, to the Sea Coast, or to such other place in Georgia as the exigencies of the service may require...."[272]

September 28, 1861 (Saturday)

Governor Brown wrote to Vice President Stephens regarding the upcoming gubernatorial election in Georgia. The governor tried to clear the waters mudding his relationship with the Confederate government.

> Our state is happily a unit (or so nearly so that the opposition amounts to nothing) in the support of President Davis and yourself, and I shall be the last man in Georgia to attempt to create any division on that subject. In my published documents and in my speeches to troops I have invariably said that you ought both to be elected by unanimous acclamation. I thought so then; I think so now. It is true I did not think the President did full justice to the Georgia brigade and I was independent enough to say so, but at the same time I have said that his acts generally have met my highest

---

[270] Candler, *Confederate Records of the State of Georgia*, 3:128–29.

[271] Ibid., 2:64–65.

[272] Ibid., 2:57.

approval and that I should support him warmly and heartily and oppose all opposition to him. All will tell you that I have been your constant advocate and supporter.[273]

September 29, 1861 (Sunday)

Secretary Benjamin requested information on the various military camps in Georgia from the governor.

> I have now the honor to request Your Excellency to furnish to this Department a statement of the location of these camps of instruction, the names by which they are called, the post-offices by which they may be addressed, and the number and organization of the troops there encamped under the call referred to. I would also respectfully request the favor of Your Excellency to furnish, so far as may be within your knowledge, a similar list of any other camps of instruction which may have been established within your State.[274]

September 30, 1861 (Monday)

Brigadier General Robert Toombs wrote of President Davis to Vice President Stephens, "I never knew as incompetent [an] executive officer. As he has been to West Point...I suppose he necessarily knows everything about it. The army is dying. I don't mean the poor fellows who go under the soil on the roadside, but the army as an army is dying, and it will not survive the winter. Set this down in your book, and set down opposite to it its epitaph, "died of West Point."[275]

October 1, 1861 (Tuesday)

Secretary Benjamin had requested "engines and cars...on the Western and Atlantic." Brown responded today, promising to "write you fully our embarrassed condition about engines and cars. I think you could get them from the Central Railroad at Savannah, from the South Carolina Railroad at Charleston, or from the Memphis and Charleston."[276]

October 2, 1861 (Wednesday)

Georgians went to the polls and elected Governor Brown for another term. Brown received 46,493 votes, Judge Nisbet 32,802.

Flag Officer Louis Goldsborough ordered Captain Hugh Purviance to the coast of Georgia. "You will proceed with the *St. Lawrence* off St. Simon's Sound, Georgia, and closely blockade the entrances to it until further orders, or until it is absolutely necessary for you to return to this place [Hampton Roads] for supplies."[277]

October 3, 1861 (Thursday)

Governor Brown worked to ensure Georgia soldiers had adequate accommodations. "Drafts drawn on the Bank of Commerce of Savannah to quarter and subsist State Troops

---

[273] Toombs, Stephens, and Cobb, *Correspondence*, 577.

[274] Candler, *Confederate Records of the State of Georgia*, 3:131.

[275] Toombs, Stephens, and Cobb, *Correspondence*, 577.

[276] Candler, *Confederate Records of the State of Georgia*, 3:132.

[277] T. Bryan, *Confederate Georgia*, 36; *ORN*, ser. I, vol. 6:280–81.

till regular means be perfected to place funds for such purposes in Savannah, will be responded to by the State."[278]

October 4, 1861 (Friday)

The Confederate War Department threatened to take martial control of the Western and Atlantic. Governor Brown, always protective of the State Road, stood firm in his response to Secretary Benjamin.

> Have given to you...reason why I can not spare cars and engines from State road. He writes from Chattanooga that he has orders to impress them. I presume he has not received your countermanding order. I hope you will telegraph him, as I shall certainly resist the impressment by military force if necessary. The Southern route, only a few hours longer, will carry promptly to extent of our capacity all freights sent, but will not suspend the working of our own road to enable another line to carry all the freight.[279]

October 5, 1861 (Saturday)

Governor Brown's office sent orders for "Capt. T. M. Bradford, Military Store Keeper at Milledgeville, to ship to Savannah...all the arms embraced in the within schedule. Also, a quantity of cartridges sufficient for and suitable to all the arms, sending...1,600 blank Maynard cartridges cases, and...10,000 Sharps primes. Also some 50,000 percussion Caps for muskets." The weapons in the schedule: "20,000 Sharps Cartridges, 15,000 Buck & Ball & 15,000 Ball Cartridges, for Muskets...5,000 or 10,000 Cartridges for Minnie Muskets, if on hand."[280]

October 6, 1861 (Sunday)

Captain George A. Mercer wrote on camp conditions around Savannah. "The city is quite sickly, the prevailing diseases being bilious and intermittent fevers, with some cases of congestive chills and a few cases of yellow fever. At Tybee, where the earth has not been disturbed, the camp has been remarkably healthy."[281]

October 7, 1861 (Monday)

At the request of the board of directors for the Brunswick & Florida Railroad, Governor Brown issued the following statement.

> I have, as Governor of Georgia and Commander-in-Chief of the army and navy of this State, and of the Militia thereof, taken charge of said railroad, to hold and manage the same, and to repair, run and place upon it in addition to what the company already has, such motive power, rolling stock and machinery, as the business of the road may from time to time require, and the exigencies of the public service may, in my opinion, demand, until such time as I may think proper to again leave the

---

[278] Candler, *Confederate Records of the State of Georgia*, 2:58.

[279] Ibid., 3:134.

[280] Ibid., 2:58–59.

[281] Mercer, "George Anderson Mercer Diary," October 6, 1861.

management of said road to said company, and to hold and conduct the same in such way as I deem compatible with the public service.[282]

October 8, 1861 (Tuesday)

The postmaster of Thompson, Connecticut, wrote to Navy Secretary Gideon Welles.

> My letter to you...relative to the arrival of the new screw steamer *Bermuda* at Savannah, was written in great haste for the closing mail.... I presume, however, sufficient was written to give you some information valuable...this same young man is in possession of much valuable information relative to the coast of Georgia and its inlets; likewise in relation to two or more prizes which were taken to Savannah by other rebel pirates; also of the defenses of that harbor and other points along the coast, together with much other information, perfectly reliable, obtained by him from a year's residence on said coast while in possession of the full confidence of that population, which, if not already known by the Government, must be invaluable. Mr. [George] Davis, for such is his name, is willing to impart other knowledge in his possession to the proper authorities if it is desired by them.[283]

October 9, 1861 (Wednesday)

Civilian George M. Barnard of Boston wrote to Secretary Welles regarding Savannah.

> As the Government must...rely on the merchants for the funds to carry on the war, we feel that we have a right to demand protection of our interests...therefore...I am prepared to form a company here which will give bonds, if required, to close the port of Savannah so that not a wherry [cargo boat] can get out or in. I can prove to the satisfaction of anyone that hulks loaded with granite blocks, heavy enough to prevent their rising on the swell, will remain stationary and impassable twenty years. I shall await your reply in the hope of a decision satisfactory to the mercantile interests of the North.[284]

October 10, 1861 (Thursday) ◐

Vice President Stephens received a letter from Thomas W. Thomas with harsh words toward President Davis.

> All governments are humbugs and the Confederate government is not an exception. Its President this day is the prince of humbugs and yet his nomination for the first permanent presidency meets with universal acceptance, and yet I do know that he possesses not a single qualification for the place save integrity. I know nothing to the contrary of his having that. Imbecility, ignorance and awkwardness mark every feature of his management of this army. He torments us, makes us sick and kills us by appointing worthless place-hunters to transact business for us on which depends our health, efficiency and even our lives. I could demonstrate all this to you in an hour's

---

[282] Candler, *Confederate Records of the State of Georgia*, 2:64.

[283] *ORN*, ser. I, vol. 6:300.

[284] Ibid., 302.

conversation. He would make a good ordinary of a county in Georgia and his capacity is not above that; but he is king, and here where we are fighting to maintain the last vestige of republicanism on earth we bow down to him with more than eastern devotion.[285]

October 11, 1861 (Friday)

People in Savannah received notice of a special need for Georgia soldiers in Richmond. "Associations and individuals contributing to the hospitals in Virginia, are reminded that a pressing want is one hundred and fifty cotton mattresses, six and a half feet long, thirty inches wide, and one and a half to two inches thick, to be used on the straw beds, which are rather hard."[286]

October 12, 1861 (Saturday)

Secretary Welles informed Flag Officer Goldsborough of a change in naval structure, one, which impacted the coast of Georgia for the balance of the war. "Upon the departure of Flag-Officer S. F. Du Pont from Hampton Roads you will consider the Atlantic Blockading Squadron divided at the junction of North and South Carolina, and the northern division under your command will be known as the North Atlantic Squadron. Let the *Susquehanna* and *Roanoke* exchange places [*Roanoke* then at Charleston, *Susquehanna* in Hampton Roads] and the above named vessels will, for the present, form part of the South Atlantic Squadron."[287]

October 13, 1861 (Sunday)

Naval Commander Edward Yard notified Flag Officer Goldsborough of a bagged prize. "I captured...the schooner *Specie*...from Savannah (via Wassaw Sound), bound for Havana with a cargo of rice...I put on board Mr. H. R. Billings, master's mate, as prize master, and five men, together with the late master, and...a passenger, and dispatched...for Philadelphia. The remainder of the crew...I have retained on board as prisoners."[288]

October 14, 1861 (Monday)

George Davis, a civilian from Thompson, Connecticut, wrote Secretary Welles with a very detailed description of the defenses on Georgia's coast.

> I left Savannah, Ga., on the 18th September last, after a residence of nearly one year in Darien, Ga., engaged as a private tutor. Darien being a seaboard town, I then became somewhat acquainted with the Georgia coast, and saw something of the defenses which were erected and in process of erection. With a chart of the Georgia coast made out by the U. S. Coast Survey before you the places of which I shall speak will be recognized. The city of Savannah is in a tolerable state of defense, although by no means invulnerable. Besides Forts Pulaski and Jackson there are land batteries thrown up on Tybee Island, mounting some ten guns, some of them 10-inch

[285] Toombs, Stephens, and Cobb, *Correspondence*, 580–81.

[286] "Associations and Individuals," *Savannah Daily Morning News*, October 11, 1861, sec. 1, https://gahistoricnewspapers.galileo.usg.edu/lccn/sn82015886/1861-10-11/ed-1/seq-1/.

[287] *ORN*, ser. I, vol. 6:313–14.

[288] Ibid., 317. Occasionally, Wassaw was misspelled as "Warsaw."

columbiads. These guns are mounted behind simple embankments of sand which nature has provided in the shape of sand dunes, and are manned by some 250 men. Besides there is a battery of flying artillery stationed there. In case the garrison is overpowered it has facilities of retreating to Fort Pulaski. The full complement of guns for this fort is 139, of which about 60 are mounted. The most of those mounted are heavy columbiads, which, being well served, would doubtless do much execution. This fort can be shelled from Tybee, and is, in fact, commanded by it, I am not able to state how many men are stationed in Fort Pulaski, but doubtless a sufficient garrison. Fort Jackson has a few guns mounted, but not much dependence is placed in its protection to Savannah. In case the Georgia coast was invaded there would be no lack of men to repel the invaders, but a very large portion of these men are nearly or quite destitute of arms, and if the inland navigation was cut off it would be next to impossible to provision these troops, having it understood that the 500,000 bushels of rice are not left for them to feed upon.[289]

October 15, 1861 (Tuesday)

Flag Officer Goldsborough notified Lieutenant Daniel Braine to "proceed off Savannah, Ga., with the *Monticello*, and report to the senior naval officer for such duty as he may assign you in blockading that port."[290]

October 16, 1861 (Wednesday)

Flag Officer Goldsborough moved other ships around to compensate for blockading the coasts of South Carolina and Georgia. "I have this day dispatched the *Susquehanna* to blockade off Charleston. By the *Rhode Island*, which left yesterday, I sent orders for the *Roanoke* to go off Beaufort, N. C., as soon as the *Susquehanna* should appear off Charleston; and I also sent orders for the *Monticello*, now off Charleston, to go off Savannah immediately. As soon as…Du Pont can assign a vessel to take the place of the *Monticello* on that service, I shall want her back…."[291]

October 17, 1861 (Thursday)

Lord Lyons wrote to Secretary Seward regarding British ships entering Southern ports: "as I am very anxious to avoid all risk…I…ask you whether I am right in understanding that you have no objection to my sending to the blockade ports, by her Majesty's ships of war, not only British official correspondence with British authorities, but also the official correspondence of other powers, friendly to the United States, with the agents of the same powers in the Southern States."[292]

October 18, 1861 (Friday) ●

Governor Brown ordered, "That Joseph T. Lumpkin, of the county of Clarke, be, and he is, hereby appointed Aide-de-Camp to the Commander-in-Chief, of the Second Brigade

---

[289] Ibid., 320–22.

[290] Ibid., 329.

[291] Ibid., 331.

[292] Ibid., 506.

and Third Division G. M. [Georgia Militia]."[293]

October 19, 1861 (Saturday)

Working to equip soldiers raised in the state, Governor Brown raised a question regarding their uniforms. He wrote to Secretary Benjamin for clarification. "Where a State shall clothe her own troops, will the clothing be required in uniforms, or will any substantial woolen clothing do? How is the money value of clothing to be ascertained and agreed upon, and what evidence will be required of its delivery by the State? Will it be paid for to the State furnishing it on delivery to the commanding officer…?" The enormous numbers of Georgians who volunteered magnified the problem of uniforms and other supplies.

After writing Benjamin, Brown issued a statewide proclamation. "In obedience to my Proclamation issued the 9th of September last to the people of Georgia, calling for volunteers for the coast defense, a number much larger than the exigencies of the service require have patriotically and promptly tendered their services. I therefore issue this my Proclamation, giving notice that no more tenders of service will be accepted…."[294]

October 20, 1861 (Sunday)

Early in the war, the Confederate government made a conscious decision to withhold cotton from foreign mills. An editor in Augusta questioned the attempt to ship cotton overseas. "We acknowledge that we are under great necessity to sell cotton; but is the necessity *absolute* to sell abroad? If so, and we acknowledge it, Lincoln has only to seal our ports, while our cotton customers in Europe stand idly by, and we are undone."[295]

October 21, 1861 (Monday)

The appointment of surgeons to the army proved the order of the day for Governor Brown.

> Dr. William Ashley, of Lowndes County, as Surgeon…Dr. T. M. Howard, of Campbell county, as Assistant Surgeon to the First Regiment; Dr. T. J. Young, of Catoosa County, as Surgeon, and Dr. James W. Curry, of Cass county, as Assistant Surgeon to the Second Regiment…Dr. J. C. C. Blackburn, of Pike County, as Surgeon, and Dr. W. J. Nichols, of [Clinch] County, as Assistant Surgeon to the Third Regiment in Gen. George P. Harrison's Brigade; and that each report for duty to the Col. commanding his Regiment, at Camp Harrison.[296]

October 22, 1861 (Tuesday)

Governor Brown dealt with financial issues in a letter to the Georgia Railroad & Banking Company. "Any reasonable extension which may be given by your bank for the payment of the twenty thousand dollars, (or any part of it which is unpaid,) the Bank advanced to the Confederate States on my guarantee as Governor…for subsistence of troops at Camps

---

293 Candler, *Confederate Records of the State of Georgia*, 2:67.

294 Ibid., 3:135; 2:69.

295 "Shall Cotton Be Exported?," *Augusta Chronicle*, October 20, 1861, sec. 2, Genealogybank.com.

296 Candler, *Confederate Records of the State of Georgia*, 2:70–71; Nichols information from Huxford, *History of Clinch County, Georgia*, 145.

McDonald and Stephens, will meet my approval; and the States guarantee shall still exist."[297]

October 23, 1861 (Wednesday)

Secretary Benjamin wrote to Governor Brown, "Can you find me some secure place in your State where I could hold safely a few hundred prisoners? Will pay a fair rent for the property." Brown responded quickly, "Your dispatch to Atlanta just received. Headquarters here now. Have no safe place here to keep prisoners. Will inquire and inform you if I can get a place in the State."[298]

October 24, 1861 (Thursday)

Captain T. W. Brantley updated the governor on a potential location for Secretary Benjamin's prisoners. "I made inquiries to-day concerning a secure place for the confinement or retention of prisoners. 1 found one place large enough for the accommodation of 200, and it is the only one that can be procured in this place I think. For particulars...apply to Messrs. Adams & Reynolds, of this city. The place...is at present occupied by Davis Smith as a negro mart."[299]

October 25, 1861 (Friday)

Secretary Benjamin discussed another issue the governor raised regarding soldiers from Georgia. "It is not required that clothing furnished by States shall be uniform in order to be accepted. Commutation is allowed for clothing furnished at the rate of $25 for six months, payable to the captains of companies (or commanding officers) upon vouchers rendered to the Quartermaster-General's Department that their men are furnished with clothing according to regulation for the time specified."[300]

October 26, 1861 (Saturday) ◐

Secretary Benjamin, via Special Orders, No. 190, designated, "The State of Georgia will hereafter constitute a separate department, to be designated the Department of Georgia, the command of which is assigned to Brigadier-General [Alexander] Lawton, headquarters Savannah, Ga."[301]

October 27, 1861 (Sunday)

The good people of Augusta learned when mailing letters in the future, the experience would prove a little more enjoyable. "Postmaster...informs us that he is daily expecting the arrival of the new Confederate postage stamps at the Augusta office. Our people will hail their appearance with pleasure, as relieving them from the present inconvenient method of paying postage."[302]

October 28, 1861 (Monday)

Governor Brown and Secretary Benjamin exchanged messages today regarding Georgia soldiers. Brown wrote first: "I am just informed by private source, having no official

---

[297] Candler, *Confederate Records of the State of Georgia*, 2:72.

[298] Ibid., 3:135–36.

[299] Ibid., 3:137.

[300] Ibid., 3:138.

[301] *OR*, ser. I, vol. 6:297.

[302] "Postage Stamps," *Augusta Chronicle*, October 27, 1861, sec. 3, Genealogybank.com.

information, that you have ordered the troops at Camp Stephens and Camp McDonald, and probably other regiments to Virginia. We are expecting an invasion of Georgia every day. You have nearly all Georgia army and over 20,000 of her troops in Virginia. In the name of the State and as an act of justice to the troops, I feel it my imperative duty to enter my solemn protest against the removal."

Benjamin's response: "The troops ordered here are unarmed and are required for urgent service in the public defense. They cannot be armed in Georgia, but can be armed by the general in command of the Army of the Potomac. I will have them clad here comfortably. I should fail in a solemn public duty if I neglected to re-enforce to my utmost ability our army, now confronted with greatly superior numbers and in daily expectation of attack."[303]

October 29, 1861 (Tuesday)

Brigadier General Lawton, in Savannah, learned of a promotion from the Confederate War Department. "Colonel [Hugh] Mercer was appointed brigadier-general to-day. The enemy's fleet sailed South this morning; destination unknown."[304] The United States Navy officially designated the South Atlantic Blockade Squadron. Beginning on this day, and continuing for the balance of the war, vessels in this command patrolled the coasts of South Carolina, Georgia, and Florida.

October 30, 1861 (Wednesday)

Brigadier General Lawton, at Camp Stephens, learned of confusion in the state. Colonel Thomas Warthen of the 20th Georgia Volunteers notified the general, "But a few hours since I received a communication from his excellency the governor, stating that he had not been advised by the Secretary of War of the action of the Department in ordering this regiment to Virginia, and, moreover, stating that he had just written to the Department protesting, in the name of the State, against this and other regiments being removed from the State."[305]

October 31, 1861 (Thursday) (All Hallow'e'en)

Florida's Governor John Milton wrote to Governor Brown on a proposed realignment of military territories.

> I have this day recommended to the President and Secretary of War the establishment of a military department, to be composed of the following counties in Georgia, Alabama, and Florida, lying on or near the Chattahoochee River, Viz: In Georgia : Decatur, Thomas, Miller, Early, Baker, Clay, Calhoun, Randolph, Quitman, Stewart, and Muscogee. In Alabama: Henry, Dale, Barbour, and Russell. I respectfully invite your consideration and approval of the measure proposed. Georgia and Alabama derive even more commercial advantages from Apalachicola than Florida herself, and both these States are deeply interested in its defense.[306]

November 1, 1861 (Friday)

---

[303] Candler, *Confederate Records of the State of Georgia*, 3:138–39.

[304] *OR*, ser. I, vol. 6:299.

[305] *OR*, ser. I, vol. 6:305.

[306] Candler, *Confederate Records of the State of Georgia*, 3:140.

As the South Atlantic Blockading continued to form, Commander John Missroon sent orders to Lieutenant Daniel Braine of the USS *Monticello*. "You will please now occupy the position which I indicated yesterday, at the northwest extremity of the curve of deep soundings, in order to prevent any attempt that may be made by vessels to pass from Savannah, abreast of Hilton Head Island, toward the channel from Port Royal Sound by day or by night, and especially at night."[307]

November 2, 1861 (Saturday)

The U.S. Treasury office responded to an inquiry regarding the supplying of ships participating in the South Atlantic blockade. The Treasury's assistant secretary George Harrington confirmed,

> receipt of your letter of the 1st instant concerning the application of certain merchants of Boston for permission to send a vessel to the blockading squadron laden with stores and comforts such as they have reason to believe many of the officers and men have need of and would gladly purchase at fair prices. You express the opinion that such a project might be allowed under proper restrictions and a limited number of vessels, and that its results, if faithfully carried out, would be highly beneficial. I beg you to indicate what restrictions should be placed upon the proposed trade, and to what extent it should be allowed.[308]

November 3, 1861 (Sunday)

Citizens in Augusta received a plea to supply a much-needed medical item. "We observe that the army surgeons in some of the Confederate States are calling on the citizens for all the empty vials they have to spare, to be used in dispensing medicines to the sick soldiers. In ordinary times empty vials were comparatively valueless, but now, when they cannot be bought, they are worth cleansing and preserving."[309]

November 4, 1861 (Monday)

The Officers of the Baldwin County Militia received a directive from Governor Brown. "You are hereby instructed to excuse from the performance of militia duty, till further order, all students engaged in a course of study in Oglethorpe University, upon the certificate of Rev. Dr. [Samuel K.] Talmadge, the President of the University, that they are students under his care, and the instruction of the faculty of the University."[310]

November 5, 1861 (Tuesday)

The Confederate War Department issued Special Orders, No. 206. "The coasts of South Carolina, Georgia, and East Florida are constituted a military department, and General R. E. Lee, C. S. Army, is assigned to its command."[311]

November 6, 1861 (Wednesday)

On a day when Georgians went to the polls to vote for Jefferson Davis and Alexander

---

307 *ORN*, ser. I, vol. 12:231.

308 Ibid., 253.

309 "Save Your Empty Vials," *Augusta Chronicle*, November 3, 1861, Genealogybank.com.

310 Candler, *Confederate Records of the State of Georgia*, 2:73.

311 *OR*, ser. I, vol. 6:309.

Stephens as the chief executives of the Confederacy, Governor Brown sent his annual message to the General Assembly during their opening session in Milledgeville. Of the conflict, Brown suggested "But one alternative is left us and but one response can be given to the inquiry as to our future policy. That response is on the tongue of every freeman, it is felt from breast to breast, and heard from lip to lip, reverberating from the hill tops to the mountains and from the mountains to the vallies, *Victory over the invader, or death to the last man sooner than acknowledge that we are vanquished.*"[312]

November 7, 1861 (Thursday)

Regarding the appointment of General Lee to command the district covering Georgia's coast, Governor Brown wrote a brief message to President Davis: "I am much gratified at the information contained in your telegram. General Lee has my highest confidence and shall have my cordial co-operation and support."[313]

November 8, 1861 (Friday)

General Lee issued General Orders, No. 1.

> In pursuance of instructions from the War Department, General R. E. Lee, C.S. Army, assumes command of the military department composed of the coasts of South Carolina, Georgia, and East Florida. Capt. T. A. Washington, C. S. Army, is announced as adjutant-general of the department; Capt. Walter H. Taylor, Provisional Army, as assistant adjutant-general; Capt. Joseph C. Ives, C. S. Army, as chief engineer; Lieut. Col. William G. Gill, Provisional Army, as ordnance officer, and Mr. Joseph Manigault as volunteer aide-de-camp to the commanding general.[314]

November 9, 1861 (Saturday) ◑

Governor Brown issued a military proclamation, hopeful "no citizen of the State having a good gun will hesitate a moment to carry or send it into the service."

> The invaders having landed a force upon the soil of our sister State of South Carolina near the borders of Georgia, where they now hold position and menace the city of Savannah; and it being thought advisable to increase our force for the defence of the coast, I issue this my Proclamation, giving notice that I will accept, in addition to the number of volunteers already accepted, the services of the thirty companies which will first tender their services and report to me their readiness to march.[315]

November 10, 1861 (Sunday)

General Lee quickly went to work in his new department, writing to Secretary Benjamin, "Am I at liberty to employ troops in South Carolina and Georgia passing through the States to Virginia?"[316]

---

[312] Candler, *Confederate Records of the State of Georgia*, 2:82. Italics in original.

[313] *OR*, ser. I, vol. 53:184.

[314] *OR*, ser. I, vol. 6:312.

[315] Candler, *Confederate Records of the State of Georgia*, 2:131–32.

[316] *ORN*, ser. I, vol. 6:314.

November 11, 1861 (Monday)

Governor Brown sent two proposed commissions to the General Assembly. "I have appointed George P. Harrison a Brigadier-General under the Act of the Legislature, assented to on the 18th day of December, 1860, to command the first Brigade of Georgia Volunteers for the defence of the State; and I have appointed Francis W. Capers a Brigadier-General to command the Second Brigade. I respectfully ask the advice and consent of the Senate in confirmation of these appointments."[317]

November 12, 1861 (Tuesday)

Governor Brown's request to return Georgia soldiers from Virginia met with disapproval from the Confederate War Department. Secretary Benjamin asserted,

> There are reasons of public policy which would make it suicidal to comply with your request to withdraw Georgia troops from the enemy's front at this moment. This Government will co-operate with all its power for the defense of your State, but it must do so in the manner it deems most certain to produce the desired effect of repulsing the enemy at all points, and cannot scatter its armies into fragments at the request of each Governor who may be alarmed for the safety of his people. Be assured that no effort will be spared to aid you, and be good enough to communicate your confidence in this assurance to your people, thus allaying all needless panic.[318]

November 13, 1861 (Wednesday)

The *Fingal* ran the blockade and brought "12,500 Enfield rifles and 10 rifled cannon, with 150 tons powder, clothing, etc." into Savannah.[319]

November 14, 1861 (Thursday)

Governor Brown tried to get weapons, which had arrived in Savannah, allocated to Georgia soldiers in the state. He wrote to Secretary Benjamin, "I trust you will let us have as many of the guns as possible. They landed here and cannot be needed worse elsewhere. There are four rifled cannon. Do let us have two of them for fort, which lacks heavy guns." Benjamin quickly responded, "I have assigned half to General [R. E.] Lee's command and the other half to General A. S. Johnston...Lee will therefore have 4,500 which, when added to the 1,100 brought in for Georgia, makes 5,600 arms for the defense of Charleston and Savannah. As soon as I get the account of the cannon on board I will appropriate to the same purpose every piece that I can fairly assign to your coast."[320]

November 15, 1861 (Friday)

Observing a day of "Fasting, Humiliation and Prayer," the Reverend Henry H. Tucker delivered a special message to the Georgia General Assembly. He closed the sermon avowing, "My countrymen, we are certain of success in this war if we but use the right means. But those means which are the last that men think of, and the last that they adopt, are the

---

[317] Candler, *Confederate Records of the State of Georgia*, 2:133–34.

[318] Ibid., 3:142–43.

[319] *ORN*, ser. I, vol. 12:380.

[320] Candler, *Confederate Records of the State of Georgia*, 3:144–45.

first in order and the first in importance in the Divine estimation. The first and last and only thing that men are apt to do, is to gather together the implements of war and prepare for battle."[321]

November 16, 1861 (Saturday)

Governor Brown sent a promotion to the General Assembly for their approval. "I hereby nominate and propose, with the advice and consent of the Senate, to appoint Gen. Henry R. Jackson, a Major General to command the First Division of Georgia Volunteers now being organized for the defence of the State."[322]

November 17, 1861 (Sunday) ●

The governor responded to Secretary Benjamin regarding the War Department's plans for the weapons Brown sought to keep in his state. "I am satisfied that your proposed division of the rifles between the coast and Kentucky is just. You have over 9,000. Shall be greatly gratified if two of the rifled cannon can be placed on Fort Pulaski, which lacks sufficient long-range guns."[323]

November 18, 1861 (Monday)

General R. E. Lee, in Savannah, wrote to his wife in Virginia, "This is my second visit to Savannah. Night before last, I returned to Coosawhatchie, South Carolina, from Charleston, where I have placed my headquarters, & last night came here, arriving after midnight. You probably have seen the operations of the enemy's fleet. Since their first attack they have been quiescent, apparently confining themselves to Hilton Head, where they are apparently fortifying."[324]

November 19, 1861 (Tuesday)

The General Assembly received a message from Governor Brown: "My own opinion is that it is not now the time to stop to count the cost, but that we should call out as many troops as may be necessary to repel the invader, should he appear either upon the sea coast or upon the borders of Tennessee, whether it may take ten thousand or twenty thousand men, or whether it may cost five or ten millions of dollars."[325]

November 20, 1861 (Wednesday)

The governor instructed Captain E. M. Field to "proceed to the cities of Macon, Columbus and Atlanta, and at either or all of those cities, seize for the use of the army of Georgia any salt which is being removed...beyond the limits of the State, or any found in large quantities for which more than five dollars per sack with usual freight from Savannah to such city is demanded; that which is held on speculation and not offered for sale at all."[326]

November 21, 1861 (Thursday)

General Lee, writing in Savannah, updated General Cooper on the military-state of defenses along the coast.

---

[321] Tucker, "God in the War," 23.

[322] Candler, *Confederate Records of the State of Georgia*, 2:138.

[323] Ibid., 3:145.

[324] R. E. Lee, *Wartime Papers*, 87.

[325] Candler, *Confederate Records of the State of Georgia*, 2:144.

[326] Ibid., 2:145.

I have just returned to this city after having inspected the batteries and posts along the coast from Charleston to Fernandina, Florida. The guns from the less important points have been removed, and are employed in strengthening those considered of greater consequence. The entrance to Cumberland Sound & Brunswick and the water approaches to Savannah & Charleston are the only points which it is proposed to defend. At all of these places there is much yet to be done, but every effort is being made to render them as strong as the nature of the positions and the means at hand will permit. They ought, after their completion, to make a good defence against any batteries that are likely to be brought against them. More guns could be usefully employed if available for this service. Those at hand have been placed in the best positions, and the troops so distributed so as to work them to advantage, the batteries are tolerably supplied with ammunition, having about 50 rounds to the gun. This amount it would be well to have increased to 100 rounds. The greatest difficulty to be contended with is the want of artillerists, and proper officers as instructors. I have been able to learn nothing of any movements of the enemy's fleet along the coast of Georgia or Florida, and am inclined to believe that they have not yet made any further demonstrations of attack.[327]

November 22, 1861 (Friday)

In a letter to his daughters, written from Savannah, General Lee noted, "This is my second visit to Savannah. I have been down the coast as far as Amelia Island to examine the defences. They are poor indeed & I have laid off work enough to employ our people a month. I hope our enemy will be polite enough to wait for us. It is difficult to get our people to realize their position."[328]

November 23, 1861 (Saturday)

Flag Officer Du Pont updated Brigadier General Thomas Sherman on naval operations on Georgia's coast. "He [Commander John Rodgers] has been sounding the Savannah Bar, and left again to-day with three vessels to continue his work up to Tybee. If the forts there have really been abandoned, which I shall know to-morrow, I will cork up Savannah like a bottle by placing a frigate in the roads opposite Tybee and out of range from Pulaski."[329]

November 24, 1861 (Sunday)

General Lee reported on worsening conditions near Savannah, writing to the War Department in Richmond, "the enemy crossed Savannah Bar with five of his vessels, and made a lodgment on Tybee Island...three other vessels joined...and the force on Tybee Island was re-enforced. Five vessels, one of them a frigate, said to be the *Sabine*, now...inside of the bar north of Tybee Island. The force...is reported to be large, but I am unable to state it. No demonstration of their purpose has yet been made further than the occupation of the island."[330]

November 25, 1861 (Monday) ◐

[327] R. E. Lee, *Wartime Papers*, 87–88.

[328] Ibid., 89.

[329] *ORN*, ser. I, vol. 12:324.

[330] *OR*, ser. I, vol. 6:32.

A beacon on the coast readied for illumination. Brigadier General Thomas Sherman reported, "It having been learned by a reconnaissance sent to the neighboring island that the forts on Tybee Island had been deserted by the rebels, I informed Commodore DuPont of the same, whereupon he…started some gunboats down there, and discovered it to be a fact. We have therefore another light-house, which should be relighted at once."[331]

November 26, 1861 (Tuesday)

Commander John Goldsborough and the crew of the USS *Florida* repulsed an attack from Commodore Josiah Tattnall's "Mosquito Fleet," which consisted of the *Savannah, Resolute, Sampson,* and the *Lady Davis.* The naval officer recounted the action.

> To-day, about 12 meridian, Commodore Tattnall, in the steamer *Everglade* as his flagship, having a hulk of about 200 tons lashed alongside, mounting one heavy gun and accompanied with steamers *Resolute* and *Sampson,* weighed anchor from under the guns of Fort Pulaski, and, standing down a short distance toward us, opened a fire with the gun on the hulk, his shot falling at least from one-fourth to one-half mile short. They were directed toward the *Pocahontas.* We all returned his salutation, but the firing from the *Seneca* and *Pocahontas*'s XI-inch was beautiful. One or two of their shells exploded nearly over him. In a very short time he resumed his former anchorage, where I left him.[332]

November 27, 1861 (Wednesday)

A Confederate Ordnance Officer, Lieutenant Colonel William Gill, reported on the artillery positioned at various locations along the coast. For Fort Pulaski, he counted

> five 10-inch columbiads *en barbette*; six 8-inch columbiads *en barbette*; two 10-inch mortars *en barbette*; three 8-inch columbiads in casemate; two 42-pounder guns in casemate; twenty 32-pounder guns in casemate; one 24-pounder gun, plank casemate. The guns and carriages are in excellent condition; have an abundance or all kinds of implements, fuses, &c. Each gun has about 120 rounds of shot and shell. Some of the fuses are imperfect; these I am renewing with new ones from the Augusta Arsenal."[333]

November 28, 1861 (Thursday)

Flag Officer Du Pont informed his squadron, "The general commanding [Brigadier General Thomas Sherman] has decided to make a complete reconnoissance of Tybee Island, which will take place to-morrow or next day, after which I shall be able to speak more positively upon the further plans in respect to that place, which in the meantime will be held by the vessels."[334]

November 29, 1861 (Friday)

A newspaper editor offered an "Aspect of the War at Present." He suggested, "Whether

---

[331] Ibid., 190.

[332] *ORN*, ser. I, vol. 12:362–63; Avery, *History of the State of Georgia*, 216.

[333] *OR*, ser. I, vol. 6:332. Italics in original.

[334] *ORN*, ser. I, vol. 12:364.

Savannah or Charleston is to be attacked is yet unknown, but in either case there will be a struggle bold, bitter and bloody. No where on earth could two hostile forces meet, where fighting will be done with so much pleasure, and with a persistence on our side...we entertain no serious fears as to the result, still aware of the odds against us, we confess to great anxiety while awaiting the shock of arms."[335]

November 30, 1861 (Saturday)

Some things never change. Advertising, for example: "Persons wanting situations of any kind; persons desiring situations filled; merchants having anything for sale on legitimate terms; inventors, or dealers, or manufacturers, having any articles of necessity or use throughout the Confederate States, will find their interests promoted in a careful attention to, and a judicious use of, the advertising columns of the TIMES."[336]

December 1, 1861 (Sunday)

Captain Quincy Gillmore with the Engineer Corps reported to Brigadier General Thomas Sherman on the status of a Confederate fortification on the coast.

> There are now probably at Fort Pulaski 700 good troops. About 200 landed yesterday, and the Navy officers informed me that at least 500 have entered the fort within the last three days, while some (probably raw recruits or portions of the Home Guard) have gone away. It may be their design to land on Tybee and hold the west end of it, to prevent the erection of batteries against the fort. I therefore recommend the immediate occupation of Tybee Island by one good regiment until the question of attempting the reduction of Fort Pulaski be determined.[337]

December 2, 1861 (Monday)

Brigadier General Thomas Sherman's report to Flag Officer Du Pont on continuing activity at Fort Pulaski: "But to know how large a force it would be judicious to place on Tybee Island I think a knowledge of the position of the enemy's battery south of it is necessary, as well as the force he has there. Captain Gillmore reports that he was unable to ascertain whether the enemy's battery is on the South Tybee Island or farther south, but that the indications are, from the top of a derrick in sight, that it is on the former."[338]

December 3, 1861 (Tuesday)

A group of soldiers at Camp Harrison in Wayne County, upon learning the General Assembly had passed a resolution to "transfer the Georgia State volunteers to the service of the Confederate States," provided their own declaration to Governor Brown. If the state took action to enforce this law, the unit would "at once abandon the field and return to

---

[335] "Aspect of the War at Present," *Rome Weekly Courier*, November 29, 1861, https://gahistoricnewspapers.galileo.usg.edu/lccn/sn82014071/1861-11-29/ed-1/seq-4/.

[336] "Persons Wanting," *Columbus Daily Times*, November 30, 1861, https://gahistoricnewspapers.galileo.usg.edu/lccn/sn82015388/1861-11-30/ed-1/seq-1/. Caps in original.

[337] *OR*, ser. I, vol. 6:195.

[338] *ORN*, ser. I, vol. 12:383–84.

our homes."[339]

December 4, 1861 (Wednesday)

Brigadier General Thomas Sherman reminded the U.S. War Department of opportunities for his command. "The reduction of Fort Pulaski will require an armament from the North...which I beg may be forwarded to Tybee Island at the earliest practicable moment, in charge of an active and experienced ordnance officer, if a suitable artillery officer cannot be obtained; for I repeat from former communications...this command being composed of raw volunteers and a dearth of experienced and instructed officers, an impossibility now exists of obtaining proper hands to direct."[340]

December 5, 1861 (Thursday)

Federal naval efforts to sink ships along the Georgia coast, in an attempt to block passages for blockade runners, continued. Commander John Missroon reported on the "stone fleet," noting "there have arrived near this place seventeen ships and barks...up to this time... many more are on their way, and may be daily expected. They are all laden with stone; but few good vessels among them, and all badly found in every respect, especially in ground tackle, few having more than one chain and anchor...." Commander C. R. P. Rodgers returned "to Tybee Roads at 1 o'clock, I landed and made a reconnoissance on foot with the marines of the *Savannah* and detachments of small-arms men from that ship and the *Ottawa*."[341]

December 6, 1861 (Friday)

Cass County name changed to Bartow County, in honor of fallen Brigadier General Francis Bartow. Bartow fell during the Battle of First Manassas/Bull Run.[342]

December 7, 1861 (Saturday)

General Lee continued to inspect the fortifications along the coasts of South Carolina and Georgia, while also looking to the health of his department.

> The recent inspection by the medical director of the department discloses the existence of much sickness among the troops. No special means can be devised for banishing measles, but catarrhal affections, pneumonia, and rheumatic complaints are produced, in many instances, by bad selection of sites for camps. They should always be located on high and dry ground, exposed to the healthful influences of the sun. It is believed that typhoid disease is developed by the close air of tents, the want of personal cleanliness, the neglect of proper police, and the prolonged occupation of the same ground of encampment. Commanding officers are particularly desired to establish proper sinks, remote from the tents, and to cause the daily removal of all garbage and offal. The tents must be frequently emptied and ventilated and the bedding thoroughly aired and cleansed. A proper attention to these measures on the part

[339] Candler, *Confederate Records of the State of Georgia*, 2:168–69.

[340] *OR*, ser. I, vol. 6:193.

[341] *ORN*, ser. I, vol. 12:419, 386.

[342] Krakow, *Georgia Place-Names*, 15.

of commanding and medical officers will do much to mitigate disease and promote the health and efficiency of the men.[343]

December 8, 1861 (Sunday)

Secretary of War Benjamin encouraged General Lee to take immediate action in arming troops within his department. "I am firm in my purpose not to give a musket to a man enlisted for less than the war (or three years, which is the same thing), and therefore I beg that you will inform Governors Pickens and Brown that if they have no 'war' troops ready to receive the arms you still retain in your hands, you will at once arm the other regiments mentioned in your letter…."[344]

December 9, 1861 (Monday)

Flag Officer Du Pont sent Commander Charles Steedman and his USS *Bienville* to the coast of Georgia. "Please proceed with all convenient dispatch and assume the blockade of St. Simon's Sound. I am induced to believe that since the more effectual blockade of Charleston and Savannah that St. Simon's Sound is more resorted to in order to forward cargoes from Brunswick. Please collect all the information you can in reference to the coast defenses, the feelings of the people, etc."[345]

December 10, 1861 (Tuesday)

Brigadier General Thomas Sherman reported "that Tybee Island is now in the occupancy of one regiment, and that an armament is being prepared sufficient to cover the channel leading into Savannah River. This armament, however, is independent of that required for the reduction of Fort Pulaski."[346]

December 11, 1861 (Wednesday)

Commander C. R. P. Rodgers of the USS *Wabash* "left Tybee Roads before daylight…with the *Ottawa*, *Seneca*, *Pembina*, and *Henry Andrew*—and crossed the bar at Ossabaw soon after 8 o'clock. Entering and passing up Vernon River, we discovered on the eastern end of Green Island a fort mounting eight guns, apparently of heavy caliber. Near it is an encampment, where we saw about seventy-five tents…a barrack near the fort…."[347]

December 12, 1861 (Thursday)

Flag Officer Du Pont informed the U.S. Department of the Navy of a captured blockade runner: "The *Admiral* was captured by the USS *Alabama*, Commander [Edmund] Lanier…about 12 miles to the southward of Tybee."[348]

December 13, 1861 (Friday)

In updating the Confederate War Department, Governor Brown informed officials, "Georgia has several thousand State troops mustered into her service for six months, organized into…division, brigades, regiments, battalions and companies. Many of the companies

---

343 *OR*, ser. I, vol. 6:339.

344 Ibid., 340.

345 *ORN*, ser. I, vol. 12:392.

346 *OR*, ser. I, vol. 6:198–99.

347 *ORN*, ser. I, vol. 12:396.

348 Ibid., 397.

consist of less than sixty men, including officers. Will you accept them for local service as organized, if tendered? If you will not, appropriation will be made for their future support by the State. If not, the State must provide for their support."[349]

December 14, 1861 (Saturday)

The General Assembly approved an act allowing soldiers to vote in the field. Enacted: "That all volunteers and other troops, citizens of this State, who are now, by law, entitled to vote, or who may at the time of such election, be entitled to vote at any election in this State, except such elections as are not returnable to the Executive Department, be and they are hereby entitled to assemble at such place as they may be stationed at, or in service, and cast their votes as though they were in their proper counties, at such elections."[350]

December 15, 1861 (Sunday)

Augusta residents learned a local merchant "just received a supply of fine French material…to furnish at short notice [flags] of all sizes, such as are used by Military companies as well as on houstops and poles. Also, streamers, revenue flags, pennants, state flags, signals, Confederate Jacks, and flags of all nations."[351] It seems J. B. Platt, the local merchant, covered all occasions; those celebrating a birthday, or local units mustering for the war!

December 16, 1861 (Monday)

General R. E. Lee wrote to Secretary Benjamin regarding a concern over troops and weapons. Lee believed some "companies that have been mustered into the Confederate States service for the war, will absorb all the arms intended for Georgia troops. There are several companies in this State organized for the war…that will require so many arms, as not to leave more than sufficient for one regiment. Could more arms be had for the troops for the war, as I believe, there would be no difficulty in procuring men."[352]

December 17, 1861 (Tuesday) ●

Flag Officer Du Pont ordered Captain James Lardner to Georgia's coast. Lardner prepared to "proceed with the *Susquehanna* under your command and assume the blockade of St. Simon's, remaining underway or at anchor as you may deem best. Many vessels are expected from England just now to run the blockade somewhere on the coast, and St. Simon's may be resorted to."[353]

December 18, 1861 (Wednesday)

Flag Officer Du Pont continued to assemble ships to blockade Georgia's coast. To Commander John Missroon he reported the dispatch of "the armed steamer *Henry Andrew*… followed by the *Ellen*….Please accept my commendation for your great zeal, and remain assured that I am fully impressed with the difficulties of holding Tybee Island."[354]

---

[349] Candler, *Confederate Records of the State of Georgia*, 3:146.

[350] *Journal of the Public and Secret Proceedings of the Convention of the People of Georgia, held in Milledgeville and Savannah*, December 14, 1861, 31.

[351] "Flags! Flags!," *Augusta Chronicle*, December 15, 1861, Genealogybank.com.

[352] *OR*, ser. I, vol. 6:346.

[353] *ORN*, ser. I, vol. 12:403.

[354] Ibid., 407.

December 19, 1861 (Thursday)

Brigadier General Thomas Sherman updated Major General George B. McClellan on military maneuvering in Georgia. "Already the Georgians are making serious threats on Tybee, and I had to send [Brigadier] General [Horatio] Wright down there yesterday with another regiment, and DuPont has sent three of his gunboats, in addition to two vessels he had there. [Captain Josiah] Tat[t]nall is busy reconnoitering with his fleet, and Pulaski has been filled with men during the past few days. They may probably make a desperate effort to retake it before our guns are up, but every care will be taken that they do not."[355]

December 20, 1861 (Friday)

Flag Officer Du Pont grew increasingly frustrated with blockade runners getting out of Georgia. He ordered Commander John Missroon to "act immediately, viz, closing effectually Wassaw Inlet, which has been troubling me. The *Susquehanna* has orders to send the *Alabama* there; the *Fingal* must not get out."[356]

December 21, 1861 (Saturday)

Brigadier General Thomas Sherman noted to Secretary of War Simon Cameron. "We have no cavalry yet, and are not sufficiently supplied with field artillery. The point of Savannah is now the point, but, to say nothing of the public interest, my own professional reputation would not permit me to make dashes without object and without lasting result. The work before us is a great one. It requires thought, system, and prudence."[357]

December 22, 1861 (Sunday)

Greedy individuals surfaced in Augusta as the first year of the war ended. "There is scarcely a shadow of doubt that some people, who ought to be engaged in the defence of the South from the inroads of Lincoln's minions, are engaged in schemes for enriching themselves in a manner which the Vigilance Committee of this city, very properly concluded had proceeded to such a stage as to demand their interference."[358]

December 23, 1861 (Monday)

Flag Officer Du Pont issued new "rules" for vessels in his blockading squadron. "Every vessel proceeding toward a blockaded port is to be boarded and examined, and if on such examination any irregularity appears in her papers, or there are discovered any suspicious circumstances attending her position or her cargo, and particularly if she had any knowledge of the blockade, such vessel is to be seized and sent in for adjudication."[359]

December 24, 1861 (Tuesday) ◐

General R. E. Lee notified Brigadier General Alexander Lawton in Savannah of artillery en route. Lee noted he had "been informed that three 32-pounders are on their way from New Orleans, and as they will probably be sent by Augusta…desirous that you should make

---

[355] *OR*, ser. I, vol. 6:207–208.

[356] *ORN*, ser. I, vol. 12:415.

[357] *OR*, ser. I, vol. 6:209.

[358] "The Vigilance Committee and 'Domestic Enemies,'" *Augusta Chronicle*, December 22, 1861, sec. 1, Genealogybank.com.

[359] *ORN*, ser. I, vol. 12:426–27.

arrangements to have them forwarded from that place to Savannah."[360]

December 25, 1861 (Wednesday) (Christmas Day)

Flag Officer Du Pont took a break from blockading Georgia's coast to pen a Christmas letter to his family. After sending his warmest greetings for the holy day, he wrote of festivities onboard his flagship. "Our ship looks so nice today, and I have given the squadron Christmas. A sprig of fir is on all the guns; I never saw this before in all my service and it looks beautifully. I never told you of our prayer meetings; they hold them near the cabin door in the evenings and open with a hymn, sweet beyond description, for I never heard such voices in a man-of-war before."[361]

December 26, 1861 (Thursday)

Brigadier General Thomas Sherman received a report from Du Pont outlining the importance of Savannah. "I have decided, after a careful examination of the subject, that it would be expedient, so far as the blockade only is concerned, to block up Wilmington River, the second entrance to Savannah, as effectually as Savannah River itself is blocked up, by sinking one or more of the stone ships at the place where the former empties into Wassaw Sound."[362]

December 27, 1861 (Friday)

Flag Officer Du Pont notified Commander John Gillis of intelligence gained regarding approaches to Savannah. Du Pont wrote, "there seems to be a passage from the Savannah River to Wassaw Sound near Little Tybee. I learn from the prisoners now on board that the *Everglade*, Commander Tattnall's steamer, has recently gone through this passage, the prisoners being on board the *Everglade* at the time. It becomes important, not alone for securely blocking up the *Fingal*, but to prevent the ingress of the pilot boats now employed for the transshipment of cargoes at Wassaw, to have this passage examined."[363]

December 28, 1861 (Saturday)

In a letter to friend William Whetten, Du Pont painted a visual picture of the Savannah coast. "The enemy have left the coast defenses they put up and have fallen back on their railroads for their base, while the topography of the country between these railroads and the seacoast is most peculiar a perfect network of water: rivers, creeks, estuaries, sounds, inlets, cuts, etc."[364]

December 29, 1861 (Sunday)

Atlanta almost experienced the flames three years before Sherman arrived. "A small wooden building between the Trout House and the Masonic Hall, occupied by Messrs. Mecaslin & Rodes, as a Family Grocery, was destroyed this morning, at about 6 o'clock, by fire.... Had the wind prevailed in a different direction, we doubt whether our gallant Firemen, with all their exertions, could have saved the Trout House from the devouring and fierce

---

360 *OR*, ser. I, vol. 6:351.

361 Du Pont, *Civil War Letters*, 1:289.

362 *ORN*, ser. I, vol. 12:434.

363 Ibid., 438.

364 Du Pont, *Civil War Letters*, 1:292.

element. As it was, they were successful in their untiring efforts, and thus saved perhaps a lar[g]e portion of our city."[365]

December 30, 1861 (Monday)

Lieutenant William Harden needed powder in Brunswick; he requested a supply from Captain R. M. Cuyler in Savannah. "By General Mercer's direction I write to urge upon you the necessity of sending us more powder. It is his belief…that we can whip off the fleet upon the first attack; but that if it is renewed the next day, as in all probability it would be, our powder would be exhausted, and they could pass us without our being able to fire a gun. I want 20 barrels large grain and 30 barrels fine grain, in all 5,000 pounds, cannon powder."[366]

December 31, 1861 (Tuesday)

Thomas Thomas wrote to Vice President Stephens from Elberton regarding social feelings in Georgia. "Since I have been here and seen what the state of public feeling is, how dispirited, uneasy and apprehensive the people are I am in much doubt as to whether I ought to retire or even change my theatre for any provocation whatever. Mr. Davis and the peculiar people he trusts have given sufficient cause to every gentleman in the army to mutiny, but if any, even the smallest, further depletion be caused in the public pulse it looks to me that our affairs will be desperate."[367]

---

[365] "Fire!," *Atlanta Daily Intelligencer*, December 29, 1861, sec. 3, https://gahistoricnewspapers.galileo.usg.edu/lccn/sn82014304/1861-12-29/ed-1/seq-3/.

[366] *OR*, ser. I, vol. 6:362–63.

[367] Toombs, Stephens, and Cobb, *Correspondence*, 586.

Chapter 2

1862

Moon Stage Legend: ◐ first quarter; ○ full, ◑ last quarter, ● new

January 1, 1862 (Wednesday)

Responding to the Georgia House of Representatives, Governor Brown stated, "I sent both Houses a special message on the subject of our coast defences, having relation more particularly to our State troops, who are under arms in the field for our defence, and for whose support no adequate provision had been made, though the Legislature had then been in session thirty days."[1]

January 2, 1862 (Thursday)

Writing to Major General George B. McClellan, Brigadier General Thomas W. Sherman proposed a plan for approaching Fort Pulaski. "I want to make a great dash on the north side of Savannah River, thus occupying the road to that city, the whole country between Broad River and Savannah River, and the southern end of the railroad, and at the same time, if found practicable, the islands in this river north of Pulaski."[2]

January 3, 1862 (Friday)

Residents of Savannah learned—from the front page of the *Daily Morning News*—of a Federal naval landing near Port Royal in South Carolina. General Robert E. Lee, still in Georgia inspecting coastal fortifications, "left the city for the scene of the action…."[3]

January 4, 1862 (Saturday)

The editors of the *Southern Confederacy* newspaper in Atlanta opined on the upcoming year. "This year will, in all probability be one of most momentous interest. The war with the United States may be prosecuted by both parties with vigor, and on a scale of imposing grandeur, that will eclipse any war of modern times."[4]

January 5, 1862 (Sunday)

Civilians continued to worry about military action along the coast of Georgia, and the day's edition of the *Southern Confederacy* newspaper brought an update from the front. "Your patriotic Governor, alarmed for the safety of the State, called on her sons to meet the exigency of a coast invasion, and most nobly have they responded. But not alone is that quarter in danger. Georgia will not be seriously invaded until the enemy has well secured the land

---

[1] Candler, *Confederate Records of the State of Georgia*, 2:71.

[2] *OR*, ser. I, vol. 6:214.

[3] "Forward Movement of the Enemy in Carolina," *Savannah Daily Morning News*, January 3, 1862, https://gahistoricnewspapers.galileo.usg.edu/lccn/sn82015886/1862-01-03/ed-1/seq-1/.

[4] "The Year 1862—What Will Be Its History?," *Atlanta Southern Confederacy*, January 4, 1862, https://www.newspapers.com/image/604727881/.

approaches to her territory."[5]

January 6, 1862 (Monday)

In Columbus, citizens read of the recent patents awarded to various industrious Georgians. Among the inventors were "Henry C. Goodrich of Augusta for camp cots; J.H. Van Houton from Savannah for breech-loading guns; and John Schley, also of Savannah, for horse-power."[6]

January 7, 1862 (Tuesday) ◐

Reporting on conditions along the coast, a Milledgeville newspaper informed their readers of the following. "Matters remain very much the same in the vicinity of Tybee. There were only four Yankee vessels inside yesterday afternoon—a large frigate, a three masted steamer and two sloops riding quietly at anchor."[7]

January 8, 1862 (Wednesday)

Reporting to General Samuel Cooper on conditions from his new post in Savannah, General Lee painted a glum scenario. "Our works are not yet finished. Their progress is slow. Guns are required for their armament, & I have not received as many troops from South Carolina & Georgia as at first expected. The forces of the enemy are accumulating, & apparently increase faster than ours."[8]

January 9, 1862 (Thursday)

In Atlanta, Sam Richards offered thoughts on recent events, especially President Lincoln's December 26, 1861, decision to release two captured representatives from the Confederacy. James Mason, Confederate envoy to Great Britain, and John Slidell, Confederate envoy to France, were aboard the British vessel *Trent* between the Bahamas and Cuba when it was intercepted by the USS *San Jacinto*. Skipper Captain Charles Wilkes apprehended and detained the two diplomats. Richards wrote, "Our hopes of war between Old Abe and England are destroyed by the prompt surrender of Mason and Slidell upon the peremptory demand of England, and the Commissioners are again en route for England where they will probably be somewhat lionized by the Britishers on account of the fuss they have been the cause of."[9]

January 10, 1862 (Friday)

A recruiter in Atlanta sent a patriotic plea for new volunteers. "Georgians, I make an earnest appeal to you for help! Give me a battalion or a regiment to go wherever the danger is most imminent. You have done well in the past campaign. Let its glorious recollections stimulate

---

[5] "The War," *Atlanta Southern Confederacy*, January 5, 1862, 3, https://www.newspapers.com/image/604727896/.

[6] "Confederate Patents," *Daily Sun*, January 6, 1862, https://gahistoricnewspapers.galileo.usg.edu/lccn/sn82014939/1862-01-06/ed-1/seq-1/.

[7] "From Tybee," *Milledgeville Southern Federal Union*, January 7, 1862, https://gahistoricnewspapers.galileo.usg.edu/lccn/sn87062317/1862-01-07/ed-1/seq-2/.

[8] R. E. Lee, *Wartime Papers*, 101.

[9] Richards, *Civil War Diary*, 88.

you to further exertions."[10]

January 11, 1862 (Saturday)

Much of the military focus in the state remained along the coast as the new year got underway. Flag Officer Samuel Du Pont notified the U.S. Navy Department of achievements, noting "I have taken seven ports, and now actually hold five ports, of which three are in South Carolina and two in Georgia, and of which five ports, three are held by us in connection with the Army."[11]

January 12, 1862 (Sunday)

As the combatants continued to engage on the front lines, folks at home had additional worries—salt! "Salt at $20 per sack, as it is selling now, is not near so extortionate as the present price of factory goods, wheat, flour, corn and various other articles of as prime necessity as salt, even."[12]

January 13, 1862 (Monday)

Secretary of the U.S. Navy, Gideon Welles, wrote to Flag Officer Du Pont of a potential source of shipbuilding supplies. "It has been represented to the Department that there are large quantities of ship timber prepared for market, some afloat and some ashore, in the creeks and inlets of the South Carolina and Georgia coasts, and it is desirable, therefore, that an examination should be made as soon as convenient to ascertain the fact."[13]

January 14, 1862 (Tuesday)

The Confederates continued to focus resources along the coast. "The troops which were stationed at Screven, Appling County, have all been removed to Savannah. All persons having business with Col. Wright will address him at Savannah."[14]

January 15, 1862 (Wednesday)

As the war entered the second year, the deployment of troops continued across the state. "The Georgia Flying Artillery, Captain H. N. Hollifield, have received orders to be in readiness to go into active service on the 22nd instant. Their battery will consist of six as fine guns as are in the service. The company goes to the coast in the service of the State, and will receive a few more recruits."[15]

January 16, 1862 (Thursday)

Brigadier General T. W. Sherman notified Flag Officer Du Pont of conditions of the approaches to Savannah. "I have before learned, the only land battery that can now be served

---

[10] "The War—To the People of Georgia," *Atlanta Southern Confederacy*, January 10, 1862, https://gahistoricnewspapers.galileo.usg.edu/lccn/sn82014677/1862-01-10/ed-1/seq-2/.

[11] *ORN*, ser. I, vol. 12:477.

[12] "Salt Again," *Atlanta Southern Confederacy*, January 12, 1862, https://gahistoricnewspapers.galileo.usg.edu/lccn/sn82014677/1862-01-12/ed-1/seq-2/.

[13] *ORN*, ser. I, vol. 12:481.

[14] "Col. Wm. F. Wright's Regiment," *Atlanta Southern Confederacy*, January 14, 1862, https://gahistoricnewspapers.galileo.usg.edu/lccn/sn82014677/1862-01-14/ed-1/seq-3/.

[15] "Georgia Flying Artillery," *Sandersville Central Georgian*, January 15, 1862, https://gahistoricnewspapers.galileo.usg.edu/lccn/sn85034105/1862-01-15/ed-1/seq-2/.

against an assailing party in the Savannah River above Pulaski is Fort Jackson. A battery has been constructed on the very lower end of Hutchinson's Island, near Fig Island, and the guns are there, but on Saturday last had not been mounted." Sherman closed his report with a request for further orders. "A large battery has been under construction on the island immediately opposite Fort Jackson during the past, ten or fourteen days, but no guns had been sent there on last Saturday. It appears to me that if the Savannah River is to be entered, now is the time, before these batteries can be completed. Will it not be possible to go in there now with a sufficient force to make it a profitable job?[16]

January 17, 1862 (Friday)

Major Edward C. Anderson wrote to General Cooper from Savannah with alarming news. "By a communication from the commandant of Saint Simon's Island I am informed that the port of Brunswick is continually blockaded by a heavy side-wheel steamer, and that the enemy's gunboats have been cruising inside of Sapello [*sic*] and the adjacent inlets. The entrance to Warsaw [*sic*] is effectually sealed; a vessel is permanently anchored inside."[17]

January 18, 1862 (Saturday)

Naval Commander John Rodgers updated Flag Officer Du Pont of the various river approaches to Fort Pulaski, and problems with the several explored methods. "For a vessel to get ashore at high water, for her to be left twelve hours aground and part of the time nearly dry, under the fire of the rifled guns of Fort Pulaski, would entail her destruction. The attempt, then, is not advisable until after the channel shall be staked or buoyed."[18]

January 19, 1862 (Sunday)

General Robert E. Lee, writing in a letter to one of his sons, explained the defensive conditions along the coasts of Florida, Georgia, and South Carolina. "I have just returned from a visit to the coast as far as Fernandina [Florida]. Our defences are growing stronger, but progress slowly. The volunteers dislike work & there is much sickness among them besides. Guns too are required, ammunition, & more men. Still on the whole matters are encouraging & if the enemy does not approach in overwhelming numbers we ought to hold our ground."[19]

January 20, 1862 (Monday)

Brigadier General T. W. Sherman revised his earlier suggestion of a joint operation, one, which might afford the Federals the occasion to secure Savannah. "Reconnaissances of Savannah River had led me to the belief that Savannah might be taken by a combined operation of the Army and Navy by operating in the river itself, which would save the slow and expensive process of bombarding Pulaski by cutting it from Savannah, and also the slow process of besieging Savannah from the south…." Sherman also summarized a discussion with Du Pont, one where the two officers conceived a plan "particularly calculated to the cutting off of Fort Pulaski…I believe, effectually."[20]

---

16 *ORN*, ser. I, vol. 12:485.

17 *OR*, ser. I, vol. 6:368–69.

18 *ORN*, ser. I, vol. 12:492–93.

19 R. E. Lee, *Wartime Papers*, 106.

20 *OR*, ser. I, vol. 6:219.

January 21, 1862 (Tuesday)
The *Southern Reporter* in Milledgeville reported on a situation affecting the delivery of mail within the state. The delays occurred, according to the suspicion of the writer, because "letters address[ed] to this place 'Manassas' are sent to Virginia. Will you please put a request in a conspicuous place in your paper, and request other papers to do so for a few times, that letters be directed to "Manassas, Bartow county, Georgia." By writing the *County* and *Georgia* without abbreviation, mistakes will be avoided." The confusion resulted when citizens in Cass County opted to rename the county (in December 1861) after Georgian Colonel Francis S. Bartow, who fell at First Manassas/Bull Run. Another name change effort, one renaming Cassville to Manassas, did not meet favor with the postal service in Washington.[21]

January 22, 1862 (Wednesday)
Governor Brown telegraphed the Confederate Secretary of the Treasury Christopher Memminger, suggesting Georgia "would pay from one to two millions of the War Tax if seven per cent. would be allowed in advance."[22]

January 23, 1862 (Thursday) ◑
Governor Brown wrapped up a visit to Savannah after a favorable inspection of fortifications made locals especially proud. The *Daily Morning News* reported, "His Excellency, Governor Brown…left in the train for Milledgeville yesterday, at noon. We understand that the Governor expresses himself much pleased with the military preparations in our vicinity, and the condition of the State troops. Governor Brown is determined to leave nothing undone on his part that will tend to the complete and efficient organization of the State forces and the successful defence of the State."[23]

January 24, 1862 (Friday)
Responding to a plea from another newspaper suggesting, "It is high time for the journals of the South to be making arrangements for a permanent, and at the same time, more economical news agency," the *Southern Confederacy* called for a mid-March meeting in Atlanta.[24]

January 25, 1862 (Saturday)
Secretary of the Navy Gideon Welles reminded Flag Officer Du Pont of the significance of strengthening the blockade. Welles noted, "The importance of a rigorous blockade at every

[21] "Manassas, Georgia," *Milledgeville Southern Recorder*, January 21, 1862, sec. 2, https://gahistoricnewspapers.galileo.usg.edu/lccn/sn82016415/1862-01-21/ed-1/seq-2/; Krakow, *Georgia Place-Names*, 143.

[22] "Finances of Georgia," *Columbus Daily Morning News*, sec. 2, January 22, 1862, https://gahistoricnewspapers.galileo.usg.edu/lccn/sn82015886/1862-01-22/ed-1/seq-2/.

[23] "His Excellency, Governor Brown," *Savannah Daily Morning News*, January 23, 1862, sec. 2, https://gahistoricnewspapers.galileo.usg.edu/lccn/sn82015886/1862-01-23/ed-1/seq-2/.

[24] "A Convention of Editors and Proprietors of the Newspapers in the Confederate States," *Atlanta Southern Confederacy*, January 24, 1862, sec. 2, https://gahistoricnewspapers.galileo.usg.edu/lccn/sn82014677/1862-01-24/ed-1/seq-2/.

point under your command can not be too strongly impressed or felt. By cutting off all communication we not only distress and cripple the States in insurrection, but by an effective blockade we destroy any excuse or pretext on the part of foreign governments to aid and relieve those who are waging war upon the Government."[25]

January 26, 1862 (Sunday)

A Federal combined reconnaissance began toward the Wilmington Narrows section of the Georgia coast. This operation would continue through January 28. Brigadier General Horatio Wright reported on the opening movements. "I proceeded on the morning of the 26th, with the transports carrying my command, in company with the gunboats, to Wassaw Sound, Georgia, where we arrived and anchored about 2 o'clock the same day. Wright detailed the naval flotilla accompanying his infantry troops and indicated Captain Charles H. Davis's ships included "the gunboats *Ottawa*...*Seneca*...*Isaac Smith*...*Potomska*...*Ellen*...and *Western World*...and two armed launches, with their crews, from the *Wabash*, under the command of Captain C. R. P. Rodgers, U.S. Navy."[26]

January 27, 1862 (Monday)

Even during a time of war, normal activities continued away from the front lines. "The Confederates States Bible Convention will assemble in Augusta, on the 19th of March. Notice with reference to Railroad accommodations will be given at an early day."[27]

January 28, 1862 (Tuesday)

Confederate Flag Officer Josiah Tattnall navigated his five steamers along the Little Tybee River, received fire from Federal naval ships in the morning, and then engaged again in the early afternoon. Federal Captain Charles Davis reported on the action, observing, "as a demonstration, the appearance of the naval and military forces in Wilmington and Wassaw Sound has had complete success. Savannah was thrown into a state of great alarm, and all the energies of the place have been exerted to the utmost to increase its military defenses, for which purpose troops have been withdrawn from other places."[28]

January 29, 1862 (Wednesday) ●

Arriving in Savannah, General Robert E. Lee updated the Confederate War Department with intelligence he had collected on the status of the coasts of South Carolina and Georgia. Of Georgia, Lee observed, "If the enemy succeed in removing the obstacles in Wall's Cut and Wilmington Narrows there is nothing to prevent their reaching the Savannah River, and we have nothing afloat that can contend against them. The communication between Savannah and Fort Pulaski will then be cut off...we must endeavor to defend the city...I have caused to be sunk in Wilmington Narrows the floating dock of this city."[29]

January 30, 1862 (Thursday)

---

[25] *ORN*, ser. I, vol. 12:522.

[26] Ibid., 526–27.

[27] "The Confederate States Bible Convention," *Columbus Daily Sun*, January 27, 1862, sec. 2, https://gahistoricnewspapers.galileo.usg.edu/lccn/sn82014939/1862-01-27/ed-1/seq-2/.

[28] *ORN*, ser. I, vol. 12:525.

[29] Ibid., 505.

Confederate Secretary of War, Judah P. Benjamin, telegraphed General Lee in Savannah. "I send you tomorrow three heavy guns, two of them 10-inch and one 8-inch, equipped complete. Will send three more in three or four days. They are all we can give you. We have no iron carriages, and send wooden carriages."[30]

January 31, 1862 (Friday)

Garrison troops in Fort Pulaski needed supplies, and efforts continued in Savannah to get rations to the soldiers. "The steamer *Leesburg* left the city yesterday morning...with a quantity of provisions. She reached the fort without any difficulty, and, although the two Yankee vessels at Wall's cut saw her, they did not open fire upon her."[31]

February 1, 1862 (Saturday)

Flag-Officer Samuel Du Pont issued General Orders No. 7, which stipulated his expected behavior of officers and sailors. "The commanding officers of the vessels attached to this squadron will give special attention to all intercourse between the men under their command and the various plantations in their vicinity. No stock or provisions of any kind must be taken without paying a fair price for the same to the negroes."[32]

February 2, 1862 (Sunday)

Calling on "Atlanta Volunteers," the *Southern Confederacy* ran this announcement: "Several of our patriotic citizens have nobly come forward and authorized Capt. A. M. Wallace to draw on them for provisions and rations for all who may volunteer, until they are mustered into service, and can draw from the Government." After reminding readers "bounty of $50 will be paid so soon as sixty-four names are enrolled," the notice closed with a call to arms. "Come! come!!! Wake from your lethargy!!! Let every able-bodied man who can possibly leave his home enrol [*sic*] his name at once."[33]

February 3, 1862 (Monday)

Naval activity along the coast continued to capture the attention of most Georgians. "We have not a word of news to report from below this morning. The Yankee vessels still remain in Wall's Cut, but none are visible on the south side of the river. It has been ascertained that the obstructions in Wilmington Narrows are untouched, and some suppose that the vessels which were there some days ago have gone round to Port Royal...."[34]

February 4, 1862 (Tuesday)

General Lee wrote to Brigadier General John C. Pemberton detailing plans if the Federals advanced toward Savannah. "It seems probable...the enemy is meditating an advance from New River to the banks of the Savannah, and General [Brigadier Thomas] Drayton has

---

[30] *OR*, ser. I, vol. 6:371.

[31] "From Fort Pulaski," *Savannah Daily Morning News*, January 31, 1863, sec. 1, https://gahistoricnewspapers.galileo.usg.edu/lccn/sn82015886/1862-01-31/ed-1/seq-1/.

[32] *ORN*, ser. I, vol. 12:532-33.

[33] "Atlanta Volunteers," *Atlanta Southern Confederacy*, February 2, 1862, sec. 3, https://gahistoricnewspapers.galileo.usg.edu/lccn/sn82014677/1862-02-02/ed-1/seq-3/.

[34] "From the Savannah News," *Columbus Daily Sun*, February 3, 1862, sec. 1, https://gahistoricnewspapers.galileo.usg.edu/lccn/sn82014939/1862-02-03/ed-1/seq-1/.

been directed to take up a line removed beyond the reach of the gunboats on New River to intercept him; should the enemy land too large a force for him to cope with, he has been directed to notify you. In that event you are desired to send to his support such of your available force as may be necessary…and to take command of the whole operation."[35]

February 5, 1862 (Wednesday)

Frustrated with a slow-moving navy, Brigadier General T. W. Sherman vented with Quartermaster General Montgomery Meigs. "My firm conviction is that if the gunboats could have been induced to enter the river as early as the 17th or 18th of last month, when Wall's Cut was then opened, and the enemy had no guns mounted at Savannah but those on Fort Jackson, Savannah would have fallen without a resistance of five hours duration, but it could not have been taken by the land force alone in that way." Sherman closed with a new target. "As Savannah seems out of our grasp for the present, we shall go down to Fernandina as soon as the Navy is ready."[36]

February 6, 1862 (Thursday) ◐

Headquartered in Savannah, General Lee grew increasingly concerned with the struggle to fill the ranks. He wrote to the War Department and Secretary Judah Benjamin, and outlined the situation. "The replacing [of] the troops in the Confederate service in this State is matter of serious consideration. The period of service of several companies, serving the batteries for the defence of the city of Savannah is about to expire. The loss of these companies at this time will be a serious injury to the defence of the city, as artillerists cannot be made on the eve of a battle." Lee closed with an appeal for Benjamin's intervention. "But the prospective injury to the service, I fear, will be equally great, as neither the sentiment of the people, or the policy of the State seems to favor the organization of troops for Confederate service."[37]

February 7, 1862 (Friday)

Continuing to plan for an advance on Fort Pulaski, Brigadier General T. W. Sherman queried Du Pont on his strategy. "Can we not we get into the Savannah River at once and effect our object? That is, erect our batteries, so as to see how the thing works before starting on the second expedition. This, I confess, was my plan, and am sorry we have not brought the matter to a test ere this." Du Pont acted. He notified Commander John Rodgers of the naval plan. "The commanding general [T. W. Sherman] is now on board in reference to the erection of the battery on Jones Island. I have agreed to his earnest suggestion that this should be done, although it must retard other operations. You will therefore dispose of the forces under your command and enter the Savannah River, if necessary, to accomplish this."[38]

February 8, 1862 (Saturday)

Continuing work along the coast, Du Pont filed a report on recent navigable decisions

---

[35] *ORN*, ser. I, vol. 12:506.

[36] *OR*, ser. I, vol. 6:221.

[37] R. E. Lee, *Wartime Papers*, 110.

[38] *ORN*, ser. I, vol. 12:498.

regarding a feint approach toward Savannah. The officer hoped this would mask his actual target—the port of Fernandina in Florida. "At this stage of the proceedings it was found expedient to send one or more gunboats into Wright's River to make a careful survey of the passage around Cunningham's Point into Savannah River, and a survey also of Mud River."[39]

February 9, 1862 (Sunday)

From Port Royal Harbor, Du Pont reported the capture, on February 5, of the schooner *Mars*. Numbered among the vessel's cargo were "notes on banks of South Carolina and Georgia, amounting to $53; of certificates of deposit in the Mechanics' Loan and Saving Association, of Savannah, from 5 cents to 50 cents, amounting to $6.25."[40]

February 10, 1862 (Monday)

General Lee, after working to strengthen the fortifications along Georgia's coast, wrote Governor Brown regarding the necessity of evacuating the more vulnerable positions. "I have had the honor to receive your letter of the 8th instant in reference to the withdrawal of the batteries from Saint Simon's & Jekyl [*sic*] Islands. No one can regret the apparent necessity of such a measure more than I do, & so great is my repugnance to yield any point of our territory to our enemies, that I have endeavored from the time of my arrival to give strength to the defences of Brunswick." Lee informed the governor of orders passed to Brigadier General Mercer to "withdraw the troops & guns from the islands to the main[land], should he, upon a reconsideration of the subject, hold to the opinion as to the inability of the batteries to contend with the enemy's fleet."[41]

February 11, 1862 (Tuesday)

Answering the call to supply 12 additional regiments to the Confederate service, Governor Brown issued a public address. In addition to detailing where the called-up soldiers should report for training, he reminded the citizens of the state of their patriotic duties. Brown avowed, if failing to respond "while there is a man in the State able to bear arms, a lady able to work to clothe him, and a dollar with which to support him in the field, we have degenerated and are unworthy our ancestors. Nay, more, we are unworthy the sacrifices which have been made for our protection by the noble sons of our State...."[42]

February 12, 1862 (Wednesday)

Major General George B. McClellan, from his headquarters in Washington, telegraphed Brigadier General T. W. Sherman for information on Fort Pulaski and Savannah. "I have been daily expecting to hear more definite accounts of what can be done in the Savannah River and of the possibility of starving out Fort Pulaski. While the rebels are pushed so much in other quarters, I would suggest for your consideration whether, by reducing your garrisons to the minimum, a successful combined attack cannot be made on Savannah so

---

[39] Ibid., 523.

[40] Ibid., 537.

[41] R. E. Lee, *Wartime Papers*, 113.

[42] Candler, *Confederate Records of the State of Georgia*, 2:189–90.

soon as Pulaski has fallen."[43]

February 13, 1862 (Thursday)

Responding to a call for supplying 12 additional regiments to the Confederate service, Governor Brown wrote to Secretary Benjamin, "I have apportioned the troops you require among the different counties of the State. Please suspend the issue of commissions to raise independent organizations till the requisition is filled, as the two do not harmonize, and confusion is the result."[44]

February 14, 1862 (Friday) (Valentine's Day)

Major General McClellan communicated with Brigadier General T. W. Sherman about Savannah. McClellan remained undecided as to the opportune time for Sherman's troops to advance. He suggested in the interim, "it is my advice and wish that no attempt be made upon Savannah, unless it can be carried with certainty by a coup de main. Please concentrate your attention and forces upon Pulaski and Fernandina. Success attends us everywhere at present."[45]

February 15, 1862 (Saturday)

Confederate gunboats attacked a Federal position in the Savannah River, and Brigadier General Egbert Viele recapped the action. "I have the honor to report that the batteries on Venus Point were attacked at 3 o'clock p.m.…by four rebel gunboats with a view of effecting a passage from Fort Pulaski for the rebel steamer then at that place. After an engagement of one hour the rebels were driven off, the flag steamer being disabled and taken in tow, and the steamer that attempted the passage of the river returning to Fort Pulaski." The general made specific mention of the unit engaged. "The guns were manned by the Third Rhode Island detachment, under Captain [John] Gould, and effectively worked. There was no loss on our side."[46]

February 16, 1862 (Sunday)

Brigadier General Hugh Mercer reported from Brunswick of the actions performed as a result of General Lee's recommendations to redeploy certain defenses away from the view of the U.S. Navy. "The guns have all been removed from the islands and brought to this place, with the exception of one 32-pounder, which 1 expect up in the course of the day. One 12-pounder and eight 32-pounders have been shipped to Savannah by rail, and I hope to get off to-day and tomorrow the columbiads and the remaining 32s, reserving four 32s to be sent to Fernandina."[47]

February 17, 1862 (Monday)

General R. E. Lee continued work in Savannah to ensure the Federal approaches to the city remained guarded. He wrote to Colonel Charles Olmstead, offering specific details on work the colonel needed to complete. "From the position the enemy has taken in the Savannah

---

[43] *OR*, ser. I, vol. 6:224.

[44] Candler, *Confederate Records of the State of Georgia*, 3:156.

[45] *OR*, ser. I, vol. 6:225.

[46] Ibid., 90–91.

[47] Ibid., 386.

River, it becomes necessary that you look to your defense in that direction. I therefore recommend that, if necessary for that purpose, you shift some of your barbette guns to the gorge of the work, and. the casemates m the northwest angle, which bear up the river, be provided with guns." Lee closed with one last piece of instruction: "I would also recommend that the parapets of the mortar batteries be carried all around, so that the mortars can be protected from the fire up the river as well as from Tybee Island, and that everything be done to strengthen the defenses of your work in the rear."[48]

February 18, 1862 (Tuesday)

Preparations continued, under General Lee's guidance, to fortify the coastal areas of the state. Lee updated General Samuel Cooper on the work completed thus far and noted special concern for Brunswick. "The nature of the ground prevents the possibility of holding of Brunswick, as the gunboats of the enemy can unmolested ascend the river within four miles of the railroad at Waynesville & about 25 miles in the rear of Brunswick. Brunswick would prove a convenient & healthy position, if occupied by the enemy, affording shelter and comfort, quarters for the troops & hospitals for the sick."[49]

February 19, 1862 (Wednesday)

Brigadier General T. W. Sherman took action to prevent a backdoor attack from Confederate boats. "I have ascertained that the *Ida* got through to Savannah by Lazaretto Creek and Wilmington Narrows...gunboats can come down through there and take our batteries in Savannah River almost in reverse. This will give me a great deal of trouble at a time when least expected. I am taking measures to blockade that passageway to the best of our ability."[50]

February 20, 1862 (Thursday) ◑

Federal Major General Quincy Gillmore took command of the forces on Tybee Island. During the evening of his arrival in Tybee, Gillmore's troops started moving artillery toward Fort Pulaski, which included "a second battery, consisting of one 8-inch siege howitzer, one 30 pounder Parrott, one 20-pounder Parrott, and three 12-pounder James rifles...established on Bird Island, just above Long Island...the flats, with the guns, ammunition, &c., on them, being towed up Mud River and across the Savannah by rowboats."[51]

February 21, 1862 (Friday)

Governor Brown wrote to General Lee in Savannah and detailed his thoughts on acceptable measures to prevent the Federals from capturing certain targets. "God grant that they may enable you to drive the enemy's gunboats from the river when the attack comes. I have to say that if my own house were in Brunswick I would certainly set fire to it, when driven from it by the enemy, rather than see it used by them as a shelter. We should destroy whatever the military necessities require. I am therefore prepared to sustain any order which in

---

[48] Ibid., 389.

[49] R. E. Lee, *Wartime Papers*, 115.

[50] *ORN*, ser. I, vol. 12:555.

[51] *OR*, ser. I, vol. 6:153.

your opinion it is necessary to have executed." Brown closed with the assertion, "Private property and private rights must yield to the great public interests now at stake. The question of compensation will be one which will address itself to the State. When the war is over, justice to sufferers will no doubt be done."[52]

February 22, 1862 (Saturday)

General Lee continued work in Savannah to strengthen the defenses and transportation network in the region. In a letter to Governor Brown, Lee called the governor's attention "to the importance to the defence of the cities of Charleston, Augusta, & Savannah, as well as to the states of Georgia & South Carolina, of connecting the Augusta & Savannah Railroad with the Georgia or South Carolina Railroad at Augusta." Funding might not prove an obstacle for the state, as Lee submitted "I am informed that the Augusta & Savannah Railroad Company is willing to build the connection at its own expense, provided they be allowed to take the route which they would prefer, & which the president of the road, Dr. [Francis T.] Willis, informs me is but ¼ of a mile in distance."[53]

February 23, 1862 (Sunday)

Taking an opportunity in Savannah to write a letter to his wife, Mary, General Lee informed her of conditions in Georgia. "Here the enemy is progressing slowly in his designs, & does not seem prepared, or to have determined when or where to make his attack. His gunboats are pushing up all the creeks & marshes of the Savannah, & have attained a position so near the river as to shell the steamers navigating it." Lee brought her up to date on his present activities, stating, "I am engaged in constructing a line of defence at Fort Jackson which, if time permits & guns can be obtained, I hope will keep them out. They [The Federal Navy] can bring such overwhelming force in all their movements that it has the effect to demoralize our new troops."[54]

February 24, 1862 (Monday)

Florida Governor John Milton received unwelcomed news from General Lee in Savannah. "The Governor of Georgia has been obliged to refuse my recent application to him for two regiments...for the purpose of preventing an advance of the enemy through Florida into the southwest portion of Georgia."[55]

February 25, 1862 (Tuesday)

The editor of a Milledgeville newspaper, envisioning what might await citizens of Georgia, urged a state of readiness. "To conceal from the people the danger in which we are involved, would be both unwise and criminal. There are some, indeed, who would speak only in smooth and consoling words. The people will now be aroused, they say and the danger will be arrested. There is therefore no need of anxiety. And we must be quiet lest the enemy

---

[52] Ibid., 396.

[53] R. E. Lee, *Wartime Papers*, 117.

[54] Ibid., 118–19.

[55] Ibid., 120.

shall think that we are all frightened."[56]

February 26, 1862 (Wednesday)

Thomas R. R. Cobb called on Georgians to respond to the "successful armies of the North…at the doors of our State." Cobb detailed instructions on the time he planned to spend in Athens, and how "additional troops" could muster "into my Legion."[57]

February 27, 1862 (Thursday)

Preparing to navigate from Port Royal, South Carolina, to Georgia, Rear Admiral Du Pont communicated his intentions to the army via a dispatch to Brigadier General T. W. Sherman. "I have been much tried by the weather. The delay, however, brought my ammunition, but it was under hay and oats, and in spite of all I could do I have to leave my gunboats to receive it. They will follow, lest I miss the tide. I leave with the coming tide, and shall be off Wassaw to-night or to-morrow morning."[58]

February 28, 1862 (Friday) ●

"The deserters just in from Savannah say there are about 65,000 troops in and about the city, which is well fortified both on the land and river sides. They are moving heaven and earth for a secure defense. So far as I can ascertain some of the smaller forts on the coast are being stripped of artillery with which to protect Savannah. The abandonment of Brunswick is an evidence of it."[59] Brigadier General T. W. Sherman's report to McClellan on conditions in his military territory.

March 1, 1862 (Saturday)

In Savannah, General Lee directed orders to an officer in Florida detailing the importance of guarding riverine approaches into Georgia. "The recent disasters in Tennessee (Forts Henry and Donelson) forces the government to withdraw forces employed in the defence of the seaboard. The only troops to be retained in Florida are such as may be necessary to defend the Apalachicola River, by which the enemy's gunboats may penetrate far into the State of Georgia."[60]

March 2, 1862 (Sunday)

In Savannah, General Lee wrote two letters; the first updated his wife on events transpiring near Fort Pulaski. "They [Federals] have worked their way across the marshes, with their dredges, under cover of their gunboats, to the Savannah River, above Fort Pulaski. I presume they will endeavour to reduce the fort & thus open the way for their heavier vessels up the river. But we have an interior line they must force before reaching the city." Lee's second letter, a response to President Jefferson Davis, who telegraphed, inquiring, "If

---

[56] "The People Must Awake," *Milledgeville Southern Federal Union*, February 25, 1862, sec. 2, https://gahistoricnewspapers.galileo.usg.edu/lccn/sn87062317/1862-02-25/ed-1/seq-2/.

[57] "Georgians!," *Athens Southern Banner*, February 26, 1862, sec. 3, https://gahistoricnewspapers.galileo.usg.edu/lccn/sn82014069/1862-02-26/ed-1/seq-3/.

[58] *ORN*, ser. I, vol. 12:570.

[59] *OR*, ser. I, vol. 6:236.

[60] R. E. Lee, *Wartime Papers*, 121.

circumstances will, in your judgment, warrant your leaving, I wish to see you here with the least delay." Lee's response: "If possible, I will leave Tuesday morning; if prevented will inform you."[61]

March 3, 1862 (Monday)

As he prepared to depart Savannah for Richmond, General Lee left final instructions for Brigadier General Alexander Lawton. "I shall be compelled to leave Savannah this evening on duty. Every effort must be made to retard, if not prevent, the further progress of the enemy up the river. If he attempts to advance by batteries on the marshes or islands, he must be driven back, if possible. It is of the utmost importance that the work at every point should be pushed forward with the utmost vigor and the closest attention given to the whole subject of the defense of the city."[62]

March 4, 1862 (Tuesday)

The waters churned along the coasts of Florida and Georgia, as naval efforts to secure key positions continued. Commander Percival Drayton, aboard the USS *Pawnee*, recapped the post-capture of Fernandina in Florida. "Soon after [Fernandina] Commander [Christopher Raymond Perry] Rodgers, with the *Ottawa*, proceeded to occupy the town of St. Mary's, Ga., a small place on the St. Mary's River, distant 10 miles from here, and where we supposed some of the guns removed from Fort Clinch had been taken."[63] Upon General Lee's departure from Savannah, Major General John C. Pemberton took command of the Department of South Carolina, Georgia, and East Florida.

March 5, 1862 (Wednesday)

St. Simons Island served as a focal point for Federal naval officers, especially after a report indicated the Confederates may have left the stronghold. Du Pont updated Commander Sylvanus Godon. "Before leaving Port Royal information reached me that the preparations of this expedition had caused the abandonment of the fort at St. Simon's Island, a very strong work, and that thirty cannon had been taken to Savannah. This has been confirmed by two sources since." Godon received orders to report his findings to Du Pont after "ascertaining the true condition of things" in the area."[64]

March 6, 1862 (Thursday)

Keeping tabs on events in Georgia, Major General McClellan telegraphed Brigadier General T. W. Sherman suggesting, "if it will not interfere with any operation of greater importance that you may now have on hand, the General-in-Chief hopes that you will be able to arrange with Commodore DuPont for the prompt occupation of Fernandina, in accordance with the original plan of the expedition." McClellan insured Sherman remained focus on the major objective in closing the dispatch. "It is supposed that this operation will not interfere with the reduction of Fort Pulaski, which is regarded as a matter of very great importance."[65]

---

[61] Ibid., 122–23; Davis telegraph in *OR*, ser. I, vol. 6:400.[**Lee's response as well?**]

[62] *OR*, ser. I, vol. 6:401–402.

[63] *ORN*, ser. I, vol. 12:577; Pemberton in *OR*, ser. I, vol. 6:402.

[64] *ORN*, ser. I, vol. 12:581. Italics in original.

[65] *OR*, ser. I, vol. 6:238.

March 7, 1862 (Friday)

Federal naval operations continued along the coast, as an expedition got underway in the Savannah River toward Elba Island. Lieutenant T. H. Stephens issued an address to civilians in the area. He announced, "the U. S. gunboat *Ottawa*, is authorized by Flag- Officer Du Pont to assure the peaceable citizens living on the St. Mary's River that they will be protected in their persons and property; that it is his desire they should return to their homes, where nobody will come near to harm them."[66]

March 8, 1862 (Saturday)

An amphibious landing on St. Simons Island took place as part of Du Pont's orders to secure the area. Lieutenant George Balch of the USS *Pocahontas* recounted the day. Balch's vessel, "armed with a howitzer, and the second cutter of this ship, with the marines and an armed cutter from the *Mohican*, to take possession of St. Simon's Island, on which we landed, instantly throwing out pickets, and taking every precaution against surprise. This done, I took formal possession of St. Simon's Island, hoisting the American flag on one of the batteries thrown up by the rebels."[67]

March 9, 1862 (Sunday)

Du Pont reported to the Navy Department on operations from the South Atlantic Blockading Squadron. "I may say in confidence that I have no doubt we have entire possession of the whole coast of Florida, as well as that of Georgia. I have just communicated with the gunboats. Lieutenant Commanding [Thomas] Stevens reports three batteries at the mouth of St. John's River with guns in them, but deserted."[68]

March 10, 1862 (Monday)

The Federals occupied Brunswick, and Lieutenant George Balch of the USS *Pocahontas* reported on the occasion. "I have the honor to report that I proceeded this day in obedience to your order with the launches, armed with howitzers, and the boats of the *Mohican* and *Pocahontas*, covered by the battery of the *Potomska*...to land and take possession of the town of Brunswick, Ga., which we did, meeting with no resistance whatever. We hoisted the American flag on the Oglethorpe House...."[69]

March 11, 1862 (Tuesday)

Seizing the area on the previous day, Lieutenant Balch conducted reconnaissance near Brunswick. "Along the banks of Turtle River we could see the embankments of a railroad and a train from Brunswick passing over it as we ascended the river. The Coast-Survey chart which I had was found very accurate as far as it went but did not take us up the whole distance."[70]

March 12, 1862 (Wednesday)

A Savannah newspaper reported on the differences between folks in the two sections of the

---

[66] *ORN*, ser. I, vol. 12:585; Elba Island information in Mosocco, *Chronological Tracking*, 49.

[67] *ORN*, ser. I, vol. 12:590.

[68] Ibid., 589.

[69] Ibid., 591.

[70] Ibid., 595.

country. "Whilst the Northern people are waging war, nominally for Southern subjugation, but really for the sole benefit of favorite contractors and greedy harpies who speculate upon the necessities of Lincolndom, the Southern people, almost as one man, are engaged in defending their liberties without respect to private inconvenience or pecuniary sacrifice."[71]

March 13, 1862 (Thursday)

Commander Sylvanus Godon with the USS *Mohican* near St. Simons Sound reported, "I have the honor to report that the *Pocahontas* and *Potomska*...returned without accident. Soon after the return of those vessels...a boat from the *Pocahontas* landed some distance outside the town to procure fresh beef; their work was done, and the boat had already left the beach, when some 40 or 50 soldiers made their appearance and fired upon the boat, killing 2 men and wounding several others."[72]

March 14, 1862 (Friday)

The Confederate War Department, via Special Orders, No. 59, announced, "Maj. Gen. John C. Pemberton is assigned to the command of the Department of South Carolina and Georgia." General Lee wrote Pemberton on the same day, offering advice on certain officers in the department, and suggesting Pemberton "will require the aid of every good citizen of your department to contribute to its defense."[73]

March 15, 1862 (Saturday) ◯

The U.S. War Department made a change to their military structure that affected the Federals in Georgia. "The States of South Carolina, Georgia, and Florida, with the expedition and forces now under Brig. Gen. T. W. Sherman, will constitute a military department, to be called the Department of the South, to be commanded by Major General [David] Hunter.[74]

March 16, 1862 (Sunday)

Commander Godon reported on conditions along the coast. "Darien has been deserted, as was Brunswick. This we learned from some contrabands who came off to us, a company of horsemen only remaining in town, with the intention of firing the place should we approach it."[75]

March 17, 1862 (Monday) (St. Patrick's Day)

Commander Godon directed one of his ships to enter Jekyll Creek and navigate to "Dubignon's place, where I discovered a deserted battery of three guns to command that stream and the remains of a camp of some two hundred men. A considerable quantity of cattle remains on the island, but very wild on our approach."[76]

March 18, 1862 (Wednesday)

---

[71] "North and South—A Contrast," *Savannah Daily Morning News*, March 12, 1862, sec. 1, https://gahistoricnewspapers.galileo.usg.edu/lccn/sn82015886/1862-03-12/ed-1/seq-1/.

[72] ORN, ser. 1, vol. 12:609–10.

[73] *OR*, ser. I, vol. 6:407.

[74] Ibid., 248.

[75] *ORN*, ser. I, vol. 12:614.

[76] Ibid., 633.

The Confederate Congress approved a measure to provide for war widows. The Committee on Military Affairs received the assignment to: "inquire into the expediency of paying, during the continuance of the present war, the pensions allowed by the laws of the United States to the widows of deceased officers and soldiers of the Army whose husbands, at the time of their decease, were citizens of any one of the States comprising this Confederacy, said widows now being citizens of the Confederate States; and report by bill or otherwise."[77]

March 19, 1862 (Tuesday)

Major General Henry Wayne, charged with the affairs of Georgia militia forces, received instructions from Major General John Pemberton. Wayne read Pemberton "approves of your idea of ordering out the militia in that part of your State invaded by the enemy; but before inaugurating a system of guerrilla warfare he would recommend that all women and children be removed before such operations are commenced on our part."[78]

March 20, 1862 (Thursday)

President Lincoln addressed naval issues in a letter to Congress. "I cordially recommend that Captain Samuel F. Du Pont receive a vote of thanks of Congress for his services and gallantry displayed in the capture, since the 21st of December, 1861, of various points on the coasts of Georgia and Florida, particularly Brunswick, Cumberland Island and Sound, Amelia Island, the towns of St. Mary's, St. Augustine, Jacksonville, and Fernandina."[79]

March 21, 1862 (Friday)

Lieutenant Clark H. Wells, onboard his ship *Unadilla*, gained intelligence of an operation, reportedly underway in Savannah. "This morning I had a conversation with the two deserters from Pulaski, and they say that an ironclad boat was being built at Savannah for the purpose of running by the batteries and then engage our vessels." Wells also shared information gained from Federal Brigadier General Egbert Viele, which indicated, "Some eight flat-bottom scows, capable of containing 400 men each, are to be towed down by the rebel steamers, to be landed where our troops are, in case the ironclad boat should be successful."[80]

March 22, 1862 (Saturday) ◑

Governor Brown corresponded with President Davis concerning Georgia's contribution of troops. Responding to the president's call on the state for twelve additional regiments, Brown noted the state "now tenders you thirteen regiments and three battalions. There are six regiments and one battalion, which will, it is believed, soon recruit to a regiment, at Camp McDonald; three regiments and a battalion and one artillery company at Camp Stephens, and four regiments and battalion of nine companies, which will no doubt soon be filled up as a regiment, at Camp Davis."[81]

March 23, 1862 (Sunday)

Outside Savannah, Brigadier General T. W. Sherman filed a scouting report of the

---

[77] *Journal of the Confederate Congress*, March 19, 1862, 2:76.

[78] *OR*, ser. I, vol. 6:410.

[79] *ORN*, ser. I, vol. 12:617.

[80] Ibid., 653.

[81] Candler, *Confederate Records of the State of Georgia*, 3:167–68.

Savannah River to naval officers. "I do not know how many gunboats you have there at present, but I would respectfully and earnestly suggest that any light-draft gunboats or armed tugs which can get through the creek which you may have on hand he sent there at once." Sherman noted the importance "that [Brigadier] General [Egbert] Viele's rear be guarded by gunboats, as it is to be presumed that if the attack expected by General Viele be made in the Savannah River, it will be accompanied with a serious one by the way of New River. I am anxious that the enemy be not allowed to make an attack in that direction, and it can only be prevented by gunboats." In closing, the general suggested, "An attack on Savannah River can hardly be prevented if the enemy chooses to make it, and we will meet it with all the means in our possession; but this in the rear it is of the highest importance to prevent."[82]

March 24, 1862 (Monday)

Governor Brown faced a dilemma and sought assistance from Secretary of War Judah Benjamin. "The term of service of the State troops expires very soon; one regiment goes out in a week. Can you place 8,000 Confederate troops in their places for the defense of Savannah? If the State troops leave and their places are not filled immediately Savannah must fall into the hands of the enemy. Shall I attempt to detain the State troops, or what is your wish?"[83]

March 25, 1862 (Tuesday)

Governor Brown wrote to Secretary Benjamin on the importance of protecting Savannah. "Our whole coast is now virtually in possession of the enemy, except the city of Savannah. The city is the key to the State, and...should be defended at all hazards. I wish to urge upon your earliest attention the importance of placing at Savannah, without delay, at least 8,000 troops, in addition to the Confederate troops now there for the defense of the city."[84]

March 26, 1862 (Wednesday)

An escaped "contraband...of Savannah," described conditions in the city to Commander John Gillis. "They [Confederates] had given up the idea of defending the Savannah River by torpedoes, because one of the principal men who were sinking them got drowned while down in a diving bell, and [they] now talk of piling the river across."[85]

March 27, 1862 (Thursday)

Concern over the receipt of firearms shipped to Savannah prompted Major General Pemberton to ask General Samuel Cooper for clarification. "I have the honor to acknowledge the receipt of a telegram from the Secretary of War, dated March 26,1862, in relation to a complaint from the governor of Georgia that certain arms imported in the Gladiator and landed at Savannah had been seized by the Confederate officers. The Secretary directs, if this be so, the arms shall be released." Pemberton received a telegraph containing an update on the situation and included in the Cooper communique: "The arms were

[82] *ORN*, ser. I, vol. 12:652.

[83] Candler, *Confederate Records of the State of Georgia*, 3:169.

[84] Ibid., 3:170.

[85] *ORN*, ser. I, vol. 12:665.

not seized, but came into the hands of the ordnance officer with Confederate arms and without any notice of the State's claim until they were shipped."[86]

March 28, 1862 (Friday)

Major Oliver T. Beard reported on a Federal exploration outside Savannah. Beard conducted "a reconnaissance of the land about the mouth of Saint Augustine Creek. The best view was obtained from the summit of the upper Coast Survey station, on Elba Island. I send you a sketch of observations. The only rebel pickets about the mouth of Saint Augustine are stationed at the points indicated. In case of an attempt to cut them off their only chance of escape would be by swimming the bayou."[87]

March 29, 1862 (Saturday)

Flag Officer Du Pont queried Brigadier General T. W. Sherman on actions of the army. "The naval blockade of Savannah River is established at Tybee Roads; the vessels in Wright's and Mud rivers are there at your request to assist the batteries, as I understand it; having them there formed no part of a plan of mine. Will you do me the favor, general, to write me what your wishes are on the subject?"[88]

March 30, 1862 (Sunday) ●

Various engagements—on land and water—took place near Wilmington and Whitemarsh Islands. Colonel Rudolph Rosa, with the 46th New York Infantry, reported on his action of the day, noting he "made a reconnaissance on [the] Islands, pushing in both cases out to Thunderbolt and Saint Augustine Creeks, opposite to Thunderbolt and Carston Bluff batteries. Nothing remarkable occurred, excepting that the small stern-wheel steamer did show herself near to our boats left at Gibson's, in the Oatland Creek, which is not spiked, and turned back after receiving three of our musket shots from a point of land."[89]

March 31, 1862 (Monday)

Commander Godon of the USS *Mohican* reported on conditions near St. Simons Sound. He planned to instruct a subordinate to "remove the railroad iron from the Jekyl Island fort, although I do not believe the rebels would attempt to occupy the place other than as sharpshooters and as a means of attack upon boats. The rails are valuable and I will have them cared for, to be removed when convenient. The battery I will direct to be blown up."[90]

April 1, 1862 (Tuesday) (April Fools' Day)

Brigadier General Quincy Gillmore informed his naval counterparts of activity at Wilmington Island. "From dispatches received from the hulk *Montezuma*, anchored in Lazaretto Creek, 1 learn that the enemy are very active in the neighborhood of Wilmington Island. Yesterday a boat guard sent out from the hulk could not be found when the relief [was] sent for it. A captured contraband informs me that they were taken by the enemy on

---

[86] *OR*, ser. I, vol. 6:419.

[87] Ibid., 112.

[88] *ORN*, ser. I, vol. 12:673.

[89] *OR*, ser. I, vol. 6:121.

[90] *ORN*, ser. I, vol. 12:689.

Monday."[91]

April 2, 1862 (Wednesday)

One year later, and Governor Brown continued to quarrel with the War Department, albeit with a new secretary—George W. Randolph. The secretary responded to Brown, noting, "I fully appreciate the noble efforts of your gallant State in the common cause, and would most gladly ease the burden she has imposed upon herself. For the present, however, we must rely upon her constancy for the defense of her coast, as we find ourselves so pressed by invading armies along our northern frontier and on the seacoast that it is impossible to send troops to your assistance."[92]

April 3, 1862 (Thursday)

Commander Godon, operating in the Wilmington Narrows, had a hectic day. "This morning...we steamed up to Shads [Shad River], passing within 2 miles of Fort Pulaski, which threw a shot at us, good line, but falling 400 yards short. Having gone far enough to decide that no one could be about the marsh...returned to the hulk again, receiving a shot from Pulaski, but falling 200 yards or more short of us."[93]

April 4, 1862 (Friday)

Federal Brigadier General Egbert Viele scouted along the Savannah River and reported the information he gathered during the mission. Viele stated, "the guns on Long Island can be put in position at once. I have one 8-inch and one 10 inch mortar which I can use. The rebels were busy all night last night moving troops towards Wilmington Island. They have evidently something on the *tapis* [under consideration]."[94]

April 5, 1862 (Saturday)

What belonged to Georgia, stayed in Georgia...the doctrine of Governor Brown. While attempting to have arms returned to the state, the governor worked with Secretary Randolph. The head of the War Department responded to Brown's request. "I regret exceedingly the interference with your arms; will use every exertion to recover and restore them, or to return others of equal value. The arms sent to Richmond were, many of them, stopped at Raleigh and turned aside to Goldsborough, for the purpose of arming three Georgia regiments called for by General Lee. It may be that those were your arms."[95]

April 6, 1862 (Sunday)

Brigadier General Viele reported a rumor swirling about Savannah. "A negro from Fort Pulaski came in last evening. He says that Colonel [Charles] Olmstead, at the fort, read a letter on parade...saying that the preparations were completed for relieving the garrison, and that it would be done in a few days with their entire force of 30,000 men if necessary. They are to attack the batteries on the river simultaneously with those on Tybee."[96]

---

[91] Ibid., 701.

[92] Candler, *Confederate Records of the State of Georgia*, 3:176.

[93] *ORN*, ser. I, vol. 12:700.

[94] *OR*, ser. I, vol. 6:265. Italics in original.

[95] Candler, *Confederate Records of the State of Georgia*, 3:180.

[96] *ORN*, ser. I, vol. 12:717.

April 7, 1862 (Friday)
Women across the South continued their work in supplying various supplies for the soldiers. The ladies of Georgia proved no different, especially for Captain George Atkinson and his company, the Columbus Rebels. "The Ladies' Soldiers' Friend Society earnestly request contributions of blankets for the…company by Tuesday, the 8th inst."[97]

April 8, 1862 (Tuesday)
The construction of railroads in Georgia during the 1840s and 1850s (and the lack of connecting lines) presented a problem in a time of war, as indicated in Major General Pemberton's orders to Brigadier General Thomas Drayton. "Proceed…to the city of Augusta, Ga…confer with the mayor…in relation to the immediate connection through Augusta of the Waynesborough and Augusta and South Carolina Railroads. You will explain to the city authorities…of the railroad companies…this measure is a military necessity…I trust those interested will acknowledge."[98]

April 9, 1862 (Wednesday)
Captain C. R. P. Rodgers reported on the work of positioning Federal artillery on the Tybee Island approach to Fort Pulaski. "There are 35 mortars and cannon in battery at Tybee. There is a serious want of fuzes, and I have told the general that I was sure you would aid him to the extent of your resources. Our batteries are very well placed, the mortars are superb, the guns excellent, but I do not think much of the defenses against the enemy's shot."[99]

April 10, 1862 (Thursday)
The Federals attacked Fort Pulaski, and Captain Quincy Gillmore noted the effectiveness of their artillery against a brick-and-mortar fortification. "By 1 o'clock in the afternoon…it became evident that the work would be breached, provided our breaching batteries did not become seriously disabled by the enemy's fire. By the aid of a powerful telescope it could be observed that the rifled projectiles were doing excellent service, that their penetration was deep and effective, and that the portion of the wall where the breach had been ordered was becoming rapidly honey-combed."[100]

April 11, 1862 (Friday)
Confederate Brigadier General Lawton reported the fall of Fort Pulaski. The garrison had to surrender, because "a breach was made in the wall at the southeast angle, nearest the Tybee Island…this breach was wide enough to drive a four-horse team through; that the wall, which embraced seven casemates in succession, was nearly all knocked down, and that all the barbette guns which could play on their batteries at Tybee (Island) had been disabled; that several shots had been fired into the magazine."[101]

April 12, 1862 (Saturday)

---

[97] "Columbus Rebels, Capt. Atkinson," *Columbus Daily Sun*, April 7, 1862, sec. 1, https://gahistoricnewspapers.galileo.usg.edu/lccn/sn82014939/1862-04-07/ed-1/seq-1/.

[98] *OR*, ser. I, vol. 6:428.

[99] *ORN*, ser. I, vol. 12:725.

[100] *OR*, ser. I, vol. 6:158.

[101] Ibid., 167.

James Andrews, a civilian, had convinced Brigadier General Ormsby Mitchel to authorize a scheme to steal a locomotive, travel north toward Chattanooga, and cut telegraph lines and damage railroad bridges along the way. Boarding the first northbound train out of Atlanta, Andrews, along with one civilian and nineteen soldiers from various Ohio regiments, boarded the *General.* A breakfast-stop in Big Shanty [modern-day Kennesaw] marked ground zero for Andrews's plan. Conductor William Fuller and his crew—Anthony Murphy and Jeff Cain—had no intention of letting their beloved engine steam away. After starting pursuit on foot and borrowing several other locomotives on the Western & Atlantic, a chase of 87 miles ended near Ringgold. Fuller returned with his engine.[102]

April 13, 1862 (Monday)

Surgeon George Cooper reported the Federal casualties from the attack on Fort Pulaski: "[killed] Thomas Campbell, private, Company H, Third Rhode Island Artillery. There were a few slight injuries received by the cannoneers during the action, but none were reported as unfitting the men for the performance of their duties."[103]

April 14, 1862 (Sunday)

Major General David Hunter issued General Orders, No. 7 from Fort Pulaski. "All persons of color lately held to involuntary service by enemies of the United States in Fort Pulaski and on Cockspur Island, Ga., are hereby confiscated and declared free in conformity with law, and shall hereafter receive the fruits of their own labor. Such of said persons of color as are able bodied and may be required shall be employed in the quartermaster's department…."[104]

April 15, 1862 (Tuesday)

Flag Officer Du Pont notified Lieutenant Alexander Semmes to take his ship to the coast of Georgia. "You will please proceed with the U.S.S. *Wamsutta* under your command to St. Simon's Sound [Brunswick] and report to Commander [Edmund] Lanier, of the *Alabama,* for duty in the inland waters connected with the sound."[105]

April 16, 1862 (Thursday)

Brigadier General Viele again worked with his naval counterparts. This time, he sought assistance from Lieutenant Collins. "I purpose, if I can obtain your kind cooperation, to sink the hulk I have at Cooper River across the channel of Mud River, above the dock at Jones Island. This will relieve the gunboat at that point. After that a gunboat in the Savannah, between Jones and Long islands, and one near the mouth of New River, will be all sufficient to hold this position against the whole State of Georgia, now that the fort has been returned to its rightful owner."[106]

April 17, 1862 (Wednesday)

The U.S. Army and Navy continued to work together in the attempt to secure Georgia's

---

[102] For an excellent study of the raid, see Bonds, *Stealing the General.*

[103] *OR,* ser. I, vol. 6:166.

[104] *OR,* ser. II, vol. 1:815.

[105] *ORN,* ser. I, vol. 12:745.

[106] Ibid., 752–53.

coast. Lieutenant Napoleon Collins reported from his ship, the *Unadilla*. "General [Egbert] Viele has requested that the gunboats here may be moved into the Savannah River, to offer additional inducements to the rebels for more effectually obstructing the channel, which has been partially done since the fall of Pulaski."[107] Reports indicated skirmishing on Whitemarsh Island.

April 18, 1862 (Good Friday)

Former enslaved persons began settling the islands along the coast, as detailed in this report from Commander Edmund Lanier, U.S. Navy. "The colony on St. Simon's has largely increased...now consists of 60 men, 16 women, and 13 children; total, 89. They have planted at this time about 80 acres of corn...several acres of potatoes and beans. As yet the colony has been no expense to the Government."[108]

April 19, 1862 (Saturday)

In a document addressed to "The Militia of Georgia," Governor Brown informed the troops of a change in military reporting structure. "I have been notified by the Secretary of War that all persons in State service between the ages of 18 and 35 are to be enrolled as conscripts in the Confederate armies...it has been deemed expedient...to turn over to the Confederate General all the State troops, as well those who are, as those who are not conscripts, till the end of their respective terms of enlistment."[109]

April 20, 1862 (Easter Sunday)

A newspaper in Augusta carried a report from a recent visitor to the coast. "Savannah is in danger, and...Georgia has got to defend RIGHT HERE. No human power can rally a reliable army in the State, for State defence, if once these guns are taken, these lines broken, and the veterans who have drilled and worked so long and well to meet the foe, have felt the humiliation of defeat."[110]

April 21, 1862 (Monday) ◑

The salt of the earth might need to come from Virginia, and rail transportation provided the most expedient manner to bring the mineral to Georgia. Governor Brown addressed the issue. "I am informed that a number of gentlemen of Atlanta...have associated themselves together for the purpose of bringing into the State from the salt works in Virginia, a supply of that much needed article. This I respectfully...ask...our people who are not actually destitute of and suffering for want of salt are compelled...to pay enormous and exorbitant prices for it."[111]

April 22,1862 (Tuesday)

The Conscription Act brought out the lion in Governor Brown, and he snarled disapprovals toward President Davis. In documenting the willingness of the state to cooperate with

---

[107] Ibid., 747; skirmish information in Mosocco, *Chronological Tracking*, 58.

[108] *ORN*, ser. I, vol. 12:756.

[109] Candler, *Confederate Records of the State of Georgia*, 2:215.

[110] "Letter from Savannah," *Augusta Daily Constitutionalist*, April 20, 1862, sec. 2, Genealogybank.com. Caps in original.

[111] Candler, *Confederate Records of the State of Georgia*, 2:216.

the Confederate war effort, Brown highlighted contributions thus far. "Georgia has promptly responded to every call made upon her by you for troops, and has always given more than you asked. She has now about 60,000 in the field. Had you called upon her Executive for 20,000 more (if her just quota), they would have been furnished without delay."[112]

April 23, 1862 (Wednesday)

Georgians received a plea for assistance from the Confederate government in Richmond. "The War Department has ordered that the C. S. Ordnance Department at Savannah, Georgia, solicit contributions of Lead from all parts of the State. Any persons having any, never mind how small the amount, will please leave the same at the Quartermaster's Office, Broad street, Columbus, Ga."[113]

April 24, 1862 (Thursday)

Gertrude Thomas went shopping in Atlanta and found inflation had visited the Gate City. "I have been out several times in the street a good many times on Whitehall the principal street, and have made several purchases…three pair of shoes…at $1.25 apiece. Black silk thread at 5 and 10 skeins, black flax at 10 cts pr skein. Everything I have bought I gave less for it than it could be bought in Augusta. A good many of the things are higher."[114]

April 25, 1862 (Friday)[Appears to be from April 1863.]

Residents of Savannah learned Major John L. Hardee intended to form "a regiment of volunteers for the war and invites volunteers to join him singly or by companies, to compete the organization of his regiment." The major reminded potential recruits they could "relieve themselves from the operation of the conscript law…."[115]

April 26, 1862 (Saturday)

Commander John Goldsborough of the USS *Florida* reported on his sailors advance toward Dorchester. "Having proceeded about 30 miles up the river and within 1½ or 2 miles of Dorchester, opposite to which the brig was at anchor, they discovered her to be on fire and learned from some captured contrabands that the rebels had scuttled and fired her and that she was burned to the water's edge." The squad, on returning from their mission, "were attacked by a company of dismounted cavalry, concealed in the woods and thick underbrush on Woodville Island, during which the *Wamsutta* lost two of her crew."[116]

April 27, 1862 (Sunday)

The Western & Atlantic Railroad, especially after the Andrews raiders paid a visit, warranted a military presence. "The Superintendent of the State Road…has been energetic in providing for the protection of the State Road, and the bridges over it. At his earnest

---

[112] Ibid., 3:193.

[113] "Lead! Lead! Lead!," *Columbus Daily Sun*, April 24, 1862, sec. 3, https://gahistoricnewspapers.galileo.usg.edu/lccn/sn82014939/1862-04-24/ed-1/seq-3/.

[114] Thomas, *Secret Eye*, 204–205.

[115] "Volunteers for the War," *Savannah Daily Morning News*, April 25, 1862, sec. 2, https://gahistoricnewspapers.galileo.usg.edu/lccn/sn82015886/1862-04-25/ed-1/seq-2/.

[116] *ORN*, ser. I, vol. 12:776.

request, we are advised Gen. [Brigadier General Danville] Ledbetter, who commands the Confederate forces at Chattanooga, has detailed a sufficient guard to protect all the bridges of the Road from that point to Atlanta."[117]

April 28, 1862 (Monday) ●

Confusion continued over selecting officers among the units from Georgia mustering into Confederate service. President Davis weighed in on the matter with Governor Brown. Davis wrote, "With regard to the mode of officering the troops now called into the service of the Confederacy, the intention of Congress is to me, as to you, to be learned from its acts, and from the terms employed it would seem that the policy of election by the troops themselves is adopted by Congress."[118]

April 29, 1862 (Tuesday)

Tense conditions in St. Simons Sound presented Federal naval officers with an unending challenge. Flag Officer Du Pont instructed Commander Goldsborough to "do all in your power to guard all accessible points, for, with the more stringent blockades elsewhere, every attempt will be made to find weak points, as they (the rebels) are becoming quite desperate."[119]

April 30, 1862 (Wednesday)

Salt remained the prime mineral receiving focus in Georgia. As the blockade started to reduce supplies, seeking additional sources served as a pastime for some. "Salt Springs: There are a number of these in Cobb county, near Sweet Water Creek...it appears evident that they could be worked to great profit. We hope some of our enterprising capitalists, will take an early opportunity of testing the water of these springs."[120]

May 1, 1862 (Thursday)

Governor Brown, concerned over an increasing number of Federal troops in the vicinity of Chattanooga, urged Secretary of War Randolph to take immediate action. "When Georgia has sent so many troops to the field, it is injury to leave her vital points exposed with no adequate protection. The President has her men and her guns, and she looks to him."[121]

May 2, 1862 (Friday)

President Davis responded to Governor Brown's request for additional soldiers in the region around Chattanooga. "The six regiments called from Camp McDonald were with difficulty armed. Every effort was made to do so, that they might serve to defend the country to which you refer. They were removed without previously consulting me, and I have not been able to supply their place." Davis hinted at Brown's possible willingness to move

---

117 "Protection of the State Road," *Augusta Daily Constitutionalist*, April 27, 1862, sec. 3, Genealogybank.com.

118 Candler, *Confederate Records of the State of Georgia*, 3:200–201.

119 *ORN*, ser. I, vol. 12:788.

120 "Salt Springs," *Macon Georgia Journal and Messenger*, April 30, 1862, sec. 3, https://gahistoricnewspapers.galileo.usg.edu/lccn/sn85038491/1862-04-30/ed-1/seq-3/.

121 Candler, *Confederate Records of the State of Georgia*, 3:204.

troops from the coast and indicated "if a brigade can be spared…General Pemberton will be directed to send it to Chattanooga."[122]

May 3, 1862 (Saturday)

The *Savannah Daily Morning News* included this announcement: "The 'Savannah Volunteer Guards' having been mustered for the war, are authorized to increase the rolls of their Companies without limit, and invite accessions to their ranks. Applications received at their Armory, corner of York and Bull street, from 9 o'clock A.M. to 6 P.M."[123] See the unit's flag image, which accompanied this recruiting announcement. Skirmishing reported at Watkins' Ferry.

May 4, 1862 (Sunday)

A terrible incident occurred in Augusta, one injuring several civilians. "One of the small rolling or incorporating mills, at the Powder Works near this city, exploded about 7 o'clock this morning, severely wounding four men—two of whom were in the mill and two outside. The mills are so constructed that an explosion in one will not affect the other—nor do a great deal of injury to the mill in which the explosion occurs."[124]

May 5, 1862 (Monday)

Responding to a reply from Secretary Randolph—one questioning certain state officers—Governor Brown detailed his confidence in each man. "I express but the opinion of half a million Georgians when I say that these Generals will compare most favorably with many now in Confederate service, occupying the rank held by them, respectively, while in State service."[125] The generals in question were Henry R. Jackson, W. H. T. Walker, and Francis W. Capers.

May 6, 1862 (Tuesday) ◐

Pondering scenarios if the capital of Milledgeville fell into Federal occupation, a newspaper editor expected a disappointment for the captors. "If the City be Captured, what then? Well, saving the discredit to our cause, and its effect of the West and beyond the Atlantic, and will be to the enemy a [t]oothless victory and will get no cotton. A part of it has been already destroyed…the remainder will not be less certain—what else can *the enemy get?*"[126]

May 7, 1862 (Wednesday)

What Governor Brown wanted, most often, the executive obtained. Today, he desired his rifles! In a letter to Secretary Randolph, Brown enclosed "a copy of your dispatch to me…in

---

[122] Ibid., 3:205.

[123] "Savannah Volunteer Guards!," *Savannah Daily Morning News*, May 3, 1862, sec. 2, https://gahistoricnewspapers.galileo.usg.edu/lccn/sn82015886/1862-05-03/ed-1/seq-2/; skirmish information in Mosocco, *Chronological Tracking*, 61.

[124] "Explosion of a Powder Mill," *Augusta Daily Constitutionalist*, May 4, 1862, sec. 1, Genealogybank.com.

[125] Candler, *Confederate Records of the State of Georgia*, 3:209.

[126] "If the City Be Captured, What Then?," *Milledgeville Southern Federal Union*, May 6, 1862, sec. 2, https://gahistoricnewspapers.galileo.usg.edu/lccn/sn87062317/1862-05-06/ed-1/seq-2/. Italics in original.

which you promise to punish any Confederate officer who again knowingly interferes with the State's arms imported by me. I am informed that twelve boxes of my Enfield rifles were received…[in] Nashville and that they have been ordered by General Lee to General E. K. Smith, of East Tennessee." The governor sought to "simply state the case and remind you of your promise, not doubting that you will act properly in the premises. When may I expect all that have been seized to be returned? I shall regret to be compelled to resort to counter seizures as the only mode of redress against these arbitrary wrongs of your officers."[127]

May 8, 1862 (Thursday)

Governor Brown clarified his disagreement with the Confederate Conscription Act in asserting his resistance in a letter to President Davis. As a bonus, Brown included a discourse on the U.S. Constitution.

> I can consent to do no act which commits Georgia to willing acquiescence in their [Confederate Congress] binding force upon her people. I cannot therefore consent to have anything to do with the enrollment of the conscripts in this State; nor can I permit any commissioned officer of the militia to be enrolled, who is necessary to enable the State to exercise her reserved right of training her militia, according to the discipline prescribed by Congress, at a time, when to prevent troubles with her slaves, a strict military police is absolutely necessary to the safety of her people.[128]

May 9, 1862 (Friday)

Major General David Hunter issued General Orders, No. 11.

> The three States of Georgia, Florida and South Carolina, comprising the Military Department of the South, having deliberately declared themselves no longer under the protection of the United States of America and having taken up arms against the said United States it becomes a military necessity to declare them under martial law. Slavery and martial law in a free country are altogether incompatible; the persons in these three States—Georgia, Florida and South Carolina—heretofore held as slaves are therefore declared forever free.[129]

May 10, 1862 (Saturday)

Uniforms made the news, as an editor in Savannah specified regulation attire for soldiers and officers. Of the officers, he noted, "The officers, though—who serve under commissions from the Confederacy—come under a different rule. In their case, as well as for regular soldiers, a uniform is prescribed by law, and no man has a right to depart from it. In doing so he violates regulations which he is under obligations to respect and support, and is amenable for it as an offense."[130]

---

[127] Candler, *Confederate Records of the State of Georgia*, 3:211.

[128] Ibid., 3:220.

[129] *OR*, ser. II, vol. 1:818.

[130] "Uniforms of Confederate Officers," *Savannah Weekly Republican*, May 10, 1862, sec. 1, https://gahistoricnewspapers.galileo.usg.edu/lccn/sn85038498/1862-05-10/ed-1/seq-1/.

May 11, 1862 (Sunday)
The South needed additional troops, but one group could avoid duty in the field—at least for the present. "The Cadets of the Georgia Military Institute are exempt from the operation of the Conscript Act. Gov. Brown has written to Maj. [John] Richardson, Acting Superintendent Ga. Military Institute, informing him that the Cadets of the Institute will not be subject to the Conscript Act."[131]

May 12, 1862 (Monday)
The *Daily Sun* in Columbus carried an announcement of a promotion involving a Georgia officer. "Capt. G. [George] W. Ross, of the Floyd Rifles, is elected Major of the 2d Ga. [Infantry] Battalion."[132]

May 13, 1862 (Tuesday)
Pemberton, contemplating an attack on Savannah, wrote to the Mayor Thomas Purse that "should it become necessary and…practicable to defend the city…in the event of the enemy's successfully passing the obstructions and batteries, the presence of women and children will not prevent it." Therefore, Pemberton advised "that they be gradually withdrawn from the city, without however creating unnecessary alarm. There are certain houses in front of the batteries on Bay Bluff which it is necessary should be removed."[133]

May 14, 1862 (Wednesday)
Confederate authorities named Atlanta a military post. General Order No. 1 clarified the selection. "For the purpose of guarding the Government stores, to preserve order in and around Atlanta, and for the protection of all loyal citizens, and the punishment of all disorderly conduct…. The officer commanding earnestly invokes the aid and co-operation of…the Mayor…City Authorities, and all citizens in preserving good order…."[134]

May 15, 1862 (Thursday)
Addressing the military districts encompassing South Carolina and Georgia, General R. E. Lee offered his advice to local officials: "I regret…the state of affairs which exists at Charleston. Your suggestion to relieve General [Roswell] Ripley of all direct control by General Pemberton could not be adopted as long as General Pemberton retained command of the Department…. The defense of the two cities, Charleston and Savannah, is so closely associated, that it is deemed unadvisable to constitute each of the two States a separate department under a separate commander."[135]

May 16, 1862 (Friday)
"This day having been set apart by proclamation of the President to be observed by the

[131] "Papers of the State Will Please Copy," *Atlanta Southern Confederacy*, May 11, 1862, sec. 2, https://gahistoricnewspapers.galileo.usg.edu/lccn/sn82014677/1862-05-11/ed-1/seq-2/.

[132] "Election of Major of the Second Georgia Battalion," *Columbus Daily Sun*, May 12, 1862, sec. 2, https://gahistoricnewspapers.galileo.usg.edu/lccn/sn82014939/1862-05-12/ed-1/seq-2/.

[133] *OR*, ser. I, vol. 14:501.

[134] Garrett and Martin, *Atlanta and Environs*, 526.

[135] *OR*, ser. I, vol. 14:504.

people of the Confederate States as a day of prayer, no paper will be issued from this office on Saturday."[136]

May 17, 1862 (Saturday)

Residents of Augusta received news regarding a special meeting in the evening. "The Election for Commissioned Officers of the Mounted Rangers will take place this evening at the Georgia Engine Room at 8 o'clock."[137]

May 18, 1862 (Sunday)

Another military unit formed in Georgia, this time, an artillery unit. "This company increased till it contained nearly 250 members. It then divided into two companies, and our fellow-citizen B. F. Wyly, was chosen Captain of the new company without opposition."[138] The unit under report eventually mustered in as Company E, 9th Georgia Light Artillery Battalion.

May 19, 1862 (Monday)

General R. E. Lee wrote to Pemberton about the number of troops in Pemberton's department. "Your whole effective force…must be about double the…enemy. Please inform me whether you have any reliable information of the strength of the enemy…I presume he will not…attack either Charleston or Savannah unless provided with iron boats, and I fear we are losing the service of troops important to us at this place [Virginia] by retaining them where they are not required."[139]

May 20, 1862 (Tuesday) ◗

Secretary Randolph notified Governor Brown of the mustering in of Georgia regiments. "I informed you by telegraph I was authorized to accept them, and have just received your letter of the 5th instant tendering them to the Confederate States Government. They will be in all respects on the same footing as regiments raised under the authority of the War Department."[140]

May 21, 1862 (Wednesday)

Major General Pemberton sent a telegraph to General Lee's headquarters regarding the defenses of Georgia and South Carolina. "Unless positively directed to send another brigade from this department I do not feel authorized to do so. At this time we need every man we have for the defense of the cities of Charleston and Savannah. I do not imagine that the season will prevent the enemy's attack when he is otherwise prepared to make it."[141]

May 22, 1862 (Thursday)

---

[136] "Day of Prayer," *Savannah Daily Morning News*, May 16, 1862, sec. 2, https://gahistoricnewspapers.galileo.usg.edu/lccn/sn82015886/1862-05-16/ed-1/seq-2/.

[137] "The Election for Commissioned Officers," *Augusta Chronicle*, May 17, 1862, sec. 1, Genealogybank.com.

[138] "The Leyden Artillery," *Atlanta Southern Confederacy*, May 18, 1862, sec. 3, https://gahistoricnewspapers.galileo.usg.edu/lccn/sn82014677/1862-05-18/ed-1/seq-3/.

[139] *OR,* ser. I, vol. 14:505–506.

[140] Candler, *Confederate Records of the State of Georgia*, 3:227.

[141] *OR,* ser. I, vol. 14:510.

Federal Brigadier General Henry Benham wrote to naval Commander Augustus Baldwin regarding continuing joint operations. Benham noted his pleasure in learning "of the prospect of your having two gunboats disposable for service in the Savannah and Cooper rivers...I trust one...may be able to go up the Savannah as far as...the upper part of Jones Island...I would suggest...the commander of the boat for the Savannah River...see Brigadier-General [Alfred] Terry, commanding at Fort Pulaski...with whom, on knowing our plans more fully, he can act most advantageously in concert."[142]

May 23, 1862 (Friday)

General Pemberton received an order to provide reinforcements for Richmond. "Send a good brigade selected from troops of upper part of Georgia and South Carolina that could not stand summer's campaign on coast; a brigadier-general selected by you to report here without delay. Very respectfully, R. E. LEE."[143]

May 24, 1862 (Saturday)

Pemberton replied to General Lee's request for additional troops in Virginia. "General [Roswell] Ripley, with [John V.] Moore's South Carolina and [Colonel William] Gibson's Georgia regiments, ordered to Richmond. Enemy's gunboats reported in Waccamaw River, have ordered a regiment and section of artillery on line of Manchester and Wilmington Railroad to protect bridges, &c. Gunboats in Stono; shall probably attack. I need more brigadier-generals in this department."[144]

May 25, 1862 (Sunday)

Commander George Prentiss of the USS *Albatross* reported on Confederate supplies he might destroy. "Large quantities of rice are stowed along the banks of the river, and the armies at Charleston and Savannah are constantly supplied from them. If you will send me the means (small steamers and vessels for transportation), I can capture immense quantities, but to do this it will be necessary to seize the mills at the same time, for when we commence seizing they will commence burning them."[145]

May 26, 1862 (Monday)

Making his thoughts on conscription known, Governor Brown clarified his position in a letter to Secretary Randolph. "I view the conscription act not only as unnecessary as to Georgia, but as unconstitutional as to all the States...considering the exigencies of the times...I determined to throw no obstacles in the way of its being carried out in Georgia further than might become absolutely necessary to preserve intact the State Government in all its department, civil and military."[146]

May 27, 1862 (Tuesday)

Major General Pemberton relayed a report on the defenses of the Chattahoochee River and enclosed information from "Col. W. E. Boggs, State Engineer of Georgia...[on] a military

[142] *ORN*, ser. I, vol. 13:24–25.

[143] *OR*, ser. I, vol. 14:518.

[144] Ibid., 519.

[145] *ORN*, ser. I, vol. 13:23.

[146] Candler, *Confederate Records of the State of Georgia*, **[vol?]**228–29.

reconnaissance of the Chattahoochee River, with a view to obstructing the most advantageous point and for the establishment of a battery for its defense.... It is not in my power to furnish the 8-inch guns asked for by Colonel Boggs. I have myself...a higher opinion of the long-range 32-pounder...and I am clearly of the opinion...Fort Gadsden is the best site on the river to combine the obstructions and defense."[147]

May 28, 1862 (Wednesday) ●

Issuing General Orders, No. 21, Pemberton reclassified the various districts under his command, including Georgia. He named a new district the "Second Division District of Georgia, and declared the "Georgia troops now in South Carolina and the Louisiana troops in Georgia will for the present be attached to the brigades within the military district in which they are respectively located, but will not be considered as forming a part of the permanent organization of such brigades."[148]

May 29, 1862 (Thursday)

Ironically, one year to the day after Brown and Davis exchanged pleasantries, the relationship between the two continued to deteriorate. Davis responded to a previous letter from the governor, which outlined Brown's opposition to conscription. In a lengthy letter, Davis responded on this day. Addressing the legality of conscription, Davis stated, "it is obvious, that if Congress have power to draft into the armies raised by it any citizens at all...the power must be co-extensive with the exigencies of the occasion, or it becomes illusory; and the extent of the exigency must be determined by Congress; for the Constitution has left the power without any other check or restriction than the Executive veto."[149]

May 30, 1862 (Friday)

Governor Brown continued his efforts to secure matériel to keep Georgia safe. "Received of Joseph E. Brown, Governor of Georgia, one bond of the Confederate States of one thousand dollars, to be used in payment at par of sums due for articles manufactured for the Ordnance Department.—Lachlan H. McIntosh, Chief of Ordnance, State of Georgia."[150]

May 31, 1862 (Saturday)

Secretary Stanton learned from Major General Hunter of points along the coast vulnerable to Federal attack. "The Navy have also possession of Saint Simon's Island, Ga., where they have a flourishing negro colony, and Captain Godon, of the Navy, who has command there, can at any time occupy Brunswick: With the necessary steamers, now almost entirely taken from us, and a few thousand additional troops, we could soon have Charleston, Georgetown, Bull's Bay, Brunswick, Savannah, Saint Mary's, and Jacksonville."[151]

June 1, 1862 (Sunday)

A newspaper in Atlanta reported on the presence of Confederate soldiers and their officer.

---

[147] *OR*, ser. I, vol. 3:507.

[148] Ibid., 523.

[149] Candler, *Confederate Records of the State of Georgia*, 3:242.

[150] Ibid., 2:221.

[151] *OR*, ser. I, vol. 14:348.

"Col. [George W.] Lee, with the well-drilled and well-seasoned troops under his command who are now at this place, has been ordered to a place where their services will perhaps be needed in making peace with Yankees, and Col. [Elisha] E. P. Watkins, whose regiment is now encamped at Camp McDonald, has been ordered here with his regiment...."[152]

June 2, 1862 (Monday)

President Davis telegraphed Major General Pemberton with an urgent request. "General Lee is in the field. Needs re-enforcements. Can you give them?" Pemberton responded with a willingness to comply but offered a warning. "Twenty vessels are in and off the Stono and increasing in number. If they attack it will be by land and water. If you say risk it, I will order 5,000 men from Savannah, but I think it will be dangerous. 1 am now in the field. I have ordered them to be ready."[153]

June 3, 1862 (Tuesday)

After requesting "two more regiments" from Brigadier General Lawton, Pemberton notified Secretary Randolph on "strong indications of a general attack on Charleston. I shall be obliged to draw largely on Savannah for troops. Can I get any from North Carolina?" Telegraph messages passed along the wires, one moving northward, the other to the south. While Pemberton called on Lawton, General Lee wrote Pemberton, "General Lawton desires to come to Virginia with troops from Georgia. I hear the enemy in Virginia are drawing re-enforcements from forces opposed to you."[154]

June 4, 1862 (Wednesday)

Pemberton replied to President Davis's request for reinforcements in Virginia. "Have just received your dispatch. Shall order three regiments from Savannah. Am drawing re-enforcements from there for Charleston also. The enemy is re-enforcing also, both in gunboats and troops. I may have to abandon one city or the other. Shall meet all your requirements promptly."[155]

June 5, 1862 (Thursday) ◐

Continuing his discussion with President Davis, and with both evaluating changing conditions in Virginia and Georgia, Pemberton countermanded an order to Lawton in Savannah. "Delay the movement of the troops heretofore ordered to Richmond until further orders, but hold them ready to move should they be required."[156]

June 6, 1862 (Friday)

Promotions in Pemberton's military district proved the order of the day, as the general announced, via Special Orders, Nos. 24 and 25. "Lieut. Col. [Thomas] T. M. Wagner, First Regiment South Carolina Artillery, is hereby announced as chief of ordnance of the Department of South Carolina and Georgia. Captain [William] Echols, Engineer Corps,

---

[152] "Col. G. W. Lee," *Atlanta Southern Confederacy*, June 1, 1862, sec. 2, https://gahistoricnewspapers.galileo.usg.edu/lccn/sn82014677/1862-06-01/ed-1/seq-2/.

[153] *OR*, ser. I, vol. 14:534–35.

[154] Ibid., 535–36.

[155] Ibid., 539.

[156] Ibid., 550.

Provisional Army of the Confederate States, is hereby announced as chief engineer of the department."[157]

June 7, 1862 (Saturday)

James Andrews, the mastermind behind the raid to steal the *General,* hanged today in Atlanta. "He was carried out Peachtree street road, accompanied by three clergymen, and escorted by a guard. A considerable crowd followed to witness the execution. He seemed to be very penitent—was composed till he came on the scaffold, when a slight tremor was perceptible."[158] Andrews and seven other raiders who eventually stretched the rope, rest in Chattanooga's National Cemetery.

June 8, 1862 (Sunday)

Concern of receiving the dreaded news on the loss of a loved one on some distant battlefront occupied the minds of many. Apprehension on crossing the road worried others. "We ask the attention of whoever it may concern to the fact that the locomotive trains run too fast through the city, and that they are not provided, as they should be, by flagmen to give warning of the approaching train."[159]

June 9, 1862 (Monday)

Governor Brown brokered a deal to obtain salt from the works in Saltville, Virginia. "I have...secured a lease on such interest in the Virginia Salt Works as will enable me to have made...a large quantity of salt during the summer....The absolute necessity for salt makes it important that all be done which can be to secure a supply for the people of the State."[160]

June 10, 1862 (Tuesday)

Pemberton notified Mayor Purse in Savannah, "Charleston is threatened; have therefore drawn troops from Savannah. If Savannah is threatened, shall draw troops from Charleston. With means at my disposal shall defend both to the best of my ability. Expect to send two regiments back to-morrow."[161]

June 11, 1862 (Wednesday)

A newspaper in Sandersville carried a notice of a local unit needing additional gunners. "The Sam Robinson Artillery want a few more recruits...they have received five...guns and will receive the other soon, which will make their battery complete. With such drill officers as we know Lieut. Howell and others of the company to be, we know the men cannot fail to understand well how to use their guns with telling effect whenever opportunity shall offer." An added incentive: "This company now offers a fine opportunity to those who

---

[157] Ibid., 552.

[158] "Execution of Andrews the Engine Thief," *Atlanta Southern Confederacy*, June 10, 1862, sec. 3, https://gahistoricnewspapers.galileo.usg.edu/lccn/sn82014677/1862-06-10/ed-1/seq-3/.

[159] "Running Trains Too Fast," *Augusta Daily Constitutionalist*, June 8, 1862, Genealogybank.com.

[160] Candler, *Confederate Records of the State of Georgia*, 2:223.

[161] *OR*, ser. I, vol. 14:557.

wish to avoid the *Conscript law*."[162]

June 12, 1862 (Thursday)

President Davis wrote to South Carolina Governor Francis Pickens regarding a potential new commander for the military district. "Perhaps Beauregard would be glad, under the circumstances, to take charge of the Department of South Carolina and Georgia. If you will be satisfied with that arrangement it might be well for you to propose it to him."[163] A little time would pass, but Davis would get his way.

June 13, 1862 (Friday)

A newspaper editor in Rome weighed in on the differences between the warring sections. "The North and the South are distinct races of people. There is no fraternity in their views, feelings and character—though both speak the same language, there is emphatically a difference in the *manner* of speaking it."[164]

June 14, 1862 (Saturday)

The *Banner and Baptist* newspaper lamented the loss of Georgia soldiers on distant battlefields. "This war—what sorrows lie hidden beneath the blood-stained mantle that envelops us, nationally! Many sad faces are mirrors to the sad scenes enacted on Old Virginia's noble grounds. Many a warm hearted, impulsive and patriotic Southerner has filled a grave, that adds new honor to his name—that of a soldier's mound."[165]

June 15, 1862 (Sunday)

Major General Pemberton announced an addition to his military district. "Brig. Gen. [Nathan "Shanks"] N. G. Evans, Provisional Army of Confederate States, is hereby assigned to duty in First Division First Military District of Department South Carolina and Georgia. He will exercise the command thereof until further orders."[166]

June 16, 1862 (Monday)

The Confederate Conscription Act adopted in April 1862 targeted men between the ages of eighteen and thirty-five as eligible for conscription [draft]. Governor Brown would frequently exempt certain classes of folks from various trades he deemed critical to Georgia. On this day, he typified his position in a letter to Captain G. W. Hunnicut of Canton, Georgia. "Having been informed that your name has been enrolled as a conscript by a Confederate officer…you are hereby directed, in case any enrolling officer attempts to arrest you, or any other commissioned officer under you, who is acting in obedience to said General Orders, to call out immediately such military force as you may need for

---

[162] "Wednesday, June 11, 1862," *Sandersville Central Georgian*, June 11, 1862, sec. 1, https://gahistoricnewspapers.galileo.usg.edu/lccn/sn85034105/1862-06-11/ed-1/seq-1/. Italics in original.

[163] *OR*, ser. I, vol. 14:561.

[164] "Is It Possible That the Union Can Be Restored?," *Rome Weekly Courier*, June 13, 1862, sec. 1, https://gahistoricnewspapers.galileo.usg.edu/lccn/sn82014071/1862-06-13/ed-1/seq-1/.

[165] "Rambling Thoughts," *Atlanta Banner and Baptist*, June 14, 1862, sec. 1, https://gahistoricnewspapers.galileo.usg.edu/lccn/sn89053822/1862-06-14/ed-1/seq-2/.

[166] *OR*, ser. I, vol. 14:566.

the purpose, and place such enrolling officer under arrest and detain him till you can report the case to me...."[167] Brown exercised his authority as governor to exempt certain classes from conscription, as he did for Captain Hunnicut.

June 17, 1862 (Tuesday)

Governor Brown delivered an ultimatum to Secretary of War Randolph. "Your...officers have enrolled several of the State officers of the militia, who will not be permitted to be carried away from their commands. You stated...no State officer is liable to enrollment, and asked me to call your attention to it if done. Please send...an order for release of all...stop the enrollment of State officers, or I shall order the arrest of each officer who arrests a State officer."[168]

June 18, 1862 (Wednesday) ◑

Found guilty of their role in stealing the locomotive *General* in Big Shanty, seven of the raiders hanged outside Atlanta's City Cemetery. William Campbell, Samuel Robertson, Marion A. Ross, John Scott, Perry G. Shadrach, Samuel Slavens, and George D. Wilson now rest at the National Cemetery in Chattanooga.[169]

June 19, 1862 (Thursday)

Men continued to answer the call to arms and prepared for military training. "The first squad from Richmond county of involuntary volunteers under the Conscription Act...left for Camp McDonald this morning. They were eleven in number."[170]

June 20, 1862 (Friday)

Major General Kirby Smith, headquartered in Knoxville, Tennessee, notified Governor Brown of a dilemma involving Georgia troops.

> The following regiments and battalions of troops from your State are now under my command in this department, viz.: Thirty-ninth Georgia Regiment (Colonel [Joseph] McConnell) Infantry; Forty-second Georgia Regiment (Colonel [Robert] Henderson) Infantry; Fifty-second Georgia Regiment (Colonel [Wier] Boyd) Infantry; Third Georgia Battalion (Lieutenant-Colonel [Marcellus] Stovall) Infantry; Fortieth Georgia Regiment (Col. [Abda] A. Johnson) Infantry; Forty-third Georgia Regiment (Colonel [Skidmore] Harris) Infantry; 36th Georgia Regiment (Colonel [Jesse] Glenn) Infantry; Ninth Battalion (Major [Joseph] Smith) Infantry; First Regiment (Colonel [James] Morrison) Cavalry. The regiments have now been reduced, chiefly by sickness, to an average effective strength of about 400 men. Can you not take measures for adding to them from conscripts and by calling upon all absentees who

---

[167] Candler, *Confederate Records of the State of Georgia*, 2:224.

[168] Ibid., 3:248.

[169] See Bonds, *Stealing the General*.

[170] "Conscripts," *Columbus Daily Sun*, June 19, 1862, sec. 1, https://gahistoricnewspapers.galileo.usg.edu/lccn/sn82014939/1862-06-19/ed-1/seq-1/.

are now able for duty to rejoin their regiments, so that the muskets be kept constantly in use?[171]

June 21, 1862 (Saturday)
Still early in the war, various Georgia communities continued to raise companies for Confederate service, like the Rome Works Artillery. "This company is now thoroughly organized and in process of active drill. To all who may wish to aid in the defence of the city, in case of necessity, invitation is extended to become members of the company. The members of this company are active, intelligent men, who are now engaged in making the weapons they will use…the company now numbers over fifty men."[172]

June 22, 1862 (Sunday)
Shortages mounted throughout the South, and in Georgia, wool proved a hot commodity. "The Confederate Government requires Wool to clothe the troops now in the field, and will purchase it at a fair market value, in any quantity offered. For the convenience of the Planters, and others, the wool can be delivered to the Quartermasters, at the following named places: Savannah, Columbus, Macon, Griffin, Atlanta, Marietta, Calhoun, Rome and Augusta, Ga."[173]

June 23, 1862 (Monday)
Perhaps spotting a glimmer of light at the end of the tunnel—and hopeful the Davis Express did not prove the source—Governor Brown wrote an encouraging message to Secretary Randolph. "I agree with you fully that…should unite all our energies to drive out the common enemy and not make war among ourselves. I am most happy…the Confederate Government has decided to respect the constitutional rights of the State…not to force her to…permitting any department of her constitutional government to be disbanded and destroyed, or to defend the existence and integrity of her government by force."[174]

June 24, 1862 (Tuesday)
In an article titled "The Great Object of the War," an editor in the state's capital offered a warning to all Georgians. "Will the Yankees spare a dollar of the property of the South, if they get the power over us? No, indeed. Southern men, we tell you, poverty and slavery will be your lot if you are conquered. Stretch every nerve, then, to win your country's independence."[175]

June 25, 1862 (Wednesday)
Major General Kirby Smith notified Governor Brown of trouble in east Tennessee. "I request that you will place such regiments of infantry…at some point on the Western and

---

[171] Candler, *Confederate Records of the State of Georgia*, 3:250–51.

[172] "Rome Works Artillery," *Rome Tri-Weekly Courier*, June 21, 1862, sec. 2, https://gahistoricnewspapers.galileo.usg.edu/lccn/sn85034102/1862-06-21/ed-1/seq-2/.

[173] "To the Planters and Others of the State of Georgia," *Augusta Daily Constitutionalist*, June 22, 1862, sec. 1, Genealogybank.com.

[174] Candler, *Confederate Records of the State of Georgia*, 3:283.

[175] "The Great Object of the War," *Milledgeville Southern Federal Union*, June 24, 1862, https://gahistoricnewspapers.galileo.usg.edu/lccn/sn87062317/1862-06-24/ed-1/seq-3/.

Atlantic Railroad convenient to Chattanooga...arms will be immediately forwarded to me, which will enable me to bring the troops you may place at my disposal promptly in the field to resist every demonstration that may threaten Chattanooga, the key to Northern Georgia."[176]

June 26, 1862 (Thursday)

Commander Godon delivered an update on happenings near Savannah. "I have...given directions to Lieutenant Commanding [Pendleton] Watmough to visit Ossabaw Sound and the Ogeechee River with proper precaution and when he can do so without neglecting his other posts. For...weeks I have had parties of from twenty to thirty men scouting the island...I...report three deserters from the rebel army at Savannah...request...orders concerning them."[177]

June 27, 1862 (Friday) ●

Georgian military officials learned of a potential influx of needed matériel. "It is currently rumored on the streets this morning that two more Confederate steamers have run the blockade, landing safely with heavy cargoes of guns, ammunition, &c."[178]

June 28, 1862 (Thursday)

Howell Cobb received an update from Major John C. Whitner in West Point, Georgia, on the efforts to organize important papers. "It has been nearly a week since I wrote you that the boxes containing the papers relating to proceedings of Provisional Congress had arrived, and yet I am not prepared to begin writing nor even to make a full report of what the papers are. I write merely to advise you of progress. The papers were in great disorder...as I am rather green in such matters...it took me some time to even begin straightening up."[179]

June 29, 1862 (Sunday)

Relief efforts continued through the South. Many women, such as these in Atlanta, worked on behalf of wounded soldiers. "The ladies in town and in the country surrounding, are requested to send to the store room of the Ladies' Soldiers' Relief Society vegetables, chickens, butter and milk. These articles are greatly needed by our sick soldiers, and will be carefully distributed to the different Hospitals."[180]

June 30, 1862 (Monday)

Major General Hunter announced a new appointment: "Surg. Charles H. Crane, U. S. Army, being the senior medical officer of the department, is hereby appointed and announced as medical director of the Department of the South...."[181]

July 1, 1862 (Tuesday)

---

[176] Candler, *Confederate Records of the State of Georgia*, 3:284.

[177] *ORN*, ser. I, vol. 13:143.

[178] "Rumor," *Columbus Daily Sun*, June 27, 1862, sec. 1, https://gahistoricnewspapers.galileo.usg.edu/lccn/sn82014939/1862-06-27/ed-1/seq-1/.

[179] Toombs, Stephens, and Cobb, *Correspondence*, 596.

[180] "Attention!," *Atlanta Southern Confederacy*, June 29, 1862, sec. 3, https://gahistoricnewspapers.galileo.usg.edu/lccn/sn82014677/1862-06-29/ed-1/seq-3/.

[181] *OR*, ser. I, vol. 14:361.

Naval Lieutenant Pendleton Watmough onboard his USS *Potomska* exchanged fire with a Confederate battery in Ossabaw Sound. "After an hour's ebb I started up, looking out for a battery of five guns that I heard was hereabouts, with piles across the river under the guns. There are six heavy guns mounted. Approaching nearer, to within a mile and a half, I fired a shot at the battery which was promptly returned with three or four shot, some of which were good ones and showed we were fairly within their range."[182]

July 2, 1862 (Wednesday)

Navy Secretary Welles sent orders to Flag-Officer Du Pont's department. "Amongst the persons known as contrabands, who have sought the protection of the United States, please ascertain if there are any men physically competent who are willing to enlist in the Navy for service in the Pacific at landsmen's wages. If so, a vessel will be sent to take 150 of them to the Isthmus."[183]

July 3, 1862 (Thursday)

Flag Officer Du Pont responded to the recent activity in Ossabaw Sound in a message to Commander Enoch Parrott. "I have received your interesting communication of yesterday, and was not surprised at the information it contained, having always had an impression that the rebels might make use of Ossabaw Sound. I will send a vessel there so soon as I have one at command."[184]

July 4, 1862 (Friday) (Independence Day) ◐

General Cooper dispatched Major General G. W. Smith in White Sulphur Springs, Virginia, with the offer of a new assignment. After General Joseph E. Johnston received a severe wound during the Battle of Fair Oaks/Seven Pines, Smith had not fared well during his hours-long stint in command of the Confederate army in northern Virginia. Another officer, General R. E. Lee, soon received permanent command of the army. So, Smith may have faced uncertainties as he read Cooper's message. "The President desires to know if you consider your health sufficiently good to take command of the Department of South Carolina and Georgia, fixing your headquarters in Charleston or such other place in the vicinity as you may deem proper."[185]

July 5, 1862 (Saturday)

Concerned over reported Confederate activity along the Ogeechee River, Du Pont ordered action from Commander John Goldsborough. "Having every reason to believe, from information received from Acting Lieutenant Commanding [Pendleton] Watmough, that Ossabaw is resorted to by the rebels, and that a fort has been constructed on the Ogeechee River, I have determined to place the *Potomska* there for the present. On the receipt of this you will…order Acting Lieutenant Commanding Watmough to Ossabaw to enforce the blockade of that sound."[186]

---

182 *ORN*, ser. I, vol. 13:161.

183 Ibid., 165.

184 Ibid., 167.

185 *OR*, ser. I, vol. 14:578–79.

186 *ORN*, ser. I, vol. 13:169.

July 6, 1862 (Sunday)

Colonel James Morrison—in Kingston, Tennessee—continued to recruit troopers for service in his 1st Georgia Cavalry Regiment; a notice in the *Southern Confederacy* announced his effort. "CAVALRY WANTED: One company will be received…this corps has been assigned the position to operate on the line of Georgia and Tennessee."[187]

July 7, 1862 (Monday)

Life continued even during a time of war, especially for young ladies ready for higher education. An announcement from the Washington Seminary in Washington, Georgia, publicized plans to "open its first session for 1862, the 1st MONDAY in August," and declared the institution "is located in a healthy region, safe and secure from many disadvantages connected with education in larger places, and is accessible by Railroad."[188]

July 8, 1862 (Tuesday)

Once conscription started, some would seek any remedy to escape service. "We are sorry to learn that one able bodied young man, of this county [Lumpkin], mutilated himself, by chopping his fingers off from one hand to avoid conscription. It should avail him nothing."[189]

July 9, 1862 (Wednesday)

Georgia's coast raised the interest of Flag Officer Du Pont, to the point he ordered an inspection of the area. He ordered Commander Charles Steedman to conduct a reconnaissance "of Ossabaw Sound, coast of Georgia. I believe it may be used as an exit from Savannah by small vessels through Romerly Marshes…I learn there is a fort up the Ogeechee…. You can feel this fort with your long-range guns and destroy it if you can, but as there is no military operation involved this must be done with sound discretion and without unnecessary loss."[190]

July 10, 1862 (Thursday)

A newspaper editor in Rome called for Georgians to maintain a resilient attitude. "As public opinion is the tribunal before which this case is to be tried, patience should be exercised, until the *denouement*, which is yet to come off, in either victory or retreat, and the evidence, in the shape of full particulars, is laid before the public, and then let the verdict be made up. Let us be careful about hasty condemnation."[191]

July 11, 1862 (Friday)

A newspaper in Columbus reported on the work accomplished, when a dedicated group—

---

187 "Cavalry Wanted," *Atlanta Southern Confederacy*, July 6, 1862, sec. 3, https://gahistoricnewspapers.galileo.usg.edu/lccn/sn82014677/1862-07-06/ed-1/seq-3/.

188 "Washington Seminary," *Savannah Republican*, July 7, 1862, sec. 2, https://gahistoricnewspapers.galileo.usg.edu/lccn/sn85038496/1862-07-07/ed-1/seq-2/. Caps in original.

189 "The Dahlonega Signal Says," *Columbus Daily Sun*, July 8, 1862, sec. 1, https://gahistoricnewspapers.galileo.usg.edu/lccn/sn82014939/1862-07-08/ed-1/seq-1/.

190 *ORN*, ser. I, vol. 13:186.

191 "There Seems to Be a Dissatisfaction," *Rome Tri-Weekly Courier*, July 10, 1862, sec. 2, https://gahistoricnewspapers.galileo.usg.edu/lccn/sn85034102/1862-07-10/ed-1/seq-2/.

Ladies Association for the Construction of a Gunboat or an Ironclad Floating Battery—raised the needed funds to build the vessel. "To your patriotic and noble efforts, Ladies of Georgia, is the port of the city of Savannah indebted for this powerful engine [CSS *Georgia*] for its defence against the hateful foes who are committing depredations upon our defenceless coasts."[192]

July 12, 1862 (Saturday)

Flag Officer Du Pont notified Acting Master Jonathan Baker to navigate the USS *Unadilla* from South Carolina to Georgia. "You will proceed to Ossabaw and join Commander [Charles] Steedman in the expedition up the Ogeechee. Mr. Rufus Murphy, a refugee sent up by Captain [Enoch] Parrott, represents himself as familiar with the waters from Brunswick to Savannah and calls himself a pilot. Captain Parrott is favorably impressed. Please send and get him and try him."[193]

July 13, 1862 (Sunday)

The *Southern Confederacy* newspaper in Atlanta ran an announcement from an Alabama newspaper praising the Georgia daily. "Atlanta enjoys superior advantage for obtaining the *latest and most reliable news* from all quarters, and especially so from North Alabama, Tennessee, and Kentucky. The *Confederacy* gives fuller reports of the movements in our armies in those States than any other page we have seen, and we take pleasure in commending it to the patronage of our readers."[194]

July 14, 1862 (Monday)

The Columbus Depot provided uniforms and other matériel to Confederate forces in the field. A newspaper editor offered "some idea" of the magnitude of the enterprise. "The amount of Clothing manufactured for the Confederate army in this city may be derived from the fact that about 240 boxes, averaging, we suppose, 3 feet square, and estimated to make 12 or 14 car loads, have been packed here within a few days past for a portion of Gen. Bragg's army."[195]

July 15, 1862 (Tuesday)

Conscription took more young men from home and into the army, casualties mounted, and folks on the home front worried about aspects of everyday life, especially education. "Hundreds of our talented young men…have fallen…hence, many important offices both of State and Church, will be vacated. Now, the inquiry is, who shall refill these offices? The history of the world demonstrates, that ignorance and cruelty go hand in hand. Yet, this

---

[192] "To the Ladies of Georgia," *Columbus Daily Sun*, July 11, 1862, sec. 1, https://gahistoricnewspapers.galileo.usg.edu/lccn/sn82014939/1862-07-11/ed-1/seq-1/.

[193] *ORN*, ser. I, vol. 13:190.

[194] "The Southern Confederacy," *Atlanta Southern Confederacy*, July 13, 1862, https://gahistoricnewspapers.galileo.usg.edu/lccn/sn82014677/1862-07-13/ed-1/seq-1/.

[195] "Clothing Made in Columbus," *Columbus Daily Sun*, July 14, 1862, sec. 2, https://gahistoricnewspapers.galileo.usg.edu/lccn/sn82014939/1862-07-14/ed-1/seq-2/.

may be the case, if our schools are suspended, until the war closes."[196]

July 16, 1862 (Wednesday)

Naval officials in Washington received a report on conditions in St. Simon's Sound from Commander John Goldsborough. "Their [Confederates] seacoast guards have been increased, their pickets multiplied on the mainland, and notwithstanding the vessels under my command are judiciously stationed…to prevent a landing by the rebels under cover of a dark night, I strongly recommend that military possession be at once taken and a force of one or two hundred soldiers or marines landed."[197]

July 17, 1862 (Thursday)

The U.S. Congress passed the Second Confiscation Act; enforcement would impact Georgia.

> That every person who shall hereafter commit the crime of treason against the United States, and shall be adjudged guilty thereof, shall suffer death, and all his slaves, if any, shall be declared and made free; or, at the discretion of the court, he shall be imprisoned for not less than five years and fined not less than ten thousand dollars, and all his slaves, if any, shall be declared and made free; said fine shall be levied and collected on any or all of the property, real and personal, excluding slaves, of which the said person so convicted was the owner at the time of committing the said crime, any sale or conveyance to the contrary notwithstanding.[198]

July 18, 1862 (Friday) ◑

Flag Officer Du Pont notified officials of plans for captured Confederate vessels. "The *Courier*, which leaves here in a few days, takes to New York the first cutter of the *Savannah*, which was stove while that vessel was aground on the bar when leaving Port Royal. It might soon be repaired at the navy yard. Also the barge belonging to Commodore Tattnall, captured in Wassaw…I beg your acceptance of as a prize memorial of our quondam [former] friend."[199]

July 19, 1862 (Saturday)

Casualties mounted, and many Confederate wounded received rail transportation. The post surgeon, John M. Johnson, welcomed them to the city. "When you arrive in Atlanta, go to the hospitals and have your wounds dressed, and get food and rest yourselves. The following hospitals are near the car shed—the farthest not more than one hundred and fifty yards—Gate City, City Hotel, Alexander, and Concert Hall."[200]

---

[196] "Education," *Columbus Daily Sun*, July 15, 1862, https://gahistoricnewspapers.galileo.usg.edu/lccn/sn82014939/1862-07-15/ed-1/seq-2/.

[197] *ORN*, ser. I, vol. 13:195.

[198] "The Second Confiscation Act," http://www.freedmen.umd.edu/conact2.htm.

[199] *ORN*, ser. I, vol. 13:199.

[200] "To the Wounded Soldiers from Richmond and Other Places," *Atlanta Southern Confederacy*, July 19, 1862, sec. 3, https://gahistoricnewspapers.galileo.usg.edu/lccn/sn82014677/1862-07-19/ed-1/seq-3/.

July 20, 1862 (Sunday)

A newspaper in Atlanta, despite a misspelling, praised a local officer. "Our well known fellow-citizen, Col. [Robert] Mattox [Maddox], of the 42d Georgia Regiment, has been at home some time on a sick furlough. We are glad to see that he has so far recovered as to be able to go out on our streets. He informs us that he will retain to his regiment in a few days, if he continues to improve. He has sacrificed as much as any man in this community to go into the service of his country."[201]

July 21, 1862 (Monday)

In a very lengthy letter to President Davis, Governor Brown maintained his disagreement with conscription, and then offered Davis a lesson in the Constitution.

> Entertaining, as I do, the highest regard for your opinion and those of each individual member of your Cabinet, it is with great diffidence that I express the conviction, which I still entertain, after a careful perusal of your letter, that your argument fails to sustain the constitutionality of the Act; and that the conclusion at which you have arrived is maintained by neither the contemporaneous construction put upon the Constitution by those who made it, nor by the practice of the United States Government, under it, during the earlier and better days of the Republic, nor by the language of the instrument itself, taking the whole contex [*sic*], and applying to it the well established rules by which all constitutions and laws are to be construed.[202]

July 22,1862 (Tuesday)

As the war progressed, counterfeit currency spread across Georgia. Early on, the process proved challenging, but with time, the forged currency looked of better quality than the real thing. As one newspaper reported, "We are informed that counterfeit Confederate notes of the denomination of ten dollars are in circulation. The engraving is coarsely done, purporting to be done by the Southern Bank Note Company, and they are printed in black and red ink. A little care will enable all to detect the spurious note, so the public need not necessarily be losers."[203]

July 23, 1862 (Wednesday)

Flag Officer Du Pont submitted a listing of the various vessels under his command in Georgia waters: "Wassaw Sound, the steamer *Flag* and bark *Braziliera*. In Ossabaw, the steamers *Unadilla* and *Potomska*. In St. Simon's, Altamaha, and *Sapelo* are the steamers *Florida*, *Wamsutta*, *Madgie*, and *E. B. Hale*."[204]

July 24, 1862 (Thursday)

Commander James Strong reported recent intelligence to Du Pont. "To-day the *Unadilla*

---

[201] "Lt. Col. R. F. Mattox," *Atlanta Southern Confederacy*, July 20, 1862, https://gahistoricnewspapers.galileo.usg.edu/lccn/sn82014677/1862-07-20/ed-1/seq-3/.

[202] Candler, *Confederate Records of the State of Georgia*, [vol?]251–52.

[203] "Counterfeit Confederate Notes," *Weekly Augusta Chronicle & Sentinel*, July 22, 1862, https://gahistoricnewspapers.galileo.usg.edu/lccn/sn82014777/1862-07-22/ed-1/seq-2/.

[204] *ORN*, ser. I, vol. 13:206.

came in...to inform me...there was a large steamer at the railroad station, loading. I mentioned to Lieutenant Commanding [Napoleon] Collins that I had seen the *Darlington* going out. He then told me that it could not be, as she was down the coast, but that it must have been a rebel steamer, and that he had been away all day...had I known that he had left...I could have taken the steamer, as she was evidently slow; probably the...*Kate*."[205]

July 25, 1862 (Friday)

Wishing to purge coastal Georgia of Confederate positions, Du Pont ordered Commander Steedman to "proceed with the *Paul Jones* under your command to Ossabaw...I desire you to make a reconnoissance [*sic*] in force, and if you are satisfied that you can destroy or silence the fort without too much risk of life I wish you to do so. In case you pass the fort you will continue to the railroad and destroy or capture the steamer."[206]

July 26, 1862 (Saturday) ●

Commander Goldsborough informed Du Pont of possible activity in Ossabaw Sound. "I have this moment been informed that a bark-rigged steamer, supposed to be the *Nashville*, loaded with cotton, is in Ossabaw trying to get out, or, rather, waiting for an opportunity."[207]

July 27, 1862 (Sunday)

A resident returned to Augusta; locals welcomed him and extended compliments on his accomplishments. "We had the pleasure of a visit...from our townsman, Maj. [Lawrence D.] Lallerstedt, of the 22d Georgia Regiment...his gallant bearing on the field of battle and his constant devotion to duty have won for him this promotion. We tender him our congratulations, and hope it may be a step to still further advances."[208]

July 28, 1862 (Monday)

Du Pont sent several vessels in pursuit of the *Nashville*. "I have the *Huron*, *Paul Jones*, and *Unadilla* after the *Nashville* in the Ogeechee. A steamer got out the other day, midday, from Ossabaw, [Lieutenant Napoleon] Collins having deliberately left his station."[209]

July 29, 1862 (Tuesday)

Commander Charles Steedman led four ships on an attack upon Fort McAllister. He recapped the day's action in his official report.

> At 10 o'clock a. m. we came within range of a battery mounting seven or eight guns on the left bank of the river (ascending) and on high ground commanding the approaches from 1½ to 2 miles. So soon as I got within range I commenced a cannonade, which was followed by the other gunboats with their rifles and occasionally XI-inch guns. The enemy answered with spirit, most of their shots striking near, and several passing over me. A spirited fire was kept up on both sides for an hour and a half (firing slowly and deliberately), when, becoming satisfied from the range of the

[205] Ibid., 211.

[206] Ibid., 212.

[207] Ibid., 217.

[208] "Major Lallerstedt," *Augusta Daily Constitutionalist*, July 27, 1862, sec. 1, Genealogybank.com.

[209] *ORN*, ser. I, vol. 13:219.

enemy's fire and weight of metal that if I attempted to ascend the river I would have to do so at a great sacrifice of life and perhaps the sinking of one or more of the gunboats, I concluded to withdraw from the contest, for had we continued we would have had to steam up, head on, a distance of more than a mile and a half, with only one gun from each vessel to return their fire; besides this, the river is "piled" across below and in point-blank range of the fort, effectually obstructing the passage, and to remove a sufficient number (if possible) to permit passing would require sacrifices not warranted.[210]

July 30, 1862 (Wednesday)

Rumors of a Confederate vessel on Georgia's coast prompted Du Pont to dispatch an order to Lieutenant John Bankhead. "I have received information that the rebels intend to run the blockade either by the Savannah River or Wassaw, and I desire to increase the force at Wassaw, as the *Seneca* has very little steam power. There is also some information, apparently reliable, that a ram is completed at Savannah."[211]

July 31, 1862 (Thursday)

Major General David Hunter notified Secretary Stanton regarding a recent order to send reinforcements to the Army of the Potomac. Sharing his concerns for various positions on the coast of South Carolina, Hunter suggested, "It is in my judgment extremely important that both these positions should be reoccupied, and also that strong posts should be established at Georgetown, Brunswick, and Saint Simon's Island. I have therefore to request that re-enforcements may be sent to this department as soon as possible, not only with a view to future operations, but also for the further security of our present positions and depots."[212]

August 1, 1862 (Friday)

Lieutenant Daniel Ammen of the USS *Seneca* reported to Du Pont from Wassaw Sound. "We continue to see the smoke of rebel steamers that come down daily beyond Skiddaway Island.... I made an examination yesterday up Tybee River as far as some old wharves without seeing traces of the enemy. To-morrow I shall send the gig through the creek to Pulaski to get mails and for a further examination...."[213]

August 2, 1862 (Saturday) ◐

A newspaper editor in Columbus, writing of the "Impressment of Slaves," reported that "The order of General [Hugh] Mercer authorizing the impressment of slaves to work on the fortifications at Savannah, seems to have created some dissatisfaction among the planters in some portions of the State. Some of the objections urged appear to be extremely frivolous." The reasons put forth included "the climate of Savannah is not congenial to negroes of the Northern and interior portions of the State [and] that Savannah should take care of her own fortifications, and let the balance of the State do the same...[a third

---

210 Ibid., 221.

211 Ibid., 222.

212 *OR*, ser. I, vol. 14:366.

213 *ORN*, ser. I, vol. 13:228.

reason]...the only rational objection urged, is in behalf of the *fodder* crop."[214]

August 3, 1862 (Sunday)

Major General David Hunter corresponded with Flag Officer Du Pont regarding a report from Fort Pulaski. "Three negroes have arrived here from Savannah and report the rebel ram a failure. She leaks and her engines are not of sufficient power. I have telegraphed to have the negroes sent down here...will give them a strict examination...as their escape into our lines at such a time, and the story they tell, would seem to render it quite possible that they have been sent for the purpose of misleading."[215]

August 4, 1862 (Monday)

Lieutenant Napoleon Collins of the USS *Unadilla* netted a prize in Ossabaw Sound. "I have the honor to report that we seized the British steamer *Lodona* at 12:30 p.m. this day, in Hell Gate, between the Ogeechee and Vernon rivers, Ossabaw Sound, for violating the blockade." He also noted, "they attempted to run into Savannah last night, but were driven off by the guns at the martello tower, Tybee Island, one shell from which penetrated and exploded in her cabin...they were running the blockade and were taken bloody handed."[216]

August 5, 1862 (Tuesday)

Brigadier General Horatio Wright reported his troop strength and locations to Secretary Stanton. "At Fort Pulaski...six companies. The cavalry is of little service in the department, and should be withdrawn if needed elsewhere."[217]

August 6, 1862 (Wednesday)

A newspaper in Macon reported on the promotion of a Georgia officer. "Lieut. J. L. Adderton, of the Zollicoffer Rifles, has been promoted to the office of Captain of the 'Granberry Guards,' by the Confederate Government. This is a new company raised in Americus, and now on duty at the Oglethorpe Encampment in this city. Capt. A. is a most worthy gentleman and citizen, and we trust will prove himself to be equally so as a soldier."[218] This unit would serve in the 10th Georgia Infantry Battalion.

August 7, 1862 (Thursday)

Flag Officer Du Pont received intelligence from an individual working under the pseudonym "Unionist." The operative reported, "I sent you a communication...in which I told you that the steamer *Nashville* was in the Ogeechee River. I afterwards learned that the steamer *Sue* was also there. General Pemberton visited this place on the 3d instant to select a suitable location for batteries. He said that he would erect one at Frazier Point and one at Mayrant's Bluff as soon as he could get the men and guns."[219]

---

[214] "Impressment of Slaves," *Columbus Daily Sun*, August 2, 1862, sec. 2, https://gahistoricnewspapers.galileo.usg.edu/lccn/sn82014939/1862-08-02/ed-1/seq-2/.

[215] *ORN*, ser. I, vol. 13:231.

[216] Ibid., 237.

[217] *OR*, ser. I, vol. 14:369.

[218] "Granberry Guards," *Macon Georgia Journal and Messenger*, August 6, 1862, https://gahistoricnewspapers.galileo.usg.edu/lccn/sn85038491/1862-08-06/ed-1/seq-2/.

[219] *ORN*, ser. I, vol. 13:338.

August 8, 1862 (Friday)
The more things change, the more they remain the same, and the postal service proved no exception. "We hope the present rates of postage will be reduced. The rates were increased, no doubt, with a view to increasing the income and making the Department self-sustaining. We have no doubt the revenue has been lessened instead of increased, without reducing the expenses a cent."[220] The rate to mail a letter had recently increased to ten cents.

August 9, 1862 (Saturday)
Opining on the issue of rights, an editor in Savannah wrote,

> Everybody talks of rights, but some people have very strange and inconsistent notions of the true import of the term. There are some citizens of Georgia, a very few we hope, who deny the right of the government to call upon them and demand the use of their property for the public service and defense; and yet these very same people utter not a murmur when the government impresses them and their sons and relatives, however indispensable they may be to the support of their wives and little ones at home, and, by force, takes them to any portion of the broad land where they may be needed as food for gunpowder![221]

August 10, 1862 (Sunday)
Rear Admiral Du Pont dispatched Commander William Le Roy to navigate his ship to the Georgia coast. "You will proceed in the morning with the *Keystone State* to sea, and cruise along the coast from Tybee and St. Andrew's to Charleston, maintaining an outer blockade. You are authorized to communicate with any of the points on this line where an inside blockade is established, giving and receiving every information."[222]

August 11, 1862 (Monday)
General Braxton Bragg, via Special Field Orders, No. 148 declared, "Martial law is hereby established within the corporate limits and environs of the town of Atlanta, Ga."[223] Bragg feared unrest in the city would obstruct troops moving through the area.

August 12, 1862 (Tuesday)
From West Point, Georgia, John Whitner sought the assistance of Howell Cobb. "There is one thing I wish you would do—write to Secy. of War to give me and those I have to employ to assist me some showing of exemption from conscription. The poppinjays employed as enrolling officers and the defeated army officers appointed to command the camps delight in harassing and putting to expense everybody."[224]

---

[220] "Postage," *Columbus Daily Sun*, August 8, 1862, sec. 2, https://gahistoricnewspapers.galileo.usg.edu/lccn/sn82014939/1862-08-08/ed-1/seq-2/; Civil War Philatelic Society, "Basic Rates."

[221] "Rights," *Savannah Republican*, August 9, 1862, sec. 1, https://gahistoricnewspapers.galileo.usg.edu/lccn/sn85038496/1862-08-09/ed-1/seq-1/.

[222] *ORN*, ser. I, vol. 13:247.

[223] *OR*, ser. I, vol. 16, pt. 2:754.

[224] Toombs, Stephens, and Cobb, *Correspondence*, 603.

August 13, 1862 (Wednesday)

On the last day of July, Major General Hunter had requested additional troops from the War Department in Washington, specifically boots on the ground in Brunswick and other coastal areas of Georgia. Today, Hunter received his answer. Assistant Adjutant-General John Kelton wrote, "The general-in-chief directs me, in reply to your communication of the 31st ultimo, addressed to the Secretary of War, to inform you that no re-enforcements can at present be sent to the Department of the South."[225]

August 14, 1862 (Thursday)

A status report from Du Pont addressed a vessel in Georgia waters. "The Savannah ram, not at all the *Fingal*, is more of a floating battery, doubtless with X-inch guns (eight of them), but she has a list, leaks, and has not power to go against the stream. She may be used to cover vessels running the blockade by putting herself between them and the forts, if entering Savannah River."[226]

August 15, 1862 (Friday)

Wounded soldiers increasingly made their way to the growing number of hospitals in Atlanta. Extra patients required added care. Surgeon J. P. Logan wrote, "The Hospitals in this city require an additional force of attendants for the sick already in the Wards. I am notified that five hundred more will arrive in the next twenty-four hours. It is hoped that persons owning or having control of negroes will promptly present them for hire at the various Hospitals, and that we shall not be compelled to call upon the military authorities for aid."[227]

August 16, 1862 (Saturday)

Ossabaw Sound served as the focus of the day for Rear Admiral Du Pont, as he provided instructions to Lieutenant-Commander John Davis. "So soon as you are ready you will proceed with the steamer *Vixen*, under your command, to Ossabaw Sound, Georgia, and report to Commander A. G. Clary, of the *Dawn*, for blockading duty in those waters. I intend the *Vixen* to relieve the *Pembina* for the present, and orders will be sent by you to Commander [Albert] Clary."[228] General Bragg appointed James M. Calhoun as "civil governor" of Atlanta.

August 17, 1862 (Sunday) ◑

"The Atlanta Hospital Association gratefully acknowledge a large lot of coffee received from Col. John H. Morgan, through Mrs. E. M. Bruce. The refreshment will be doubly grateful to our poor sick soldiers when they know it is presented by the gallant Partizan Chief of Kentucky, and is a small portion of the spoils he recently and so bravely won from the

---

[225] *OR*, ser. I, vol. 14:374.

[226] *ORN*, ser. I, vol. 13:254.

[227] "Negroes Wanted," *Atlanta Southern Confederacy*, August 15, 1862, sec. 3, https://gahistoricnewspapers.galileo.usg.edu/lccn/sn82014677/1862-08-15/ed-1/seq-3/.

[228] *ORN*, ser. I, vol. 13:262; Garrett and Martin, *Atlanta and Environs*, 527.

enemy." Caffeine, caffeine, a most welcome treat from the "Thunderbolt"![229]

August 18, 1862 (Monday)

President Davis informed the Confederate Congress of potential action regarding the ages of those eligible for conscription. "The very large increase of forces recently called into the field by the President of the United States may render it necessary hereafter to extend the provisions of the conscript law so as to embrace persons between the ages of 35 and 45 years. The vigor and efficiency of our present forces, their condition, and skill and ability which distinguish their leaders, inspire the belief that no further enrollment will be necessary."[230] Having already read the casualty lists from several battles, one can imagine several "older" Georgia men did not receive this news with open arms.

August 19, 1862 (Tuesday)

Acting Lieutenant John Barnes received a new assignment from Du Pont. "You are hereby detached from the *Wabash* and will proceed to Ossabaw Sound and relieve Commander A. G. Clary in the command of the U.S.S. *Dawn*, now blockading those waters. I have asked the Department to approve of this appointment, as eminently due to your faithful and gallant services in this ship and squadron since the very commencement of the war."[231]

August 20, 1862 (Wednesday)

The economic impact of the war, coupled with declining resources, began to worry Georgians. "The subject of bread for the people in the future, is one of vast importance.... For clothing we can possibly manage...but the same cannot be said of bread. Day by day, a new supply must be had, and at greatly advanced prices upon former years. While provisions have advanced at least one hundred per cent, wages have remained stationary. At the present rate of prices four dollars per day for labor, is about equal to two before the war."[232]

August 21, 1862 (Thursday)

In Richmond, General cooper issued General Orders, No. 60.

> Ordered, That Major-General [David] Hunter and Brigadier-General [John] Phelps be no longer held and treated as public enemies of the Confederate States, but as outlaws; and that in the event of the capture of either of them, or that of any other commissioned officer employed in drilling, organizing, or instructing slaves, with a view to their armed service in this war, he shall not be regarded as a prisoner of war, but held in close confinement for execution as a felon at such time and place as the President shall order.[233]

August 22, 1862 (Friday)

---

[229] "The Atlanta Hospital Association," *Atlanta Southern Confederacy*, August 17, 1862, sec. 3, https://gahistoricnewspapers.galileo.usg.edu/lccn/sn82014677/1862-08-17/ed-1/seq-3/. Morgan's nickname was the "Thunderbolt" of the Confederacy.

[230] *Journal of the Confederate Congress*, August 18, 1862, 2:228.

[231] *ORN*, ser. I, vol. 13:266.

[232] "Bread vs. Wages," *Columbus Daily Sun*, August 20, 1862, https://gahistoricnewspapers.galileo.usg.edu/lccn/sn82014939/1862-08-20/ed-1/seq-2/.

[233] *OR*, ser. I, vol. 14:599.

Perhaps fearing ramifications from General Cooper's order the previous day, Hunter decided to lay low for a while. Major General Henry Halleck issued Special Orders, No. 202: "Maj. Gen. D. Hunter, U.S. Volunteers, has on his own application a leave of absence for sixty days. He will turn over the command of his department to the officer next in rank [Brigadier General John M. Brannan].[234]

August 23, 1862 (Saturday)

A report of yet another possible attempt to run the blockade prompted Rear Admiral Du Pont to notify his various squadron vessels near the Ogeechee River. To Commander Daniel Ammen of the USS *Sebago*, he wrote, "From information received to-day there is reason to believe that the *Nashville*, loaded with cotton, is endeavoring to run the blockade. She is either in the Ogeechee or Vernon River. You will please keep careful watch on her and another steamer called the *Emma*; the latter; will probably attempt to escape through Wassaw." Du Pont received this intelligence courtesy of "Three deserters from Savannah…say that she was below Fort Jackson prepared to run the blockade."[235]

August 24, 1862 (Sunday)

A resident of Atlanta returned for a visit but probably wished the call had occurred under other circumstances. "J. M. Clarke, [Edward Y. Clarke] Esq., Adjutant of Col. [F. M.] Nix's…regiment of [16th] Georgia Partisan Rangers, is now in our city…. We regret to learn that he is quite unwell—though he hopes to be so far recovered as to…return to regiment in about ten days. We learn that he was with the regiment when it took Huntsville, Tennessee, a few days ago, and greatly distinguished himself for his intrepidity, coolness, and good judgment."[236]

August 25, 1862 (Monday) ●

Commander Ammen responded to Du Pont's orders to guard against a blockade run on the coast of Georgia. "I have the honor to acknowledge your note…in relation to the steamers *Nashville* and *Emma*. I hope the latter may endeavor to run the blockade at this point, as I think there is not the least probability of her success. The *Sebago* [Ammen's ship] is anchored in the evening near the inner buoy; this gives us command of the Tybee River channel, as well as that of Wilmington River. I think it impossible that any vessel can evade us."[237]

August 26, 1862 (Tuesday)

Colonel George Washington Lee, the provost marshal of Atlanta, issued General Orders No. 9.

> Having been informed that a large quantity of bills of the denominations of Fifty Dollars and One Hundred Dollars, purporting to be Confederate notes, which are supposed by some to be counterfeits, are being thrown into circulation in this city; It

---

[234] Ibid., 380.

[235] *ORN*, ser. I, vol. 13:278.

[236] "Adjutant E. Y. Clarke," *Atlanta Southern Confederacy*, August 24, 1862, sec. 2, https://gahistoricnewspapers.galileo.usg.edu/lccn/sn82014677/1862-08-24/ed-1/seq-2/.

[237] *ORN*, ser. I, vol. 13:282.

is hereby ordered that all persons holding any of said bills, hold them until they have been subjected to a proper test and announced either genuine or spurious. The object of the above order being obvious, it is hoped that all loyal citizens will contribute to its thorough observance.[238]

August 27, 1862 (Wednesday)

Coastal Georgia received great attention, especially during the first three years of the war. "We are glad to see that several counties...are responding promptly to the call for aid in completing these defences [at Savannah]. Among them, are those of Sumter (whose quota has already gone), Monroe and Houston. Houston county sends a physician with the compensation of five hundred dollars, and an overseer at two hundred and fifty. Other counties are also moving in the matter."[239]

August 28, 1862 (Thursday)

Parents had enough worries over their sons on the front lines; problems with younger siblings proved challenging at home. "It is a rare thing to see a train, or even the engine and tender pass, that small boys are not jumping on and off to the great danger of their lives...we saw a half dozen boys swinging on to the rear of a train, and one little fellow made us shudder by amusing himself in running from car to car when the train was in full motion." A Savannah paper urged that "Conductors of trains should be made, under a penalty, to see to it that boys are kept off. If some effective steps are not taken promptly, it will not be many days before some doting father and mother are called on to weep bitter, bitter tears, over the mangled remains of their child. Let the warning be heeded."[240]

August 29, 1862 (Friday)

Secretary of War Randolph issued Special Orders, No. 202. "General G. T. Beauregard, C. S. Army, is assigned to the command of the Department of South Carolina and Georgia."[241]

August 30, 1862 (Saturday)

A call instilling Christian principles into the young men learning the art of war. "While our officers are training their men in discipline, in movement, in arms, if they would also impress upon them the great necessity of a moral tone, we should soon be beyond all danger from our foes. It is wrong to neglect moral power while we are cultivating physical power."[242]

August 31, 1862 (Sunday)

---

[238] "General Orders No. 9," *Atlanta Southern Confederacy*, August 26, 1862, sec. 3, https://gahistoricnewspapers.galileo.usg.edu/lccn/sn82014677/1862-08-26/ed-1/seq-3/.

[239] "The Defences of Savannah," *Macon Georgia Journal and Messenger*, August 27, 1862, https://gahistoricnewspapers.galileo.usg.edu/lccn/sn85038491/1862-08-27/ed-1/seq-2/.

[240] "A Timely Warning," *Savannah Republican*, August 28, 1862, sec. 2, https://gahistoricnewspapers.galileo.usg.edu/lccn/sn85038496/1862-08-28/ed-1/seq-2/.

[241] *OR*, ser. I, vol. 14:601.

[242] "To the South," *Atlanta Banner and Baptist*, August 30, 1862, sec. 1, https://gahistoricnewspapers.galileo.usg.edu/lccn/sn89053822/1862-08-30/ed-1/seq-1/.

Major General Hunter sent Rear Admiral Du Pont information on a vessel near Fort Pulaski. "The officers of the…*Cosmopolitan*, just from Fort Pulaski, report that at daylight this morning a large steamer was discovered aground in the [Savannah] River…3 miles above the fort. She was fired upon from the fort, when boats were seen to leave her and soon after she was discovered to be on fire. The captain of the *Cosmopolitan* feels confident that she is the *Nashville*."[243]

September 1, 1862 (Monday)

Governor Brown shared concerns over his political opinions with Vice President Stephens. "I have already come…into conflict with the Confederate authorities in vindication of what I have considered the rights of the State and people of Georgia, and I was fearful, as no other governor seems to raise these questions, that I might be considered by good and true men in and out of Congress too refractory for the times."[244]

September 2, 1862 (Tuesday) ◐

News of new army vocabulary passed to the citizens of Floyd County. "In all 'General Orders' of the army of the West, whenever occasion is had to refer to the Northern army, it is now styled the 'Abolition army of the North,' and 'Abolition General,' instead of using the word 'Federal.' The change is very pertinent."[245]

September 3, 1862 (Wednesday)

Athens received a visitor from the Army of Northern Virginia. "[Lieutenant] Vardy P. Sisson…is now at home recruiting his health—shattered by fever while in camp. He has been in Gen. Johnston's army from the time of the evacuation of Harper's Ferry till the present—has used the 'shooting stick' in many battles and skirmishes without receiving a scratch."[246] Sisson served in the 8th Georgia Infantry.

September 4, 1862 (Thursday)

Major Hermann Hirsch from the Quartermaster Department, ran a notice in a Savannah newspaper seeking "Horses & Mules." The officer wanted "a number of Horses and Mules, suitable for Artillery Service, for which the best prices will be paid. Partics wishing to sell will deliver their stock at the Government Stables, on West Broad street, near the Central Railroad Depot, for inspection."[247]

September 5, 1862 (Friday)

Folks in Rome read of seasoning as they perused the broadsheet over breakfast. "A meeting will be held at 2 P.M., to-day at the City Hall, for the purpose of forming a Salt Company. Share $100—Capital 30,000. The importance of this movement is palpable to every

---

[243] *ORN*, ser. I, vol. 13:297.

[244] Toombs, Stephens, and Cobb, *Correspondence*, 605.

[245] "In All General Orders," *Rome Tri-Weekly Courier*, September 2, 1862, sec. 2, https://gahistoricnewspapers.galileo.usg.edu/lccn/sn85034102/1862-09-02/ed-1/seq-2/.

[246] "We Had the Pleasure," *Athens Southern Banner*, September 3, 1862, sec. 3, https://gahistoricnewspapers.galileo.usg.edu/lccn/sn82014069/1862-09-03/ed-1/seq-3/.

[247] "Horses & Mules," *Savannah Republican*, September 4, 1862, sec. 4, https://gahistoricnewspapers.galileo.usg.edu/lccn/sn85038496/1862-09-04/ed-1/seq-4/.

person, and we hope the citizens will give the matter the attention it deserves."[248]

September 6, 1862 (Saturday)

Lieutenant-Commander William Truxton of the USS *Alabama* reported from coastal Georgia. "I regret to say I find myself very much hampered among these narrow creeks by the want of proper boats and boat equipments. The ship has not one really good boat and no boat guns."[249]

September 7, 1862 (Sunday)

Seeking a break from the stresses of daily life during war, residents of Augusta prepared for a night on the town. "The Queen Sisters and Palmetto Band will commence their second week in this city at Concert Hall to-morrow, Monday, evening with an attractive bill. Pay them a visit."[250]

September 8, 1862 (Monday)

Vice President Stephens wrote to James Calhoun, the newly appointed "civil Governor of Atlanta." Stephens, a strict Constitutionalist, did not pull any punches in his correspondence with Calhoun, or anyone else. "Gen Bragg had no more authority for appointing you civil Governor of Atlanta, than I had; and I had, or have, no more authority than any street walker in your city. Under his appointment, therefore, you can rightfully exercise no more power than if the appointment had been made by a street walker. We live under a Constitution…made for war as well as peace."[251]

September 9, 1862 (Tuesday)

"We learn from persons connected with the Macon & Western Railroad, in this city [Milledgeville], that several hundred sacks of salt have passed over that Road, within the past, week, consigned to Agents…at Macon, Savannah &c. These Agents are charged with the duty of selling out this salt at prime cost, to certain classes of our fellow-citizens, commencing first with soldiers' families."[252] The supply of salt continued to lessen, placing greater attention on the needed commodity.

September 10, 1862 (Wednesday)

Major General Pemberton responded to General Cooper in Richmond on recruiting of partisan units in Georgia. Pemberton declared "no individual has applied for or received my approval, as required by Article V, General Orders, No. 30. If authority has been obtained for such organizations in that State it must either have been on the approval of

---

[248] "September 5, 1862," *Rome Weekly Courier*, September 5, 1862, sec. 2, https://gahistoricnewspapers.galileo.usg.edu/lccn/sn82014071/1862-09-05/ed-1/seq-2/.

[249] *ORN*, ser. I, vol. 13:300.

[250] "The Queen Sisters," *Augusta Daily Constitutionalist*, September 7, 1862, sec. 3, Genealogybank.com.

[251] "Hon. James M. Calhoun, Atlanta, Ga.," *Atlanta Southern Confederacy*, September 28, 1862, sec. 2, https://gahistoricnewspapers.galileo.usg.edu/lccn/sn82014677/1862-09-28/ed-1/seq-2/.

[252] "Salt for the People of Georgia," *Milledgeville Southern Federal Union*, September 9, 1862, sec. 3, https://gahistoricnewspapers.galileo.usg.edu/lccn/sn87062317/1862-09-09/ed-1/seq-3/.

Brigadier-General Lawton, without reference to myself as department commander, or by authority granted directly from the Department of War. It is very certain that these troops ought to be disbanded…."[253]

September 11, 1862 (Thursday)

Georgia residents learned of another opportunity for prayer and reflection: "The Proclamation of President Davis setting apart Thursday the 18th inst. as a day of thanksgiving and prayer by the people of the Confederate States will command approving attention. Let our business houses be closed on that day, and let all unite in thanksgiving to the Allwise Governor of the Universe for blessings vouchsafed to an infant government."[254]

September 12, 1862 (Friday)

In Richmond, the Confederate Congress approved a motion regarding a Savannah native, when considering "the nomination of John C. Nicoll to be district attorney for the State of Georgia. On the question, Will the Senate advise and consent to the appointment of John C. Nicoll? It was determined in the affirmative."[255]

September 13, 1862 (Saturday)

Select religious denominations, like the Quakers, claimed a status of "conscientiously opposed to fighting." An editor in Savannah declared opposition "to all exemptions for [these] reasons," noting that, "war is a political state that imposes its burdens on *every* citizen of a country."[256]

September 14, 1862 (Sunday)

Farmers, caretakers of the land and suppliers of foodstuffs for families and regiments. "Mr. A. Barksdale, living near Albany…has sold ten thousand bushels of Corn to the Government, delivered at the railroad at 75 cents per bushel—the Government furnishing the sacks. This is probably a larger price than will be paid hereafter, and has been done to insure its early delivery."[257] At least Barksdale benefited from his hard work.

September 15, 1862 (Monday) ◑

Captain William Barton, 48th New York Infantry, informed his superiors of an incident near Fort Pulaski. "Lieutenant [Christopher] Hale…the bearer of the flag of truce sent from this fort…was stopped at the picket station near Four-Mile Point, the officer in charge of which…sent him through the obstructions in the river, some 2 miles within the enemy's lines, to a second picket, where he was detained for over twenty-four hours, entirely without food and almost without shelter, and even after permission was given him to return to

---

[253] *OR*, ser. I, vol. 14:603.

[254] "The President's Proclamation," *Columbus Daily Sun*, September 11, 1862, sec. 2, https://gahistoricnewspapers.galileo.usg.edu/lccn/sn82014939/1862-09-11/ed-1/seq-2/.

[255] *Journal of the Confederate Congress*, September 12, 1862, 2:279.

[256] "Exemptions from Military Service," *Savannah Weekly Republican*, September 13, 1862, sec. 2, https://gahistoricnewspapers.galileo.usg.edu/lccn/sn85038498/1862-09-13/ed-1/seq-2/. Italics in original.

[257] "New Corn," *Augusta Daily Constitutionalist*, September 14, 1862, sec. 3, Genealogybank.com.

Pulaski the boat was brought to by a shot from Fort Jackson and kept waiting two hours in a heavy rain."[258]

September 16, 1862 (Tuesday)

Flag Officer Tattnall notified Lieutenant Thomas Pelot of a new assignment. "By authority of the Secretary of the Navy, you are hereby appointed to the command of the C.S.S. *Savannah*."[259] Pelot skippered the gunboat, not the ironclad of the same name launched in 1863.

September 17, 1862 (Wednesday)

In Richmond, Secretary of War Randolph issued Special Orders, No 218. "Maj. Gen. J. C. Pemberton, on being relieved in command of the Department of South Carolina and Georgia by General Beauregard, will repair to this city and report for further orders."[260]

September 18, 1862 (Thursday)

Presenting an editorial on "The Present Campaign—Temper of the North," a newspaper editor offered a warning. "We should bear in mind that the North is in earnest in this matter. It matters little to us whether the Yankees are all abolitionists or whether there be in their midst an element of 'States' Rights Democracy'; they are all for the 'Union,' and that means subjugation or extermination. The abolition party is in power; its power is supreme; it controls the civil and military departments of the Government…."[261]

September 19, 1862 (Friday)

The Ordnance Department in Richmond received a request for artillery from Major General Pemberton. The officer noted, "as the complement of heavy guns promised for this department cannot be had from Rome, you have the goodness of providing them from Richmond, over and above the 10-inch columbiads which are to come from there…General Beauregard, who has not yet assumed command, [requested] that the guns you supply from Richmond in lieu of those expected from Rome, Ga., be 10 inch instead of 8-inch columbiads…."[262]

September 20, 1862 (Saturday)

Major General Ormsby Mitchel notified Halleck, "I have assumed command of the Department of the South. The moral and military effect of the capture and occupation of Charleston and Savannah, in my opinion, cannot be overestimated. Every day that passes adds to the strength of the defenses in process of construction by the enemy before these two important cities."[263]

September 21, 1862 (Sunday)

---

[258] *OR*, ser. I, vol. 14:381.

[259] *ORN*, ser. I, vol. 13:807.

[260] *OR*, ser. I, vol. 14:603–604.

[261] "The Present Campaign—Temper of the North," *Columbus Daily Sun*, September 18, 1862, sec. 2, https://gahistoricnewspapers.galileo.usg.edu/lccn/sn82014939/1862-09-18/ed-1/seq-2/.

[262] *OR*, ser. I, vol. 14:604.

[263] Ibid., 383.

General Beauregard spent the day inspecting "the defenses of Savannah." His observations led him to conclude "Savannah thoroughly defended from a naval attack, and when its line of land defenses will be completed, with a proper garrison of about 15,000 men, may be considered impregnable until the enemy shall bring against it an overwhelming force, which it is not probable they will ever attempt, as the result, if favorable, will not compensate them for the expense and trouble."[264]

September 22, 1862 (Monday)

Major General Pemberton wrote to Brigadier General Hugh Mercer in Savannah. "The rapid completion of the gunboat at Savannah is of the greatest importance. You will therefore furnish every assistance in the way of mechanics which the authorized agent of the Navy Department may call for. If necessary ordinary routine must be temporarily dispensed with to facilitate this object."[265]

September 23, 1862 (Tuesday) ●

Secretary Randolph gave Brigadier General Mercer thoughts on Savannah defenses.

> Colonel [Edward] Anderson thinks it important to have a permanent artillery organization for the defense of Savannah. If you concur with him you may convert unattached infantry companies, with their consent, into heavy artillery, or unattached companies may with their own consent and that of their colonels be detached and converted into artillery, and their places in the infantry regiment supplied by new companies or by conscripts, or you may organize the existing heavy artillery companies into a battalion, fill the companies to their maximum, and organize new companies from the excess above the minimum. The minimum of an artillery company is 70 and the maximum 150 privates. Nominate field officers for the battalion when organized. A regimental organization for heavy artillery is not convenient; two battalions will be better.[266]

September 24, 1862 (Wednesday)

Beauregard assumed command of the Department of South Carolina and Georgia and issued several dispatches. To the army: "In entering upon my duties, which may involve at an early day the defense of two of the most important cities in the Confederate States against the most formidable efforts of our powerful enemy, I shall rely upon the ardent patriotism, the intelligence, and unconquerable spirit of the officers and men under my command to sustain me successfully." Beauregard read a final report from Pemberton, which listed "10,000 infantry, 1,200 heavy artillery, 2,000 cavalry, [and] 8 field batteries" at Savannah. To this, the new chieftain stated, "Approved as the minimum force required...."[267]

September 25, 1862 (Thursday)

---

[264] Ibid., 612.
[265] Ibid., 605.
[266] Ibid., 608.
[267] Ibid., 609.

Beauregard sent the War Department a listing of the troops and their locations within his department. For Georgia, Brigadier General Hugh Mercer oversaw 124 various units, including soldiers in Savannah, at Oglethorpe Barracks, at the Savannah River batteries, in Darien, along the Little Ogeechee River, and in Macon.[268]

September 26, 1862 (Friday)

From St. Andrew's Sound, Lieutenant-Commander Robert Scott of the USS *Florida*, reported on the capture of blockade runner the *Agnes*. "The crew consists of a captain, mate, and four men. Two passengers were also found on board, one of whom…had succeeded in running the blockade from Savannah in the *Agnes* with a cargo of cotton on the 5th of July, 1862, and was captured three days later off Hole in the Wall by the *Huntsville*. I have placed a prize crew on board and sent her to Philadelphia for adjudication…."[269]

September 27, 1862 (Saturday)

The Confederate Congress approved the Second Conscription Act, which extended the age of those eligible for service from eighteen to forty-five.[270]

September 28, 1862 (Sunday)

For readers of the *Southern Confederacy*, "X" no longer marked the spot! "For the present we have quit notifying daily subscribers of the expiration of their subscription, by sending the red 'X.' Subscriptions are mostly by the quarter, and the time, being short, will generally be remembered by subscribers. As usual, papers will be discontinued at the end of subscriptions."[271]

September 29, 1862 (Monday)

"Must our soldiers continue to battle for our country's freedom half naked, while thousands of able-bodied young men are permitted to remain at home, it would seem, for the express purpose of oppressing their indigent families. Is ours a speculator's government, or is it a government of the people?"[272] Criticism like this editorial from Columbus would intensify as the war progressed.

September 30, 1862 (Tuesday) ◐

Colonel William Barton's command left Fort Pulaski "at 1 o'clock on the morning…with armed steamers *Planter* and *Starlight*, having on board five companies Forty-eighth New York State Volunteers, under command of Capt. D. W. Strickland, and a detachment of Company G, Third Rhode Island Artillery, in charge of Capt. John H. Gould."[273] On this mission, the Federals targeted saltworks along the May River in South Carolina.

October 1, 1862 (Wednesday)

---

[268] Ibid., 625.

[269] *ORN*, ser. I, vol. 13:346–47.

[270] *Journal of the Confederate Congress*, H.R. 15, September 27, 1862.

[271] "The Red 'X,'" *Atlanta Southern Confederacy*, September 28, 1862, sec. 3, https://gahistoricnewspapers.galileo.usg.edu/lccn/sn82014677/1862-09-28/ed-1/seq-3/.

[272] "Destitution in Our Army," *Columbus Daily Sun*, September 29, 1862, sec. 2, https://gahistoricnewspapers.galileo.usg.edu/lccn/sn82014939/1862-09-29/ed-1/seq-2/.

[273] *OR*, ser. I, vol. 14:125.

Captain Sylvanus Godon filed a report on activity in Ossabaw Sound. "Captain [W. R.] Taylor…had…sent north…William H. Gladding, a pilot…attempting to pass the blockade…too dangerous a man to be allowed to be adrift. I have just heard from Lieutenant-Commander [John] Barnes, now at Ossabaw, that he learns from contrabands at that place that the *Nashville* is ready to go to sea from the Ogeechee River, and is waiting only the arrival of this same Gladding to pilot her out."[274]

October 2, 1862 (Thursday)

Lieutenant-Commander Alexander Semmes of the USS *Wamsutta* reported from St. Simon's. "I send by the *Massachusetts* the mate, three of the crew, and two passengers of the schooner *Agnes*, taken by the *Florida*…whilst running the blockade of St. Andrew's Sound."[275]

October 3, 1862 (Friday)

Beauregard, responding to a need for reinforcements in Florida, wrote Secretary Randolph, "Two regiments ordered to [Brigadier] General [Joseph] Finegan will be sent from Georgia, the War Department assuming the responsibility of detaching them at this time from Georgia, where the troops are already prostrated by disease, as [Brigadier] General [Hugh] Mercer reports."[276]

October 4, 1862 (Saturday)

Philanthropy proved the order of the day for the Roswell Factory. "This company, in view of the necessities of the poor, have made a gratuitous distribution of 1,000 bunches of cotton yarn to ten counties specified, which is equal to $4,000 for the relief of needy families. We commend the example to all other Cotton Factories in the State."[277]

October 5, 1862 (Sunday)

The Etowah Iron Works needed additional crews to keep needed supplies available for the trains traversing the rail. "We ask special attention to the cards of the Etowah Manufacturing and Mining Company. They want to hire one hundred stout negro men, and two hundred men to chop wood, Good wages and steady employment given."[278]

October 6, 1862 (Monday)

Secretary Randolph reconsidered the request of Beauregard to send reinforcements to Florida. "If you think Savannah endangered by detaching two regiments to General Finegan you will retain them. It was not intended to deprive you of discretion in the matter."[279] Beauregard recalled the soldiers.

---

[274] *ORN*, ser. I, vol. 13:354.

[275] Ibid., 347.

[276] *OR*, ser. I, vol. 14:617.

[277] "Roswell Factory," *Columbus Daily Sun*, October 4, 1862, sec. 2, https://gahistoricnewspapers.galileo.usg.edu/lccn/sn82014939/1862-10-04/ed-1/seq-2/.

[278] "Etowah Iron Works—Negroes and Wood Choppers Wanted," *Atlanta Southern Confederacy*, October 5, 1862, sec. 3, https://gahistoricnewspapers.galileo.usg.edu/lccn/sn82014677/1862-10-05/ed-1/seq-3/.

[279] *OR*, ser. I, vol. 14:629.

October 7, 1862 (Tuesday)
The Confederate War Department, via Special Orders, No. 234, announced, "The States of South Carolina, Georgia, and that part of Florida east of the Apalachicola River will constitute the department under the command of General G. T. Beauregard. The Department of East and Middle Florida is hereby constituted a district, and will form a part of the department under General G. T. Beauregard."[280]

October 8, 1862 (Wednesday)
Beauregard assessed his expanded responsibilities and notified General Cooper in Richmond of the region, which required most of Beauregard's attention. "It is proper for me to say that the more urgent importance of the defense of the ports of Charleston and Savannah must necessarily occupy so much of my time that I cannot be absent long enough to visit and make myself acquainted personally with the defensive resources and capabilities of Florida, and hence must rely entirely on the local commander."[281]

October 9, 1862 (Thursday)
In Savannah, Flag Officer Tattnall ordered Lieutenant Thomas Pelot to "[p]roceed with the steamer *Savannah* under your command to the anchorage between Forts Jackson and Cheves, and be ready at all times to man the naval battery [Fort Cheves] with the crew of the *Savannah.*"[282]

October 10, 1862 (Friday)
Lieutenant-Colonel William D. Mitchell received orders from Brigadier General Joseph Finegan to "…move with the Twenty-ninth and Thirtieth Georgia Regiments under his command with all possible dispatch to Savannah and report to Brigadier-General Mercer for duty. The quartermaster will furnish transportation via Monticello."[283]

October 11, 1862 (Saturday)
The Confederate Congress authorized "the exemption of one white man per plantation with twenty or more slaves, the so-called Twenty-Slave Law."[284] Many folks in the South started referring to the war as "a rich man's war, a poor man's fight."

October 12, 1862 (Sunday)
Members of the Oglethorpe Artillery received notice of those "absent from camp are hereby notified that the Company will be in Augusta about the 15th inst., en route for Charleston, S.C., and each absentee, convalescents included, are hereby required to report in person…all furloughs are now revoked, and members not reporting…will be considered DESERTERS…."[285]

---

[280] Ibid., 630.

[281] Ibid., 631.

[282] *ORN*, ser. I, vol. 13:812.

[283] *OR*, ser. I, vol. 14:635.

[284] S. Lee, "Twenty-Slave Law," https://www.encyclopediavirginia.org/twenty-slave_law#start_entry.

[285] "Oglethorpe Artillery, Attention!," *Augusta Daily Constitutionalist*, October 12, 1862, sec. 2, Genealogybank.com. Caps in original.

October 13, 1862 (Monday)
Governor Brown met difficulties while trying to contract with one individual to make spirits within the state. In a case of one bad grain spoiling the entire barrel, Brown issued a directive to the officers of the state militia. "I…direct the seizure of all stills which may be found running in any part of the State, under any pretended Government contract, unless the person so distilling has a contract direct from the proper officer of the Government at Richmond, for the manufacture of a specific quantity, with a certificate of such officer that it is absolutely necessary for the hospitals or other indispensable purposes of the army."[286]
The Confederate Congress suspended "the writ of habeas corpus in any city, town, or military district, whenever in his [President Davis] judgment the public safety may require it."[287]
October 14, 1862 (Tuesday)
Beauregard notified Brigadier General Mercer in Savannah: "There are indications that the Abolition commander at Port Royal may undertake some raid into the Third Military District. I…direct you to hold in readiness about 2,000 infantry of your command for detached service at a moments notice…three days' cooked rations…40 rounds of ammunition…and a reserve supply of 60 rounds of ammunition and two days' subsistence…."[288]
October 15, 1862 (Wednesday) ◑
A newspaper editor in Athens opined on the condition of the Confederacy. "It is said that the war has visited us so long; but it is pleasant to receive the encomiums and the applause which have been elicited by the skill and courage of our generals and soldiers and the wisdom of our rulers. The world is praising us!"[289]
October 16, 1862 (Thursday)
Beauregard issued Special Orders, No. 195, regarding artillery in his department. "Commanders of forts and batteries will examine forthwith their magazines, in order to ascertain whether they have any projectiles not suited to their armament. All such as may be found will be immediately returned to the ordnance depot, stating their number and caliber."[290]
October 17, 1862 (Friday)
Fearful of the defenses of Savannah, and the resulting problems if the Federals captured the city, Governor Brown issued a notice "To the Planters of Middle and Southwestern Georgia." Brown appealed "to each planter in the portion of the State above mentioned, which from its location and its large number of slaves, is most deeply interested, to tender to [Brigadier] General [Hugh] Mercer, immediately, one-tenth of all his working hands. He

---

[286] Candler, *Confederate Records of the State of Georgia*, 2:235.

[287] Confederate Congress, "CHAP. LI.—An Act authorizing the suspension of the writ of habeas corpus" (October 13, 1862), 84.

[288] *OR*, ser. I, vol. 14:639.

[289] "The Praises We Have Won—Our Duty Now," *Athens Southern Banner*, October 15, 1862, sec. 2, https://gahistoricnewspapers.galileo.usg.edu/lccn/sn82014069/1862-10-15/ed-1/seq-2/.

[290] *OR*, ser. I, vol. 28, pt. 2:379.

will accept only the number needed; but as prompt action is necessary, I trust five thousand, in place of five hundred, will be tendered in ten days."[291]

October 18, 1862 (Saturday)

Passage of the Second Conscription Act served as fuel for Governor Brown's flames cast toward President Davis. In a lengthy letter to the president, Brown hammered his disapproval of the act. "If you deny this rightful privilege to those between 35 and 45, and refuse to accept them as volunteers with officers selected by them in accordance with the laws of their State, and attempt to compel them to enter the service as conscripts, my opinion is, your orders will only be obeyed by many of them when backed by an armed force which they have no power to resist."[292]

October 19, 1862 (Sunday)

A newspaper editor in Augusta offered thoughts on President Lincoln's preliminary Emancipation Proclamation: "God demands justice; the President offers to compromise by giving the Lord a note payable in ninety days, provided that his efforts to suppress the rebellion do not succeed in spite of Providence within that time. Endorse the note who please, we have had enough of federal paper currency, and will have nothing to do with it."[293]

October 20, 1862 (Monday)

Beauregard inspected the defenses of Savannah. In his report, he noted the following conditions.

> Fort Jackson, 3 miles below the city…is a very weak work, mounting two 8-inch columbiads, seven 32-pounders, one 18-pounder—ten guns. Its masonry walls are almost entirely exposed to the enemy's fire…Battery Lee, near and just below Fort Jackson, is a water battery of three 10-inch mortars, two 10-inch columbiads, three 8-inch columbiads, one 42-pounder, and one 32 pounder, in all seven guns; a good position, but its rear is entirely open to Carston's Bluff, about 1¼ miles off. If the latter were occupied by an enemy with rifled or heavy guns both of these works could not be held more than one or two hours. The magazines of Battery Lee are worse than useless, being so damp (or wet rather) that powder cannot keep in them. I then visited Lawton's Battery of seven guns (two 10-inch columbiads, two 8-inch columbiads, one 42 pounder, one 32-pounder, and one 32-pounder rifled) across the river and a little above Fort Jackson. It is not entirely completed, but appears to have good traverses between every gun. Its new magazine is not yet constructed; the old one is small and quite damp. I then visited the naval battery, on a small island not far from Lawton's Battery. It has nine guns (seven 32-pounders, two 24 pounders, Blakely). It is unprovided with sufficient traverses, and can be enfiladed from beyond the obstructions. I have ordered one of its guns to be removed and a large traverse constructed in its place. On a small island near the city there is a small three-gun battery

---

[291] Candler, *Confederate Records of the State of Georgia*, 2:236–37.

[292] Ibid., 3:296.

[293] "The Following Is Given," *Augusta Daily Constitutionalist*, October 19, 1862, sec. 3, Genealogybank.com.

(three 32-pounders), Hutchinson Island Battery, enfilading the river, and Screven's Causeway, on the South Carolina side. It occupies an advantageous position, but apparently low and damp.[294]

October 21, 1862 (Tuesday)

Beauregard continued his inspection of the defenses of Savannah. He noted "an unfortunate mistake was made in locating the obstructions and defenses at Savannah River. The two are too far apart...and those defenses are entirely under the control of batteries placed by an enemy on bluffs from Fort Boggs to Carston's Bluff; so that if any one of the line of outworks was to fall into his hands the series of them would necessarily have to be evacuated, and the enemy would then have the way open to establish the batteries...commanding the defenses on the river."[295]

October 22, 1862 (Wednesday)

Residents of Savannah may have received a surprise with the morning news, as they read "many soldiers are in the practice of selling the shoes which they draw from the Quartermaster's Department to citizens. The shoes supplied by the Government are of a superior quality—they are issued to the soldiers at $2.50 a pair, and are readily sold to outsiders at $6 and $8.—Shoes of equal quality cannot be purchased from the stores for less than double these prices."[296]

October 23, 1862 (Thursday) ●

Beauregard notified General Cooper on conditions near Savannah. "I must call the attention of the department to the necessity for more troops from Rantowles Creek to Savannah River, a distance of 75 miles, only about 2,500 men being available for that purpose. Colonel [William S.] Walker deserves promotion for meritorious services, and, moreover, when reenforcements are sent to him he is ranked by the colonel commanding them."[297]

October 24, 1862 (Friday)

Reporting on military action near Coosawhatchie, South Carolina, Colonel Claudius C. Wilson focused on Georgians. "On receiving orders...to return I turned the command over to Lieutenant-Colonel [F. Hay] Gantt, Eleventh South Carolina Infantry, and have now the honor to report that the entire Georgia forces returned...without casualty, and are now in their several camps."[298] Governor Brown always fretted whenever state soldiers left their native soil, so this information surely pleased the executive.

October 25, 1862 (Saturday)

Rear Admiral Du Pont filed a report to Secretary Welles, one, containing intelligence gained from a Confederate deserter, which indicated "the *Nashville* is laid up, having been entirely unloaded of her cotton, and is moored at the railroad bridge, 15 miles from

---

[294] *OR*, ser. I, vol. 14:645–46.

[295] Ibid., 14:646–47.

[296] "Soldiers Selling Their Shoes," *Savannah Daily Morning News*, October 22, 1862, sec. 2, https://gahistoricnewspapers.galileo.usg.edu/lccn/sn82015886/1862-10-22/ed-1/seq-2/.

[297] *OR*, ser. I, vol. 14:652.

[298] Ibid., 188.

Savannah. Large quantities of cotton are collecting in Savannah, all baled for storage. Four thousand contrabands are at work round Savannah; all would leave and come to the coast if they a dared."[299]

October 26, 1862 (Sunday)

Reporting on "Salt in Virginia," one Augusta newspaper informed readers of activity in Saltville, Virginia. "The Governor of Virginia [John Letcher] and Committee...have released all salt purchased by individuals...furnaces belonging to the Georgia Salt Manufacturing Company are turning out two hundred bushels per day. They have a large pile on hand, which will be forwarded to Georgia as soon as transportation is renewed."[300] Getting the mineral out of Virginia grew increasingly difficult with the worsening condition of the railroads.

October 27, 1862 (Monday)

Major General Ormsby Mitchel—who approved the Andrews Raid in April 1862—contracted yellow fever, and his command passed to another officer. "In consequence of the temporary illness of the major-general commanding Brig. Gen. J. M. Brannan will assume command of the Department of the South. By command of Maj. Gen. O. M. Mitchel."[301] Mitchel died three days later.

October 28, 1862 (Tuesday)

Governor Brown seasoned his offer to secure an important mineral. "There is the greatest necessity for salt in this State. If we can not increase the supply, it will be impossible to save half the meat of the State. I will agree to take all that Messrs. Graves & Goldsmith can deliver in Atlanta, at $7.50 per bushel of fifty pounds till the 1st of March, to be distributed amongst the people of the State at cost."[302]

October 29, 1862 (Wednesday) ◐

Commander Charles Steedman ordered Lieutenant William Budd, "So soon as the tide serves" to "proceed with the *Potomska* under your command to Sapelo Sound. Take the *Braziliera* in tow and tow her to St. Catherine's, anchoring her in the most suitable place for a sailing vessel to blockade. Having accomplished this, you will blockade Sapelo Sound."[303]

October 30, 1862 (Thursday)

An article in a Savannah newspaper promoted recruits for a "Siege Artillery Battalion." Offering a public relations charm, young men learned "[v]olunteers entering these corps will escape the disabilities of conscription, and besides the bounty of fifty dollars, will receive one dollar per month more than is paid to infantry. As heavy artillery, employed in maintaining our line of defence, they will not be ordered to distant points while our own

---

[299] *ORN*, ser. 1, vol. 13:417.

[300] "Salt in Virginia—The Georgia Salt Manufacturing Company," *Augusta Daily Constitutionalist*, October 26, 1862, sec. 3, Genealogybank.com.

[301] *OR*, ser. I, vol. 14:387.

[302] *OR*, ser. I, vol. 2:237–38.

[303] *ORN*, ser. I, vol. 13:421.

seaboard is threatened."[304]

October 31, 1862 (Friday) (All Hallow'e'en)

Beauregard updated Confederate Navy Secretary Mallory on conditions in the Department of South Carolina and Georgia.

> On my return yesterday from Savannah I found here your letter of the 20th instant. I thank you for the prompt and favorable support you have given me in the desire to construct one of Capt. [Francis] F. D. Lee's marine torpedo rams, which I think is destined ere long to change the system of naval warfare, for it is evident that if ships are constructed invulnerable above water they must be attacked under it, where most vulnerable. I confidently believe that with three of these light-draught torpedo rams and as many iron-clad gunboat-rams this harbor [Charleston] could be held against any naval force of the enemy, who could never bring here seaworthy iron-clad gunboats or steamers of light draught that could withstand the destructive effects of our harbor rams. The same means can also be used (with one less of each class) for Savannah and Mobile.[305]

November 1, 1862 (Saturday)

Governor Brown issued a call to Georgia planters to provide labor for Brigadier General Mercer in Savannah. "After you have been repeatedly notified of the absolute necessity for more labor to complete the fortifications adjudged by the military authorities in command to be indispensable to the defence of the key to the State, will you delay action till you are compelled to contribute means for the protection, not only of all your slaves, but of your homes, your firesides and your altars?"[306]

November 2, 1862 (Sunday)

Lieutenant-Commander John Davis of the USS *Wissahickon* reported on an engagement.

> At 12 [p.m.] discovered a boat up the river pulling downstream. Sent an armed boat to meet her, the strange boat having five men in her. When she turned and pulled rapidly upstream, fired the 20-pounder rifle to bring her to. The boat continued on; got underway and steamed up the river; fired another shot but failed to bring her to. She succeeded in getting under guns of Genesis battery; recalled the boat when about 2 miles off the battery. Let go the port anchor to bring the ship to, when we fired another shot which exploded directly over the battery. They fired five shots in return, but they fell short of us.[307]

November 3, 1862 (Monday)

Reporting on the opening stage of a mission down the coast to destroy salt supplies, Lieutenant Colonel Oliver Beard, 48th New York Infantry, moved "with the steamer

---

[304] "Siege Artillery Battalion," *Savannah Daily Morning News*, October 30, 1862, https://gahistoricnewspapers.galileo.usg.edu/lccn/sn82015886/1862-10-30/ed-1/seq-2/.

[305] *OR*, ser. I, vol. 14:661.

[306] Candler, *Confederate Records of the State of Georgia*, 2:239.

[307] *ORN*, ser. I, vol. 13:427.

Darlington, having on board Captain Trowbridge's company of colored troops (62)...proceeded up Bell River, Florida, drove in the rebel pickets...and destroyed their place of rendezvous...proceeded and destroyed the salt-works, and all the salt, corn, and wagons which we could not carry away, besides killing the horses; thence proceeded to Saint Mary's, and brought off two families of contrabands, after driving in the enemy's pickets."[308]

November 4, 1862 (Tuesday)

The Federal expedition to destroy various saltworks continued. Lieutenant Colonel Beard again reported on the work of the day. "I proceeded to King's Bay, Georgia, and destroyed a large salt-work on a creek about a mile from the landing, together with all the property on the place. Here we were attacked by about 80 of the enemy, of whom we killed 2."[309]

November 5, 1862 (Wednesday)

Secretary Randolph ensured the mayor of Columbus, James Bozeman, the Confederate authorities understood the significance of the city. Randolph confirmed, "the department is fully aware of the importance of defending the Chattahoochee River and the city of Columbus, and has taken the necessary steps to provide for their defense. The country...has been thrown into a military district, which General Howell Cobb will command. The experience, energy, and stake in the country of that officer afford the best guarantees that he will neglect nothing for its defense."[310]

November 6, 1862 (Thursday) ◐

The meeting of the General Assembly began in Milledgeville, and as customary, the delegates received the governor's written address. Brown expressed his concern for folks on the home front. "So large a number of our arms bearing men have already gone into the military service of the Confederacy, and so many more may soon be required, that we have comparatively a small number left in each county, and in some localities where the slave population is very large, scarcely enough to direct their labor remain with them. Our women and children are, therefore, left at home almost entirely without protection."[311]

November 7, 1862 (Friday)

Lieutenant William Budd and his USS *Potomska* had a busy day on the coast.

> 9:55 a.m. stopped at a plantation on Sapelo River...10:40 anchored off King's plantation...12 to 4 p.m.: the captain with ten men, armed, went on board the Darlington and went up the river to a plantation. In passing a bluff they were fired upon by the rebel soldiers; returned the fire...2:20 steamer returned; got underway and proceeded down the river, shelling the woods as we went...2:05 got aground. Fired 36 shells from broadside guns and 4 stands grape; fired 27 shells from Parrott...4 to 6 p.m:...4:50 floated steamer down the river...5 opened fire on the enemy's pickets at

[308] *OR*, ser. I, vol. 14:191.

[309] Ibid.

[310] Ibid., 666.

[311] *OR*, ser. I, vol. 2:273–74.

Setaliman's Bluff; the enemy in large numbers concealed in rifle pits. At 5:30 discovered the buildings on fire from our shell.[312]

November 8, 1862 (Saturday)

Governor updated the General Assembly on the contract to obtain salt from Saltville, Virginia. He noted a recent "the well known character of Governor [John] Letcher for liberality, justice and patriotism, I think fully justify the conclusion that he will not interfere with either the works put up by this State or by her citizens with her sanction, for the supply of consumers without speculation."[313]

November 9, 1862 (Sunday)

Lieutenant-Commander A. K. Hughes of the USS *Mohawk* "proceeded with this vessel on an expedition to the town of St. Mary's...anchoring close by, and fired several shells into it...I concluded to return...but...several musket shots were fired at us from different portions of the town. I...came to anchor...under a fire from musketry, when I opened our battery upon the place...firing shell and canister, which drove the rebels completely out of the town and set fire to several buildings."[314]

November 10, 1862 (Monday)

Beauregard issued a circular to all officers in his Department of South Carolina and Georgia. "To prevent unnecessary alarm and suppress sensational reports the commanding general enjoins upon all commanding officers to take and report the names of all persons who may communicate important intelligence of the movements of the enemy. In certain cases, at the discretion of the officer to whom communication is made, the person who shall communicate such information will be secured until further orders from these headquarters."[315]

November 11, 1862 (Tuesday)

The Georgia Supreme Court ruled to support conscription.[316]

November 12, 1862 (Wednesday)

Attempting to avoid a logjam, Brigadier General Rufus Saxton wrote to Rear Admiral Du Pont: "I am going to send the steamers *Darlington* and *Ben De Ford* to a place near Darien, Ga., to procure lumber. If the gunboats now on that station could be permitted to accompany those vessels, as a safeguard against an attack while the lumber is being loaded, I should esteem it as a very great favor."[317]

November 13, 1862 (Thursday)

Governor Brown provided Colonel Ira Foster with several new hats, as he announced the officer "is hereby authorized and directed to take charge of the Pay Department of this State, not only as relates to the duties heretofore imposed upon him, but to include the

---

[312] *ORN*, ser. I, vol. 13:438.

[313] Candler, *Confederate Records of the State of Georgia*, 2:309.

[314] *ORN*, ser. I, vol. 13:442.

[315] *OR*, ser. I, vol. 14:675.

[316] T. Bryan, *Confederate Georgia*, 87.

[317] *ORN*, ser. I, vol. 13:444.

Commissary General, Chief of Ordnance with theirs and his commissioned assistants."[318]

November 14, 1862 (Friday) ◐

Attempting to ensure Georgians had enough food crops for the upcoming year, a representative introduced a resolution in the General Assembly, requesting "the planters of Georgia…not to plant cotton the ensuing year only sufficient for home consumption as the production of a surplus of that valuable staple of the South would be highly impolitic (not to say unpatriotic) and invite aggression from the enemy and tend to protract this unnatural and iniquitous war against the rights of the Southern people, and the most sacred dictates of humanity."[319]

November 15, 1862 (Saturday)

A commissary officer alerted Confederate officials of a problem in his district. "The people of Albany are very anxious that it [corn] should be seized. Some course must be pursued or the Army will suffer for bread. You have no idea the number of corn-buyers in Southwestern Georgia, mostly on speculation. This must be stopped in some way or our Army will suffer. I expect we shall be forced to haul our corn or go without."[320]

November 16, 1862 (Sunday)

Readers of the *Southern Confederacy* learned of a thankful regiment. "Capt. L. P. Thomas…represents the greatful [*sic*] soldiers of the 42d Ga. Regiment, in returning their thanks to the kind ladies of Wilkes county…clothing and shoes lately furnished to soldiers in this regiment afford as much relief and comfort as such necessaries ever could bring to soldiers under any circumstances…they are more resolved on meriting the very favorable considerations of the patriotic ladies of Wilkes and the State of Georgia."[321]

November 17, 1862 (Monday)

Beauregard received a letter from Governor Brown. "I have the honor this morning to acknowledge the receipt of your note…relative to a proposed conference between the Governors of the Southern States and those of the Northwestern States. As the General Assembly is now in session, I have that subject under consideration."[322]

November 18, 1862 (Tuesday)

Colonel Jeremy Gilmer of the Confederate Engineer Bureau corresponded with Captain Theodore Moreno in Columbus. "The necessary implements, carriages, &c., to put the ordnance now on the [Chattahoochee] river in a complete state of efficiency can…be obtained from the arsenal at Macon…and it would be well for you to suggest to the senior captain of the two artillery companies mentioned in your letter to make the necessary requisition on the officer in charge of the arsenal, subject to the approval of the general commanding the department."[323] Skirmish reported along the Doboy River.

---

[318] Candler, *Confederate Records of the State of Georgia*, 2:317.

[319] *Journal of the Senate of the State of Georgia…1862*, November 14, 1862, 94.

[320] *OR*, ser. I, vol. 14:683.

[321] "Thanks," *Atlanta Southern Confederacy*, November 16, 1862, https://gahistoricnewspapers.galileo.usg.edu/lccn/sn82014677/1862-11-16/ed-1/seq-3/.

[322] Candler, *Confederate Records of the State of Georgia*, 3:302–303.

[323] *OR*, ser. I, vol. 14:682; skirmish in Mosocco, *Chronological Tracking*, 104.

November 19, 1862 (Wednesday)

Lieutenant-Commander John Davis of the USS *Wissahickon* supplied superiors with his engagement on the day.

> This morning I moved up the river with this vessel, the *Dawn*, and mortar schooner No. 5, and opened fire on the battery at Genesis Point at 8:15. Advancing from the first position about a quarter of a mile with this vessel and the *Dawn*, continued firing, when the enemy disappeared as though they had deserted the battery; all this time they fired no guns. I again advanced about a quarter of a mile, with the *Dawn* in company to the bend of the river in the direction of the battery and about 1¾ miles from it, when the enemy opened fire, at 9:45, and I regret to say the first shot struck this vessel abreast the XI-inch gun and about 4 feet below the water line, causing a serious leak; failing to gain on it with the pumps, and apprehensive of the necessity of putting the vessel ashore, I reluctantly dropped down, beyond their range, and succeeded in partially stopping the leak so that the pumps would keep her free. At 2:30 p.m. we ceased firing and returned to our usual anchorages. No casualties occurred during the day on our side. The practice of the vessels was to all appearances entirely satisfactory.[324]

November 20, 1862 (Thursday)

Rear Admiral Du Pont clarified military versus civilian targets for Lieutenant Commander Hughes of the USS *Mohawk*. "I am in receipt of your communication...giving some details of an expedition to St. Mary's, though I could not quite make out from your dispatch the object of it. In reference to the destruction of the sawmill, as mentioned by you, it is my desire to avoid destroying private property unless used for pickets or guard stations and other military purposes. Of course if fired upon from any place, it is your duty, if possible, to destroy it."[325]

November 21,1862 (Friday) ●

In Athens, Brigadier General Howell Cobb received a notice from Beauregard regarding the need of soldiers in more locations than either officer can fill. So, as Beauregard suggested, "The means at our command for the defense of my Department (South Carolina and Georgia and Florida to the Chattahoochee) are very limited, so much so that I am unable to spare one man from South Carolina and Georgia for Florida at present, but I hope after the fall campaign in Virginia troops will be sent for the defense of my department. Meanwhile we must do the best we can by calling on the State authorities for all the assistance they can furnish us."[326]

November 22, 1862 (Saturday)

Officials in Florida, political and military, had concerns over reported action in Georgia. Brigadier Joseph Finegan notified officials in Georgia: "The mayor of Columbus, under

---

[324] *ORN*, ser. I, vol. 13:454.

[325] Ibid., 443.

[326] *OR*, ser. I, vol. 14:684.

direction of the city council, is arranging to obstruct the Apalachicola River below our batteries at Alum Bluff, and desires protection and permission to proceed with the work. Governor [John] Milton, of this State, protests against the obstructions being placed in the river, unless done under direction of the proper military authorities of the Confederate States."[327]

November 23, 1862 (Sunday)

Ensign George Wood received orders from Commander Charles Steedman. "You will proceed with the U.S. schooner *Norfolk Packet* under your command to Doboy Sound, when, on your arrival, you will relieve Acting Master [Frank] Meriam, of the *Madgie*, in blockading the entrance of that sound."[328]

November 24, 1862 (Monday)

Governor Brown wrote to President Davis requesting him to "direct the Chief of Ordnance to give me an order upon Colonel [Washington] Rains, of Augusta, for the powder. We anticipate trouble with our slaves during the approaching holidays and fear we shall need the powder. Most of the powder mentioned in the resolution was furnished by the State to supply Fort Pulaski before it fell into the hands of the enemy and to supply our batteries along the coast and around Savannah."[329]

November 25, 1862 (Tuesday)

In the General Assembly, the Senate approved and passed to the House, an amendment that would allow the governor to "advertise and call for volunteers above the age of forty years and below eighteen, stating where said companies will be located or expected to perform duty."[330] Across the Confederacy, as more and more youngsters and the aged answered, many suggested President Davis—and other officials—took men "from cradle to grave."

November 26, 1862 (Wednesday)

Governor Brown, along with the other officials of each Confederate state, received a letter from President Davis.

> The repeated defeats inflicted on the Federal forces in their attempt to conquer our country have not yet sufficed to satisfy them of the impossibility of success in their nefarious design to subjugate these States. A renewal of the attempt on a still larger scale is now in progress; but with manifest distrust of success in a warfare conducted according to the usages of civilized nations, the United States propose to add to the enormous land and naval forces accumulated by them, bands of such African slaves of the South as they may be able to wrest from their owners, and thus to inflict on the non-combatant population of the Confederate States all the horrors of a servile

---

[327] Ibid., 686.

[328] *ORN*, ser. I, vol. 13:459.

[329] Candler, *Confederate Records of the State of Georgia*, 3:303.

[330] *Journal of the Senate of the State of Georgia…1862*, November 25, 1862, 154.

> war, superadded to such atrocities as have already been committed on numerous occasions by their invading forces.[331]

November 27, 1862 (Thursday)

General Cooper attempted to quell the concerns of Florida's governor regarding navigation on the Chattahoochee River. "The command of General [Howell] Cobb has been enlarged to include that part of Georgia which embraces the navigable waters of Chattahoochee and Flint Rivers, and has been instructed to use his best efforts to obtain forces from that State."[332]

November 28, 1862 (Friday)

The General Assembly dealt with "An act to incorporate the Empire State Iron and Coal Mining Company." The body heard from Governor Brown, who opposed the issue. Brown stated,

> Patriotism alone seldom prompts the investment of capital; nor, indeed, is there more patriotism in the manufacture of iron than there is in making corn or wheat. These are as necessary as iron; and iron can no more be made without them, than they can without iron. We compel the planter who attempts to make money by raising grain and fails, to pay his debts. Why then should he who invests his surplus in an iron foundry and fails, be exempt from the payment of his debts?[333]

November 29, 1862 (Saturday)

Governor Brown notified Beauregard of a new piece of legislation in Georgia.

> The General Assembly of this State has just passed an act authorizing me to place obstructions in the navigable streams of this State against incursions of the enemy and to hire or impress slaves to perform the necessary labor. As I desire to preserve and cultivate the most cordial relations between yourself as the commander of the military department in which Georgia is embraced and myself in carrying out the provisions of said act, I propose to furnish the laborers by hiring or impressing them as contemplated in the act, and putting them under officers and engineers detailed by you for that duty, and to give the whole planning, supervision, control, and execution of the work to such officers and engineers as you may order on such duty.[334]

November 30, 1862 (Sunday)

Beauregard inquired of Brigadier General Mercer in Savannah, "Please inform me the condition of enemy's fleet at Fort Pulaski. If all be quiet, discharge cars [trains] collected."[335]

December 1, 1862 (Monday)

In a letter to Linton Stephens (brother of the Confederate vice president), Robert Toombs aired his thought on military and political issues confronting Georgia and the South. "It

---

[331] Candler, *Confederate Records of the State of Georgia*, 3:305.

[332] *OR*, ser. I, vol. 14:689.

[333] *Journal of the Senate of the State of Georgia...1862*, November 28, 1862, 175.

[334] Candler, *Confederate Records of the State of Georgia*, 3:307.

[335] *OR*, ser. I, vol. 14:693.

was and is now my opinion that I could best serve the public cause in the army and I intend to stay there as long as I can with honor, and life lasts; but I am well aware that that scoundrel Jeff Davis will avail himself of any opportunity [to] drive me from it, with dishonor if he could—but that part of it is in my own hands, I thank God, not in his."[336]

December 2, 1862 (Tuesday)

Beauregard updated Governor Brown about the need to obstruct certain Georgia rivers as a defensive measure. "After full inquiry and mature consideration I decided a few days ago to obstruct the Altamaha River at a favorable military position, Lake Bluff, about 1½ miles below the Albany and Savannah Railroad. Any of the streams Your Excellency should consider ought to be obstructed would be reconnoitered as soon as an engineer officer could be selected for that object."[337]

December 3, 1862 (Wednesday)

William Wadley, a New Hampshire native who moved to Georgia as a young man, remained in his new adopted home at the outbreak of war, and took on added responsibilities on this day. General Cooper, via General Orders, No. 98, announced, "Col. William M. Wadley, assistant adjutant-general, is hereby specially assigned to take supervision and control of the transportation for the Government on all the railroads in the Confederate States." Among Wadley's responsibilities, empowerment "to make contracts for transportation with said railroads, or any of them, and such negotiations and arrangements with them as may be requisite or proper to secure efficiency, harmony, and co-operation on the part of said railroads, or any proper number of them, in carrying on the transportation of the Government."[338]

December 4, 1862 (Thursday)

Brigadier General Mercer sent an "Ahoy!" to General Cooper in Richmond. "The Navy here [Savannah] is in urgent need of seamen. I have a number of volunteers from the Army ready and anxious to enter that service. Can I not transfer them at once without further formality?"[339]

December 5, 1862 (Friday)

The General Assembly considered, but took no immediate action on, a resolution

> for the support of indigent widows and orphans of soldiers who have died or been killed in the service of this State or of the Confederate States; for the support of the indigent families of soldiers who may be in the public service, and for the support of indigent soldiers who may be disabled by wounds or disease in the service of this State or the Confederate States, for and during the year 1863; to provide for raising funds

---

[336] Toombs, Stephens, and Cobb, *Correspondence*, 608.

[337] Candler, *Confederate Records of the State of Georgia*, 3:311.

[338] *OR*, ser. IV, vol. 2:225.

[339] *OR*, ser. I, vol. 14:698.

to carry into effect said appropriation, and to provide for the application of the same to the purposes aforesaid.[340]

December 6, 1862 (Saturday)

The Senate passed a resolution to the house. "Therefore be it Resolved by the General Assembly of the State, That the President of the Central Rail Road, and the authorities controlling the Savannah, Albany and Gulf Rail Road, be and they are hereby earnestly solicited and requested to forward, and with the least practicable delay, all salt in their respective depots to its final destination."[341]

December 7, 1862 (Sunday)

Atlantans learned of recent impressment activity in the city. "The Government Agent here seized the woollen goods, Osnaburg, Shoes, Thread, Hats and such articles as come under their bill of instructions. So far as we have heard, some of the agents who were employed to perform this duty, have performed it in a gentlemanly way, and softened its *hard* places by courtesy and a willingness to give us as little trouble as possible."[342]

December 8, 1862 (Monday)

Governor Brown worked diligently to arm Georgia soldiers. In addition to rifles and other armaments, Brown also had a fondness for a unique weapon. On this day, he received a report from his chief of ordnance, which indicated that through mid-September 1862 the state had paid for 7,099 "Joe Brown Pikes"![343]

December 9, 1862 (Tuesday)

To halt reported misconduct of soldiers in Georgia, the General Assembly resolved

> That the Commanding General of the Confederate army be respectfully requested, without delay, to arrest and put a stop to such ruinous and cruel policy, whether the same is or not authorized by the military authorities of that district, and that, if it be absolutely necessary to make such impressments, it be done only in such cases where a surplus may be found, and that the people of the country be not driven to starvation and ruin by such cruel procedure.[344]

December 10, 1862 (Wednesday)

The Senate took up a report from the Committee on the Georgia Military Institute.

> They [the committee] find from the facts referred to them that the wooden dormitories for the Cadets are wholly insufficient for the accommodation of the corps, and are also in a dilapidated condition; that the increasing patronage of the Institute demands largely increased accommodations. They further find that there are no buildings upon the Institute grounds for the residence of the Superintendent and the Commandant of the Cadets, both of whom should reside upon the campus for the

---

[340] *Journal of the Senate of the State of Georgia…1862*, December 5, 1862, 217.

[341] Ibid., December 6, 1862, 231.

[342] "Our Markets, & c.," *Atlanta Southern Confederacy*, December 7, 1862, https://gahistoricnewspapers.galileo.usg.edu/lccn/sn82014677/1862-12-07/ed-1/seq-3/. Italics in original.

[343] Candler, *Confederate Records of the State of Georgia*, 2:353.

[344] *Journal of the Senate of the State of Georgia…1862*, December 9, 1862, 249.

effectual enforcement of the discipline. They further find that a lot of land comprising eight acres, lying immediately south of the campus and running up to the buildings of the Institute, is important to the Institute, first, as a garden for the production of vegetables for the use of the corps; secondly, for the erection of kitchens and other necessary out-houses; and lastly, for the removal therefrom of individuals whose proximate positions to the corps has given trouble in their management. They recommend that to erect suitable brick barracks for the accommodation of two hundred and fifty cadets—for the erection of suitable dwellings for the Superintendent and Commandant, and for the purchase of said eight acres of land, the sum of fifty thousand dollars be appropriated, to be used by the Board of Inspectors for such purposes only, on such terms as his Excellency the Governor may direct.[345]

December 11, 1862 (Thursday)

Governor Brown informed his quartermaster-general of the governor's refusal to approve resolutions passed in the General Assembly regarding the seizure of factories and tanners "for the purpose of clothing our self-sacrificing troops in the Confederate service from this state." The resolution allowed the seizures to continue until December 20; Brown did not believe this afforded enough time. He instructed the quartermaster department to "proceed to execute the orders…with such variations only as may be necessary to conform prices to the orders…."[346]

December 12, 1862 (Friday)

Governor Brown wrote to the General Assembly regarding the ability of units to elect their own officers. "The right of the State to appoint the officers to command her militia now employed in the service of the Confederate States, is therefore admitted by the President and Secretary of State, and has been decided by the General Assembly, and is too clear for doubt or cavil. Yet this right is denied by the Conscription Act, and our troops are deprived of its benefits. In the whirl of revolution, whither are we drifting?"[347]

December 13, 1862 (Saturday)

Brigadier General Hugh Mercer, headquarters in Savannah, received the following telegraph from Beauregard: "Hold about 2,500 infantry, including Screven's battalion, in readiness for transportation to this place [Charleston], with four days' cooked provisions, with 40 rounds of ammunition in cartridge box and 60 in reserve, in light marching order, with cooking utensils, and two tents per company and two for the field and staff of each regiment or battalion."[348]

December 14, 1862 (Sunday) ◑

Confederate soldiers started leaving Savannah, as Beauregard order Brigadier General Mercer to "Put the troops ordered (about 2,500) from your district in motion for this place [Charleston] at once. Report when started."[349]

---

[345] Ibid., December 10, 1862, 263.

[346] Candler, *Confederate Records of the State of Georgia*, 2:332–34.

[347] Ibid., 2:342–44.

[348] *OR*, ser. I, vol. 14:711.

[349] Ibid., 713.

December 15, 1862 (Monday)

Deliver the mail or the minié? A Savannah newspaper article posed the question. "All Postmasters whose commissions exceeded one thousand dollars for the year ending 30th June, 1862, are appointed by the President, and are not subject to military duty under the Conscript Act; but those whose commission did not amount to that sum, are appointed by the Postmaster General, and are subject to military duty if they are not exempt by age."[350]

December 16, 1862 (Tuesday)

Rear Admiral Du Pont notified Secretary Welles as to the location of various vessels of the South Atlantic Blockading Squadron along Georgia's coast. "Wassaw Sound, U.S.S. *Conemaugh*. Ossabaw Sound, U.S. steamers *Wissahickon* and *Dawn* and schooner *C.P. Williams*. Guarding St. Catherine's, Sapelo, Doboy, and St. Simon's sounds, U.S. steamers *Paul Jones*, *Potomska*, *Madgie*, bark *Braziliera*, and schooner *Norfolk Packet*."[351]

December 17, 1862 (Wednesday)

Colonel Thomas R. Cobb fell mortally wounded during the December 13 Battle of Fredericksburg. A citizen of Augusta wrote of the loss to the colonel's brother—Howell Cobb. "In performing the sad office of having sent to you today a dispatch…informing you of the death of your noble and gallant brother, I cannot refrain from expressing to you my heartfelt sympathy in this terrible bereavement. His death has cast a gloom over this city. How valued should be the liberties purchased with such precious blood. May God console you and protect you."[352]

December 18, 1862 (Thursday)

Troopers in the 3rd Georgia Cavalry, near Columbus, learned of a call to report "on Monday 22d inst. By 12 o'clock M., ready to march without fail. All who are absent without proper vouchers will be advertised as deserters."[353]

December 19, 1862 (Friday)

General Beauregard issued General Orders, No. 127, which announced the appointment of a general staff. Among those listed, as "chiefs of subsistence in the States in which they are respectively stationed…Maj. [Joseph] J. L. Locke, State of Georgia…."[354]

December 20, 1862 (Saturday) ●

A bleak holiday awaited many folks in Georgia. "Owing to the difficulty of running the blockade, that friend of juvenility, Santa Claus, finds it hard to obtain his usual varieties of 'goodies' and 'pretties,' for his little friends for the coming Christmas."[355]

---

350 "All Postmasters," *Savannah Daily Morning News*, December 15, 1862, sec. 1, https://gahistoricnewspapers.galileo.usg.edu/lccn/sn82015886/1862-12-15/ed-1/seq-1/.

351 *ORN*, ser. I, vol. 13:480.

352 Toombs, Stephens, and Cobb, *Correspondence*, 609.

353 "Attention, 3d Georgia Cavalry!," *Columbus Daily Sun*, December 18, 1862, https://gahistoricnewspapers.galileo.usg.edu/lccn/sn82014939/1862-12-18/ed-1/seq-2/.

354 *OR*, ser. I, vol. 14:727.

355 "Santa Claus," *Rome Tri-Weekly Courier*, December 20, 1862, sec. 2, https://gahistoricnewspapers.galileo.usg.edu/lccn/sn85034102/1862-12-20/ed-1/seq-2/.

December 21, 1862 (Sunday)
The editor of the *Daily Constitutionalist* in Augusta ran an advertisement promoting his newspaper. "The *Constitutionalist* is one of the best papers published in the South. The *Constitutionalist* is Thoroughly Southern, and adheres, under our new Government, to its old principles of State Rights and Strict Construction. It advocates the Admission, into the Confederacy only, of those States which recognize Property in Slaves as a part of their Social System."[356]

December 22, 1862 (Monday)
"Messrs. Spiller & Burr are manufacturing a fine article of Colt's Revolvers in Atlanta, Georgia…the pistols are well finished, mounted in white metal, and had every appearance of being as good as the original Colt's. This begins to look like independence."[357] Spiller and Burr, after relocating to Macon, produced firearms for the Confederacy until late 1864.

December 23, 1862 (Tuesday)
A newspaper article attempted to lift spirits of folks in Milledgeville and elsewhere. "If our forces are sometimes overpowered, the disaster should not cause us to despond. Think of the defeats the enemy has sustained since the beginning of last summer. We cannot always be successful, and perhaps, it is best for us to get an occasional drubbing. Continued success causes over confidence, and over confidence begets neglect."[358]

December 24, 1862 (Wednesday)
Christmas did not serve as a joyous occasion for all Georgians. "It is ordered that during the Christmas holidays and until the 5th day of January, 1863, all negroes living out of the corporate limits of the city, who are found in said limits shall be taken up and confined in the Guard House, provided, such negroes are not specially sent to the city, by order of and on business for their employer."[359]

December 25, 1862 (Thursday) (Christmas Day)
Lieutenant-Commander William Gibson learned he would spend Christmas working. Du Pont ordered him to "proceed with the *Seneca* under your command to Ossabaw and relieve Lieutenant-Commander J. L. Davis, of the *Wissahickon*, in the charge of the blockade of those waters."[360]

December 26, 1862 (Friday)
After a brief pause for Christmas, newspaper editors busied themselves in scolding civilians

---

356 "The Constitutionalist," *Augusta Daily Constitutionalist*, December 21, 1862, sec. 4, Genealogybank.com.

357 "Pistol Manufactory in Atlanta," *Columbus Daily Sun*, December 22, 1862, sec. 2, https://gahistoricnewspapers.galileo.usg.edu/lccn/sn82014939/1862-12-22/ed-1/seq-2/.

358 "No Cause to Despond," *Milledgeville Confederate Union*, December 23, 1862, https://gahistoricnewspapers.galileo.usg.edu/lccn/sn85034083/1862-12-23/ed-1/seq-3/.

359 "Notice to Planters and Citizens Living out of the Corporate Limits of the City," *Columbus Daily Sun*, December 24, 1862, https://gahistoricnewspapers.galileo.usg.edu/lccn/sn82014939/1862-12-24/ed-1/seq-2/.

360 *ORN*, ser. I, vol. 13:488.

for various shortcomings. "Unless our people soon get to making iron in larger quantities, we shall have an iron famine equal to the salt famine. There is no difficulty in procuring a bountiful supply, if those who have means will go into the business. No country on earth is richer in ores of the finest quantities than ours, and especially in Georgia."[361]

December 27, 1862 (Saturday)

Folks in Augusta learned of pleasant and profitable holiday: "Christmas Day was very generally observed by our citizens as a holiday. Notwithstanding the existence of war, everybody seemed to enjoy it considerably, and a universal good feeling seemed to prevail. This feeling was augmented by the gratifying news which had been received for the days previous [Battle of Fredericksburg]. The confectionary and toy stores were crowded almost constantly, and a great deal of money must have changed hands."[362]

December 28, 1862 (Sunday) ◐

In General Orders, No. 132, Beauregard announced the subdivisions of his department. "The District of Georgia, Brig. Gen. [Hugh] H. W. Mercer commanding, embraces the State of Georgia, excluding the defenses of the Apalachicola River and its main affluents."[363] Brigadier General Howell Cobb held responsibility for the Apalachicola.

December 29, 1862 (Monday)

"We feel satisfied that our readers will share with us the regret we feel in announcing that this will be the last night that the Queen Sisters, who have ministered so acceptably to the tastes of our theatre-going people, will appear in our city, at least for the present." A popular form of entertainment—a break from the weariness of war news—came to an end in Savannah.[364]

December 30, 1862 (Tuesday)

An "Abstract of Field Return" indicated Brigadier General Mercer had a strength of "8,890 Aggregate present."[365]

December 31, 1862 (Wednesday)

Brigadier General John Brannan reported the specific units composing the garrison of Fort Pulaski: "48th New York, Col. [William] W. B. Barton. 3d Rhode Island Artillery, Company G, Capt. [John] J. H. Gould. 1st New York Engineers, Company F, Capt. [Samuel] S. C. Eaton."[366]

---

361 "Unless Our People," *Rome Weekly Courier*, December 26, 1862, sec. 1, https://gahistoricnewspapers.galileo.usg.edu/lccn/sn82014071/1862-12-26/ed-1/seq-1/.

362 "Christmas Day," *Augusta Daily Constitutionalist*, December 27, 1862, sec. 1, Genealogybank.com.

363 *OR*, ser. I, vol. 14:736.

364 "Theater," *Savannah Republican*, December 29, 1862, sec. 2, **[link?]**

365 Ibid., 740.

366 Ibid., 390.

Chapter 3

1863

Moon Stage Legend: ◐ first quarter; ○ full, ◑ last quarter, ● new

January 1, 1863 (Thursday)

President Abraham Lincoln's Emancipation Proclamation goes into effect, but newspapers in Georgia carried a different pronouncement. The *Daily Sun* noted, "The future looks far brighter than it did twelve months ago. Then our armies were weak, undisciplined, driven back, and partially demoralized. Now they are strong, well disciplined and victorious to a degree almost beyond human credulity, certainly beyond human expectation."[1] President Jefferson offered a speech in Atlanta (see January 5 entry).

January 2, 1863 (Friday)

A Columbus newspaper carried a frontpage article titled "Run the Blockade!" "Green tea, Rio coffee, carbonate of soda, soap, [and] sugars" numbered among the various goods that made their way into Columbus and John N. Birch offered for sale to the public.[2]

January 3, 1863 (Saturday)

The Federal troops garrisoning Fort Pulaski played a baseball game inside the fortification. New Yorkers dominated the field, as the 48th NY Infantry bested the 47th; final score: 20-7.[3]

January 4, 1863 (Sunday) ○

Espousing on the results of the war through early 1863, editors of the *Augusta Chronicle* suggested, "The time can not be far distant when they [the U.S.] will eagerly accept peace upon our terms, or will compel their Government to make propositions for pacification. To continue their attempts to crush the rebellion will be the height of madness, and of that, these frequent defeats must go far to convince them."[4]

January 5, 1863 (Monday)

Recounting President Davis's New Year's Day visit to Atlanta, the Columbus newspaper summarized the president's comments. "He spoke with deep feeling of admiration of the conspicuous part Georgia had borne in the contest now waging for the subjugation of our country. He reminded his auditory that Georgia was the mother of two States, Alabama and Mississippi, and that therefore there should on the one side exist the feeling of maternal

---

[1] "Editorial," *Columbus Daily Sun*, January 1, 1863, https://gahistoricnewspapers.galileo.usg.edu/lccn/sn82014939/1863-01-01/ed-1/seq-2/.

[2] *Columbus Daily Sun*, January 2, 1863, 1, https://gahistoricnewspapers.galileo.usg.edu/lccn/sn82014939/1863-01-01/ed-1/seq-2/.

[3] Guss, *Fort Pulaski*, 78.

[4] "The Results of the Victory," *Augusta Chronicle*, January 4, 1863, Genealogybank.com.

affection, and on the other that of filial regard."[5]

January 6, 1863 (Tuesday)

General P. G. T. Beauregard sent the following dispatch to Brigadier General Hugh Mercer's Savannah headquarters. "Send back troops here recently at Wilmington properly provided for the field except means of transportation—four days' rations (two days' cooked); also camp equipage. Answer."[6]

January 7, 1863 (Wednesday)

Colonel Charles C. Jones Jr., stationed in Savannah, wrote to his mother and father, giving them insight on his military duties. "I cannot say to you how busy I have been of late...difficult for me to recall a leisure moment during the past two weeks. On Friday of this week I have ordered in five of my light batteries in order that I may give General Mercer an inspection and review. I trust the parade and review will be attractive, and assure the general commanding of the efficiency of the light batteries in this command, and of their preparedness at any moment for actual service."[7]

January 8, 1863 (Thursday)

Colonel Jones wrote to his mother and father. His letter carried a focus on cotton. "Please, Father, let me know how many bales of cotton can be delivered at No. 3 from all the plantations named, in order that I may at once communicate with the purchasers. By the arrangement proposed we save all the expenses of freight to Savannah, drayage, commissions, etc., which form no small item in the aggregate." Jones closed the correspondence in refocusing on military activity at hand and sending his best to loved ones at home. "Tomorrow I expect to have a grand review by General Mercer of five of my light batteries. With warmest love to self, my dear father, to my dear mother, and many kisses for my precious little daughter, I am ever Your affectionate son, Charles C. Jones, Jr."[8]

January 9, 1863 (Friday)

Colonel Jones, in Savannah, received a letter from his father—the Reverend Charles C. Jones. "Today is your grand review. Nothing prevented my being present but my weakness and Mother's indisposition. It would have afforded me unfeigned pleasure to have witnessed it. I never saw the like. Rivers rising and railroads open. Stirring times are upon us. We have only to stand the braver and trust in God more perfectly."[9]

January 10, 1863 (Saturday)

George Harrington, acting secretary of the treasury, notified Gideon Welles, U.S. secretary of the navy, of a blockade running situation at Savannah. "SIR: I have the honor to transmit to you a copy of a letter from...acting collector of customs at Port Royal...relating to the steamer *Emma*, now ashore near Fort Pulaski, having on board a valuable cargo of cotton

---

[5] "President Davis Visit to Atlanta," *Columbus Daily Sun*, January 5, 1863, 2, https://gahistoricnewspapers.galileo.usg.edu/lccn/sn82014939/1863-01-05/ed-1/seq-2/.

[6] *OR*, ser. I, vol. 14:743.

[7] Myers, *Children of Pride*, 1008.

[8] Ibid., 1011.

[9] Ibid., 1012.

and turpentine, which, with the machinery of the steamer, can be saved..." Harrington closed his dispatch in requesting "such instructions may be given to the officer in command of the naval forces at Port Royal as you may deem proper in the premises."[10]

January 11, 1863 (Sunday)

Feeling the pain of many on the home front who had lost husbands, sons, brothers, and fathers during the war, editors of the *Southern Confederacy* published a poem titled "From the Spirit Land" to offer some relief to the discomforted. The first stanza reads, "Weep not, dear sister, for my fate, for I am with the blest / Mine were a soldier's life and death, be mine a soldier's rest: / The highest seats in blissful realms by Heaven's laws, / Are given to the virtuous brave who die in Freedom's cause."[11]

January 12, 1863 (Monday) ◑

The *Daily Sun* carried the casualties the 5th Georgia Infantry Regiment incurred during the Battle of Stone's River/Murfreesboro. Learning of the killed or wounded, whether in the "Clinch Rifles, Griffin Light Guards, Irish Volunteers, McDuffie Rifles, Dawson Volunteers, Cuthbert Rifles, Schley Guards, Hardee Rifles, Georgia Grays, or the Upson Guards,"[12] the broadsheet of the day brought tearful news to many.

January 13, 1863 (Tuesday)

Possibly casting a thought toward a future increase in use, the newspaper in Rome carried a report on the hospitals in the area. "We think that our hospitals are a credit to our city. An examination shows that they have been put on foot with experience and sound judgment, and are being conducted in the proper way. The rooms are kept clean and warm, and we doubt not but the little bunks look inviting to the weary, war-worn soldier, that has slept so often on the cold ground, with naught perhaps to shelter him from the storm but a blanket."[13]

January 14, 1863 (Wednesday)

General Beauregard issued General Orders No. 7, detailing procedures for conscription. "Pursuant to orders from the War Department, hereafter persons liable to conscription will be allowed to join any particular company and regiment requiring recruits in this command."[14]

January 15, 1863 (Thursday)

An outbreak of smallpox in the state busied reporters in communicating the danger. "We regret to state...that this loathsome disease is prevailing in many sections of our State, and that Atlanta is now infected with the pestilence to an extent which should cause our citizens

---

[10] *ORN*, ser. I., vol. 13:508.

[11] "From the Spirit Land," *Atlanta Southern Confederacy*, January 11, 1863, https://gahistoricnewspapers.galileo.usg.edu/lccn/sn82014677/1863-01-11/ed-1/seq-3/.

[12] "List of Killed and Wounded—5th Georgia Regiment," *Columbus Daily Sun*, January 12, 1863, https://gahistoricnewspapers.galileo.usg.edu/lccn/sn82014939/1863-01-12/ed-1/seq-2/.

[13] "Our Hospitals," *Rome Tri-Weekly Courier*, January 13, 1863, https://gahistoricnewspapers.galileo.usg.edu/lccn/sn85034102/1863-01-13/ed-1/seq-2/.

[14] *OR*, ser. I, vol. 14:749.

to be watchful, and use every precaution to prevent its spreading to any greater extent among us."[15]

January 16, 1863 (Friday)

Acting on his duties as commander of the Confederate forces in Savannah, Brigadier General Hugh Mercer requested additional artillery from the War Department in Richmond. He received a response on this date from C. H. Lee, the assistant adjutant general. "The within statement exhibits all the artillery sent to the department of General Beauregard lately; more will be sent as it can be spared. General Beauregard must make such disposition of it as he deems best." The ordnance officer recapped the artillery previously sent to Savannah. "The Department of South Carolina and Georgia has received full three-fourths of the heavy armament prepared within the last three months: Fifteen 10-inch columbiads, two 42-pounder rifled and barbette, two Napoleons, two Ellsworth rifles (captured), one 3.67-inch rifled and barbette, six 10-inch mortars."[16] Mercer would have to wait.

January 17, 1863 (Saturday)

Rear Admiral Du Pont responded to a report from Captain Joseph Green expressing concerns on behalf of the U.S. Navy toward the blockade runner *Rattlesnake* (formerly the CSS *Nashville*). "I am in receipt of your dispatch of yesterday and in accordance with your suggestion that another gunboat is necessary in Ossabaw to guards the passes which [the] *Nashville* may take, I am sending at daylight the *Water Witch*, with orders for the *Seneca* to return to her station at Ossabaw. The *Marblehead* will take her place in Wassaw."[17]

January 18, 1863 (Sunday)

An appeal went out to the women of Atlanta, and beyond, to offer their assistance for injured soldiers. "The Ladies of the Hospital Association are earnestly requested to cook for the wounded soldiers now in the Hospitals the coming week. The committee will remain as it now stands. Provisions to be furnished at the store room."[18]

January 19, 1863 (Monday) ●

Inflation continued to escalate throughout the Confederacy, as the effectiveness of the Federal blockade increased, as reflected in a Savannah newspaper. "There was a scarcity of beef in the market on Saturday last, and prices, we learn, which started in the morning at 25¢ per lb., suddenly rose to 40 cts. This may suit long purses, but the poor are not able to stand such figures."[19]

January 20, 1863 (Tuesday)

Confederate Secretary of War James Seddon reminded Brigadier General Howell Cobb of

---

[15] "Smallpox in Atlanta," *Rome Tri-Weekly Courier*, January 15, 1863, https://gahistoricnewspapers.galileo.usg.edu/lccn/sn85034102/1863-01-15/ed-1/seq-1/.

[16] *OR*, ser. I, vol. 14:750–51.

[17] *ORN*, ser. I, vol. 13:514.

[18] "Ladies!! Ladies!!," *Atlanta Southern Confederacy*, January 18, 1863, sec. 3, https://gahistoricnewspapers.galileo.usg.edu/lccn/sn82014677/1863-01-18/ed-1/seq-3/.

[19] "Telegraphic," *Savannah Republican*, January 19, 1863, sec. 2, https://gahistoricnewspapers.galileo.usg.edu/lccn/sn85038496/1863-01-19/ed-1/seq-2/.

items requiring Cobb's attention in Georgia. "The First Georgia Regiment...reduced in numbers, was sent...to Georgia, to be recruited by conscripts, and...ordered to report to you for service. It is thought by the President important that this regiment should be recruited full, as he thinks it would prove more effective than raw troops, and you had better take care that enough conscripts be first obtained to accomplish this before you recommend expansion over too large a surface."[20]

January 21, 1863 (Wednesday)

Federal naval officers near Savannah continued to harbor thoughts of the *Nashville*, or *Rattlesnake*. Captain J. F. Green alerted Lieutenant Commander William Gibson to "station the vessels composing the naval force in Ossabaw Bar as follows: The *Seneca* and *Wissahickon*, in the Ogeechee in a depth of water that will not admit of the *Nashville* approaching them for the purpose of running them down, and in the best position to intercept that vessel should she attempt to proceed to sea."[21]

January 22, 1863 (Thursday)

Rear Admiral Du Pont dispatched the following plan: "I am sending the ironclad *Montauk*, Commander [John] Worden, to Ossabaw to ascend the Ogeechee, if she can, to capture the fort at Point Genesis and to burn the *Nashville*."[22]

January 23, 1863 (Friday)

A Federal naval flotilla left Beaufort, South Carolina, navigating toward Georgia via the St. Marys River. Ships involved included "the steamers, *John Adams*, *Planter*, and *Ben De Ford*."[23]

January 24, 1863 (Saturday)

Commander Charles Steedman received the following orders from Rear Admiral Du Pont. "You will please proceed...to St. Johns River...making a reconnaissance of the St. John's as far as you may deem necessary. You can, if convenient, stop at St. Simon's on your way south, delivering the mails there, but after your reconnaissance up the St. John's you will return to St. Simon's and take charge of the blockade there and the adjoining waters."[24]

January 25, 1863 (Sunday)

The Federal navy, preparing to launch an attack on Fort McAllister, continued exploring various waterways in the vicinity of the stronghold. Captain J. F. Green reported on recent intelligence. "The *Fingal* dropped down to [St.]. Augustine Creek last Monday for the purpose of taking advantage of the high tides and going through that creek if possible, otherwise by Fort Pulaski and proceed by sea to rescue the *Nashville*. For some unknown reason she did not attempt it, as the contraband [the man who had related his observations to Green] saw her off the mouth of the creek last Friday."[25]

---

[20] *OR*, ser. I, vol. 53, 277.

[21] *ORN*, ser. I, vol. 13:522–23.

[22] Ibid., 531.

[23] Mosocco, *Chronological Tracking*, 120.

[24] *ORN*, ser. I, vol. 13:534.

[25] Ibid., 536.

January 26, 1863 (Monday)

Various Federal navy ships moved into position for a January 27 attack on Fort McAllister. Commander John Worden, onboard the *Montauk*, made this log entry. "At 1:30 p.m. started up the Ogeechee River. At 7 saw a light over the marsh in the direction of Coffee Bluff. At 7:45 two boats on expeditionary duty passed up from the fleet."[26]

January 27, 1863 (Tuesday)

Commander Worden provided an account of the naval attack on Fort McAllister. "At 7:35 a.m. we opened fire on the fort. After firing our XI and XV-inch guns once the enemy opened a brisk fire upon us. Their practice was very fine, striking us quite a number of times, doing us no damage. Most of their shot struck inside of 15 feet from us." The commander halted the attack "At 11:15 a.m., all our shells being expended and finding our solid shot not seriously affecting the enemy...."[27]

January 28, 1863 (Wednesday)

General P. G. T. Beauregard provided General Samuel Cooper with an update on Fort McAllister. "Two enemy's gunboats and three steamers attacked for several hours yesterday Fort [McAllister], Genesis Point, on Great Ogeechee. Attack repulsed; nobody hurt in fort. Two steamers went out this harbor safely last night and one came in with various army supplies."[28]

January 29, 1863 (Thursday)

Commander Worden, outside Savannah, continued to conduct various naval scouting missions. "The dispatch boat *Daffodil* arrived at 8:30 a.m. with ammunition for the vessels. We received ours, and were employed during the day in filling shells and shifting fuzes. At 9:30 p.m. two boats, under the charge of Lieutenant-Commander [Charles H.] Cushman, of this vessel, went up the river on a reconnoissance, but discovered no material change in the enemy's position."[29]

January 30, 1863 (Friday)

Newspaper editors in Rome commented on the increasing inflation in the region. "We have not reported the markets because the prices of articles changed so rapidly, and the supplies so limited that it was not deemed worth while to make a report." A listing of various goods followed—"Apples—'Played out' entirely; Bacon—None in market. Last we heard of was 50 to 60 cents." After continuing to report on various staple goods, the editor lamented, "Our business affairs are in a miserable condition."[30]

January 31, 1863 (Saturday)

General Beauregard submitted his field return from the Department of South Carolina, Georgia, and Florida. He listed totals for the District of Georgia: Infantry, 99 officers and

---

[26] Ibid., 547.

[27] Ibid., 544.

[28] *ORN*, ser. I, vol. 14:198.

[29] *ORN*, ser. I, vol. 13:628.

[30] "Rome Markets," *Rome Weekly Courier*, January 30, 1863, sec. 2, https://gahistoricnewspapers.galileo.usg.edu/lccn/sn82014071/1863-01-30/ed-1/seq-2/.

1,279 soldiers; Cavalry, 93 officers, 1,554 troopers; Artillery, 123 officers and 1,856 gunners. "Aggregate present and absent, 7,344."[31]

February 1, 1863 (Sunday)

Military action in Georgia remained concentrated along the coast, as the Federal navy again attacked Fort McAllister. Confederate Brigadier General Hugh Mercer reported, "A Yankee ironclad is anchored about 200 yards from the obstructions. Four other gunboats and one mortar boat are opposite…[Genesis Point, Fort McAllister]. Our parapet in front of the 8-inch gun is entirely demolished, though the detachments are still at their guns. We will hold the battery to the last extremity and blow her up before we will surrender. The attack is severe, but the men are in fine spirits."[32]

February 2, 1863 (Monday)

Reporting on the aftermath of the attack on Fort McAllister, Beauregard provided details to Confederate officials. "The movements of the enemy seem to indicate Savannah as their future objective point. The battery at Genesis Point, on the Great Ogeechee, has twice been unsuccessfully attacked with an iron-clad (a monitor), four gunboats, and one mortar boat, to which the battery could oppose only two effective guns—an VIII-inch columbiad and a 32-pounder, rifled. The result must be very encouraging to us for the defenses of this harbor."[33]

February 3, 1863 (Tuesday)

The officer in charge of the gunboat *Seneca*, Lieutenant Commander William Gibson, recounted his part in the attack on Fort McAllister. "We opened fire at 7:20 a.m. and continued the cannonade four hours and forty minutes…the enemy fired at us with at least two guns as well as with the mortar, but he was mainly occupied with the ironclad. The fort has been enlarged and strengthened with huge traverses within a recent period, and though but an earthwork, is now really colossal of its kind."[34]

February 4, 1863 (Wednesday)

Newspaper headlines called "the attention of the citizens of Savannah, old and young—all who are able and willing to bear arms in defense of their firesides and altars—to the earnest and eloquent appeal of Gen. [Brigadier Hugh] Mercer…. The object of this call is to induce a prompt organization of all arms-bearing citizens not now connected with the military corps, in order that they may be ready in the hour of need."[35]

February 5, 1863 (Thursday)

Rear Admiral Du Pont communicated the following advice to Commander Worden: "I have nothing official to write but to be careful of your ammunition. I am glad you made

---

[31] *OR*, ser. I, vol. 14:757.

[32] *ORN*, ser. I, vol. 13:633.

[33] Ibid., 819.

[34] Ibid., 629–30.

[35] "Organization for Home Defense," *Savannah Daily Morning News*, February 4, 1863, sec. 2, https://gahistoricnewspapers.galileo.usg.edu/lccn/sn82015886/1863-02-04/ed-1/seq-2/.

the second attack, because it will add to your experience of the powers of your vessel. The fort [McAllister] is strong, and of that description which may stand long hammering."[36]

February 6, 1863 (Friday)

Rewarding the troops defending Fort McAllister, Beauregard, via General Orders No. 23, declared, "The thanks of the country are due to this intrepid garrison, who have thus shown what brave men may withstand and accomplish, despite apparent odds. 'Fort McAllister' will be inscribed on the flags of all the troops engaged in the defense of the battery."[37]

February 7, 1863 (Saturday)

The Emancipation Proclamation went in effect January 1, 1863. Just over one month later, Confederate officers in the field witnessed early results, as Beauregard's chief of staff reported. "In connection with the course of your present situation, I have only to say that were the language of President Lincoln's proclamation of doubtful import, the meaning would be made clear by the fact that there are now at Hilton Head or that vicinity [Charleston] fugitive slaves who have recently been employed in armed expeditions against the people of Georgia and South Carolina."[38]

February 8, 1863 (Sunday)

Writing to South Carolina Governor Milledge L. Bonham, Beauregard delivered alarming news. "Every indication is that Charleston or Savannah will soon be attacked by an overwhelming force. Not much assistance can be expected from Confederate Government, and no chance of even temporary success should at this moment be allowed the enemy."[39]

February 9, 1863 (Monday)

In Savannah, Brigadier General Hugh Mercer received an unusual order from Beauregard. "Send all 15-inch shell thrown by enemy at Fort McAllister to Charleston."[40]

February 10, 1863 (Tuesday)

Brigadier General William S. Walker informed Beauregard of concerns on his ability to resist an attack on Savannah: "A very probable and feasible programme of the enemy's operations would be to take the entire force at their command for the purpose of occupying the railroad and destroying it, and after its destruction to use the same force for operating on Savannah." Walker also suggested "that troops should be ready in Savannah to cross the river and march down the Screven's Ferry road. In that event I should think it advisable to have works near the river on this side; under which we could retire and check the advance of the enemy if we were driven from our first position."[41]

February 11, 1863 (Wednesday) ◐

Citizens of Savannah may have smiled when perusing the morning newspaper and reading of a recent discovery. "We have in our possession a little pamphlet edition of Old Abe's

---

[36] *ORN*, ser. I, vol. 13:644.

[37] Ibid., 638.

[38] *OR*, ser. I, vol. 13:562.

[39] *OR*, ser. I, vol. 14:768.

[40] Ibid., 771.

[41] Ibid.

Emancipation Proclamation, which was left at St. Mary's, Ga., by the Yankees on their recent vandal visit to that place. The pamphlet is no doubt designed for circulation South, where it was erroniously [*sic*] supposed by the author it would not find currency through the press."[42]

February 12, 1863 (Thursday)

Lamenting the intrusion of government officials, the editor of Rome's *Tri-Weekly Courier* suggested, "It is to be deeply regretted that the Government deemed it to its interest, to occupy almost the entire city as a Hospital. Nine-tenths of the important business houses are now occupied, and laid off into four distinct Hospitals, to wit: 'The Lumpkin,' 'The Bell,' 'The Quintard,' and 'The ________' Hospitals, all crowded to overflowing with inmates."[43]

February 13, 1863 (Friday)

Soldiers in the 8th Georgia Infantry, stationed in Fredericksburg, Virginia, wrote to the newspaper editor in Rome: "Current events in Abolitiondom all point to the fact that the great crisis of the war is now rapidly approaching. Lincoln...has made his last mad leap in his Abolition proclamation; the iron-grasp with which he crushed freedom of speech and an untrammeled press has been broken, and now, not only disaffection, but outright opposition, to his tyrannous rule, spreads like wild fire throughout the length and breath [*sic*] of his...almost enslaved dominions."[44]

February 14, 1863 (Saturday) (Valentine's Day)

Columbus citizens received an opportunity to assist in the defenses of Savannah; an evening out awaited some. "Every citizen of Columbus, and its vicinity, who is willing, at a moment's warning, to go to Savannah and aid in defending it against an attack by the enemy is requested to be at Temperance Hall to night at 7½ o'clock."[45]

February 15, 1863 (Sunday)

Rear Admiral Du Pont provided orders for Lieutenant John Kittredge: "You will proceed with the U.S.S. *Wamsutta* under your command to St. Simon's and report for blockading duty to Commander [Charles] C. Steedman, senior officer present, delivering mails and packages intended for the vessels there."[46]

February 16, 1863 (Monday)

---

42 "Telegraphic," *Savannah Daily Morning News*, February 11, 1863, sec. 2, https://gahistoricnewspapers.galileo.usg.edu/lccn/sn82015886/1863-02-11/ed-1/seq-2/.

43 "Rome and Her Hospitals," *Rome Tri-Weekly Courier*, February 12, 1863, sec. 2, https://gahistoricnewspapers.galileo.usg.edu/lccn/sn85034102/1863-02-12/ed-1/seq-2/. The unnamed hospital in the article may be the Polk; see "A Guide to the Samuel Hollingsworth Stout Papers," https://legacy.lib.utexas.edu/taro/utcah/00042/cah-00042.html.

44 "Camp 8th GA. Regiment," *Rome Weekly Courier*, February 13, 1863, https://gahistoricnewspapers.galileo.usg.edu/lccn/sn82014071/1863-02-13/ed-1/seq-2/.

45 "Defence of Savannah," *Columbus Daily Sun*, February 14, 1863, sec. 2, https://gahistoricnewspapers.galileo.usg.edu/lccn/sn82014939/1863-02-14/ed-1/seq-2/.

46 *ORN*, ser. I, vol. 13:664.

The CSS *Chattahoochee*, a twin-screw schooner, built in Early County, Georgia, launched; she would have a short life.[47]

February 17, 1863 (Tuesday) ●

Beauregard, in Savannah, corresponded with Governor Brown regarding the general's plans for the Federals. "I have ordered all State troops sent here to be subsisted. I hope to give the Abolitionists a warm reception."[48]

February 18, 1863 (Wednesday)

A query from Beauregard to Governor Brown on a busy day, as the general scrambled to get reinforcements: "Enemy collecting large land and naval forces at Port Royal to attack this place or Charleston. Can any State troops or militia be furnished for the defense of Savannah: if so, how many?"[49] In Macon, workers laid the cornerstone for an armory.

February 19, 1863 (Thursday)

During the naval assault on Fort McAllister earlier in the month, Commander Worden and his *Montauk* took part in the bombardment. After an inspection of the *Montauk*'s damage, Rear Admiral Du Pont found "the effect of shot on the pilot house, causing by concussion or percussion, the large nuts screwed on to the bolts inside to fly off with great violence, wrenching off the end of the bolt itself; they cross the pilot house and rebound from the opposite side. We are…preparing a screen of boiler iron to go around the pilot house."[50]

February 20, 1863 (Friday)

Two governors worked with Beauregard to shore-up his troop strength. Governor Brown promised two regiments, yet the general believed "more could be had in this State and South Carolina. If they could be armed they would answer well behind fortifications."[51]

February 21, 1863 (Saturday)

Rear Admiral Du Pont ordered Commander William Le Roy to "proceed to St. Simon's with the *Keystone State* under your command and report to Commander [Charles] Steedman, senior officer present, for blockading duty in those waters, taking with you the mails, if any."[52]

February 22, 1863 (Sunday)

"Organizations of companies or battalions for the defense either of Charleston or Savannah will remain in Augusta, drilling and perfecting themselves in the use of arms, prepared and ready to move to either of the first-named cities on short notice."[53] Beauregard's report of

---

[47] U.S. Naval History Division, *Civil War Naval Chronology*, 6:208; "February in Georgia History."

[48] *OR*, ser. I, vol. 14:781.

[49] Ibid., 784; Matthew, "Confederate States Armory at Macon, Georgia," http://www.csarmory.org.

[50] *ORN*, ser. I, vol. 13:672.

[51] *OR*, ser. I, vol. 14:787.

[52] *ORN*, ser. I, vol. 13:673.

[53] *OR*, ser. I, vol. 14:788.

the day highlighted preparations for defending key cities in his department.

February 23, 1863 (Monday)

U.S. gunboats captured the *Glide*, a blockade-runner, in Wassaw Sound. An officer with the U.S. Coast Survey detailed his involvement. "This morning at daybreak a vessel was reported to me as being aground on the shoal off the end of Little Tybee Island, which appeared to be a blockade runner. I immediately started with an armed boat and seven men to board her. Found her to be the *Pembroke*, a Savannah pilot boat (now sailing under the name of the *Glide*). She was loaded with 72 bales of cotton, bound for Nassau."[54]

February 24, 1863 (Tuesday)

As the effectiveness of the Federal blockade intensified, the resultant matériel shortages pushed Georgia officials to act, so the opening of a new uniform provider made news. Under the heading "Georgia Soldiers' Clothing Bureau of Augusta," readers learned the bureau served as an "auxiliary to the facilities afforded by the Confederate Government, and will, it is believed alleviate any want of clothing that may, from any cause, exist among the Georgia troops."[55]

February 25, 1863 (Wednesday) ◐

General Beauregard made an "appeal to the people of South Carolina and Georgia, [to] brush up your fowling piece and prepare to meet the Northern hirelings, the moment they set foot on Georgia soil."[56]

February 26, 1863 (Thursday)

"Governor Brown has ordered all officers holding commissions in the State Militia to repair immediately to Savannah, and report to General Beauregard, for service in the defence of the city. This patriotic act of the Governor will be heartily approved by the people of the State, and, we trust, promptly responded to by all those to whom the order is directed." The *Savannah Daily Morning* editorial continued the discourse, explaining why this did not serve as an attempt from the governor to avoid conscription of Georgia militia forces. "It remains for those who hold commissions in the militia to prove to the country that they seek no such certificates of exemption from the ranks in the hour of danger."[57]

February 27, 1863 (Friday)

Naval action continued along the coast; Lieutenant Commander John Barnes logged his report. "The rebel steamer *Nashville* came down the Ogeechee River on a reconnaissance. The *Seneca* ran up to Genesis Point and exchanged shots with Fort McAllister."[58] Barnes

---

[54] *ORN*, ser. I, vol. 13:686.

[55] "Georgia Soldiers' Clothing Bureau of Augusta," *Milledgeville Southern Recorder*, February 24, 1863, sec. 2, https://gahistoricnewspapers.galileo.usg.edu/lccn/sn82016415/1863-02-24/ed-1/seq-2/.

[56] "Wednesday, Feb. 25, 1863," *Sandersville Central Georgian*, February 25, 1863, sec. 2, https://gahistoricnewspapers.galileo.usg.edu/lccn/sn85034105/1863-02-25/ed-1/seq-2/.

[57] "The Officers of the Militia Ordered into Service," *Savannah Daily Morning News*, February 26, 1863, sec. 2, https://gahistoricnewspapers.galileo.usg.edu/lccn/sn82015886/1863-02-26/ed-1/seq-2/.

[58] *ORN*, ser. I, vol. 13:705.

did not realize, until seeing during reconnaissance the following day, that the *Nashville* had run aground above Fort McAllister.

February 28, 1863 (Saturday)

Federal naval vessels attacked Fort McAllister and sank the CSS *Nashville*; Commander John Worden submitted the following report of the action.

> I have the honor to report that yesterday evening the enemy's steamer *Nashville* was observed by me in motion above the battery known as Fort McAllister. A reconnoissance immediately made proved that in moving up the river, she had grounded in that portion of the river known as the Seven-Mile Reach. Believing that I could, by approaching close to the battery, reach and destroy her with my battery, I moved up at daylight this morning, accompanied by the blockading fleet in these waters…by moving up close to the obstructions in the river I was enabled, although under a heavy fire from the battery, to approach the *Nashville*, still aground, within the distance of 1,200 yards. A few well-directed shells determined the range, and soon [we] succeeded in striking her with XI-inch and XV-inch shells. The other gunboats maintained a fire from an enfilading position upon the battery, and the Nashville at long range. I soon had the satisfaction of observing that the Nashville had caught fire from the shells exploding in her in several places, and in less than twenty minutes she was caught in flames forward, aft, and amidships. At 9:20 a.m. a large pivot gun mounted abaft her foremast exploded from the heat; at 9:40 her smoke chimney went by the board, and at 9:55 her magazine exploded with terrific violence, shattering her in smoking ruins. Nothing remains of her.[59]

March 1, 1863 (Sunday)

Congratulations from Rear Admiral Du Pont reached Commander Worden. One can imagine the delight of the crew when they received Du Pont's "commendation for their good conduct, not only on this occasion, but during the previous attacks of the *Montauk* on the fort [McAllister], and their services generally in the Ogeechee."[60]

March 2, 1863 (Monday)

The Federal fleet prepared for another assault on Fort McAllister, and U.S. Secretary of Navy Gideon Welles sent a telegram, dispatching "the *Courier*, with stores, immediately to Port Royal. They are very much needed."[61]

March 3, 1863 (Tuesday)

Another naval attack on Fort McAllister resulted in failure to destroy the bastion. Naval records indicate "8 a.m. the *Passaic*, *Patapsco*, and *Nahant* underway and steaming slowly up the Ogeechee River. At 8:05 mortar schooners underway in tow of the tug *Dandelion*. At 8:25 a.m. mortar fleet in position. At 8:31, battery opened fire on the ironclads." Captain John McCrady filed the damage report from the fort. "Earthwork.—No material

---

[59] Ibid., 697–98.

[60] Ibid., 706.

[61] Ibid., 710.

damage, nor any that could not be repaired in one night. Guns.—One gun carriage scattered; two traverse wheels broken. Men.—Two men slightly wounded."[62]

March 4, 1863 (Wednesday)

Brigadier General Robert Toombs resigned his commission and returned to his home in Washington, Georgia.[63] After the recent attack on fort McAllister, Rear Admiral Du Pont evaluated the outcome, and surmised, "The results have been of great service in testing not only the resisting, but the aggressive, powers of the ironclads, which will be of much use in future operations.

March 5, 1863 (Thursday)

Federal inspectors took a close look at the USS *Montauk*'s damage after the attack on Fort McAllister. Their findings in indicated the "explosion took place beneath the back end of the port boiler, under a part where the ship's bottom is very flat." Completing their investigation, and finding several sections of damage, the engineers suggested the ship "be beached and a soft patch tap bolted to the inside of the cracked plate: that the floors be straightened and refastened to the frames, and that a wrought-iron pipe be put in place of the cast-iron one which broke."[64]

March 6, 1863 (Friday)

Providing a status report to Washington, Rear Admiral Du Pont recapped the recent attack on Fort McAllister. Du Pont desired, "before entering upon more important operations, to subject the various mechanical appliances of the ironclads to the fullest test of active service and to give the advantage of target practice to the officers and men with their new ordnance. For this purpose I had ordered a concentration in the Ogeechee of such of these vessels as were ready to attack Fort McAllister and secure or destroy the *Nashville*."[65]

March 7, 1863 (Saturday)

Work continued to repair the hull damage the USS *Montauk* incurred during the attack on Fort McAllister. Du Pont notified Secretary Welles he had "the honor to enclose the report of the survey on the *Montauk*, injured by the explosion of a torpedo on the 28th ultimo after the destruction of the Nashville. Drawings are also forwarded herewith."[66]

March 8, 1863 (Sunday)

Front page news of the day: "The telegraph informs us that the enemy has abandoned his enterprise at Fort McAllister—for the present at least. Are the Yankees becoming distrustful of their all powerful rams?"[67]

March 9, 1863 (Monday)

Commander J. R. Madison Mullany, onboard the USS *Bienville*, reported capture of a

---

[62] Ibid., 723, 732–33.

[63] Warner, *Generals in Gray*, 307; Du Pont's observation in *ORN*, ser. I, vol. 13:725.

[64] *ORN*, ser. I, vol. 13:707–708.

[65] Ibid., 716.

[66] Ibid., 707.

[67] "From the Coast," *Columbus Daily Sun*, March 8, 1863, sec. 1, https://gahistoricnewspapers.galileo.usg.edu/lccn/sn82014939/1863-03-08/ed-1/seq-1/.

suspected blockade-runner, the schooner *Lightning*. "The proximity of the vessel to the coast of Georgia and South Carolina, the nature of her cargo, and the fact that she was entirely out of her course if bound to Beaufort, N.C., and that there was no endorsement on her papers by our consul at Nassau, New Providence, convinced me that it was my duty to seize her."[68]

March 10, 1863 (Tuesday)

Naval action along Georgia's coast left many pondering the fate of future days. "Fort McAllister, it seems, has been given over. The 'rebels' are still in the undisputed possession of the Ogeechee and Abraham's terrible rams have departed in peace. What next? We shall see, what we shall see."[69]

March 11, 1863 (Wednesday)

The threat of Federal naval attacks remained foremast in the minds of seaboard folks, and rumors mixed with truth. "We hear of no vessels on our immediate coast. The enemy are probably waiting for the arrival of more iron-clads, the departure of some of which from Northern ports have been announced before making their grand attack on Charleston or Savannah, or both."[70]

March 12, 1863 (Thursday) ◑

Suggesting "Our Greatest Disaster" lay ahead, the editor of a Savannah newspaper penned the following forecast: "The North is preparing for another desperate attempt to subjugate the south. If Lincoln succeeds in harmonizing the discordant elements among her people (and it is wiser that we should act upon the presumption that he will), the war is to be waged with intenser fury than ever before."[71]

March 13, 1863 (Friday)

Colonel William Barton of the 48th New York Volunteers submitted intelligence obtained when three Confederate deserters fled to Fort Pulaski. "The *Atlanta* (ram) is lying some half mile from the *Georgia*, and nearer Fort Jackson. A third ironclad is so far completed as to be ready for her armament…one or two more are commenced. A large earthwork is in process…near Causton's Bluff, which Beauregard pronounces the key to the possession of the city. But seven guns are as yet mounted on it. It is proposed to mount twenty-seven to thirty. Great fear is felt that the city will be attacked and taken."[72]

March 14, 1863 (Saturday)

Residents of Rome welcomed the influx of Confederate soldiers into the region, despite reports of disgruntled civilians in other towns. "We have had much complaint against

---

[68] *ORN*, ser. I, vol. 13:744.

[69] "What Next?," *Columbus Daily Sun*, March 10, 1863, sec. 1, https://gahistoricnewspapers.galileo.usg.edu/lccn/sn82014939/1863-03-10/ed-1/seq-1/.

[70] "The Yankee Fleet at Port Royal," *Savannah Daily Morning News*, March 11, 1863, sec. 1, https://gahistoricnewspapers.galileo.usg.edu/lccn/sn82015886/1863-03-11/ed-1/seq-1/.

[71] "Our Greatest Danger," *Savannah Daily Morning News*, March 12, 1863, sec. 1, https://gahistoricnewspapers.galileo.usg.edu/lccn/sn82015886/1863-03-12/ed-1/seq-1/.

[72] *ORN*, ser. I, vol. 13:750.

soldiers at various places, where they were stationed, as being troublesome, and in some instances disrespectable and insulting to the citizens. It affords us pleasure to say that the citizens of this place have had no cause to complain of those whose lot has cast them here. The officers are men of high standing, polite and agreeable to all."[73]

March 15, 1863 (Sunday)

Responding to an inquiry from Beauregard regarding additional artillery for his department, Colonel Ambrosio Gonzales submitted the following report. "There is no record in the ordnance or artillery offices relative to the applications of General Pemberton for heavy guns for this department. I am positive about one thing…he went to Richmond to apply…for such heavy guns and obtained the promise of ten 10-inch columbiads, and several 8-inch which were to have been cast in Rome, Ga."[74]

March 16, 1863 (Monday)

Georgia's Adjutant General Henry Wayne offered counsel to Brigadier General Hugh Mercer on dealing with the state's governor. "As men not military do not understand the relations and connection of responsibilities of military grades and rank…let me suggest to you some arrangement with General Beauregard by which your responsibility to him and at the same time your position as the military commander in the State of Georgia may be understood by the Governor, and a conflict of authority engendered in his mind prejudicial to the public interests be prevented." Wayne delivered an additional observation: "I am aware that you do not stand upon points, but I can see in the ignorance of the Governor in military affairs, contentious as he constitutionally is, the germs of difficulties with you all and with the Confederate Government."[75]

March 17, 1863 (Tuesday) (St. Patrick's Day)

Special Orders, No. 75 stipulated "In compliance with paragraph IV, Special Orders, No. 64, Department of South Carolina, Georgia, and Florida, the board of general officers therein constituted will assemble at Oglethorpe Barracks at 10 a. m., 17th instant, and daily thereafter until adjournment. Capt. W. W. Gordon, assistant adjutant-general, is hereby appointed as recorder. By order of Brigadier-General [Hugh] Mercer."[76]

March 18, 1863 (Wednesday)

Governor Brown believed General Braxton Bragg had plans to take military possession of the Western & Atlantic Railroad. Brown, questioning Bragg's motives, wrote President Davis. Davis responded, reassuring Brown he need not fear Bragg taking such action. Brown wrote back to Davis today, noting, "Your dispatch of yesterday is quite satisfactory for the assurance it contains."[77]

March 19, 1863 (Thursday) ●

---

[73] "Saturday Morning, March 14, 1863," *Rome Tri-Weekly Courier*, March 14, 1863, sec. 1, https://gahistoricnewspapers.galileo.usg.edu/lccn/sn85034102/1863-03-14/ed-1/seq-2/.

[74] *OR*, ser. I, vol. 14:828.

[75] Ibid., 836.

[76] Ibid., 865.

[77] Candler, *Confederate Records of the State of Georgia*, 3:330.

Sailors defected from the Confederate Navy, and Federal navy Captain John Rodgers reported on visitors to a nearby post. "I have the honor herewith to submit the result of an examination of five deserters from the Confederate transport *Savannah*, who, being on picket duty, secured the arms of their officer, a master's mate, and brought him prisoner to Fort Pulaski."[78]

March 20, 1863 (Friday)

Captain Arthur Kinzie, Major General Hunter's aide-de-camp, provided a written overview of his reconnaissance of Savannah; Hunter supplied the report to Rear Admiral Du Pont. "There are no obstructions, such as torpedoes...in the North Channel this side of the *Georgia.* From personal observation...I am confident that two of our ironclads could destroy the *Georgia* in two or three hours. The people of Savannah have no confidence in the defenses of the city and are ready at any moment, if we make a vigorous attack, to seek safety in flight."[79]

March 21, 1863 (Saturday)

A board of officers met in Savannah to identify the number and battery location of available artillery pieces. In the summary of their report, the officers declared, "There are now nominally upon these city lines forty-six guns, but of these four have been taken for the siege train. Four more are to be taken for the siege train and seven are old guns, very unsafe and likely to burst, being 24-pounders reamed out to 30-pounders. These fifteen guns should be replaced by ten 32-pounders and five 8-inch siege howitzers."[80]

March 22, 1863 (Sunday)

Brigadier General Hugh Mercer, commanding the District of Georgia, submitted his troop returns. Mercer indicated his force included the following, present for duty, forces: infantry 5,361; cavalry, 1,836; and 2,740 artillerymen.[81]

March 23, 1863 (Monday)

Secretary William Seward received a request from abroad, as Lord Lyons wanted information on shipping protocol given the Federal blockade. "A British subject has written to ask me to enquire from you whether you will grant permits to British subjects to load ships with cotton in the Savannah River below the Confederate obstructions. Will you be so kind as to tell me what answer I should make?"[82]

March 24, 1863 (Tuesday)

Beauregard shared—with Brigadier General Mercer commanding in Savannah—thoughts on how to best manage Governor Brown. The governor, facing an upcoming election, balked at impressing more enslaved persons to assist in building fortifications. "I have not had time until now to answer your letter of the 19th instant, inclosing one from [Major General Henry] Wayne to you. I think you are both right in your views, for what we want

---

[78] *ORN*, ser. I, vol. 13:767.

[79] Ibid, 776.

[80] *ORN*, ser. I, vol. 14:867.

[81] Ibid., 840.

[82] *ORN*, ser. I, vol. 13:781.

are the means of defending the State of Georgia, and those can evidently be had only by a thorough good understanding between the Confederate and State Governments or authorities; hence I will accept any reasonable measures to attain that desirable end."[83]

March 25, 1863 (Wednesday)

Calling the General Assembly to reconvene in Milledgeville on this date, the delegates received the governor's proclamation. Brown highlighted various subjects needing the attention of the Assembly and shared his thoughts on the prevailing mood in the state. "We can never be conquered by the arms of the enemy. We may be by hunger, if we neglect to husband all the resources for the supply of provisions, which a kind Providence has placed within our reach...the great question in this revolution is now a question of bread. The army must be fed...or the sun of liberty will soon set in darkness and blood, and the voice of freedom will be forever hushed in the silence of despotism."[84] In Washington, six of the participants in the Andrews Raid received the Medal of Honor. Secretary Stanton presented the first to Jacob Parrott. Then Elihu Mason, William Pittenger, William Reddick, William Bensinger, and Robert Buffum received their medals before meeting President Lincoln.

March 26, 1863 (Thursday)

The Georgia General Assembly passed a resolution, which recommended "the Confederate Congress to levy at once a tax that will raise money enough to place the credit and currency of the Confederate Government beyond doubt or contingency."[85]

March 27, 1863 (Friday) ◐

Gideon Welles clarified the earlier inquiry from Lord Lyon regarding the shipping of cotton in Savannah. "In reply I would state that I am aware of no authority to grant permits for shipment of cotton in the blockaded region. Port Royal is the only place in the vicinity of Savannah from which such shipments can legally be made."[86] People across the South observed—as President Davis had proclaimed—a day of fasting.

March 28, 1863 (Saturday)

Brigadier General Hugh Mercer received the following order from Beauregard's office in Charleston. "If Yankee letters plainly indicate future attack on Fort McAllister then suspend removal of 10-inch guns; not otherwise."[87]

March 29, 1863 (Sunday)

The Federal naval officers continued to redeploy ships to strengthen the blockade. "Proceed with the *Wamsutta* under your command to Wassaw to relieve the *Marblehead*. You will please, when there, take the most suitable position to enable you to pass out should you be threatened by any superior force."[88]

---

[83] *OR*, ser. I, vol. 14:836, 842.

[84] Candler, *Confederate Records of the State of Georgia*, 2:370; Medal of Honor from Bonds, *Stealing the General*, 320–22.

[85] *Journal of the Senate at an Extra Session...March 25th, 1863*, March 26, 1863, 33.

[86] *ORN*, ser. I, vol. 13:786.

[87] *OR*, ser. I, vol. 14:848.

[88] *ORN*, ser. I, vol. 13:793–94.

March 30, 1863 (Monday)
The board of Confederate officers evaluating the artillery in the vicinity of Savannah revised their report. "The official report of 'Guns applied for by General G. T. Beauregard for the defense of Savannah' was submitted to the board, showing an aggregate of fifty-four pieces of heavy ordnance, instead of twenty-five pieces, as heretofore stated."[89]

March 31, 1863 (Tuesday)
Confederate Major General Benjamin Huger reviewed the cannon emplacements along the coast. "I report for the information of the War Department that I have inspected the artillery and ordnance stores at this place. I transmit herewith...a tracing of Savannah and its environs, on which is marked in red [heavy black] the positions of the different works."[90]

April 1, 1863 (Wednesday) (April Fools' Day)
The General Assembly, meeting in Milledgeville passed a resolution authorizing Governor Brown to take action at Savannah. Their decree stated the governor "is hereby authorized and instructed to fill the requisition of the Confederate General at Savannah for fifteen hundred negroes for ninety days according to the resolutions of this General Assembly...that the Governor shall, as far as practicable impress first such negroes as are engaged in other than agricultural pursuits; Provided the impressment shall not be made from necessary house servants."[91]

April 2, 1863 (Thursday)
Captain Charles Steedman ordered Lieutenant Commander Gustavus H. Scott to redeploy his vessel. "You will proceed with the U.S. gunboat *Marblehead* under your command and take a position in the Savannah River for the purpose of keeping a vigilant lookout as to the movements of the enemy in that vicinity. You will use your discretion in remaining at anchor in the river above Fort Pulaski during the night."[92]

April 3, 1863 (Good Friday)
Confederate Secretary of the Navy Stephen Mallory directed Commander Richard Page in Savannah to begin submitting a quarterly report. Specifically, Mallory wanted the "number of times each gun is fired, with the weight and kind of projectile and charge of powder, stating also the number of each gun and other distinguishing marks upon it."[93]

April 4, 1863 (Saturday)
The General Assembly delegates listened to the reading of a new resolution.

> Georgia respectfully declines to accede to any of the plans which have been proposed by some of her sister States, or to any plan for the assumption or endorsement of Confederate debt by the several States; not because she feels any distrust of the success of the Confederate Government, for she entertains a firm confidence in the invincibility of a nation determined to be free; nor because she feels any indifference towards

[89] *OR*, ser. I, vol. 14:871.

[90] Ibid., 853.

[91] *Journal of the Senate at an Extra Session...March 25th, 1863*, April 1, 1863, 63.

[92] *ORN*, ser. I, vol. 13:805.

[93] Ibid., 822.

the common cause of independence, for she regards her own honor and existence as inseparable from the triumph of that cause, but because she is convinced that the credit of the Confederate Government is to be maintained, not by indorsements, but by payments, by the inauguration of such a system of payment as will inspire confidence in the early reduction of the public debt, and in its ultimate entire redemption.[94]

April 5, 1863 (Easter Sunday)

Federal ships circumnavigated between Charleston and Savannah, and Beauregard notified Brigadier General Mercer in Savannah of a pressing order. "All monitors are outside. Send movable column immediately to stop on Savannah turnpike, 2½ miles from new bridge across Ashley River. Siege train will come afterward or via Augusta. Inform when troops leave."[95]

April 6, 1863 (Monday)

Naval attacks continued in Charleston, and Beauregard sought a response from Georgia. "Enemy's ironclads (nine) have all crossed the bar, and are moving in as if to engage us. Can not the naval commander [at] Savannah be induced to make a descent at once on Port Royal and effect a diversion?"[96]

April 7, 1863 (Friday)

The General Assembly, per Governor Brown's request, addressed the issue of soldier pay. The body voted for Georgia's elected officials in Richmond "to bring this question before the Congress of the Confederate States, and to do all in their power, by their influence and their votes to procure the passage of an act to raise the monthly pay of privates in the army to twenty dollars per month, and of non-commissioned officers in like proportion...."[97]

April 8, 1863 (Wednesday)

In Charleston, Beauregard informed Brigadier General Mercer in Savannah to send surplus to South Carolina. "So long as enemy's monitors are here [Charleston] within this bar your position can be in no danger nor can you be attacked without notice. Send spare columbiad carriages here soon as possible."[98]

April 9, 1863 (Thursday)

The General Assembly heard the reading of a new resolution. This act would have "authorized and required" Governor Brown to "furlough all the troops now in the State service, except such portion as may be necessary to guard the bridges on the State Road, after the first of June until the first of January next, unless the position of the enemy and the defense of the State should, in his judgment, require them to be called out at an earlier day."[99]

April 10, 1863 (Friday) ◑

---

[94] *Journal of the Senate at an Extra Session...March 25th, 1863*, April 4, 1863, 79.

[95] *OR*, ser. I, vol. 14:881.

[96] *ORN*, ser. I, vol. 13:824.

[97] *Journal of the Senate at an Extra Session...March 25th, 1863*, April 7, 1863, 92.

[98] *OR*, ser. I, vol. 14:890.

[99] *Journal of the Senate at an Extra Session...March 25th, 1863*, April 9, 1863, 107.

Adjutant General Wayne directed the 33rd Regiment of Georgia Militia to work as military police. "A lawless mob is now engaged in pillaging the stores of the merchants of Milledgeville, and...city authorities...are either unable or indisposed to preserve the order and peace... assemble at once such portion of your regiment as can be immediately warned...[report] to the Mayor of Milledgeville, to act, under his orders, as a *posse comitatus* for the suppression of the riot and for the recovery and restoration of the goods pillaged to their respective owners."[100]

April 11, 1863 (Saturday)

President Davis received a vote of approval from the Georgia General Assembly, as they passed a resolution, which clarified the state's stance on Davis's conduct. Resolved: "That the ability and success...the Chief Magistrate of the Confederate States...has discharged the duties devolved upon him by his high and responsible office, have commanded the admiration and secured the confidence of his countrymen...Georgia hereby pledges herself to furnish all the means at her disposal to enable him to bring to a successful termination the cruel and unjust war now being waged upon her citizens."[101]

April 12, 1863 (Sunday)

An editor in Columbus offered a tongue-in-cheek commentary on generals thus far in the war. "We have Lees, Jacksons, Hills, Johnsons, and Beauregards, but no 'young Napoleons,' or 'fighting Joe Hookers,' or 'dashing Popes,' whose valor is so renowned that their presence causes their antagonists to change their front, and exhibit only their 'backs.'"[102]

April 13, 1863 (Monday)

The Joint Committee on Salt Supply delivered a report to the General Assembly. The committee stated they "are informed that on the first of April instant, there was as much as 40,000 bushels of salt at Saltville, Virginia, made for supply of Georgians and awaiting transportation. The daily manufacture at that place for consumption in this State is large, say about 1500 bushels...if successful transportation arrangements are accomplished...we will get for consumption in Georgia from that source, during the approaching season, as much as 275,000 bushels."[103]

April 14, 1863 (Tuesday)

Soldier remuneration served as the focus of Governor Brown's letter to President Davis. The General Assembly had passed a measure requesting an increase in pay for privates from eleven dollars to twenty dollars. Brown relayed the message to Davis and included this opening: "In conformity to the request of the General Assembly of this State, I have the honor herewith to transmit to you a copy of resolutions just passed, recommending an increase of pay to the privates and non-commissioned officers in the service of the

---

[100] Candler, *Confederate Records of the State of Georgia*, 2:440.

[101] "*Journal of the Senate at an Extra Session...March 25th, 1863*, April 11, 1863, 111.

[102] "Greatness vs. Grandeur," *Columbus Daily Sun*, April 12, 1863, sec. 2, https://gahistoricnewspapers.galileo.usg.edu/lccn/sn82014939/1863-04-12/ed-1/seq-2/.

[103] *Journal of the Senate at an Extra Session...March 25th, 1863*, April 13, 1863, 127.

Confederate States."[104]

April 15, 1863 (Wednesday)

In the General Assembly, the Senate approved a bill that would "authorize and empower the Mayor and Council of every city and town in this State to purchase land inside or outside of their corporate limits for cemeteries, and other public uses of said corporations."[105]

April 16, 1863 (Thursday)

The Georgia House of representatives passed a bill, which the Senate heard read today. "A bill to be entitled an act to provide for the suppression of domestic insurrection within the limits of the State of Georgia, and in the enforcement of the laws by establishing a State guard throughout the State and to abrogate all commissions heretofore granted to militia officers in this State."[106]

April 17, 1863 (Friday) ●

Members of the General Assembly spent the day dealing with myriad financial issues, including a "bill to increase and fix the compensation of the employees of the Penitentiary of this State during the present war between the United States and Confederate States."[107]

April 18, 1863 (Saturday)

Governor Brown acted on a resolution from the General Assembly, which sought to facilitate cotton trade with foreign nations. The commission bestowed upon C. G. Baylor, the right to serve as commissioner to the "Government of her Britannic Majesty, Victoria, Queen of Great Britain, to the Government of his Imperial Majesty, Napoleon III., Emperor of France, and the Governments and Empires respectively of Belgium, Prussia, The Hollands, Spain, Austria, Switzerland, Sardinia, Portugal, Russia, Norway, Sweden and Denmark, with powers, and charged with the duties set forth in the Instructions and Joint Resolution of the General Assembly of Georgia."[108]

April 19, 1863 (Sunday)

An appeal for help in securing the fortifications in Savannah reached Beauregard. "Captain McCrady (chief engineer of Georgia) has but 132 negroes engaged upon the earthworks near Savannah. Of these 102 will be discharged this week. The Legislature of Georgia...is much opposed to making another impressment, and is inclined to leave it to yourself or Brigadier-General [Hugh] Mercer to make a military impressment in accordance with the recent act of Congress." The dispatch closed, "This would lead to delay and might compromise the safety of Savannah, as the works for which the labor is required are important for her defense."[109]

April 20, 1863 (Monday)

Captain William Hazzard of the 4th Georgia Cavalry left a note for Federal officials on St.

---

[104] Candler, *Confederate Records of the State of Georgia*, 3:332.

[105] *Journal of the Senate at an Extra Session...March 25th, 1863*, April 15, 1863, 127.

[106] Ibid., April 16, 1863, 157.

[107] Ibid., April 17, 1863, 161.

[108] Candler, *Confederate Records of the State of Georgia*, 2:442.

[109] *OR*, ser. I, vol. 14:902.

Simons Island; at least the letter contained his signature as the writer. Complaining of atrocities former Federal troops had performed in the region, the dispatch detailed acts of "bushwhacking, shooting sentinels on posts," and a litany of other offenses. Naval Commander William Le Roy reported the found letter on this day and added his own observations. "From information that has reached me, I am fearful the complaint of the writer is but too true. I have been told that the negro troops who were at one time stationed upon this island committed grave outrages, firing upon the church, pulpit, gravestones, etc., conduct that can not be too highly reprobated."[110]

April 21, 1863 (Tuesday)

Commander Le Roy updated his dispatch of the previous day, indicating he could report "a boat from the *Potomska* came to me...through the inland passage and reported finding the wharf at Gascoins Bluff...on fire...it had burned sufficiently long to destroy the wharf. There being no residents at Gascoins Bluff, I can only come to the conclusion some of the rebel troops from the main landed during the night and committed the ravages...."[111]

April 22, 1863 (Wednesday)

After more than two years of war and the increasing effectiveness of the Federal blockade, newspapers and the editors found obtaining paper for printing as difficult a task as selecting the headline for the next edition. "Are our friends saving for us all the rags they can gather up? Save them and send them on by the earliest opportunity. We will pay cash for all clean linen and cotton rags that may be delivered to us—from 5 to 6 cents per pound."[112]

April 23, 1863 (Thursday)

Commander Andrew Drake's crew captured a sloop in Wassaw Sound. Drake stated one of his picket boats "chased upon the reef a small sloop, apparently loaded with cotton. She has no name, and no papers of any kind were found on board other than a few Southern newspapers of a late date, which I forward to you. The crew escaped to the shore in a small boat."[113]

April 24, 1863 (Friday)

The Confederate Congress passed a Tax Act, which would impact every entity in Georgia and the other Confederate states. "Each farmer or planter, after reserving twenty bushels of peas or beans, but not more than twenty bushels of both, for his own use, shall deliver to the Confederate Government, for its use, one-tenth of the peas, beans and ground peas produced and gathered by him during the present year."[114]

April 25, 1863 (Saturday) ◐

The war, well into the third year, placed a strain on supplies of most everything in Georgia. Looking ahead, Governor Brown took steps to gather matériel for soldiers. He wrote to

[110] *ORN*, ser. I, vol. 14:150.

[111] Ibid., 151.

[112] "Rags! Rags!," *Athens Southern Watchman*, April 22, 1863, sec. 2, https://gahistoricnewspapers.galileo.usg.edu/lccn/sn82014669/1863-04-22/ed-1/seq-2/.

[113] *ORN*, ser. I, vol. 14:158.

[114] *OR*, ser. IV, vol. 2:521.

Colonel Ira Foster in the Georgia Quartermaster Department. "Fearing that Georgia troops in Confederate service will suffer for want of shoes and clothing...you are hereby directed to draw your requisition for two millions of dollars...and you are further directed so to use said funds as will enable you to furnish next winter, if needed by Georgia troops, forty or fifty thousand pairs of shoes, and about thirty thousand suits of clothes."[115]

April 26, 1863 (Sunday)

Residents of Savannah received word Brigadier General Alexander Lawton prepared to leave the city. "This gallant Georgian, who has done so much to illustrate his State on the battlefield, is now in the city en-route for his command in Virginia. With the exception of stiffness in the limb and a paralysis of a portion of the foot...he has entirely recovered from the painful wound received in the battle of Sharpsburg."[116] Griffin hosted a missionary mass meeting, whose delegates determined the best ways to secure and distribute religious tracts, Bibles, and other items to the soldiers.

April 27, 1863 (Monday)

A newspaper editor questioned the sustainability of the state's leader. "Why must Governor Brown's reputation as Commander-in-Chief of our State forces grow less and less? Because in all his military reputation, he is obliged to *Wayne*."[117] This reference to Georgia's adjutant general Henry Wayne leaves one curious how Wayne found himself on the shelf in the newspaper office.

April 28, 1863 (Tuesday)

The Southern rail network continued to present challenges for generals in the field. Major General Pemberton wrote the war department regarding "the importance of connecting through Savannah the Albany, Gulf and Georgia Central Railroad. I have endeavored to impress upon the officers of the company the risk they run in neglecting to have this work done. This road is doing very little business, and might readily spare some of its rolling stock to other roads not so well supplied. If the war continues we shall need every locomotive in the Confederacy."[118]

April 29, 1863 (Wednesday)

Major General Hunter corresponded with Flag Officer Du Pont regarding a combined effort along the Savannah River. "In our last interview I had the honor of submitting to you a suggestion that a joint demonstration on the Savannah River, even though merely a demonstration, would have the good effect of keeping the enemy's coast in alarm and tending to prevent any large withdrawal of his forces to reinforce his other armies in Virginia or

---

[115] Candler, *Confederate Records of the State of Georgia*, 2:445.

[116] "Gen. A. R. Lawton," *Savannah Republican*, April 26, 1863, sec. 2, https://gahistoricnewspapers.galileo.usg.edu/lccn/sn85038496/1863-04-26/ed-1/seq-2/; Avery, *History of the State of Georgia*, 266.

[117] "April 27, 1863," *Savannah Republican*, April 27, 1863, sec. 2, https://gahistoricnewspapers.galileo.usg.edu/lccn/sn85038496/1863-04-27/ed-1/seq-2/.

[118] *OR*, ser. I, vol. 14:484.

the West."[119]

April 30, 1863 (Thursday)

The newspaper in Rome dispelled a rumor, which stated Federal Major General William Rosecrans hailed from Georgia. The news had passed, and as gossip often does, with each retelling of the account, the connection to Georgia grew stronger, even including the general's marriage to a lady from Roswell. Finally, Confederate chaplain Charles Qunitard laid rest to the story. "The statement is absolutely untrue. Miss Bullock…of Roswell, Cobb County Georgia, married Theodore Rosevelt [*sic*] Esq., a merchant of New York."[120]

May 1, 1863 (Friday)

Before adjourning their session, the Confederate Congress passed a resolution, offering "the thanks of Congress…to the officers and soldiers engaged in the defence of Fort McAllister, Georgia, on the first of February and third of March last, for the gallantry and endurance with which they successfully resisted the attacks of the ironclad vessels of the enemy."[121]

May 2, 1863 (Saturday)

Confederate officials reported on military action in north Alabama. "A cavalry force of the enemy, estimated at 1,000, has moved from Corinth, Miss., across Northern Alabama…[and on this date] destroyed the depot at Gadsden, Ala., and was threatening Rome, Ga., and the Georgia Railroad. General Forrest was pursuing them, and it is thought that they may endeavor to return through East Tennessee to their own lines."[122] The party referenced in this report were troopers (many on mules) under the command of Colonel Abel Streight.

May 3, 1863 (Sunday)

General Bragg summarized the culmination of Streight's Raid. "Between Rome and Gadsden, a party of 1,600 of the Federal Army surrendered to General [N. B.] Forrest, after several days' fighting…." Streight, in his post-campaign report, explained the forces behind his decision to surrender.

> After some maneuvering, Forrest sent in a flag of truce, demanding the surrender of my forces. I called a council of war…our ammunition was worthless, our horses and mules in a desperate condition, the men were overcome with fatigue and loss of sleep, and we were confronted by fully three times our number, in the heart of the enemy's country, and, although personally opposed to surrender…I yielded to the unanimous voice of my regimental commanders, and at once entered into negotiations with

---

[119] *ORN*, ser. I, vol. 14:164.

[120] "Gen. Rosencranz Not a Citizen of Georgia," *Rome Tri-Weekly Courier*, April 30, 1863, sec. 2, https://gahistoricnewspapers.galileo.usg.edu/lccn/sn85034102/1863-04-30/ed-1/seq-2/.

[121] *Statutes at Large of the Confederate States of America, Passed at the Third Session of the First Congress; 1863*, May 1, 1863, 170.

[122] *OR*, ser. I, vol. 23, pt. 2:814.

Forrest to obtain the best possible terms I could for my command, and at about noon...we surrendered as prisoners of war.[123]

May 4, 1863 (Monday)

The heavy fighting in Virginia, where many Georgians served in the Army of Northern Virginia, put a strain on facilities for convalescing soldiers. One agency acted. "It is stated that the Georgia Relief and Hospital Association have secured the St. Charles Hotel building, on Main street, in Richmond, which has been fitted up as a 'Wayside Home,' where Georgia soldiers will be received and made comfortable, and whose wholesome food and clean apartments the Georgia soldiers sojourning in Richmond are invited and expected to enjoy."[124]

May 5, 1863 (Tuesday, Cinco de Mayo)

"Such a jubilee, Rome has never experienced. Such raptures over Gen. Forrest and his brave men." The citizens of Rome continued to celebrate the capture of Colonel Streight and shouted, "Great Victory! Great Joy! The Yankees in Rome at Last."[125]

May 6, 1863 (Wednesday)

Governor Brown's message to General R. E. Lee, after Pemberton had enforced the measure in Charleston: "If the authorities of Augusta and Savannah desire martial law and General Pemberton thinks it a military necessity I have no objection."[126]

May 7, 1863 (Thursday)

The capture of Streight's troopers continued to make news, especially when a movement of the prisoners occurred. "Seventeen hundred prisoners, captured near Rome, arrived here [Atlanta] this evening. They are stalwart men."[127]

May 8, 1863 (Friday)

Major General Pemberton spent the day pleading for martial law in Savannah. To General R. E. Lee, he wrote, "The mayor and aldermen of Savannah do not wish martial law proclaimed. I think it should be." In a letter to Governor Brown, the general stated, "I am asked from Richmond whether the authorities wish martial law proclaimed in Savannah. I desire it. Answer."[128]

May 9, 1863 (Saturday)

Bring another big gun to the coast; Commander John Mercer Brooke planned to do so and notified Commander Richard Page in Savannah. "The 7-inch rifle, No. 1740 (Reg. No. 40), leaves Richmond for Savannah to-day. This gun is intended to replace 7-inch rifle No.

---

[123] *OR*, ser. I, vol. 23, pt. 1:294; Streight quote, 292.

[124] "Wayside Home," *Savannah Daily Morning News*, May 4, 1863, sec. 2, https://gahistoricnewspapers.galileo.usg.edu/lccn/sn82015886/1863-05-04/ed-1/seq-2/.

[125] "Great Victory! Great Joy!," *Rome Tri-Weekly Courier*, May 5, 1863, sec. 2, https://gahistoricnewspapers.galileo.usg.edu/lccn/sn85034102/1863-05-05/ed-1/seq-2/.

[126] Candler, *Confederate Records of the State of Georgia*, 3:210.

[127] "Forrest's Prisoners Arrived at Atlanta," *Savannah Daily Morning News*, May 7, 1863, sec. 2, https://gahistoricnewspapers.galileo.usg.edu/lccn/sn82015886/1863-05-07/ed-1/seq-2/.

[128] *OR*, ser. I, vol. 14:495–96.

1641, now mounted as bow gun of the *Atlanta*. The latter you will please place on shore in charge of the ordnance officer to await further orders. Equipments accompanying No. 1740 and not required on board will also be put in store."[129]

May 10, 1863 (Sunday) ◗

"After almost innumerable failures in military operations of an extensive character, it seems now to be the purpose of the enemy to give over his favorite scheme of conquest by 'Grand Army" movements, and resort to a sort of guerilla warfare. Their only remaining course is a predatory warfare."[130] This notion, which a newspaper editor offered, did not transpire.

May 11, 1863 (Monday)

Beauregard, updated Secretary of War Seddon on operations near Savannah. "With my cavalry I shall make a show of occupation of the…Districts and the line of the Charleston and Savannah Railroad; but it must not be lost sight of that my communications with Savannah can be cut by the enemy…and when that is done he will get possession of a large extent of rich rice lands, and large stores of rice…which would be a heavy loss."[131]

May 12, 1863 (Tuesday)

Beauregard informed Secretary Seddon of the available troop strength in his department. "Have ordered to General Pemberton, contrary to my opinion, [Brigadier General Nathan] Evans' brigade and one regiment, amounting to 2,700 men, leaving only 6,000 infantry available in whole South Carolina and Georgia; the other 1,000 will await further orders of Department."[132]

May 13, 1863 (Wednesday)

Along the Savannah River, Commander Richard Page transferred his control to Commander William Webb. "I am directed to transfer to you the command afloat on this station. The vessels are the following, viz: The ironclad steamer *Atlanta*, ironclad steamer *Georgia*, gunboat *Isondiga*, steamer *Oconee*, steamer *Resolute*, and steamer *Firefly* (tender). The *Isondiga* is now cruising in the waters between [St.] Augustine Creek and Wassaw Sound."[133]

May 14, 1863 (Thursday)

Confederate officials offered an opinion regarding the citizenry of Georgia, one calling for them to remain ready to take up arms. "Enroll every citizen, without regard to age, who is able to shoulder a gun. Divide those enrolled into ten companies…[plus] a company of mounted men…to act as scouts…[and] a battery of at least six pieces. It is not contemplated by this plan to require the citizens to drill, or to lose any time from their daily

---

[129] *ORN*, ser. I, vol. 14:695.

[130] "The Future—The Enemy's Programme," *Columbus Daily Sun*, May 10, 1863, sec. 2, https://gahistoricnewspapers.galileo.usg.edu/lccn/sn82014939/1863-05-10/ed-1/seq-2/.

[131] *OR*, ser. I, vol. 14:935.

[132] *OR*, ser. I, vol. 14:938.

[133] *ORN*, ser. I, vol. 14:697.

avocations."[134]

May 15, 1863 (Friday)

F. H. Morse, the U.S. consulate in London, wrote of concerns abroad regarding the blockade. "The rumor of an impending attack by a Confederate force on…our blockading squadrons has again reached me through different channels…now the necessitous circumstances of the Confederates may drive them to…attempt to break the blockade at some leading port, say Charleston, Wilmington, or some port on the Georgia or Florida coast, or possibly Mobile."[135]

May 16, 1863 (Saturday)

A newspaper account, or wake-up call, alerted folks in Muscogee County. "In view of the recent movements of the enemy in the west, and his daring raids through Alabama and Georgia, it is getting high time our citizens should begin to prepare for emergencies. Let every man in the county put his name to the paper and signify his willingness to defend his home when the hour of danger arrives."[136]

May 17, 1863 (Sunday) ●

The Etowah Iron Works received a new supervisor. "We are gratified to learn that this distinguished gentleman has been appreciated in Georgia and assigned to the control of an important interest. Ha has been chosen President of the Etowah Iron Mining Company, in Bartow county, who have one among the finest works of the kind in the country."[137] The new employee—Major General G. W. Smith.

May 18, 1863 (Monday)

An Augusta newspaper reported on Federal prisoners in the city, and the open confines they enjoyed. "The freedom of the city is one of the highest courtesies that can be extended to distinguished strangers, and this many of our blue-coated guests seemed to enjoy, roaming about the streets at pleasure, mingling freely with our citizens and servants, arguing trite political questions with some, and indulging in insolent swagger in the presence of others."[138]

May 19, 1863 (Tuesday)

Farmer-turned-soldier seemed the method needed to prevent further destruction of property and the theft of livestock and other goods. "Every town, every county, every settlement should be a camp of minute men," the *Confederate Union* argued. "The Yankee raids to

---

[134] "How to Organize the Citizens for Defence," *Atlanta Southern Confederacy*, May 14, 1863, sec. 2, https://gahistoricnewspapers.galileo.usg.edu/lccn/sn82014677/1863-05-14/ed-1/seq-2/.

[135] *ORN*, ser. I, vol. 14:234.

[136] "Local Defense," *Columbus Daily Sun*, May 16, 1863, sec. 2, https://gahistoricnewspapers.galileo.usg.edu/lccn/sn82014939/1863-05-16/ed-1/seq-2/.

[137] "Gen. Gustavus W. Smith," *Savannah Republican*, May 17, 1863, sec. 1, https://gahistoricnewspapers.galileo.usg.edu/lccn/sn85038496/1863-05-17/ed-1/seq-1/.

[138] "The Yankee Prisoners at Augusta," *Savannah Daily Morning News*, May 18, 1863, sec. 2, https://gahistoricnewspapers.galileo.usg.edu/lccn/sn82015886/1863-05-18/ed-1/seq-2/.

plunder burn and destroy would cease, and the contest would have to be settled on the great battle fields."[139]

May 20, 1863 (Wednesday)

Confederate naval Commander William Webb ensured his ship, the CSS *Atlanta*, and other vessels would receive needed fuel. His order to Engineer J. L. McCarthy stated, "You will keep the C.S. steamer *Resolute* filled with wood (leaving room for 80 or 100 tons of coal to supply the ironclads), and always be ready to move at a moment's notice."[140]

May 21, 1863 (Thursday)

Georgians learned of a change in military command involving Georgia soldiers, officers, and a battalion. "Lt. Col. M. A. Stovall having been promoted to a Brigadier Generalship, the Colonelcy of his old regiment devolves upon Maj. A. F. Rudler. Col. R. will be remembered as one of Gen. Walker's men in the Nicaragua affair, several years ago. Maj. Jas. T. Smith, of the 9th Ga., succeeds to the Lt. Colonelcy; he is a. native of Elbert county, Ga."[141]

May 22, 1863 (Friday)

Beauregard notified Brigadier General Mercer in Savannah of support needed in Mississippi. "General J. E. Johnston has just telegraphed for three good light batteries. I have ordered two from Charleston to report to him forthwith at Canton, Miss. You will please order one to do likewise from your district."[142]

May 23, 1863 (Saturday)

Commander Webb of the CSS *Atlanta* wrote to officers in charge of training camps in various Georgia locales. "I have directed Midshipman [William D.] Goode, who will deliver this letter, to proceed to the camps of instruction near Macon and Atlanta for the purpose of obtaining conscripts for the Navy. I shall be much obliged if you will afford him such assistance as may be in your power to expedite his orders."[143]

May 24, 1863 (Sunday)

An effective general needs artillery, and Brigadier General Ripley took action to pad his military coffers. "After several ineffectual efforts to have some arrangements made by which heavy guns can be rifled and banded at the arsenal (there being nobody at that establishment capable of the work), I have arranged with Mr. Cameron to put up a furnace himself, that the business can be proceeded with, and have ordered the iron from Atlanta."[144]

May 25, 1863 (Monday) ◐

Beauregard submitted an abstract of troop strength in the District of Georgia: 1,868

---

[139] "What Armed Citizens Can Do," *Milledgeville Confederate Union*, May 19, 1863, sec. 4, https://gahistoricnewspapers.galileo.usg.edu/lccn/sn85034083/1863-05-19/ed-1/seq-4/.

[140] *ORN*, ser. I, vol. 14:698.

[141] "Third Ga. Battalion—First GA. Regiment," *Columbus Daily Sun*, May 21, 1863, sec. 1, https://gahistoricnewspapers.galileo.usg.edu/lccn/sn82014939/1863-05-21/ed-1/seq-1/.

[142] *OR*, ser. I, vol. 14:347.

[143] *ORN*, ser. I, vol. 14:699.

[144] *OR*, ser. I, vol. 14:1022.

infantry soldiers, 1,812 cavalry troopers, and 2,206 artillery gunners.[145]

May 26, 1863 (Tuesday)

Commander Webb had requested guards from Captain Josiah Tattnall's command along the coast of Savannah. Tattnall's response: "There are but 36 marines…on this station unattached; 26 of these are in a course of drill for the ironclad *Savannah*, leaving but 10 for other service. If you wish a guard of 10 men at once for the *Georgia* in their present condition, you can have them, but I suggest the advantage of their remaining in barracks for a short time for the purpose of drill…."[146]

May 27, 1863 (Wednesday)

The CSS *Chattahoochee*, a ship constructed in Saffold, Georgia, exploded near Blounsttown, Florida. During the next year, officials hauled the remains of the vessel to Columbus, where she underwent repair. Captain Theodore Moreno recounted the tragic event, as the ship's "boiler exploded, killing 10 men almost instantly, wounding severely 8 more, and losing by drowning 4 more, who had jumped overboard immediately after the explosion."[147]

May 28, 1863 (Thursday)

Georgians, certainly those living in Macon, learned of a rumored Federal invasion from the coast. "There are reports from the coast of incipent [*sic*] movements for a raid from Brunswick. We place no faith in them, but it is well to be faithless."[148] News such as this often appeared in the local papers across Georgia and most other states. Editors, quick to grab an exclusive, often printed information with no foundation.

May 29, 1863 (Friday)

Commander Andrew Drake and his USS *Cimarron* captured a blockade runner in Wassaw Sound. Drake noted, "this morning, a small sloop was discovered standing down Wassaw Sound, which soon after hoisted a flag of truce, when I sent a boat to communicate. On the sloop's coming to the ship, she proved to be the *Evening Star*, with a crew of three white men…and laden with 9 bales of cotton. The accompanying papers were handed me by F. W. Rose, who claims to be the master of the sloop."[149]

May 30, 1863 (Saturday)

Rear Admiral Du Pont, eyes on the coast of Georgia, directed yet another ship to the area. He instructed Commander Alexander Rhind, "please proceed with the *Paul Jones* under your command to St. Simon's and take charge of the blockade of that sound and the adjacent waters, relieving Commander [William] Le Roy, who will give you such information as his experience may suggest. You will, on your way down, touch at Sapelo,

[145] Ibid., 953.

[146] *ORN*, ser. I, vol. 14:699.

[147] U.S. Naval History Division, *Civil War Naval Chronology*, 6:208; *OR*, ser. I, vol. 14:954.

[148] "Telegraphic," *Macon Daily Telegraph*, May 28, 1863, sec. 1, https://gahistoricnewspapers.galileo.usg.edu/lccn/sn82016437/1863-05-28/ed-1/seq-1/.

[149] *ORN*, ser. I, vol. 14:220.

communicating with the blockading vessel stationed there."[150]

May 31, 1863 (Sunday)

On the previous day, the CSS *Georgia* ran aground in St. Augustine Creek. Today, Commander Webb William Webb notified Secretary Mallory of what went awry. "I left my anchorage…above the obstructions in the Savannah River…and proceeded…about one-fourth of a mile…when, having passed all the most dangerous shoals and bars, and on making a short turn around a point of marsh, the main steam valve of the forward engine crushed…entirely disabled the engine, and the tide taking the vessel on the bow swung her into the marsh, where she is at present."[151]

June 1, 1863 (Monday)

Acting Master Edward Moses, USS *Fernandina*, reported on information gleaned from "two contrabands that escaped out of the Altamaha River, near Darien….. They state that the rebels are cotton-cladding three steamers near Darien, preparatory to making an attack in this vicinity; there is no doubt but what this can be relied upon. I am aware they have two steamers in that river previous to this."[152]

June 2, 1863 (Monday)

The citizen-soldiers of Floyd County received a call to action! "The various companies that have recently been organized in this county, will meet in Rome today, for the purpose of forming a Legion. Let everybody come, and help to perfect the *organization.*"[153]

June 3, 1863 (Wednesday)

Via Special Orders, No. 249, Major General Halleck notified Hunter of a change in Federal command, one, which included the military district encompassing Georgia. "By direction of the President Major-General Hunter is temporarily relieved from command of the Department of the South, and will report to the Adjutant-General for special duty in Washington. Brig. Gen. [Quincy] Q. A. Gillmore is assigned by the President to the temporary command of the Department of the South."[154]

June 4, 1863 (Thursday)

A combined operation left Georgia and moved to attack Bluffton, South Carolina. Naval Lieutenant Commander George Bacon reported,

> I proceeded to Fort Pulaski and reported to Colonel Barton, the commander of the fort, as officer in command of naval forces for the attack on Bluffton. He immediately gave orders that the army gunboat *Mayflower* should be placed under my command. I left…and came to anchor off the south end of Hilton Head Island and awaited the

---

[150] Ibid., 222.

[151] Ibid., 704.

[152] Ibid., 227.

[153] "For Home Defenc.," *Rome Tri-Weekly Courier*, June 2, 1863, sec. 2, https://gahistoric-newspapers.galileo.usg.edu/lccn/sn85034102/1863-06-02/ed-1/seq-2/.

[154] *OR*, ser. I, vol. 14:464.

arrival of the army gunboat and transports, which were of lighter draft, and were to join me at 11.30 p.m."[155]

June 5, 1863 (Friday)

Certain unscrupulous individuals continued their efforts to profit from the war. "To obtain monopoly, so as to control prices as heretofore, these heartless speculators and extortioners are willing to risk a good deal in order to save themselves, if possible. The people can have no sympathy whatever with such operators, whose God is Mammon, and whose country is their own narrow hearts."[156]

June 6, 1863 (Saturday)

Secretary Seddon notified Governor Brown of a new call upon Georgia. "I am instructed by the President...to make on you a requisition for 8,000 men...for service therein, for the period of six months from August 1 next, unless in the intermediate time a volunteer force, organized under the law for local defense and special service, of at least an equal number be mustered and reported as subject to his call for service within your State."[157]

June 7, 1863 (Sunday)

Glancing toward the future, and optimistic of Confederate victory, a newspaper editor in Columbus offered thoughts on the border states. "After the North shall have fought us long enough to understand that 'reconstruction' is an absurdity, and that the only road to an honorable and permanent peace consists in the unconditional acknowledgment of our independence, a very important question will arise as to boundary lines." The writer suggested, "Maryland, Kentucky and Missouri, will still remain disputed territories. To settle this dispute will be secondary only to the settlement of the controversy now going on between the eleven Confederated States of the South and the States of the old Federal Union."[158]

June 8, 1863 (Monday) ◐

Captain William Hazzard with the 4th Georgia Cavalry reported on an affair near Brunswick. "[C]ouriers reached camp about 10 o'clock with information that two gunboats and one transport towing two large boats loaded with troops had started from Saint Simon's Island in the direction of Brunswick. Previous information justified the belief that a temporary landing in Brunswick would be attempted...the heavy boom of cannon gave assurance...the Brunswick pickets, had disputed a landing." Hazzard detailed events as they unfolded, "The firing was incessant for about three-quarters of an hour, when the boats withdrew. After firing some fifty shots the one threatening the salt works returned and joined the other at Brunswick. We lost one horse...but were blessed in losing no one; not

---

[155] *ORN*, ser. I, vol. 14:238.

[156] "Wheat Speculation," *Savannah Republican*, June 5, 1863, sec. 2, https://gahistoricnewspapers.galileo.usg.edu/lccn/sn85038496/1863-06-05/ed-1/seq-2/.

[157] Candler, *Confederate Records of the State of Georgia*, 3:343–44.

[158] "The Border States," *Columbus Daily Sun*, June 7, 1863, sec. 2, https://gahistoricnewspapers.galileo.usg.edu/lccn/sn82014939/1863-06-07/ed-1/seq-2/.

even a wound was inflicted."[159]

June 9, 1863 (Tuesday)

A Confederate naval officer made a few changes in the skippers of the various ships in his flotilla. Lieutenant Thomas Pelot received orders to take his *Oconee* to Savannah and "report to Flag-Officer Tattnall, and inform him that you are ordered to turn over to him the steamer *Oconee* and the officers and crew…after you have deliverd [*sic*] the officers and crew and the steamer to Commander Tattnall…return…and take charge of the steamer *Resolute*, lying off Thunderbolt."[160]

June 10, 1863 (Wednesday)

Rear Admiral Du Pont learned of a possible sneak attack from the Confederates. "Information has just been received from five deserters, who arrived this morning at Fort Pulaski from Savannah, that the rebel ironclad *Atlanta* is now lying at Thunderbolt battery, and will probably to-night attack the *Cimarron*, after which, it is said, she will proceed to Ossabaw." The officer ordered Lieutenant Commander L. Howard Newman to "on receipt of this communication, withdraw the *Dawn*, and lie outside the bar and maintain an outside blockade."[161]

June 11, 1863 (Thursday)

Destruction in Darien provided the news for the day, as Federal boats shelled the town, and soldiers disembarked from the ships to do additional damage. Soldiers under the commands of colonels James Montgomery and Robert Gould Shaw, including United States Colored troops (USCT), attacked the town. Captain William A. Lane of the 20th Georgia Cavalry Battalion reported that "Two steamers and two gunboats made their appearance in Doboy Sound…proceeded…southward along the channel known as the inland pass from Savannah to Brunswick…in a few minutes were vigorously shelling our pickets…in thirty minutes…Darien was being burned…I suppose that 300 or 400 landed. They remained until the town was consumed, when they (the vessels) went out into the sound."[162]

June 12, 1863 (Friday)

Anniversaries of important days—whether a wedding, the birth of a child, or change in military responsibility—are when each person celebrates their own special occasions. On this day, Brigadier General Quincy Gillmore, perhaps, made note of his special time as the new Federal commander of the district encompassing Georgia. He wrote to Halleck, stating "Major-General Hunter relinquished and I assumed command…I shall…make a full report by next steamer."[163]

June 13, 1863 (Saturday)

Colonel Shaw, in a letter to his family, wrote of the countryside near Darien, where the

---

[159] *OR*, ser. I, vol. 14:315.

[160] *ORN*, ser. I, vol. 14:709–10.

[161] Ibid., 249.

[162] *OR*, ser. I, vol. 14:318. For more information on the destruction of Darien, see S. King, *Darien: The Death and Rebirth of a Southern Town.*

[163] *ORN*, ser. I, vol. 14:246.

officer and his 54th Massachusetts Infantry Regiment remained. "A deserted homestead is always a sad sight, but here in the South we must look a little deeper than the surface, and then we see that every such overgrown plantation, and empty house, is a harbinger of freedom to the slaves, and every lover of his country, even if he have no feeling for the slaves themselves, should rejoice."[164]

June 14, 1863 (Sunday)

A call for home defense beckoned folks in Columbus to respond. "The people of Georgia and Alabama have been urged, time and again, to organize themselves into military companies for Home Defence. These exhortations should be the more forcible when we consider the recent predatory mode of Yankee warfare. It would seem that we have had sufficient experience already to arouse us to action."[165]

June 15, 1863 (Monday)

As one studies history, evidence grows that some things never change. Governor Brown struggled to get the wealthiest Georgians to pay their income taxes, so he acted. "You are, therefore, directed to order the Tax Collectors of the respective counties of this State to assess and collect a tax of $50,000 from each person or body corporate in this State who shall fail or refuse to make a return of his, her or their profits, made or realized as aforesaid."[166]

June 16, 1863 (Tuesday) ●

One year later, and the governor continued to seek clarification from the Confederate War Department on Georgia soldiers. "The privilege of organizing companies for local defence, and of tendering them to the President for acceptance, is allowed to the people by the act of Congress. I am not authorized to restrict or deny it. If you will undertake to direct such organizations, and can thus obtain the whole number required in Georgia for the purpose explained, I will thankfully accept your aid, and from this time leave the matter in your hands for execution."[167]

June 17, 1863 (Wednesday)

Naval action in Wassaw Sound dominated the day's events in Georgia. Captain John Rodgers of the USS *Weehawken* reported on his prize catch. "At 5:15 [a.m.], being distant from him about 300 yards, we commenced firing. At 5:30 the enemy hauled down his colors and hoisted the white flag, we having fired five shots; steamed near the ironclad and ordered a boat to be sent alongside. At 5:45 Lieutenant [Joseph] Alexander came on board to surrender the Confederate ironclad *Atlanta*." Commander Webb of the CSS *Atlanta* noted, "All this time we were hard and fast aground. The tide did not rise high enough for an hour and a half to float the ship, and seeing the effects of the *Weehawken*'s shot, and the position she and the monitor *Nahant* had assumed on each quarter of the *Atlanta*, where my guns

---

[164] Shaw and Duncan, *Blue-Eyed Child of Fortune*, 345.

[165] "Home Defence," *Columbus Daily Sun*, June 14, 1863, sec. 2, https://gahistoricnewspapers.galileo.usg.edu/lccn/sn82014939/1863-06-14/ed-1/seq-2/.

[166] Candler, *Confederate Records of the State of Georgia*, 2:455.

[167] Ibid., 3:354.

could not be brought to bear on them, to save life I was induced to surrender."[168]

June 18, 1863 (Thursday)

A group of men in eastern Georgia took out newspaper notices to assist in their efforts to recruit new militia units. "We respectfully invite our fellow-citizens of Scriven county, to meet in Sylvania, on the first Monday in July next, for the purpose of forming a military organization in each militia district, in order to protect ourselves against threatened Yankee raid."[169]

June 19, 1863 (Friday)

Secretary Seddon wrote to Governor Brown and detailed his plan for mustering in Georgia soldiers.

> As far as I can gather your wishes, you prefer organizations under State authority and their acceptance as State troops. I do not deem it desirable, chiefly on account of the limited term of their proposed service engagement (six months), that they should be mustered and received as militia; but if you can organize State volunteer organizations of equal duration and equal liability to call for special service as emergency may demand and tender them for acceptance to the Confederate Government, they will be cheerfully accepted and put on like footing as constituting when in service part of the Provisional Army.[170]

June 20, 1863 (Saturday)

A newspaper editor in Rome alerted folks of the changing nature of raids. "In war 'raids' are understood to be 'hostile incursions,' but as now practiced by the Federals, they are, 'incursions,' for the purpose of robbing, stealing, murdering, burning, destroying, devastating and raping. Friends, are you ready for these things? Are you ready to meet the Northern Comanchees [*sic*]?"[171]

June 21, 1863 (Sunday)

Rear Admiral Du Pont congratulated Captain John Rodgers and the crew of the USS *Weehawken*. "I take great pleasure in acknowledging your official report of the capture of the rebel ironclad steamer *Atlanta*, and congratulate you at having deprived the enemy of their most powerful vessel of war. You will please express to your officers and men…my commendation of their gallant services in this as on all other occasions."[172]

June 22, 1863 (Monday)

One year before Sherman's forces entered Georgia, Governor Brown offered an astute projection to all Georgians. "It is not doubted that our enemies are increasing their cavalry

---

[168] *ORN*, ser. I, vol. 14:265, 291.

[169] "Attention Scriven County," *Savannah Republican*, June 18, 1863, sec. 2, https://gahistoricnewspapers.galileo.usg.edu/lccn/sn85038496/1863-06-18/ed-1/seq-2/; see Krakow, *Georgia Place-Names*, 206, for history of the spelling of the county.

[170] Candler, *Confederate Records of the State of Georgia*, 3:357–58.

[171] "Raids," *Rome Tri-Weekly Courier*, June 20, 1863, sec. 2, https://gahistoricnewspapers.galileo.usg.edu/lccn/sn85034102/1863-06-20/ed-1/seq-2/.

[172] *ORN*, ser. I, vol. 14:271.

force and making preparations to send raids of mounted men through Georgia, as well as other States, to burn all public property in our cities, destroy our railroad bridges, workshops, factories, mills and provisions, leaving our country, now the home of a happy people, little better than a desolate waste behind them."[173]

June 23, 1863 (Tuesday)

Continuing to endorse the horrid institution of slavery, a newspaper editor encouraged,

> Rest assured, People of Georgia, and of the Confederate States, God will not permit such a People to subjugate you, and destroy an Institution sanctioned, more than two thousand years ago, under his own unchangeable and irreversible seal. Do not despond therefore, when your loved ones die—when your property is taken away—when you witness the destruction of your cities and towns, and hear the mad ravings of the infuriated foe. Watch on, wait on. Let every man and boy keep bis gun and his ammunition in good order and ready for use.[174]

June 24, 1863 (Wednesday) ◐

The U.S. Navy received notice of a new commander for the South Atlantic Blockading Squadron, which encompassed the coast of Georgia. Secretary Wells informed Du Pont that "Rear-Admiral [Andrew] Foote being unable from sickness to proceed to Port Royal, Rear-Admiral [John] Dahlgren, who was a pointed next in command, has been ordered to repair thither and relieve you of the command...you will turn over to him all unexecuted orders."[175]

June 25, 1863 (Thursday)

Confederate fortunes in Vicksburg grew bleak, and President Davis telegraphed Beauregard for reinforcements, asking, "Can you give him [General Johnston] further aid, without the probable loss of Charleston and Savannah? I need not state to you that the issue is vital to the Confederacy." Beauregard responded from his headquarters in Charleston, South Carolina. "Telegram is received. No more troops can be sent away from this department without losing railroad and country between here and Savannah. Georgetown district would have also to be abandoned."[176]

June 26, 1863 (Friday)

Governor Brown continued to bicker with the Confederate War Department regarding the appointment of officers in Georgia regiments. Brown believed he enjoyed this prerogative; President Davis disagreed. Secretary Seddon hoped the most recent problem, which involved the 51st Georgia Infantry, might find a peaceful resolution. "It is to be regretted that this difference of opinion should have existed, and that the expression of your views should have been given such direction as may possibly excite some dissatisfaction among

---

[173] Candler, *Confederate Records of the State of Georgia*, 2:456.

[174] "Will Any Man or Woman Despond?," *Milledgeville Confederate Union*, June 23, 1863, sec. 3, https://gahistoricnewspapers.galileo.usg.edu/lccn/sn85034083/1863-06-23/ed-1/seq-3/.

[175] *ORN*, ser. I, vol. 14:296.

[176] *OR*, ser. I, vol. 28, pt. 2:162–63.

the officers of that gallant regiment. It is hoped that upon reconsideration you will concur with the views herein expressed." Seddon referenced the recent Conscription Act, specifically the clause "all vacancies shall be filled by the President...."[177]

June 27, 1863 (Saturday)

Beauregard verified the Federal command change in the navy and indicated the positions of his opponent's various vessels. "Major-General Hunter has been relieved of the command of the Federal troops in this department by Brigadier-General Gillmore, the officer who conducted the operations that resulted in the reduction of Fort Pulaski. At present, three of the enemy's iron-clads are in the North Edisto and two at Hilton Head, leaving one still in Warsaw [Wassaw]_Sound."[178]

June 28, 1863 (Thursday)

Secretary Mallory in the Confederate Naval Department received news from Flag Officer William W. Hunter in Savannah. "I respectfully report to you that I have this day arrived at this place, in obedience to your order of the 22d instant, received by me at Richmond, Va., on the 23d instant." Hunter issued General Orders, No. 1, which stipulated, among other points, "The national flag adopted by the late Congress will be hoisted on all vessels under my command on the 1st of July next, or as soon thereafter as it can be procured."[179]

June 29, 1863 (Monday)

Rear Admiral Du Pont updated work on the recently captured Confederate ironclad. "Drawings and descriptions of the *Atlanta* have been prepared and...forwarded to the Department. Inventories of all articles found on board have been made and a board of competent officers, having no pecuniary interest in the capture, has been appointed to appraise the vessel, her equipments, etc.... Repairs have already been made in part and are still progressing...."[180]

June 30, 1863 (Tuesday)

Commandant Josiah Tattnall notified Flag Officer William Hunter of a new boat. "The ironclad steamer *Savannah* being completed in all respects and ready for service, with the exception of her officers, in which she is deficient, I have the pleasure to transfer her to your command with the wish that her services prove honorable to yourself and advantageous to the Confederacy."[181]

July 1, 1863 (Wednesday)

Work on taking inventory of the CSS *Atlanta* and assessing a price on the ironclad ended. Captain William Taylor reported the "Hull $250,000, Machinery 80,000," and various other components onboard brought the total value to "$350,829.26."[182] Adjusted for

[177] Candler, *Confederate Records of the State of Georgia*, 359–60.

[178] *OR*, ser. I, vol. 28, pt. 2:170.

[179] *ORN*, ser. I, vol. 14:712.

[180] Ibid., 302.

[181] Ibid., 713.

[182] Ibid., 277; Friedman, "The Inflation Calculator," https://westegg.com/inflation/infl.cgi?money=350829&first=1863&final=2019.

inflation to modern day, the CSS *Atlanta* would be valued at $7,384,081.33.

July 2, 1863 (Thursday)

A man from Elberton wrote Vice President Stephens seeking the Confederate official's intervention on behalf of the gentleman's brother. "There are some people in Lincoln and Wilkes who have never been to the war and who never intend to go, trying to have him [the brother] conscripted for what reason I am unable to say except that he attends strictly to his own business and will fight if he is pushed upon. Can you do anything for him without subjecting yourself to any thing unpleasant!"[183]

July 3, 1863 (Friday)

Major Edward Anderson of the 24th Georgia Cavalry Battalion reported on an expedition to Ossabaw Island. "With a party of 9 men, I landed there just about daylight.... We scouted it carefully up to McDonald's place, where we arrived about 12 m., without seeing any sign of the enemy, excepting a few abandoned picket posts."[184]

July 4, 1863 (Saturday) (Independence Day)

Major Anderson and his force continued to scout Ossabaw Island. "We left our lair before day; but on our way Captain (R. H.) Wylly, of Company C, was taken suddenly and violently sick, and we had to return without accomplishing it. On our way back, however, we paid a formal visit to McDonald's, and surprised and captured there a Yankee picket post of 2 men; also, we captured 8 negroes."[185]

July 5, 1863 (Sunday)

Having finished taking inventory of the CSS *Atlanta*, Du Pont, in one of his final acts before turning command of the South Atlantic Blockading Squadron over to Dahlgren, released a prisoner. "So soon as the wounded men of the captured ironclad steamer *Atlanta* can dispense with the services of Assistant Surgeon Robert R. Gibbes, formerly of that steamer, he is to be sent by flag of truce either to Charleston or Savannah."[186]

July 6, 1863 (Monday)

Secretary Mallory afforded greater authority to Flag Officer William Hunter in Savannah: "You are hereby authorized to appoint master's mates for your vessels should their services be required, subject to the approval of this Department. It may afford an opportunity of promoting deserving men."[187]

July 7, 1863 (Tuesday) ◑

Searching for reinforcements to fill ranks of Confederate armies in other areas, General Cooper telegraphed Beauregard. "Any disposable force would be of most essential service. If you conclude any can be spared, prepare them for movement, and report at once by telegram."[188]

---

183 Toombs, Stephens, and Cobb, *Correspondence*, 620.

184 *OR*, ser. I, vol. 28, pt. 1:193.

185 Ibid.

186 *ORN*, ser. I, vol. 14:268–69.

187 Ibid., 717.

188 *OR*, ser. I, vol. 28, pt. 2:181.

July 8, 1863 (Wednesday)

The fighting continued, and casualties mounted. Officers worked tirelessly to keep men at arms, both at the state and national level. "All those who desires to Volunteer in the defense of the State, are hereby notified that a list will be opened on t-morrow, at the City Sheriff's office, in the Court House, for the purpose of forming a company. A citizen of Savannah will pay a bounty of Twenty-Five Dollars to each Volunteer as soon as the Company is organized."[189]

July 9, 1863 (Thursday)

Flag Officer William Hunter wrote General Cooper of a deed that forced him to discipline an officer. "A writ of habeas corpus has been served on the commanding officer of the *Georgia* [Lieutenant Thomas Pelot] for the discharge of one of her crew, which will determine a precedent to discharge the whole of this crew, who are a body of well-drilled men and constitute a very important part of my naval defense here."[190]

July 10, 1863 (Friday)

The Confederate War Department converted an officer from land to sea. "Lieutenant [Washington] Gwathmey, C. S. Navy, now serving with the Army, will proceed without delay to Savannah, Ga., and report to Flag-Officer W. W. Hunter, commanding naval squadron, etc... for assignment to duty."[191] Gwathmey would command the CSS *Georgia.*

July 11, 1863 (Saturday)

On the heels of defeat at Gettysburg and the loss of Vicksburg, Georgians worried about their future. A newspaper editor proposed a plan for reinforcing the Confederate armies in the field. "The three thousand militia officers, heretofore foolishly kept out of service, might, if properly organized, successfully defend Georgia from Yankee raids. Will they now throw themselves into the breach and show themselves men? We have reason to hope they will. They have a personal interest, in common with their fellow citizens already in the field, in the defense of our State."[192]

July 12, 1863 (Sunday)

Fearing threat of a Confederate vessel, Rear Admiral Dahlgren ordered Commander John Downes to take the USS *Nahant* to Wassaw Sound. "In consequence of information received respecting the probable movement of the rebel ironclad *Savannah*, you will please proceed at once to Wassaw Sound, Georgia, and assume charge of the blockade in those waters."[193]

July 13, 1863 (Monday)

---

[189] "Military Service, under the Call of the Gov. of Georgia," *Savannah Republican*, July 8, 1863, sec. 2, https://gahistoricnewspapers.galileo.usg.edu/lccn/sn85038496/1863-07-08/ed-1/seq-2/.

[190] *ORN*, ser. I, vol. 14:715.

[191] Ibid., 724.

[192] "Necessity for Action," *Columbus Daily Sun*, July 11, 1863, sec. 2, https://gahistoricnewspapers.galileo.usg.edu/lccn/sn82014939/1863-07-11/ed-1/seq-2/.

[193] *ORN*, ser. I, vol. 14:337.

Regiments North and South needed chaplains; shortages continued throughout the war, robbing many young men from hearing the word of God. Georgia tried. "The Domestic board has appointed six additional missionaries to the army—four of whom are pastors who have volunteered to spend a few months in the service, the Board meeting their expenses. How many will go? Has not Georgia some that she could spare?"[194]

July 14, 1863 (Tuesday)

Robert Toombs wrote to Vice President Stephens from Washington, Georgia. "I see by the papers you are in Richmond. I hope you will stay there, if your advice will be received. We are gloomy and in great trouble; North, South, East and West the clouds look dark and threatening. I feel but little like going into civil life; we must fight this thing out, and I shall try to be with the militia of Georgia in the prospective defense of our homes."[195]

July 15, 1863 (Wednesday) ●

The Confederate Navy Department notified Flag Officer Hunter of new assignments in his squadron. "Commander [Robert] R. F. Pinkney and Lieutenants [Lewis] L. R. Hill and William E. Hudgins have been ordered to the *Savannah*; Lieutenant [Washington] Gwathmey to the command of the *Georgia*, and Third Assistant Engineer John C. Phillips to the same vessel; Lieutenant [Hamilton] Dalton to the squadron."[196]

July 16, 1863 (Thursday)

Flag Officer Hunter notified Secretary Mallory on action taken against a sailor. "The writ of habeas corpus in the case of one of the crew of the *Georgia* has been decided against the Government. This, as a precedent, will cause most of the crew to be discharged."[197]

July 17, 1863 (Friday)

A dispatch from Flag Officer Josiah Tattnall to Flag Officer Hunter: "Supposing that the attack on Charleston was to be made immediately, and that the absence of the party sent from Savannah would be limited, I ordered Lieutenant C. B. Oliver, the ordnance officer of this station, to report to you for duty. His services here are absolutely necessary, and as there appears no apprehension of an immediate assault on Charleston I request you to order his return to his duties at Savannah."[198]

July 18, 1863 (Saturday)

Tattnall, writing from Savannah, got straight to the point in his dispatch to Flag Officer William Hunter. "You will direct the detachment of officers and men and arms sent you from my command to be returned to me immediately."[199]

July 19, 1863 (Sunday)

"The Yankees, always up to tricks, think everybody as mean and treacherous as themselves.

---

[194] "Army Missionaries," *Washington [Georgia] Christian Index*, July 13, 1863, https://gahistoricnewspapers.galileo.usg.edu/lccn/2001233946/1863-07-13/ed-1/seq-2/.

[195] Toombs, Stephens, and Cobb, *Correspondence*, 621.

[196] *ORN*, ser. I, vol. 14:726.

[197] Ibid., 716.

[198] Ibid., 727.

[199] Ibid.

They are now trying to create the impression that Mr. Stephens was sent to Washington, not for the purpose avowed, but in order to 'declare the Jeff. Davis government' when he got there.—The suggestion is as cowardly as it is false. It is very well for them to begin framing excuses, for their failure to treat on so sacred a question as the humanities of war."[200] On behalf of the Confederate government, Vice President Stephens had attempted a trip to Washington to discuss prisoner exchanges; President Lincoln refused to meet.

July 20, 1863 (Monday)

Flag Officer Hunter worked to regain his reinforcements sent previously to Charleston and asked Secretary Mallory for "early action on this subject, from the fact that the greater part of the *Georgia* crew are about to be discharged under a writ of habeas corpus, and the detachment of my command now at Charleston leaves the steamers *Savannah* and *Isondiga* nearly stripped of officers, men, and small arms."[201]

July 21, 1863 (Tuesday)

Concerned over the vulnerability to Federal approach in Savannah, Brigadier General Hugh Mercer wrote to Secretary of War John Seddon in Richmond.

> While all the principal points around the city have been as well fortified as the amount of labor hitherto procurable has permitted, at least two flank approaches of the highest importance have been necessarily neglected. First. The Georgia Central Railroad, the principal artery of communication with the interior, can be cut by the enemy whenever he shall have succeeded in forcing one of our outposts, and, this effected, Savannah will be in a condition of regular investment and siege. Second. Fort Bartow, at Causton's Bluff, my principal reliance for holding the Savannah River batteries, will itself prove ineffective, unless the peninsula in its rear be defended. This peninsula cannot be held, with all the troops I can hope to obtain, unless fortified, and once in the possession of the enemy, he would be enabled (1) to reduce Fort Bartow by siege, and (2) to shell out the river batteries by a reverse fire. I consider it certain that no number of troops we can possibly obtain in the present circumstances of the Confederacy can possibly hold these two vital points without the assistance of fortifications.[202]

July 22, 1863 (Wednesday)

People in Athens learned of an attempt to repair arms in their city. "The Sheriff and his deputy be authorized to receive all guns that need repairs, from such persons as have joined companies for home defence; that these guns be turned over to Cook & Bro.; who propose to repair them—the owner paying the actual cost to the workman doing the repairs."[203]

---

[200] "Mr. Stephens' Mission," *Savannah Republican*, July 19, 1863, sec. 2, https://gahistoricnewspapers.galileo.usg.edu/lccn/sn85038496/1863-07-19/ed-1/seq-2/; J. Davis, *Papers*, 9:244–45.

[201] *ORN*, ser. I, vol. 14:730.

[202] *OR*, ser. I, vol. 28, pt. 2:215.

[203] "Arms for Home Defence," *Athens Southern Watchman*, July 22, 1863, sec. 2, https://gahistoricnewspapers.galileo.usg.edu/lccn/sn82014669/1863-07-22/ed-1/seq-2/.

July 23, 1863 (Thursday) ◐
"I have this day transferred to the *Georgia*, under your command, all the available men at my disposal, that you may therewith prepare and keep in readiness the *Georgia* for immediate service. You will cause her crew to be stationed, drilled, and instructed in their duties at the battery as soon as possible, and in every respect keep your command in the best condition for service."[204] An order to Lieutenant Gwathmey received from Flag Officer Hunter in Savannah.

July 24, 1863 (Friday)
A Confederate staff officer wrote to Savannah Mayor Thomas Holcombe of military activity in Charleston and the importance of success in South Carolina on Savannah. The officer reminded the mayor "every effort made toward an effectual defense of Charleston is really the surest way to defend Savannah. A successful war cannot be carried on without a concentration, at the proper time, of all the available forces at command, on the decisive point."[205]

July 25, 1863 (Saturday)
Secretary Seddon notified the governor on the status of a Georgia regiment. "Your Excellency must perceive that the Fifty-first Georgia regiment stands upon exactly the same footing as the troops tendered by the States or volunteering under this Act [February 1861 act to raise provisional forces], and that this Act contains not the slightest intimation that the troops received under it were received as State militia. There is a direct provision that a portion of the officers shall be appointed by the President."[206]

July 26, 1863 (Sunday)
Citizens in Columbus honored the Wilkes County native who received a mortal wound during the Battle of Gettysburg: "We understand that an arrangement has been made, with the pastors of the several Churches, to suspend services in all the Churches this morning except those at the Presbyterian Church, in order that our people may have an opportunity of listening to the funeral sermon by Dr. Higgins at the latter Church commemorative of the death of [Brigadier] Gen. Paul J. Semmes."[207]

July 27, 1863 (Monday)
Secretary Seddon responded to Brigadier General Mercer's request to "impress negro labor." "The power to impress in such exigency must be given," the secretary consented, "but the terms of the law should be strictly pursued. It is very desirable the impressment should be made under the authority of the State of Georgia, but, in case of the Governor's refusal, the general must act under the Congressional law."[208]

July 28, 1863 (Tuesday)

---

[204] *ORN*, ser. I, vol. 14:733.

[205] *OR*, ser. I, vol. 28, pt. 2:224–25.

[206] Candler, *Confederate Records of the State of Georgia*, 3:379.

[207] "Church To Day," *Columbus Daily Sun*, July 26, 1863, sec. 2, https://gahistoricnewspapers.galileo.usg.edu/lccn/sn82014939/1863-07-26/ed-1/seq-2/.

[208] *OR*, ser. I, vol. 28, pt. 2:215–16.

Growing increasingly concerned of a Federal incursion into the heart of the state, Governor Brown notified officials in Milledgeville. "In case of attack," he wrote, "it will be the duty of the State House officers and clerks to see that the Treasury, the Public Records, Papers and other valuable articles in the State House are removed to places of safety."[209]

July 29, 1863 (Wednesday)

Continuing to create exemptions to keep certain occupations out of the war, Governor Brown notified officials in Baldwin County: "You will exempt from the draft on the 4th day of August next, should one become necessary in your county, the editors and all other persons connected with, and necessary to the publication of, each and all newspapers in your county, upon their furnishing to you evidence that they have united themselves with one of the companies formed under the orders already issued for the local defence of the county of Richmond."[210]

July 30, 1863 (Thursday)

Colonel Gorgas informed the governor of South Carolina of regulations to receive ordinance from Georgia. "Please to cause requisitions to be addressed by colonels of regiments, showing the strength of the command, to Col. [George Washington] G. W. Rains, commanding C. S. Arsenal, Augusta, Ga. Requisitions must be approved by the mustering officer of the Confederate service."[211]

July 31, 1863 (Friday)

Commander John Beaumont received orders to relocate his USS *Nantucket* from Port Royal to the coast of Georgia. Commander William Reynolds informed Beaumont, "You will be taken in tow by the *Prometheus* when you are ready for sea, and you will proceed to Wassaw and relieve Commander [John] Downes, who will give you a copy of his instructions from the admiral and all the information which he possesses concerning the situation at Wassaw. You can communicate with me by way of Fort Pulaski, from whence to this place there is a telegraph."[212]

August 1, 1863 (Saturday)

Acting Master Woodbury Polley's USS *Madgie* started taking on water in St. Catherine's Sound. "The leak has steadily increased till at present she leaks from 4 to 6 inches. We have only the deck pumps to keep her free, as the donkey pump has given out and the engineer reports he is not able to repair it, and her engine is so bad that she will not steam ahead in a head sea and will only go 3 knots in still water."[213]

August 2, 1863 (Sunday)

Beauregard worked to obtain reinforcements for Savannah. In a note to General Cooper he stated, "Transports filled with troops reported going south from Stono, probably intended to operate against Savannah. Cannot some of my troops sent to General [Joseph E.]

---

[209] Candler, *Confederate Records of the State of Georgia*, 2:469.

[210] Ibid.

[211] *OR*, ser. I, vol. 28, pt. 2:609.

[212] *ORN*, ser. I, vol. 14:411.

[213] Ibid., 412.

Johnston be ordered back immediately, for the defense of this city?" Cooper responded quickly, ordering Johnston to send "[Brigadier General Nathan] Evans' brigade, without delay, to Savannah, Ga., retaining the artillery and horses for the present."[214]

August 3, 1863 (Monday)

Beauregard notified Brigadier General Mercer of actions regarding one regiment and news of reinforcements. Mercer learned "the detachment of 78 men belonging to the Sixty-third Georgia Volunteers, having become very much reduced by casualties and sickness, has been ordered to return to Savannah. Brig. Gen. N. G. Evans has been ordered to take position with his brigade at Savannah."[215]

August 4, 1863 (Tuesday)

The increased Federal intensity near Charleston promoted Beauregard to notify Brigadier General Mercer in Savannah: "No danger whatever of surprise now. We must know what the enemy is doing before moving troops. It is still very doubtful whether he will attack both places [Charleston and Savannah] at once."[216]

August 5, 1863 (Wednesday)

Brigadier General Hugh Mercer wrote to Beauregard from Savannah. "I have the honor to acknowledge the receipt of a letter of the 3d instant informing me that Brigadier-General [Nathan] Evans...had been ordered to Savannah...as General Evans is my senior in rank, I will turn over the command of this military district to him, relinquishing a responsibility which I never sought and am not unwilling to resign."[217]

August 6, 1863 (Thursday) ◑

In Savannah, Brigadier General Mercer received most pleasant news. "[Brigadier] General Howell Cobb has been ordered to send to Savannah, to report to you, 500 infantry and one light battery."[218]

August 7, 1863 (Friday)

More news of blockade running attempts out of Savannah went to Rear Admiral Dahlgren. Acting Master C.J. Van Alstine, onboard the USS *Stettin*, reported on "two persons who had made their escape from Savannah. These persons have been doing business in Savannah as tanners, and are quite intelligent men. They represent that a steamer is fitting out in Savannah loading with cotton, and to carry out a large number of armed men to be put on board of a vessel at Nassau or Havana, if they succeed in getting through the blockade."[219]

August 8, 1863 (Saturday)

A British Consul in Savannah, Allan Fullarton, obtained a reply from Governor Brown to resistance on the part of British subjects living in Georgia who took an oath "that they will not, under any circumstances, take part in the contest now raging in this country by taking

---

[214] *OR*, ser. I, vol. 28, pt. 2:250.

[215] Ibid., 253.

[216] Ibid., 256.

[217] Ibid., 259.

[218] Ibid., 260.

[219] *ORN*, ser. I, vol. 14:429.

up arms on either side. In reply to this, permit me to remind you that no such self-imposed obligation can free the subjects of Her Majesty who choose to remain in this State from the higher obligation which, by the laws of nations, they are under to the State for protection while they remain within its limits."[220]

August 9, 1863 (Sunday)

Lending some authenticity to a report received previously, Dahlgren learned from Lieutenant Commander Austin Pendergrast, "I have received two refugees from Savannah on the 5th instant. They inform me that there are two ironclads building; one is on the stocks, the other has one-half of her armature on one side. I understand that the *Savannah*, or *Everglade*, is now at Thunderbolt, loaded with cotton, with the intention of running the blockade at the first opportunity."[221]

August 10, 1863 (Monday)

Summertime in the South—hot, humid, mosquito-infested regions, especially along the coast, made life miserable (and unhealthy) for sailors. Rear Admiral Dahlgren issued an order regarding safeguarding measures for his squadron. "The weather most trying to our men and most likely to engender the fevers of this region is upon us. Commanding officers and others will therefore be careful to expose the men to the sun as little as possible. The medical officers will report to me promptly, through their commanding officers, the first sign of contagious disease, so that suitable measures may be taken."[222]

August 11, 1863 (Tuesday)

"Since Gov. Brown has turned over the Major Generals, the Brigadier Generals, Colonels, Majors, Captains and Lieutenants, of Georgia Militia, to the Confederate service for State defence, and since most of them are now in volunteer companies, or have been drafted, or have rendered a satisfactory excuse, we hope that some other topic will be discussed, and that we shall not be under the necessity of again filling our columns with the old hackneyed subject."[223] A frustrated editor in Milledgeville shared his thoughts on previous quarrels between Governor Brown and the Confederate War Department over who held responsibility for assigning officers.

August 12, 1863 (Wednesday)

A problem with the swapping of prisoners made news. "The number of officers held by us is an interesting fact in connection with the refusal of the Yankees to respect the cartel of exchange. The number in our custody now is five hundred and twenty-three, all commissioned."[224]

August 13, 1863 (Thursday)

---

[220] Candler, *Confederate Records of the State of Georgia*, 3:388.

[221] *ORN*, ser. I, vol. 14:432.

[222] Ibid., 434.

[223] "The Militia Officers," *Milledgeville Southern Recorder*, August 11, 1863, sec. 2, https://gahistoricnewspapers.galileo.usg.edu/lccn/sn82016415/1863-08-11/ed-1/seq-2/.

[224] "Telegraphic," *Savannah Daily Morning News*, August 12, 1863, sec. 1, https://gahistoricnewspapers.galileo.usg.edu/lccn/sn82015886/1863-08-12/ed-1/seq-1/.

Secretary Mallory wrote to Flag Officer William Hunter in Savannah. "Your letter of the 8th instant, relative to arming the *Firefly*, etc., has been received, and Flag-Officer [Josiah] Tattnall has been requested to have all necessary work done to fit out and arm the vessel as you recommend."[225]

August 14, 1863 (Friday) ●

Residents of Savannah awoke to a story on page one of the *Savannah Republican*. "From England we may expect nothing, and ought to ask nothing. She has never forgotten her old animosities, being the first to throw those firebrands of discord that have kindled a cruel war. The abolition of slavery has been her steady purpose. By subjugation we will lose that domestic institution, the real cause of the war."[226]

August 15, 1863 (Saturday)

"Capt. C. B. Mims, commandant of this military Post, has placed in our hands, the sum of fifty dollars...as a private donation for the benefit of the indigent families of deceased soldiers from this county...there is a good deal of suffering among some of those, whose natural protectors have fallen in battle, or died in the service.... Here is a fine field for active benevolence...prompted by true patriotic and Christian motives."[227] Generous individuals always rose to the occasion, and a military officer leading the way set a great example.

August 16, 1863 (Sunday)

Past the mid-point of the war, units continued to organize in Georgia. "Attention, Ivey Guards: You are hereby ordered to meet at Warnock & Salisbury's Warehouse, TUESDAY MORNING, Aug. 18th, at 10 o'clock. The object of the meeting is to assist in the organization of a Regiment or Battalion, and elect Field Officers. By order of Lieut. L. B. Duck, commanding company."[228]

August 17, 1863 (Monday)

Consul Fullarton responded to the governor's letter regarding British subjects residing in Georgia taking up arms in defense of the state. "Such service might be rendered by them in the event of a war by a foreign power, but not in a civil war like that which now rages on this continent."[229]

August 18, 1863 (Tuesday)

General Beauregard responded to a letter from Brigadier General Quincy Gillmore regarding African American soldiers in the Confederate officer's Department of South Carolina, Georgia, and Florida. "You knew...there existed an order of the President of my Government...which expressly exclude armed negroes from recognition by Confederate States

---

[225] *ORN*, ser. I, vol. 14:749.

[226] "How to Close the War," *Savannah Republican*, August 14, 1863, sec. 1, https://gahistoricnewspapers.galileo.usg.edu/lccn/sn85038496/1863-08-14/ed-1/seq-1/.

[227] "Commendable," *Columbus Daily Sun*, August 15, 1863, sec. 2, https://gahistoricnewspapers.galileo.usg.edu/lccn/sn82014939/1863-08-15/ed-1/seq-2/.

[228] "Attention, Ivey Guards," *Columbus Daily Sun*, August 16, 1863, sec. 2, https://gahistoricnewspapers.galileo.usg.edu/lccn/sn82014939/1863-08-16/ed-1/seq-2/. Caps in original.

[229] Candler, *Confederate Records of the State of Georgia*, 3:391–92.

officers as legitimate means of war. You know…in accordance with this position of the constituted authorities…I had uniformly refused to receive or communicate in this department with flags of truce borne by officers or escorted by men of negro regiments in your service."[230]

August 19, 1863 (Wednesday)

Secretary of War Seddon requested the assistance of Richard R. Cuyler, president of the Georgia Central Railroad.

> I feel assured I shall be excused for appealing to your sense of patriotic duty to render all the efficient aid in your power to the transportation of necessary supplies in Southern Georgia, on which we must mainly depend for the support of our army, as well in Virginia as in Tennessee and South Carolina. For the next sixty days there must be great strain on the resources of transportation to give even a moderate support to those armies. Your own energy and ability, as well as the resources of the road under your charge, encourage me to hope that, if you will devote especial attention to the accomplishment of the end, it will be successfully attained.[231]

August 20, 1863 (Thursday)

Reporting on an engagement along the coast, Acting Master Woodbury H. Polleys described the action. "At 9:15 [a.m.], on the 20th, a boat was reported coming around the east end of St. Catherine's Island, about a mile distant from us…. In a few moments two more came around full of men. We commenced firing on them as soon as the guns would bear and continued until they got out of range…having succeeded in fetching one boat…the others escaping."[232]

August 21, 1863 (Friday) ◐

Southrons observed a Day of Humiliation, Fasting, and Prayer. Residents of Savannah had an opportunity to attend Christ Church and listen to a special sermon marking the day from Reverend Stephen Elliott. The pastor reminded everyone of the need to maintain faith.

> Forward, my hearers, forward, with our shields locked and our trust in God, is our only movement now. It is too late even to go backward. We might have gone backward a year ago, when our armies were victoriously thundering at the gates of Washington and were keeping at successful bay the Hessians of the West, had we been content to bear humiliation for ourselves and degradation for our children. But even that is no longer left us. It is now victory or unconditional submission; submission not to the conservative and christian [*sic*] people of the North, but to a party of infidel fanatics, with an army of needy and greedy soldiers at their backs. Who shall be able to restrain them in their hour of victory?[233]

---

[230] *OR*, ser. I, vol. 28, pt. 2:45.

[231] Ibid., 295–96.

[232] *ORN*, ser. I, vol. 14:492.

[233] Elliott, "Ezra's Dilemna [*sic*]."

August 22, 1863 (Saturday)
Nurse Kate Cumming wrote from a hospital outside Ringgold, "The enemy are shelling Chattanooga; all the hospitals are leaving there. I can not help, from looking round and thinking, that perhaps ere many days we may be compelled to leave here."[234]
August 23, 1863 (Sunday)
Many facilities in Georgia produced various matériel for the war. The Columbus Leather Cloth Manufactory was one example. "The company is manufacturing large quantities of enameled cloth of various kinds. They are like wise manufacturing the first quality of lamp-black—an article very much in demand at this time. Perhaps the most interesting part of their work is their manufacture of cartridge boxes, belts, haversacks, &c. They are manufacturing an article of cartridge boxes equal in appearance (and we doubt not in durability also) to any made in Yankeedom."[235]
August 24, 1863 (Monday)
Meals on the hoof occupied the governor's considerations in a letter to President Davis. "There are a great many wild cattle in lower Georgia. Florida cow-drivers cannot be had in that country, nor do the people care to sell cattle for currency at present prices. I beg to suggest that you order details from the force under Brig.-General Howell Cobb to drive them out immediately and pay the people very liberal compensation for them."[236]
August 25, 1863 (Tuesday)
Many folks received the blessing of large families, perhaps several sons and daughters to start, and over the years, marriages solidified household unity. Parents in Columbus welcomed a new opportunity for their sons and daughters to attend the Slade Institute, reopening under the tutelage of new president, Dr. E. LeCompte. The school's mission: "to impart a sound, practical education, based upon the most useful theoretical studies."[237] One can only imagine how, during a time of war, young minds absorbed knowledge, which shaped future teachers, doctors, quality engineers, and myriad other vocations. Thankfully, education remained a concern across Georgia.
August 26, 1863 (Wednesday)
Colonel D. Wyatt Aiken reported on the importance of Macon, and preparations to raise companies to protect the valuable "arsenal, armory, and laboratory…." Aiken detailed the formation of "three companies, under charge of Colonel Cuyler, who has them regularly drilled in the school of the company." Finally, the officer noted the importance of the city. "Macon is the focus of three important railroads, which, with their branches, ramify every section of the State. The throngs in the streets, the numerous scapegraces [rascally persons] picked up here, and the evident unstable sentiment of the population, in my humble

---

[234] Cumming, *Kate*, 131.

[235] "Columbus Leather Cloth Manufactory," *Columbus Daily Sun*, August 23, 1863, https://gahistoricnewspapers.galileo.usg.edu/lccn/sn82014939/1863-08-23/ed-1/seq-2/.

[236] Candler, *Confederate Records of the State of Georgia*, 3:402.

[237] "The Slade Female Institute," *Columbus Daily Sun*, August 25, 1863, sec. 2, https://gahistoricnewspapers.galileo.usg.edu/lccn/sn82014939/1863-08-25/ed-1/seq-1/.

judgment, calls loudly for the establishment of martial law, at least here, if not throughout the Confederacy."[238]

August 27, 1863 (Thursday)

As the war progressed, mounting casualties pressed Georgians into action. Ministers often led the way, as this appeal from Chaplain T. C. Stanley indicates. "I have been detailed to visit the several counties where the 46th Ga. Vols. were enlisted, and solicit donations for a Hospital Fund to be applied for the benefit of the sick of the command. Much privation and suffering have been endured for the want of such a fund, and I feel well assured that an appeal to the friends of the soldier, and especially to those of this command, will not go unanswered."[239]

August 28, 1863 (Friday)

As the Federals under the command of Major General William Rosecrans in the Army of the Cumberland prepared to move from forward into northwest Georgia, Rome residents readied. "Tis not likely that active operations will be much longer delayed along the Tenn. River line. The enemy have already showed great restlessness, and the feint at Chattanooga last Friday, and renewed again on Saturday, as it is rumored, will doubtless prove the precursor of movements on a more extensive scale. Let all the companies for State defence be ready to rally at a moments warning."[240]

August 29, 1863 (Saturday)

The Army of the Cumberland began crossing the Tennessee River into Georgia as the opening of the Chickamauga Campaign got underway. Cavalry Colonel William N. Estes reported to Major General Joe Wheeler. "Enemy crossed the Tennessee River 10 miles below Bridgeport this morning, by fording, in a large cavalry force. We are gradually falling back on Trenton. We have fallen back 1 mile since last skirmish."[241]

August 30, 1863 (Sunday)

General Braxton Bragg sent a report to General Cooper in Richmond on developing conditions in northwest Georgia. "The enemy's forces are apparently moving for a union or within supporting distance on the other side of the river. Against this, we cannot possibly hold our long line from Virginia to Georgia. We shall accordingly concentrate as far as necessary in front of our supplies. Traitors have already broken the railroad and telegraph beyond Knoxville. Have sent paroled prisoners to Atlanta. Arms for them should be sent

---

[238] *OR*, ser. I, vol. 28, pt. 2:307.

[239] "Hospital Fund for 46th Ga. Reg't," *Columbus Daily Sun*, August 27, 1863, sec. 2, https://gahistoricnewspapers.galileo.usg.edu/lccn/sn82014939/1863-08-27/ed-1/seq-2/. This regiment mustered soldiers from Upson, Schley, Harris, Muscogee, Chattahoochee, Webster, Marion, and Talbot counties (National Park Service, "46th Regiment, Georgia Infantry").

[240] "Hasten on the Preparations," *Rome Weekly Courier*, August 28, 1863, sec. 1, https://gahistoricnewspapers.galileo.usg.edu/lccn/sn82014071/1863-08-28/ed-1/seq-1/.

[241] *OR*, ser. I, vol. 30, pt. 4:564. For a comprehensive treatment of the campaign, see Powell, *Chickamauga Campaign*.

there by eastern route."[242]

August 31, 1863 (Monday)

Rosecrans's advance, coupled with Major General Ambrose Burnside's approach on Knoxville, prompted Secretary Seddon to notify Governor Brown. "We are advised that a formidable force of the enemy is advancing on East Tennessee. Cannot the local troops organized by you be thrown to aid?"[243]

September 1, 1863 (Tuesday)

Major General Joe Wheeler received news—from Bragg's Adjutant General Kinloch Falconer—of Federals advancing into Georgia. "The enemy are reported to have crossed in force into Will's Valley, at Trenton. The general wishes a report immediately from you as to the truth of this report, and any facts in regard to the number of the enemy."[244]

September 2, 1863 (Wednesday)

Wheeler notified his subordinates of planned action if the Army of the Cumberland attacked. "In case of an advance of the enemy all cavalry commanders…will be instructed to report the fact to headquarters Army of Tennessee, to these headquarters, and to the officers commanding the bridge guards at Resaca and Etowah."[245]

September 3, 1863 (Thursday)

Federal cavalry Brigadier General Robert Mitchell reported on Confederates near Alpine; skirmishing also indicated at this location. "Wheeler encamped at Alpine, on the Gadsden and Chattanooga road, last night; he marched from there this morning at sunrise in the direction of Chattanooga, supposed to be going to Trenton."[246]

September 4, 1863 (Friday) ◐

General Bragg worked to deploy elements of the Army of Tennessee to various locations in northwest Georgia. He reported in a dispatch to Lieutenant General D. H. Hill, "Wheeler is gone… to Rome to head them [Federals] off from our communication." Bragg then directed Hill to "Consult Cleburne. He is cool, full of resources, and ever alive to a success. Then give me your views, or call with [Major General Patrick] Cleburne and see what our resources are."[247]

September 5, 1863 (Saturday)

Federal cavalry officer Colonel Robert Minty reported on the movements of Bragg, which moved Rosecrans to believe Bragg indeed continued to fall back through Georgia. "I believe that Macon, Ga., is the position to which Bragg is falling back. At Calhoun, on Thursday last, General Buckner ordered that all able-bodied negroes should be sent to Macon to work on the fortifications."[248] Skirmish near Alpine.

---

[242] *OR*, ser. I, vol. 30, pt. 4:566.

[243] Candler, *Confederate Records of the State of Georgia*, 3:409.

[244] *OR*, ser. I, vol. 30, pt. 4:580.

[245] Ibid., 584–85.

[246] *OR*, ser. I, vol. 30, pt. 3:331.

[247] *OR*, ser. I, vol. 30, pt. 4:594.

[248] *OR*, ser. I, vol. 30, pt. 3:372; skirmish in Mosocco, *Chronological Tracking*, 166.

September 6, 1863 (Sunday)

General Bragg ordered the evacuation of Chattanooga. "In order to meet the enemy and strike him…this army will move immediately toward Rome in four columns. Lieutenant-General Polk will move on the La Fayette road via Rossville, Snow Hill, and La Fayette to Summerville…General [D. H.] Hill will follow Polk's column. [Major] General [W. H. T.] Walker will move via Graysville…. All men from hospitals and all stores will be immediately sent to the rear. The hospitals as low down as Resaca will be vacated."[249] Skirmishes at Stevens Gap and Summerville.

September 7, 1863 (Monday)

Major General James Negley, near McKaig's Springs, dispatched the headquarters of the XIV Army Corps with a request. "I trust to have reliable information from these gaps…tomorrow morning….I…request that a secret-service fund of at least $1,000 be placed in the hands of my quartermaster. I am compelled to advance money for this purpose from private funds. These people are so poor and dependent that when employed upon this business (which they appear to be willing to undertake) they should be paid at once. There are several trustworthy loyalists in this vicinity."[250]

September 8, 1863 (Tuesday)

As the Federals penetrated Georgia, skirmishing occurred near Alpine. The Confederate War Department, via Special Orders, No. 213, took steps to safeguard Atlanta. "Brig. Gen. Howell Cobb is assigned to the duty of organizing at Atlanta the Georgia militia, and such of the local force from that State as have been ordered to that point by His Excellency the Governor of Georgia for service in the Confederate States."[251]

September 9, 1863 (Wednesday)

On a day with skirmishing at Lookout Mountain, the Federals occupied Chattanooga. Rosecrans reported, "Chattanooga is ours. Our movement on the enemy's flank and rear goes on." Bragg continued to maneuver the Army of Tennessee, as reinforcements under the command of Lieutenant General James Longstreet left Virginia for Georgia. After Burnside secured Knoxville, the only rail route open for Confederate officials resulted in a lengthy trip down the coast. Longstreet wrote, "we were obliged to make the circuit through the Carolinas to Augusta, Georgia, and up by the railroad, thence through Atlanta to Dalton and Ringgold."[252]

September 10, 1863 (Thursday)

Skirmishing reported at Summerville, and Federal forays toward Rome and La Fayette; lastly, an affair at Pea Vine Creek near Graysville. Of this action, Confederate Brigadier General John Pegram reported, "near Graysville…when, being out on a reconnaissance with the Sixth Georgia Cavalry (Colonel [John] Hart), it was reported the enemy had

---

[249] *OR*, ser. I, vol. 30, pt. 4:610–11; skirmish in Mosocco, *Chronological Tracking*, 167.

[250] *OR*, ser. I, vol. 30, pt. 3:409.

[251] *OR*, ser. I, vol. 30, pt. 4:625; skirmish in Mosocco, *Chronological Tracking*, 167.

[252] *OR*, ser. I, vol. 30, pt. 3:499; Longstreet, *From Manassas to Appomattox*, 374; skirmish in Mosocco, *Chronological Tracking*, 167.

thrown himself between Colonel [John] Scott and myself…I ordered Colonel Hart to charge the enemy with two companies of his regiment. This he most gallantly did, and brought out 59 prisoners (being the skirmishers of [Major General John] Palmer's division) from within sight of the masses of the enemy."[253]

September 11, 1863 (Friday)

Colonel John T. Wilder reported on a hard day of fighting for his "Lightning Brigade." He noted, "I have driven the enemy from Ringgold to a point 2 miles beyond Tunnel Hill, and will picket strongly on the front. While I write, my advance is skirmishing briskly. The enemy disputed every inch of the way stubbornly. I have come over ground hard to advance on when disputed as it was to-day." Skirmishing reported at Blue Bird Gap, Rossville, Lee and Gordon's Mills, Davis' Cross-Roads, near Ringgold, and a Federal scouting party headed toward Rome.[254]

September 12, 1863 (Saturday) ●

The intensity of military activity increased in northwest Georgia, with skirmishes reported at Alpine, Dirt Town, Leet's Tan-yard, and along the La Fayette Road. From his post near La Fayette, Captain A.T. Fielder, with the 12th Tennessee Infantry "marched off under a burning sun over a good part of the same road over which we had traveled yesterday back in the direction of Chattanooga…we were halted about 3 oclk. formed line of battle stacked arms and ordered to break ranks but told not to scatter off [.]' Fielder could hear "our Cavelry [*sic*] skirmishing with the enemy in front of us scattering artilary [*sic*] is also to be heard prisoners are occasionally being brought by going to the rear." He closed, "The indications are that we shall have a general engagement soon, may God give us the victory and as bloodless a one as possable [*sic*] nevertheless not my will but thine be done."[255]

September 13, 1863 (Sunday)

Skirmishing continued in northwest Georgia, with action reported at La Fayette, Lee and Gordon's Mills, and near Summerville. Early-morning orders went out: "Major-Generals [Ben] Cheatham, [Thomas] Hindman, and [W. H. T.] Walker will push forward a brigade each on the Gordon's Mills, Pea Vine, and Ringgold roads respectively, following the cavalry, in order to develop the enemy."[256]

September 14, 1863 (Monday)

Lieutenant George A. Mercer in Savannah watched events in the northwest section of the state. "The news to night is anything but cheering; Bragg's whole army has fallen back into north western Georgia, and all of East Tennessee, including Chattanooga, is in the hands of the enemy. A defeat suffered by our army now opens upper Georgia to his savages." Skirmishing reported near La Fayette.[257]

---

[253] *OR*, ser. I, vol. 30, pt. 2:528; skirmishes in Mosocco, *Chronological Tracking*, 168.

[254] *OR*, ser. I, vol. 30, pt. 3:546; skirmishes in Mosocco, *Chronological Tracking*, 168.

[255] Cathey, *Captain T. A. Fielder's Civil War Diary*, 260–61.

[256] *OR*, ser. I, vol. 30, pt. 4:645; skirmishes in Mosocco, *Chronological Tracking*, 168.

[257] Mercer, *George Anderson Mercer Diary*, September 14, 1863; skirmishes in Mosocco, *Chronological Tracking*, 169.

September 15, 1863 (Tuesday)

In Atlanta, Colonel Moses Wright updated Bragg on the status of reinforcements. "[Brigadier General Jerome] Robertson's brigade went up 8 p. m., 14th instant, to Resaca, 1,300 strong. [Brigadier General Henry] Benning's (1,200 strong) and [Brigadier General Evander] Law's (2,000 strong) go up at 7 p. m. to-day. Benning compelled to stop to ration and get shoes, for barefooted men." Skirmishing at Catlett's Gap, Pigeon Mountain, Summerville, and at Trion Factory.[258]

September 16, 1863 (Wednesday)

The Army of the Cumberland continued to position themselves in various locations in preparation for battle. Skirmishing reported at Lee and Gordon's Mills and near Alpine. Major General Thomas Wood reported from Lee and Gordon's Mills. "One of my scouts…just returned reports that…the bulk of the enemy's force is about La Fayette and in the vicinity. He says it is commonly understood that the enemy is not going to leave this region of country without a fight…. He reports that it is said [Major General Simon] Buckner's force is at Shields' Gap, and that it is commonly said he is to attack and take Gordon's Mills." Bragg issued Special Orders, No. 245, which directed his army to occupy the following positions.

> Buckner's corps and Walker's reserves…from Pea Vine Church, north along Pea Vine Creek. Polk's corps…take post on Buckner's left, and occupy the ground to near Glass' Mill…Forrest's cavalry will cover the front and flank of both these movements. Wheeler's cavalry…will pass through Dug to Catlett's Gap, press the enemy…and join our flank near Glass' Mill. Reed's Bridge, Byram's Ford, Alexander's Bridge, and the fords next above, will be seized and held by our cavalry. [Lieutenant General D.H.] Hill's corps will occupy the gaps across Pigeon Mountain and observe the road to the south, and be ready to move at a moment's notice. All extra wagon trains will be sent across Taylor's Ridge, near Ringgold.[259]

September 17, 1863 (Thursday)

Military preparations continued near Chickamauga Creek, and officials on both sides took steps to ensure clarity in orders for their commands. Lieutenant General D. H. Hill's General Orders, No. 48, serves as one example. "Most of our disasters have been the result of a want of promptness. We must make up by the celerity of movement what we lack in numbers and equipments. Regiments will be expected to move in ten minutes, brigades in twenty, and divisions in thirty from the time of the receipt of the order." Skirmishing at Owen's Ford and Ringgold; the Federals left Rossville on a scouting mission.[260]

September 18, 1863 (Friday)

Battle lines continued to develop along Chickamauga Creek. Skirmishing reported at Pea Vine Bridge, Alexander's Bridge, Reed's Bridge, Dryer's Ford, along Spring Creek, and

---

[258] *OR,* ser. I, vol. 30, pt. 4:652; skirmishes in Mosocco, *Chronological Tracking,* 169.

[259] *OR,* ser. I, vol. 30, pt. 3:681; *OR,* ser. I, vol. 30, pt. 4:657; skirmishes in Mosocco, *Chronological Tracking,* 169.

[260] *OR,* ser. I, vol. 30, pt. 4:661–62.

near Stevens Gap. Major General Wheeler received the following update. "Owens' Ford was lost to-day. [Brigadier General Frank] Armstrong is now picketing with some 60 men from Childress' Ford to Glass' Mill, a distance of 2½ miles. Lieutenant-General [D. H.] Hill begs you will relieve him with your cavalry to-morrow morning, as he does not wish to scatter [Major General John C.] Breckinridge's division, which should be concentrated at Glass' Mill."[261]

September 19, 1863 (Saturday)

The Army of Tennessee struck the left flank of the Army of the Cumberland; the Battle of Chickamauga opened. Hard fighting failed to turn the Federal left flank, but the day ended on a better note for General Bragg. Late in the evening Longstreet and the lead elements of his reinforcements from Virginia arrived. Bragg created two wings from his army, giving Longstreet the left wing, and Lieutenant General Polk the right. Captain Samuel Foster in Cleburne's command captured the action in his diary.

> The fireing [sic] is very heavy on our right and left, and the Yank[s] are blazing away at us like fury. Some heavy pine timber here—While lying down here today one man is shot in the head and killed so dead that the man next to him did not know it until we had to move, and moving here was an awful bad piece of business; bullets fly like the wind you can hear them zip zip zip but you cant see them. You know they are passing very thick and that is all. The fireing gradually slackens up as dark comes on; for here when it gets dark, it is very dark. In the night we are moved to the right lots of others troop going to the right.[262]

September 20, 1863 (Sunday) ◐

Day two of the Battle of Chickamauga again produced heavy fighting. Longstreet's troops advanced as Rosecrans ordered Major General Thomas Wood to pull his division out of line to plug a gap elsewhere. No gap existed but the one Wood's Division created, thus swinging a giant barn door open, which allowed the Confederates to break the Federal line. The right half of Rosecrans's command started a pell-mell retreat to Chattanooga. On the left of the Federal line, Major General George Thomas's command held firm. Thomas earned the nickname "Rock of Chickamauga," as his men stalled the attacking Confederates long enough to afford the balance of the Army of the Cumberland safe retreat to Chattanooga. A Pyrrhic victory for the Confederates, the battle produced the second highest casualty count of the war, as Rosecrans lost 16,170, and Bragg suffered 18,454 dead, wounded, and missing.[263] A member of the 125th Ohio Infantry stood his ground along with the other "Tigers," as "Gen. Thomas had said, 'This position must be held.' We could but die, we must not yield, and for long hours we beat back the enemy, almost single handed, and did hold our own."[264]

---

[261] Ibid., 666.

[262] Foster, *One of Cleburne's Command*, 53.

[263] "Chickamauga," https://www.battlefields.org/learn/civil-war/battles/chickamauga.

[264] Baumgartner, *Yankee Tigers II*, 97. For the definitive account of Thomas, see B. Wills, *George Henry Thomas*, 1.

September 21, 1863 (Monday)

A Texas soldier wrote of the immediate aftermath of the Battle of Chickamauga as he and comrades toured the battlefield. "We saw men cold and stiff in death, and yet holding on to their gun; some with the ramrod yet in their hand; some with paper yet between their teeth, just as they had bitten it from the cartridge for loading, and the cartridge yet held by their thumb, middle and forefinger as if in the act of emptying the powder into their gun. By noon…the stench from dead men and horses was getting to be sickening." Skirmishing continued at Rossville, Lookout Church, and in Dry Valley.[265]

September 22, 1863 (Tuesday)

Acting Master G. W. Ewer onboard the USS *Seneca*, reported his action on the day. Tonight "in obedience to your order, I proceeded up the river with an armed boat's crew for the purpose of destroying the salt works, known as the Hudson Place Salt Works, situated near Darien, Ga. I. have to report the demolition of the works, and that for all purposes of salt manufacture they are now completely useless, the principal boilers being stove in, engine blown up, vats, etc., cut down."[266]

September 23, 1863 (Wednesday)

Governor Brown, seldom a supporter of initiatives from the Confederate government, also disliked impressment. Today, he issued a proclamation to the "Civil and Military Officers of Georgia." In the document, Brown informed "the citizens of this State that it is their right and duty to resist all impressments of their property by persons who cannot show legal authority to make the impressment, and to use all the force, in such cases, which is necessary to the protection of their persons and property."[267]

September 24, 1863 (Thursday)

Private John Compton with the 105th Ohio Infantry, wrote of the aftermath of Chickamauga. "We have ben in a very hard fight last friday saturday, and Sunday We fought the enimy with Superior number our loss was grate While the enimy was grater… We are very heavy fortifying here [outside Chattanooga] then we will try them…."[268]

September 25, 1863 (Friday)

Governor Brown responded to a conference offer from President Davis. "I regret to inform you that heavy press of office business will deny me that pleasure [meeting with Davis] for the present. As the late splendid victory which the army under the command of General Bragg has won upon the bloody fields of Chickamauga—'the stream of death'—has driven the enemy from the soil of this State, an interview is less important than it might otherwise have been."[269]

---

[265] Collins, *Chapters from the Unwritten History of the War Between the States*, 162, 164; skirmishes in Mosocco, *Chronological Tracking*, 170.

[266] *ORN*, ser. I, vol. 14:670.

[267] Candler, *Confederate Records of the State of Georgia*, 2:475.

[268] "Letter—John Compton, 24 September 1863 [to his sister Margaret]," https://phparchives.wordpress.com/2020/09/14/letter-john-compton-24-september-1863/.

[269] Candler, *Confederate Records of the State of Georgia*, 3:418.

September 26, 1863 (Saturday)

"The course of Gen. Bragg in not permitting the Press Association to remain in the front has deprived the public of the reliable reports from the field of Chickamauga, 'The Stream of Death,' to which it is entitled, and which the press had made arrangements to have sent."[270] It seems Bragg occupied a spot on the list of generals who preferred that press members stay away from military camps.

September 27, 1863 (Sunday)

"It is astonishing how some men can change their opinions. Only two weeks ago we heard some men in this city launching forth their artillery of censure on Gen. Bragg, and to our amazement, since the battle of Chickamauga, they have been foremost in praise of him. 'Och ye are a decateful set of spalpeens [rascals]!'"[271] How quickly success on the field of battle could amend the thoughts of many.

September 28, 1863 (Monday)

A graduate of the Georgia Military Institute in Marietta, Pierce Manning Butler Young, received promotion to the rank of brigadier general in the Confederate army.[272]

September 29, 1863 (Tuesday)

Major General Howell Cobb sought direction and support from General Cooper in Richmond.

> I submit for the decision of the department the proper mode of filling vacancies in the companies and regiments of the State troops. Governor Brown insists with great earnestness that all vacancies should be filled under the State laws. He discriminates between these troops and those in the regular Confederate service, and claims that vacancies, including field officers, should be filled by election, as required by the laws of the State. Whilst I am utterly opposed to all elections in the army, and regard them as the fruitful sources of trouble, I would recommend, if consistent with the President's view of the law, that the concession should be made and the vacancies be filled under the laws of the State. It is an evil, I know, but perhaps a lesser one than a conflict with the State authorities on the point.[273]

September 30, 1863 (Wednesday)

Secretary of War Seddon, via Special Orders, No. 232, stipulated, "The Fifty-seventh Georgia Regiment, [Major General Carter] Stevenson's division, will repair to Savannah, Ga., and report for duty to Brigadier-General [Hugh] Mercer."[274]

October 1, 1863 (Thursday)

---

[270] "Incidents from the Battle-Field," *Rome Tri-Weekly Courier*, September 26, 1863, sec. 1, https://gahistoricnewspapers.galileo.usg.edu/lccn/sn85034102/1863-09-26/ed-1/seq-1/.

[271] "Our City," *Atlanta Daily Intelligencer*, September 27, 1863, sec. 3, https://gahistoricnewspapers.galileo.usg.edu/lccn/sn82014304/1863-09-27/ed-1/seq-3/.

[272] Eicher and Eicher, *Civil War High Commands*, 585.

[273] Candler, *Confederate Records of the State of Georgia*, 3:420.

[274] *OR*, ser. I, vol. 28, pt. 2:385.

Dr. John R. Cheves notified Beauregard in Savannah of his work on a new artillery shell.

> I have received the shells to he prepared with incendiary materials, and have them in the hands of the workmen. I find that a very large quantity of powder is used as a bursting charge. I must beg that you will designate some department or officer in Savannah, by whom the shells may be received when finished, and who will refund to me the cost on delivery. Supposing, then, that 1,000 pounds of phosphorus can be obtained, it will serve for 6,000 12-pounder shells, or about 2,000 32-pounder rifled shells.[275]

October 2, 1863 (Friday)

"It is stated that some of the Yankee prisoners, captured at Chickamauga, had a large stock of counterfeit Confederate money, and bills of exploded banks, which they are passing off on unsuspecting people along the railroad. Served them right, for they have no business to be trading with these precious scoundrels."[276]

October 3, 1863 (Saturday)

The *Daily Intelligencer* of Atlanta reported on a new unit in the field.

> The appointment of Gen. Henry R. Jackson to command the First Brigade of Georgia State Troops, and which is now in active service, we are gratified to learn, is received with favor by the command, as we felt it would be when it was made by the President. If military experience…military skill and chivalric bearing up on the field, with generous consideration for…his command, will endear a General to his men, we are satisfied this first brigade of our State troops will come out of the service with the highest appreciation of and confidence in, their commander, and who, "native and to the manor born" doubtless feels honored in being appointed to his present command, composed, as it is, of Georgians.[277]

October 4, 1863 (Sunday) ◑

The *Columbus Daily Sun* reported, "We understand that the four companies from this city…which left for Atlanta on Wednesday…have been ordered back. It is stated that it was not intended troops from this section should have been ordered to other points, as it is deemed necessary that a city of such importance to the Confederacy as Columbus, should always be prepared to repel any raid the enemy may attempt to make on it…."[278] One can imagine the folks in Columbus rested a bit easier.

October 5, 1863 (Monday)

Secretary Seddon continued dialogue with Major General Howell Cobb regarding Georgia

---

[275] Ibid., 386.

[276] "It Is Stated," *Rome Tri-Weekly Courier*, October 2, 1863, sec. 2, https://gahistoricnewspapers.galileo.usg.edu/lccn/sn82014071/1863-10-02/ed-1/seq-2/.

[277] "First Brigade of State Troops," *Atlanta Daily Intelligencer*, October 3, 1863, sec. 2, https://gahistoricnewspapers.galileo.usg.edu/lccn/sn82014304/1863-10-03/ed-1/seq-2/.

[278] "To Return," *Columbus Daily Sun*, October 4, 1863, sec. 2, https://gahistoricnewspapers.galileo.usg.edu/lccn/sn82014939/1863-10-04/ed-1/seq-2/.

troops. He suggested when troops "have not been organized under the Confederate laws, but as militia, then there can be no doubt...the appointments will be with the Governor.... When the organizations have been under the Confederate Acts for local defense, then, if before...tendered they are organized into regiments, the field officers may be...elected by the men, and then, as regiments organized, they may be tendered and accepted by the Confederate authorities."[279]

October 6, 1863 (Tuesday)

Lieutenant General Leonidas Polk wrote to President Davis from Atlanta. Polk stated Bragg had suspended him and ordered him "to this place." This order was based on alleged disobedience in not attacking the enemy at day-light on Sunday the 20th ult. For the delay charged cannot feel myself responsible. And let it be observed, by whomsoever caused, it did not occasion any failure in our success in the battle, for the enemy was clearly beaten at all points along my line and fairly driven from the field.[280]

October 7, 1863 (Wednesday)

Colonel Robert Anderson, 5th Georgia Cavalry, wrote to Beauregard with a proposal to realign the troopers.

> There are now stationed in the District of Georgia, under the command of Brigadier-General [Hugh] Mercer, the Fourth Regiment of Georgia Cavalry, Colonel [Duncan] Clinch; the Fifth Regiment of Georgia Cavalry, Col. R. H. Anderson; Lieutenant-Colonel [John] Millen's battalion of six companies, Maj. [Edward] E. C. Anderson's battalion of three companies, and an independent squadron, under Captain [J. L.] McAllister; making in all thirty-one companies, with an aggregate of at least 2,500. I very respectfully suggest that the above organizations be brigaded, and that an energetic and competent cavalry officer be appointed brigadier-general, and assigned to the command of all this cavalry.[281]

October 8, 1863 (Thursday)

Wounded Confederate soldiers after Chickamauga flooded Georgia's medical system, prompting Beauregard to notify General Cooper of a problem. "But one hundred and forty-five ambulances in whole department, which are in constant use with troops and hospitals for my command and General Bragg's wounded, at Augusta, Macon, &c. [Colonel Robert H.] Anderson left yesterday with five ambulances. Nearly 4,000 negroes working on fortifications of First District cannot be supplied with any. I await further orders."[282]

October 9, 1863 (Friday)

During his visit to Georgia, President Davis made speeches at several stops along the rail. Today, he spoke in Marietta. A newspaper account stated he "appeared on the platform of the car, and was greeted with cheers." Davis "complimented the ladies of Georgia for their

---

[279] Candler, *Confederate Records of the State of Georgia*, 3:421.

[280] J. Davis, *Papers*, 10:12.

[281] *OR*, ser. I, vol. 28, pt. 2:401.

[282] Ibid., 403.

exertions in behalf of the wounded in the late battle [Chickamauga]; also the citizens of the Empire State, in the celerity with which they responded to the call for troops, and the readiness manifested by the people to rally to the defence of our borders." Preparing to depart, "Generals Longstreet, Pemberton and Breckinridge, Senator Cobb, Gov. Brown…and [the president's] staff" joined Davis in boarding the train.[283]

October 10, 1863 (Saturday)

Armand Beauregard, the general's brother, arrived at the Army of Tennessee with President Davis. After speaking with Bragg, Armand wrote to his brother, noting Bragg

> alluded to the battle of Chickamauga and to the arrest of General Polk, who…had invariably delayed operations by modifying instructions given him and executing them too late. In the last battle both he Polk) and [D. H.] Hill had jeopardized the successful annihilation of Rosecrans' whole army. The first is under arrest…the latter to be relieved from command. General Pemberton…accompanied the President, expecting to be the successor of General Polk, but abandoned his pretensions upon learning the opposition raised by the troops."[284]

October 11, 1863 (Sunday)

Dr. Samuel Stout wrote Surgeon General S. P. Moore in Richmond of hospital quandaries in Georgia. "From the diagram herewith it will be seen that I am confined to narrow limits in providing hospital accommodations for a very large army. I have no hospitals of a permanent character north of Kingston and Rome. In the event of a retreat southward of our army the hospitals at Rome, Kingston, Cassville, and Marietta will probably have to be removed south of Atlanta."[285]

October 12, 1863 (Monday) ●

Secretary Mallory notified Flag Officer William Hunter in Savannah, "Flag-Officer [John] Tucker has been called upon to return the men belonging to the squadron under your command, unless it is absolutely essential to the public interests that they should be further retained [near Charleston]."[286]

October 13, 1863 (Tuesday)

General Beauregard clarified the deployment of soldiers within his military District of South Carolina, Georgia, and Florida. "District troops are intended also for defense of department, and those of department for defense of Confederacy. Circumstances control where they shall be located and by whom commanded."[287]

October 14, 1863 (Wednesday)

President Davis addressed the Army of Tennessee.

---

[283] "Marietta GA, October 9," *Charleston Daily Courier*, October 10, 1863, sec. 1, https://www.newspapers.com/image/604536592#.

[284] *OR*, ser. I, vol. 30, pt. 4:735.

[285] *OR*, ser. I, vol. 30, pt. 5:736.

[286] *ORN*, ser. I, vol. 15:692.

[287] *OR*, ser. I, vol. 28, pt. 2:416.

> A grateful country has recognized your arduous service, and rejoiced over your glorious victory on the field of Chickamauga. When your countrymen shall more fully learn the adverse circumstances under which you attacked the enemy—though they cannot be more thankful—they may admire more the gallantry and patriotic devotion which secured your success. I fervently hope that the ferocious war, so unjustly waged against our country, may be soon ended, that, with the blessing of peace, you may be restored to your homes and the useful pursuits; and I pray that our Heavenly Father may cover you with the shield of His protection in the hours of battle, and endow you with the virtues which will close your trials in victory complete.[288]

October 15, 1863 (Thursday)
"Georgians! the recent great victory which drove back the enemy from your borders was won, in part by barefooted men! Think of that—you that have tanyards, and you also that have money to buy leather. If you want to ride rough-shod over the enemy—shoe the defenders of the Confederacy."[289] Shortages of matériel continued to mount as the blockade tightened, and Federal armies captured key manufacturing centers across the South.

October 16, 1863 (Friday)
Responding to "defects referred to in the Blakely projectiles," Beauregard ordered his ordnance chief to "Send extract relating to rifling of guns, &c., to Colonel [Washington] Rains, of Augusta Arsenal, for his views and such instructions as he thinks ought to be given on the subject."[290]

October 17, 1863 (Saturday)
Via Special Orders, No. 212, Beauregard announced, "Brig. Gen. [Raleigh] R. E. Colston, having reported for temporary service in this department, is assigned to duty in the District of Georgia, and will report to Brigadier-General [Hugh] Mercer, commanding."[291]

October 18, 1863 (Sunday)
Major General U. S. Grant issued General Orders, No. 1, declaring his appointment to "command of the Military Division of the Mississippi, embracing the departments of the Ohio, of the Cumberland, and of the Tennessee. The headquarters of the Military Division of the Mississippi will be in the field, where all reports and returns required by Army Regulations and existing orders will be made."[292]

October 19, 1863 (Monday) ◐
Ladies in Savannah went to work to raise funds women on the home front. "We…call attention to the ball that will be given this evening by the German Ladies' Association, for the benefit of the German soldiers' wives. The ball take place at the Turner's Hall…we trust will be well patronized by our liberal and patriotic citizens. The object is a charitable

---

[288] *OR*, ser. I, vol. 30, pt. 4:744–45.

[289] "Barefoot Soldiers," *Rome Tri-Weekly Courier*, October 15, 1863, sec. 2, https://gahistoricnewspapers.galileo.usg.edu/lccn/sn85034102/1863-10-15/ed-1/seq-2/.

[290] *OR*, ser. I, vol. 28, pt.2:379.

[291] *OR*, ser. I, vol. 28, pt. 2:423.

[292] *OR*, ser. I, vol. 30, pt. 4:450–51.

one, and well worthy of patronage. The ladies...have some twenty destitute families under their care...."[293]

October 20, 1863 (Tuesday)

Attempting to quell reports of soldiers deserting their posts in Savannah, Brigadier General Mercer wrote to Secretary Seddon.

> The troops composing this command are as loyal and patriotic as in any portion of the Confederacy. There have been many absent without leave from this as from all our armies, but I am happy to say that very many returned in consequence of the President's proclamation, and very many in consequence of vigorous measures adopted since to enforce their return. The absentees have always plead distress in their families, and avowed every disposition to fight for their country.[294]

October 21, 1863 (Wednesday)

Quartermaster General Alexander Lawton wrote to Secretary Seddon with a cotton concern. "All the sea transportation...of this bureau is now being availed of to send out cotton, and procure in return quartermaster's supplies. This is done for the benefit of all the military departments...I see no good to result from a partial arrangement.... It will not increase the resources of the bureau, and will lead to conflict and confusion."[295]

October 22, 1863 (Thursday)

Beauregard wrote to Longstreet, who occupied a position outside Chattanooga. "Enemy's movements indicate an early attack on Pocotaligo or Savannah. Please send forthwith [Brigadier General George] Anderson's brigade to latter city."[296]

October 23, 1863 (Friday)

Major General Gillmore learned he would not receive additional weapons to increase the firepower of his department. Halleck stated, "All conscripts from States represented in your command were some days ago ordered to be sent to you until the regiments are filled. There are not sufficient Spencer rifles manufactured to supply your requisitions, but all that can be obtained will be sent to you in preference to any one else."[297]

October 24, 1863 (Saturday)

A newspaper editor in Rome wrote of conditions not far from the front lines at Chattanooga. "Our Hospitals are full of sick and wounded soldiers...all appear to be doing well—very few deaths. The convalescents give no trouble but remain quietly within their proper limits. The Floyd Legion stick close their posts of duty, like good soldiers, some of them have almost become strangers in the city. Such men will do for soldiers. They don't spoil

---

[293] "German Ball," *Savannah Daily Morning News*, October 19, 1863, sec. 2, https://gahistoricnewspapers.galileo.usg.edu/lccn/sn82015886/1863-10-19/ed-1/seq-2/.

[294] *OR*, ser. I, vol. 28, pt. 2:412.

[295] Ibid., 418.

[296] Ibid., 440.

[297] Ibid., 112.

much paper in writing furloughs."[298]

October 25, 1863 (Sunday)

Folks in Columbus, with an eye on the weather, had concerns far more severe than a thunderclap. "Heavy rains Friday and Friday night. Cool and cloudy all day yesterday. The atmosphere continues damp and chilly. Considerable sickness in town."[299] Fears over a potential outbreak of smallpox dampened morale.

October 26, 1863 (Monday)

From near Chickamauga, General Bragg wrote to Beauregard on requested reinforcements for the coasts of South Carolina and Georgia. "Your dispatch to General Longstreet referred to me. Cannot spare troops from here. Have ordered [Major] General [Howell] Cobb, at Atlanta, to aid you. He can do it sooner and better."[300]

October 27, 1863 (Tuesday)

Secretary Seddon responded to Major General Howell Cobb's letter. "I regret that there is a conflict of views on this question between the Confederate authorities and the Governor, but the course of the Department is clear. The call for the militia was made, in the event that the quota of the State should not be filled up by volunteers under the Confederate law, for local defense and special service."[301]

October 28, 1863 (Wednesday)

Seeking reinforcements in Charleston, Beauregard asked Major General Jeremy Gilmer to consider "the matter before you, to investigate whether these companies may not be replaced...and ordered here without material risk of exposing Savannah to fall by a *coup de main*."[302]

October 29, 1863 (Thursday)

President Davis made a stop in Atlanta on his return to Richmond. A reporter noted the executive "spent the day in the city...as the guest of Mr. William Knox."[303]

October 30, 1863 (Friday)

During a stop in Macon, President Davis addressed the citizens. According to a report from the *Macon Telegraph*, Davis

> responded to his welcome in a very felicitous speech-in compliment to Georgia and Georgia soldiers-in brief exposition of the issues involved in this mighty war, which he contrasted with those of the first war of independence in glancing at its present aspects and certain fruition in complete political and commercial independence. He

---

[298] "Local," *Rome Tri-Weekly Courier*, October 24, 1863, sec. 2, https://gahistoricnewspapers.galileo.usg.edu/lccn/sn85034102/1863-10-24/ed-1/seq-2/.

[299] "The Weather," *Columbus Daily Sun*, October 25, 1863, sec. 2, https://gahistoricnewspapers.galileo.usg.edu/lccn/sn82014939/1863-10-25/ed-1/seq-2/.

[300] *OR*, ser. I, vol. 28, pt. 2:444.

[301] Candler, *Confederate Records of the State of Georgia*, 3:425.

[302] *OR*, ser. I, vol. 28, pt. 2:454. Italics in original.

[303] "The President," *Columbus Daily Sun*, October 30, 1863, sec. 1, https://gahistoricnewspapers.galileo.usg.edu/lccn/sn82014939/1863-10-30/ed-1/seq-1.

thought the signs of the times justified him in saying to every one "be of good cheer." But the cause still demanded the utmost energies of the people. Every man who could bear arms should be in the ranks, and those who could not should labor in the common cause by sustaining the armies in every way possible. He closed with a beautiful tribute to the ladies and an impressive invocation of the smile of Heaven upon the hearth-stones made desolate in this cruel and unjustifiable war, and upon the cause and the country.[304]

October 31, 1863 (Saturday) (All Hallow'e'en)

The Army of Tennessee needed additional food and Secretary Seddon called upon Governor Brown. "The difficulties in…supplies surpass any conception you can have, and it has become a question of the gravest doubt whether the army of General Bragg can be maintained…in its present position. Under these circumstances will Your Excellency pardon me for pressing on your consideration earnestly the importance…of removing all impediments to the free action of commissary officers and of giving them the countenance of your influence?"[305]

November 1, 1863 (Sunday)

The *Daily Sun* in Columbus reported on the cotton market. "There has been a good demand for cotton since our last report, and prices have advanced about two cents per pound. On Tuesday last, sixteen hundred bales were sold. Since then there has been but little cotton on the market."[306]

November 2, 1863 (Monday)

Robert Toombs wrote to Vice President Stephens from Washington, Georgia.

> Mr. Davis's present policy will overthrow the revolution in six months if the enemy only (give) him time enough to stand still and do nothing. I shall do what I can to avert so dire a calamity. Of course in adopting the proposed course towards Davis I am fully aware of the nature of the contest. We shall both fight under the same flag…with this difference: I shall avow it and he will quote scripture, say "God bids us do good for evil" and thus clothe (his) naked villainy in old odd ends stole forth from holy writ and seem a saint when he plays the devil.[307]

November 3, 1863 (Tuesday) ◗

A newspaper in Atlanta ran a story explaining how "Col. M. H. Wright" would offer "employment to one hundred boys and girls, to do light work at the C. S. Laboratory, at the old race track." The editor suggested, "There are a great many boys and girls in Atlanta, the children of poor parents, who, if industriously inclined, could earn enough money to aid,

---

[304] J. Davis, *Papers*, 10:43.

[305] Candler, *Confederate Records of the State of Georgia*, 3:426–27.

[306] "Our Markets," *Columbus Daily Sun*, November 1, 1863, https://gahistoricnewspapers.galileo.usg.edu/lccn/sn82014939/1863-11-01/ed-1/seq-2/.

[307] Toombs, Stephens, and Cobb, *Correspondence*, 630.

in a great measure, their indigent mothers. Let the parents of these boys and girls send their children to the Laboratory, where they can be made useful besides averting the evils that threaten the poor this winter."[308]

November 4, 1863 (Wednesday)

Major General Phil Sheridan filed a report on intelligence gleaned from eight Confederate deserters. "The enemy are fortifying at different points on the railroad between Chickamauga Station and Atlanta. Their works at Atlanta are said to be extensive. The troops have nothing now but corn-bread and bad meat. No salt meat is being issued."[309]

November 5, 1863 (Thursday)

The General Assembly gathered in Milledgeville and received Governor Brown's annual (printed) address. The governor endorsed the institution of slavery, multiple times, and reminded the elected delegates of the stakes.

> Again, our form of government is emphatically the poor man's best government; and he loses all his political rights, if he permits it to be overthrown. If our government were monarchical, and wealth and honors, with the right to govern, descended by the laws of the kingdom in the same family from generation to generation, the poor man would have but little interest in it, and but little inducement to fight for it. But under our form of government, wealth and honors are the exclusive prerogatives of no particular family. Like the waves of the ocean they are constantly changing place, and are transferred as generations pass, from one family to another.[310]

November 6, 1863 (Friday)

Action from the General Assembly "was to count out and add the returns of the several counties of this State, and the votes of citizens of this State in the military service of the Confederate States, and the State of Georgia; upon which it appeared that Joseph E. Brown was duly elected Governor of Georgia, for the ensuing two years, and was so declared by the presiding officer."[311] Brown received 35,558 votes, Joshua Y. Hill 18,222, and Timothy M. Furlow 3,148.

November 7, 1863 (Saturday)

Despite some misgivings among several Georgians, they would stick with Governor Brown for another term. "His Excellency Joseph E. Brown, of the county of Cherokee, elected by the people for the Fourth Term, on the first Wednesday in October last, Governor and Commander-in-Chief of the Army and Navy of this State, and the Militia thereof, for two years next ensuing, was this day, at 12 o'clock M., inaugurated in the Representative Chamber, at the Capitol, and being conducted by a Committee to the Executive Office, entered

[308] "Employment for the Poor," *Atlanta Daily Intelligencer*, November 3, 1863, https://gahistoricnewspapers.galileo.usg.edu/lccn/sn82014304/1863-11-03/ed-1/seq-3/.

[309] *OR*, ser. I, vol. 31, pt. 3:41.

[310] Candler, *Confederate Records of the State of Georgia*, 2:484–85.

[311] *Journal of the Senate of the State of Georgia…1863*, November 6, 1863, 40; Bass, "The Georgia Gubernatorial Elections of 1861 and 1863," 167–88.

upon the discharge of his duties."[312]

November 8, 1863 (Sunday)

An editor in Columbus informed citizens of the various types of artillery shot the gunners used. "Grape consists of nine shots arranged in three layers, which vary in size according to the calibre of the gun....Canister for a gun contains twenty-seven small cast iron balls, in four layers....Shrapnel consists of a very thin shell, which is filled with musket balls...."[313]

November 9, 1863 (Monday)

Robert Toombs addressed the General Assembly during an evening session. After praising the patriotic women of the South, he closed with, "Gentle woman [women], realize and accept the grand truth that liberty in its last analysis is but the blood of the brave."[314]

November 10, 1863 (Tuesday)

Governor Brown occasionally issued a permit, which allowed an individual to distill spirits for the use of the military. Today, he revoked one such certificate. "Ordered...said license issued...to said Andrew Dunn of said county of Monroe, authorizing him to distill in said county, twenty thousand gallons of whiskey for said Commissary Department...the same is, hereby revoked and annulled...."[315]

November 11, 1863 (Wednesday) ●

Beauregard wrote to Brigadier General Mercer regarding the coast of Georgia. "It is the wish of the War Department that ports favorable for the use and resort of a small class of sea-going steamers, engaged in running the blockade, shall be opened, if possible, in your district. Please have the matter thoroughly examined into, and make a detailed report to these headquarters...with such details and information as may assist the views of the Government...."[316]

November 12, 1863 (Thursday)

Governor Brown reported on the arrival of the new state seal, ordering "That said new Great Seal be adopted and used, on and after this day, as the Great Seal of the State of Georgia...."[317]

November 13, 1863 (Friday)

Secretary Seddon wrote of Major General Howell Cobb's responsibilities in Georgia, specifying the officer "was authorized in the district of country where the conscription act was suspended to form new organizations. In good faith those begun should be completed; then the suspension of the conscription law recalled, and the conscript officer put to work. I

---

[312] Candler, *Confederate Records of the State of Georgia*, 2:536.

[313] "Military Terms—The Difference between Grape, Canister, Shrapnell and Shell," *Columbus Daily Sun*, November 8, 1863, https://gahistoricnewspapers.galileo.usg.edu/lccn/sn82014939/1863-11-08/ed-1/seq-1/.

[314] "Speech of Hon. Robert Toombs," *Atlanta Daily Intelligencer*, November 13, 1863, https://gahistoricnewspapers.galileo.usg.edu/lccn/sn82014304/1863-11-13/ed-1/seq-2/.

[315] Candler, *Confederate Records of the State of Georgia*, 2:537.

[316] *OR*, ser. I, vol. 28, pt. 2:500.

[317] Candler, *Confederate Records of the State of Georgia*, 2:539.

concur in the policy of this."[318]

November 14, 1863 (Saturday)

Beauregard reported on the condition of several Confederate vessels in his department.

> Our gunboats are defective in six respects. First. They have no speed, going only from 3 to 5 miles an hour, in smooth water and no current. Second. They are of too great draught to navigate our inland waters. Third. They are unseaworthy, by their shape and construction, as represented by naval officers. Fourth. They are incapable of resisting the enemy's 15-inch shots at close quarters, as shown by the *Atlanta*, in Warsaw Sound last spring. Fifth. They cannot fight at long range, their guns not admitting an elevation greater than from 5° to 7°, corresponding to 1¼ to 1½ miles range. Even at long range, naval officers are of opinion that the oblique sides and flat decks of our gunboats would not resist the plunging shots of the enemy's 200 and 300 pounders. Sixth. They are very costly, warm, uncomfortable, and badly ventilated, consequently sickly.[319]

November 15, 1863 (Sunday)

General Bragg complained about the use of the Western and Atlantic Railroad to General Cooper. "For three weeks I have been striving to bring forward from Atlanta two battalions of troops intended for this army. My orders have been repeated over and over, without result, whilst passenger trains loaded with citizens have left that city twice every day. The transportation quartermaster there is stationed by the War Department, and not under my control."[320]

November 16, 1863 (Monday)

The General Assembly believed President Davis needed a vote of confidence, so they committed to provide one. Resolving: "the State of Georgia fully appreciating the onerous trials, and arduous duties devolving upon, the chief magistrate of the Confederate States, and realizing his patriotic devotion to the whole country and his self-denying sacrifices, tenders to him the assurances of unabated confidence, and an unalterable determination to sustain him in his efforts to conquer an honorable peace and maintain the liberties of the nation."[321]

November 17, 1863 (Tuesday) ◐

In the General Assembly, the Committee on the Judiciary made a report on various bills under their consideration, including one they did not recommend for adoption.

> A bill to be entitled an act to compensate the citizens of this State, where slaves have died from neglect while in the service of the State or of the Confederate States, by any agreement or contract with this State, where such slaves have been contributed by, or impressed from such citizens to work on the defences of Savannah, in

---

318 *OR*, ser. I, vol. 28, pt. 2:483.

319 Ibid., 503.

320 *OR*, ser. I, vol. 31, pt. 3:698.

321 *Journal of the Senate of the State of Georgia…1863*, November 16, 1863, 72.

> conformity to any resolution of the General Assembly of this State, and to point out the mode of trial for ascertaining the fact of the death of such slaves from neglect, and of the value of such slaves and for other purposes....[322]

November 18, 1863 (Wednesday)

The Georgia General Assembly voted down a "bill to make the refusal to take or receive Treasury notes of the Confederate States at par value in payment of debts, dues, or demands, or for articles bought, a test of loyalty to this State and to the cause of the Confederate States, in the war now being waged against the said Confederate States by the United States, and to punish for such refusal as an act of disloyalty as aforesaid." Skirmish reported at Trenton.[323]

November 19, 1863 (Thursday)

The Senate received for consideration, "A bill to authorize all persons in the military service of this State, or the Confederate States, including those in hospitals and detailed service, to vote at municipal elections."[324]

November 20, 1863 (Friday)

Governor Brown asked the General Assembly to pass a resolution regarding taxes.

> Requesting our Senators and Representatives in Congress to use all their influence and do all in their power to procure the speedy repeal of the law which provides for the imposition and collection of a tax in kind, and to procure such modifications of the impressment act as will compel the government to pay the market value as just compensation for property impressed by it. And to urge the passage of such laws as will require the tax in future to be collected in currency, and will absorb any redundancy of the currency caused by the payment of just compensation for property purchased by the government.[325]

November 21, 1863 (Saturday)

A hostile group confronted Rear Admiral Du Pont, and they did not wear gray clothing! Reporting to Secretary Welles, the officer indicated, "The Department is making every effort to hasten the completion of the ironclads now building, and regrets to state that the recent strike among the mechanics has caused a partial suspension of the work, and will create still further delay."[326]

November 22, 1863 (Sunday)

Colonel James T. Wheeler reported to Lieutenant General Hardee of his brigade's action in northwest Georgia. "I now hold Johnson's Crook, the enemy having retreated back to and below Trenton. Their strength was about 1,500 infantry and 200 cavalry, six pieces of artillery, and fifteen wagons. They burned Cureton's and Penn's Mills. Early part of last

---

322 Ibid., November 17, 1863, 79.

323 Ibid., November 18, 1863, 83; skirmish in Mosocco, *Chronological Tracking*, 185.

324 *Journal of the Senate of the State of Georgia...1863*, November 19, 1863, 91.

325 Candler, *Confederate Records of the State of Georgia*, 2:544–45.

326 *ORN*, ser. I, vol. 15:134.

night their forces were visible near Trenton."[327]

November 23, 1863 (Monday)

Flag Officer William Hunter received a word of caution from the Confederate Navy Department. "The frequency of...desertions to the enemy enjoins the necessity of great caution in the selection of men, as well as officers, for the performance of all such duties, as well as the propriety of having more than one officer in the guard boat."[328]

November 24, 1863 (Tuesday)

Captain W. S. Winder received instructions from the Confederate War Department. "The Secretary of War directs that a prison for the Federal prisoners shall be established in the State of Georgia...proceed without delay to select a site for that purpose in the neighborhood of Americus or Valley Ford. You will go by way of Milledgeville to consult Governor Brown, and also by way of Atlanta to consult General [Howell] Cobb. You will hold yourself in readiness to return to these headquarters as soon as ordered."[329]

November 25, 1863 (Wednesday)

The Army of Tennessee, routed off Missionary Ridge, left Tennessee and fell back into Georgia. Governor Brown reported to the legislature that several Georgia regimental flags had found their way back to the "Empire State of the South." Brown listed the colors of the 4th, 12th, 14th, and 20th Georgia Regiments, as well as the "Federal Battery Flag captured with the guns of the enemy at the battle of Chancellorsville, by the 4th Georgia Regiment. Two Battery Flags, captured at the battle of Gettysburg by [Brigadier] Gen. [George] Doles' Georgia Brigade."[330]

November 26, 1863 (Thursday)

Private P. D. Stephenson of the Washington Artillery, part of Major General Patrick Cleburne's command, joined his comrades as they "marched...to near the town of Ringgold and turned off along the road and camped. If such thing could be called 'camping.' No fires (too near the enemy), no tents, no supper...we threw ourselves at once on the ground and sank into slumber...with the depressing sense of disgraceful rout weighing on our hearts like lead." Skirmish reported near Graysville.[331]

November 27, 1863 (Friday)

Major General Patrick Cleburne's men blocked Ringgold Gap, presenting a barrier to the approaching force of Major General Joe Hooker's Corps. Hooker tried to manage his eager soldiers, noting, "the greatest difficulty I experienced with my new command, and the one which caused me the most solicitude, was to check and curb their disposition to engage, regardless of circumstances, and, it appears, almost of consequences." Cleburne's command repulsed the piece-meal attacks from the Federals long enough to allow the Army of

---

[327] *OR*, ser. I, vol. 31, pt. 3:738.

[328] *ORN*, ser. I, vol. 15:107.

[329] *OR*, ser. II, vol. 6:558.

[330] Candler, *Confederate Records of the State of Georgia*, 2:552.

[331] Stephenson, *Civil War Memoir*, 144; skirmishes in Mosocco, *Chronological Tracking*, 186.

Tennessee to safely occupy the defenses of Dalton. A Confederate soldier holding the gap, watched as Cleburne "allowed the head of the enemy's column to come within 100 feet or so of us! Indeed it did not look more than that. On they came! Down the railroad track carelessly, not in line of battle but in marching column, no skirmishers thrown out, no sign of seeing us or suspecting our presence! What a sight that was! What a moment!" Federal casualties, 507; Confederates, 221.[332]

November 28, 1863 (Saturday)

Taking to the bottle (figuratively), Governor Brown wrote to the General Assembly, "For the accommodation of the Confederate authorities, I recommend such change in the law as will remove the restriction…to the extent that the distiller who has already been licensed to make whiskey for the government shall not be prohibited from distilling corn furnished to him by the government, nor shall he be required to know where the government purchased the corn."[333]

November 29, 1863 (Sunday)

General Bragg commented on the defeat at Missionary Ridge and offered to take what he deemed to be the appropriate action. "My first estimate of our disaster was not too large, and time only can restore order and morale. All possible aid should be pushed on to Resaca, and I deem it due to the cause and to myself to ask for relief from command and an investigation into the causes of the defeat."[334]

November 30, 1863 (Monday)

The Confederate army in Dalton learned of a new chieftain when General Cooper responded to Bragg's appeal. "Your request to be relieved has been submitted to the President, who, upon your representation, directs me to notify you that you are relieved from command, which you will transfer to Lieutenant-General Hardee, the officer next in rank and now present for duty."[335]

December 1, 1863 (Tuesday)

From Dalton, Bragg wrote to General Cooper, "I shall relinquish command to-morrow. It will not do for me to remain, and I request to be ordered to Newnan or La Grange, Ga., or that vicinity. Please reply promptly."[336]

December 2, 1863 (Wednesday) ◑

Lieutenant General Hardee addressed the soldiers in the Army of Tennessee.

> General Bragg having been relieved from duty with this army, the command has devolved upon me. The steady purpose, the unflinching courage, and the unsullied patriotism of the distinguished leader who has shared your fortunes for more than a year,

---

[332] *OR*, ser. I, vol. 31, pt. 2:322; Stephenson, *Civil War Memoir*, 145–46; National Park Service, "Ringgold Gap," https://www.nps.gov/civilwar/search-battles-detail.htm?battleCode=GA005.

[333] Candler, *Confederate Records of the State of Georgia*, 2:552–53.

[334] *OR*, ser. I, vol. 31, pt. 2:682.

[335] Ibid.

[336] OR, ser. I, vol. 31, pt. 3:771.

> will be long remembered by this army and by the country he has served so well. I desire to say, in assuming command, that there is no cause for discouragement. Our losses were small and will be rapidly replaced. The country is looking to you with painful interest. I feel that it can rely upon you. Only the weak and the timid need to be cheered by constant success. Let the past take care of itself; we can and must secure the future.[337]

December 3, 1863 (Thursday)

With Georgia on his mind, General R. E. Lee wrote to President Davis.

> I have considered with some anxiety the condition of affairs in Georgia and Tennessee. My knowledge of events has been principally derived from the public papers and the impressions I have received may be erroneous, but there appears to me to be grounds to apprehend that the enemy may penetrate Georgia and get possession of our depots of provision and important manufactories. I see it stated that General Bragg has been relieved from command, and that General Hardee is only acting until another commander shall be assigned to that army. I know the difficulties that surround this subject, but if General Beauregard is considered suitable for the position, I think he can be replaced at Charleston by General Gilmer. More force, in my opinion, is required in Georgia, and it can only be had, so far as I know, from Mississippi, Mobile, and the Department of South Carolina, Georgia, and Florida.[338]

December 4, 1863 (Friday)

Lieutenant General Hardee submitted his field return, which indicated an aggregate present of 39,463 Confederate infantry and artillery in the vicinity of Dalton. A soldier in Cobb's Legion wrote to his wife from Kingston, "I hope you and Sammie are well. Don't let him forget his Daddy. I have a strong hope that these sad days will be shortened & that we will yet be happy together again. May God sanctify the troubles of these days to our eternal good. Be sure to write to me. Love to all. God bless you my dear wife & also our precious boy."[339]

December 5, 1863 (Saturday)

President Davis had contemplated sending General R. E. Lee to the Western Theater. On this day, he again broached the subject with Lee. "Could you consistently go to Dalton, as heretofore explained?" Federal scouting mission between Rossville and Ringgold reported.[340]

December 6, 1863 (Sunday)

Folks in Columbus read an editorial on General Bragg leaving Dalton.

> Who are they that now labor to revive the Bragg controversary? Have the so called "enemies" of that unfortunate officer manifested the least disposition to drag his

---

[337] Ibid., 776.

[338] Ibid., 779.

[339] Ibid., 783; Burney, *Southern Soldier's Letters Home*, 257.

[340] *OR*, ser. I, vol. 31, pt. 3:785; scout in Mosocco, *Chronological Tracking*, 189.

misfortunes before the public, at a time when delicacy and good sense both suggest the impropriety of such a course? Do toadies imagine that the demand upon the part of the army and people for Bragg's removal proceeded from motives of personal animosity merely? If so, they are even more ignorant than we had imagined them to be.[341]

December 7, 1863 (Monday)

General R. E. Lee responded to President Davis's inquiry regarding the general's willingness to take command in Georgia.

> I have had the honor to receive your dispatch, inquiring whether I could go to Dalton. I can if desired, but of the expediency of the measure you can judge better than I can. Unless it is intended that I should take permanent command, I can see no good that will result, even if in that event any could be accomplished. I also fear that I would not receive cordial co-operation, and I think it necessary if I am withdrawn from here that a commander for this army be sent to it. I hope Your Excellency will not suppose that I am offering any obstacles to any measure you may think necessary. I only seek to give you the opportunity to form your opinion after a full consideration of the subject. I have not that confidence either in my strength or ability as would lead me of my own option to undertake the command in question.[342]

December 8, 1863 (Tuesday)

President Lincoln issued a Proclamation of Amnesty and Reconstruction. The president offered, if

> in any of the States of Arkansas, Texas, Louisiana, Mississippi, Tennessee, Alabama, Georgia, Florida, South Carolina, and North Carolina, a number of persons, not less than one tenth in number of the votes cast in such state at the presidential election of [1860], each having taken the oath aforesaid, and not having since violated it, and being a qualified voter by the election law of the state existing immediately before the so-called act of secession, and excluding all others, shall reëstablish a state government which shall be republican, and in nowise contravening said oath, such shall be recognized as the true government of the state, and the state shall receive thereunder the benefits of the constitutional provision which declares that "the United States shall guaranty to every state in this Union a republican form of government, and shall protect each of them against invasion; and on application of the legislature, or the executive, (when the legislature cannot be convened,) against domestic violence."[343]

December 9, 1863 (Wednesday)

In the General Assembly, the Senate approved a resolution (House had previously approved) dealing with the Georgia battle flag issue from Governor Brown's earlier report.

---

[341] "December 6, 1863," *Columbus Daily Sun*, December 6, 1863, https://gahistoricnewspapers.galileo.usg.edu/lccn/sn82014939/1863-12-06/ed-1/seq-2/. Italics in original.

[342] *OR*, ser. I, vol. 31, pt. 3:792.

[343] Lincoln, "Proclamation of Amnesty and Reconstruction," http://www.freedmen.umd.edu/procamn.htm.

That the State of Georgia accepts with just pride these evidences of the courage and patriotism of her sons illustrated in a cause involving every principle of right, interest and honor, dear to the hearts of freemen. That the Adjutant and Inspector General, be directed, under the supervision of the Governor, to arrange said flags in some conspicuous place in the Capitol building, where they may forever remain a public testimonial of Georgia's appreciation of gallant and heroic deeds, and a public incentive to her children of future generations to emulate great and noble examples. That the Adjutant and Inspector General, be directed to make a similar disposition of all such flags as may have been heretofore, or may hereafter be received by the State.[344]

December 10, 1863 (Thursday) ●

President Davis inquired of Hardee in Dalton, "What information have you in regard to the movements and probable purposes of the enemy? Use all means to obtain full and accurate information, and keep me regularly advised. This information is necessary to guide me in the distribution of troops."[345]

December 11, 1863 (Friday)

The General Assembly worked to safeguard the coast. "Resolved...the Committee on the State Republic, are hereby instructed to consider what action it may be prudent and proper for the authorities of Georgia to take, for the encouragement of the organization of a Volunteer Navy, for the service of the Confederacy, and to increase the number of vessels and seamen engaged in the Naval service; and to report by bill or otherwise, as early as practicable upon the subject."[346]

December 12, 1863 (Saturday)

Colonel Louis D. Watkins reported on a cavalry skirmish near La Fayette. Watkins and "a force of 200 men from the Fourth and Sixth Kentucky Cavalry...charged into the town of La Fayette, capturing 18 prisoners, 6 of whom were officers of the rebel signal corps, and some 30 animals. Two hours before we arrived...the Second Kentucky (rebel) Cavalry had left the town, greatly to the regret of myself and all my command."[347]

December 13, 1863 (Sunday)

In Atlanta, Colonel Moses Wright notified the "Cook & Brother" firearms manufacturing concern in Athens of acts needed in the event of a threat from Federal forces. "It will be impossible to spare any force from here, as no doubt, if a raid should be attempted at all, so far down, this place or Augusta would certainly be the object, rather than Athens, but you should be vigilant. Call on the company in Walton County if any aid is needed. Should it be possible, we will gladly aid you." Skirmish at Ringgold.[348]

December 14, 1863 (Monday)

On a day when the Federals conducted a scouting mission between Rossville and La

---

[344] *Journal of the Senate of the State of Georgia...1863*, December 9, 1863, 189.

[345] *OR*, ser. I, vol. 52, pt. 2:575.

[346] "Resolution in Reference to a Volunteer Navy," no. 28 in *Acts of the General Assembly of the State of Georgia...November and December, 1863*, December 11, 1863, 112.

[347] *OR*, ser. I, vol. 31, pt. 1:604.

[348] *OR*, ser. I, vol. 31, pt. 3:816; skirmish in Mosocco, *Chronological Tracking*, 190.

Fayette, Captain Thomas Key spent a quiet day encamped in Dalton.

> After the day's labor was over, and while I was lying under a fly before a log heap of hickory wood roasting my feet and drowsily meditating over past happy days and thinking of my dear wife and sweet children, a band of string and brass instruments struck up inspiring music which sent thrills of joy and sacred reminiscences through every avenue of my heart. Among the pieces that the band played was that dear old tune "Home Sweet Home," around which clusters sacred memories of father, mother, sisters, and the hallowed family hearthstone. How freshly it brought to mind my interesting little family and how sincerely did I pray that God would soon return me to my happy home. While the music was pealing softly out upon the still, cold air, the peaceful moon seemed to put on a sad face and keep harmony with the music and my emotions. And even the tall pines stood motionless as if enchanted by the strains of soft music which all nature was drinking in.[349]

December 15, 1863 (Tuesday)

The General Assembly passed legislation dealing with desertion. Enacted, "That any person who shall hereafter conceal a deserter from the army or navy of the Confederate States, or from the militia or State forces of this State, while in actual service, knowing him to be a deserter, shall be guilty of a misdemeanor; and on conviction, thereof, shall he punished by fine or imprisonment in the common jail of the county, or both, in the discretion of the Court; fine not to exceed five hundred dollars, nor the imprisonment to exceed six months."[350]

December 16, 1863 (Wednesday)

General Joseph E. Johnston named commander of the Army of Tennessee. President Davis notified him, "You will turn over the immediate command of the Army of the Mississippi to Lieutenant-General [Leonidas] Polk, and proceed to Dalton and assume command of the Army of Tennessee. Give to Lieutenant-General Polk full information as to the condition of the department, and leave with him the officers of the general staff. A letter of instruction will be sent you at Dalton."[351]

December 17, 1863 (Thursday) ◐

Hardee—in Dalton—outlined to General Cooper his thoughts on the status of the Army of Tennessee. "The moral effect of inaction will be to dispirit the army and shake the confidence of the public mind. To enable this army to take the field, re-enforcements are necessary. I would respectfully suggest that the force of this army could be increased by the withdrawal of troops from other points, without materially injuring the defenses of those localities."[352]

---

[349] Key and Campbell, *Two Soldiers*, 11; scout in Mosocco, *Chronological Tracking*, 191.

[350] "An Act to punish any person who may hereafter conceal, or assist any deserter in resisting a legal arrest in this State," no. 61 in *Acts of the General Assembly of the State of Georgia...November and December, 1863*, December 15, 1863, 63.

[351] *OR*, ser. I, vol. 31, pt. 3:835–36.

[352] Ibid., 840.

December 18, 1863 (Friday)
Secretary Seddon provide Johnston with "fuller instructions" as the president had promised two days prior.

> It is apprehended the army may have been by recent events somewhat disheartened and deprived of ordnance and material. Your presence, it is hoped, will do much to inspire hope and re-establish confidence, and through such influence, as well as by the active exertions you are recommended to make, men who have straggled may be recalled to their standards, and others, roused by the danger to which further successes of the enemy must expose the more southern States, may be encouraged to recruit the ranks of your army. It is desired that your early and vigorous efforts be directed to restoring the discipline, confidence, and prestige of the army and to increasing its numbers, and that at the same time you leave no means unspared to restore and supply its deficiencies in ordnance, numbers, and transportation. The movements of the enemy give no present indications of a purpose to attack your army...as soon as the condition of your forces will allow it is hoped you will be able to assume the offensive.[353]

December 19, 1863 (Saturday)
A Union sympathizer from East Tennessee, A. G. W. Puckett, provided valuable intelligence to Colonel John Parkhurst in Chattanooga.

> The rebel General Hardee is strengthening his position and fortifying between Tunnel Hill and Dalton, and also at Resaca, near Oostenaula River, on the Western and Atlantic Railroad, and also at the river near the Allatoona Mountains. This last place is a very formidable position for the rebels, as the river is near where the railroad passes through the mountains. These mountains will be hard to pass through, as they are all cut up with sharp hills and deep ravines, and but few pass-ways through them, and these pass-ways being a good piece apart on our left, from 10 to 20 miles apart, and not much better on the right. I am reliably informed that they intend to make a stand at this point, as they think they cannot be flanked in these mountains. The Georgia militia are now on Hardee's left at Dirt Town, this side of Rome.

Sections of northeast Georgia—Rabun, Gilmer, Union, and other counties—harbored bands of Union sympathizers and deserters starting in late 1862. Jeff Anderson numbered among the leader of these gangs.[354]

December 20, 1863 (Sunday)
In Dalton, Captain Thomas Key enjoyed "the Holy Sabbath and it affords me a deep, quiet pleasure to sit by my dirt jambs and peruse the letters addressed to me by my Savior."[355]

December 21, 1863 (Monday)
Beauregard sent a telegraph to Major General Jeremy Gilmer in Savannah. "Can you not

---

[353] Ibid., 842–43.

[354] Ibid., 447; Avery, *History of the State of Georgia*, 257.

[355] Key and Campbell, *Two Soldiers*, 13.

manage to get from Gorgas or the Secretary of War a few heavy guns, 10-inch columbiads and others, for the defense of Savannah? It seems to me that at least six should be furnished at once. Two 10-inch columbiads have already been promised me, but they have not yet been sent." Federal scout from Rossville to La Fayette reported.[356]

December 22, 1863 (Tuesday)

Prior to General Johnston arriving in Dalton, Hardee offered a Christmas present to the soldiers in the Army of Tennessee.

> In order to give to our brave soldiers an opportunity to visit their homes and provide for their families during the winter, the following system of furloughs is announced: For every 30 men of each regiment actually present in camp for duty, 1 man may be furloughed for any period not exceeding thirty days, conditioned that the same be approved by the proper company and regimental commanders certifying that no man of the same company furloughed under this order remains absent without leave, and the application shall then be approved at brigade, division, corps, and army headquarters.[357]

December 23, 1863 (Wednesday)

President Davis wrote to General Johnston on expectations for future military action.

> This is addressed under the supposition that you have arrived at Dalton [Johnston had not] and have assumed command of the forces at that place. The intelligence recently received respecting the condition of that army is encouraging, and induces me to hope that you will soon be able to commence active operations against the enemy. You will not need to have it suggested that the imperative demand for prompt and vigorous action arises, not only from the importance of restoring the prestige of the army, and averting the dispiriting and injurious results that must attend a season of inactivity, but from the necessity of reoccupying the country, upon the supplies of which the proper subsistence of our armies materially depends. It is my desire that you should communicate fully and freely with me concerning your proposed plan of action, that all the assistance and co-operation may be most advantageously afforded that it is in the power of the Government to render.[358]

December 24, 1863 (Thursday)

Hardee informed the War Department on the condition of the Army of Tennessee.

> The troops are in comfortable winter quarters, and the health of the men unprecedentedly good. A general and liberal system of furloughs "has been adopted, which, it is believed, will be productive of much good. Our losses in artillery and artillery horses have been replaced, old batteries have been refitted and new ones obtained, and the army is again provided with a sufficiency of serviceable field artillery. I feel

---

[356] *OR*, ser. I, vol. 28, pt. 2:568; scout in Mosocco, *Chronological Tracking*, 192.

[357] *OR*, ser. I, vol. 31, pt. 3:855.

[358] Ibid., 856–57.

great pleasure in turning over the command to General Johnston in the fine condition above exhibited.[359]

December 25, 1863 (Friday) (Christmas Day)

In Dalton, Captain Thomas Key and comrades enjoyed Christmas Day. "Before breakfast the Doctor made some eggnog, a worthy luxury that is seldom enjoyed in the army. Had sausages for breakfast, quite a treat, the first within the last twelve months. Ralph Bailey and Willie Smith called at my cabin about eleven o'clock, when Bailey made the second eggnog. All went smoothly in the battery. Out in the open air some of the men were hopping to the notes of an old fiddle, trying to be merry."[360]

December 26, 1863 (Saturday)

Hardee issued General Orders, No. 229, his final as provisional commander of the Army of Tennessee.

> The commander of the forces sees with pain the leniency with which crimes and offenses of an aggravated nature are treated by courts-martial. Adequate, prompt, and certain punishment for commission of offenses is essential to the preservation of the discipline, morale, and efficiency of the army. The frequent occurrence of disobedience of orders or inactivity in the execution of them, desertion from the service, the embezzlement of public stores, show conclusively that so long as guilt remains unpunished disorders and crimes will abound. The fact should deeply enter the mind of the army and country, that in time of active war, where the safety of the Confederacy is at stake, all who have neglected their duty and have deserted their colors should be punished as they deserve. Inadequate punishments for such offenses are neither just nor humane. The commander of the forces announces that in future the law will be faithfully and promptly enforced. Courts-martial will therefore proceed diligently to the trial of all cases which may be brought before them. Their proceedings will be promptly rendered, and the execution of their sentences promptly carried into effect. It shall be the duty of the inspectors-general of each corps, division, and brigade of the army to see after every muster that all stoppages of pay ordered by courts-martial or the military courts are entered on the muster-rolls.[361]

December 27, 1863 (Sunday)

In Dalton, General Johnston issued General Orders, No. 1. "In obedience to the orders of His Excellency the President, [I have] the honor to assume command of the Army of Tennessee."[362]

December 28, 1863 (Monday)

General Johnston offered his initial assessment of the Army of Tennessee. To Secretary Seddon, he reported ,"This army is now far from being in condition to resume the

---

[359] Ibid., 860.

[360] Key and Campbell, *Two Soldiers*, 15.

[361] *OR*, ser. I, vol. 31, pt. 3:869–70.

[362] Ibid., 873.

offensive. It is deficient in numbers, arms, subsistence stores, and field transportation. Let me remind you that I have little if any power to procure supplies for the army. Having no power to procure means of feeding, equipping, or moving the army, I am also released from corresponding responsibilities."[363]

December 29, 1863 (Tuesday)

Tennessee Senator Gustavus A. Henry wrote to General Johnston in Dalton. "We are all greatly rejoiced to know that you are in command of the Army of Tennessee. I discover from my correspondence you possess the entire confidence of this whole country as you do mine. Whip the invaders before you, and you will break the power of the enemy and secure the independence of our country. The country looks to you for great results."[364]

December 30, 1863 (Wednesday)

Captain Thomas Key offered his opinion on Major General Patrick Cleburne's "views...upon...calling into the field 300,000 negroes and also upon the question of emancipating the negroes." Key suggested, "The idea of abolishing the institution at first startles everyone, but when it is viewed as the means of giving us victory or closing the war, every person with whom I have conversed readily concurs that liberty and peace are the paramount questions and is willing to sacrifice everything to obtain them. All, however, believe the institution a wise one and sanctioned by God."[365]

December 31, 1863 (Thursday)

Gertrude Thomas, in her home outside Augusta, closed the year "in the sitting room before a fire which is almost out and the rain which has been falling steadily all last night and today still continues.... I could look into the fire and listening to the rain drops as they fall, reflect upon the disappointment of our sanguine hopes for the coming of peace with the closing of the year. But I will strive against such feelings and hope that the close of 1864 may find us an Independent Nation upon the face of the earth but while I hope so I confess that there is more hope than trust. Our prospects are extremely gloomy."[366]

---

[363] Ibid., 874.

[364] Ibid., 878–79.

[365] Key and Campbell, *Two Soldiers*, 18–19.

[366] Thomas, *Secret Eye*, 219.

Chapter 4

1864

Moon Stage Legend: ◐ first quarter; ○ full, ◑ last quarter, ● new
January 1, 1864 (Friday) ◑
Military officials reported a skirmish near Dalton.[1] Writing from Mansfield, Dolly Lunt Burge noted in her diary, "A new year is ushered in but peace comes not with it. A bloody war is still decimating our nation & thousands of hearts are to day bleeding over the loss of loved ones."[2]
January 2, 1864 (Saturday)
Before the heat of military action warmed the spring, Georgians struggled with unusually chilly weather. Atlanta diarist Sam Richards shared, "I am told the thermometer said 8° only and it was so cold we could hardly keep comfortable in bed."[3] Dolly Lunt Burge, perhaps suffering from fingers too cold for extensive writing, asserted, "Coldest day I have ever known in Georgia."[4] Confederate generals gathered in Dalton to listen to a proposal from Major General Patrick Cleburne. The native Irishman proposed arming enslaved males. "The immediate effect of the emancipation and enrollment of negroes on the military strength of the South would be: To enable us to have armies numerically superior to those of the North, and a reserve of any size we might think necessary; to enable us to take the offensive, move forward, and forage on the enemy."[5]
January 3, 1864 (Sunday)
Sam Richards lamented on shortages after nearly three years of war, exclaiming, "O dear me! Last year I didn't like turnips, and now I do!"[6]
January 4, 1864 (Monday)
Anticipating the upcoming spring military campaign season, the *Columbus Daily Times* carried an editorial on what might lay in the future for Georgia, especially along the coast. "The point against which the power of the enemy will be concentrated and hurled is not yet determined, but we think it more than probable that Charleston or Savannah, or lines connecting those two cities, before the winter closes, will feel its pressure."[7]
January 5, 1864 (Tuesday)

---

[1] Irvine, *Military Operations of the Civil War*, 4:163.
[2] Burge, *Diary*, 142.
[3] Richards, *Civil War Diary*, 215.
[4] Burge, *Diary*, 143.
[5] *OR*, ser. I, vol. 52, pt. 2:590.
[6] Richards, *Civil War Diary*, 215.
[7] "The Coast," *Columbus Daily Times*, January 4, 1864, 2, https://gahistoricnewspapers.galileo.usg.edu/lccn/sn82015388/1864-01-04/ed-1/seq-2/.

Issuing a call "To the People of the Southern Confederacy," a Milledgeville newspaper reprinted a plea, which originally appeared in the *Columbus Sun*. "The country needs all that every man can do. The safety of your property, your liberties and your lives, requires at your hands all that you can do. If you are in a position of have the means to do more than others, be not afraid of doing too much, but be thankful that you can do so much."[8]

January 6, 1864 (Wednesday)

One year later, Beauregard continued to correspond with Confederate officials in Savannah. This time, Major General of Engineers Jeremy Gilmer stood on the receiving end: "Reports from the enemy say he intends attacking Savannah via Ogeechee River. May not be true, but have an eye in that direction. Are any encampments visible along this coast?"[9]

January 7, 1864 (Thursday)

In Camden County, Julia Johnson Fisher's diary entry captured hardships on the home front, even for those living far from the front lines. "There has been great destruction of property here by the pickets as well as the enemy. Instead of a protection they are a great injury; and nuisance—not one raised a finger to save any property from the fire, and no person has been near us. We are in a desolated region. Should the enemy burn us out we know not where to go."[10]

January 8, 1864 (Friday)

General Joseph E. Johnston issued General Orders No. 5 from his headquarters in Dalton (see Appendix 5).

January 9, 1864 (Saturday) ●

General Johnston, concerned over the flow of matériel to his army, wrote to President Davis, suggesting, "the difficulty in supplying us comes from the employment of a large number of cars in transporting Government cotton to Wilmington. Rolling-stock and roads necessary for transporting our supplies are thus used to such an extent as to make it difficult to furnish daily rations. I beg you to consider this."[11]

January 10, 1864 (Sunday)

Writing from Warm Springs, Georgia, General Braxton Bragg shared his fond hopes for the future of the Army of Tennessee. "I shall follow you and your noble comrades with prayers as fervent and hopes as strong as when I shared the toils and honors of the field, and no one of you will rejoice more than myself at the success which I trust awaits you, and at the future award of honors already won."[12]

January 11, 1864 (Monday)

Nurse Kate Cumming, working at a hospital in Newnan, wrote of a recent meal with

---

[8] James N. Bethune, "To the People of the Southern Confederacy," *Milledgeville Southern Recorder*, January 5, 1864, 2, https://gahistoricnewspapers.galileo.usg.edu/lccn/sn82016415/1864-01-05/ed-1/seq-2/.

[9] *OR*, ser. I, vol. 35, pt. 1:509.

[10] Fisher, *Diary, 1864*, 3.

[11] *OR*, ser. I, vol. 32, pt. 2:537.

[12] Ibid., 543.

Confederate cavalry troopers and offered her opinion on morale away from the front lines. "We had five of Scott's cavalry dine with us to-day. They are very hopeful of our cause, but we seldom meet a soldier down-hearted. It is only the home folks who grumble."[13]

January 12, 1864 (Tuesday)

Savoring an early meal during his winter encampment in Dalton, Private John Jackman, with the Orphan Brigade from Kentucky, noted in his diary, "Foggy this morning. Had hot biscuits, butter, molasses and stewed peaches for breakfast. Quite an improvement on our general bill of fare. Damp—appearance of snow."[14]

January 13, 1864 (Wednesday)

Continuing to resupply the Army of Tennessee, General Joseph E. Johnston remained frustrated with the rail network. His letter to Georgia's Adjutant General Henry Wayne detailed, in Johnston's opinion, the problem. "I beg you to represent to the Governor the importance of immediate reform in the management of the railroad from Atlanta to Dalton. It seems to be entirely unmanaged. Unless the State authorities act promptly in this matter we shall be compelled to march back to our sources of supply. I addressed the Governor yesterday on this subject."[15] Brigadier General William Wofford received reassignment from the Army of Northern Virginia to take command of the Department of North Georgia.[16]

January 14, 1864 (Thursday)

Quartermaster General Alexander Lawton reiterated General Johnston's message regarding the railroads supplying his army in Dalton. "General Johnston considers the supply of his army as seriously endangered by the condition of the Western and Atlantic Railroad. The want of fuel and condition of rolling-stock present serious obstacles. I beg to call your attention earnestly to this matter, as the fate of Georgia may depend on that road. Can this Department assist in any arrangement you desire to make?"[17]

January 15, 1864 (Friday) ◐

Remaining in their winter encampment in Dalton, the Confederate soldiers struggled to ward off cold, wet weather. Various newspapers printed their solicitations for items from home. "Company C, 9th Ga. Batt. Art., is, at this time, standing greatly in need of Clothing, Shoes, and Blankets. The weather is very severe, and it is impossible for soldiers to serve their country in the absence of these comforts. The snow covers the face of the earth in this region, and the suffering is great, and will continue to augment, if not relieved by kind friends at home."[18]

January 16, 1864 (Saturday)

---

[13] Cumming, *Kate*, 186–87.

[14] Jackman, *Diary of a Confederate Soldier*, 103.

[15] *OR*, ser. I, vol. 32, pt. 2:552.

[16] Hannings, *Every Day of the Civil War*, 391.

[17] Candler, *Confederate Records of the State of Georgia*, 3:453.

[18] "To the Citizens of Columbus and Surrounding Country," *Columbus Daily Sun*, January 15, 1864, https://gahistoricnewspapers.galileo.usg.edu/lccn/sn82014939/1864-01-15/ed-1/seq-1/.

Sam Richards had received a notice informing him of pending conscription, a situation he sought to avoid. After trying to obtain an exemption as a printer, Confederate enrollment officials notified him a trip to Decatur, and a plea to officials there, might prove satisfactory. As he lamented his uncertain future, Richards wrote,

> So all I can do now, will be to go to Head Quarters at Decatur and see what...the Chief Enrolling Officer will do about it. If am forced to serve just because I put in a substitute when I was already exempt without, thinking that I was thereby benefitting the country as well as myself, I shall always feel as though I was doubly cheated and injured, and cannot be expected to serve with much love and zeal a government that has acted in such a way.[19]

January 17, 1864 (Sunday)

Private John Daniels and his comrades in the 13th Michigan Infantry received orders to prepare for departing Savannah. "We have orders to march but do not know where to but we suppose somewhere to the North East of this place. Perhaps to Charleston S.C. or to Augusta Ga. or north west of this place to Macon, Ga. We are ordered to be ready with four days rations."[20]

January 18, 1864 (Monday)

"The winter is wearing away, and soon our battle flags will have to be unfurled to the breezes of spring, and the lines of gray will have to be drawn up a living wall, against which the tide of invasion, it is hoped, will beat in vain." Private John Jackman, 9th Kentucky Infantry, looked toward the upcoming campaign in writing a letter to a newspaper editor.[21]

January 19, 1864 (Tuesday)

Saddened by the absence of her husband—a loneliness many ladies across the South shared—Kate Peddy wrote to her spouse, George, a surgeon in the 56th Georgia Infantry, who was wintering in Dalton. "If I could only find language expression enough to convey you an idea of the love that fills my heart for you," she wrote, "such burning words of affection would be penned as never a mortal being saw before, but I have so often tried to tell you and then made a most miserable failure, it is almost useless to try."[22]

January 20, 1864 (Wednesday)

General Johnston issued General Orders No. 14, which dealt with reenlistments. "In the regiments re enlisted for the war, furloughs will be granted at the rate of 1 to every 10 men present for duty. These furloughs will be granted until the season of active operations begin. The certificates of commanders will conform accordingly."[23]

January 21, 1864 (Thursday)

---

[19] Richards, *Civil War Diary*, 216.

[20] Daniels, *Marching through Georgia*, n.p.

[21] Jackman, *Diary of a Confederate Soldier*, 104.

[22] Peddy, *Saddle Bag and Spinning Wheel*, 197.

[23] *OR*, ser. I, vol. 32, pt. 2:582. Researchers can find a listing of the various units composing the Army of Tennessee in this same section of the *OR*.

A Federal regiment, the 28th Kentucky Mounted Infantry, under the command of Colonel William P. Boone, moved deeper into Georgia. Boone reported on the movement of the day. "Started from Rossville…with 220 men and 11 officers…and 211 men and 4 officers of the Fourth Michigan Cavalry; total, 446. Moved through McLemore's Cove to a point between Blue Bird and Dug Gaps, 25 miles south of Chattanooga."[24]

January 22, 1864 (Friday)

Brigadier General Alfred Iverson reported from Rome, on a skirmish earlier in the day. "Dispatch received states enemy surprised [Colonel A. B.] Culberson's command (Georgia State Guards) last night, 7 o'clock. Thinks they retired toward La Fayette."[25]

January 23, 1864 (Saturday)

Reporting various pieces of military information to President Davis, General Johnston communicated the improved conditions of the railroad servicing his army in Dalton. "The management of the railroad is much improved…we are much better supplied. We have now on hand provision and forage (corn) for several days. Our horses and mules are in very poor condition…from the effect of cold weather, short allowance of corn, and want of long forage, all… having been exhausted in December. Our prospects are better for the future, the chief quartermaster thinks."[26]

January 24, 1864 (Sunday)

General Johnston issued a circular to the troops in the Army of Tennessee regarding the judicious use of rations. "The great and growing scarcity of meat demands that no lot should be condemned as unfit for issue without close and minute examination. Brigade commanders are directed to select a board of three experienced and competent field officers, whose duty it shall be to inspect all stores in the brigade reported as unfit for issue. If parts of a joint only are affected they will see that the unsound is removed and the remainder furnished to the troops."[27]

January 25, 1864 (Monday)

Surgeon Peddy wrote to his wife, Kate, from Dalton, sharing his optimism for the coming campaign season. "Our troops are in good spirits and are ready for the conflict to begin. I think they will be more fighting this year than any year of the war. The Lincoln Government are going to send their legions which they are now fitting out against us from all quarters and all directions. If every one will do their duty, you need not fear to hear from the result." A Federal scout headed toward Rome in search of rations.[28]

January 26, 1864 (Tuesday)

Julia Fisher, writing from Camden County, lamented the war's impact on inflation. "So far as we can ascertain people seem certain that the confederacy is short lived; that this year must terminate the war. Confederate money is almost valueless. Worth only five cents on

---

[24] *OR*, ser. I, vol. 32, pt. 2:198.

[25] *OR*, ser. I, vol. 32, pt. 1:112.

[26] *OR*, ser. I, vol. 32, pt. 2:603.

[27] Ibid., 609.

[28] Peddy, *Saddle Bag and Spinning Wheel*, 201–202; Mosocco, *Chronological Tracking*, 209.

the dollar."[29]

January 27, 1864 (Wednesday)

Seeking additional infantry soldiers, not troopers in the saddle, General Johnston wrote to President Davis from Dalton in response to the latest information regarding recruiting efforts from Brigadier General John Hunt Morgan.

> I think that much discontent in the infantry would be produced by authorizing [Joseph] Lewis' brigade to mount themselves. We want infantry, and all our infantry wish to be cavalry. The troops from Texas, Arkansas, and West Tennessee are as eager to be mounted as the Kentuckians. Men professing to have authority are recruiting in Georgia and Alabama for Forrest and Morgan illegally. I beg that such authority may be revoked. They prevent recruiting infantry.[30]

January 28, 1864 (Thursday)

Military orders emanated from Dalton, as General Johnston issued General Orders Nos. 15 and 17. The first dealt with furloughs for troops "volunteering their services for the war." The second order involved a reduction in various matériel for the army, and specified the field transportation regulations at the corps, division, brigade, and regimental levels. For regiments, "(counting those consolidated as one): Officers' baggage, including desks, money boxes, and medicine chests, 1 6-horse wagon • every 300 enlisted men present for duty, 1 wagon and 1 ambulance; battalion of sharpshooters, 1 wagon."[31]

January 29, 1864 (Friday)

Captain A.T. Fielder, with the 12th Tennessee Infantry, wrote of camp conditions in Dalton. "Cloudy with appearance of falling weather Health good wound improving. All quiet in Camp The day was Cloudy and warm. Nothing going on but the Common routine of duties of a soldier in Camp Night had prayer meeting Lt. Lane left on furlough rained lightly after prayers lay down about 9½ oclk (finished and sent off the letter beginning yesterday)."[32]

January 30, 1864 (Saturday)

Reports of skirmishing along Chickamauga Creek occurred during the day, while in Dalton, Private Lorenzo Sanders—with the 30th Tennessee Infantry—participated in a corps review.[33]

January 31, 1864 (Sunday) ◐

An officer with the 10th South Carolina Infantry, writing from winter quarters in Dalton, told his fiancée of reenlistments underway in the Army of Tennessee. "The great majority of this Brigade, I am glad to say, has re-enlisted unconditionally for the war. All men re-enlisting are entitled to furlough in the proportion of one furlough to ten men re-enlisted,

---

[29] Fisher, *Diary, 1864*, 5.

[30] *OR*, ser. I, vol. 32, pt. 2:621.

[31] Ibid., 631–32.

[32] Cathey, *Captain T. A. Fielder's Civil War Diary*, 304.

[33] Harrison, "The Diary of an 'Average' Confederate Soldier," 266.

a great many are now going off under this order, and which by the way, is quite a stimulus to the good work. I don't think legally it will amount to anything, but I like to see the spirit shown."[34]

February 1, 1864 (Monday)

Julia Fisher commented on the reported prices of various goods in Savannah. Where one person "paid $6.00 a yard for calico in Savannah—it is now selling at $10.00. Only $100.00 for a calico dress—a fine state of things! Confederate money is hardly worth picking up." She then turned her focus on upcoming military campaigning season. "They are collecting an army of 80,000 to have a finishing battle in the Spring. God speed the right!"[35]

February 2, 1864 (Tuesday)

Captain Fielder spent part of his day enjoying the "clear and pleasant" weather in Dalton and participating in "Regimental drill & Dress parade." As evening approached, the temperature dropped and the winds fluttered the flaps of Fielder's tent, as "after prayers [he] lay down about 9 oclk."[36]

February 3, 1864 (Wednesday)

Lieutenant General Leonidas Polk requested reinforcements from the Army of Tennessee to assist in protecting vital locations in Alabama. General Johnston responded, "The enemy, much more than double my number, is in motion in my front. I have not cavalry enough to observe him, so that it is impossible for me to promise further than that I will at any time give you all aid in my power, but do not see now that I can help you."[37]

February 4, 1864 (Thursday)

Gertrude Clanton Thomas finally got to meet Brigadier General John Hunt Morgan. Writing from Burke County, she penned a detailed description of the officer, who didn't look like what she had imagined. She found Morgan a "handsome, light haired, fair complexioned man...he wears a mustache and goatee and has a genial smile which irradiates his whole face."[38] Morgan came to Georgia to recruit new troopers for his cavalry command.

February 5, 1864 (Friday)

A big day for the Army of Tennessee, one that Private Jackman enjoyed. "Grand review of the army by Gen'l Johnston to-day. A beautiful day for the occasion. This review took place in a large field south of town, half a mile. The troops were formed in three parallel lines, each nearly, or quite two miles in length. After the Gen'l rode up and down the lines, going in front and rear of each, he took his station at a point for all to pass on review." Jackman took pride, as his "brigade did finely...."[39]

February 6, 1864 (Saturday)

The passing days brought thoughts of spring to many on the home front. Julia Johnson

---

[34] Walker, *Great Things Are Expected of Us*, 96–97.

[35] Fisher, *Diary, 1864*, 6.

[36] Cathey, *Captain T. A. Fielder's Civil War Diary*, 305.

[37] *OR*, ser. I, vol. 32, pt. 2:662.

[38] Thomas, *Secret Eye*, 221.

[39] Jackman, *Diary of a Confederate Soldier*, 106.

Fisher journaled, "The weather is now delightful and summer like. All are busy planting and clearing the land. Oh! how we all long for a time of peace and plenty, for our once happy land that was flowing with milk and honey."[40] In Atlanta, Sam Richards attended a welcoming ceremony for Brigadier General Morgan.[41]

February 7, 1864 (Sunday) ●

A revival occurred during the winter of 1863–1864, which affected armies North and South. Dalton served as the epicenter of religious activity for the Confederates in the Western Theater, as Captain A.T. Fielder with the 12th Tennessee Infantry attended two worship services. "The morning Clear and Cool—Health good wound doing well—at 11 oclk heard the Chaplin of the 13th & 154th Tenn Regts. Subject the fall of man and cited to the 3rd Chap. of Gen. for a foundation—at 2½ oclk. P.M. preaching by our Chaplin subject the Ten Commandments together with the Lords Prayer and the paralell run between them…night after prayers lay down awhile after 9 oclk."[42]

February 8, 1864 (Monday)

The Federals conducted reconnaissance missions in preparation for a movement toward Dalton, and skirmishes occurred near Ringgold.[43]

February 9, 1864 (Tuesday)

The Confederate War Department issued Special Orders No. 33. "Lieut. Gen. J. B. Hood will proceed without delay to Dalton, Ga., and report to General Joseph E. Johnston, commanding, for assignment to the command of an army corps."[44]

February 10, 1864 (Wednesday)

Family news saddened the day for Dolly Lunt Burge. "Little did I think while writing the above that away in Maine my native state friends & relatives were laying in the grave my father & stepmother. By a letter received through 'flag of truce' I learn they both died the last day of the old year. Of what disease I know not. Oh this cruel war that has deprived me of being with them & ministering to their wants. I step into my parents place & will soon follow them to the grave."[45]

February 11, 1864 (Thursday)

Lieutenant William E. Readick, Company B, 63rd Georgia Infantry, reported from Thunderbolt Battery outside Savannah. "This company was ordered to picket Whitemarsh Island…therefore proceeded to that place and arrived there the same day, a distance by water of some three miles to Point of Rocks, which was…Headquarters."[46]

February 12, 1864 (Friday)

President Davis wrote to Johnston with a request for the general to assist Lieutenant

---

[40] Fisher, *Diary, 1864*, 6.

[41] Richards, *Civil War Diary*, 218.

[42] Cathey, *Captain T. A. Fielder's Civil War Diary*, 306.

[43] Mosocco, *Chronological Tracking*, 205.

[44] *OR*, ser. I, vol. 32, pt. 2:699.

[45] Burge, *Diary*, 143.

[46] Hewett, *Supplement to the Official Records*, pt. 2, vol. 7:175.

General Polk's beleaguered force outside Jackson, Mississippi; from Dalton, Johnston responded. "I have, by telegraph, expressed to His Excellency the opinion that I cannot effectually reenforce General Polk without making this army too weak to resist an advance of the enemy; so that we cannot aid General Polk without leaving the way into Georgia open. Not being able to do both I am waiting for further instructions."[47]

February 13, 1864 (Saturday)

Rear Admiral John Dahlgren notified Lieutenant Commander Austin Pendergrast of needed investigation along the coast of Georgia. "It is rumored that two or three steamers are in the river near Darien, watching an opportunity to escape. You will please give me all the information you can collect about them, and also your opinion as to the practicability of capturing them."[48]

February 14, 1864 (Sunday) (Valentine's Day) ◐

Preparing for an advance on Dalton, Major General George Thomas wrote to Major General U. S. Grant. "As I am desirous of using a portion of [Major General John] Logan's force in the movement on Dalton, I think it will be better for his whole train to come here. As yet no one knows of the direction of the movement. I therefore have great hopes of its success."[49]

February 15, 1864 (Monday)

The war entered the third year amid an ever-tightening blockade. Shrinking supplies of matériel prompted Governor Brown to seek additional supply outlets. An agency in Wilmington, North Carolina, received a request: "Reposing special trust and confidence in your capacity and integrity, I hereby commission you as agent of the State of Georgia, to act for her in Wilmington in receiving and storing, and under my instructions, exporting cotton for said State and receiving, storing and forwarding supplies for soldiers' clothing, blankets, military equipments, etc., imported for said State."[50]

February 16, 1864 (Tuesday)

Captain A.T. Fielder, with the 12th Tennessee Infantry in Dalton, busied himself with paperwork to ward off the winter chill. "Clear and verry Cold having been one of the Coldest nights of the season health good wound improving—I went before the board of Surgeons who recommended that I have a furlough on account of my wound The Company payrolls were sent round to be filled out for the months of Nov. & Decr. I was engaged a part of the evening at work upon them."[51]

February 17, 1864 (Wednesday)

Via General Orders No. 22, General Johnston informed the Army of Tennessee of a new policy. "The system of cavalry tactics prepared by Major-General Wheeler is adopted for

---

[47] *OR*, ser. I, vol. 32, pt. 2:727.

[48] *ORN*, ser. I, vol. 15:322.

[49] *OR*, ser. I, vol. 32, pt. 2:389.

[50] Candler, *Confederate Records of the State of Georgia*, 2:574.

[51] Cathey, *Captain T. A. Fielder's Civil War Diary*, 308–309.

the use of the cavalry of the Army of Tennessee."[52]

February 18, 1864 (Thursday)

Skirmishing occurred in northwest Georgia. Captain William C. Harris with the 38th Illinois Infantry reported, "A detachment was also sent to Ellidge's Mill, where they found a picket station, and captured 6 men, among the number a lieutenant."[53]

February 19, 1864 (Friday)

Gathering intelligence on an opponent's position and strength proved challenging, often dangerous, and sometimes rewarding. Major General Thomas received such a gift from a returning surgeon, earlier held captive. Using this information, he updated Major General Grant in Nashville with intelligence, which placed "Cleburne's division at Tunnel Hill; Stewart's division between Tunnel Hill and Dalton; Walker 2 miles out from Dalton, toward Spring Place; Cheatham at Dalton, and Stevenson's and Bate's divisions to the west of Dalton 2 miles. He saw all of the camps, and estimates their force, between 30,000 and 40,000."[54]

February 20, 1864 (Saturday)

Moving his regiment from Dalton to Demopolis, Alabama, to reinforce the area, Captain A.T. Fielder penciled events of the day in his diary. "This morning found us on the Cars and a little after sun rise we reached LaGrange Ga. where we remained until 9 oclk. awating some trains to pass when we left. Clear & verry white frost Health good wound a little sore we reached West Point at 11 oclk. Night still cold we lay down early layover all night."[55]

February 21, 1864 (Sunday)

Preparing for an advance on Dalton, Grant wrote to Thomas inquiring, "Do your troops move to-morrow? It is important that at least a demonstration be made at once." Thomas replied, "Your dispatch, of this morning received. The troops will move to-morrow morning by daylight."[56]

February 22, 1864 (Monday)

The Federals began advancing during an operation, which would take the name Demonstration on Dalton. The first day out, Major General Thomas, and others, seemed genuinely concerned with the whereabouts of Major General Cleburne. Thomas penned two dispatches on the subject. The first, to Major General John Palmer: "If Cleburne is really moving toward Demopolis you had better give your entire attention to Dalton." The next message, to Major General Joe Hooker, related, "A scout has just come in and reports Cleburne's division at La Fayette with the intention of moving into McLemore's Cove this morning. He may intend to make a demonstration in this direction, or he may intend to attack the railroad between this and Bridgeport. Warn your troops to be on the lookout,

52 *OR*, ser. I, vol. 32, pt. 2:759.

53 *OR*, ser. I, vol. 32, pt. 1:407.

54 *OR*, ser. I, vol. 32, pt. 2:429.

55 Cathey, *Captain T. A. Fielder's Civil War Diary*, 309–10.

56 *OR*, ser. I, vol. 32, pt. 2:442–43.

and have the country observed in their front as far as possible."[57]

February 23, 1864 (Tuesday)

William Bate received promotion to the rank of major general, but the Confederates found the day occupied in skirmishing with the advancing Federals. Bate would have to wait for his party. General Johnston acted to turn Lieutenant General Hardee's troops, marching to reinforce Polk in Alabama, around and urged their rush back to Dalton. Johnston closed, emphatically stating, "The enemy is advancing; is now in force at Tunnel Hill. Lose no time." Skirmishing took place at Catoosa Station, Dalton, and Tunnel Hill.[58]

February 24, 1864 (Wednesday)

Skirmishing took place at Buzzard Roost, Rocky Face Ridge, and Tunnel Hill, as the Federals continued the press on Dalton. Private John Jackman with the 9th Kentucky Infantry, despite the nearby skirmishing, spent the day at ease. "We are quietly resting on arms not having heard a hostile gun yet. The news from the front is, that the enemy is advancing in strong force, slowly, and are about Tunnell Hill, the main body having camped at Ringgold last night. Our troops are still coming up from the rear, and are in fine spirits. Things don't look so much like a retreat now-more like 'fight.'"[59] The first prisoners arrived at Camp Sumter in Andersonville.

February 25, 1864 (Thursday)

From Dalton, General Johnston reported, "We have been skirmishing all day successfully." During a day that produced a military encounter near Frick's Gap, Federal Major General John Palmer issued orders to Brigadier General Charles Cruft. "You will push forward with your column toward Dalton. Attack any force you may meet. I am on my way to join you. General [Absalom] Baird's division is marching to your support."[60]

February 26, 1864 (Friday)

Major General Thomas updated Grant on his actions of the day. "It is not possible to carry the place [Dalton] by assault. Palmer made the attempt to turn it yesterday with Baird's and Cruft's divisions, but was met by an equal force, exclusive of their cavalry, and in an equally strong position as at Buzzard Roost. After expending nearly all his ammunition he retired during the night to Catoosa Platform." Thomas closed his dispatch indicating depletion of matériel might lead to a cease in the advance. "Our transportation is poor and limited. We are not able to carry more than 60 rounds per man. Artillery horses so poor that Palmer could bring but sixteen pieces. The country is stripped entirely of subsistence and forage. The enemy's cavalry is much superior to ours. Prisoners taken yesterday report that a portion of Cleburne's division has returned. I will await the developments of this

---

[57] Ibid., 445.

[58] Ibid., 799; date of Bate's promotion and skirmish information in Mosocco, *Chronological Tracking,* 208.

[59] Jackman, *Diary of a Confederate Soldier,* 107; skirmish information in Mosocco, *Chronological Tracking,* 209; "Dates at Andersonville," https://www.nps.gov/ande/learn/historyculture/feb24.htm.

[60] *OR,* ser. I, vol. 32, pt. 2:466:803.

day, and advise you further."[61]

February 27, 1864 (Saturday)

The Demonstration on Dalton ended with skirmishing near Catoosa Platform, and Thomas penned Grant the results of the exercise. "My troops, after ceaseless labor under the greatest embarrassment for want of transportation, reached within 3 miles of Dalton, where they were received by the enemy, strongly posted, and in force fully equal to my own in infantry. His artillery and cavalry was not only in better condition as regards horses, but was at least two to our one in pieces and men." Concerned about the rations and fodder needed to continue, Thomas noted the lack of sustenance in the region. "We found the country entirely stripped of everything like forage, and our mules being in such poor condition that double the number of teams we now have could not supply the troops, I thought it best to come back to Ringgold, and, if workmen can be found…to go to work deliberately to repair the railroad and advance as it progresses." Thomas closed with a statement of conviction. "Johnston has no idea of leaving Dalton until compelled, and having a force greater than what I now have under my immediate command I cannot drive him from that place."[62]

February 28, 1864 (Sunday)

Major General Thomas updated Grant on conditions in the aftermath of the Federal advance on Dalton. "I have caused a thorough examination of the railroad between this [Chattanooga] and Tunnel Hill to be made. The officer reports that with 400…construction corps the road can be put in complete running order in six weeks from the time they commence. The road from Cleveland to Dalton can be finished in a week, provided we can get the necessary rails." Meanwhile, Johnston telegraphed Lieutenant General James Longstreet in East Tennessee, keeping Pete updated on the recent attack on Dalton. "The enemy fell back night before last to Ringgold."[63] On the Confederate officer front, Lieutenant General John Bell Hood received command of the Army of Tennessee's 2nd Corps.

February 29, 1864 (Monday)

General Johnston submitted a return to the War Department in Richmond of his troop strength in Dalton. He tallied an "'Aggregate present' in Hardee's Corps of 18, 470; Hood's Corps 21,881; 6,084 in cavalry; 815 in reserve artillery; and 565 as misc," resulting in a total of 48,010 officers and soldiers and 123 pieces of artillery.[64]

March 1, 1864 (Tuesday) ◑

Lieutenant General Hood issued General Orders No. 31, in which he introduced himself to the Army of Tennessee. Hood stated although "he comes among them a stranger he trusts they will not be strangers long. He has come to share their hardships and their dangers, their pleasures and their triumphs. To fight it successfully in the day of action is his

---

[61] Ibid., 480.

[62] Ibid., 482.

[63] Ibid., 489–90, 812; Hood's assignment information in Mosocco, *Chronological Tracking*, 209.

[64] *OR*, ser. I, vol. 32, pt. 2:820.

highest ambition, but the history of war teaches that two-thirds of the elements of success in battle consist in preparation for it." He closed, setting clear expectations for the troops under his command and avowing he will "expect from all prompt and cheerful compliance with orders and the requirements of discipline, and a cordial co-operation with him in his efforts to carry this corps to the highest point of military efficiency."[65]

March 2, 1864 (Wednesday)

A deserter from the Army of Tennessee provided Major General Oliver O. Howard with information on the navigable rivers in the region. "The Connesauga and Coosawattee Rivers are fordable at several places above Resaca; the trains of the enemy crossing at these fords. The Oostenaula is not fordable, having very high banks. The Coosa River is navigable to Greensport." Howard also learned, "The rebels have a foundry and machine-shop at that place [Rome], casting and preparing guns."[66]

March 3, 1864 (Thursday)

Colonel Moses H. Wright questioned a recent message from General Johnston concerning Brigadier General Marcus J. Wright and the defenses of Atlanta. Writing from Atlanta, Moses begged "to be informed if the order is to be interpreted as relieving me from duty, inasmuch as nothing of the kind appears on the face of the order. I was assigned to duty in command of the troops and defenses of Atlanta." The colonel requested confirmation, as "I have been anxious to be relieved for some time and have so expressed myself, but the order assigning General Wright does not do it, except by implication, he being superior in rank, though I was never assigned to duty in command of the post. An early reply will greatly oblige me, as I will then know whether I am to turn over public property to General Wright or not."[67]

March 4, 1864 (Friday)

Colonel Moses Wright updated General Johnston on the defensive status of Atlanta. "Effective strength of garrison at this place, two companies of artillery and 13 men of another; in all, 135 men. Local troops from our shops, &c., about 500 strong when called out. Many of the local troops failed to re-enlist in February. The troops from the convalescent camps cannot be relied upon…forces entirely inadequate to defense of place."[68]

March 5, 1864 (Saturday)

Captain A.T. Fielder received disappointing news in Dalton. Fighting the chilly wind, which magnified the pain in his hip (from a wound received at Missionary Ridge), Fielder deepened the grief of the day in his diary. "The application which I sent up for furlough Come back approved by all but Gen. Johnston, and disapproved by him on account of the locality where I wished to go, deemed unsafe…." Skirmishing occurred at Leet's Tanyard.[69]

---

[65] *OR*, ser. I, vol. 32, pt. 3:575.

[66] Ibid., 12.

[67] Ibid., 581–82.

[68] Ibid., 584.

[69] Cathey, *Captain T. A. Fielder's Civil War Diary*, 314; skirmish information in Mosocco, *Chronological Tracking*, 211.

March 6, 1864 (Sunday)
Private Jackman spent the Sabbath attending worship services in Dalton, and "heard a very good sermon by the Rev. Dr. [John Berry] McFerrin, formerly editor of the *Methodist Christian Advocate*, Nashville. Went again at night: Rev. [Charles C.] Weaver of Ga. spoke. Eight or ten soldiers joined the church. Nothing of interest in the military line this week. Latter part of the week, weather clear nights cool."[70]

March 7, 1864 (Monday) ●
General Braxton Bragg, settling into his new position as military adviser to President Davis, wrote to the commander of his old army. "Communicate your wants to me freely, and I will do all I can to give you strength and efficiency. We must necessarily encounter privations and hardships and run some risk, but the end will justify the means."[71]

March 8, 1864 (Tuesday)
Private Jackman, whiling away the day in Dalton, closed March 8 in attending a preaching service. "Received a letter from home by flag of truce, dated feby. 10th, and answered it immediately. Went to church at night and heard Dr. McFerrin speak."[72]

March 9, 1864 (Wednesday)
A great revival spread through the army in Dalton, and Private Jackman, although probably not aware his observations offered an eye-witness account of the event, continued to drill, write, and pray. "Did not send my letter home until to-day. Went to church again to-night and heard Dr. McF. The church (Baptist) is crowded full of soldiers every night. Many are joining. Set in raining & I had to come home through it." While Jackman attended church, skirmishing continued a few miles to the west. Brigadier General Absalom Baird dispatched Major General Thomas: "Colonel [Thomas] Harrison has arrived here. He reconnoitered Nickajack and the other gaps this morning, and found the rebels in larger force than before since the raid. Whether they will move out again I cannot tell. Harrison's command is 4 miles south of this, picketing beyond."[73]

March 10, 1864 (Thursday)
An army marches on its stomach and treading along on a decent roadway also helps keep soldiers moving. To create roads, where none existed, the Federals and Confederates deployed soldiers in pioneer units. In addition to cutting a path through the wilderness, these men also built bridges, pontoon bridges, etc., anything requiring an axe instead of a musket. One such soldier in the Army of Tennessee, Hiram Williams, became part of a Pioneer Corps on this day in Dalton. He wrote of his new comrades, "There is seven in my mess, of as clever sociable fellows as you would wish to meet with...they are clean, a great consideration in camp. The rations are a little more plentiful [and] a little better in quality here than at camp. First, have no drill. Secondly, roll call but once-a-day, in camp three times, with all one's accoutrements on. To be sure we have to work now and then, but I do not

[70] Jackman, *Diary of a Confederate Soldier*, 109.

[71] *OR*, ser. I, vol. 32, pt. 3:592.

[72] Jackman, *Diary of a Confederate Soldier*, 109.

[73] Ibid.; Baird dispatch in *OR*, ser. I, vol. 32, pt. 3:46.

engage in any battle."[74]

March 11, 1864 (Friday)

Captain William Dixon of the Republican Blues wrote of conditions in Fort McAllister. "I am Officer of the Day. The *Republican* [Savannah newspaper] is out today with two colums [*sic*?] and a half about the late fight at this Post. If am not too lazy tonight I will copy it. It is not a very correct account but is about as near as they generally get of such things."[75]

March 12, 1864 (Saturday)

General Orders, No. 98, issued from the U.S. War Department, announced, "Maj. Gen. W. T. Sherman is assigned to the command of the Military Division of the Mississippi, composed of the Departments of the Ohio, the Cumberland, the Tennessee, and the Arkansas."[76] Thus, the stage was set for the officer who would lead the Federal armies into Georgia for much of 1864.

March 13, 1864 (Sunday)

Hiram Williams did not have to wait long for his first assignment as a pioneer. "We have orders to build two dams, so as to overflow the valley of Taylor's Creek and we have to get the lumber at Tilton, a small RR station 9 miles below Dalton. We left our camp at Mill's Gap this morning at daylight [and] walked to Dalton (3½ miles) where we took the train and came on to Tilton. Soon after our arrival, we went out to repair the roads...."[77]

March 14, 1864 (Monday)

Reporting of intelligence gained regarding the movement of Confederate forces, Major General John Logan dispatched his account: "I have reliable information that all the rebel troops sent in the direction of Sherman and Mobile have returned to Dalton, and all the squads of home guards, &c., except pickets on the river, are ordered there...the enemy are certainly concentrating for some purpose."[78]

March 15, 1864 (Tuesday) ◐

His body in Savannah but the heart at home, Lieutenant Marcus Bethane Ely wrote to his wife Martha. "I went before the Board again on Monday but I have heard nothing from it. They promised to send up another application—but I suppose they intend to deceive me. I am looking everyday for my Uniontown furlough. love to Children & yourself darling Don't forget to write."[79]

March 16, 1864 (Wednesday)

Lieutenant General John Bell Hood believed the troops in his corps needed clarification of expected operating procedures. Through General Orders, No. 40, the soldiers gained a better understanding of military protocol.

I. Guns and colors captured from the enemy in time of battle, being the most valuable trophies of war, as establishing the valor of the troops capturing them, the following

---

[74] Williams, *This War So Horrible*, 34.

[75] Dixon, *Blues in Gray*, 146.

[76] *OR*, ser. I, vol. 32, pt. 3:58.

[77] Williams, *This War So Horrible*, 34.

[78] *OR*, ser. I, vol. 32, pt. 3:69.

[79] Ely and Ely, *Just and Holy Cause?*, 101.

instructions are given for the guidance of divisions, brigades, and regimental commanders:
II. When guns are captured one or more slightly wounded men should be detailed to remain with them to prevent their being claimed by troops not engaged in their capture.
III. When colors are captured and the troops are still pressing forward they should be torn from the staff and tied around the waist of one of the men, or sent to the rear by a wounded man.
IV. Commanding officers should see that captured colors are not lost or mislaid, but that they are placed in the capital of the Confederate States, or the capital of the State to which the captors belong, as a proud memorial to future generations of their heroic achievements.[80]

March 17, 1864 (Thursday) (St. Patrick's Day)

John Beauchamp Jones, a clerk in the Confederate War Department, noted a report from Georgia. "Letters from Lieut.-Gen. Hood to the President, Gen Bragg, and the Secretary of War, give a cheering account of Gen. Johnston's army at Dalton. The men are well fed and well clothed. They are in high spirits, 'and eager for the fray.' The number is 40,000. Gen. H. urges, most eloquently, the junction of Polk's and Loring's troops with these, making some 60,000…."[81] In Nashville, Grant and Sherman met and planned the campaigns for 1864, which included Federals advancing into Georgia.

March 18, 1864 (Friday)

Issuing General Orders, No. 1, from Nashville, Sherman declared he "assumes command of the Military Division of the Mississippi, embracing the Departments of the Ohio, Cumberland, Tennessee, and Arkansas; headquarters in the field, with an office at Nashville, Tenn., where all returns and reports will be addressed." In Dalton, Johnston focused on Sherman and Grant in a telegraph to Bragg, writing, "Grant is at Nashville. Sherman by last accounts at Memphis. Where Grant is we must expect the great Federal effort. We ought therefore to be prepared to beat him here. He has not come back to Tennessee to stand on the defensive. His advance, should we be ready for it, will be advantageous to us."[82]

March 19, 1864 (Saturday)

The Confederate War Department, via Special Orders, No. 66, announced an officer assignment to the Army of Tennessee. "Brig. Gen. F. A. [Francis Asbury] Shoup is relieved from present duty and will report to General Joseph E. Johnston, commanding, &c., at Dalton, Ga., for assignment to artillery duty."[83]

March 20, 1864 (Sunday)

The soldiers in Dalton passed another Sabbath tending to camp chores and going to church services. Private Jackman attended "the Baptist church in forenoon to hear Brig. Genl

---

[80] *OR*, ser. I, vol. 32, pt. 3:644.

[81] Jones, *Rebel War Clerk's Diary*, 2:154; Grant and Sherman in *OR*, ser. I, vol. 32, pt. 3:85.

[82] *OR*, ser. I, vol. 32, pt. 3:86:649.

[83] Ibid., 657.

[William] Pendleton, Chief of Artillery in Lee's army, preach. He is Episcopal. An old, gray beard, and stoutly built. Gen'ls Johnston and Hardee were present, with many other generals. House very much crowded. Went to Bap. chch [*sic*] at night.—All quiet in military circles, the past week."[84]

March 21, 1864 (Sunday)

Captain Thomas Key, and artillery officer with the Army of Tennessee in Dalton, enjoyed a special occasion in his military career. "Today assumed command of my company. Numbers of friends visited me to hear news from Arkansas. I told them of my 'difficulties in the pursuit of pleasures,' and what their friends were doing, etc."[85]

March 22, 1864 (Tuesday)

Winter weather paid a visit to Dalton, leaving a blanket of white, where soon, crimson would dot the landscape. The soldiers in the Army of Tennessee took advantage of the snow to hone their military skills. Instead of skirmishing with Federal forces, they staged a giant snowball fight! "Early in the morning, the 4th Ky…got up a snow fight…and all the other regiments in our brigade went to reinforce the 4th. After fighting awhile, our brigade and [Brigadier General Robert] Tyler's 'made friends' and both went over to [Brigadier General Jesse] Finley's Fla. brigade of our division, and charged the camp. Finley was soon 'cleaned out.' I got several bruises." Private Jackman participated again in the afternoon, when "a courier came over from Tyler's brigade, stating that all of [Major General A. P.] Stewart's division was advancing on our division. We formed our lines in a range of hills, and waited for the enemy…had not been in line long, when we could see the red banners of the advancing hosts, contrasting beautifully with the white snow. They came steadily forward, and soon the air was full of snow-balls." In the evening, Jackman retired, a happy but bruised soldier. "I recd. a wound in the left eye…to-night I feel 'terribly' sore."[86]

March 23, 1864 (Wednesday)

Captain Key had an unsuccessful session with General Johnston, as the artillery officer sought to replenish his batteries after the Battles of Chickamauga and Missionary Ridge. Key asked Johnston "if he would not transfer some of the 15th Arkansas Regiment who were desirous of being attached to my battery. The General remarked that all his army would go into cavalry and batteries if it were allowed, and that he would not transfer a soldier drilled in infantry to make a bad cannoneer." Johnston's decision left Key resorting "to other sources to fill my depleted ranks."[87]

March 24, 1864 (Thursday)

Kate Cumming, working at a hospital in Newnan, observed soldiers "constantly passing to reinforce Johnston's army. They are mainly troops from Mobile. I have been told that the Seventeenth and Twenty-ninth Alabama Regiments are among them."[88] Both the

---

[84] Jackman, *Diary of a Confederate Soldier*, 110.

[85] Key and Campbell, *Two Soldiers*, 64.

[86] Jackman, *Diary of a Confederate Soldier*, 110–11.

[87] Key and Campbell, *Two Soldiers*, 64.

[88] Cumming, *Kate*, 193.

regiments Cumming heard about did indeed serve with the Army of Tennessee.

March 25, 1864 (Good Friday)

A massing of Federal troops alerted General Johnston, who wrote to General Bragg for assistance. "The enemy is rapidly receiving re-enforcements at Ringgold. A scout, an officer, reported last night that he saw four trains of troops arrive there night before, and citizens told him they had been arriving so for five days, agreeing with Louisville papers. We should be re-enforced immediately. Further delay will be dangerous."[89]

March 26, 1864 (Saturday)

Recovering from the recent snowball skirmish, Captain Key experienced an unexpected inspection. "Last night I received a note to come to Captain Kearn's, and it was so dark and wet that I did not get back until after reveille. Major [Thomas] Hotchkiss, for the first time since he has been commanding the battalion, came to the company at roll call and found Lieutenant [likely James G.] Marshall asleep and me absent. He arrested the Lieutenant and as soon as I returned sent for me to lecture me."[90]

March 27, 1864 (Easter Sunday)

The Sabbath morn greeted Hiram Williams in Dalton. "I got up to find a cloudless sky above me, and soon the sun bathed the mountain tops above us in golden light. It is a lovely day, after our week of cold and snow and rain. A pleasant contrast, and I love to dwell upon it. It reminds me of our Country. The past week has been what our Country now is, this day what it will be when Peace smiles upon us again."[91]

March 28, 1864 (Monday)

From Columbus, Dr. George B. Douglas wrote to Dr. Samuel Stout regarding the overcrowded conditions of local hospitals. "I have this day telegraphed you requesting that no more sick or wounded be sent here until those already here can be properly cared for. During the past 24 hours, over 700 have been sent to this post for whom no adequate preparations have been made and it will require several days to provide quarters for them."[92]

March 29, 1864 (Tuesday)

General William Pendleton reported on his visit with the Army of Tennessee to preach, but especially to inspect the readiness of Johnston's artillery. After detailing the condition of the guns and horses, Pendleton summarized his findings. "This state of things did not strike me as existing to a greater extent in the Army of Tennessee than in other commands at all similarly situated. The prevalent condition of the forces is nearly, if not quite, up to the average seen at this season in most of our artillery animals on the fronts, where hard service and hard fare occur together." Federal scouts reported in the vicinity of Deer Head Cove.[93]

---

[89] *OR*, ser. I, vol. 32, pt. 3:674.

[90] Key and Campbell, *Two Soldiers*, 65.

[91] Williams, *This War So Horrible*, 41.

[92] Toalson, *No Soap, No Pay*, 131.

[93] *OR*, ser. I, vol. 32, pt. 3:685–86; scouting information in Mosocco, *Chronological Tracking*, 216.

March 30, 1864 (Wednesday)

General Johnston continued in his efforts to supply the Army of Tennessee. In a dispatch to Bragg, Johnston noted, "We have now field transportation for about 100 rounds of ammunition for small-arms, and food and forage for five days. One hundred and thirty-five wagons have been prepared for the bridge equipage, and 1,000 mules (about 800 of them are for those wagons) are reported on the way from Mississippi." The federals started a foray into the vicinity of McLemore's Cove.[94]

March 31, 1864 (Thursday)

Drilling in Dalton! Captain Key and his battery participated in a mock battle. "The batteries were harnessed and moved upon a large field to be carried through the maneuvers of a sham battle. All of General Hardee's corps was present and the dark lines of men made a grand display as they moved in battle array, their guns glittering in the sunlight. There were many ladies on a distant hill to witness our fight." Intent on performing for the onlookers, Key noted, "One line representing the Southerners threw out their skirmishers and drove back the Yankee line, and in turn the Yankees brought up their skirmishers and drove the Southerners skedaddle. The sham battle was over and we returned to camp expecting to have it renewed the following day with bloody carnage."[95]

April 1, 1864 (Friday) (April Fools' Day)

Captain Key enjoyed a light moment on the special day. "This being All Fool's Day, jokes opened upon Dr. [Peter R.] Ford of my mess. The men of the company had their many hearty laughs over 'April Fool.' The sham fight, which we expected to transpire today, was postponed from the fact that the ground was quite wet and rain still falling. Spent the day in my tent writing."[96]

April 2, 1864 (Saturday)

General R. E. Lee wrote to President Davis, after Lee discussed the status of conditions in Georgia with Brigadier General Pendleton. "Other preparations might also be made, but if, after a full consideration of the subject by General Johnston, there should not be, in his opinion, reasonable grounds for expecting success I would not recommend its execution. He can better compare the difficulties existing to a forward movement with the disadvantages of remaining quiet, and decide between them."[97]

April 3, 1864 (Sunday)

A change in the leadership structure occurred in the Army of Tennessee, as General Johnston announced, via General Orders, No. 29, "Brig. Gen. F. A. Shoup, assigned by the President, will take command of the artillery of the army." Along the Ducktown Road, skirmishers exchanged fire during the day.[98]

---

[94] *OR*, ser. I, vol. 32, pt. 2:714; McLemore's Cove information in Mosocco, *Chronological Tracking*, 216.

[95] Key and Campbell, *Two Soldiers*, 66.

[96] Ibid., 67. Ford's full name from Sibley, *Confederate Artillery Organizations*, 107.

[97] *OR*, ser. I, vol. 32, pt. 3:737.

[98] Ibid., 742; skirmish information in Mosocco, *Chronological Tracking*, 217.

April 4, 1864 (Monday)

Grant outlined his plan to Sherman for the 1864 spring campaigns. "You I propose to move against Johnston's army, to break it up and to get into the interior of the enemy's country as far as you can, inflicting all the damage you can against their war resources. I do not propose to lay down for you a plan of campaign, but simply to lay down the work it is desirable to have done, and leave you free to execute in your own way."[99]

April 5, 1864 (Tuesday)

Struggling to combat pneumonia and scurvy, Private Grant Taylor with the 40th Alabama Infantry wrote his wife, Malinda, from the Newsom Hospital in Cassville. "I once more attempt to write you a few lines. Thank God I am still mending but it is very slowly. I am getting so I can sit up right smart but my side has a dead feeling which I fear will be some time in getting well. I feel very thankful that it is no worse. The patients die up here pretty fast. 3 have died since I came here."[100]

April 6, 1864 (Wednesday) ●

Harboring a dislike of the branch of service consisting of troops in the saddle, Lieutenant Colonel Irvine Walker, with the 10th South Carolina Infantry, wrote to his wife from Dalton. The officer's spouse had a friend in the infantry, who contemplated requesting a change to a cavalry regiment. "You read of the Cavalry having tremendous battles, hard fighting all day, heavy loss in killed and wounded, and down at the bottom of the dispatches you will see one man killed ten wounded. Why I assure you that we would not put upon our battle flags a victory such as the most important ever won by Cavalry in this war."[101]

April 7, 1864 (Friday)

A nineteenth-century form of spectator sports occurred in Dalton, and Captain Key provided the commentary. "This morning all were prepared for the great sham fight which was to come off. I managed Major Hotchkiss' battalion on the field. The fight…sounded very much a true battle. There were thousands of spectators, among whom were ladies said to be from Atlanta and other cities. They occupied a lofty hill which gave them a commanding view." Key ended his entry declaring, "The battle was grand and interesting to those who do not see it in its bloody reality. It is said two soldiers were wounded—one losing an eye. I regretted to see such a waste of ammunition (all to gratify the wives of two Generals) when our forces on the west side of the river have almost no ammunition whatever."[102]

April 8, 1864 (Friday)

On a Day of Fasting in the Confederacy, Lieutenant Marcus Ely, with the 54th Georgia Infantry, wrote to his wife of conditions from his post along the coast. "I am at the Savannah River Trestle and likely to remain here for some time. I am very well satisfied have no one to trouble me being nine miles from the company. I frequently get on the train and go

---

[99] *OR*, ser. I, vol. 32, pt. 3:246.

[100] G. Taylor, *This Cruel War*, 108.

[101] Walker, *Great Things Are Expected of Us*, 109.

[102] Key and Campbell, *Two Soldiers*, 68–69.

down to the Savannah river Bridge which is about three miles from the foot of the trestle. The Trestle is a vast framework for the train to run on twenty feet high passing through a dismal swamp…."[103]

April 9, 1864 (Saturday)

Captain Key enjoyed a rare day off, as he obtained an eight-hour leave. The artillery officer decided "to visit Calhoun, Georgia, to have a coat cut and made, I jumped aboard the cars two miles from Dalton, where I was camped, and was soon at that town. I called at the tailor's shop and had to pay $130 to have a coat and pants made—I to furnish the cloth and trimmings except buttons, which were $4 each. Oh, how this world is given to extortion!"[104]

April 10, 1864 (Sunday)

Major General Sherman's response to Grant's directive for the spring campaign displays Sherman's penchant for adhering to plans. "Should Johnston fall behind Chattahoochee I would feign to the right, but pass to the left, and act on Atlanta, or on its eastern communications, according to developed facts. This is about as far ahead as I feel disposed to look, but I would ever bear in mind that Johnston is at all times to be kept so busy that he cannot, in any event, send any part of his command against you or [Major General Nathaniel] Banks." While Sherman pondered the future, some of his troops scouted into Georgia. Colonel Robert Minty of the 4th Michigan Cavalry filed a report on the action. "At 3.30 this a.m. I sent out a party under command of Captain Warner, Fourth Ohio Cavalry, to endeavor to capture a rebel picket of 50 men, stationed near the Dedmon Trace. In consequence of the want of knowledge of their actual position Captain Warner struck the picket from the north instead of the east, and succeeded in capturing but 4 of them, privates of the Second and Fourth Tennessee Cavalry."[105]

April 11, 1864 (Monday)

Federal troops conducted a reconnaissance from Rossville to La Fayette. Colonel Carter Van Vleck and his 78th Illinois Infantry "left camp soon after daylight…and marched to within 1 mile of La Fayette. I heard nothing of the enemy, excepting 4 scouts, who came from the direction of La Fayette, and passing through Catlett's Gap came to a point near Crawfish Spring and returned."[106]

April 12, 1864 (Tuesday)

General Thomas submitted an account of conditions in northwest Georgia. "Wheeler still remains at Tunnel Hill, supported by infantry (either a division or brigade, the scouts cannot say which), between Tunnel Hill and Buzzard Roost. A dam has been built across the gap at Buzzard Roost, so that the wagon road can be flooded. I think this will prove advantageous to us and to their disadvantage, if we succeed in routing their forces this side of Tunnel Hill." Meanwhile, the Confederates noted, "Scouts report that two regiments of

---

[103] Ely and Ely, *Just and Holy Cause?*, 109–10.

[104] Key and Campbell, *Two Soldiers*, 69–70.

[105] *OR*, ser. I, vol. 32, pt. 3:313–14; Minty report in *OR*, ser. I, vol. 32, pt. 1:658.

[106] *OR*, ser. I, vol. 32, pt. 1:662.

Yankee infantry, 800 or 1,000 strong, entered La Fayette at 7 a. m. to-day and camped half mile from the town, on the Dug Gap road."[107]

April 13, 1864 (Wednesday) ◐

Lieutenant Ely with the 54th Georgia Infantry tried to cheer his wife from his position on the Savannah River Trestle. "You know there can not be sunshine all the time. Occasionally a lowering cloud will obscure the bright clouds of our existence—occasionally the sea of life is rendered turbulent by the winds of adversity."[108]

April 14, 1864 (Thursday)

General Johnston outlined plans for the spring campaign season to Colonel Benjamin Ewell in Richmond, writing, "Assuming offensive must depend on relative forces. I shall be ready to do it whenever they warrant it. It will be a month or six weeks before we can expect the necessary transportation. I cannot foresee what force the enemy may then have. I do not think our present strength sufficient for defensive since Longstreet's withdrawal. No one is more anxious than I for offensive operations by this army." Skirmishing reported at Taylor's Ridge.[109]

April 15, 1864 (Friday)

Disease and sickness bivouacked in countless camps North and South. Captain Key did not elude the unwelcomed visitors, indicating he

> was not well, so hoarse that I could scarcely talk...[spent] most of my time...examining chemistry. I discovered the reason why tight doors are unhealthy. Anyone who sleeps in a close room with a fire will arise in the morning feeling stupid, heavy, and wearied, but in camp I have never felt that dull, sluggish depression, for I am sleeping under a fly or often under a tree where the winds sweep over and my room is the whole heavens.[110]

April 16, 1864 (Saturday)

An unusual circular, one from General Johnston informing his troops of an opportunity to grow their sea legs. "Lieut. William W. Carnes, C. S. Navy, is authorized to select 170 men of this army to be transferred to the naval service. Commanding officers are hereby directed to afford him the necessary aid for the discharge of this duty. In making these selections no organization must be destroyed, and as far as practicable seamen will be taken."[111]

April 17, 1864 (Sunday)

Soldiers with a green thumb, pursued a new hobby while on garrison duty. "The 63d Georgia at Thunder Bolt battery near Savannah have determined to raise vegetables for themselves. It would be well for all stationary troops to follow this example. They could live

---

[107] *OR*, ser. I, vol. 32, pt. 3:352:775.

[108] Ely and Ely, *A Just and Holy Cause?*, 110–11.

[109] *OR*, ser. I, vol. 32, pt. 3:781; skirmish information in Mosocco, *Chronological Tracking*, 220.

[110] Key and Campbell, *Two Soldiers*, 71.

[111] *OR*, ser. I, vol. 32, pt. 3:789.

much more comfortably thereby."[112]

April 18, 1864 (Monday)

News reached Savannah and Captain William Dixon of a pending redeployment of some of the Confederate soldiers. "We received orders today stopping all furloughs. It is said that a call was made by the Sec of War on Gen Beaurigard [*sic*] to hold ten thousand troops ready to move for Virginia or Northern Georgia. If they are sent I expect to be among them."[113]

April 19, 1864 (Tuesday)

Captain Edgeworth Bird of the 15th Georgia Infantry—at Granite Farm in Hancock County while on leave from Virginia—wrote to his daughter, Saida. "Circumstances have so transpired that I still breathe the flower scented air of Granite Farm, to the great joy of Mama and no small gratification to myself. Recent movements of Longstreet's Corps have quite changed our plans. Only the night before I was to set out to join the party at Washington, Col. [Dudley] DuBose's boy reached here, telling me of the late army news and the change in programme."[114]

April 20, 1864 (Wednesday)

From his camp near Dalton, Lieutenant Colonel Irvine Walker with the 10th South Carolina Infantry wrote his wife, Orie, of his expectations for the upcoming campaign. "Active preparations will, I suppose, begin…very soon now. Today we hear a report that the enemy is moving round to Huntsville, Ala. Leaving only a Corps in front of Chattanooga. If this is so, this Army, or a great part of it, will go to North Alabama. I think they intend making a simultaneous move on Richmond and Atlanta. And I trust that God will give us strength to hurl back the invading columns." Walker ended, "I am very sanguine of a great victory gained by our Army and a summer in Tennessee and possibly in Kentucky. I pray God to grant us victory and to spare me through the dangers and perils of the coming campaign."[115]

April 21, 1864 (Thursday)

Lieutenant General Hardee issued specifications for the standards in his corps. "The battle-flags of this corps, known as 'the Virginia battle-flag,' will have inscribed on them the number of the regiment and the State to which it belongs; the number in the upper angle formed by the cross and the name of the State in the lower angle."[116]

April 22, 1864 (Friday)

Captain Key paid a visit to the Army of Tennessee's new artillery chieftain. "Called on General Shoup to represent to him the reduced condition of my battery, caused by the two battles of Chickamauga and Missionary Ridge, and to ask him to aid me in getting more

---

[112] "Gardening in Camp," *Columbus Daily Sun*, April 17, 1864, sec. 2, https://gahistoricnewspapers.galileo.usg.edu/lccn/sn82014939/1864-04-17/ed-1/seq-2/.

[113] Dixon, *Blues in Gray*, 206.

[114] E. Bird and S. Bird, *Granite Farm Letters*, 162.

[115] Walker, *Great Things Are Expected of Us*, 112.

[116] *OR*, ser. I, vol. 32, pt. 3:802.

men. Found him very agreeable and courteous. He told me that he had telegraphed General Bragg for conscripts to fill up his batteries, and that he would do all he could for my company."[117]

April 23, 1864 (Saturday)

The Confederates attacked a cavalry force near Ringgold. Colonel Eli Murray reported casualties of "5 killed and 10 wounded, and Lieutenant [Horace] Scovill and 12 men taken prisoners." Murray explained the surprise assault. "A regiment of dismounted rebel cavalry sneaked over Taylor's Ridge, getting in rear of our picket-post at Leet's farm. A charge of three companies of rebel cavalry attacked our advance vedettes, drove them to the reserve of the post at Nickajack, which reserve was ready to receive them, which it did, fighting the three companies and following back until they were attacked in rear by the dismounted men, who had come over the ridge." The colonel praised his soldiers, noting, "They then made a stand against both parties. Attacked as they were, our men did all they could. They were found vigilant and active."[118]

April 24, 1864 (Sunday)

Colonel Smith Atkins with the 92nd Illinois Infantry insinuated acts of atrocity occurred in the region. "I beg to call especial attention to the brutal murder of our men while in the enemy's hands and disarmed. The evidence is conclusive (the best possible)—the statements of men, fatally wounded, just before their death. There is no room for doubt in the premises, and a terrible retribution should follow this damnable outrage upon brave men." On the same day, Colonel Charles Smith called on "430 men of Tenth Ohio Volunteer Cavalry." Leaving Ringgold at 3:00 p.m., the troopers "proceeded via Leet's Mill to La Fayette…arrived at 11 p.m.…with intention of capturing the rebel pickets (posted at Smith's and Mattock's Gaps through Taylor's Ridge)."[119]

April 25, 1864 (Monday)

The garrison troops in Savannah received orders to prepare for redeploying. "Command very much surprised on receipt of orders calling all detached companies of 1st Regt of Ga to prepare at once to join their Regiment at Savannah to march to Dalton Ga. Gen Mercer is ordered there and we go as part of his Brigade. The company is pleased as they are tired of Battery work."[120]

April 26, 1864 (Tuesday)

Private Grant Taylor with the 40th Alabama Infantry, still hospitalized in Cassville, wrote to his wife of information from the army in Dalton. "Yes there is some good news. I hear of great revivals going on in parts of Johnston's army. Nearly entire companies in some instances have joined the church. May God continue the good work until our entire army shall have been converted."[121]

---

[117] Key and Campbell, *Two Soldiers*, 73.

[118] *OR*, ser. I, vol. 32, pt. 1:679.

[119] Ibid., 680–81, 685–86.

[120] Dixon, *Blues in Gray*, 207.

[121] G. Taylor, *This Cruel War*, 245.

April 27, 1864 (Wednesday)
A Confederate force attacked Brigadier General Judson Kilpatrick's cavalry pickets outside Ringgold. Kilpatrick reported, "The enemy attacked our pickets on Taylor's Ridge...they succeeded in getting between the outpost and reserve of the second post from camp on old Alabama road, and attacked the outpost but did not succeed in capturing any of them. They captured 5 out of 7 of the horses that were on the outpost. All quiet on the line."[122]
April 28, 1864 (Thursday) ◗
One sentence, thirteen words, started an avalanche of blue across Georgia. Grant telegraphed Sherman: "Get your forces up so as to move by the 5th of May."[123]
April 29, 1864 (Friday)
Engaging Federals near Tunnel Hill, Brigadier General W. Y. C. Humes and his cavalry had a busy day on their hands! An early dispatch from Humes read, "The enemy are pressing us with infantry, cavalry, and artillery on the Ringgold road." Sometime later, he updated conditions, writing, "The enemy are extending their lines on our right, and indications of a strong force. I am falling back to Tunnel Hill slowly." Finally, his after-action report: "The enemy from Ringgold this morning were about 1,500 infantry, 2 pieces artillery, 300 cavalry. They have withdrawn to Ringgold Gap, and our pickets have been reestablished. Our loss near 20 killed, wounded, and missing."[124]
April 30, 1864 (Saturday)
Action began heating up in northwest Georgia, as Sherman's three armies prepared to begin the campaign of 1864. Brigadier General Absalom Baird, near Ringgold, notified his superiors of Confederate activity. "There are indications that the enemy are gathering in force on my right flank. The cavalry near Nickajack trail has largely increased, and our pickets in that vicinity have heard drums beating in the valley east of Taylor's Ridge. A scout also reports tents there, which he thinks belong to infantry. I shall probably learn nothing more until morning."[125]
May 1, 1864 (Sunday)
Sherman made final preparations before beginning the campaign to occupy General Johnston. He updated Grant on his progress. "Schofield...will move to Cleveland. Thomas will concentrate at Ringgold, and McPherson's troops are all in motion toward Chattanooga, and by May 5 I will group them at Rossville and Gordon's Mills. The first move will be: Thomas, Tunnel Hill; Schofield, Catoosa Springs, and McPherson, Villanow." The general added, "Enemy has a general idea of our plans, and are massing about Richmond and Dalton. Weather fine; roads very good...we will all go out on the 5th. I will expect further notice from you, but will agree to draw the enemy's fire within

---

[122] *OR*, ser. I, vol. 32, pt. 1:687.
[123] *OR*, ser. I, vol. 32, pt. 3:521.
[124] *OR*, ser. I, vol. 32, pt. 1:691–92.
[125] *OR*, ser. I, vol. 32, pt. 3:542.

twenty-four hours of May 5." Skirmishing in the vicinity of Stone Church in Catoosa County.[126]

May 2, 1864 (Monday)

From Dalton, Lieutenant General Hood sent a circular to the soldiers in his corps. "As there is a prospect of an early advance of the enemy, and of the troops being called upon to move at any time, it is desired that commanding officers cause all rations on hand to be placed in the haversacks of the men whenever they are ordered under arms."[127] Skirmishing at Lee's Cross-Roads.

May 3, 1864 (Tuesday)

Skirmishing reported near Catoosa Springs, along Chickamauga Creek, and at Red Clay. Lieutenant Colonel Horace Lamson with the 4th Indiana Cavalry described action at Red Clay, stating, "the brigade, 1,031 strong, marched…from Cleveland, and camped for the night at Red Clay. Late in the day, and just before going into camp, 1 of the division scouts, a member of the First Wisconsin Cavalry, was killed while in the advance with a few of his comrades."[128]

May 4, 1864 (Wednesday)

Sherman notified Grant things had moved into place to launch his advance into Georgia the following day. "Thomas' center in Ringgold, left at Catoosa, right at Leet's Tan-yard. Schofield closing up on Thomas. All move to-morrow, but I hardly expect serious battle till the 7th. Everything very quiet with the enemy. Johnston evidently awaits my initiative. I will first secure the Tunnel Hill, then throw McPherson rapidly on his communications, attacking at same time in front cautiously and in force." Meanwhile, Johnston informed Bragg, "The movements of the enemy in our front…satisfy me that he will immediately attack with his united forces." Skirmishing along the Varnell's Station Road.[129]

May 5, 1864 (Thursday) ●

The Atlanta Campaign began with skirmishing at Tunnel Hill; Major General John Palmer reported on the action. "Brigadier-General [James] Morgan, with one of his regiments, drove the rebel pickets from the two hills to the right of the Tunnel Hill road without firing a shot, paying no attention to the few shots fired by them." Johnston dispatched Wheeler, questioning, "Did General Palmer come within your picket-lines and reconnoiter without being reported by your picket?[130]

May 6, 1864 (Friday)

Federal movements, and the accompanying skirmishing near Tunnel Hill, prompted Hood to instruct Major General A. P. Stewart to prepare earthworks. "Construct an abatis in

---

[126] *OR*, ser. I, vol. 32, pt. 4:3; skirmish information in Mosocco, *Chronological Tracking*, 224.

[127] *OR*, ser. I, vol. 32, pt. 4:658; skirmish information in Mosocco, *Chronological Tracking*, 224.

[128] *OR*, ser. I, vol. 38, pt. 2:780; skirmish sites in Mosocco, *Chronological Tracking*, 225.

[129] *OR*, ser. I, vol. 38, pt. 4:25:659–60; skirmish in Mosocco, *Chronological Tracking*, 225.

[130] *OR*, ser. I, vol. 38, pt. 4:36:664.

front of your works at Mill Creek Gap; also at any point along your line on Rocky Face Ridge where you think the enemy could climb, so that your line may be held with a small force, should it be necessary."[131]

May 7, 1864 (Saturday)

The pace of action increased as Sherman's forces moved into Georgia. Sherman reported to Major General Henry Halleck in Washington City, "Thomas is at Tunnel Hill. Enemy at Buzzard Roost Gap. McPherson is moving toward Villanow and Resaca. Skirmishing, but no real fighting yet." Bragg received an update from Johnston: "The enemy are between Tunnel Hill and Dalton, about five miles from Dalton, and are advancing. We hold Mill Creek Gap. They have also troops in observation this side of Varnell's Station on the Cleveland road." Skirmishing at Nickajack Gap, along with the places Sherman and Johnston mentioned.[132]

May 8, 1864 (Sunday)

On a day with skirmishing at various locations (Rocky Face Ridge, Buzzard Roost, Mill Creek Gap, and Dug Gap), Hiram Williams and his pioneer comrades occupied ringside seats. "Had to go and assist some artillery to get on the top of Buzzard Roost. Had a hard time of it. When on the top of the mountain, we had a fine view of the field below us. The enemy's skirmishers were advancing across the fields in plain view. It was a grand sight, and I could have looked for hours at them had not other work interfered." Williams learned some of his regiment "was put out on skirmish this morning...one of our boys was instantly killed."[133]

May 9, 1864 (Monday)

Sherman deployed Major General McPherson and the Army of the Tennessee as his quick-strike force to penetrate Snake Creek Gap and cut off Johnston's supply line. After successfully maneuvering through the gap, McPherson, upon spotting Confederates south of his position, withdrew his army. He wrote to Sherman, "The enemy have a strong position at Resaca...they displayed considerable force, and opened on us with artillery. After skirmishing till nearly dark...I decided to withdraw the command..." Sherman later regretted letting Johnston slip out of his net. "Such an opportunity does not occur twice in a single life, but at the critical moment McPherson seems to have been a little cautious." While the Army of the Tennessee penetrated the gap, skirmishing played out at Varnell's Station and Dalton.[134]

May 10, 1864 (Tuesday)

Captain Samuel Foster with the 24th Texas Cavalry wrote of the day's activity in and around Dalton. "This morning...ordered to 'fall in' when We go back to the gap.... As

---

[131] Ibid., 669.

[132] *OR*, ser. I, vol. 38, pt. 4:56:672; skirmish in Mosocco, *Chronological Tracking*, 227.

[133] Williams, *This War So Horrible*, 58; skirmish sites in Mosocco, *Chronological Tracking*, 227.

[134] *OR*, ser. I, vol. 38, pt. 4:106; Sherman, *Memoirs*, 500; skirmish sites in Mosocco, *Chronological Tracking*, 228.

soon as we get down in the valley, instead of going back to Dalton we go…towards Resaca…until we get to another gap, having been on a forced march. After remaining…about half an hour, just long enough to rest we are started back the road we came and by night we are back at Dug Gap…after having traveled about 38 miles today All hands being tired."[135]

May 11, 1864 (Wednesday)

Temperatures continued to rise, accompanying the increasing friction between the combatants at Dalton. General Johnston notified General Cooper, "there has been skirmishing and many partial engagements brought on by their [Federals'] attempts to gain the passes and commanding positions on the mountains. They have thus far failed in all their attempts. The enemy now making strong demonstrations on Resaca. Lieutenant General Polk has been directed to concentrate his troops at Resaca."[136]

May 12, 1864 (Thursday)

Among the engagements near Dalton on the day, one involved Brigadier General Kilpatrick's force against elements of Wheeler's cavalry; Kilpatrick received a wound during this action. "General Kilpatrick is out on the Resaca road about four miles, very near the junction with the Lay's Ferry and Dalton road; quite a sharp skirmishing. The general sent a brigade of cavalry out on the road from Sugar Valley to Dalton; just received news from it; the enemy's pickets were driven in for four miles, when the rebels showed quite a strong force."[137] As a result of this action, coupled with other fighting in the area, General Johnston ordered the Confederates to fall back to Resaca.

May 13, 1864 (Friday) ◐

Maneuvering, and skirmishing at Tilton and other locales proved the acts of the day, as the Army of Tennessee fell back toward Resaca. Private J. P. Cannon with the 27th Alabama Infantry, positioned at Resaca, had little time before "skirmishing began…at 3 p.m. our pickets were driven in and we could see a dark line of blue moving toward us. Raising a hurrah, they started at a double-quick, but one volley broke their line and they fell back in confusion. In a short time, the same movement was repeated and a second repulse followed. The third time they rallied, but we poured such a storm of shot and shell into them that their ranks were broken and they fell back disheartened." As the smoke of battle dissipated, Cannon and comrades "got picks and spades and went to work with a determination to be better prepared for an assault that might reasonably be expected in the morning."[138] The ball had opened in Resaca!

May 14, 1864 (Saturday)

Fighting opened in earnest during the Battle of Resaca; this affair served as the second most costly battle of the entire Atlanta Campaign: both sides suffered approximately 2,800 casualties. Private A. B. Clonts with the 40th Georgia Infantry noted, "There has been a

---

[135] Foster, *One of Cleburne's Command*, 73.

[136] *OR*, ser. I, vol. 38, pt. 4:692.

[137] Ibid., 150.

[138] Cannon, *Bloody Banners and Barefoot Boys*, 65.

continual roar of cannon and small arms…for two days. The Yanks are shelling Calhoun today, and it may be we will have to fall back still (further). I think it will be a close race between us and the Yanks to Atlanta."[139]

May 15, 1864 (Sunday)

Day two of the battle at Resaca produced the heaviest fighting on the Confederate right flank, which Lieutenant General Hood's troops occupied. The Federals came under heavy artillery fire from Captain Max Van den Corput's Cherokee Battery. Colonel Benjamin Harrison's soldiers in the 70th Indiana Infantry, along with other regiments, charged into the havoc. Harrison reported his "men moved on with perfect steadiness and without any sign of faltering up the hillside and to the very muzzles of the enemy's artillery, which continued to belch their deadly charges of grape and canister, until the gunners were struck down at their guns. Having gained the outer face of the embrasures, in which the enemy had four 12-pounder Napoleon guns, my line halted for a moment to take breath." Later in the evening, under cover of darkness, the Hoosiers captured the battery. Skirmishing reported in the vicinity of Rome.[140]

May 16, 1864 (Monday)

Skirmishing reported at Calhoun, Floyd's Spring, and near Rome. Major Tom Taylor with the 47th Ohio Infantry noted his movements on the day. "Woke up about half past three…saw (railroad) bridge burning. Slept until near five and then got up and washed. Twenty minutes to seven moved across to the river Oostonaula [*sic*]…Captured a few prisoners…moved back to Calhoun Ferry road where we drew rations & recd. baggage. At four P.M. moved down the road, crossed the river and at dark camped on a hill about two miles from the river." Major General Dan Sickles, serving as an observer with Sherman's armies, wrote to President Lincoln after the fighting at Resaca: "I have accompanied General Sherman's army in the successful campaign from Chattanooga to Resaca, witnessing the retreat of the enemy from successive lines of fortified positions, through forty miles of mountains. If Georgia cannot be defended on its northern frontier, it cannot be defended anywhere."[141]

May 17, 1864 (Tuesday)

The Army of Tennessee approached Adairsville during a day, which also produced skirmishing near Rome. On the Adairsville front, various probing actions from the Federals prompted Major General Patrick Cleburne to dispatch Hardee. "I supposed that to-day my division would be rested, but the firing of the enemy approaches and every one is moving by, so I believe I will be left in rear again; if so I would like to have a line of battle selected and be informed of the state of affairs in my front and on my flanks. My men are very tired and need rest much." On the Federal side, Sherman updated Halleck, reporting,

---

[139] Mills, *Dear Mother*, 292; casualties from National Park Service, "Resaca," https://www.nps.gov/civilwar/search-battles-detail.htm?battleCode=GA008.

[140] *OR*, ser. I, vol. 38, pt. 2:371; skirmish in Mosocco, *Chronological Tracking*, 230.

[141] T. Taylor, *Tom Taylor's Civil War*, 117; skirmish in Mosocco, *Chronological Tracking*, 230; Daniel E. Sickles telegram to A. Lincoln, May 16, 1864, *Lincoln Papers*.

"I start in person now for Adairsville. I think everything has progressed and is progressing as favorably as we could expect; but I know we must have one or more bloody battles, such as have characterized Grant's terrific struggles. Johnston has Hardee's, Hood's, and Polk's corps, with irregulars and militia on his lines of communication. His cavalry outnumbers ours, but acts on the defensive."[142]

May 18, 1864 (Wednesday)

General Johnston received a message from President Davis on a day his soldiers engaged the Federals at Cassville Kingston, and along Pine Log Creek. Davis held some hope for the army in Georgia. "Your dispatch of 16th received; read with disappointment. I hope the re-enforcements sent will enable you to achieve important results."[143]

May 19, 1864 (Thursday)

In Cassville, General Johnston issued orders for an attack; a late-night council of war with his subordinate officers convinced Johnston to rescind the order.

> Soldiers of the Army of Tennessee, you have displayed the highest quality of the soldier—firmness in combat, patience under toil. By your courage and skill you have repulsed every assault of the enemy. By marches by day and by marches by night you have defeated every attempt upon your communications. Your communications are secured. You will now turn and march to meet his advancing columns. Fully confiding in the conduct of the officers, the courage of the soldiers, I lead you to battle. We may confidently trust that the Almighty Father will still reward the patriots' toils and bless the patriots' banners. Cheered by the success of our brothers in Virginia and beyond the Mississippi, our efforts will equal theirs. Strengthened by His support, those efforts will be crowned with the like glories.[144]

May 20, 1864 (Friday)

There was skirmishing along the Etowah River in Cartersville during a day Governor Brown wrote a lengthy letter to Major General Howell Cobb—almost a legal brief—defending his belief in the unconstitutionality of conscription.

> I am perfectly willing that the hardy, wayworn veterans of Georgia who are kept in the front, and have no comfortable office, and no command in the rear, who left their wives and little ones to defend your large inheritance, as well as their own log cabins, to whom, when naked and barefoot in the dreary storms of winter, I have sent clothes and shoes when they could get none from the Confederacy, and whose poor, helpless wives and little ones I have labored day and night to procure appropriations, and get up supplies to feed and clothe, when suffering for food and raiment, shall judge whether my services have been more valuable in my present position than they could have been in the field, however a good soldier I might have been able to make; and

---

[142] *OR*, ser. I, vol. 38, pt. 4:721:219; skirmish in Mosocco, *Chronological Tracking*, 231.
[143] *OR*, ser. I, vol. 38, pt. 4:725; skirmish sites in Mosocco, *Chronological Tracking*, 231.
[144] Ibid., 728.

whether I have indeed been their friend, or, as you would intimate, only their "pretended friend."[145]

May 21, 1864 (Saturday)

Updating superiors proved the order of the day for Sherman and Johnston. Sherman telegraphed Halleck, "Weather very hot and roads dusty. We, nevertheless, by morning, will have all our wagons loaded and be ready for a twenty days' expedition. I allow three days to have the army grouped about Dallas, whence I can strike Marietta, or the Chattahoochee, according to developments. You may not hear from us in some days, but be assured we are not idle or thoughtless." Johnston wrote to President Davis, "I have earnestly sought an opportunity to strike the enemy. The direction of the railroad to this point has enabled him to press me back by steadily moving to the left and by fortifying the moment he halted. He has made an assault upon his superior forces too hazardous, and in making this retrograde march we have [not] lost much by straggling or desertion."[146]

May 22, 1864 (Sunday)

Spending a day of calm before the storms formed on the horizon to the west, Private Robert Patrick with the 4th Louisiana Infantry noted conditions in camp near Big Shanty. He wrote, "All quiet in camp. Lying on our oars. This country affords fine water in abundance. The whole country is covered with pennyroyal. On the hills and in the valleys, in the fields and in the woods, in the shade and in the sunshine, the ubiquitous pennyroyal may be seen. Sometimes in lifting up a loose stone, I am somewhat astonished to find it nearly as heavy as a cannon ball."[147]

May 23, 1864 (Monday)

Sherman makes final preparations to break from his supply line, the Western & Atlantic, and slide his three armies westward into Paulding County. His plan. Get into the rear of the Army of Tennessee, cut the railroad, and force General Johnston to fight or lose Atlanta. A quartermaster officer reported, Sherman "is provided with twenty days' supplies of all kinds. No more forage will be required at this point...and you will have ample time...to fill this depot with everything that may be wanted. Make yourself entirely easy. The emergency has passed. Sherman expresses himself as highly pleased, and says no army in the world is better provided." Skirmishing reported at Stilesborough.[148]

May 24, 1864 (Tuesday)

There was skirmishing at Burnt Hickory, Cass Station, Cassville, and near Dallas, as Sherman's armies began to move into Paulding County. Johnston's cavalry scouts detected the maneuvers, and Johnston sidled his army westward. Hardee notified "Bishop" Polk, "I put my corps in motion this morning at 2 a. m. My orders, to get in the main Dallas and Atlanta road, to take up a position and defend it. I am also instructed to keep in communication with you."[149]

---

[145] *OR*, ser. IV, vol. 3:433; skirmish in Mosocco, *Chronological Tracking*, 232.

[146] *OR*, ser. I, vol. 38, pt. 4:274:736.

[147] Patrick, *Reluctant Rebel*, 168–69.

[148] *OR*, ser. I, vol. 38, pt. 4:299; skirmish in Mosocco, *Chronological Tracking*, 233.

[149] *OR*, ser. I, vol. 38, pt. 4:739; skirmish sites in Mosocco, *Chronological Tracking*, 233.

May 25, 1864 (Wednesday)

Opening a series of affairs in Paulding County, the Battle of New Hope Church began with a blaze and ended amid tornado conditions. Mother Nature may have joined the fray as various soldier reports indicate witnessing destruction typical of a twister. If the fighting did not prove enough, the storm resulted in the Federal troops calling the entire region the "Hell Hole." An officer with the 15th Ohio Infantry, 1st Lieutenant Alexis Cope witnessed the storm, later writing, "A thunderstorm was coming up…and the thunder from the clouds mingled with that of our cannon. In the midst of the din there was one mighty peal of thunder—so loud, so deep, so profound that we were awestricken. It made our heavy guns sound like the snapping of matches in comparison. It was comforting…for it made us remember that God was on His throne and still watching over His world. No one who heard that peal of thunder could ever forget it." During the battle, Major General Joe Hooker's XX Corps attacked portions of Hood's command and suffered 1,665 casualties to the Confederate loss of 400.[150]

May 26, 1864 (Thursday)

After a day of fighting at New Hope Church, the soldiers under Sherman and Johnston fortified their positions in Paulding County. Mounting tensions developed in Dallas, as both sides—McPherson's boys against those of Hardee—pondered what the future might offer. Captain Charles Wills with the 103rd Illinois Infantry noted in his diary, "We started at 8 this morning, and have not made more than one and one-half miles. Soldiers from the front say that Hardee's Corps fronts us two miles ahead, and that he proposes to fight. I have heard no firing that near this morning, but have heard artillery eight or ten miles east. A number of prisoners have been sent back, who all report Hardee at Dallas."[151]

May 27, 1864 (Friday)

Fighting continued in Paulding County. Sherman attempted to move a portion of his command—Brigadier General Thomas Wood's division, back to the east in attempt to locate, and strike, the Confederate right flank. Confederate officials, wise to Sherman's activity, redeployed troops to their right, where they established a defensive line at Pickett's Mill. The Federal attack, designed to launch in three successive waves, faltered. Once the fighting drew to a close, and darkness settled over the field of battle, Brigadier General Hiram Granbury requested permission to advance his Texans into the ravine, where the Federal advances had halted. Major General Patrick Cleburne agreed with Granbury's request. After charging through the darkness (and netting several prisoners), Cleburne commented, "It needed but the brilliancy of this night attack to add luster to the achievements of Granbury and his brigade in the afternoon." The Federals casualties included 1,600 killed, wounded, or missing during the Battle of Pickett's Mill; the Confederate casualties totaled 450.[152]

---

[150] Strayer and Baumgartner, *Echoes of Battle*, 108; casualties from American Battlefield Trust, "New Hope Church," https://www.battlefields.org/learn/civil-war/battles/new-hope-church.

[151] C. Wills, *Army Life of An Illinois Soldier*, 247–48.

[152] *OR*, ser. I, vol. 38, pt. 3:726; casualties from National Park Service, "Pickett's Mill," https://www.nps.gov/civilwar/search-battles-detail.htm?battleCode=GA012.

May 28, 1864 (Saturday) ◑

Sherman had already started sliding his troops back to the east to reconnect with his supply line and end the days of disappointment in Paulding County. The Confederates near Dallas, under Hardee's command, believed the Federals across the way had started withdrawing too, but McPherson's soldiers remained in their trenches. The Confederate attack order went out quickly, but the news to cancel the advance traveled so slowly that about half the attackers did not receive the word to fall back. It was a dreadful day to wear the gray. The Battle of Dallas produced 1,500 Confederate casualties and 380 Federal dead, wounded, or missing. Private Sam Watkins with the 1st/27th Tennessee Consolidated Infantry witnessed a ghastly sight: "It was the grandest spectacle I ever witnessed. We could see the smoke and dust of battle, and hear the shout of the charge, and the roar and rattle of cannon and musketry. We can see the line of dead and wounded along the track over which he passed, and finally we see our battle flag planted upon the Federal breastworks."[153]

May 29, 1864 (Sunday)

After three battles in Paulding County, both sides rested. Sherman informed Halleck, "I give him to-day (Sunday) to gather in the wounded and bury the dead of both sides, and to night and to-morrow will endeavor to gain ground to our left three or four miles. I have no doubt Johnston has in my front every man he can scrape…."[154]

May 30, 1864 (Monday)

Major General Cleburne, writing from along the Dallas Road, queried Hardee as to his next course of action. "General [Daniel] Govan is in reserve in rear of General [States Rights] Gist 100 yards; [Lucius] Polk is in the line. General [William] Bate thinks the line cannot be held if Polk is removed. I desire to know if I am to withdraw Polk at the hazard of losing the line. We have had no sleep to-night. The attacks at this place, though believed to be only a demonstration, are increasing in intensity and boldness."[155]

May 31, 1864 (Tuesday)

Holding a position near Dallas, Captain Samuel Foster noted during the horrors of war: "We seem to be held in reserve for any thing that may come up, any where on the line—We remained on the branch all night, and from the firing in our front we seem to be about opposite the centre of the army. The heavy fireing [*sic*] on our left was the Yanks firing on their own pickets. Their pickets came over to our line for protection from their own men—They reported that they were all drunk over there."[156]

June 1, 1864 (Wednesday)

Spreading like the branches of a tree, the various Federal forces under Sherman's command continued to advance south and east. A report of skirmishing near Kingston, and the capture of Allatoona Pass numbered among the day's events. Reporting from Allatoona Pass,

---

[153] National Park Service, "Dallas," https://www.nps.gov/civilwar/search-battles-detail.htm?battleCode=GA011; Watkins, *Company Aytch*, 200.

[154] *OR*, ser. I, vol. 38, pt. 4:343.

[155] Ibid., 748.

[156] Foster, *One of Cleburne's Command*, 90.

Major General George Stoneman notified Sherman, "We arrived at 5 p.m. without molestation to the advance, and the rear will be up in an hour. We have a strong position and can hold it against any reasonable force."[157]

June 2, 1864 (Thursday)

Signal Officer Samuel Sample notified Major General John Logan of what his flagmen had witnessed earlier in the day: "One piece of artillery and 2,100 infantry passed rebel signal station, moving to our left and south of east, toward Marietta. They had no knapsacks, and were accompanied by litter-bearers."[158]

June 3, 1864 (Friday)

Action, on both land and water, continued in Georgia. Confederate Flag Officer William Hunter notified authorities of the capture of a Federal vessel. "I have the honor to report that an expedition from my command, under Lieutenant [Thomas] T. P. Pelot, C. S. Navy...carried, by boarding, the U.S.S. *Water Witch*, near Ossabaw Sound, after a hard fight. Our loss is, killed, the gallant Lieutenant Pelot, Moses Dallas (colored), pilot, and 3 men. From 10 to 12 wounded."[159]

June 4, 1864 (Saturday) ●

The armies continued to maneuver. As Sherman again attempted to turn Johnston's flank, the Confederate general prepared to move into earthworks under construction in Cobb County. Johnston notified Bragg in Richmond, "In consequence of the enemy's movements to his left we have taken this position [Lost Mountain]; our line nearly parallel to the Chattahoochee, more than two-thirds of it to the right of the mountain."[160]

June 5, 1864 (Sunday)

Sherman reported from Allatoona on the movement of the Confederate forces and forecast how events might unfold. "It has been raining hard for three days...the construction party is at work on the Etowah bridge, and should repair it in five days, when I will move on to Marietta. I expect the enemy to fight us at Kenesaw Mountain, near Marietta, but I will not run head on his fortifications. An examination of his abandoned lines here shows an immense line of works, all of which I have turned with less loss to ourselves than we have inflicted on him."[161]

June 6, 1864 (Monday)

Acworth received visitors, and the scene turned from gray to blue. Sherman reported to Halleck, "I am now on the railroad at Acworth Station, and have full possession forward to within six miles of Marietta." Sergeant Lyman Widney with the 34th Illinois Infantry, near Acworth, noted of the day, "We followed our line of works toward the left...in the afternoon we were led at a rapid rate until many dropped from the ranks exhausted and there were several cases of sunstroke. This proved to be the hottest day of our campaign. The air

---

[157] *OR*, ser. I, vol. 38, pt. 4:379.

[158] Ibid., 390.

[159] *ORN*, ser. I, vol. 15:495.

[160] *OR*, ser. I, vol. 38, pt. 4:759.

[161] Ibid., 408–409.

was sultry and the sun shone with a fierce, strong heat. At 5:00 P.M. we halted two and a half miles from the railroad and six miles from Marietta."[162]

June 7, 1864 (Tuesday)

Lieutenant General Hood, preparing to engage the Federals in Cobb County, issued a circular detailing actions need to protect innocent civilians. Hood tasked his subordinates "to make inquiry of any families who may be near enough the lines to be in danger, and learn if they wish to move. Those families who desire to move, and have not the means of doing so, will be furnished with wagons to transport them and their effects out of danger."[163]

June 8, 1864 (Wednesday)

Eyes on Sherman's armies, Johnston reported the Federal movements to General Cooper in Richmond. "Our scouts report the enemy extending to our right and massing on the railroad between Acworth and Big Shanty. We are moving to meet this, and our line, extended across the railroad, runs from Gilgal Church to north of the Kenesaw Mountain." Meanwhile, Sherman developed his own plans in Acworth. "To-morrow I will feel forward with cavalry," he wrote, "and follow up with infantry the moment the enemy develops his designs. If he fight [*sic*] at the Kenesaw Mountain I will turn it; but if he select the line of the Chattahoochee then I must study the case a little more before I commit myself."[164]

June 9, 1864 (Thursday)

Sherman issued Special Field Orders, No. 21, which dictated the avenue of approach each of his three armies would use in moving forward, beginning at 6:00 the next morning. "Major-General Thomas the center, on the Burnt Hickory and Marietta road and such other roads as he may choose between it and the Acworth and Marietta road...Major-General McPherson will move by the Acworth and Marietta road, with a column following the railroad and his cavalry well to the left, after passing Big Shanty." Finally, for the Army of the Ohio, "Major-General Schofield will cover his wagons well about Mount Olive Church, and feel well with cavalry and skirmishers down the road past Hardshell Church, to ascertain the enemy's strength about Lost Mountain and the ridge connecting it with Kenesaw Mountain." Hood reported early movements of the Federals, "the enemy are advancing in force in our front, along the railroad and the Big Shanty and the Marietta dirt road...."[165]

June 10, 1864 (Friday)

Brigadier General Lawrence "Sul" Ross and his Confederate horsemen kept tabs on the advancing Federals. Ross reported, "The enemy have not retired from their position in front of Davis' house, but occupy the same ground as before their advance yesterday evening. My pickets are re-established at the posts held by them before being driven in. I have had no report this morning from my scouts on the left (or enemy's right). So far as my pickets can discover, no change has occurred in enemy's line to the left or west of Davis'

---

[162] Ibid., 418; Widney, *Campaigning with "Uncle Billy,"* 239.

[163] *OR*, ser. I, vol. 38, pt. 4:763.

[164] Ibid., 763, 433.

[165] Ibid., 445, 765.

house."
Skirmishing reported near Calhoun.[166]

June 11, 1864 (Saturday)

Sherman, writing from Big Shanty, provided an update to Halleck in Washington. "Johnston is intrenched on the hills, embracing Lost Mountain, Pine Hill, and Kenesaw...it has rained so hard...the ground is so boggy...we have not developed any weak point or flank. The Etowah bridge is done...supplies will now be accumulated in Allatoona Pass.... One of my chief objects...to give full employment to Johnston...makes...little difference where he is, so he is not on his way to Virginia."[167]

June 12, 1864 (Sunday)

Private Jackman and his Kentucky comrades spent the Sabbath at rest in Cobb County. "Sunday. Am lying around loose. All quiet save sharpshooting. Our division seems to be holding Sherman's troops in check, while our main army is fortifying 2 miles to the rear of us, and Kenesaw Mountain."[168]

June 13, 1864 (Monday)

Captain William Dixon, entrenched near Lost Mountain, noted in his diary, "Our Regiment has been on Picket all day. Our cavalry on the flanks were drove from their position this morning. They moved like lot of scared sheep. The Yanks are in force in our front."[169]

June 14, 1864 (Tuesday)

Concerned over the exposed position of Major General William Bate's Division, early on this day, Lieutenant General Leonidas Polk joined Johnston and Hardee for an inspection at Pine Mountain. Riding to the crest of the peak, the three officers dismounted and viewed a sea of blue along their front. Close to the base of Pine Mountain, Captain Peter Simonson and the 5th Indiana Light Artillery Battery prepared to execute orders from Sherman and throw a shell or two in the direction of the Confederate position. The gunners readied their pieces and fired. Johnston and Hardee quickly got out of view; Polk lingered behind. The second artillery shell cut Polk in half. Johnston notified the Army of Tennessee of the incident. "Polk fell to-day at the outpost of this army, the army he raised and commanded, in all of whose trials he shared, to all of whose victories he contributed. In this distinguished leader we have lost the most courteous of gentlemen, the most gallant of soldiers. The Christian patriot soldier has neither lived nor died in vain. His example is before you; his mantle rests with you."[170]]

June 15, 1864 (Wednesday)

Confederate soldiers occupied the Gilgal Church line, as skirmishing continued in the vicinity of Pine Mountain and the new position of the Army of Tennessee. Sherman, writing

---

[166] *OR*, ser. I, vol. 38, pt. 4:768; skirmish in Mosocco, *Chronological Tracking*, 237.

[167] *OR*, ser. I, vol. 38, pt. 4:454–55.

[168] Jackman, *Diary of a Confederate Soldier*, 138.

[169] Dixon, *Blues in Gray*, 218.

[170] *OR*, ser. I, vol. 38, pt. 4:776. For an excellent study of the Atlanta Campaign, see Castel, *Decision in the West*.

from Big Shanty, delivered Secretary Stanton a brief update. "We killed Bishop Polk yesterday, and have made good progress to-day, of which I will make a full report as soon as one of my aides comes from the extreme right flank. General Grant may rest easy that Joe Johnston will not trouble him, if I can help it by labor or thought."[171]

June 16, 1864 (Thursday)

Private Sam Watkins participated in the Battle of Gilgal/Golgatha Church, and recalled the thick fighting, as Federals attacked Cleburne's position. Watkins saw "the Yankee line came in close proximity," and tried to hunker down as "cannon balls were ripping and tearing through the bushes." Watkins noted, "Every few moments, a raking fire from the Yankee lines would be poured into our lines, tearing limbs off the trees, and throwing rocks and dirt in every direction; but I never saw a soldier quail, or even dodge. While in this position…shrapnel and grape-shot, came ripping and tearing through our ranks, wounding [Brigadier] General Lucius E. Polk, and killing some of his staff."[172]

June 17, 1864 (Friday)

The Army of Tennessee began occupying the Mud Creek Line, a position they would hold for about two days. Sergeant Rice C. Bull and his comrades in the 123rd New York Infantry "made a general advance. We found the enemy's works deserted; they had retreated during the night. We advanced in line for another mile until we reached another range of hills. There again we found them well fortified. At one o'clock we halted in an open field on quite a high point. While we were at rest we were opened on by a battery located a long distance away." As the lines grew closer, the intensity of the action increased. "Most of their shot and shell fell short, but one solid shot that carried farther than the rest did us some damage. The shot was nearly spent and traveled so slow we could hear it coming and knew from the sound it would strike near us. It struck at the right of the Regiment, bounding like a ball, passed over the heads of the men in five companies and struck the ground in the center of Company K, wounding five men."[173]

Junc 18, 1864 (Saturday)

Private Benjamin Chapman with the 19th Alabama Infantry wrote to his wife from a line of battle outside Marietta. "Sarah, have had a hard time since I left Dalton. We've been skirmishing and fighting and marching to and fro ever since we left Dalton and part of the time we have had some disagreeable weather to go through and the prospects are very good to continue for several days yet. The enemy charge our men on our left the other day and then drove them with greater slaughter, then our turn. They are skirmishing and cannonating [*sic*] every day somewhere on the lines." Skirmishes reported at Acworth and Allatoona.[174]

June 19, 1864 (Sunday)

---

[171] *OR*, ser. I, vol. 38, pt. 4:480.

[172] Watkins, *Company Aytch*, 186.

[173] Bull, *Soldiering*, 127.

[174] McCurdy, *"Yours Truly Husband until Death…,"* June 18, 1864, n.p.; skirmishes from Mosocco, *Chronological Tracking*, 240.

The Army of Tennessee began occupying the Kennesaw Mountain Line. A soldier in Major General W. H. T. Walker's Division, 1st Lieutenant Hamilton Branch with the 54th Georgia Infantry, described the retrograde movement to the new defensive works. "We were moved about 3/4 mile to the right and put into the front trenches near the Marietta road. my company was then ordered out on picket but Genl Hardee considering it dangerous for us to go out in the day ordered us to wait until night fall...the enemy then commenced shelling us and shelled us very heavyly [*sic*] for about 1 hour."[175]

June 20, 1864 (Monday)

Brigadier General Lawrence Ross reported engaging a Federal force. "The Yankee cavalry are now at the bridge on Powder Springs road, fighting my pickets. The bridge is three miles from this place [Cheney House]. All my scouts were driven out before the cavalry and could not pass behind them for the high water. Every creek is swimming and the fields and woods very boggy. Nothing but cavalry has been seen by my scout." Brigadier General Jacob Cox delivered a Federal account: "Tell [Major] General [George] Stoneman that Colonel [Silas] Adams reports some force of enemy's cavalry approaching in vicinity of Powder Springs."[176]

June 21, 1864 (Tuesday)

Troops continued maneuvering along the Kennesaw Mountain Line. J. R. Boyle of the 111th Pennsylvania wrote, "the Second and Third brigades were posted on the right of the First, and the One Hundred and Eleventh Pennsylvania and One Hundred and Thirty-seventh New York were sent out under Colonel Cobham to reconnoiter the Marietta and Powder Springs road They encountered a strong skirmish line three fourths of a mile down the road at Grier's plantation...engaged and pressed it back one fourth of a mile...action...continued throughout the day."[177]

June 22, 1864 (Wednesday)

Concerned that Sherman was preparing to turn the left flank of the Army of Tennessee, Johnston redeployed Hood's Corps from the right to the left flank. Hood's boys began arriving around the Kolb farmhouse, when Hood spotted Federals in his front and ordered and attack. Going in blind, absent any reconnaissance, Hood incurred 1,000 casualties as Federal artillery unleashed their fury on the advancing soldiers in gray. Major General Joe Hooker's troops received the bulk of the attack, and Hooker reported, "Our artillery did splendid execution among them." Verifying Hooker's statement, a declaration from Major General Carter Stevenson, whose soldiers advanced into the inferno. "The artillery of the enemy, which was massed in large force and admirably posted, was served with a rapidity and fatal precision which could not be surpassed." The Federals incurred an estimated 300 killed, wounded, or missing during the Battle of Kolb's Farm.[178]

---

[175] Joslyn, *Charlotte's Boys*, 251.

[176] *OR*, ser. I, vol. 38, pt. 4:783:540.

[177] Boyle, *Soldiers True*, 222–23.

[178] *OR*, ser. I, vol. 38, pt. 4:563; Strayer and Baumgartner, *Echoes of Battle*, 156; McMurry, *Road past Kennesaw*, 24.

June 23, 1864 (Thursday)
After participating in the Battle of Kolb's Farm, Major Frederick C. Winkler, 26th Wisconsin Infantry, noted the following day, "We have got into a new position somewhat in advance of the one we held before. It is a very important position, as it holds one of the principal roads leading back to Marietta. A good many rebel deserters have come into our lines during the last night; they are all very much discouraged."[179]
June 24, 1864 (Friday)
Via Special Field Orders, No. 28, Sherman outlined plans that would result in battle three days later. "The army commanders will make full reconnaissances and preparations to attack the enemy in force on the 27th instant, at 8 a.m. precisely. The commanding general will be on Signal Hill, and will have telegraphic communication with all the army commanders." He then charged each of his three primary subordinates with the work ahead. Skirmishing reported near La Fayette.
I. Major-General Thomas will assault the enemy at any point near his center, to be selected by himself, and will make any changes in his troops necessary by night, so as not to attract the attention of the enemy.
II. Major-General McPherson will feign by a movement of his cavalry and one division of infantry on his extreme left, approaching Marietta from the north, and using artillery freely, but will make his real attack at a point south and west of Kenesaw.
III. Major-General Schofield will feel well to his extreme right and threaten that flank of the enemy with artillery and display, but attack some one point of the enemy's line as near the Marietta and Powder Springs road as he can with prospect of success.[180]
June 25, 1864 (Saturday)
The Federals continued to maneuver into position for the attack of the 27th. The incessant rainfall made the task of moving artillery and supply wagons more difficult, as the dirt roads turned into quagmires. Captain A.T. Fielder and his Tennesseans tried to keep their powder dry while strengthening the earthworks on the Kennesaw Mountain Line. "Rained verry hard during the night and still raining this morning—health good—Early this morning apart of our Brigade went out to the front while an other part went out to work on the fortifications It rained nearly all the forenoon—the 11th Regt. of our Brigade which went out to the front in the morning returned in the evening near night appearance of Clearing off. Night lay down about 10 oclk." Skirmishing reported at Allatoona and Spring Place.[181]
June 26, 1864 (Sunday) ◑
One day before battle, Hood demonstrated his effectiveness in predicting the intentions of his opponent. "The lieutenant-general commanding directs me to say that he desires you to have the abatis in front of your position made very formidable, so as to enable your troops to repulse any force of the enemy that may he brought against them...General Hood

[179] Winkler, *Letters*, 136.
[180] *OR*, ser. I, vol. 38, pt. 4:588; skirmish from Mosocco, *Chronological Tracking*, 242.
[181] Cathey, *Captain T. A. Fielder's Civil War Diary*, 233; skirmishes from Mosocco, *Chronological Tracking*, 242.

anticipates that the enemy will assault our works, and thinks it well (to) be prepared for such contingency."[182] Skirmishing along Olley's Creek during the day.

June 27, 1864 (Monday)

Sherman, hoping to break through the center of the Confederate position along the Kennesaw Mountain Line, ordered the attack. McPherson feigned an assault on Big Kennesaw Mountain, while Schofield demonstrated on the Confederate right flank. Once these two operations commenced, Thomas and the Army of the Cumberland hit the center. The Federals encountered stubborn resistance from the soldiers in Major General Benjamin Franklin Cheatham's Division. The advancing Federals, those in the warmest part of the fight—on an already hot morning—lost Brigadier General Charles Harker almost immediately. Colonel Dan McCook led his troops to near the salient position of the gray line but could not break through. McCook received a mortal wound and died several days later at his home in Ohio. Sergeant Nixon B. Stewart with the 52nd Ohio Infantry, who struggled below the salient, noted a defilade protected his wounded comrades. "Probably one-half of our regiment that were unharmed, lay within twelve feet of the earth works and not in a position to load and fire," Stewart wrote. "One by one our men crawled back to the new line below, while many of us, with the dead and seriously wounded, lay near the works." Captain W. J. McMurray, 20th Tennessee Infantry (CSA), painted the scene of the attacking Federals: "The Yankees were seven lines deep and led by gallant officers; they came forward with a rush like a great cloud of Egyptian flies. Their front lines began to melt from their first step, but onward they came over their dead and dying." Sherman suffered 3,000 casualties, while the Confederate loss approximated 1,000 in the Battle of Kennesaw Mountain.[183]

June 28, 1864 (Thursday)

Captain Samuel Foster, serving in Cleburne's Division, spent the day after battle maneuvering to strengthen the Confederate line. He noted, "The firing kept up all night as usual. Our Brigade moved to the left…just the length of one Regiment. The small arms are still firing this morning, intermixed with Artillery, all along the line in front of us. This evening the fireing [*sic*] has ceased in our front, there being temporary suspension, for the Yanks to bury their dead."[184]

June 29, 1864 (Wednesday)

A soldier in the 105th Ohio Infantry wrote of the ceasefire to recover the dead lining the field beneath the Confederate defenses. "After the assault we kept on digging and fighting. There was an armistice from one o'clock until eight o'clock, p. m., on the 29th, for the purpose of burying the dead.… Then the fight began again, and we worked our way closer and closer to the Confederate entrenchments until, in some places the lines were not more

---

[182] *OR*, ser. I, vol. 38, pt. 4:794–95; Irvine, *Military Operations of the Civil War*, 4:36.

[183] Baumgartner and Strayer, *Kennesaw Mountain*, 161; Luvaas and Nelson, *Guide to the Atlanta Campaign*, 285; casualties from National Park Service, "Kennesaw Mountain," https://www.nps.gov/civilwar/search-battles-detail.htm?battleCode=GA015.

[184] Foster, *One of Cleburne's Command*, 98.

than thirty yards apart. A head or a hand that showed above the works was sure to bring a shot."[185]

June 30, 1864 (Thursday)

On a day with skirmishing at Acworth, Allatoona, and La Fayette, Sherman wrote to his wife Ellen. In the letter—perhaps influenced from the recent setback at Kennesaw—Sherman shared thoughts on fighting. "I begin to regard the death & mangling of a couple thousand men as a small affair, a kind of morning dash—and it may be well that we become so hardened. I suppose the people are impatient why I dont push or move rapidly to Atlanta but those who are here are satisfied with the progress."[186]

July 1, 1864 (Friday)

Sherman ordered Thomas and McPherson to "Let your artillery and skirmishers stir up the enemy a little this evening and to-morrow morning. I fear they are getting too strong on General Schofield, who has gone farther toward Ruff's Mill than I contemplated." Skirmishing at Howell's Ferry, Allatoona, and Lost Mountain.[187]

July 2, 1864 (Saturday)

Wagon wheels wrapped, canteens muffled, and no talking among the soldiers, the Army of Tennessee quietly slipped-away from their positions along the Kennesaw Mountain Line. Earlier in the day, Johnston issued a circular detailing the redeployment to prevent Sherman's forces from turning the Confederate left flank.

> The army will change position to-night. 1. The Army of Mississippi will withdraw its artillery at dark and its infantry at 10 p. m. 2. Hardee's and Hood's corps will move their artillery at dark, their infantry at 11 p. m. 3. Each corps commander will leave on the lines such rear guard as he may think proper until 1 a. m., then to be withdrawn and followed by the skirmish line. 4. The corps will move by routes already indicated to the commanders of each, and take position in two lines on the new line indicated. 5. The reserve artillery will be protected by the corps in whose line it is serving and take the route of the corps. 6. Wheeler's cavalry will cover the infantry from General Hood's left to General Loring's right. 7. Corps commanders will send their spare carriages of every description to the rear at or before sunset. 8. General Johnston will move with the center column.[188]

July 3, 1864 (Sunday)

William King watched as troops fell back through Marietta. "About 6 o'clock the last of our infantry had passed, and our Cavalry skirmishers were collecting in the yard, they informed me that a detachment of our Cavalry had formed in an open field a few hundred yards south, to check the advance of the Federal Cavalry." Soon, Federal cavalry forces

---

[185] Tourgée and Luebke, *Story of a Thousand*, 305.

[186] Sherman, *Sherman's Civil War*, 660; skirmishes from Mosocco, *Chronological Tracking*, 243.

[187] *OR*, ser. I, vol. 38, pt. 5:5; skirmishes from Mosocco, *Chronological Tracking*, 244.

[188] *OR*, ser. I, vol. 38, pt. 5:860.

arrived; the infantry followed, and King went in search of additional guards for his property. During his absence, a guard left from Major General Joe Hooker's Corps "was the first to commence the robbing, he broke in the first door soon after I left, multitudes followed him, every room, closet, wardrobe, and trunk was forced open, nothing escaped their examination, and almost everything of value which they could remove was taken...."[189]

July 4, 1864 (Monday) (Independence Day)

The Confederates continued to fall back, as General Johnston tasked Hood with fighting a delaying action, which would allow the balance of the Army of Tennessee to safely occupy the Chattahoochee River Line. This action from Hood played out during the day as heavy artillery fire rattled the ground along the Smyrna/Ruff's Mill Line. In his post action report, Colonel P. Sidney Post of the 59th Illinois Infantry noted, "The day was extremely hot and the men suffered dreadfully from thirst and exposure to the sweltering sun on that open field, but the position was held, and during the night the foe again fled." Private Sam Watkins found himself in fear of life and limb, writing, "I cannot now remember a more severe artillery duel. Two hundred cannon were roaring and belching like blue blazes. It seemed that the earth was frequently moved from its foundations, and you could hear it grate as it moved." Sherman noted of the action, "We celebrated our Fourth of July, by a noisy but not a desperate battle, designed chiefly to hold the enemy there till Generals McPherson and Schofield could get well into position below him...near the Chattahoochee crossings." Skirmishes at Neal Dow Station and along Rottenwood Creek.[190]

July 5, 1864 (Tuesday)

Daybreak along the Chattahoochee River revealed a series of Confederate fortifications in varying states of readiness. The unique design of the fortifications—brainchild of the Army of Tennessee's artillery chief, Brigadier General Francis A. Shoup—presented challenges for soldiers, blue and gray. Depending upon the position along the six-mile stretch, one's eyes viewed works in different states of readiness. Shoup's concept called for placing above-ground fortifications (akin to three-sided log cabins without a roof) between 60 and 175 yards apart, depending on the terrain. "The nature of the line was quite novel," he recorded. "It was not a system of earth works, but a line of detached log redoubts packed in with earth. They were entirely enclosed, of this form in ground plan, each intended to be defended by one company of about eighty men. They were nearly perpendicular on the outer faces, ten or twelve feet in height, and the front faces about twelve feet thick, while the backs were only five or six feet through." Skirmishes at Howell's Ferry, Turner's Ferry, Isham's Ford, and Pace's Ferry.[191]

July 6, 1864 (Wednesday)

Federal cavalry moved eastward in Cobb County. Brigadier General Kenner Garrard reported the action to Sherman: "Roswell was occupied by my command with but small

---

[189] W. King, *Diary*, 4.

[190] *OR*, ser. I, vol. 38, pt. 1:431; Watkins, *Company Aytch*, 201; Sherman, *Memoirs*, 535; skirmishes from Mosocco, *Chronological Tracking*, 244.

[191] Shoup, "Dalton Campaign," 263; skirmishes from Mosocco, *Chronological Tracking*, 245.

opposition, the few hundred rebels on the roads falling back before my advance, and burning the bridge after crossing. There is a good ford at this place, so I am informed (the shallow ford), but as the opposite banks command this one, and pickets lie on the other side, I have not crossed any of my men." Private George Lea, with the 7th Mississippi Infantry, held a position in the river defenses, writing, "I have nothing of importance to write to you we are either fighting or building breast works all the time[.] Our Division is on the left of the line resting on the Chattahoochee River[.] Some of our forces are on the other side[.] I expect Enemy will try to cross the River if they can and I expect they will[;] they are trying to avoid an open field fight with us[,] they will have to come on us in our works and they know that will not pay."[192]

July 7, 1864 (Thursday) ●

Federal occupation of Roswell resulted in destruction and the taking of prisoners. Sherman updated Halleck:

> General Garrard reports to me that he is in possession of Roswell, where were several valuable cotton and woolen factories in full operation, also paper-mills, all of which, by my order, he destroyed by fire. They had been for years engaged exclusively at work for the Confederate government, and the owner of the woolen factory displayed the French flag; but—as he failed also to show the United States flag, General Garrard burned it also. The main cotton factory was valued at a million of United States dollars. The cloth on hand is reserved for use of United States hospitals, and I have ordered General Garrard to arrest for treason all owners and employees, foreign and native, and send them under guard to Marietta, whence I will send them North. Being exempt from conscription, they are as much governed by the rules of war as if in the ranks. The women can find employment in Indiana. This whole region was devoted to manufactories, but I will destroy every one of them. Johnston is maneuvering against my right, and I will try and pass the Chattahoochee by my left. Ask Mr. Stanton not to publish the substance of my dispatches, for they reach Richmond in a day, and are telegraphed at once to Atlanta. The Atlanta papers contain later news from Washington than I get from Nashville. Absolute silence in military matters is the only safe rule. Let our public learn patience and common sense.[193]

Captain David Conyngham, a part-time reporter for the *New York Herald*, wrote of the scene in Roswell, "There were at the time about three hundred female operators employed in it, and it was a feeling to witness how they wept, as this, their only means of support, was consigned to destruction. They were sent north, or wherever they chose. This factory worked over four thousand spindles, and was certainly the most important in this section of country."[194]

July 8, 1864 (Friday)

Blockade runners worked to get in and out of the tightening net along the coast. On this

---

[192] *OR*, ser. I, vol. 38, pt. 5:68; Lea and Skellie, *May Angels Guard Thee*, 103–104.

[193] *OR*, ser. I, vol. 38, pt. 5:73.

[194] Conyngham, *Sherman's March*, 145.

day, one vessel did not successfully make the run outward. Rear Admiral Dahlgren indicated "the U.S.S. *Sonoma*, Lieutenant-Commander [Edmund] Matthews, captured the small side-wheel steamer *Ida*, which vessel left Sapelo…bound to Nassau. She had on board 54 bales of upland cotton, 10 men, and a captain named [William] Postell, who, I am told, was formerly a midshipman in the Navy."[195] In Cobb County, the Federals prepared to initiate a crossing of the Chattahoochee River near Sope Creek: "Half past three o'clock in the afternoon was the time set for the crossing. The signal to advance was given. A single cannon-shot was fired from the enemy's outpost…but so completely was it now covered by the rifles of [Colonel Robert] Byrd's men, that no one could aim it or fire. The mounted men, conscious of their inability to cope with the force before them, galloped away to carry the news."[196]

July 9, 1864 (Saturday)

His right flank now turned, with increasing numbers of Federal troops crossing the Chattahoochee River in Roswell and at Sope Creek, General Johnston held a position no longer tenable, so the Army of Tennessee left Shoup's defenses. The architect of the River Line paused to look "at the works into which my heart had gone to such a degree, and felt that the days of the Confederacy were numbered. I could not…see why the position should not have been held indefinitely."[197]

July 10, 1864 (Sunday)

The Confederates burned the railroad and wagon bridges over the Chattahoochee River as they fell back. Johnston informed Cooper, "we crossed at and below the railroad, and are now about two miles from the river, guarding the crossings."[198] Private P. D. Stephenson with the 5th Company of the Washington Artillery wrote of the scene on the Atlanta side of the river: "The morning sun…witnessed two great armies reposing on opposite sides of the Chattahoochee. The river like a winding ribbon ran between them and each side seemed disposed to accept it as a temporary bar. Both commands might well be pardoned for doing so after a two month death grapple. Repulse after repulse, and fearfully bloody, had been the fate of every front attack of our antagonist."[199]

July 11, 1864 (Monday) ◐

Prisoners at Camp Sumter in Andersonville finally rid themselves of the notorious "Raiders," a band of prisoners who robbed from their fellow inmates. After a trial, which found six of the Raiders guilty, the hanging took place today. One of the prisoners, John Ransom, a quartermaster with the 9th Michigan Cavalry, observed the execution and noted, "At about eleven o'clock they were all blindfolded, hands and feet tied, told to get ready, nooses adjusted and the plank knocked from under. It was an awful sight to see, still a necessity."[200]

---

[195] *ORN*, ser. I, vol. 15:562.

[196] Cox, *Atlanta*, 139.

[197] Shoup, "Dalton Campaign," 264.

[198] *OR*, ser. I, vol. 38, pt. 5:873.

[199] Stephenson, *Civil War Memoir*, 206.

[200] Ransom, *Andersonville Diary*, 114–15.

Sherman, updating Washington on the status of conditions in Georgia, wrote, "The enemy is now all beyond the Chattahoochee, having destroyed all his bridges. We occupy the west bank for thirty miles...we now commence the real game for Atlanta, and I expect pretty sharp practice, but I think we have the advantage, and propose to keep it."[201]

July 12, 1864 (Tuesday)

Jefferson Davis bantered about the notion of firing Johnston and replacing him with Hood. In typical Davis fashion, he sought input on the matter from General Lee. Lee suggested, "It is a bad time to release the commander of an army situated as that of Tenne. We may lose Atlanta and the army too. Hood is a bold fighter. I am doubtful as to other qualities necessary."[202]

July 13, 1864 (Wednesday)

After exercising his patience with Johnston to the breaking point, President Davis sent Bragg to Atlanta for a visit with the general. When his boots once again hit Georgia ground, Bragg quickly telegraphed Davis. "Have just arrived without detention. Our army all south of the Chattahoochee, and indications seem to favor an entire evacuation of this place. Shall see General Johnston immediately." Later in the day, Bragg updated the president. "Our army is sadly depleted...I find but little encouraging."[203]

July 14, 1864 (Thursday)

Hood provided Bragg with his assessment of the campaign, and his thoughts Johnston's lack of aggressiveness.

> I have, general, so often urged that we should force the enemy to give us battle as to almost be regarded reckless by the officers high in rank in this army, since their views have been so directly opposite. I regard it as a great misfortune to our country that we failed to give battle to the enemy many miles north of our present position. Please say to the President that I shall continue to do my duty cheerfully and faithfully, and strive to do what I think is best for our country, as my constant prayer is for our success.[204]

July 15, 1864 (Friday)

Bragg visited with Johnston and provided a status update to President Davis. Bragg noted Johnston treated him "courteously and kindly. He has not sought my advice, and it was not volunteered. I cannot learn that he has any more plan for the future than he has had in the past. It is expected that he will await the enemy on a line some three miles from here, and the impression prevails that he is now more inclined to fight. The morale of our army is still reported good."[205]

July 16, 1864 (Saturday)

The discord between General Johnston and President Davis did not bode well for

---

[201] *OR*, ser. I, vol. 38, pt. 5:113–14.

[202] R. E. Lee, *Dispatches*, 282.

[203] *OR*, ser. I, vol. 38, pt. 5:878.

[204] Ibid., 880.

[205] Ibid., 881.

Confederate efforts during the Atlanta Campaign. Often, Johnston would respond to an inquiry from the president with language vague enough to equate to no response at all. Davis, after reading Johnston's latest, felt akin to a blind man in a corn maze and requested "to hear from you as to present situation, and your plan of operations so specifically as will enable me to anticipate events." "My plan of operations must, therefore, depend upon that of the enemy," Johnston replied. "It is mainly to watch for an opportunity to fight to advantage. We are trying to put Atlanta in condition to be held for a day or two by the Georgia militia, that army movements may be freer and wider."[206]

July 17, 1864 (Sunday)

Snap, crackle, and pop! Not the sounds Johnston heard over breakfast, but those of the final straw breaking the camel's back. General Cooper served the news: "Hood has been commissioned to the temporary rank of general under the late law of Congress. I am directed by the Secretary of War to inform you that as you have failed to arrest the advance of the enemy to the vicinity of Atlanta, far in the interior of Georgia, and express no confidence that you can defeat or repel him, you are hereby relieved from the command of the Army and Department of Tennessee…."[207]

July 18, 1864 (Monday)

Most of the soldiers in the Army of Tennessee thought highly of "Old Joe," so word of his termination shocked many of them. Others, though, approved. Private P. D. Stephenson noted, "At the time of Johnston's dismissal his reputation among us had sunk to its proper level. He had gained no laurels during the campaign; on the contrary, what he had were tarnished by the unpleasant gossip among us as to his headiness and to speak plainly, arrogance and self sufficiency." Jefferson Davis would concur. Skirmishing reported near Buckhead.[208]

July 19, 1864 (Tuesday)

As the Army of the Cumberland approached Peach Tree Creek, skirmishing broke out in the area. Meanwhile, Hardee issued a circular informing his soldiers of the new commander's plan. "By direction of General Hood you will cause the banks of Peach Tree Creek to be thoroughly examined in front of your division; place a strong skirmish line there, and cause the best defenses that can be made to be placed there. The object is to enable a small force to resist the enemy's crossing for some time."[209]

July 20, 1864 (Wednesday)

At the Battle of Peach Tree Creek, Hood ordered Hardee's Corps to attack as soldiers in the Army of the Cumberland crossed the creek. Seeking to strike before they could establish earthworks, the gray line advanced piecemeal. Major General Thomas directed reinforcements along his lines and repulsed the attack. Federal casualties in the victory were 1,710.

---

[206] Ibid., 882–83.

[207] Ibid., 885.

[208] Stephenson, *Civil War Memoir*, 210; skirmishes from Mosocco, *Chronological Tracking*, 249.

[209] *OR*, ser. I, vol. 38, pt. 5:894.

In his first battle as commander of the Army of Tennessee, Hood lost, based on recent scholarship, a number reduced to 2,500.[210]

July 21, 1864 (Thursday)

After Peach Tree Creek, both armies maneuvered, each seeking an advantage in terrain. Unbeknownst to the officers at the time, one Federal unit secured exceptionally good ground. McPherson reported, "Brigadier-General [Mortimer] Leggett...advanced his lines and captured a hill, quite a commanding position, this forenoon.... The [Bald] hill is two and a quarter miles from Atlanta, and a portion of the enemy's works around the town are in view." Grant wrote to Sherman regarding the change in command of the Army of Tennessee and indicated the firing of Johnston proved of "much to the surprise of the army and public; also that this change indicates that there will be no more retreating, but that Atlanta will be defended at all hazards and to the last extremity." On the Confederate side, Assistant Adjutant-General A. P. Mason notified Brigadier General Marcus Wright he "must be prepared to-night for an evacuation of Atlanta, should it become necessary. You will, therefore, without saying anything about it, be prepared to move when Lieutenant-General [A. P.] Stewart's troops move into town, should the evacuation take place."[211]

July 22, 1864 (Friday)

Hardee received orders from Hood to march his corps southward through Atlanta, then make a northeastward maneuver, and position his force in the rear of McPherson's Army of the Tennessee. Marching at night, on hot, dusty roads slowed Hardee. Realizing he could not position his corps in the rear of the Federal army to attack at the appointed hour, Hardee requested and received permission from Hood to make a frontal assault. Hardee's soldiers advanced, and Cheatham troops joined the fray. During the Battle of Atlanta—the costliest of the entire Atlanta Campaign—the Federals held. The high ground Leggett gained the previous day proved instrumental in McPherson's men holding their lines; victory produced a loss for Sherman, as McPherson fell mortally wounded. Federal casualties totaled 3,722 to the Confederate loss of 5500.[212]

Second Lieutenant Richard Tuthill, 1st Michigan Light Artillery, looked out from his position on

> an open field containing not more than 20 acres. Beyond this were woods. Pat Cleburne's Texans...desperate and mad, were to make an attempt to wipe out the disgrace of their former defeat. Their line well formed, they emerged from their concealment in the woods, and yelling as only the steer-drivers of Texas could yell, charged upon our division. On came the Texans, but they were met by a continuous volley of musketry and shrapnel, shell and canister from our six rifled Rodmans and Cooper's howitzers. It seemed as if no man of all the host who were attacking us could escape alive; and yet, still yelling, they persisted in their desperate undertaking. Their

[210] S. Davis, *Texas Brigadier to the Fall of Atlanta*, 298.

[211] *OR*, ser. I, vol. 38, pt. 5:219:211, 900.

[212] S. Davis, *Texas Brigadier to the Fall of Atlanta*, 329.

> line was reformed, and again and again they attempted the impossible to drive the 3rd Division from the line it had decided to hold.[213]

July 23, 1864 (Saturday)

Post-battle reports proved the order of the day. Hood wrote to Secretary of War Seddon, "In the engagement of yesterday we captured 18 stand of colors instead of 5, and 13 guns instead of 22, as previously reported. Brigadier-General [Hugh] Mercer not wounded. All quiet to-day except skirmishing, and the enemy occasionally throwing shell into the city. The army is in good spirits." Sherman, in two different messages to Halleck, recapped the battle of July 22, and reported, "Our left, though refused somewhat, is still within easy cannon-range of Atlanta. The enemy seems to man his extensive parapets and, at the same time, has to spare heavy assaulting columns; but to-day we will intrench our front lines, which will give me troops to spare to meet these assaults." Sherman's second message informed of a successful cavalry raid through Alabama and into western Georgia. "[Major] General [Lovell] Rousseau reports from Marietta yesterday his safe return from Opelika, having destroyed that depot, 30 miles of railroad toward Montgomery, 3 miles toward Columbus, and 2 toward West Point. His entire loss 12 killed and 30 wounded. He brings in 400 mules and 300 horses."[214]

July 24, 1864 (Sunday)

Major General John "Black Jack" Logan took command of the Army of the Tennessee after McPherson fell during the battle of July 22 and turned in a stellar performance that would have gained him permanent command in another man's army. Sherman, however, did not believe in promoting officers to lead an army if they had not attended West Point. So, another officer received the nod, and Logan retained command of his corps. In a message to Halleck, Sherman wrote, "The sudden loss of McPherson was a heavy blow to me. I can hardly replace him, but must have a successor. After thinking over the whole matter, I prefer that Maj. Gen. O. O. Howard be ordered to command the Army and Department of the Tennessee. If this meets the President's approval, notify me by telegraph, when I will put him in command and name others to fill the vacancies created."[215]

July 25, 1864 (Monday) ◑

From Cobb County, William King wrote of rumors in Atlanta.

> Another day of trial and anxiety has come, all nature seems cheerful, the skies bright and clear and the weather very cool for the season, and after Breakfast as I could not go to town I walked to the Picket station near the Graveyard, gave one of them a letter to take to the P.O. for me and asked him to inquire for letters there for me.... I met two Federal officers, there I learnt that the report of the Federal Army having

---

[213] Strayer and Baumgartner, *Echoes of Battle*, 236.

[214] *OR*, ser. I, vol. 38, pt. 5:903:234–35.

[215] Ibid., 240–41.

entered Atlanta some days ago was untrue, and that they were still out of it up to yesterday evening.[216]

July 26, 1864 (Tuesday)

Sherman notified the War Department of his initial plans to cut the rail lines serving Atlanta.

> I send by the right a force of about 3,500 cavalry, under [Brigadier] General [Edward] McCook, and round by the left about 5,000 cavalry, under Stoneman, with orders to reach the railroad about Griffin. I also have consented that Stoneman (after he has executed this part of his plan), if he finds it feasible, may, with his division...go to Macon and attempt the release of our officers, prisoners there, and then to Anderson[ville] to release the 20,000 of our men, prisoners there.[217]

July 27, 1864 (Wednesday)

Skirmishing reported along Snapfinger Creek, as Private W. L. Truman with 1st Missouri Light Artillery wrote from the defenses of Atlanta.

> The Ga. State Melitia [*sic*], are coming in and taking their places in the trenches, many old men and boys, but we old soldiers feel that they will do good fighting, if attacked in their works, but we do not expect Sherman to attack us in our breastworks. We build works to protect ourselves, from his shells and bullets, fired at us from behind his own works, and not from his attacks. Every battery man that can be spared from the guns is ordered to take a musket and get in the trenches close by and do his duty in case of an attack.[218]

July 28, 1864 (Thursday)

Once again Hood took the aggressive action, developing a sound battle plan that called for Lieutenant General S. D. Lee's Corps to advance out the Lickskillet Road until he located the Federal troops, entrench, and await Lieutenant General A. P. Stewart's Corps, which would follow Lee. Once Stewart went behind Lee's line and positioned his soldiers on the flank of the Federals, both units would attack. Lee's command moved westward. Spotting boys in blue ahead, Lee launched his attack in piecemeal fashion. When Stewart arrived, the Battle of Ezra Church had ended. The Army of Tennessee suffered around 3,000 casualties, while the Federal force engaged, primarily Major General O. O. Howard's Army of the Tennessee, lost 632 killed, wounded, or missing. While the fighting played on at Ezra Church, reports of skirmishing at Campbellton, Flat Rock Bridge, and Lithonia occupied officers on both sides. Private Edwin Smith with the 54th Ohio Infantry noted his involvement in the battle: "Charge after charge was made by the massed rebel forces on our single line, but were met and repulsed by the undaunted coffee-coolers with a fearful slaughter. Our guns would get so hot that we could not hold them. Three times when the rebels

---

[216] W. King, *Diary*, 36.

[217] *OR*, ser. I, vol. 38, pt. 5:260–61.

[218] Truman, "Memoirs," http://www.cedarcroft.com/cw/memoir/index.html; skirmish from Mosocco, *Chronological Tracking*, 252.

were driven back we let them cool, and twice poured water in them to clean them out."[219]

July 29, 1864 (Friday)

McCook and Stoneman continued their respective raids, Stoneman southeast of Atlanta and McCook to the southwest. Skirmishing near Lovejoy Station resulted in slight damage to the Macon & Western Railroad. Hood requested assistance from Governor Brown. "Just have information that the enemy have struck the Macon road six miles below Jonesborough. General Hood desires you to give all possible assistance to repair the damage. Troops have been sent from here to prevent its destruction as far as possible. Please communicate with Captain [George] Hazlehurst, who is somewhere below, gathering railroad iron. I send this letter by Captain Shoup, my aide-de-camp."[220]

July 30, 1864 (Saturday)

William King, venturing out in Marietta, met Federal troops and had a change of opinion after speaking with young men who shared King's desires. "What a joyful day will it be to me when peace returns. God grant that it may not be far distant; all the Federal soldiers I converse with seem as anxious as I am for peace, that they may be allowed to their families & domestic enjoyments at Home—all the feelings they express seem kind & sympathizing with us. My intercourse with them has greatly elevated my opinion of the character & feelings of the Federal Army."[221] There was skirmishing at Newnan, along Clear Creek, and near Macon, Clinton, and Hillsborough. Major General Wheeler described the fighting at Brown's Mill, where his troopers routed the Federal cavalry with Brigadier General Edward McCook. "I pressed rapidly down the road upon their flank," he wrote, "cutting off nearly two entire regiments, which surrendered in a body with all their artillery, wagons, and ambulances. The entire column was thrown into disorder, and a number of prisoners, arms, horses, and 2 stand of colors were captured in the pursuit which ensued. Some 300 [Confederate] prisoners...captured the previous day, were also recaptured by our troops." Skirmishing reported along Clear Creek.[222]

July 31, 1864 (Sunday)

Brigadier General Alfred Iverson's force blocked Major General Stoneman's attempt to rejoin Sherman's armies. The Battle of Sunshine Church did not turn out well for Stoneman and his force. Stoneman reported to Sherman,

> A portion of this brigade I sent to hold a cross-road and keep the enemy from getting between me and the main force, pack train, &c. This also gave way and followed the rest, so that near the end of the day I found myself with about 200 of the Fifth Indiana Cavalry and the section of artillery. I insisted on continuing the contest and, if taken prisoners at all, upon being taken fighting, but the officers with me protested that, being without ammunition and surrounded, our escape was next to impossible; that there was no use in fighting longer; that we had accomplished our object in covering

---

[219] Casualties from S. Davis, *Texas Brigadier to the Fall of Atlanta*, 358; skirmishes from Mosocco, *Chronological Tracking*, 252; Smith quote in Strayer and Baumgartner, *Echoes of Battle*, 261.

[220] *OR*, ser. I, vol. 38, pt. 5:930.

[221] W. King, *Diary*, 45.

[222] *OR*, ser. I, vol. 38, pt. 3:956; skirmish from Mosocco, *Chronological Tracking*, 252.

> the retreat of the rest of the command until it was well under way, and that in justice to all concerned we should surrender. My own horse had been shot under me and I was scarcely able to mount the worn-down one and the only one I could find to replace the one I had lost, and our chances of escape were so small that I consented to be taken prisoners of war, and as such our treatment has been everything that could have been expected. Our loss in killed and wounded was quite large. I feel better satisfied with myself to be a prisoner of war, much as I hate it, than to be amongst those who owe their escape to considerations of self-preservation.[223]

August 1, 1864 (Monday)
Days earlier, Sherman had ordered an artillery bombardment of Atlanta. Sam Richards wrote of what resulted in a daily occurrence. "We have had shelling semi-occasionally but thus far none of the deadly missiles have reached our house and we could look upon them at a safe distance with composure. For fear that they should ever reach us I have done several hard days' work preparing a 'pit' in our cellar, to retreat to for shelter."[224]

August 2, 1864 (Tuesday) ●
W. A. Chapman, 19th Alabama Infantry, wrote to his sister from the defenses around Atlanta. He informed her of the death of her husband, Benjamin, during the Battle of Ezra Church and provided her with information on his unit's location. "We are now in our trenches and skirmishing with the Yanks. expecting a fight at any time," he told her. "Yet our prospects look gloomy. It does truly appear that we must part with our best friends and at last be conquered. But the battle is not always to the strong so we live in hope. I can add no more now but remain as ever your friend and brother." Federal naval expedition to McIntosh County.[225]

August 3, 1864 (Wednesday)
Captain David Conyngham noted of the day, "General Schofield, having gained the north side of Utoy Creek, prepared to make a lodgment there. The creek is a deep, narrow channel, running east and west, four miles south of Atlanta. The banks of the creek are very steep, and their sides are tangled with vines and bushes." Meanwhile, Hood dispatched Major General William T. Martin, asking his cavalry officer for "definite information of the enemy's left…not only where it is, but what forces are there. Use every means in your power to ascertain." Skirmishing along Mulbery [Mulberry?] Creek and at Jug Tavern.[226]

August 4, 1864 (Thursday)
Quarreling generals slowed the Federal advance toward Utoy Creek and afforded the Confederates additional time to entrench. Sherman wrote to Major General John Palmer, "You will during the movement against the railroad report to and receive orders from General Schofield. Obey his orders and instructions." "I am General Schofield's senior," Palmer

---

[223] *OR*, ser. I, vol. 38, pt. 2:914.

[224] Richards, *Civil War Diary*, 229.

[225] McCurdy, *"Yours Truly Husband until Death…,"* August 2, 1864, n.p.; expedition in Mosocco, *Chronological Tracking*, 254.

[226] Conyngham, *Sherman's March*, 201; *OR*, ser. I, vol. 38, pt. 5:942.

replied. "We may co-operate but I respectfully decline to report to or take orders from him." Later in the day, Palmer yielded out of "courtesy."[227]

August 5, 1864 (Friday)

Captain John C. Van Duzer with the U.S. Military Telegraph Service in Washington City updated Major Thomas Eckert (working in the same service) on events near Utoy Creek. "Operations to-day complete failure, or worse. Schofield and Palmer were ordered to carry a point which would command railroad south of Atlanta…the attacking force moved early, and the whole line was engaged, but when Schofield and Palmer found the enemy they stopped and intrenched. There they stay yet, while they make no progress, and the rebels have time to mass men and throw up earth works, or to evacuate as they choose."[228]

August 6, 1864 (Saturday)

The Federal gears engaged as they launched an attack against the Confederates of, primarily, Major General William Bate's Division. Time lost in squabbling proved detrimental to the Federal attack. Major James T. Holmes with the 52nd Ohio Infantry and his comrades absorbed a destructive fire, as they "never were shelled so before...but here, they poured them thick and fast upon us." Hood notified Secretary Seddon, "The enemy made two assaults to-day on [Brigadier General Jesse] Finley's and [Brigadier General Joseph] Lewis' brigades, of Bate's division, in [Lt. Gen. S. D.] Lee's corps, both of which were handsomely repulsed, with loss to them." Federal casualties of 400 killed, wounded, or missing; Confederate loss at 225 during the Battle of Utoy Creek.[229]

August 7, 1864 (Sunday)

Captain William Nugent of the 28th Mississippi Cavalry, homesick for his wife, wrote to his her from his post outside Atlanta.

> When your letters are delayed…I grow moody and disappointed and am only revived when some friendly hand brings a missive from the darling of my bosom. I am too far off and too strongly bound by regulations to fly to your relief and minister to your comfort; and it is this thought which adds to the poignancy of feeling. I sometimes am inclined to kick at the laws which effect a compulsory separation between man and wife and to esteem it all wrong. Still, my own precious Nellie, what can I do? A cruel, relentless war is waged for our annihilation, and unless we present a bold front to the enemy, contesting every inch of ground, we may expect nothing but vassalage and slavery all our lives.[230]

August 8, 1864 (Monday)

A busy day for the Federals outside the defenses of Atlanta. First, Major General Thomas informed Sherman, "The 4½-inch guns have not yet arrived. They are not due until

---

[227] *OR*, ser. I, vol. 38, pt. 5:354–55.

[228] Ibid., 388.

[229] Holmes, *52d O. V. I. Then and Now*, 255–56; Hood quote from *OR*, ser. I, vol. 38, pt. 5:947; casualties from National Park Service, "Utoy Creek," https://www.nps.gov/civilwar/search-battles-detail.htm?battleCode=GA019.

[230] Nugent and Nugent, *My Dear Nellie*, 196.

tomorrow. I have selected a very good point for them on [Brigadier General John W.] Geary's left, where you can get a fair view of the town, and half a mile nearer than any other position. It was reported that they were to leave Chattanooga at 8 a.m.; to-day. The position selected enfilades White Hall street, upon which is General Hood's headquarters, and the battery is being built to-night." A few hours later, Sherman dispatched his three subordinates. "Orders for to-morrow, August 9: All the batteries that can reach the buildings of Atlanta will fire steadily on the town to-morrow, using during the day about fifty rounds per gun, shell and solid shot."[231]

August 9, 1864 (Tuesday)

Young Carrie Berry, age ten, penned her daily diary entry from her home in Atlanta. "We have had to stay in the cellar all day the shells have ben falling so thick around the house. Two have fallen in the garden, but none of us were hurt. Cousin Henry Beatty came in…and wanted us to move, he thought that we were in danger, but we will try it a little longer."[232]

August 10, 1864 (Wednesday) ◐

For months, General Johnston had badgered the Confederate War Department to send Major General Nathan Bedford Forrest and his troopers to north Georgia to sever Sherman's supply line—the Western and Atlantic Railroad. Officials in Richmond urged Johnston to use the cavalry already present with the Army of Tennessee to accomplish the task. Johnston never tried. Hood did. He sent Major General Joe Wheeler and his troopers out today, with orders to "move upon the enemy's line of communications, destroy them at various points between Marietta and Chattanooga; then cross the Tennessee River, break the line of communication on the two roads running from Nashville to the army; to then leave 1,200 men to continue their operations on those roads; to then return again striking the railroad south of Chattanooga, and join the main army."[233]

August 11, 1864 (Thursday)

Captain Henry Potter, 4th Michigan Cavalry, wrote to his sister from near Decatur. "I told you of my promotion in my last [letter]—have not received my commission yet. My men are all very well pleased. I have some as good fighting men as there are in the regiment trusty and true as steel and I will stand by them to the last."[234] The 4th Michigan served in Colonel Robert Minty's First Brigade, Brigadier General Kenner Garrard's 2nd Division, in Thomas's Army of the Cumberland.

August 12, 1864 (Friday)

General Hood issued General Field Orders, No. 14, from Atlanta. Among other things, the order stated, "The lawless seizure and destruction of private property by straggling soldiers in the rear and on the flanks of this army has become intolerable. It must come to an end. Officers are held responsible that their men conduct themselves properly. Hereafter

---

[231] *OR*, ser. I, vol. 38, pt. 5:419:431.

[232] Berry, *Confederate Girl*, 9.

[233] *OR*, ser. I, vol. 38, pt. 3:957.

[234] Ruddy, ed., "Letters of Henry Albert Potter," http://freepages.rootsweb.com/%7Emruddy/genealogy/letters5.htm.

all cavalry horses must be branded." And finally, "Citizens are warned not to purchase from or exchange horses with soldiers, except when the authority for the transaction is previously had from the company and regimental commanders." Offering a textbook example as to how officers created maps in the field, Sherman's dispatch to Schofield: "Meet Generals Thomas and Howard at my headquarters at 10 a. m. [to-morrow]. Collect to-night the names of as many resident farmers as you can, as I have copy of a rebel map with names on it and ruled to lots. I will have copies made enough for us all. The name of the man who lived at the house we were in this evening will enable us to locate our line exactly."[235]

August 13, 1864 (Friday)

General Hood issued a circular to the Army of Tennessee.

> General Hood desires that you impress upon your officers and men the absolute necessity of holding the lines they occupy, to the very last. He feels perfectly confident that, with the obstructions in their front, and the artillery to break his masses, the enemy cannot carry our works, however many lines he may advance against them, and however determined maybe his assaults, so long as the men occupy the trenches, and use their rifles. Let every man remember that he is individually responsible for his few feet of line, and that the destiny of Atlanta hangs upon the issue.

Sherman, in his daily report to Halleck suggested, "If I should ever be cut off from my base, look out for me about Saint Mark's, Fla., or Savannah, Ga." Hours later, Sherman received disturbing news from Acworth, courtesy of the work of Wheeler and his troopers. "Train No. 2, first section, engine 25, was fired upon one mile south of Acworth; the road entirely torn up for 8 rods; engine 25 badly off; ties all burnt and iron bent."[236]

August 14, 1864 (Sunday)

Continuing their northward raid on Sherman's supply line, Wheeler's troopers approached Dalton. Colonel Bernard Laiboldt commanded the Federal garrison of the town. Wheeler outnumbered the Federals (5,000 to around 300) and sent Laiboldt a surrender request. "To prevent the unnecessary effusion of blood, I have the honor to demand the immediate and unconditional surrender of the forces under your command at this garrison." The colonel responded, "I have been placed here to defend this post, but not to surrender." The Confederates attacked and drove the garrison "back to the earth-works erected…on a hill east of the railroad depot and commanding the city, but unprotected by artillery. General Wheeler again sent a flag of truce, which I refused to accept, having the bearer notified that at another advance of such a flag it would be fired upon… the enemy brought up two pieces of artillery and fired several rounds…[they] kept up their firing continually during the night."[237]

August 15, 1864 (Monday)

Captain Samuel Foster, 24th Texas Cavalry, made the following observations in his diary

---

[235] *OR*, ser. I, vol. 38, pt. 5:960:478.

[236] Ibid., 962, 482, 487.

[237] *OR*, ser. I, vol. 38, pt. 1:324.

entry. "Not much canonading yesterday nor today near us—Very warm in the forenoon. Rain in the afternoon. We are still in reserve. The impression is that the Yanks are moving some way or other else why are they so still. We are between East Point and the Chattahoochee river kee[p]ing the Yanks from extending their lines to the West Point R.R." Skirmishing at Sandtown and Fairburn.[238]

August 16, 1864 (Tuesday)

Colonel Emerson Opdycke wrote from "still in sight of Atlanta," on the consolidation of several Federal regiments due to attrition. "The 125th [Ohio Infantry] will join me tomorrow morning…the regiments that are going are the inferior ones of this brigade.... It is sad to break up old and cherished associations, but it cannot be avoided [Brigadier General Charles] Harker lives not, and the 125th leaves it. God bless it; but I cannot predict a very brilliant future for it, unless other regiments are added to it."[239]

August 17, 1864 (Wednesday)

Soldiers continued to engage near Atlanta, while along the coast, the Federal navy landed troops outside South Newport. Commander George Colvocoresses, from the USS *Saratoga*, filed a report summarizing the results. The commander's force captured "a lieutenant and 28 privates of Company F, Third South Carolina Cavalry…30 Enfield rifles, 54 sabers, 3 shotguns, 3 rifles, 1 revolver, and 2,000 rounds of cartridges; burned their encampment and stables, destroyed two of the largest salt works on the coast…destroyed the large bridge (South Newport River) on the main Savannah road…also captured the mail…altogether, we captured 107 persons." Regarding casualties, the officer stated, "There were no casualties on our side, and I am not aware that there were any on the enemy's, for we surrounded them and seized their arms before they had time to recover from their fright and surprise."[240]

August 18, 1864 (Thursday)

Sherman informed Halleck of his next plan to cut the remaining railroads servicing Atlanta. Once again, he would send his cavalry. "To-night General Kilpatrick will start for the Macon road with five brigades of cavalry, which can whip all the enemy's cavalry present, and to-morrow I will demonstrate along my whole line to give General Kilpatrick time to make a good break in that road [Macon & Western], so vital to Hood. We all feel confident we can succeed, and for that reason do not regret that Wheeler has gone up to East Tennessee." Skirmishing at Camp Creek.[241]

August 19, 1864 (Friday)

Kilpatrick's railroad raid continued, as skirmishes occurred at Red Oak, along the Flint River, and near Jonesborough. Captain Joseph G. Vale with the 7th Pennsylvania Cavalry participated in the day's skirmishing and wrote of the intensity of the action.

---

[238] Foster, *One of Cleburne's Command*, 121; skirmishes in Mosocco, *Chronological Tracking*, 259.

[239] Opdycke, *To Battle for God and the Right*, 214.

[240] *ORN*, ser. I, vol. 15:631.

[241] *OR*, ser. I, vol. 38, pt. 5:569–70; skirmish in Mosocco, *Chronological Tracking*, 259.

> By orders of General Kilpatrick...marched at dusk...reaching at day-break of the 19th, the Montgomery and Atlanta railroad, at Red bank [Red Oak], west of Atlanta. While the First brigade was crossing the railroad, a battery of rebel artillery posted on the hills east and parallel to the line of march, and supported by a brigade of mounted infantry, suddenly assailed with great fury on the left flank. The rebels, under cover of the mist, pushed up to within two hundred yards of the marching column, opening with artillery and musketry on the Seventh Pennsylvania, then passing. Companies G and M. although exposed to the full force of, and consequent confusion resulting from, the unexpected attack, were held firmly in place, and, closing ranks, pushed through the heavy fire, and finding a rebel force barring their way at the junction of the Sandtown with the Jonesboro' road, charged and scatted, and drove them several hundred yards in the direction of Atlanta....[242]

August 20, 1864 (Saturday)

Brigadier General Lawrence Ross and his mounted Texans proved a constant nuisance to Kilpatrick's force. On this day, with support from the soldiers of Brigadier Generals Daniel Reynolds and Frank Armstrong, they struck at Lovejoy's Station. Escaping a near entrapment, Kilpatrick made his way back to the Federal lines and reported he had damaged the Macon & Western Railroad enough to put the line out of service for several days. [Sherman reported ten days.][243]

August 21, 1864 (Sunday)

Captain Thomas Key observed a day away from his artillery battery and attended church.

> Packed up this morning and moved into the suburbs of Atlanta in order to be nearer the center of the batteries. As soon as I had selected my place of encampment I left Lieutenant Dosher to pitch my tent while I rode to church. Heard the same minister that I described last Sabbath, but neither so good a sermon nor so large a congregation. The worshipers were few because the clouds were leaking and town people are always dressed too neatly and richly to get wet. The poor soldiers are glad to go to church to keep out of the rain, as ordinarily they have to stand under a tree or a blanket stretched over a few sticks.[244]

August 22, 1864 (Monday)

Lieutenant Washington Hopkins with the Signal Corps provided a report to Brigadier General Alpheus Williams. "The enemy have had working parties engaged at different places along their line of works—on the traverses along works to right of four-gun fort, on the side of six-gun fort struck by the shells from heavy gun on our left, and along works

---

[242] Vale, *Minty and the Cavalry*, 338–39; skirmishes in Mosocco, *Chronological Tracking*, 259–60.

[243] *OR*, ser. I, vol. 38, pt. 5:634. For an excellent treatment of Sherman's various cavalry experiments in the struggle for Atlanta, see Evans, *Sherman's Horsemen: Union Cavalry Operations in the Atlanta Campaign*.

[244] Key and Campbell, *Two Soldiers*, 118.

south to 15 degrees west of south, distance three miles. There are two battle-flags flying from the line of works to left of four-gun fort not seen there yesterday."[245]

August 23, 1864 (Tuesday)

Sherman issued Special Field Orders, No. 59, dealing with trade. "All trade is prohibited near armies in the field or moving columns of troops save that necessary to supply the wants of the troops themselves. Quartermasters and commissaries will take such supplies as are needed in the countries passed through, leaving receipts and taking the articles up on their returns. No claim of private interest in it will be entertained by the military authorities."[246]

August 24, 1864 (Wednesday) ◗

Federal artillery continued the shelling of Atlanta, and a newspaper in the city detailed the effects of the bombardment.

> During the last few days that portion of Atlanta lying along Marietta street has been furiously bombarded, making the avenues of travel perfectly untenable and the destruction of property almost unprecedented; yet it only effects the ruin of property, nothing else is gained by all his furious work. The shelling process has been increased in intensity during the past four or five days. The enemy has located several large siege guns which cast their 64 and 72-pounder missiles over all portions of the city, but thus far they have rained their terrible contents down on the suffering non-combatants, however, without much fatality resulting. The city is very desolate.[247]

August 25, 1864 (Thursday)

After days of non-stop bombardment and the attendant roar of missiles zipping through the air, things grew quiet in Atlanta. Sam Richards noted, "the shelling ceased altogether and it was rumored that the enemy was retreating and it is now known that they have deserted their camps around the city and are going *some*where but what is their design it is hard to tell. I fear that we have not yet got rid of them finally, but that they have some other plan in view to molest and injure us."[248] Sherman's three armies prepared to move to the southwest of the city to destroy the last railroad servicing Atlanta.

August 26, 1864 (Friday)

Sherman began maneuvering his armies to the west of Atlanta; he updated Halleck, writing at 6:45 p.m. from near East Point. "I have moved the Twentieth Corps to the Chattahoochee bridge, where it is intrenched, and with the balance of the army am moving for Jonesborough on the Macon road. Last night we made the first move without trouble; to-night I make the second, and the third will place the army massed near Fairburn. If Hood attacks he must come out, which is all we ask. All well thus far." Skirmishing reported near the Chattahoochee River bridge, and along the river at Pace's and Turner's Ferries.[249]

---

[245] *OR*, ser. I, vol. 38, pt. 5:629–30.

[246] Ibid., 648.

[247] *Atlanta Daily Intelligencer*, quoted in Hoehling, *Last Train from Atlanta*, 359.

[248] Richards, *Civil War Diary*, 232. Italics in original.

[249] *OR*, ser. I, vol. 38, pt. 5:669; skirmishes in Mosocco, *Chronological Tracking*, 261.

August 27, 1864 (Saturday)
From along the Chattahoochee River, Major General Henry Slocum announced, "I have the honor to report that I have to-day assumed the command of the Twentieth Corps. The corps is in position as directed, at Pace's, Montgomery's, and Turner's Ferries, and intrenched. Yesterday afternoon Geary's division, at Pace's Ferry, had some sharp skirmishing with the enemy's cavalry, capturing a few prisoners. My headquarters are near the railroad bridge."[250]

August 28, 1864 (Sunday)
Sherman's armies continued to move to the west of Atlanta, as Hood's scouts provided intelligence on their positions. To Secretary Seddon in Richmond, Hood wrote, "The enemy have changed their entire position, the left of their line resting near the Chattahoochee about Sandtown, and their right extending to a point opposite and near the West Point railroad between East Point and Fairburn. They hold all the crossings on the Chattahoochee from Pace's Ferry down to Sandtown, but not with a continuous line." Meanwhile, Sam Richards spent a fearful day in church. "A shell has entered the roof of our church and passed through the back of the seat in the choir...and finally lodged somewhere in the front wall without exploding. Every thing is quiet enough now, we hear no cannon or musketry."[251]

August 29, 1864 (Monday)
Private William Oake, with the 26th Iowa Infantry, and his comrades made a "rapid march to the right cut the enemy's last line of communication, by placing his [Sherman's] army astride the railroad at Jonesboro, thirty miles in their rear. This would compel them to evacuate their present strong position at Atlanta." Skirmishing reported at Red Oak.[252]

August 30, 1864 (Tuesday)
Captain Key's Battery struck their tents and "moved to the spring at Mrs. Connally's on the Sandtown Road. General Cleburne's division moved three miles to a position south of East Point and began temporary works to meet a flanking movement of the enemy. Some skirmishing occurred two miles from the line, but it was a feint while Sherman moved upon the railroad at Jonesboro." The cannoneer noted, "Three corps drove our cavalry within a mile of that place...Hardee's corps was ordered to move for its defense. At day-dawn, after marching all night, we reached the designated position. I ordered up my omnibus and ordnance train, but the courier neglected to deliver the message or could not find them." Skirmishing reported at East Point; Brigadier General Kilpatrick described the action at the Flint River Bridge: "Here he [Confederates] made a determined resistance, with the assistance of 400 infantry. He was again driven back from one position to another till a favorable opportunity offered, when I rushed the Ninety-second Illinois forward, saved the bridge, and crossed in face of rifle-pits. Captain Estes and the officers and men of the Ninety-

---

[250] *OR*, ser. I, vol. 38, pt. 5:678.

[251] Ibid., 997; Richards, *Civil War Diary*, 233.

[252] Oake, *On the Skirmish Line*, 249; skirmish in Mosocco, *Chronological Tracking*, 262.

second Illinois are alone entitled to all the praise for this successful exploit."[253]

August 31, 1864 (Wednesday)

Lieutenant generals Hardee and S. D. Lee approached Jonesborough; they had located the Federal forces southwest of Atlanta, and Hood sent orders to attack. On this day, the first of two during the Battle of Jonesborough, Hardee's men engaged, had early success, and then, with arriving Federal soldiers, had to fall back. Lee's Corps joined with Hardee, but intelligence provided to Hood indicated a looming attack on Atlanta from the north. In the evening, Hood withdrew Lee's Corps back to Atlanta in the event the news proved true; faulty intelligence in the end. This action left Hardee's corps facing the majority of Sherman's forces. Earlier in the day, Schofield's soldiers had cut the Macon & Western Railroad near Rough and Ready, thus, in essence, making the loss of life on the morrow needless. Schofield sent a dispatch to Sherman on the accomplishment. "[Brigadier General Jacob] Cox got the railroad at 3 o'clock and [Major General David Stanley joined him about 4. We are well intrenched and have the road secure."[254]

September 1, 1864 (Thursday) ●

Fighting on day two at Jonesborough resulted in Hood's troops evacuating Atlanta. Facing superior numbers, Hardee held long enough for the balance of the Army of Tennessee and fall back to a defensive position Hardee selected at Lovejoy's Station. The casualties from the Battle of Jonesborough: Federals, 1,446; Confederates, 3,600. Hood reported, "we withdrew from Atlanta. A train of ordnance stores and some railroad stock had to be destroyed in consequence of the gross neglect of the chief quartermaster to obey the specific instructions given him touching their removal. He had ample time and means, and nothing whatever ought to have been lost."[255]

September 2, 1864 (Friday)

During the early morning hours, terror struck Atlantans. Teen Mary Rawson, "her sleep and dreams...interrupted by rapid and loud explosions," observed as "The Heavens were in a perfect glow while the atmosphere seemed full of flaming rockets, crash follows crash and the swift moving locomotives were rent in pieces and the never tiring metallic horse lay powerless while the sparks filled the air with innumerable spangles." There was skirmishing at Lovejoy's Station, and a Federal scouting mission to Sulphur Springs also took place.[256]

September 3, 1864 (Saturday)

Sherman paused in his pursuit—near Lovejoy's Station—of the Army of Tennessee long enough to telegraph Halleck in Washington City: "So Atlanta is ours, and fairly won. I shall not push much farther on this raid, but in a day or so will move to Atlanta and give

---

[253] Key and Campbell, *Two Soldiers*, 124; skirmish in Mosocco, *Chronological Tracking*, 262; *OR*, ser. I, vol. 38, pt. 5:736–37.

[254] *OR*, ser. I, vol. 38, pt. 5:735.

[255] S. Davis, *Texas Brigadier to the Fall of Atlanta*, 436; *OR*, ser. I, vol. 30, pt. 4:580.

[256] Hoehling, *Last Train from Atlanta*, 408; skirmish in Mosocco, *Chronological Tracking*, 263.

my men some rest. Since May 5 we have been in one constant battle or skirmish, and need rest." Mary Rawson managed to wax poetic even while viewing the ruins of Atlanta.

> The sun and bright azure are shut out by lowering clouds from which the rain pours in torrents.... At ten this morning Father had a visit from the provost marshal and several other officers, who wished us to give up our beautiful home for headquarters for the general. This request Father told him it was impossible to comply with for where could we find another home of any kind? They finally gave up the idea of taking it from us and seemed much pleased with our old school house instead. Oh how I felt to see the beloved old playground in front of the school covered with tents and the beautiful little shade trees cut down.[257]

September 4, 1864 (Sunday)
Sherman updated Halleck on his plans for Atlantans: "I propose to remove all the inhabitants of Atlanta, sending those committed to our cause to the rear, and the rebel families to the front. I will allow no trade, manufactories, nor any citizens there at all, so that we will have the entire use of railroad.... If the people raise a howl against my barbarity and cruelty I will answer that war is war, and not popularity-seeking. If they want peace they and their relatives must stop war."[258]

September 5, 1864 (Monday)
Hood wrote to Governor Brown from near Lovejoy's Station. "We are greatly in need of cars to transport sick and wounded. Can you not allow me to use the cars you have sent to Griffin for your purposes?" In Cobb County, William King lamented the impact of war, writing, "What a curse the professional politicians have proved to be to us. What misery their lust for party power has brought upon a happy people."[259]

September 6, 1864 (Tuesday)
The fall of Atlanta and the proximity of Federal forces prompted Confederate officials to begin the evacuation of Camp Sumter in Andersonville. Prisoner John Ransom noted in his diary, "Hurrah! Hurrah!! Hurrah!!! Can't holler except on paper. Good news. Seven detachments ordered to be ready to go at a moment's notice. All who cannot walk must stay behind. If left behind shall die in twenty-four hours. Seven detachments are going out of the gate; all the sick are left behind. The greatest excitement; men wild with joy."[260]

September 7, 1864 (Wednesday)
Sherman notified Hood of his decision regarding residents of Atlanta.

> I have deemed it to the interest of the United States that the citizens now residing in Atlanta should remove, those who prefer it to go South and the rest North. For the latter I can provide food and transportation to points of their election in Tennessee, Kentucky, or farther north. For the former I can provide transportation by cars as far as Rough and Ready, and also wagons; but that their removal may be made with as

---

[257] *OR*, ser. I, vol. 38, pt. 5:777; Hoehling, *Last Train from Atlanta*, 429.

[258] *OR*, ser. I, vol. 38, pt. 5:794.

[259] Ibid., 1022; W. King, *Diary*, 110–11.

[260] Ransom, *Andersonville Diary*, 131.

little discomfort as possible it will be necessary for you to help the families from Rough and Ready to the cars at Lovejoy's. If you consent I will undertake to remove all families in Atlanta who prefer to go South to Rough and Ready, with all their movable effects, viz, clothing, trunks, reasonable furniture, bedding, &c., with their servants,—white and black, with the proviso that no force shall be used toward the blacks one way or the other. If they want to go with their masters or mistresses they may do so, otherwise they will be sent away, unless they be men, when they may be employed by our quartermaster. Atlanta is no place for families or non-combatants and I have no desire to send them North if you will assist in conveying them South. If this proposition meets your views I will consent to a truce in the neighborhood of Rough and Ready, stipulating that any wagons, horses, or animals, or persons sent there for the purposes herein stated shall in no manner be harmed or molested, you in your turn agreeing that any cars, wagons, carriages, persons, or animals sent to the same point shall not be interfered with. Each of us might send a guard of, say, 100 men to maintain order, and limit the truce to, say, two days after a certain time appointed. I have authorized the mayor to choose two citizens to convey to you this letter and such documents as the mayor may forward in explanation, and shall await your reply.[261]

September 8, 1864 (Thursday)

Responding to Sherman's order to evacuate Atlanta, Hood tersely replied, "And now, sir, permit me to say that the unprecedented measure you propose transcends, in studied and ingenious cruelty, all acts ever before brought to my attention in the dark history of this war. In the name of God and humanity I protest, and believe you will find yourself wrong in thus expelling from their homes and firesides the wives and children of a brave people." President Lincoln sent his thanks to Sherman on the successful campaign and praised their "distinguished ability, courage and perseverance...which, under Divine favor, has resulted in the capture of the city of Atlanta. The marches, battles and sieges, and other military operations that have signalized the campaign, must render it famous in the annals of war, and have entitled those who have participated therein to the applause and thanks of the nation." Meanwhile, Mayor James Calhoun notified the residents of Atlanta of Sherman's decree, stating "you must all leave Atlanta; All persons are requested to leave their names and number in their families with the undersigned as early as possible, that estimates may be made of the quantity of transportation required."[262]

September 9, 1864 (Friday) ◐

Sherman continued to stipulate conditions of the military occupation of Atlanta. "Even sutlers must be prohibited from coming to Atlanta. I will as soon as the railroad is open make arrangements for opening and supplying three stores, one at Atlanta, one at Decatur, and one at East Point, and allow them jointly one car a day. Telegraph all parties to push

---

[261] *OR*, ser. I, vol. 38, pt. 5:822.

[262] Reed, *History of Atlanta*, 203; *OR*, ser. I, vol. 38, pt. 5:838.

Wheeler…to the death. Now is the time to strike them hard…to wipe out all guerrilla bands. Show them no mercy."[263]

September 10, 1864 (Saturday)

The exchange between Sherman and Hood intensified with each communication. Sherman wrote today, "If we must be enemies, let us be men and fight it out, as we propose to do, and not deal in such hypocritical appeals to God and humanity. God will judge us in due time, and He will pronounce whether it be more humane to fight with a town full of women, and the families of 'a brave people' at our back, or to remove them in time to places of safety among their own friends and people." Governor Brown wrote Hood, requesting "the militia of the State," given the fall of Atlanta, "be permitted, while the enemy are preparing for the winter campaign, to return to their homes [until] another campaign commences against other important points in the State." A Confederate force engaged a Federal foraging party near Campbellton.[264]

September 11, 1864 (Sunday)

Mayor Calhoun of Atlanta, along with Edward E. Rawson and S. C. Wells, wrote to Sherman, with a request to reconsider his declaration of removing all civilians from the city. "We, the undersigned, mayor and two of the council for the city of Atlanta, for the time being the only legal organ of the people of the said city to express their wants and wishes, ask leave most earnestly, but respectfully, to petition you to reconsider the order requiring them to leave Atlanta."[265]

September 12, 1864 (Monday)

Sherman responded to the mayor's request, "The use of Atlanta for warlike purposes is inconsistent with its character as a home for families. There will be no manufactures, commerce, or agriculture here for the maintenance of families, and sooner or later want will compel the inhabitants to go. Why not go now, when all the arrangements are completed for the transfer, instead of waiting till the plunging shot of contending armies will renew the scenes of the past month?" The general clarified his position on war: "War is cruelty and you cannot refine it, and those who brought war into our country deserve all the curses and maledictions a people can pour out." In closing, Sherman reminded the Atlanta officials, "Now that war comes home to you, you feel very different. You deprecate its horrors, but did not feel them when you sent car-loads of soldiers and ammunition and molded shells and shot to carry war into Kentucky and Tennessee, and desolate the homes of hundreds and thousands of good people who only asked to live in peace at their old homes and under the Government of their inheritance." Hood continued his rebuke of Sherman's action: "You say, 'let us fight it out like men.' To this my reply is, for myself, and, I believe, for all the true men, ay, and women and children, in my country, we will fight you to the death. Better die a thousand deaths than submit to live under you or your Government and your negro allies."[266]

---

[263] *OR*, ser. I, vol. 38, pt. 5:839–40.

[264] *OR*, ser. I, vol. 39, pt. 2:416; Campbellton in Mosocco, *Chronological Tracking*, 265.

[265] *OR*, ser. I, vol. 39, pt. 2:417.

[266] Ibid., 418–19, 422.

September 13, 1864 (Tuesday)

During a lull in fighting after the fall of Atlanta, Captain Tom Key spent his time thinking of family. "This morning we moved our quarters a half mile south of Jonesboro.... The ground half a century gone had been plowed by the steady farmer, but now had overgrown with thick stubby pines...I halted and under their thick foliage laid myself on the ground to restore nature and dream of home, wife, and peace. Since during the armistice I have nothing that demands all my time, I find myself listening to the words of Lord Byron entitled 'Don Juan,' spoken in verse."[267]

September 14, 1864 (Wednesday)

The exchange of festering quills between Hood and Sherman continued, as the latter responded today to a letter from Hood.

> I agree with you that this discussion by two soldiers is out of place and profitless, but you must admit that you began the controversy by characterizing an official act of mine in unfair and improper terms. I reiterate my former answer, and to the only new matter contained in your rejoinder I add, we have no "negro allies" in this army; not a single negro soldier left Chattanooga with this army or is with it now. There are a few guarding Chattanooga.... I was not bound by the laws of war to give notice of the shelling of Atlanta, a "fortified town" with magazines, arsenals, foundries, and public stores. You were bound to take notice. See the books. This is the conclusion of our correspondence, which I did not begin, and terminate with satisfaction.[268]

September 15, 1864 (Thursday)

Sherman operated with information that suggested Brown and Stephens wished an audience with the general to discuss peace. He wrote to Halleck, "All well, and troops in line, healthy camps, and supplies coming forward finely. Governor Brown has disbanded his militia, to gather the corn and sorghum of the State. I have reason to believe that he and [Vice President] Stephens want to visit me, and I have sent them a hearty invitation." The meeting did not occur. Skirmishing reported in Lumpkin County and near Snake Creek Gap.[269]

September 16, 1864 (Friday)

Private W. L. Truman with 1st Missouri Light Artillery spent the day in camp. He and his comrades agreed "to fast one day, and have our commissary to issue that days rations to the destitute people, who were driven out of Atlanta. I believe and hope the whole army will do as much." Truman proudly closed, stating, "We Missourians, have taken the lead, ever remembering our suffering people at home." Halleck congratulated Sherman on the Atlanta Campaign, and noted, "As you suppose, I have watched your movements most attentively and critically, and I do not hesitate to say that your campaign has been the most brilliant of the war. Its results are less striking and less complete than those of General Grant

---

[267] Key and Campbell, *Two Soldiers*, 133.

[268] *OR*, ser. I, vol. 39, pt. 2:422.

[269] Ibid., 381; skirmishes in Mosocco, *Chronological Tracking*, 169.

at Vicksburg, but then you have had greater difficulties to encounter, a longer line of communication to keep up, and a longer and more continuous strain upon yourself and upon your army."[270]

September 17, 1864 (Saturday)

Hardee requested a new assignment to get away from Hood, whom he disliked. Hood wrote President Davis, "By next Monday evening this army will be between Palmetto and Fairburn. Please appoint Cheatham to command Hardee's corps. This change will promote the efficiency of the army. If Hardee is relieved Cheatham takes command by seniority of rank."[271]

September 18, 1864 (Sunday)

Preparing to move the Army of Tennessee to Palmetto, Hood notified Brigadier General John Winder in Andersonville. "As the army will be in position to-morrow on the West Point railroad, it is important that the Federal prisoners, except the 2,000 to be exchanged, should be removed without delay."[272] Hood and Sherman had agreed to exchange 2,000 prisoners each.

September 19, 1864 (Monday)

General R. E. Lee wrote to President Davis from his headquarters near Petersburg. The state of affairs in Georgia occupied Lee's thoughts.

> I have had a conversation with General Beauregard with reference to the army and operations in Georgia. I have endeavored particularly to explain to him the necessity of the commander in Georgia developing the latent resources of the department, drawing to him all absentees from the army, concentrating its strength, restoring its confidence, and, in a word, creating the means with which he must operate against the enemy and the impracticability at present of giving him any extraneous aid. Of all this he is fully sensible, and while strongly impressed with the responsibility of the station and fearful of not being equal to the present emergency, being anxious to do all in his power to serve the country, he says he will obey with alacrity any order of the War Department placing him in command of that army, and do his best to expel the enemy. Should you deem, therefore, a change in the commander of the army in Georgia advantageous, and select General Beauregard for that position, I think you may feel assured that he understands the general condition of affairs, the difficulties with which they are surrounded, and the importance of exerting all his energies for their improvement.[273]

September 20, 1864 (Tuesday)

Hood, planning to move northward, sent orders to Brigadier General Ambrose Wright in Augusta. "Instruct the superintendent of the Georgia railroad to take up at once all the rails

---

[270] Truman, "Memoirs"; *OR*, ser. I, vol. 38, pt. 5:856–57.

[271] *OR*, ser. I, vol. 39, pt. 2:842.

[272] Ibid., 844; see also pg. 381, Sherman to Halleck regarding prisoner exchange.

[273] *OR*, ser. I, vol. 39, pt. 2:846.

between the Oconee River and Stone Mountain, and to destroy all bridges between those two points; the iron to be kept for future use." Skirmish reported at Cartersville.[274]

September 21, 1864 (Wednesday)

Hood requested a much-desired item for the soldiers in the Army of Tennessee from the Quartermaster Department in Richmond. "This army is very much in need of shoes; its operations render it absolutely necessary that they should be furnished at once. Dillard, at Columbus, can furnish 5,000 pairs on your order. Please give it."[275]

September 22, 1864 (Thursday) ◐

Hood, updating Bragg on the next phase of military operations in Georgia, wrote, "I shall, unless Sherman moves south, so soon as I can collect supplies, cross the Chattahoochee River, and form lines of battle near Powder Springs. This will prevent him from using the Dalton railroad and force him to drive me off or move south, when I shall fall upon his rear. I make this move, as Sherman is weaker now than he will be in future, and I as strong as I can expect to be."[276]

September 23, 1864 (Friday)

During a trip to visit Hood and the Army of Tennessee, President Davis addressed the citizens of Macon.

> What, though misfortune has befallen our arms from Decatur to Jonesboro', our cause is not lost. Sherman cannot keep up his long line of communication, and retreat sooner or later, he must. And when that day comes, the fate that befel the army of the French Empire and its retreat from Moscow will be reacted. Our cavalry and our people will harass and destroy his army as did the Cossacks that of Napoleon, and the Yankee General, like him will escape with only a body guard.[277]

September 24, 1864 (Saturday)

Sherman wrote to Major General Oliver Howard's headquarters near East Point. Sherman asserted, "I have no doubt Hood has resolved to throw himself on our flanks to prevent our accumulating stores, &c., here, trusting to our not advancing into Georgia. Some cavalry got possession of Athens, Alabama, yesterday. I think I will send a division from [Major General] Thomas to Bridgeport, and the balance of the one you have at Rome…so as to act in case the enemy puts himself up west of the Coosa. Let [Brigadier General John] Corse get all ready."[278]

September 25, 1864 (Sunday)

President Davis visited the Army of Tennessee at Palmetto. After meeting with Hood, the two inspected the soldiers. Private Robert Patrick with the 4th Louisiana Infantry watched as "President Davis reviewed the troops to-day, and as he rode down the lines there were

---

[274] Ibid., 850; skirmish in Mosocco, *Chronological Tracking*, 267.

[275] *OR*, ser. I, vol. 39, pt. 2:860.

[276] Ibid., 862.

[277] J. Davis, *Papers*, 11:61.

[278] *OR*, ser. I, vol. 39, pt. 2:463.

calls for Gen'l Johnston to be restored to command. The troops do not like Hood."[279]

September 26, 1864 (Monday)

Despite the loss of Atlanta, Governor Brown continued his work in securing and distributing salt for Georgians. "Notwithstanding the means of bringing salt from the works in [Saltville] Virginia into the State have been greatly curtailed during the present year, I have...succeeded in bringing in...from other sources...about thirty thousand bushels...which quantity is now in store ready for distribution. Although this will not be enough to supply all, it will, if distributed, relieve a great many, and the others can have assistance when more can be procured."[280]

September 27, 1864 (Tuesday)

A soldier in the 82nd Indiana Infantry wrote to his wife from Atlanta. Thoughts of the upcoming presidential election caused him concern. "I have gust Came of[f] picket this morning and feal vary Well over it but i have lost all hopes of geting to Come home to Vote. i Dont think we will get to Come home till our time is out. We have sind [signed] the pay role a gain and expect to be paid in a fiew Days.: have poot Down sixtey Dollars on the elotement [allotment] role which Will be paid at indinaplus."[281]

September 28, 1864 (Wednesday)

Two generals on the move; Hood prepared to move the Army of Tennessee across the Chattahoochee River, and one readied for a new command. Hood to President Davis from Palmetto: "I commence to change my headquarters to-morrow; hope to complete it by Friday night or early Saturday morning. I am very hopeful of good results." Via Special Orders, No. 5, soldiers learned, "By direction of the President, Lieut. Gen. W. J. Hardee is relieved from duty with the Army of Tennessee, and will proceed at once to Charleston, S.C., and assume command of the Department of South Carolina, Georgia, and Florida. He is authorized to take with him such officers of the general staff at present serving at corps headquarters as may be agreed upon by himself and Major-General Cheatham." Skirmish near Decatur.[282]

September 29, 1864 (Thursday)

Sherman reported to Halleck on the situation in Georgia, "Hood now rests twenty-four miles south, his left on the Chattahoochee, and his right on the West Point road. He is removing the iron of the Macon road. I can whip his infantry, but his cavalry is to be feared."[283]

September 30, 1864 (Friday) ●

Sherman wrote to Major General Thomas. "There is no doubt some of Hood's infantry is across the Chattahoochee, but I don't think his whole army is across. If he moves his whole force to Blue Mountain, you watch him from the direction of Stevenson, and I will do the

---

[279] Patrick, *Reluctant Rebel*, 230.

[280] Candler, *Confederate Records of the State of Georgia*, 2:729.

[281] Mabrey, *Yankee Soldier*, 138.

[282] *OR*, ser. I, vol. 39, pt. 2:880; skirmish in Mosocco, *Chronological Tracking*, 269.

[283] *OR*, ser. I, vol. 39, pt. 2:517.

same from Rome, and as soon as all things are ready I will take advantage of his opening to me all of Georgia." Skirmish reported near Camp Creek.[284]

October 1, 1864 (Saturday)

Skirmish at Salt Spring, as Hood continued to move the Army of Tennessee northward. Vice President Stephens responded, through William King, to an inquiry from Sherman.

> I have considered the message...from General Sherman...[the] message was a verbal invitation by him...to visit him at Atlanta, to see if we could agree upon some plan of terminating this fratricidal war without the further effusion of blood. But in the present instance the entire absence of any power on my part to enter into such negotiations, and the like absence of any such power on his part, so far as appears from his message, necessarily precludes my acceptance of the invitation thus tendered.[285]

October 2, 1864 (Sunday)

A busy day in Georgia! Major General Joe Wheeler to Colonel Lewis Johnson, the officer charged with the garrison at Dalton: "I have the honor to demand the immediate and unconditional surrender of the forces under your command. I have sufficient force to compel the surrender of your garrison." Lewis refused. There was skirmishing at Big Shanty, along the Flat Rock and McDonough Roads, at Sand Mountain, near Fairburn, and outside Powder Springs. President Davis visited Beauregard in Augusta and gave him additional responsibilities. Davis telegraphed Secretary Seddon of the change. "I have assigned General Beauregard to the command of the departments heretofore commanded respectively by Generals Hood and [Lieutenant General Richard] Taylor. Please telegraph to General Beauregard at this place the territorial limits of these departments, which together now form his command."[286]

October 3, 1864 (Monday)

Sherman worked to ensure he had an adequate communication infrastructure in place. Two dispatches noted, "I have messages by signal from Kenesaw and Allatoona" and "I have now telegraphic communication with Rome, Allatoona, and Marietta. All quiet." Skirmishing reported at Big Shanty and near the "Kenesaw Water-Tank."[287]

October 4, 1864 (Tuesday)

Hood ordered Lieutenant General A. P. Stewart to move. "your third division (say French's)...up the railroad and fill up the deep cut at Allatoona with logs, brush, rails, dirt, &c.... it is probable that the guard at the railroad bridge on Etowah is small, and when [Major] General [Samuel] French goes to Allatoona, if he can get such information as would justify him, if possible move to that bridge and destroy it...its destruction would be a great advantage to the army and the country." Skirmishing on the day at Acworth, Moon's Station, and near Lost Mountain.[288]

---

[284] Ibid., 532; skirmish in Mosocco, *Chronological Tracking*, 270.

[285] *OR*, ser. I, vol. 39, pt. 3:778; skirmish in Mosocco, *Chronological Tracking*, 270.

[286] *OR*, ser. I, vol. 39, pt. 3:784:782; skirmishes in Mosocco, *Chronological Tracking*, 271.

[287] *OR*, ser. I, vol. 39, pt. 3:44:47; skirmishes in Mosocco, *Chronological Tracking*, 271.

[288] *OR*, ser. I, vol. 39, pt. 1:814; skirmishes in Mosocco, *Chronological Tracking*, 271.

October 5, 1864 (Wednesday)

The Battle of Allatoona Pass. Major General Samuel French's troops moved toward the pass in the early morning hours, with the goal of destroying stockpiles of Federal supplies and damaging the railroad. Lieutenant Colonel John Tourtellotte's force held the pass and awaited reinforcements, which arrived in the form of five regiments from Rome under the command of Brigadier General John Corse. The Confederates attacked from the front and rear, as heavy fighting played beneath the Star Fort, while Tourtelotte and his men tried to hold the Eastern Redoubt. During the battle, Course communicated with Sherman via signal flags. Sherman managed the affair from atop Big Kennesaw Mountain and signaled to Corse, "hold on…working hard for you." French demanded a surrender, which Corse refused. After hours of engagement, French received a dispatch indicating the approach of Federal Forces. On departing the field of battle, French observed, "Silence, like the pall of death, rests over Allatoona; it is as lifeless as a graveyard at midnight." The Federals suffered 706 casualties, while French lost 897. Skirmishing reported near New Hope Church. [289]

October 6, 1864 (Thursday)

The Army of Tennessee, positioned in Dallas, awaited marching orders from Hood, who dispatched Lieutenant General Stewart to "communicate with Major-General French and learn if he ascertained from any prisoners taken yesterday what are the number of enemy's forces now at Rome, or what troops have been sent in that direction lately." Major General French met with Hood the day after the Battle of Allatoona. French described Hood as "a disheartened man. His countenance was sad and his voice doleful. He received me with a melancholy air, and asked no questions; did *not refer to the battle*, 'told me where my corps was, and said he would leave next day.' He seemed much depressed in spirits. Perhaps he experienced a feeling of remorse that his want of information had induced him to send me to burn the Etowah bridge, stopping an hour or two en route at the Allatoona cut…."[290]

October 7, 1864 (Friday)

Skirmishing near Dallas, as Brigadier General Absalom Baird indicated to Major General Jefferson C. Davis: "My advance went as far as…three miles and a half beyond Lost Mountain. Our cavalry is now near Dallas. Had sharp fighting near New Hope, and a few artillery shots nearer to Dallas. [Lieutenant General S. D.] Lee's and [Lieutenant General A. P.] Stewart's corps were encamped near here for three days, and the last left yesterday for the direction of Dallas. A brigade of cavalry passed here yesterday."[291]

October 8, 1864 (Saturday) ◐

Secretary Seddon wrote a scathing letter to Governor Brown that questioned many actions of the state's chief official.

> The ten thousand militia you boast to have organized, without adding to the count, those you are proceeding to organize, if incorporated with the veteran regiments prior

[289] *OR*, ser. I, vol. 39, pt. 3:97; French, *Two Wars*, 257; skirmish in Mosocco, *Chronological Tracking*, 271; National Park Service, "Allatoona," https://www.nps.gov/civilwar/search-battles-detail.htm?battleCode=GA023.

[290] *OR*, ser. I, vol. 39, pt. 3:799; French, *Two Wars*, 285.

[291] *OR*, ser. I, vol. 39, pt. 3:124.

to the 1st of May, would have been an invaluable acquisition to the army of Tennessee, and not improbably have hurled back the invader from the threshold of your State. That they, or a large proportion of them at least, were not ready for that service and other auxiliary means to its operations were not afforded, I am bound to think was due to the obstacles and embarrassments interposed by Your Excellency and the local authorities with your countenance, to the enforcement of the acts of Congress for the recruitment and maintenance of the armies.[292]

October 9, 1864 (Sunday)

Pursuing Hood's troops moving north through Georgia, Sherman stopped at Allatoona to write Grant. "I propose we break up the railroad from Chattanooga, and strike out with wagons for Milledgeville, Millen, and Savannah. Until we can repopulate Georgia, it is useless to occupy it, but the utter destruction of its roads, houses, and people will cripple their military resources. I can make the march, and make Georgia howl." Skirmish reported at Van Wert.[293]

October 10, 1864 (Monday)

In Cartersville, Sherman sent a dispatch to Colonel Tourtellotte on the need to strengthen fortifications. "I would make a good redoubt to the south of the Cartersville road and make a good abatis. Forty men in such a work would be a great protection to that flank. Such a work, with the two at the railroad cut, would be enough to hold Allatoona against a cavalry dash, which is the most that will likely occur again. I attach much importance to abatis." Hood, in Cave Spring, notified Brigadier General Iverson to "immediately destroy the railroads leading to Atlanta as close up. to the city as possible, commencing at our present breaks. Do this on all the roads." Skirmishing reported near Rome.[294]

October 11, 1864 (Tuesday)

Sherman corresponded with Grant regarding next steps in Georgia.

> I would infinitely prefer to make a wreck of the road and of the country from Chattanooga to Atlanta...send back all my wounded and worthless, and...move through Georgia, smashing things to the sea. Instead of being on the defensive, I would be on the offensive; instead of guessing at what he [Hood] means to do, he would have to guess at my plans. The difference in war is full 25 per cent. I can make Savannah, Charleston, or the mouth of the Chattahoochee. Answer quick, as I know we will not have the telegraph long.

Federal excursion to Flat Creek reported.[295]

October 12, 1864 (Wednesday)

Like most Civil War soldiers, Private James Daniel with the 9th Georgia Infantry missed his beloved wife and wrote as often as time allowed. After receiving a wound, which led to the amputation of his right leg, Daniel passed the hours in the hospital thinking of home

---

292 Candler, *Confederate Records of the State of Georgia*, 3:634–35.

293 *OR*, ser. I, vol. 39, pt. 3:162; skirmish in Mosocco, *Chronological Tracking*, 272.

294 *OR*, ser. I, vol. 39, pt. 3:189:811; skirmish in Mosocco, *Chronological Tracking*, 273.

295 *OR*, ser. I, vol. 39, pt. 3:202; federal expedition in Mosocco, *Chronological Tracking*, 273.

and writing to his wife in Sumter County. "I have never spared myself in going into a fight, as I determined long ago to get out of this war if I had to be killed out. But I would rather die than be separated forever from you and my darling children." There was skirmishing at Rome, La Fayette, and Resaca. Grant—after receiving word President Lincoln "feels much solicitude in respect to general Sherman's proposed movement"—wrote to Sherman, "It would be much better to go south than to be forced to come north. You will, no doubt, clean the country where you go of railroad tracks and supplies. I would also move every wagon, horse, mule, and hoof of stock, as well as the negroes. As far as arms can be supplied, either from surplus or by capture, I would put them in the hands of negro men. Give them such organization as you can. They will be of some use."[296]

October 13, 1864 (Thursday)

Military action occurred in several locations—Buzzard Roost, Rice Springs Farm near Rome, Tilton, and in Dalton. Hood sent the following surrender demand to Colonel Lewis Johnson in Dalton: "I demand the immediate and unconditional surrender of the post and garrison under your command, and should this be acceded to, all white officers and soldiers will be paroled in a few days. If the place is carried by assault, no prisoners will be taken." Johnson replied, "I cannot surrender the men under my command whatever the consequences may be." After discussing the situation with other officers in his command, Johnson did surrender, "deeming it my duty as a soldier to do so under the circumstances…."[297]

October 14, 1864 (Friday)

Major General George Thomas wrote to Brigadier General George Wagner in Chattanooga, "If it is not known to a certainty that the enemy are at Dalton or in that vicinity I wish you to let the troops at Ringgold, Tunnel Hill, and other points on the road remain at their posts, unless their safety depends upon their withdrawal."[298]

October 15, 1864 (Saturday)

Action again flared at Snake Creek Gap, as Lieutenant Colonel Charles Sheldon reported from there to XVII Corps headquarters. "I pushed forward as directed, but found none of our cavalry. Ran on the enemy's vedettes near Dalton and Rome road. Drove them out of the first line of works, and am now pushing for the gap and second line. Have not yet found a skirmish line, but think there is one, as the signs in the works indicated a strong reserve."[299]

October 16, 1864 (Sunday)

Sherman wrote to Grant from near Ship's Gap, where skirmishing occurred during the day.

> I got the dispatch in cipher about providing me a place to come out on salt water, but the cipher is imperfect and I cannot make out whether Savannah or Mobile be the point preferred, but I also want to know if you are willing that I should destroy Atlanta and the railroad. Hood broke eight miles of road at Big Shanty and about

---

[296] Lane, *Dear Mother*, 332; skirmishes in Mosocco, *Chronological Tracking*, 273; *OR*, ser. I, vol. 39, pt. 3:222.

[297] *OR*, ser. I, vol. 39, pt. 1:718; pt. 3:257; pt. 1:719.

[298] *OR*, ser. I, vol. 39, pt. 3:279.

[299] Ibid., 293.

> fifteen from Resaca to the tunnel. The break at Big Shanty is repaired, but the other will take some time. I have now taken position where I don't care which way he moves. I think the rebels will now go back south.

In a second dispatch, Sherman stated, "That south is nearly if not quite done and that north will be pushed with the utmost vigor. I want to make a raid that will make the South feel the terrible character of our people." Hood, near La Fayette, wrote to Lieutenant General Richard Taylor in Alabama. "We have completely destroyed the enemy's railroad from Resaca to Tunnel Hill. The main body of Sherman's army in the neighborhood of Dalton."[300]

October 17, 1864 (Monday)

A meeting of various Southern governors (Alabama, Georgia, Mississippi, North Carolina, South Carolina, and Virginia) took place in Augusta. The group passed several resolutions, including one that read, "There is nothing in the present aspect of public affairs to cause any abatement of our zeal in the prosecution of the war to the accomplishment of a peace based on the independence of the Confederate States. And to give encouragement to our brave soldiers in the field and to strengthen the Confederate authorities…we will use our best exertions to increase the effective force of our armies." Beauregard's command extends to the "Confederate Military Division of the West."[301]

October 18, 1864 (Tuesday)

Brigadier General John Corse, from his headquarters in Rome, wrote to Brigadier General John E. Smith of unfolding events. "General Sherman says the enemy are going south, at Summerville and Alpine, and he thinks will go to Gaylesville and so on down the Coosa. They may turn into Tennessee, but he thinks not. He wants Kilpatrick, near Stilesborough, advised of this fact; and that he has ordered 500,000 rations from Allatoona here for the use of his army. Please send Kilpatrick this word." Skirmishing at Summerville.[302]

October 19, 1864 (Wednesday)

Sherman outlined his plans to Halleck on a day with skirmishing at Ruff's Station, and near the Turner's and Howell's ferries.

> We must not be on the defensive, and I now consider myself authorized to execute my plan to destroy the railroad from Chattanooga to Atlanta, including the latter city…strike out into the heart of Georgia, and make for Charleston, Savannah, or the mouth of the Appalachicola. I must have alternates, else, being confined to one route, the enemy might so oppose that delay and want would trouble me, but, having alternates, I can take so eccentric a course that no general can guess at my objective. I will turn up somewhere, and believe I can take Macon and Milledgeville, Augusta and Savannah, Ga., and wind up with closing the neck back of Charleston so that they will starve out. This movement is not purely military or strategic, but it will illustrate

---

[300] Ibid., 304–305, 309, 823.

[301] "Manifesto of the Governors of the Confederate States," *Richmond Dispatch*, October 24, 1864, sec. 2, https://www.newspapers.com/image/80617934; *OR*, ser. I, vol. 39, pt. 3:824–25.

[302] *OR*, ser. I, vol. 39, pt. 3:350; skirmish in Mosocco, *Chronological Tracking*, 275.

> the vulnerability of the South. They don't know what war means, but when the rich planters of the Oconee and Savannah see their fences and corn and hogs and sheep vanish before their eyes they will have something more than a mean opinion of the 'Yanks.' Even now our poor mules laugh at the fine corn-fields, and our soldiers riot on chestnuts, sweet potatoes, pigs, chickens, &c. The poor people come to me and beg as for their lives, but my answer is, "Your friends have broken our railroads, which supplied us bountifully, and you cannot suppose our soldiers will suffer when there is abundance within reach."[303]

October 20, 1864 (Thursday)

From his headquarters in Macon, Major General Howell Cobb issued a circular calling on all to resist the Federals.

> The movements now being made to redeem every portion of Georgia from the occupation of the enemy will be attended with success if her own people will do their duty. The active and faithful discharge of this duty by every man who owes service to his country alone is necessary to accomplish the result. To effect this result at once is the object of this circular. All officers belonging to this command, especially enrolling officers, are instructed to use renewed efforts in enforcing all orders for the return of absentees to their commands, as well as sending forward those who have so far failed or refused to report. It is the fixed purpose of both Confederate and State authorities that the men who can serve the country in this critical juncture shall do it, and no effort will be spared by either to effect the result. Not only to officers, but to every good citizen is the appeal made to bring into the service every man able to do duty in the field. A few weeks of faithful service by every man in Georgia able and liable to do it would drive the last enemy from our soil and rid the State forever of their hateful presence. Georgians! the destiny of your State is in your hands. Now is the time to strike the blow, and if the enemy is not driven from your soil it will be your fault, not theirs.

Sherman informed Major General Thomas of his decision to leave Thomas's force in Tennessee, and of Sherman's discontinuing his pursuit of Hood. "To pursue Hood is folly, for he can twist and turn like a fox and wear out any army in pursuit. To continue to occupy long lines of railroads simply exposes our small detachments to be picked up in detail and forces me to make countermarches to protect lines of communication. I know I am right in this and shall proceed to its maturity."[304]

October 21, 1864 (Friday)

In a letter to his wife, Ellen, Sherman discussed his troops. "This Army is now ready to march to Mobile, Savannah or Charleston, and I am practising them in the art of foraging and they take to it like ducks to water. They like pigs, sheep, chickens, calves and sweet potatoes better than rations. We won't starve in Georgia."[305]

---

[303] *OR*, ser. I, vol. 39, pt. 3:357–58; skirmishes in Mosocco, *Chronological Tracking*, 275.

[304] *OR*, ser. I, vol. 39, pt. 3:835:378.

[305] Sherman, *Home Letters*, 313–14.

October 22, 1864 (Saturday)
Major General Howell Cobb wrote of the governor in a letter to Secretary Seddon. "You rightly suppose that Governor Brown is not only willing, but anxious to bring the Confederate authorities into disrepute with the people of Georgia, and I have no doubt it would have afforded him unalloyed pleasure to have attributed the loss of Atlanta to the withholding by the Confederate authority of detailed men from the service at that critical juncture."[306]

October 23, 1864 (Sunday)
Plans began to gel as Sherman looked to the future and a march across Georgia. To his chief quartermaster, Sherman ordered, "Send back all unserviceable stock, wagons, and stores, and keep on hand only a limited supply, just what we can pick up in our wagons and haul." To Major General Slocum, Sherman boasted, "If Georgia can afford to break our railroads, she can afford to feed us. Please preach this doctrine to men who go forth, and are likely to spread it."[307]

October 24, 1864 (Monday)
Various guerrilla and bushwhacker units operated in north Georgia throughout the war. Perhaps none posed a bigger threat than John Gatewood and his operatives. Sherman sought to eliminate this nuisance. He informed Major General David Stanley,

> There is a gang of guerrillas under one Gatewood somewhere behind us. He has about 100 men and will likely hurry to the north of our road, back to Rome. I wish you to send a brigade... scout out toward Dirt Town and Coosaville...make diligent inquiries...let all know that such fellows will be dealt with summarily. Let the people also understand that when we are in search of such fellows we take no baggage, and therefore live on the country. If they want to save what little corn and potatoes [they have], they must manage to get Gatewood disposed of, for he will bring ruin on them all.[308]

Skirmishing reported along South River.

October 25, 1864 (Tuesday)
Sherman penned an interesting communication to Secretary Stanton in Washington City.

> I do not wish to be considered as in any way adverse to the organization of negro regiments, further than as to its effects on the white race. I do wish the fine race of men that people our Northern States should rule and determine the future destiny of America; but if they prefer trade and gain, and leave to bought substitutes and negroes the fighting (the actual conflict), of course the question is settled, for those who hold the swords and muskets at the end of this war (which has but fairly begun) will have something to say. If negroes are to fight, they, too, will not be content with sliding back into the status of slave or free negro. I much prefer to keep negroes yet for some time to come in a subordinate state, for our prejudices, yours as well as mine, are not yet schooled for absolute equality. I would use negroes as surplus, but not spare a

[306] Candler, *Confederate Records of the State of Georgia*, 3:641.
[307] *OR*, ser. I, vol. 39, pt. 3:404:406.
[308] Ibid., 415; skirmish in Mosocco, *Chronological Tracking*, 276.

single white man, not one. Any white man who don't or won't fight now should be killed, banished, or denationalized, and then we would discriminate among the noisy patriots and see who really should vote. If the negroes fight and the whites don't, of course the negroes will govern. They won't ask you or me for the privilege, but will simply take it, and probably reverse the relation hitherto existing, and they would do right.[309]

October 26, 1864 (Wednesday)

Sherman continued preparations to leave Gaylesville, Alabama, and return to Atlanta. He wrote Major General James Steedman of the need to stand on the ready. "The Fourth Corps marches to-morrow for Chattanooga. Make arrangements to relieve [Brigadier General] John E. Smith's men at Resaca, and prepare to receive at Resaca and Chattanooga all the wounded and sick of this army; also be prepared when I give you notice, or when you know that I have started south, to burn the Resaca bridge, and take up all the iron back to Dalton or even to Chattanooga...." A Federal expedition left Atlanta heading toward Trickum's Cross-Roads.[310]

October 27, 1864 (Thursday)

Commenting on the U.S. Signal Corps during the campaign for Atlanta, Sherman informed Secretary Stanton of their great service. "In several instances this corps has transmitted orders and brought me information of the greatest importance that could not have reached me in any other way. When the enemy had cut our wires and actually made a lodgment on our railroad about Big Shanty, the signal officers on Vining's Hill, Kenesaw, and Allatoona sent my orders to General Corse at Rome, whereby General Corse was enabled to reach Allatoona just in time to defend it." Sherman closed in declaring, "Had it not been for the services of this corps on that occasion I am satisfied we should have lost the garrison at Allatoona and a most valuable depository of provisions there, which was worth to us and the country more than the aggregate expense of the whole signal corps for one year." Skirmishing reported at Trickum's Cross-Roads.[311]

October 28, 1864 (Friday)

Sherman began implementing his next plan and wrote to Halleck, "I have sent Stanley's corps to Chattanooga, and may also send Schofield's; but I do not want to go back myself with the whole army, as that is what the enemy wants. If you can re-enforce Thomas and enable him to hold Tennessee I will soon make Hood let go, for when I get my sick and wounded to the rear I will start for Macon. The railroad is now done."[312]

October 29, 1864 (Saturday)

Brigadier General John Smith, in Cartersville, received an update from Sherman: "I will send General Schofield's corps to Resaca from here [Rome] to-morrow, and it will relieve all your men at Adairsville and above. You will then collect your division at Kingston and

---

309 *OR*, ser. I, vol. 39, pt. 3:428–29; Avery, *History of the State of Georgia*, 292.

310 *OR*, ser. I, vol. 39, pt. 3:447–48; expedition in Mosocco, *Chronological Tracking*, 277.

311 *OR*, ser. I, vol. 39, pt. 3:461; skirmish in Mosocco, *Chronological Tracking*, 277.

312 *OR*, ser. I, vol. 39, pt. 3:476–77.

Cartersville ready to move. I must here await for the development of Hood. I think Thomas will have enough men to handle him, even if he succeeds in crossing the Tennessee."[313]

October 30, 1864 (Sunday) ●

Sherman began positioning his chess pieces on a board called Georgia. Via Special Field Orders, No. 111, subordinates received their marching orders.

> Maj. Gen. J. M. Schofield will move his corps to Resaca, and relieve all troops along the railroad belonging to the Fourteenth and Fifteenth Corps, and order them to join their proper divisions by Kingston. He will cover the railroad during the movement of the trains and report for further instructions to Maj. Gen. George H. Thomas, at Nashville, both by telegraph and letter. Bvt. Maj. Gen. Jeff. C. Davis will move his corps to Kingston and there await further orders. Maj. Gen. O. O. Howard, with the cavalry, will move his army by easy marches to Dallas and Smyrna Camp-Ground, reporting his position as often as possible en route that orders may reach him via Allatoona and Marietta. All detachments and recruits will join their respective corps at once by the most direct route. Brig. Gen. John E. Smith will assemble his division at Cartersville and Allatoona, and Brig. Gen. John M. Corse will hold his at Rome until further orders.[314]

October 31, 1864 (Monday) (All Hallow'e'en)

In Marietta, the First Georgia Volunteer Infantry Battalion formed, marking the only Federal unit during the war containing the name "Georgia."[315]

November 1, 1864 (Tuesday)

Sherman's chief engineer officer, Captain Orlando Poe, wrote from Atlanta to his wife, Nelly. The officer suggested receiving mail in the immediate future would prove problematic, as Sherman's force prepared to start "on our new campaign, which will last several weeks at least, and be made without a 'Base,' so that we will have no communication with the North. We are going to move out on our own hook, and all the news you will have of us will be from rebel newspapers."[316]

November 2, 1864 (Wednesday)

Grant unleashed his tiger! To Sherman he wrote, "I do not really see that you can withdraw from where you are to follow Hood, without giving up all we have gained in territory. I say, then, go as you propose." Sherman responded, in two different dispatches, stating in the first "I think Jeff. Davis will change his tune when he finds me advancing into the heart of Georgia instead of retreating, and I think it will have an immediate effect on your operations at Richmond." In a second message, Sherman asserted, "I am clearly of opinion that the best results will follow me in my contemplated movement through Georgia."[317]

---

[313] Ibid., 495.

[314] Ibid., 511.

[315] R. Davis, "White and Black in Blue," 367. Major General Henry Slocum commanded the Army of Georgia during Sherman's Savannah Campaign.

[316] P. Taylor, *My Dear Nelly*, 277.

[317] *OR*, ser. I, vol. 39, pt. 3:594–95.

November 3, 1864 (Thursday)
Sherman updated Halleck on the situation in Georgia. "I propose to adhere as nearly as possible to my original plan, and, on reaching the sea-coast, will be available for re-enforcing the army in Virginia, leaving behind a track of devastation, as well as a sufficient force to hold fast all that is of permanent value to our cause. When I leave Atlanta it will contain little that will be of use or comfort to the enemy." Meanwhile, Governor Brown sent his annual message to the Georgia legislature, as they started their session in Milledgeville. Brown covered myriad subjects in the lengthy address and specified continuing disagreements with the Confederate government.

> We may, as we have a right to do, differ among ourselves as to the wisdom of a certain line of policy, and of certain acts of the Confederate administration; and some of us may deplore its errors and mismanagement, while others may attempt to justify all its mistakes and defend all its errors, and may be ready in advance to approve everything it may do, and still we may all, as one man, remain true to our sacred cause and be prepared, if necessary, to expend our last dollar and shed our last drop of blood in its defense.[318]

November 4, 1864 (Friday)
Sherman issued Special Field Orders, No. 115, which outlined his plans for the rails.

> The railroad lying between Resaca and Etowah bridge will be left substantially undisturbed. The bridge at Resaca, and the iron north of it, will be removed by cars into Chattanooga and stored for future use. The railroad from the Etowah bridge into Atlanta will be destroyed. The Fourteenth Corps will be charged with the destruction of that road from Etowah, to Big Shanty, the Fifteenth and Seventeenth Corps with that from Kenesaw to Chattahoochee bridge, and the Twentieth Corps from the Chattahoochee into and including Atlanta.[319]

November 5, 1864 (Saturday)
Near Bucktown, Lieutenant Colonel John Ashworth and the 1st Georgia State Troops, a unit formed through the efforts of Unionist James George Brown, skirmished with Colonel James Findley's 1st Georgia State Cavalry Home Guards. The Southern troops captured Ashworth's force of twenty-one, and inflicted casualties of four dead and three wounded.[320]

November 6, 1864 (Sunday) ◐
Skirmishing reported along the McDonough Road outside Atlanta. Sherman provided Grant with alternate versions of the campaign he planned for Georgia.

> If, therefore, I should start before I hear further from you or before further developments turn my course, you may take it for granted that I have moved via Griffin to Barnesville; that I break up the road between Columbus and Macon good, and then,

---

[318] Ibid., 614; Candler, *Confederate Records of the State of Georgia*, 2:738.
[319] *OR*, ser. I, vol. 39, pt. 3:627.
[320] R. Davis and Kinsland, "Forgotten Union Guerrillas."

if I feint on Columbus, will move, via Macon and Millen, to Savannah, or if I feint on Macon you may take it for granted I have shot off toward Opelika, Montgomery, and Mobile Bay or Pensacola. I will not attempt to send couriers back, but trust to the Richmond papers to keep you well advised. I will give you notice by telegraph of the exact time of my departure.[321]

November 7, 1864 (Monday)

Colonel James Findley's Home Guards escorted their prisoners to Gainesville, where on this day, they rounded-up several civilians known to have supported Ashworth's soldiers; among the lot, several Confederate deserters. Twelve of these men hanged in Gainesville, in the Limestone Creek Massacre. Today, these men rest in Marietta's National Cemetery.[322]

November 8, 1864 (Tuesday)

Thanks in large part to the fall of Atlanta, President Lincoln defeated George B. McClellan for another term in office. Major Frederick C. Winkler, 26th Wisconsin Infantry wrote of the election from his post in Atlanta. "We had an election in the regiment today. This regiment is gathered, as you know, from democratic districts, and two years ago cast an almost unanimous democratic vote. Today, Lincoln received one hundred and twelve and McClellan eighty-eight votes."

From Kingston, Sherman issued Special Field Orders, No. 119:

> The general commanding deems it proper at this time to inform the officers and men of the Fourteenth, Fifteenth, Seventeenth, and Twentieth Corps that he has organized them into an army for a special purpose, well known to the War Department and to General Grant. It is sufficient for you to know that it involves a departure from our present base, and a long and difficult march to a new one. All the chances of war have been considered and provided for, as far as human sagacity can. All he asks of you is to maintain that discipline, patience, and courage which have characterized you in the past, and he hopes, through you, to strike a blow at our enemy that will have a material effect in producing what we all so much desire—his complete overthrow. Of all things the most important is that the men, during marches and in camp, keep their places and not scatter about as stragglers or foragers, to be picked up by a hostile people in detail. It is also of the utmost importance that our wagons should not be loaded with anything but provisions and ammunition. All surplus servants, non-combatants, and refugees should now go to the rear, and none should be encouraged to encumber us on the march. At some future time we will be enabled to provide for the poor whites and blacks who seek to escape the bondage under which they are now suffering. With these few simple cautions in your minds, he hopes to lead you to achievements equal in importance to those of the past.

---

[321] Skirmish in Mosocco, *Chronological Tracking*, 279; *OR*, ser. I, vol. 39, pt. 3:660–61.

[322] R. Davis and Kinsland, "Forgotten Union Guerrillas"; for additional information see Holman, "Most Criminal and Remarkable Incident."

In Macon, General Joseph E. Johnston wrote to a family member in Abingdon, Virginia. "I was removed for not attacking equal ground almost 3 times my number," he wrote. "After Hood crossed the Chattahoochee, Sherman approached him repeatedly with about equal forces. Yet the fighting general avoided battle. I wish that you would suggest to your friends a comparison of my campaign with others in this part of the world."[323]

November 9, 1864 (Wednesday)

Brigadier General John Geary reported on an engagement near Atlanta. Geary started the morning "roused by the sounds of artillery in our front...found a force of the enemy attacking my line on the East Point road...[Brigadier General Alfred] Iverson's brigade of Georgia troops...advanced within about 150 yards of our outer works, when they received a destructive fire and retreated hastily. The whole affair lasted from 7 a.m. to 8.15. The enemy left in our hands 2 dead and 2 prisoners, 1 of whom was mortally wounded. There were no casualties on our side."[324] In Kingston, Sherman issued Special Orders, No. 120, which detailed the reorganization of his force. "For the purpose of military operations this army is divided into two wings, viz, the Right Wing, Maj. Gen. O. O. Howard commanding, the Fifteenth and Seventeenth Corps; the Left Wing, Maj. Gen. H. W. Slocum commanding, the Fourteenth and Twentieth Corps." Howard would command the Army of the Tennessee, while Slocum led the newly named Army of Georgia.

November 10, 1864 (Thursday)

Making final provisions before leaving Kingston, Sherman telegraphed Colonel Amos Beckwith in Atlanta. "When I start I propose to move with great rapidity, faster than cattle can possibly gain on us. They [Army of Tennessee] are now five days behind and could not possibly catch up, as I will break the Etowah and Chattahoochee bridges in passing, and those streams are now too high to cross without bridges. We can safely rely on the country for half rations of meat. Where a million of people live, I have no fear of getting a share."[325]

November 11, 1864 (Friday)

Sherman, headquartered in Kingston, wrote "probably my last dispatch" to Halleck.

My arrangements are now all complete, and the railroad cars are being sent to the rear. Last night we burned all foundries, mills, and shops of every kind in Rome, and tomorrow I leave Kingston with the rear guard for Atlanta, which I propose to dispose of in a similar manner, and to start on the 16th on the projected grand raid. I have balanced all the figures well, and am satisfied that General Thomas has in Tennessee a force sufficient for all probabilities, and I have urged him the moment Beauregard turns south to cross the Tennessee at Decatur and push straight for Selma. I would like to have [Major] General [John] Foster to break the Savannah and Charleston road about Pocotaligo about December 1. All other preparations are to my entire satisfaction.

In Alabama, Hood wrote to Major General Cobb at Lovejoy's Station. "Should Sherman

323 Winkler, *Letters*, 169; *OR*, ser. I, vol. 39, pt. 3:701; Johnston, "Some War Letters," 324–25.

324 *OR*, ser. I, vol. 39, pt. 1:670; pt. 3:713.

325 *OR*, ser. I, vol. 39, pt. 3:728.

advance on the Augusta, Macon, or West Point railroad it is very important that the road should be taken up in his front, or if time should not permit this it should be destroyed. If you have information of a probability of his advancing on any of these roads have the iron taken up immediately."[326]

November 12, 1864 (Saturday)

Adjutant Cornelius Platter with the 81st Ohio Infantry noted the destruction as Sherman's troops headed toward Atlanta, wreaking havoc along the way. "Reached Cassville by daylight. The place was burned by our troops last Summer and presented nothing but a mass of ruins. Only two houses are standing and they are churches. Reached Cartersville at 10 AM where we halted several hours. Everything at Cartersville has been destroyed today Quite a number of wagons were burned and enough medical supplies to last a Division 3 months."[327]

November 13, 1864 (Sunday)

Entering Marietta, Major Henry Hitchcock, one of Sherman's staff officers, watched as the courthouse fire "blazed furiously, and this set other buildings on fire, across the street, and opposite hotel. Elsewhere on Square large stores etc., begun to burn, and spread. Large buildings opposite left of hotel showed smoke." Upon questioning Sherman about the inferno, Sherman responded "Can't save it—I've seen more of this sort of thing than you. I say Jeff Davis burnt them." From near Jonesborough, Major General Wheeler alerted Hood, "Enemy have been burning something in Atlanta for the last two days."[328]

November 14, 1864 (Monday)

Sergeant Alexander Downing and the 11th Iowa Infantry spent their final in Atlanta wreaking havoc. "We tore up the railroad tracks through Atlanta and burned all the public buildings. There was a fine large station here, and a splendid engine house, but both were burned."[329]

November 15, 1864 (Tuesday)

The right wing, under the command of Major General O. O. Howard, left Atlanta. As they advanced, skirmishes occurred at East Point, Jonesborough, Rough and Ready, and at Stockbridge. A soldier in the 70th Ohio Infantry regiment wrote of the morning's activities.

> From some commanding elevation the clear-toned bugle sounds out the reveille, and another and another responds, until the startled echoes double and treble the clarion calls. Intermingled with this comes the beating of drums, often rattling and jarring on unwilling ears. In a few moments the peaceful quiet is replaced by noise and tumult, arising from hill and dale, from field and forest. Amid all is the busy clatter of tongues and tools. Then the animals are hitched into the traces, and the droves of cattle relieved from the night's confinement in the corral; knapsacks are strapped; the

[326] Ibid., 740, 911.

[327] Platter diary, Saturday, November 12, 1864, 5–6.

[328] Hitchcock, *Marching with Sherman*, 52–53; *OR*, ser. I, vol. 39, pt. 3:918.

[329] Downing, *Downing's Civil War Diary*, 228–29.

men seize their trusty weapons, and as again the bugles sound the note of command, the soldiers fall into line and file out upon the road....[330]

November 16, 1864 (Wednesday)

The left wing of Sherman's force, Major General Henry Slocum's Army of Georgia, headed eastward out of Atlanta with Sherman accompanying the army. Pausing, and turning in his saddle, Sherman observed, "Behind us lay Atlanta, smouldering and in ruins, the black smoke rising high in air, and hanging like a pall over the ruined city." Skirmishing occurred at Bear Creek Station, near the Cotton River Bridge, and at Lovejoy's Station. A soldier in a Georgia unit engaged against the Federals at Bear Creek wrote, "met and encountered the overwhelming numbers of Sherman's advance, killing and wounding a great many of the advancing enemy, but we were unable to check them, as our Reg could only muster 48 guns. We were so completely run over that we were scattered in every direction, those of us who were not killed and captured."[331]

November 17, 1864 (Thursday)

A skirmish occurred near Towalia Bridge as Sherman's two armies continued marching from Atlanta. President Davis responded to a suggestion from several Georgia senators who had proposed a Georgia peace treaty with the North. Even though Davis suggested the "objection to separate State action which you present in your letter appears to be so conclusive as to admit no reply," the president outlined his adamant position against the notion in a lengthy response. Beauregard informed Governor Brown, "[Lieutenant] General [Richard] R. Taylor has been ordered to repair forthwith to Georgia and take command of all Confederate troops now operating against Sherman." In Macon, Robert Toombs notified the governor of dire straits, writing, "Things are very bad here. Sherman...is leading, say, 30,000 men against us. We are retreating as rapidly as possible, consistent with good order and efficiency. The militia are retreating in admirable order...as General Cobb reports. I believe the Legislature will grant you large and liberal powers. Tell them the country is in danger. Let all of her sons come to her rescue."[332]

November 18, 1864 (Friday)

The heat intensified in Georgia, and Brown telegraphed President Davis, "A heavy force of the enemy is advancing on Macon, laying waste the country and burning the towns. We have not sufficient force. I hope you will send us troops as re-enforcements till the exigency is passed." Davis sent orders to Major General Howell Cobb in Macon. "In addition to the troops of all kinds you should endeavor to get out every man who can render any service...employ negroes in obstructing roads by every practicable means. Colonel

[330] Connelly, *History of the Seventieth Ohio Regiment*, 125; skirmishes in Mosocco, *Chronological Tracking*, 281.

[331] Sherman, *Memoirs*, 655; soldier quote from T. Bryan, *Confederate Georgia*, 167; skirmishes in Mosocco, *Chronological Tracking*, 281.

[332] Skirmishes in Mosocco, *Chronological Tracking*, 281; J. Davis, *Papers*, 11:162; Taylor assignment in *OR*, ser. I, vol. 44:862; Toombs to Brown in Candler, *Confederate Records of the State of Georgia*, 3:673.

[Washington] Rains, at Augusta, can furnish you with shells prepared to explode by pressure, and these will be effective to check an advance. You have a difficult task, but will realize the necessity for the greatest exertion."[333] As Federal troops approached Milledgeville, the General Assembly adjourned.

November 19, 1864 (Saturday)

Brigadier General John Geary's troops neared Buck Head Station. The officer reported on the action during the day.

> I passed through Madison before daylight, and moved along the road parallel to the Georgia railroad, halting for dinner at Buck Head Station, where I destroyed the water-tank, stationary engine, and all the railroad buildings. After marching one mile beyond the station I again halted and destroyed a portion of the railroad, also a large quantity of cord wood, and other railroad material. At Buck Head Station my advance exchanged shots with the enemy's scouts. I sent on a detachment in advance of the main body to drive these scouts and whatever there might be of the enemy's cavalry in the vicinity across the Oconee, and to burn the railroad bridge across the river; also another detachment several miles above to destroy a large mill and the ferry-boats across the Appalachee. I also destroyed in all to-day about five miles of railroad and a large quantity of railroad ties and string timbers.[334]

November 20, 1864 (Sunday)

On a day with skirmishing at Clinton, Griswoldville, and along Walnut Creek, Brigadier General Judson Kilpatrick's troopers feinted toward Macon. Sergeant William Harding in the 5th Ohio Cavalry, rode out about noon. "Come to the pickets, kill 2 of them and at the RR have a sharp skirmish. Break up the RR and camp."[335]

November 21, 1864 (Monday) ◑

Sergeant Rice C. Bull and the soldiers in the 123rd New York Infantry had a wet day. As Bull described it:

> The storm made the road slippery and soft and our trains were delayed so it was late at night when we were all in and the trains parked. During the day we passed through Eatonton, quite a good-sized town but without any railroad so there were no cotton or buildings to destroy. We gave no demonstration when we went through this village; the rain had dampened our enthusiasm. Our camp was within fourteen miles of Milledgeville…night it cleared and became cold.

There was skirmishing at Clinton, Eatonton, Gordon, Griswoldville, and outside Macon.[336]

November 22, 1864 (Tuesday)

The right wing of Sherman's force bypassed Macon. Confederate officials believed the

---

[333] *OR*, ser. I, vol. 44:865; Avery, *History of the State of Georgia*, 298.

[334] *OR*, ser. I, vol. 44:270.

[335] Dougherty, *Making Georgia Howl!*, 182; skirmishes in Mosocco, *Chronological Tracking*, 282.

[336] Bull, *Soldiering*, 186; skirmishes in Mosocco, *Chronological Tracking*, 282.

Federals would surely target the powder works in Augusta, so they sent troops out of Macon in pursuit. The home guard and militia—"Joe Brown's Pets"—under the command of Brigadier General Pleasant Philips caught up with the rear guard of the Federals, under the command of Brigadier General Charles Walcutt, near Griswoldville. Philips ordered his troops to make a suicidal charge on the entrenched Federals holding the high ground. When the smoke of battle began to dissipate, a Federal officer witnessed and later described the ghastly scene: "Old gray-haired men and weakly looking men and little boys not over fifteen years old lay dead or writhing in pain."[337] Across the bloody fields of Griswoldville lay hundreds among the 650 Confederate casualties. The Federals listed sixty-two as killed, wounded, or missing. Perhaps their action on the day helped alleviate any discomfiture these soldiers suffered as they operated under the moniker of governor's pets, a name applied to many units Brown created to safeguard the state and keep some out of Confederate service.

November 23, 1864 (Wednesday)

The Federals entered Milledgeville and destroyed historic state documents, burned the volumes in the state library, and conducted a mock legislative session to vote Georgia back into the Union. Captain David Conyngham, among Sherman's soldiers in the capitol, noted, "Stacks of Georgia state money were found in the treasurer's office. There were millions of dollars there, the most of it not signed. The men loaded themselves with it; the negroes fought over it, and 'bressed de Lord, dey were richer dan poor massa now.'" Major General Slocum issued orders from his headquarters while in Milledgeville. "Should the enemy burn forage and corn on our route houses, barns, and cotton-gins must also be burned to keep them company." Skirmishing reported at Ball's Ferry and at the Georgia Central Railroad bridge.[338]

November 24, 1864 (Thursday—Thanksgiving)

The soldiers of the 68th Ohio Infantry, including Private Myron B. Loop, in the right wing of Major General Howard, spent the day acting "as guard for our supply train. We marched 12 miles [along Georgia Central Railroad] and went into camp. After supper we were ordered out on the railroad, and for a time were engaged in tearing up the track."[339]

November 25, 1864 (Friday)

Major General Joe Wheeler's troopers engaged outside Sandersville. The Confederate officer reported, "After moving three miles we were charged by the enemy, whom we met and checked, and then in turn charged and drove them back for a mile, capturing, killing, and wounding about thirty of the enemy, besides capturing several horses, mules, and one

---

[337] Bragg, *Griswoldville*, 140. Bragg's work offers an excellent study of this battle. Casualties from National Park Service, "Griswoldville," https://www.nps.gov/civilwar/search-battles-detail.htm?battleCode=GA025.

[338] Conyngham, *Sherman's March*, 254; *OR*, ser. I, vol. 44:532; skirmishes in Mosocco, *Chronological Tracking*, 282.

[339] Loop, *Long Road Home*, 180.

loaded wagon."[340]

November 26, 1864 (Saturday)

Lieutenant General Hardee, in Millen, sent an update to President Davis. "Enemy entered Sandersville to-day in force. Wheeler says Kilpatrick has gone toward Augusta, and he will pursue him with all of his force, except one brigade, which will be left in this front. Wheeler is uncertain whether Sherman is going to Augusta or Savannah." There was skirmishing in the vicinity of Sandersville.[341]

November 27, 1864 (Sunday)

Cavalry skirmished at Sylvan Grove and outside Waynesborough. Kilpatrick reported, "During this march my flanks and rear had been attacked again and again by Wheeler's cavalry, but without serious results, and did not prevent the column from steadily marching on. We passed through Waynesborough and encamped in line of battle on the railroad three miles south of the town." Wheeler wrote of the pursuit, "During the chase the enemy set fire to all corn cribs, cotton gins, and large number of barns and houses. We succeeded in driving him off in nearly half the instances in time to extinguish the flames, and frequently pressed him so rapidly as to prevent his firing a number of houses, thus saving a large amount of property."[342]

November 28, 1864 (Monday)

Skirmishing occurred at Buck Head Church, Davisborough, and again near Waynesborough. General Bragg, in Augusta, notified the Confederate War Department of events. "A running fight has continued to this time, the advantage with us. We are now driving them toward Millen. Devastation marks the enemy's route."[343]

November 29, 1864 (Tuesday) ●

Major Hitchcock, with Sherman in Wilkinson County, expressed his surprise over the previous days. "Certainly this 'is the perfection of campaigning.' Since we left Sandersville I have seen nothing of an enemy."[344]

November 30, 1864 (Wednesday)

While most Georgia eyes focused on Sherman's movement toward the southeast, a skirmish—which involved guerrilla forces operating in the region—took place in Dalton. Colonel Joshua B. Culver of the 13th Michigan Infantry reported, "The attack was easily repulsed. They captured one of my scouts. Have sent a reconnaissance out on main roads. You need not entertain any fears of my surrendering. Do not think the force exceeded 200."[345]

December 1, 1864 (Thursday)

Colonel Cyrus Briant with the 88th Indiana Infantry reported on an engagement near

---

340 *OR*, ser. I, vol. 44:407.

341 Ibid., 899; skirmishing in Mosocco, *Chronological Tracking*, 283.

342 *OR*, ser. I, vol. 44:363, 408.

343 Ibid., 902.

344 Hitchcock, *Marching with Sherman*, 110.

345 *OR*, ser. I, vol. 45, pt. 1:1193.

Millen's/Shady Grove. The Hoosiers "marched on Sebastopol and Waynesborough road, about one mile from the main road, occupying this position until wagon train all passed. My foraging party, numbering thirty-two men and one officer, were attacked some five miles out by a squad of rebel cavalry, but succeeded in getting off with a goodly supply of forage and no loss."[346]

December 2, 1864 (Friday)

Skirmishing was reported at Buck Head Creek and at Rocky Creek Church. Brigadier General Absalom Baird reported on the action: "met the enemy again at Rocky Creek, at 10 a. m., posted behind strong barricades and disposed to dispute our crossing at the ford. The Seventy fourth Indiana charged and dispersed them, and the division…went into camp."[347] Major General Howard and Slocum learn, from Sherman, their destination: Savannah.

December 3, 1864 (Saturday)

Colonel Smith D. Atkins reported on the day's skirmishing. His soldiers "marched fourteen miles and encamped at Thomas' Station. The Ninety-second Illinois Mounted Infantry Volunteers was placed on picket to cover the infantry of [Brigadier] General [Absalom] Baird in tearing up track and skirmished with the enemy nearly all night. The enemy shelled the regiment with artillery, killing two and wounding one."[348]

December 4, 1864 (Sunday)

The cavalry troopers of Kilpatrick and Wheeler clashed in the streets of Waynesborough. Kilpatrick reported, "I…drove him from one position to another, till he made a final stand in and about the town of Waynesborough. Here his lines were too long to be flanked, so we boldly charged and broke his center. He fought stubbornly for a time, but finally gave way before our flashing sabers, and in twenty minutes was retreating in great confusion through the woods, fields, and on every available road leading toward Augusta." Wheeler indicated the "Enemy made several charges upon the position which I had taken, all of which were repulsed by fire from behind breast-works and by counter-charges. Enemy's vastly superior forces, which completely enveloped my flanks, compelled me to retire toward Brier Creek. A number of officers and men were killed and wounded…."[349] Skirmishes reported along the Little Ogeechee River, and at Lumpkin's Station, Statesborough, and Station No. 5 on the Georgia Central Railroad.

December 5, 1864 (Monday)

Federal intelligence, gained from "a rebel officer who has deserted," indicated "General Sherman is within sight of Savannah, and that all of the women and children were sent out of the city last night."[350] Captain Charles Wills of the 8th Illinois Infantry, who was "Thirty-six miles from Savannah," described the countryside near the Ogeechee River. "Rather poor country, farms small, and much Pine. Negroes swarmed us to-day. Sherman's

---

[346] *OR*, ser. I, vol. 44:172.

[347] Ibid., 204. See also pgs. 602, 609 for Sherman's communication with both officers.

[348] *OR*, ser. I, vol. 44:391.

[349] Ibid., 634, 929–30; skirmishes in Mosocco, *Chronological Tracking*, 286.

[350] *OR*, ser. I, vol. 44:635–36; C. Wills, *Army Life of an Illinois Soldier*, 331–32; skirmishes in Mosocco, *Chronological Tracking*, 286.

order is not to let any more go with us than we can use and feed." Skirmishing reported at Dalton and along the Little Ogeechee River.

December 6, 1864 (Tuesday)

Federal attacks along the Charleston and Savannah Railroad on a day Grant wrote to Sherman regarding next actions, once the march on Savannah ended.

> On reflection...I have concluded that the most important operation toward closing the rebellion will be to close out Lee and his army. You have now destroyed the roads of the South, so that it will probably take three months, without interruption, to re-establish a through line from east to west. In that time I think the job here will be effectually completed. My idea now, then, is that you establish a base on the sea-coast, fortify, and leave in it all your artillery and cavalry, and enough infantry to protect them, and, at the same time, so threaten the interior that the militia of the South will have to be kept at home. With the balance of your command come here by water with all dispatch. Select yourself the officer to leave in command, but you I want in person. Unless you see objections to this plan, which I cannot see, use every vessel going to you for purposes of transportation.

Beauregard wrote to President Davis, mourning the fact "we have not thus far been more successful...but he [Sherman] will doubtless be prevented from capturing Augusta, Charleston, and Savannah and he may yet be made to experience serious loss before reaching the coast."[351]

December 7, 1864 (Wednesday)

From Savannah, Lieutenant General Hardee reported to General Cooper in Richmond. "Considerable fighting at Coosawhatchie...without definite results. The enemy hold a position near Coosawhatchie and the railroad. Heavy skirmishing at No. 2, Central railroad...large force of the enemy...have crossed the Ogeechee opposite that point. Fighting...at Cannouchee Bridge. Enemy have made their appearance...on the Savannah River."[352] Skirmishing also reported at Buck Creek, Cypress Swamp, and Jenks's Bridge. A soldier in the 113th Ohio Infantry, along with the rest of his regiment, "reached Ebenezer creek late in the evening and began to prepare to lay a bridge across the stream"

December 8, 1864 (Thursday)

Many civilians in the path of Sherman's forces endured hardships; the loss of foodstuffs and family treasures caused much pain. Frequently, the culprits wore gray, especially those gathering sustenance. Alexander Walker wrote to Governor Brown from Richmond County, regarding Wheeler's troopers, who Walker labeled as a "plundering band of horse stealing ruffians—with the exception of some Texas brigades or regiments, I know of none that do not deserve this epithet."[353]

---

[351] Federal attacks in Mosocco, *Chronological Tracking*, 286; *OR*, ser. I, vol. 44:636, 931.

[352] *OR*, ser. I, vol. 44:938; skirmishes in Mosocco, *Chronological Tracking*, 287; McAdams, *Every-Day Soldier Life*, 123.

[353] Alexander Walker to Joseph E. Brown, December 8, 1864, in Brown, *Papers*, https://repository.duke.edu/dc/brownjosephepapers-000846380/secst0339.

December 9, 1864 (Friday)

Sherman's two wings drew closer to Savannah. On the left, Major General Jefferson C. Davis, once his troops crossed the swampy waters of Ebenezer Creek, ordered the pontoon bridges cut, stranding several hundred former enslaved persons on the other side. Many jumped into the murky waters, only to disappear beneath the surface; an undetermined number perished. An officer in Davis's command stated, "The idea of five or six hundred black women, children and old men being thus returned to slavery by such an infernal copperhead as Jeff. C. Davis was entirely too much for my Democracy…I am determined to expose this act of his publicly…." Wheeler's troopers soon approached, and the Confederate officer reported "a great many negroes were left in our hands, whom we sent back to their owners." Skirmishing reported at Cuyler's Plantation, Eden Station, Pooler Station, Monteith Swamp, and along the Ogeechee Canal.[354]

December 10, 1864 (Saturday)

The marching portion of Sherman's Savannah Campaign ended, as the Federal force reached the outer defenses of the city. Sherman started ascertaining his next target and seeking ways "to open communication with our fleet in Ossabow and Wassaw Sounds." Colonel Ezra Carman, commanding a brigade in the XX Corps, moved "down to the Charleston and Savannah Railroad, and destroyed about two miles of the track, and moved on to within five miles of Savannah, where the enemy were found strongly intrenched. Formed line of battle on left of Third Division, right resting on the Savannah turnpike. A forage party under command of Captain [Henry] Gildersleeve…captured the rebel dispatch steamer *Ida* on the Savannah River." Skirmishing at Springfield and other locales outside Savannah.[355]

December 11, 1864 (Sunday)

Brigadier General Kilpatrick and his troopers "have been all day making a road out of range of the rebel guns. I have thoroughly examined the entire country…between the Ogeechee and the rebel lines. It is impossible to cross the Little Ogeechee at any point. I have been in sight of Fort McAllister; it has about 200 men and thirteen guns mounted. I have proposed to General Howard to cross the Ogeechee with my command and a force of infantry, and take the fort."[356]

December 12, 1864 (Monday)

Confederate Flag Officer William Hunter had trouble navigating through the Federal batteries along the Savannah River. "I engaged these [batteries] with the *Sampson*, *Macon*, and the *Resolute*, I leading in the *Sampson*. All the vessels were riddled by their Parrott shells, several bursting on board. The *Resolute* was disabled and taken." While Hunter dodged

---

[354] Connolly, *Three Years in the Army of the Cumberland*, 354–55; *OR*, ser. I, vol. 44:410; skirmishes in Mosocco, *Chronological Tracking*, 287.

[355] *OR*, ser. I, vol. 44:676, 235; skirmishes in Mosocco, *Chronological Tracking*, 288. For a good treatment of the entire Savannah Campaign, see Noah Andre Trudeau, *Southern Storm: Sherman's March to the Sea* (New York: Harper, 2008).

[356] *OR*, ser. I, vol. 44:690.

Federal shells, Sherman connected, visually, with the Federal vessels along the coast. Rear Admiral John Dahlgren reported, "I have just received a communication from Sherman's army. It is a few miles from Savannah, and in fine spirits. I shall bring all my available force into connection with the army."[357]

December 13, 1864 (Tuesday)

To successfully establish a link with the Federal vessels resting off the coast, Sherman needed to secure Fort McAllister. Brigadier General William Hazen received the call to take the fortification, and equipped with nine regiments, the boys in blue prepared to advance. Fort McAllister had earlier repulsed several naval attacks, but the fortification, never intended to fend off an attack from the land, lay vulnerable. Despite the efforts of Major George Anderson and a garrison of a few hundred soldiers, the fort fell in about fifteen minutes. Hazen stated, "Our charge, however, carried the whole front. Our losses, which numbered one hundred and thirty, were nearly all from torpedoes, and at close quarters. The garrison did not surrender; they fought within the works, and were overcome man by man." Hazen reported the capture of 250 Confederates. The capture of the fort prompted Sherman to consider "Savannah as already gained."[358]

December 14, 1864 (Wednesday)

Lieutenant-Commander Robert W. Scott of the USS *Sonoma* started a bombardment of Confederate positions along the coast. "I pushed up the Vernon River to feel the Rosedew and Beaulieu batteries (Fort McAllister having been taken by the forces of Major-General Sherman the evening before), and at 1:30 p.m. came within range and opened fire on Fort Beaulieu and found the works to be very strong and their practice good...."[359]

December 15, 1864 (Thursday)

From Savannah, Hardee delivered disturbing news to President Davis. "Sherman has secured a water base, and [Federal Major General John] Foster, who is already nearly on my communications, can be safely and expeditiously re-enforced. Unless assured that force sufficient to keep open my communications can be sent me, I shall be compelled to evacuate Savannah." Grant notified Halleck to "communicate with Sherman, and direct him to send no troops from his army to Virginia until plan of campaign is fully agreed upon."[360]

December 16, 1864 (Friday)

Federal troops attempting to destroy the bridge on the Savannah, Albany and Gulf Railroad met defeat at the hands of Confederate militia at Doctortown. Sherman updated Grant on the campaign. "I think Hardee, in Savannah, has good artillerists, some 5,000 or 6,000 infantry, and it may be a mongrel mass of 8,000 to 10,000 militia and fragments. In all our marching through Georgia he has not forced me to use anything but a skirmish line, though at several points he had erected fortifications and tried to alarm us by bombastic threats."

---

[357] *ORN*, ser. I, vol. 16:489, 126.

[358] Hazen, *Narrative of Military Service*, 333; *OR*, ser. I, vol. 44:95, 111, 701.

[359] *ORN*, ser. I, vol. 16:149.

[360] *OR*, ser. I, vol. 44:960, 715.

Skirmish reported near Hinesville.[361]

December 17, 1864 (Saturday)

In a dispatch to Hardee, Sherman requested the surrender of Savannah.

> You have doubtless observed from your station at Rosedew that sea going vessels now come through Ossabaw Sound and up Ogeechee to the rear of my army, giving me abundant supplies of all kinds, and more especially heavy ordnance necessary to the reduction of Savannah. I have already received guns that can cast heavy and destructive shot as far as the heart of your city; also, I have for some days held and controlled every avenue by which the people and garrison of Savannah can be supplied; and I am therefore justified in demanding the surrender of the city of Savannah and its dependent forts, and shall await a reasonable time your answer before opening with heavy ordnance. Should you entertain the proposition I am prepared to grant liberal terms to the inhabitants and garrison; but should I be forced to resort to assault, and the slower and surer process of starvation, I shall then feel justified in resorting to the harshest measures, and shall make little effort to restrain my army—burning to avenge a great national wrong they attach to Savannah and other large cities which have been so prominent in dragging our country into civil war.[362]

Hardee refused.

December 18, 1864 (Sunday)

Sherman corresponded with Grant on potential next steps in Sherman's campaign. "With Savannah in our possession at some future time…we can punish South Carolina as she deserves, and as thousands of people in Georgia hoped we would do. I do sincerely believe that the whole United States, North and South, would rejoice to have this army turned loose on South Carolina to devastate that State, in the manner we have done in Georgia…."[363]

December 19, 1864 (Monday)

Via a "Confidential Circular," Hardee outlined plans for vacating Savannah. "The troops in and around Savannah will be transferred to-night to the left bank of the Savannah River, and will proceed thence to Hardeeville." Confederate Naval Commander Thomas Brent reported his command burned the "*Water Witch*…after consultation with the commanding general and by his advice, to prevent her falling into the hands of the enemy."[364]

December 20, 1864 (Tuesday) ◑

Hardee issued his final order while still in Savannah. Referencing his "Confidential Circular" of the previous day, the general informed his command the movement "will be executed to night at the hours as originally arranged, and not as subsequently amended—that

[361] Ray, *Drifting into Darien*, 69–70; *OR*, ser. I, vol. 44:728; skirmish in Mosocco, *Chronological Tracking*, 289.

[362] *OR*, ser. I, vol. 44:737.

[363] Ibid., 743.

[364] Ibid., 967; *ORN*, ser. I, vol. 16:484.

is, Wright's division will move at 8 o'clock, McLaws' division at 10 o'clock, and Smith's division at 11 o'clock, and Wright's skirmishers will be withdrawal at 10.30 o'clock, McLaws' skirmishers at 12.30 o'clock, and Smith's skirmishers at 1 o'clock."[365]

December 21, 1864 (Wednesday)

A hectic day in Savannah! The Confederates scuttled the CSS *Georgia*, *Isondiga*, *Firefly*, and *Savannah* to prevent Federal forces from capturing the ships. Captain David Conyngham and other Federals witnessed a "a flash of light; then, as if from the crater of a volcano, an immense volume of flame shot up, illumining the heavens for miles then came the fearful report, and the rebel ram *Savannah* was no more. The concussion was fearful, rocking the city and the vessels at anchor." Colonel H. A. Barnum and the 149th New York Infantry "moved down the Augusta road, and at about half a mile from the junction of the Augusta road with the Charleston railroad was met by the mayor and a delegation of aldermen of the city with a flag of truce, who formally surrendered the city of Savannah."[366] Other Federal forces occupied Fort Jackson.

December 22, 1864 (Thursday)

William T. Sherman telegraphed to President Abraham Lincoln, "I beg to present you as a Christmas gift the City of Savannah with 150 heavy guns & plenty of ammunition & also about 25,000 bales of cotton."[367]

December 23, 1864 (Friday)

Private John Daniels with the 13th Michigan Infantry spent a less than desirable day in Savannah. "We moved camp this afternoon within mile and a half of the city. We draw scanty rations and buy rice so that we have nearly enough to eat though the meal is very bad yet. It is beef that has been driven through the swamps and rivers of Ga. and was poor when it was first foraged."[368]

December 24, 1864 (Saturday)

Dolly Lunt Burge prepared for a gloomy holiday. "This has usually been a very busy day with me preparing for Christmas. Not only for my own tables but for gifts for my servants. Now how changed no cakes, pies or confectionary, can I have. We are all Sad. No loud jovial laugh from our boys is heard. I have nothing to put even in Sadai's stocking which hangs so invitingly for Santa Claus. Poor children! Why must the innocent suffer with the guilty?"[369]

December 25, 1864 (Sunday) (Christmas Day)

Catharine Whiteland Rowland, near Waynesborough, spent a few melancholy hours thinking of brighter days.

---

[365] *OR*, ser. I, vol. 44:972; officers referenced Brigadier General Ambrose Wright, Major General Lafayette McLaws, and Major General Gustavus W. Smith.

[366] U.S. Naval History Division, *Civil War Naval Chronology*, 4:148; Conyngham, *Sherman's March through the South*, 292; *OR*, ser. I, vol. 44:310. For an interesting article on the CSS *Georgia*, see Jordan, "Recovery of CSS *Georgia*."

[367] Sherman, Simpson, and Berlin, *Sherman's Civil War*, 772.

[368] Daniels, *Marching through Georgia*, December 23, 1864, n.p.

[369] Burge, *Diary*, 166.

The greeting of "Merry Christmas" seems like a mockery, now, while there is so much trouble and suffering in our midst & I have not had the heart to give utterance to it today. What a striking contrast between this Christmas & those that were spent in former years; then it was a time of merry making, a time of joyful reunion when we were all gathered together in our happy home; now it is a season of sadness as it only recalls those joyous days that are gone, never more to return, as loved ones with us then, have passed away to meet with us again no more on earth & the brightest of our circle fallen by the hand of a savage & merciless foe. God has been most merciful unto us and my heart is full of gratitude and thankfulness for all the blessings he has given me and above all do I thank him for having spared the life of my precious husband and child.[370]

December 26, 1864 (Monday)
Sherman busied himself reading and writing letters. From President Lincoln, he received, "Many, many thanks for your Christmas gift, the capture of Savannah. When you were about leaving Atlanta for the Atlantic coast, I was anxious, if not fearful; but feeling that you were the better judge, and remembering that 'nothing risked, nothing gained,' I did not interfere. Now, the undertaking being a success, the honor is all yours; for I believe none of us went further than to acquiesce." Lincoln closed with a question, "But what next? I suppose it will be safer if I leave General Grant and yourself to decide. Please make my grateful acknowledgments to your whole army, officers and men." Sherman telegraphed Grant. "I am very glad to learn that Jeff. Davis is in the condition [sick] reported to you, and hope that before this time he is dead and out of the way. From my intercourse with the people of Georgia I think it would give great satisfaction to them generally to know that this was so. Still I shall, of course, go on with my preparations without reference to anything of the kind, and as though the Southern Confederacy possessed all the vitality which they boast of."[371]

December 27, 1864 (Tuesday)
Secretary Stanton sought to open the door while Sherman wished to shed light on the subject; both thinking of Savannah. Stanton wrote to Lieutenant General Grant, "Is there any objection, on military grounds, to the President removing the blockade of Savannah by proclamation, and opening it to public trade, except contraband of war?" Meanwhile, Sherman requested the U.S. Coast Service to "at the earliest practicable moment, take the necessary steps to have the Tybee Light-House rebuilt, put in good order, and relighted; and also that the channels leading up to Savannah be buoyed and lighted as soon as possible."[372]

December 28, 1864 (Wednesday) ●
Residents in Savannah held a meeting at the Masonic Hall and passed resolutions to "lay

---

[370] Harper, ed., *Second Georgia Infantry Regiment*, 70.
[371] *OR*, ser. I, vol. 44:809–10.
[372] Ibid., 820–21.

aside all differences [and put forth] best endeavors to bring back the prosperity and commerce we once enjoyed."[373]

December 29, 1864 (Thursday)

Major Hitchcock wrote from Savannah, "The weather is bright and lovely—a fine bracing fall day we should call it. Indications daily increase of the tremendous moral effect our campaign has had and will have in Georgia in 'knocking out the underpinning' of the C.S.A."[374]

December 30, 1864 (Friday)

Receiving promotion to the rank of major general on this day, Pierce M. B. Young achieved the highest rank among Georgia Military Institute alumni.[375]

December 31, 1864 (Saturday)

Private John Brobst, 25th Wisconsin Infantry, spent the final day of the year in Georgia thinking of home and loved ones.

> The old year will soon be gone forever. How many have gone to their long homes since one year ago today. Gay and happy one year ago today, but as sixty-four passes off in the sea of time it finds them mouldering in their cold graves. Many of my comrades that were well and promising one year ago, today sleep under the soil of Georgia, but they have filled a hero's grave. They sleep in honor of their country, and all friends to our government should feel proud of their mouldering bodies. But how many look on them with disdain and say, 'He was nobody but a soldier. We will enjoy the rights that he died for. We care not who suffers death for the good of the country. We will undo all that they can do.' But the day is fast coming when such men will have to curtail the cowardly and unruly tongues that hang in their heads or they will fill a grave more degrading than that of a soldier. Yes, a grave of disgrace and shame, a Benedict Arnold grave, the grave of a traitor.[376]

---

[373] Sholes, *Chronological History of Savannah*, 79.

[374] Hitchcock, *Marching with Sherman*, 203.

[375] Eicher and Eicher, *Civil War High Commands*, 585.

[376] Brobst, *Well Mary*, 110–11.

Chapter 5

1865—and Beyond

Moon Stage Legend: ◐ first quarter; ○ full, ◑ last quarter, ● new

January 1, 1865 (Sunday)

Prior to leaving Savannah, Major General William T. Sherman busied himself in "planning a new flank movement, visiting Hilton Head in person…, and travelling night and day during his journey to that place and back."[1]

January 2, 1865 (Monday)

Major General W. T. Sherman wrote Secretary of War Edwin Stanton from Savannah, informing Stanton of the policy Sherman had in the city regarding cotton. "I had already been approached by all the consuls and half the people of Savannah on this cotton question and my invariable answer has been that all the cotton in Savannah was prize of war, and belonged to the United States, and nobody should recover one bale of it with my consent."[2]

January 3, 1865 (Tuesday)

Brigadier General Hugh Judson Kilpatrick wrote to Sherman of scavenging operations outside Savannah. "My people are getting plenty of forage on the other side of Taylor's Creek, but are fighting for it. Colonel Atkins, with 1,500 men and two pieces of artillery, crossed this morning and will clean the rebels out. When may I expect to get some horses from the infantry! I can feed them now and am very anxious to get ready for the field."[3]

January 4, 1865 (Wednesday) ◐

Writing in his diary, while stationed in Savannah, Sergeant Alexander Downing with the 11th Iowa Infantry prepared to leave the city and move into South Carolina. "Our division, the Fourth, received orders to be ready to move in the morning," he wrote. "Our regimental quartermaster received a consignment of clothing for the men. I drew a rubber blanket, one shirt, one pair of drawers and a hat. I also purchased at one of the stores here a military cap for $6.00; I sent $200.00 home…to father."[4]

January 5, 1865 (Thursday)

Sherman spent the day ensuring final preparations continued for his troops to move north into South Carolina. He took time, however, to write his wife, Ellen. "I do think that in the Several Grand Epochs of this war my name will bear a prominent part, and not least among them the determination I took at Atlanta to destroy that place & march on this City, whilst Thomas my Lieutenant should dispose of Hood. The idea, the execution and Strategy are all good and will in time be understood."[5]

---

[1] Nichols, *Story of the Great March*, 325.

[2] Sherman, *Sherman's Civil War*, 788–89.

[3] *OR*, ser. I, vol. 47, pt. 2:13.

[4] Downing, *Downing's Civil War Diary*, 244.

[5] Sherman, *Sherman's Civil War*, 791.

January 6, 1865 (Friday)

The *Columbus Times* reported, "The quiet which has followed the occupation of Savannah by Sherman is about to be interrupted. The landing of troops on the Carolina Coast and Savannah River…means this much. Whether Sherman will advance upon Charleston or upon Augusta or Branchville is, of course, an unsolved problem."[6]

January 7, 1865 (Saturday)

Major Henry Hitchcock, anticipating responses, North and South, as Sherman's forces prepared to leave Savannah for South Carolina, wrote, "When we do move or soon after—I suspect there will be more puzzling over Sherman's plans than ever; and the rebels will brag as much louder, and fiercer, and bloodier, than during the last march, as their threats, etc., then exceeded those of the Atlanta campaign."[7]

January 8, 1865 (Sunday)

A soldier in the 113th Ohio Infantry stationed in Savannah, wrote of the day's activities. "The 98th O.V.I. [Ohio Volunteer Infantry] relieved the 113th at 11 a.m. and we returned to our former camp near the city. Our trip of five days out among the green trees and singing birds has been an enjoyable one, yet all are glad to be back."[8]

January 9, 1865 (Monday)

Captain Charles Wills of the 103rd Illinois Infantry occupied his time in final preparations before departing Savannah and remaining hopeful of a pending promotion. "The men's clothing was packed in valises, and all the eatables sold to parties who remain here, save one barrel of Irish potatoes. We leave to-morrow morning." Turning his thoughts toward a rise in the ranks, Wills wrote, "Major Willison's resignation was accepted to-day, and this evening the officers unanimously agreed to recommend me to fill the vacancy. There was not a hint towards any one else. I take it as a high compliment. I will value the recommendation more than the commission, if I get it."[9] Wills received his promotion later in the spring.

January 10, 1865 (Tuesday)

Brigadier General Alpheus Williams, with headquarters in Savannah, issued the following circular to troops in the Federal XX Corps: "The attention of division and subordinate commanders in this corps is again called to the necessity of immediately putting their commands in readiness for another campaign. The men must be thoroughly clothed and equipped. Requisitions must be at once made on the quartermasters and ordnance departments to put the command in condition for active service." Williams closed in reminding the soldiers of the necessity of haste in attending to this matter: "This must be attended to immediately, as our stay here will probably be short, and when the time arrives the command will move, whether in readiness or not."[10]

January 11, 1865 (Wednesday)

---

[6] "The News," *Columbus Times*, January 6, 1865, https://gahistoricnewspapers.galileo.usg.edu/lccn/sn86053047/1865-01-06/ed-1/seq-2/.

[7] Hitchcock, *Marching with Sherman*, 205.

[8] McAdams, *Every-Day Soldier Life*, 130.

[9] C. Wills, *Army Life of an Illinois Soldier*, 336.

[10] *OR*, ser. I, vol. 47, pt. 2:33–34.

Secretary of War Edwin Stanton arrived in Savannah to investigate complaints against Sherman regarding his treatment of African American troops under his command. Sherman refused to deploy the African American units under his command into battle, and rumors of Major General Jefferson C. Davis stranding former enslaved people at Ebenezer Creek had reached Washington. Trying to build a defense, Sherman wrote to Supreme Court Chief Justice Salmon P. Chase: "On approaching Savannah I had at least 20,000 negros, clogging my roads, and eating up our subsistence. The same number of white refugees would have been a military weakness. Now you Know that military success is what the nation wants, and it is risked by the crowds of helpless negros that flock after our armies. My negro constituents of Georgia would resent the idea of my being inimical to them, they regard me as a second Moses or Aaron."[11]

January 12, 1865 (Thursday)

Fanny Andrews, writing from near Albany, wreaked havoc with her words toward the soldiers under Sherman's command:

> If I wasn't afraid the Yankees might cut me off from home and sister, too, I would pick up and go now. Yankee, Yankee, is the one detestable word always ringing in Southern ears. If all the words of hatred in every language under heaven were lumped together into one huge epithet of detestation, they could not tell how I hate Yankees. They thwart all my plans, murder my friends, and make my life miserable.[12]

January 13, 1865 (Friday)

Moving their campsite to better ground proved the order of the day for the soldiers in the 130th Ohio Infantry still in Savannah. "We have been busy today with our quarters. Some of the materials of our former camp were carried up on our shoulders and used again here. We are on a dry site, somewhat better than the one we have just left. A number of our officers went to theater to hear Doesticks."[13]

January 14, 1865 (Saturday)

Moving out of Savannah and into South Carolina, Sergeant Downing of the 11th Iowa Infantry recorded in his diary, "Our army commenced to move at 7 this morning and by 10 o'clock the last detachment had crossed Broad river. We moved on about ten miles, driving the rebels and skirmishing with them all the way. The Iowa Brigade lost one man killed.... the expedition consists of the Seventeenth Army Corps with General Foster's command on our left."[14]

January 15, 1865 (Sunday)

---

[11] Sherman, *Sherman's Civil War*, 794.

[12] Andrews, *War-Time Journal of a Georgia Girl*, 67.

[13] McAdams, *Every-Day Soldier Life*, 131. Mortimer Q. Thomson, a nineteenth-century humorist, performed in various theaters throughout the country under the pseudonym "DoeSticks" ("Thomson, Mortimer [1832–1875]").

[14] Downing, *Downing's Civil War Diary*, 246.

Sherman, writing from Savannah, informed his wife, Ellen, of his plans for a campaign through the Carolinas. "Of course my course will be north. I will feignt [*sic*] on Augusta & Charleston, avoid both and make for Columbia, Fayetteville and Newbern N.C. Dont breathe for the walls have ears and foreknowledge published by some mischievous fool might cost many lives. We have lived long enough for men to thank me for Keeping my own counsels, and Keeping away from Armies those pests of newspapermen."[15]

January 16, 1865 (Monday)

Private John Daniels with the 13th Michigan Infantry, uncertain of the time he had left in Savannah before receiving orders to advance into South Carolina, ruminated on his time in the city, writing, "The past 20 days were spent in the common duties of camp life, drill, picket, and work on fortifications. We drew new clothing and after a while we got nearly full rations. I have had rheumatism in my legs which are now very lame. There is some prospect of our moving soon, but some think that we shall stay to guard the place."[16] The 13th Michigan received orders on the following day to break camp and prepare to move out. While Daniels busied himself with camp duties, Major General Sherman issued Special Field Orders, No. 15, from Savannah. "The islands from Charleston south, the abandoned rice-fields along the rivers for thirty miles back from the sea, and the country bordering the Saint John's River, Fla., are reserved and set apart for the settlement of the negroes now made free by the acts of war and the proclamation of the President of the United States."[17] (See Appendix 6.)

January 17, 1865 (Tuesday)

As portions of Sherman's troops began leaving Savannah, Jefferson Davis wrote to the governor of South Carolina, Andrew Magrath, "I am fully alive to the importance of successful resistance to Sherman's advance, and have called on the governor of Georgia to give all the aid he can furnish. Had you not better correspond with him on that point?"[18]

January 18, 1865 (Wednesday)

Theodore Upson with the 100th Indiana Infantry numbered among the first of Sherman's regiments to depart Savannah during the opening stage of the Carolinas Campaign. Upson wrote of the day's activities, "We landed at Beaufort about 8 in the evening and marched out a mile prehaps [*sic*] and camped on a Sandy flat. To day we marched through mud and rain, forded two streams and had a little skirmish with the Johnnys."[19]

January 19, 1865 (Thursday) ◐

Secretary of War Stanton had concluded his visit in Savannah and returned to Washington, when he received a letter from Sherman. "Delegations of the people of Georgia continue to come in, and I am satisfied that with a little judicious handling and by a little respect being paid to their prejudices, we can create a schism in Jeff Davis' dominions. All that I

---

[15] Sherman, *Sherman's Civil War*, 797.

[16] Daniels, *Marching through Georgia*, n.p.

[17] *OR*, ser. I, vol. 47, pt. 2:60.

[18] Ibid., 1018.

[19] Upson, *With Sherman to the Sea*, 147, 150.

have conversed with realize the truth that Slavery as an institution is defunct...."[20]

January 20, 1865 (Friday)

Major General Joe Wheeler and his troopers prepared to thwart, as best they could, Sherman's advancing forces. Brigadier General H. K. McCoy provided recent intelligence to Wheeler regarding the Federal cavalry near Savannah. "I have information from a very reliable source that Kilpatrick is camped at the Little Ogeechee...he has four brigades...claims to have 2,600 men in each, though he thinks this is overrated, and that 1,500 or 2,000 to each is enough. He is of opinion that the move will be on Southwest Georgia, and not on Carolina. I do not think it prudent to give the name in a dispatch; but I know the man is true and I have much confidence in his judgment."[21]

January 21, 1865 (Saturday)

Mary Jones, writing from Hart County, noted information she learned from a visitor living in Liberty County, who "Gave us various accounts of the enemy." Jones continued the account, "They encamped near his house; at one time on his premises over a thousand. They entered his dwelling day and night. They were forced to obtain a guard from the commander of the post...to protect his family. The house was repeatedly fired into under pretense of shooting rebels, although they knew that none but defenseless women and children were within."[22]

January 22, 1865 (Sunday)

Sherman, still in Savannah, wrote to his brother, Senator John Sherman. "I start today for the advance of my army at Pocataligo, but we have had such storms & rains that the whole country is under water, but I will be off as soon as possible. No one is more alive to the importance of time than I am." In closing, the Sherman reminded his brother of the officer's thoughts on new ranks in the army. "I wrote you that I deem it unwise to make another Lt. Genl. or to create the Rank of General. Let the Law Stand as now. I will accept no commission that would tend to create a rivalry with Grant."[23]

January 23, 1865 (Monday)

Major General Daniel Harvey Hill, in Augusta, requested additional matériel from Lieutenant General William Hardee. Hill indicated his need "of artillery officers, men, and harness, is very urgent. We have twelve 6-pounders, four 3-inch rifles, two 20 and two 10-pounder Parrotts, but no men or horses or harness. If you could send me a chief of artillery and some artillery officers I would try to extemporize three or four batteries and man them from the hospitals."[24]

January 24, 1865 (Tuesday)

Major General D. H. Hill sent a dispatch to Major General Wheeler concerning the safety of Augusta. "A telegram from Lieutenant-General Hardee placed the cavalry in this district

---

[20] Sherman, *Sherman's Civil War*, 801.

[21] *OR*, ser. I, vol. 47, pt. 2:1030.

[22] Myers, *Children of Pride*, 1247.

[23] Sherman, *Sherman's Civil War*, 808–809.

[24] *OR*, ser. I, vol. 47, pt. 2:1038.

temporarily under my command. This seems to me the only arrangement that can be made. If I am to be held responsible for the defense of Augusta, the troops directly defending it ought, of course, be under the responsible commander."[25]

January 25, 1865 (Wednesday)

Continuing to harbor deep resentment toward the Federal soldier, Fanny Andrews noted she had "no faith in Yankees of any sort, especially these miserable turncoats that are ready to sell themselves to either side. There isn't gold enough in existence to galvanize one of them into a respectable Confederate."[26]

January 26, 1865 (Thursday)

Entering the fourth year of the conflict, some folks still held hopes of Great Britain and France interceding on behalf of the Confederacy. "There has been a rumor going the rounds of the press for the past two weeks, that England and France propose to recognize the Confederate States immediately, if we will stipulate to emancipate our slaves within fifty years. We sincerely hope there may be some truth in the rumors."[27]

January 27, 1865 (Friday) ●

Quartermaster General Alexander Lawton reported on soldier uniform contributions from various states. Georgia, he stated, "has issued within the past year as follows: Twenty-six thousand seven hundred and forty-five jackets, 28,808 pair of pants, 37,657 pair of shoes, 7,504 blankets, 24,952 shirts, 24,168 pair of drawers, and 23,024 pair of socks...."[28]

January 28, 1865 (Saturday)

Visiting her sister, and preparing to celebrate a family birthday, Fanny Andrews, and party—which included Major General Samuel Jones—received surprise guests. Fanny watched as "a whole cavalcade of horses and government wagons came rattling up to the door, and the general and one of his aides helped two ladies and their children to alight from an ambulance in which they were traveling." Andrews and family welcomed their guests and prepared to feed and shelter them, along with additional arriving Confederate officers. "People are used to putting up with any sort of accommodations these times and they seemed very glad of shelter," Fanny recalled.[29]

January 29, 1865 (Sunday)

Sherman's forces continued moving into South Carolina, and Major General D. H. Hill, headquartered in Augusta, questioned the adeptness of his cavalry in response to the advancing Federals. He wrote to Major General Wheeler inquiring, "How is the enemy to be delayed by such operations? How are we to get information of his movements? I have known nothing in the war so remarkable as this movement. Surely it is the duty of the cavalry to delay and harass the enemy, and if this be not done the most serious disasters

---

[25] Ibid., 1042.

[26] Andrews, *War-Time Journal of a Georgia Girl*, 75.

[27] "Two Rumors of Recognition," *Albany Patriot*, January 26, 1865, sec. 2, https://gahistoricnewspapers.galileo.usg.edu/lccn/sn82014211/1865-01-26/ed-1/seq-2/.

[28] *OR*, ser. IV, vol. 3:1040.

[29] Andrews, *War-Time Journal of a Georgia Girl*, 79–80.

may and, in fact, must occur."[30]

January 30, 1865 (Monday)

Observing the movement of Federal forces away from Savannah, Major General Hill dispatched orders to Major General Carter Stevenson. "I think that there can be no doubt that Sherman is advancing in earnest and that the affair will be decided this week, I hope that you will keep your troops in motion and not wait transportation by rail. The railroad is entirely in the hands of Yankees and they delay every movement. More than half of the two advanced brigades have deserted. Can nothing be done to prevent it?"[31]

January 31, 1865 (Tuesday)

President Davis wrote to General Lee one day before Lee received notification of his promotion to general in chief. Davis updated Lee on military actions in various parts of the South; regarding Georgia, Davis stated, "I have not heard of Gen'l Beauregard's arrival in Georgia, but suppose he is now there, and hope he may be able to obtain a considerable auxiliary force through his influence over the Governor, and otherwise."[32]

February 1, 1865 (Wednesday)

Swirling rumors confused many; as Sherman's forces moved from Savannah into South Carolina, reports of Federal reinforcements prompted Brigadier General Iverson to dispatch Wheeler's adjutant: "Prisoners say that the Nineteenth Corps, commanded by Sheridan, is now in Savannah, and they say that Kilpatrick is on this side of the Savannah River. The enemy are still crossing the river, and not advancing on this side of the river. They charged and scattered my pickets day before yesterday."[33]

February 2, 1865 (Thursday) ◐

Continuing preparations for resisting Sherman's force advancing into South Carolina, Beauregard's adjutant, Colonel William Brent, notified the quartermaster's office of the general's orders. As "soon as the troops of the Army of Tennessee shall have passed, its transportation now en route to this point shall be placed on the cars and hurried forward." Beauregard dictated certain locations as collection points for subsistence, including, "at Washington, Ga., five days' rations for 10,000 men...and at Augusta, Ga., ten days' rations for 15,000 men. You will supply the necessary transportation for the supplies before mentioned to the points indicated."[34]

February 3, 1865 (Friday)

President Lincoln joined with Secretary of State William H. Seward in meeting three commissioners from the Confederate government. During the Hampton Roads Peace Conference, Lincoln and Seward met with Georgian and C.S.A. vice president Alexander Stephens, Senator Robert Hunter, and Assistant Secretary of War John A. Campbell onboard the steamer *River Queen*. Their discussions accomplished nothing as Lincoln held firm

---

[30] *OR*, ser. I, vol. 47, pt. 2, 1058.

[31] Ibid., 1062.

[32] J. Davis, *Papers*, 11:366.

[33] *OR*, ser. I, vol. 47, pt. 2, 1077.

[34] Ibid., 1082.

against the intention of Jefferson Davis's written instructions for the Southern trio, which read in part, "In conformity with the letter of Mr. Lincoln...you are to proceed to Washington City for informal conference with him upon the issues involved in the existing war, and for the purpose of securing peace to the two countries."[35] On this reference to "two countries," Lincoln could not consent.

February 4, 1865 (Saturday)

Nurse Cumming expressed her thought on the Hampton Roads Peace Conference and Vice President Stephens. "Lincoln has agreed to receive peace commissioners, and three of our ablest men...Stephens...Judge Campbell, and Senator Hunter, have gone on the mission. All seem much pleased with the selection which has been made in our commissioners. I hope Stephens is satisfied now that he has gone on the mission for which he has so long wished."[36]

February 5, 1865 (Sunday)

Wheeler and his troopers received orders from Beauregard, which detailed the expected actions of the cavalry officer. "Obey General Hardee's instructions, but should you find that the enemy intends moving in force on Columbia instead of Augusta, join your command to [Major General Wade] Hampton's to oppose his progress."[37]

February 6, 1865 (Monday)

General R. E. Lee officially assumed the position of general in chief, as Beauregard tried to determine which target of strategic significance Sherman's forces might strike. From his headquarters in Augusta, Beauregard clarified an earlier dispatch to Wheeler. "I informed you last night to follow instructions of General Hardee, looking, however, to support of Generals Hampton and Stevenson for defense of Columbia and crossings of Congaree. Columbia is more important than Augusta."[38]

February 7, 1865 (Tuesday)

In Georgia, the loss of vital rations proved telling, as Beauregard attempted to move soldiers toward North Carolina. "General Beauregard directs me by telegraph to instruct you to send the wagons by rail and the horses by land to Augusta. This is all-important." A.A.G. J.B. Eustis responded: "Telegram received. Wagons not yet arrived at this place. How are they to be shipped by rail to Augusta when there is a break of thirty-two miles?"[39]

February 8, 1865 (Wednesday)

Uncertain as to Sherman's intended targets, Colonel G. W. Rains and the crew at the Powder Works in Augusta faced a tremendous amount of work. Beauregard dispatched Rains, stating he deemed "it advisable that you commence at once the removal of your stores."[40]

February 9, 1865 (Thursday)

---

[35] *OR*, ser. I, vol. 46, pt. 2:512.

[36] Cumming, *Kate*, 254.

[37] *OR*, ser. I, vol. 47, pt. 2, 1103.

[38] Ibid., 1107.

[39] Ibid., 1112.

[40] Ibid., 1121.

Major General D. H. Hill, from his headquarters in Augusta, let his frustration seep into a dispatch to Wheeler. "It seems to me that a concentration of your cavalry upon Kilpatrick would crush him," he wrote. "I have sent an order to [Colonel Charles] Crews to unite with [Colonel James] Hagan, and probably something will then be done, as he seems to have a better command. I hope that you will keep us constantly apprised of movements. Is there any infantry moving upon Augusta? I have had no report from Hagan whatever."[41]

February 10, 1865 (Friday)

Major General James Steedman reported on skirmishing at Johnson's Crook, Georgia: "Col. Felix Prince Salm, Sixty-eighth New York Volunteers, surprised [probably William W.] Witherspoon's company, in Johnson's Crook, at 2 a. m. of the 10th instant. He killed 3, wounded 5, captured Captain [John B.] Countiss, Twenty-first Georgia Regiment, and 15 men, amongst them Witherspoon's brother; 30 stand of arms, and 23 horses. Colonel Salm returned to camp without the loss of a man."[42]

February 11, 1865 (Saturday)

Major General Wheeler and his troopers scouted the Federal troops advancing into South Carolina. Major General Frank Cheatham, writing from Augusta, notified Wheeler of reinforcements coming to the cavalry officer. "I have a force of about 3,000 men, including the Georgia militia. They are located on this side of Big Horse Creek to defend the crossing. I will send [Brigadier] General J.A. Smith, with Cleburne's division, about 1,000 men, to Graniteville to assist you in protecting that place. I will be on the road from Augusta to Graniteville."[43]

February 12, 1865 (Sunday)

Major General Hill, in Augusta, made final preparations for sending Cheatham's command into South Carolina; a refitting remained. To Cheatham: "I have ordered [Alfred] Iverson to send up his Enfields by 2 o'clock train. If you have an ordnance officer here at that hour, you can get them."[44]

February 13, 1865 (Monday)

Major General Cheatham received orders to advance his "corps at once to Columbia, S.C. The troops should be supplied, and carry with them, five days' cooked rations."[45]

February 14, 1865 (Tuesday) (Valentine's Day)

Colonel William Brent, Beauregard's adjutant, worked in Augusta to gather additional armaments for troops heading to South Carolina. "These headquarters having been informed that there are several local companies in this city armed with Enfield rifles, General Beauregard desires that you will cause their arms to be collected by Captain Finney and turned over to Cheatham's corps"; message delivered to Brigadier General Birkett Fry.[46]

---

[41] Ibid., 1136.

[42] *OR*, ser. I, vol. 49, pt. 1:39.

[43] *OR*, ser. I, vol. 47, pt. 2:1163.

[44] Ibid., 1170–71.

[45] Ibid., 1174.

[46] Ibid., 1184.

February 15, 1865 (Wednesday)
Governor Brown's message to the legislature recapped the various setbacks over the winter 1864–1865. "The army of invasion, led by a bold and skillful General, have passed through our State, laid waste our fields, burned many dwelling houses, destroyed county records, applied the torch to gin houses, cotton and other property, occupied and desecrated the capitol, and now hold the city of Savannah…."[47]

February 16, 1865 (Thursday)
Major General D. H. Hill, with headquarters in Augusta, informed Major General Edward Walthall of the possibility of interruption in moving his force forward. "I am sorry that the wagons were not sent out as ordered last night. This may delay your movement until to-morrow, and then your march so far in rear of Cheatham will be hazardous. You ought to get as near him as possible. General Young, with a strong cavalry force, is ordered to cover your movement."[48]

February 17, 1865 (Friday)
Confederate Secretary of War John C. Breckinridge notified Beauregard of issues concerning Georgia and the railroads. "Two trains belonging to the State of Georgia have been impressed to remove stores from Charleston. Georgia has cotton on the road. Return the trains to her agent unless they are employed for the removal of troops, ordnance, or other Confederate property of more importance than cotton, and return them as early as practicable in any event."[49]

February 18, 1865 (Saturday) ◐
The day following the burning of Columbia, South Carolina, Confederate officials in Augusta struggled with a different problem. "There are large numbers of officers and men in this city absent from their commands. They excuse themselves by saying they do not know where their commands are, and when informed, reply they cannot walk there. A camp of direction should be established at some suitable point for the concentration of these absentees, and there kept until they be sent to their proper commands. All such should be kept out of the city."[50]

February 19, 1865 (Sunday)
Predicting the termination of war, a newspaper article suggested the conflict "will be ended, as most rebellions are ended, *by internal disruption and collapse*. It will leave no treaty in history—no treaty in which the name of 'Jefferson Davis' and 'Abraham Lincoln' will appear as arbitrators of peace."[51]

February 20, 1865 (Monday)

---

[47] Ibid., 818.

[48] Ibid., 1206–207.

[49] Ibid., 1207.

[50] Ibid., 1218.

[51] "How the Rebellion Will End," *Columbus Daily Sun*, February 19, 1865, sec. 2, https://gahistoricnewspapers.galileo.usg.edu/lccn/sn82014939/1865-02-19/ed-1/seq-2/. Italics in original. The newspaper carried a reprint from the *New York Times*.

Beauregard ordered an engineer officer, Captain Andrew H. Buchanan, to "proceed at once to the point on the Savannah River, via Washington, Ga., where the road from Washington to Abbeville, S.C., crosses. A pontoon bridge has been ordered to be constructed at that or some eligible point near by. You will confer with the engineer in charge of the work and give him such aid as you can."[52]

February 21, 1865 (Tuesday)

The General Assembly, meeting in Macon, passed a resolution honoring "Major General G. W. Smith and the officers and men composing the first Division of Georgia militia, and to the officers and men of the Georgia State Line, for their conspicuous gallantry at Griswoldville, in this State, and especially for their unselfish patriotism, in leaving their State, and meeting the enemy in the memorable and well fought battle field at Honey Hill, in South Carolina."[53]

February 22, 1865 (Wednesday)

Writing from Albany, Fanny Andrews, tired of war-torn conditions on the home front, held hope for better days ahead. "Now that the Yanks have passed by Augusta and are making their way to Columbia and Charleston, I hope they will give Georgia a rest."[54]

February 23, 1865 (Thursday)

The Georgia General Assembly, offering "the assurances of Georgia to her sister States," discussed several resolutions, which indicated the desire to continue the fight. As a reminder to the other Confederate States, the Assembly pronounced, "If, however, we shall fail, we will have the proud satisfaction of knowing that we have exhausted the argument, and the people of the State of Georgia will stand united as one man prepared to win by our arms the just measures of our rights, or fill patriots' graves."[55]

February 24, 1865 (Friday)

Pausing to remember the soldier sacrifices over the past four years, the General Assembly introduced a special resolution, one offering: "our profoundest gratitude…to our soldiers who on many a bloody battle-field have illustrated their State by deeds of heroic valor, and that while we look to them with pride and confidence we will see that their efforts are generously sustained and that the amplest resources of the State are applied for the support and comfort of their families at home."[56]

February 25, 1865 (Saturday) ●

At the request of General Lee, General Johnston took to the field once again. Johnston issued General Orders No. 1, which stated he assumed "command of the Army of Tennessee and all troops in the Department of South Carolina, Georgia, and Florida." Trying to rally as many men as possible to slow Sherman's advance, the general encouraged "all absent soldiers of the Army of Tennessee to rejoin their regiments and again confront the enemy

---

[52] *OR*, ser. I, vol. 47, pt. 2:1229–30.

[53] *Journal of the Senate at an Extra Session…February 15th, 1865*, February 21, 1865, 36.

[54] Andrews, *War-Time Journal of a Georgia Girl*, 100.

[55] *Journal of the Senate at an Extra Session…February 15th, 1865*, February 23, 1865, 52.

[56] Ibid., February 24, 1865, 58.

they so often encountered in Northern Georgia, and always with honor."[57]

February 26, 1865 (Sunday)

As the war entered its fourth year, Sam Richards, in Atlanta, observed, "Continued success appears to attend the Yankee arms, for Charleston, Columbia and Wilmington have all been given up to them and Sherman seems to march whenever he pleases without let or hindrance. I should like very much to hear how our folks in Dixie are getting on."[58]

February 27, 1865 (Monday)

Skirmishing occurred near Spring Place, while the *Savannah Daily Herald*, operating under Northern control, reported on new burial procedures for Federal soldiers. "A thoroughly excellent plan to secure the perfect identification of the remains of our soldiers who are buried in Southern cemeteries, and other Southern lands, and are, in most cases, interred hastily, in accordance with the urgent necessities of war, has been lately recommended by the War Department and has been adopted with the most satisfactory results in the Department of Savannah."[59] The plan included placing a card containing information on the deceased inside a sealed bottle and placing it inside the coffin.

February 28, 1865 (Tuesday)

Although many across the South had surrendered notions of a successful end to the war, a call to remain fervent went out to Georgians in the *Columbus Times*: "Let the Confederacy and the United States and the world see that Georgia is not whipped and will not be whipped; but that with indomitable will and persistency, she intends to carry on this war until her rights as a land of freemen are obtained, and until the banner of her country floats gloriously and triumphantly over the heights of Independence."[60]

March 1, 1865 (Wednesday)

Citizens in Columbus managed to escape Sherman's force as they marched from Atlanta to Savannah, but activity on the home front remained busy. "Ladies in the country and city, are most respectfully invited to send their worn out cotton apparel and sheets to the Wayside Home. One hundred wounded arriving per week, require RAGS, RAGS, RAGS." Skirmishing reported at Holly Creek.[61]

March 2, 1865 (Thursday)

Meeting in Macon, the Georgia General Assembly passed an act because of Sherman's capture of Savannah. "Be it enacted...That the removal of the assets, books and effects of said

---

[57] *OR*, ser. I, vol. 47, pt. 2, 274.

[58] Richards, *Civil War Diary*, 262–63.

[59] "Burial of Union Soldiers," *Savannah Daily Herald*, February 27, 1865, sec. 2, https://gahistoricnewspapers.galileo.usg.edu/lccn/sn82014389/1865-02-27/ed-1/seq-2/; skirmish information from Mosocco, *Chronological Tracking*, 309.

[60] "Georgia's Position," *Columbus Times*, February 28, 1865, https://gahistoricnewspapers.galileo.usg.edu/lccn/sn86053047/1865-02-28/ed-1/seq-2/.

[61] "Remember the Wounded Soldier!," *Columbus Daily Sun*, March 1, 1865, https://gahistoricnewspapers.galileo.usg.edu/lccn/sn82014939/1865-03-01/ed-1/seq-2/; Holly Creek skirmish found in Mosocco, *Chronological Tracking*, 309.

[Central Railroad and Banking] Company, from Savannah to Macon, is hereby sanctioned and made lawful; and that the principal office of the said Company shall hereafter, and as long as Savannah is occupied by the enemy, be at the aforesaid city of Macon."[62]

March 3, 1865 (Friday)

Confederate cavalry skirmished with Federals near Tunnel Hill. Captain John P. Cravens with the 145th Indiana Infantry reported on the action. "I was out repairing the [telegraph] wire with a small squad…and was attacked by McDonald with double my force. He captured four of my men." Cravens also included a note he received from one of the Confederates, which stated, "I am in command of a detachment, by order of General Wheeler, C. S. Army. I am not a guerrilla, as you suppose. I now beseech you to recognize my paroles. If not, the crime of inhumanity be on your own head and not on mine. A. McDonald."[63]

March 4, 1865 (Saturday) ◐

In Macon, the General Assembly passed an act stating, "it shall not be lawful for the Mayor and Council of the city of Marietta in said State, to levy and collect a tax on the citizens and tax-payers of said city, exceeding one-fortieth of one per cent., and this Act shall continue and be inforce only for and during the present war."[64]

March 5, 1865 (Sunday)

The hardship of war and the ever-increasing inflation in the Confederacy produced hardships for civilians on the home front and local businesses. Passenger traffic on the Chattahoochee River did not escape rising fares. "Passage from Columbus to Chattahoochee $75, From Chattahoochee to Columbus $100. Freights to any point on Chattahoochee River $4 per hundred [pounds]."[65]

March 6, 1865 (Monday)

Louisa Warren Fletcher of Cobb County wrote of the hardships of war. "It is painful in the extreme to know that so many around us are suffering for food & clothing & we cannot help them without giving what we really need for ourselves O! this desolating war! when will it end! May God in mercy grant relief to the suffering poor!"[66]

March 7, 1865 (Tuesday)

The Georgia General Assembly began the day's session with the introduction of a resolution, "That the committee on Confederate relations be instructed to report back to the Senate the resolution in regard to the question of enlisting slaves in the armies of the

---

[62] "An Act to Amend an Act of the 14th of December…," no. 22 in *Acts of the General Assembly of the State of Georgia…November, 1864*, March 2, 1865, 46.

[63] *OR*, ser. I, vol. 49, pt. 1:74. Full identification of McDonald unknown.

[64] "An Act to Limit the Tax to Be Imposed upon the Citizens and Taxpayers…," no. 82 in *Acts of the General Assembly of the State of Georgia…November 1864*, March 4, 1865, 82.

[65] "Special Notices," *Columbus Times*, March 5, 1865, sec. 1, https://gahistoricnewspapers.galileo.usg.edu/lccn/sn86053047/1865-03-05/ed-1/seq-1/.

[66] Fletcher, *Journal of a Landlady*, 158.

Confederate States."[67]

March 8, 1865 (Wednesday)

Thoughts of the widows and orphans the war produced occupied the minds of the various General Assembly members, and they "took up the report of the committee upon the bill to be entitled an act to make an appropriation of two millions of dollars, in addition to the appropriation already made for the support of indigent families of Soldiers, who are in the public service, and for the support of indigent soldiers who have been or may be hereafter disabled by wounds or disease in the Confederate or State service, for the year 1865, and for other purposes."[68]

March 9, 1865 (Thursday)

Governor Brown wrote to the Georgia General Assembly, encouraging them to revoke the Conscript Act and "let us return to the principles upon which we entered the contest…let the whole country…rally around our glorious leaders, Lee, Johnston and Beauregard, who should be untrammeled by Presidential interference in the management of military campaigns, and we shall again triumph in battle and roll back the dark cloud of despondency which has so long darkened our horizon and blighted our hopes."[69]

March 10, 1865 (Friday)

Citizens across the South observed one of the Days of Fasting, which President Jefferson Davis declared as a time to pray and meditate for better days ahead. Perhaps embracing the special day even more deeply, Fanny Andrews reflected on a different concern—there was little fasting or prayer "done at Gopher Hill. A tornado passed over the Flat Pond plantation yesterday, destroying every house on it and killing fifteen negroes; a schoolhouse was blown down and several children killed…all the poultry was drowned, and two calves blown away and never came down again! So much for marvels."[70]

March 11, 1865 (Saturday)

The sound of battle struck Natural Bridge, outside Tallahassee, Florida, on March 6. Five days later, Fanny Andrews remained in the dark as to the outcome of the skirmish. She wrote, "Communication between here and Washington is so interrupted that I don't suppose they have heard yet of the reported raid into Florida…. The latest news is that the Yankees have whipped our forces at Tallahassee, but the waters are so high and communication so uncertain that one never knows what to believe. At any rate, I shall not run till I hear that the enemy are at Thomasville."[71]

March 12, 1865 (Sunday)

Sam Richards, in one diary entry, exhibited both a passion for religion and his lack of regard for humankind when he wrote, "This morning we went to Dr Westons church, and were

---

[67] *Journal of the Senate of the Extra Session of the General Assembly…February 15th, 1865*, March 7, 1865, 119.

[68] Ibid., March 8, 1865, 131.

[69] Candler, *Confederate Records of the State of Georgia*, 2:869–70.

[70] Andrews, *War-Time Journal of a Georgia Girl*, 114.

[71] Ibid., 116; Natural Bridge skirmish information in Mosocco, *Chronological Tracking*, 311.

not so well pleased as at previous attendance, for he introduced an illustration in the course of his sermon which too plainly showed his war and nigger sentiments. Tonight Mr and Mrs West came in and we had a grand concert of Sacred Music!"[72]

March 13, 1865 (Monday)

Skirmishing played out near Dalton, and Colonel Hiram Sickles with the 147th Illinois Infantry filed the post-action report. "About 4 this p.m. the guerrillas captured five railroad hands one mile from my line on Cleveland road. I mounted all the mules and horses I had, and sent them after the guerrillas. Killed 2 of the cusses, captured 1. I am sorry they did not kill him also. What shall I do with him?"[73]

March 14, 1865 (Tuesday)

Colonel Sickles remained busy near Dalton; his troops netted a surprise. "I sent out a small detachment under Major [Giles] Bush, One hundred and forty-seventh Illinois. He met seventy mounted rebels. Had a fight with them, killing and wounding several. Captured one prisoner from Lee's rebel army, Virginia. We had but one man wounded slightly. Will send the prisoner up first train."[74] One can surmise the soldier, if indeed from the Army of Northern Virginia, numbered among the increasing number of absconders in 1865.

March 15, 1865 (Wednesday)

A newspaper article offered thoughts on abolition: "The proposition to abolish slavery now, we look upon as a base surrender—the most abject *submission* to the enemy! Whatever were the *real* causes of the war, the country was assured at the outset that the object was to prevent the abolition of slavery by the Lincoln party. If we abolish it now, have we not yielded all that our leaders in 1860–'61 said they demanded?" On this same day, members of the 49th Georgia Infantry, stationed in Virginia, wrote to General R. E. Lee endorsing the arming of African Americans. The officers of the regiment requested, "That the negroes in these counties of Georgia, from which our companies hail from, be conscribed, in such numbers and under such regulations as the War Department may deem proper." The 49th contained soldiers from Irwin, Laurens, Pierce, and Pulaski, Telfair, Washington, and Wilkinson counties.[75]

March 16, 1865 (Thursday)

With the war approaching the end, most Southerners faced a gloomy horizon. Fanny Andrews did too; dreary weather merely added to the misery of the day. She lamented, "Rain, rain, rain, nothing but rain! The river is out of its banks again and all that part of the plantation overflowed. We are completely water-bound; nobody can come to us and we can go nowhere. We have not even the mail to relieve the monotony of life...."[76]

---

[72] Richards, *Civil War Diary*, 264.

[73] *OR*, ser. I, vol. 49, pt. 1:86.

[74] Ibid.

[75] "Abolition," *Athens Southern Watchman*, March 15, 1865, sec. 3, https://gahistoricnewspapers.galileo.usg.edu/lccn/sn82014669/1865-03-15/ed-1/seq-3/; Avery, *History of the State of Georgia*, 298.

[76] Andrews, *War-Time Journal of a Georgia Girl*, 117.

March 17, 1865 (Friday) (St. Patrick's Day)
A Columbus newspaper reported on destruction in Effingham County. "We are informed that the Yankee army has twice visited that section and as a consequence there is hardly anything left for subsistence of the population. In the neighborhood of Sisters Ferry the destitution is greatest."[77]

March 18, 1865 (Saturday)
Citizens of Columbus learned, from an editorial, people in the North subscribed to a notion the Confederacy stood on the precipice of disunion. "A portion of the Yankee press and people are evidently under the impression that the South is divided against herself; that, consequently, the 'rebellion' will be *felo de se* [suicidal] in a few months more, and that thus will end our boasted struggle for constitutional government."[78]

March 19, 1865 (Sunday)
A report from a commissary store in Atlanta shed light on the hardships of people left in the wake of war. The store "is almost constantly thronged with women and children begging for bread. They do not ask for meat, but are satisfied with bread alone. During the late freezing weather, females walked as far as sixteen miles in the mud and ice, for the purpose of getting meal, which they would carry home upon their shoulders."[79]

March 20, 1865 (Monday) ◑
Skirmishing near Ringgold prompted Brigadier General Henry Judah to send "five companies" of the 151st Illinois Infantry as reinforcements to Captain Achilles Chiniquy, who had dispatched Judah: "My pickets have been attacked. Guerrillas have withdrawn; expect an attack before daylight in morning. Send re-enforcements if convenient."[80]

March 21, 1865 (Tuesday)
Reporting on the number of newspaper employees exempt from conscription, a Columbus editor listed, for Georgia "Editors 12, Employees 136." The eight states contained in the report represented a total of "123 editors…672 employees."[81]

March 22, 1865 (Wednesday)
Major General James Wilson embarked upon the largest raid of the war (13,480 troopers) that terminated in Georgia. Meanwhile, President Davis wrote of his expectations for north Georgia. "I have some hope that General William Wofford will collect absentees and get recruits in Northern Georgia sufficient to constitute a force which might be effective in

---

[77] "Georgia Items," *Columbus Daily Sun*, March 17, 1865, sec. 1, https://gahistoricnewspapers.galileo.usg.edu/lccn/sn82014939/1865-03-17/ed-1/seq-1/.

[78] "Thursday Morning March 18, 1865," *Columbus Daily Sun*, March 18, 1865, sec. 2, https://gahistoricnewspapers.galileo.usg.edu/lccn/sn82014939/1865-03-18/ed-1/seq-2/. Italics in original.

[79] "Distress in Atlanta," *Columbus Daily Sun*, March 19, 1865, sec. 1, https://gahistoricnewspapers.galileo.usg.edu/lccn/sn82014939/1865-03-19/ed-1/seq-1/.

[80] *OR*, ser. I, vol. 49, pt. 1:322.

[81] "Newspaper Exempts," *Columbus Daily Sun*, March 21, 1865, sec. 1, https://gahistoricnewspapers.galileo.usg.edu/lccn/sn82014939/1865-03-21/ed-1/seq-1/.

operating on the enemy's communications through Chattanooga. General Cobb, I fear, will be able to do but little to increase the force alluded to as that which might be in hand under General Wofford...."[82]

March 23, 1865 (Thursday)

An editorial in the *Columbus Times* stated, "We are glad to learn that the absentees are coming back with great cheerfulness, as well as alacrity, and are happy at the opportunity of throwing off the terrible penalties of the law which were suspended over them, and of coming forward to perform their duties and renew their vows of devotion to their country." Unbeknownst to folks in the city, soon they would need all the troops they could muster.[83]

March 24, 1865 (Friday)

After the failed Confederate effort at Franklin and Nashville in late 1864, the remaining soldiers of the Army of Tennessee made their way eastward to join with General Johnston in North Carolina. One Georgia newspaper proudly reported that "Numbers of soldiers pass through here daily to join their commands." The editor noticed, "We have yet to see a desponding soldier, we mean a real not a 'play' vetrean [*sic*]. Let the people infuse this cheerful spirit...and all will soon be well. Have no sickening refrain of 'when this cruel war is over' but let every voice send up the stirring words of to arms! to arms!"[84]

March 25, 1865 (Saturday)

The *Daily Sun* carried a story, which the editor believed served "as a noble example worthy of the emulation of every Confederate State." The story referenced "General [Ira] Foster, the efficient Quartermaster General of the great and generous State of Georgia, has reached Richmond. He brought...10,000 suits of clothing for the Georgians in Lee's army—a most timely and acceptable present. This clothing is a gift from Georgia to her sons in the field."[85]

March 26, 1865 (Sunday)

Citizens in Columbus read a patriotic message from a newspaper editor, a man who continued to harbor hopes for a Southern victory. "Thank God! we are satisfied that Georgians will press forward and onward from generation to generation, until our religious and political equality, and the rights and sovereignty and independence of the Confederate States of America are established and acknowledged."[86]

March 27, 1865 (Monday) ●

Brigadier General Wirt Adams prepared to leave Macon; a cavalry commander needed

---

[82] *OR*, ser. I, vol. 49, pt. 2:1140; Wilson's troop count from *OR*, ser. I, vol. 49, pt. 1:404.

[83] "The Army—A Cheering Estimate," *Columbus Times*, March 23, 1865, sec. 1, https://gahistoricnewspapers.galileo.usg.edu/lccn/sn86053047/1865-03-23/ed-1/seq-1/.

[84] "Returning Soldiers," *Columbus Daily Sun*, March 24, 1865, sec. 1, https://gahistoricnewspapers.galileo.usg.edu/lccn/sn82014939/1865-03-24/ed-1/seq-1/.

[85] "Georgia," *Columbus Daily Sun*, March 25, 1865, sec. 2, https://gahistoricnewspapers.galileo.usg.edu/lccn/sn82014939/1865-03-25/ed-1/seq-2/.

[86] "The Legislature," *Columbus Times*, March 26, 1865, sec. 1, https://gahistoricnewspapers.galileo.usg.edu/lccn/sn86053047/1865-03-26/ed-1/seq-1/.

reinforcements in Alabama. "The application for transportation hence to West Point was based upon an order of Lieutenant-General [Nathan Bedford] Forrest, to send forward my command immediately and come on by the first railroad train myself. I take some members of my staff with me for the purpose of arranging for encampment, &c., before the arrival of my command."[87]

March 28, 1865 (Tuesday)

Columbus did not have visitors in blue yet, but a problem of a different type worried locals. "Our city is infested by a gang of robbers and houseburners, who ought to be ferreted out, and made to know there is yet some law in the land. Every man should be on the alert to arrest the scoundrels, and when caught, signal examples should be made."[88]

March 29, 1865 (Wednesday)

Tired of the suffering and shortages, a weakened Gertrude Thomas wept sadness into her diary. "At times I feel as if I was drifting on, on, ever onward to be at last dashed against some rock and I shut my eyes and almost wish it was over, the shock encountered and I prepared to know what destiny awaits me. I am tired, oh so tired of this war. I want to breathe free."[89]

March 30, 1865 (Thursday)

Increasingly, the blockade totally depleted most Southern stockpiles of common goods, yet commerce continued, albeit in an ad hoc manner. "A considerable traffic is carried on through the picket lines in the vicinity of Savannah. Cotton and tobacco, and perhaps provisions, are being carried in an and exchanged for articles of foreign growth and manufacture."[90]

March 31, 1865 (Friday)

Sam Richards, along with many other folks in Georgia, suffered the lasting effects of the military campaigns of 1864. "Our Monthly Expenditures seem to average about $75 now, on Rent & Provisions about $6o and the balance more or less for Furniture, Clothing &c, not including of course the outlay in first setting up our establishment. I do not suppose there are many people who live on as small a sum as that, who pretend to live in any comfort."[91]

April 1, 1865 (Saturday) (April Fools' Day)

Federal troops, under the command of Brigadier General Henry Judah, departed Dalton on a scouting mission toward Spring Place.[92]

April 2, 1865 (Sunday)

---

[87] *OR*, ser. I, vol. 49, pt. 2:1165.

[88] "Every Citizen to His Duty," *Columbus Daily Sun*, March 28, 1865, sec. 2, https://gahistoricnewspapers.galileo.usg.edu/lccn/sn82014939/1865-03-28/ed-1/seq-2/.

[89] Thomas, *Secret Eye*, 257.

[90] "From Augusta," *Columbus Daily Sun*, March 30, 1865, sec. 2, https://gahistoricnewspapers.galileo.usg.edu/lccn/sn82014939/1865-03-30/ed-1/seq-2/.

[91] Richards, *Civil War Diary*, 267.

[92] Mosocco, *Chronological Tracking*, 318.

Fanny Andrews spent another Sabbath day despairing of the hardships of war. "I went to church at Mt. Ėnon. After service we stopped to tell everybody good-by, and I could hardly help crying, for we are to leave sure enough on Tuesday, and there is no telling what may happen before we come back; the Yankees may have put an end to our glorious old plantation life forever."[93]

April 3, 1865 (Monday) ◐

In Atlanta, Sam Richards received startling information. "The news of the evacuation of Richmond and Petersburg came yesterday but we did not hear it until today. Things look very dark and hopeless for our people truly, and humanly considered, there seems no chance of success; and yet can not believe that the unjust and bloody programme of the North will be permitted to be carryed [*sic*] out to completion by a righteous God."

Colonel Werner W. Bjerd with the 147th Illinois Infantry reported skirmishing as part of the expedition, which left Dalton on April 1. Bjerd reported his command was "attacked all afternoon by the whole gang of guerillas…forces under Major [Tom Polk] Edmonson…. They made several charges upon us, but were driven back each time. In one of the charges Major E., who was in command of the gang, was killed."[94]

April 4, 1865 (Tuesday)

Visiting family in Cuthbert, Fanny Andrews described the beauty of the area between "Macon and Thomasville" and saw a train with "1,100 Yankee prisoners"; she then arrived in Cuthbert. "The village seems to be very gay," she wrote. "We found an invitation awaiting us for to-morrow night and the gentlemen in the house proposed a theater-party for this evening, to see the amateurs, but it is Lent, and I am trying to do better in the way of refraining from worldly amusements and mortifying the flesh, than I did in Montgomery last spring, so we spent the evening at home."[95]

April 5, 1865 (Wednesday)

Major General James Wilson's force took Selma on April 2; Fanny Andrews lamented the incident. "A report has come that the Yankees have taken Selma, and a raid is advancing towards Eufaula, so that puts a stop to our Chunnennuggee trip. I can't say that I am disappointed, for I don't want to turn my face from home any more…."[96]

April 6, 1865 (Thursday)

Looking toward a possibility of the war ending in Confederate defeat, an editorial provided an uninviting outlook. "Perhaps at no time since the war began, has the North been more hopeful of speedy success, or more determined in the purpose to prosecute the same until the Southern States submit to the National authority of the United States. We gather this from statements of returned prisoners, from the Northern journals, and from the increased activity of the Federal armies."[97]

---

[93] Andrews, *War-Time Journal of a Georgia Girl*, 127.

[94] Richards, *Civil War Diary*, 268; *OR*, vol. 49, pt. 1:509.

[95] Andrews, *War-Time Journal of a Georgia Girl*, 131–33.

[96] Ibid., 134.

[97] "Thursday Morning, April 6, 1865," *Columbus Daily Sun*, April 6, 1865, sec. 2, https://gahistoricnewspapers.galileo.usg.edu/lccn/sn82014939/1865-04-06/ed-1/seq-2/.

April 7, 1865 (Friday)

Major General Sam Jones, head of the Military Department of South Carolina, Georgia, and Florida, received a message from Governor Brown. "I agree with you fully in opinion on the blockade question, and inform you in this confidential manner that the cotton is to be carried down by the State on her steamers and sold to persons who have authority from the United States Government to purchase, and sell us in exchange necessaries which we cannot do without. It is also the policy in this way to accumulate some funds abroad to pay for soldiers' clothing, &c."[98]

April 8, 1865 (Saturday)

"We doubt if ever the city of Savannah experienced a more profound sensation than...when its attention was called to the...fall of Richmond. Though the occupation of this city by the federals, has for months, been a 'foregone conclusion,' the positive announcement of its fall gave to the hearts of every one, however well prepared by the late intelligence from our armies, a shock—agreeable to some, distasteful to others, but startling all."[99]

April 9, 1865 (Palm Sunday)

While General Lee prepared to meet Lieutenant General Grant in Appomattox, Sam Richards and family attended worship service in Atlanta. The Richards family did not particularly enjoy the sermon. The reverend espoused "the leaders of the rebellion should not be touched in person or liberty, but that their pride of caste should be humbled and their power to do harm taken away by confiscating their estates and disfranchising them."[100]

April 10, 1865 (Monday)

Sam Richards started his day with depressing news. "The first thing that met my eye this morning in looking over the 'News' was this startling heading: 'Surrender of Gen. Rob. E. Lee and all his army!' So now there seems to be nothing more for the South to do but make the best terms they can and give up the unequal contest, begun in too much haste and fought with such dreadful loss for four long years." Richards closed with thoughts of defeat. "It grieves me to think of what the South has suffered and lost, for what?"[101]

April 11, 1865 (Tuesday)

Fanny Andrews spent the morning with Mary Joyner in Cuthbert. "Almost every mail brings her [Mary] grateful letters from the soldiers she has nursed, or from the wives and sweethearts of those who will never need her services again. I love to hear her tell about her experiences in the Atlanta hospitals during the siege. Some of them are very funny, but more of them are sad. She was called 'the hospital angel' in Atlanta, and well deserved the name."[102]

---

[98] Candler, *Confederate Records of the State of Georgia*, 3:711.

[99] "Reception of the News in Savannah," *Savannah Daily Herald*, April 8, 1865, sec. 2, https://gahistoricnewspapers.galileo.usg.edu/lccn/sn82014389/1865-04-08/ed-1/seq-2/.

[100] Richards, *Civil War Diary*, 269–70.

[101] Ibid., 270.

[102] Andrews, *War-Time Journal of a Georgia Girl*, 141.

April 12, 1865 (Wednesday)
A report on conditions at Camp Sumter came from Early County: "The number of Yankee prisoners now confined at Andersonville is about five thousand. They are well provided for in every way, except with clothing and shoes. An old field near by has been appropriated for burial purposes. Here, over seventeen thousand Yankees [around 13,000 died] have found their resting place."[103]

April 13, 1865 (Thursday)
Amid declining spirits across the state, Governor Brown continued with his duties, issuing a certificate for the procurement of corn. "D. G. Hughes, having given bond and security, payable to the Governor of the State, for the faithful disbursement of whatever moneys may be placed in his hands to buy corn...and to purchase meat and other stores for the Commissary Department of this State, to be delivered at such times during the year as the same may be called for...is hereby appointed agent of the State."[104]

April 14, 1865 (Good Friday)
Good Friday turned bad in the evening, when John Wilkes Booth assassinated President Lincoln in Washington's Ford's Theater. In Georgia, seemingly a million miles away from the horror awaiting the nation, Nurse Cumming observed the Christian holy day. "A gloomy day. I went to church in the morning, and listened to one of the finest sermons I ever heard. The text was 'and the people stood beholding.' The vocal music was excellent; the voices were very sweet, and the contralto is one of the finest I ever listened to."[105]

April 15, 1865 (Saturday)
Major General Wilson's troopers neared Columbus, and Governor Brown ordered Major General G. W. Smith to redeploy his force to the threatened spot on the Chattahoochee River. "You are...hereby directed to order out the militia of the State...to rendezvous at Columbus, as fast as possible. All who are subject to your command under your former orders from these headquarters are embraced in this call, and all subject to militia duty under fifty years of age who fail to respond will be turned over to Confederate service."[106]

April 16, 1865 (Easter Sunday)
The Battle of Columbus and an engagement at Fort Tyler; a few of the final military engagements of the war played out in Georgia. Initially skirmishing on the Girard [present day Phenix City] Alabama, side of the Chattahoochee River, Major General Wilson noted his success. "Late in the afternoon, Upton arrived...made reconnaissances, put his troops in position, and at 8.30 p. m., with 300 dismounted men from the Third Iowa, attacked the rebel works...carried them in fine style, and with a part of the Tenth Missouri pushed the retreating rebels so closely as to save the bridges across the river; captured 1,200

---

[103] "Wednesday, April 12, 1865," *Early County News* (Blakely), April 12, 1865, sec. 2, https://gahistoricnewspapers.galileo.usg.edu/lccn/sn85034007/1865-04-12/ed-1/seq-2/.

[104] Candler, *Confederate Records of the State of Georgia*, 2:876.

[105] Cumming, *Kate*, 269.

[106] Candler, *Confederate Records of the State of Georgia*, 3:712.

prisoners, 52 field guns in position."[107]

While the fighting continued in Columbus, Colonel Oscar La Grange's cavalry captured Fort Tyler near West Point, Georgia. La Grange dispatched of his success. "We have just taken Fort Tyler by assault, capturing garrison (200 men) and armament. My command is now crossing the river on the wagon bridge. The resistance was stubborn and our loss severe. The rebel General [Brigadier General Robert] Tyler was killed. We have destroyed the railroad to this point and captured 13 engines and 150 cars, with a considerable quantity of corn and other stores."[108]

April 17, 1865 (Monday)

Wilson's troopers wreaked havoc on Columbus, destroying everything of military value. In his report, Wilson declared his cavalrymen had "destroyed the iron-clad ram *Jackson*, mounting six 7-inch rifles nearly ready for sea; burned the navy-yard, arsenal, foundry, armory, sword and pistol factory, accouterment shops, paper-mills, four cotton factories, all the bridges on the river, 15 locomotives, and 200 cars, beside 100,000 bales of cotton and an immense quantity of artillery ammunition."[109]

April 18, 1865 (Tuesday) ◐

Lead elements of Wilson's force skirmished near Double Bridges; Captain William Van Antwerp filed this post-action report. "We captured the bridges this morning at 7 o'clock and with them thirty-four prisoners. There was a detachment of forty-five men left on picket at the bridges for the purpose of burning them upon our approach, but we came upon them suddenly, and Captain Charles T. Hudson with one battalion of the Fourth Michigan charged them gallantly over and four miles beyond the bridges, capturing besides the prisoners 1 wagon and 1 caisson." The officer noted, "Had our animals been in condition for pursuit I have no doubt we could have captured many more prisoners, as I learn the road is full of stragglers. I have the bridges well guarded, and will hold them until Colonel [Robert] Minty's arrival. Will also have the factories burned."[110] Fighting also occurred along the Flint River, at Pleasant Hill, and near Barnesville.

April 19, 1865 (Wednesday)

Major General Wilson, in presenting "twenty-four stand of colors, captured from the enemy," listed among the lot, the "Flag of Dixie Rangers captured by detachment Fourth Indiana Cavalry in skirmish near Barnesville, Ga., 19th April, 1865."[111]

April 20, 1865 (Thursday)

Macon fell to Federal forces. Major General Wilson sent news of the event to Major General Sherman. "My advance received the surrender of this city this evening. General [Howell] Cobb had previously sent me under a flag of truce a copy of a telegram from General

---

[107] *OR*, ser. I, vol. 49, pt. 1:352.

[108] *OR*, ser. I, vol. 49, pt. 2:367.

[109] *OR*, ser. I, vol. 49, pt. 1:352.

[110] *OR*, ser. I, vol. 49, pt. 2:394; skirmish information in Mosocco, *Chronological Tracking*, 324.

[111] *OR*, ser. I, vol. 49, pt. 1:398–99.

Beauregard declaring the existence of an armistice between all the troops under your command and those under General Johnston. I shall therefore hold its garrison, including Major-Generals G. W. Smith and Cobb and Brigadier-General [William] Mackall, prisoners of war. Please send me orders." Skirmishing reported along Tobesofkee Creek and near Spring Hill.[112]

April 21, 1865 (Friday)

In Sparta, Fanny Andrews learned "of Lee's surrender, and of the armistice between Johnston and Sherman. Alas, we all know only too well what that armistice means! It is all over with us now, and there is nothing to do but bow our heads in the dust and let the hateful conquerors trample us under their feet. There is a complete revulsion in public feeling."[113]

April 22, 1865 (Saturday)

While in Washington, Georgia, Fanny Andrews heard the news of arriving soldiers. "Paroled men from Lee's army are expected every day now, and the town is already as full as it can hold. The only hotel has been closed and private hospitality is taxed to the utmost."[114] A portion of Wilson's troopers skirmished near Buzzard Roost.

April 23, 1865 (Sunday)

Sam Richards visited a Baptist church on 25th Street in Atlanta for perhaps the only time. He complained, "the preacher did not please us. Instead of Christ, he preached Lincoln and seemed to think one about as good as the other."[115]

April 24, 1865 (Monday)

Washington, Georgia, witnessed an influx of soldiers from Virginia. Fanny Andrews watched as the "shattered remains of Lee's army are beginning to arrive. There is an endless stream...trains are going and coming at all hours. The soldiers bring all sorts of rumors and keep us stirred up in a state of never-ending excitement. Even when they don't ask for anything the poor fellows look so tired and hungry...we feel tempted to give them everything we have."[116]

April 25, 1865 (Tuesday) ●

Fanny Andrews continued to lament the defeat of the Army of Northern Virginia. Of those residents in Washington, Georgia, Andrews observed, "Everybody is cast down and humiliated, and we are all waiting in suspense to know what our cruel masters will do with us. Think of a vulgar plebeian like Andy Johnson, and that odious Yankee crew at Washington, lording it over Southern gentlemen! I suppose we shall be subjected to every indignity that hatred and malice can heap upon us."[117]

April 26, 1865 (Wednesday)

General Johnston surrendered all troops under his command to Major General Sherman at the Bennett Place in North Carolina. After receiving the news, Major General Thomas

---

[112] Ibid., 367; skirmish information in Mosocco, *Chronological Tracking*, 324.

[113] Andrews, *War-Time Journal of a Georgia Girl*, 171.

[114] Ibid., 180–81; skirmish information in Mosocco, *Chronological Tracking*, 325.

[115] Richards, *Civil War Diary*, 272.

[116] Andrews, *War-Time Journal of a Georgia Girl*, 181–82.

[117] Ibid., 185.

wrote to Major General Wilson. "The terms of the armistice between General Sherman, U. S. Army, and General Johnston, C. S. Army, are disapproved and repudiated by the United States, and orders have been accordingly issued that all U. S. commanders push to their utmost all military operations in which they were engaged at the time of the armistice above referred to." Thomas prepped Wilson on dealing with Confederate resistance. "If General Cobb refuses to surrender Macon to you after the reception of this message, the people cannot complain, whatever may be the consequences, should you be compelled to assault the place."[118]

April 27, 1865 (Thursday)

Fanny Andrews found humor in the delivery of "seven great boxes full of papers and instruments belonging to the department...." Seems naval officers wished to locate their archives in Washington, Georgia. Andrews continued, "Father had them stored in the cellar, the only place where he could find a vacant spot, and so now, about all that is left of the Confederate Navy is here in our house, and we laugh and tell father, that he, the staunchest Union man in Georgia, is head of the Confederate Navy."[119]

April 28, 1865 (Friday)

Witnessing returning soldiers while in Washington, Georgia, Fanny Andrews's heart saddened when thinking of loss. "I blame the secession politicians myself," she wrote, "but the cause for which my brothers risked their lives, the cause for which so many noble Southerners have bled and died, and for which such terrible sacrifices have been made, is dear to my heart, right or wrong. The more misfortunes overwhelm my poor country, the more I love it; the more the Yankees triumph, the worse I hate them, wretches!"[120]

April 29, 1865 (Saturday)

Dolly Lunt Burge reflected on an exceptionally long month. "This has been a month never to be forgotten. Events of a lifetime have transpired within its limits. Two armies have surrendered. The President of the U. States has been assassinated Richmond evacuated & Davis the President of the Confederacy put to grief to flight—The old flag has been raised again upon Sumpter & an armistice accepted."[121]

April 30, 1865 (Sunday)

Nurse Cumming spent the morning of the Sabbath in church; she returned in the evening for a second service, which left her pondering the post-war future. "I knew we had peace—how, I did not understand; but certainly thought we were independent. This is a severe ordeal; may God in his mercy give us comfort through it."[122]

May 1, 1865 (Monday)

Major General Wilson received a telegraph in Macon, one with important news from Sherman in Savannah. "Supplies sent you to Augusta by boat. Johnston finally surrendered on

---

[118] *OR*, ser. I, vol. 49, pt. 2:471.

[119] Andrews, *War-Time Journal of a Georgia Girl*, 187.

[120] Ibid., 188.

[121] Burge, *Diary*, 171–72.

[122] Cumming, *Kate*, 276.

the 27th [26th] all his troops extending to the Chattahoochee. Amnesty orders sent you by land. After paroling prisoners, destroying guns and war material, move to Decatur, Ala., and report to General Thomas or myself for orders."[123]

May 2, 1865 (Tuesday) ◐

Brigadier General William Wofford notified Brigadier General Henry Judah of his willingness to stack arms. "I hereby surrender myself and the Confederate forces under my command to you upon the terms under which General Lee, C. S. Army, surrendered to Lieut. Gen. U. S. Grant." Political issues, as well as military affairs, confronted Major General George Thomas. In a communication to Secretary Stanton, he addressed politics.

> The present condition of the inhabitants of North Georgia and Alabama is extremely embarrassing to them and they are reduced to the verge of despair. I have this morning received a letter from a citizen of Ringgold, Ga., asking in the name of the people of North Georgia if the people of that section of the State properly petition the President for the appointment of a man chosen by the loyal voters of that section as military governor that their petition will be granted, and if so assured they request authority to be given them to hold an election, not only to select their military governor, but to provide for the election of county officers, so as to be prepared to reorganize and re-establish civil law in the portion of the State north of the Etowah as soon as possible.[124]

May 3, 1865 (Wednesday)

From his position near the Savannah Bridge, Secretary of War John C. Breckinridge stipulated the disbursement plan for what remained of the Confederate treasury. Breckinridge tasked Major E. C. White with taking "charge of silver (in specie and bullion) belonging to the Government, and estimated at $108,322.90." White would "distribute the specie proportionately to the troops present, upon certified returns of the strength of their command by the several brigade commanders. He will correctly estimate the value of the bullion in coin; and will pay in gold, placed in his hands for the purpose as above required for the distribution of the silver in specie."[125]

May 4, 1865 (Thursday)

Major General Wilson began enforcing the surrender of various Confederate units in Georgia. "Have sent [Major General Emory] Upton to Atlanta and Augusta; [Brigadier General Edward] McCook goes to Tallahassee to-morrow to carry out terms of convention. There is an immense amount of war material in this country which should be collected at Macon or Atlanta and guarded by infantry. Shall do all I can to get it together. The arsenal here [Macon] is very valuable."[126] Jefferson Davis arrived in Washington, Georgia.

May 5, 1865 (Friday—Cinco de Mayo)

---

[123] *OR*, ser. I, vol. 49, pt. 2:550.

[124] Ibid., 564, 569.

[125] Ibid., 1278.

[126] Ibid., 598; Avery, *History of the State of Georgia*, 324.

After holding the final Confederate cabinet meeting in Washington, Jefferson Davis's party continued to advance across Georgia; Federal scouts tried to locate their exact location. Grant wrote to Major General Thomas regarding the infrastructure of Georgia. "There is no use attempting to rebuild the road to Atlanta. A much cheaper and easier way for supplying the country where General Wilson is can be found from the sea-coast. It may not be necessary for us to keep troops in the interior." Skirmishing reported at Summerville.[127]

May 6, 1865 (Saturday)

Moving quickly to restore a form of government in the state, Governor Brown wrote to President Andrew Johnson, "The complete collapse in the currency and the great destitution of provisions among the poor makes it absolutely necessary that the Legislature meet to supply this deficiency, and with a view to the restoration of peace and order by accepting the result which the fortunes of war have imposed upon us, I have called the Legislature to meet 22d instant." Brown closed with a query. "General Wilson informs me that he cannot permit the assemblage without instructions from the Government at Washington. Does he reflect the views of the Government, or will you order that no force be used to prevent the meeting of the Legislature?"[128]

May 7, 1865 (Sunday)

President Johnson, through Secretary Stanton, issued orders to Major General Wilson in Macon. "The President directs...you immediately arrest Joseph E. Brown, who pretends to act as Governor of Georgia, and send him in close custody under sufficient and secure guard to Major-General [Christopher] Augur, at Washington [District of Columbia], and allow him to hold no communication, verbal or written, with any person but the officer having him in charge after the receipt of this order."[129]

May 8, 1865 (Monday)

In his post-campaign report, Major General Wilson recapped the accomplishments for Sherman. "In thirty days we marched over 500 miles, took 6,300 prisoners, 23 colors, and 156 guns, defeating Forrest, scattering the militia, destroying every railroad, iron establishment, and factory in North Alabama and Georgia. From Montgomery to this place [Macon], 220 miles, we marched in six days, resting one at Columbus and West Point."[130]

May 9, 1865 (Tuesday)

Governor Brown received a message from Major General Wilson noting the "collapse in...currency and...great destitution among the people of Georgia mentioned in your telegram have been caused by rebellion, treason, and insurrection against the laws of the United States, incited and carried on for the last four years by you and your confederate rebels and traitors, who alone are responsible for the waste, destitution, and want now existing in that State." Meanwhile, the Davis party rejoined—Jefferson with Varina and the children—outside Irwinville.[131]

---

[127] *OR,* ser. I, vol. 49, pt. 2:613; skirmish in Mosocco, *Chronological Tracking,* 327.

[128] Candler, *Confederate Records of the State of Georgia,* 3:718.

[129] *OR,* ser. I, vol. 49, pt. 2:647.

[130] Ibid., 663.

[131] Ibid., 681; J. Davis, *Papers,* 11:582.

May 10, 1865 (Wednesday)

Jefferson Davis and party were captured in Irwinville, and Colonel Robert Minty of the 4th Michigan Cavalry reported on the mission to apprehend the president: "Colonel [Benjamin] Pritchard found a detachment of the First Wisconsin Cavalry, under Lieutenant-Colonel [Henry] Harnden, on Davis' track ahead of him; he then took a circuitous route, and by marching until 2 a. m.…succeeded in gaining Irwinville while Davis was in camp three-quarters of a mile north of that place. He immediately surrounded the camp, and shortly before daybreak closed in and captured the entire party."[132]

May 11, 1865 (Thursday)

Federal cavalry troopers arrested Alexander Stephens. Major General Upton noted Stephens "is…in a very feeble state of health. I would suggest that he be sent by way of Augusta and Savannah, as he expresses a desire not to travel with the other party."[133]

May 12, 1865 (Friday)

In Kingston, marking one of the final surrender ceremonies east of the Mississippi River, Brigadier General William Wofford capitulated to Brigadier General Henry Judah. In his Nashville headquarters, Major General Thomas received details of the ceremony. "The terms of surrender between Generals Judah and Wofford…was fixed for the 12th proximo, and the place Kingston, in order to give General Wofford time to collect his forces. These consist, nominally, of all the Confederate and State forces in Northwestern Georgia, amounting, on paper, to about 10,000."[134]

May 13, 1865 (Saturday)

Federal officers reported Georgia's top official now numbered among the captives. "General Wilson has sent Lieutenant [William] Bayard in charge of Governor Brown, of Georgia, a prisoner, under orders to report him to Secretary of War at Washington, and that they have arrived at Dalton. Shall they be forwarded here and on to Nashville, and in what manner?"[135]

May 14, 1865 (Sunday)

Residents of Atlanta received news of the capture of Jefferson Davis. Sam Richards bemoaned the event in his diary, writing, "He is in all probability on the way to the gallows, as the present Administration seems disposed to deal harshly with the chief men of the South. If Davis is hung I think there will be another large drop of bitterness added to the hatred which the despotic course of the North has engendered in the minds of the Southern people generally, during this dreadful war."[136]

May 15, 1865 (Monday)

Fanny Andrews observed the changing social scene in Washington, Georgia, noting, "Even in our little town the streets are so full of idle negroes and bluecoats that ladies scarcely ever

[132] *OR*, ser. I, vol. 49, pt. 1:526–27.

[133] *OR*, ser. I, vol. 49, pt. 2:750.

[134] Ibid., 605.

[135] Ibid., 753.

[136] Richards, *Civil War Diary*, 274.

venture out. We are obliged to go sometimes, but it is always with drooping heads and downcast eyes. A settled gloom, deep and heavy, hangs over the whole land." Yet, she remained hopeful. "I don't believe this war is over yet. The Trans-Mississippi bubble has burst, but wait till the tyranny and arrogance of the United States engages them in a foreign war! Ah, we'll bide our time."[137]

May 16, 1865 (Tuesday)

Federal troops netted a sought-after prize. Major General Wilson informed the War Department of his catch. "I have the honor to report that I have arrested Capt. H. Wirz…notorious as commandant of the Andersonville prison, and have sent him under guard to General Thomas. I forward herewith all the records…of the prison that could be found, and…other papers relating to his cruel treatment of our men. I respectfully request that this miscreant be brought before a general court-martial in Washington, D.C.…"[138]

May 17, 1865 (Wednesday) ◑

Dolly Lunt Burge made the following diary entry relating current affairs in Georgia and elsewhere across the South. "I hear to day that our negroes are all freed by the US government. This is more than I anticipated yet trust it will be a gradual thing & not done all at once but the Disposer of All knows best & will do right—."[139]

May 18, 1865 (Thursday)

Federal soldiers paid a visit to Fanny Andrews and family in Washington, Georgia.

> Two rebel horsemen came galloping up the avenue with news that a large body of Yankee cavalry was advancing…plundering the country as they passed. We…were busy concealing valuables for father, when the tramping of horses and shouting of the men reached our ears. Then they began to pass by our street gate, with two of their detestable old flags flaunting in the breeze. Nearly all of them had bags of plunder tied to their saddles, and many rode horses which were afterwards recognized as belonging to different planters in the county. I saw one rascal with a ruffled pillowcase full of stolen goods, tied to his saddle, and some of them had women's drawers tied up at the bottom ends, filled with plunder and slung astride their horses. There was a regiment of negroes with them, and they halted right in front of our gate. Think of it! Bringing armed negroes here to threaten and insult us![140]

May 19, 1865 (Friday)

Fanny Andrews continued to observe former Confederate soldiers passing through town. "I have witnessed the breaking up of three…armies; Lee's and Johnston's have already passed through Washington, and Gen. Dick Taylor's is now in transit, but all these…thousands of disbanded, disorganized, disinherited Southerners have not committed one-twentieth part of the damage to private property…committed by the first small squad of Yankee

---

[137] Andrews, *War-Time Journal of a Georgia Girl*, 254.

[138] *OR*, ser. I, vol. 49, pt. 2:800.

[139] Burge, *Diary*, 173.

[140] Andrews, *War-Time Journal of a Georgia Girl*, 261–62.

cavalry that passed through our county."[141]

May 20, 1865 (Saturday)

Residents of Macon received notice to guard against evil spirits—not the ghostly type, but the bottled variety. "Our military authorities are particularly active in feriting [*sic*] out and punishing dealers in spiritous liquors. We have heard it said that John Barleycorn could throw down any man in a fair tussle, but Gen. Wilson is likely to prove a match for him, and will throw both John and his backers, if he comes blustering about in this neighborhood."[142]

May 21, 1865 (Sunday)

Dolly Lunt Burge again wrote of the end of the peculiar institution. "I had a long conversation with my man Elbert to day about freedom & told him I was perfectly willing but wanted direction. He says the Yankees told Maj [Augustus] Lees servants they were all free but they had better remain where they were until it was settled as it would be in a month time."[143]

May 22, 1865 (Monday)

Fanny Andrews wrote of her dad, and his sudden rise in popularity. "On account of father's always having been such a strong Union man, he is supposed to have some influence with our new masters, and is frequently appealed to by the citizens to lay their grievances before the Yankee commandant, and so he has become pretty well acquainted with him in a business way."[144]

May 23, 1865 (Tuesday)

Fanny Andrews spent "nearly all day" in bed, but rose in time to go into town. "I went to walk in the afternoon and met John Garnett just from Albany, and he says the Yankees are behaving better in South-West Georgia than anybody expected. This makes us all feel very much relieved...."[145]

May 24, 1865 (Wednesday) ●

Parading in Washington City proved the order of the day, as Sherman's soldiers who had participated in the Atlanta and Savannah campaigns received their just recognition. Things appeared a bit gloomier for those folks living on the land the armies left behind. Today, Major General Wilson learned, from Georgia's quartermaster general, Ira Foster, just how bad.

> Cobb, Fulton, Clayton, and contiguous counties in this State, by reason of both Northern and Southern armies having been quartered therein for several weeks, are totally destitute of the means for support only as supplies are shipped in from a distance. In these counties reside about 15,000 poor and penniless men, women, and

---

[141] Ibid., 263.

[142] "Look Out Whiskey Dealers!," *Macon Daily Journal and Messenger*, May 20, 1865, https://gahistoricnewspapers.galileo.usg.edu/lccn/sn87060121/1865-05-20/ed-1/seq-2/.

[143] Burge, *Diary*, 173–74.

[144] Andrews, *War-Time Journal of a Georgia Girl*, 266.

[145] Ibid., 266–67.

> children, who must, of necessity, starve unless the public shall supply their wants. The corn we have on hand cannot sustain life but a few days longer. We have no cheering prospects of getting more.[146]

May 25, 1865 (Thursday)

Responding to the plight facing civilians in Georgia, Major General Wilson went to work. "Something must be done at once to get rations to the suffering people of Georgia. The repair of the Atlanta and Chattanooga Railroad will afford the best means. I can scarcely supply my own command with corn, much less a large indigent population. Not a day should be lost in repairing the railroad."[147]

May 26, 1865 (Friday)

Major General Wilson received a telegraph from Major General Thomas indicating immediate plans for a portion of Wilson's force in Georgia. "General Grant does not approve of sending the whole of your command to Texas, but he designs that you should remain in Georgia with about 2,000 cavalry and some infantry (he does not say how much) in command of the State, I take it."[148]

May 27, 1865 (Saturday)

Fanny Andrews wrote of life for former Confederate soldiers amid the uncertainty in the immediate postwar period.

> Those who have no other clothes can still wear the gray, but must rip off the buttons and decorations. The beautiful Hungarian knot, the stars, and bars, the cords, the sashes, and gold lace, are all disappearing. People everywhere are ransacking old chests, and the men are hauling out the old clothes they used to wear before the war, and they do look so funny and old-fashioned, after the beautiful uniforms we had all gotten used to! But the raggedest soldier of the Confederacy in his shabby old clothes is a more heroic figure in my eyes than any upstart Yankee officer in the finest uniform he can get into. I feel like crying whenever I think of the change and all that it means. We are a poverty-stricken nation, and most of them are too poor to buy new clothes. I suppose we are just now at the very worst stage of our financial embarrassments, and if we can manage to struggle through the next five or six months, some sort of currency will begin to circulate again.[149]

May 28, 1865 (Sunday)

Sam Richards attended church, where he picked up a pamphlet from the U.S. Christian Commission. After perusing the booklet, he contemplated on the recent war, and his previous thoughts toward folks in the North.

> A feeling of regret and sadness came over my mind at the evidence that Christian men and women at the North were as sincere in the belief of the righteousness and justice of their cause as were the Christians of the South in their devotion to theirs. Can it

---

[146] *OR*, ser. I, vol. 49, pt. 2:890.

[147] Ibid., 891.

[148] Ibid., 910.

[149] Andrews, *War-Time Journal of a Georgia Girl*, 270–71.

be possible that the purpose of God in permitting this war was to put an end to slavery (black slavery?) No doubt many will think so, as that seems to have been one result. I can readily think that the time may have come when He sees that the curse may pass away, but at the same time I believe that hitherto that state of things has been sanctioned and sustained by the same divine authority that first instituted it. I do not believe that the war was the punishment for the sin of slavery.[150]

May 29, 1865 (Monday)

President Andrew Johnson issued a Proclamation of Amnesty, detailing how former adversaries could regain standing as a citizen of the United States. Johnson exempted several classes of individuals from this act, including "All who shall have been military or naval officers of said pretended Confederate Government above the rank of colonel in the Army or lieutenant in the Navy...all persons who held the pretended offices of Governors of States in insurrection against the United States."[151]

May 30, 1865 (Tuesday)

Arnold Elzey, a former major general in the Confederate army, visited Fanny Andrews and family. During the military occupation of the South, the Federals forced the former Confederates to remove buttons and any insignia from their uniforms. This did not sit well with Fanny, who wrote, "The general wore a gray coat from which all the decorations had been ripped off and the buttons covered with plain gray cloth, but he would look like a soldier and a gentleman even in a Boston stove-pipe hat, or a suit of Yankee blue. Some of our boys put their discarded buttons in tobacco bags and jingle them whenever a Yank comes within earshot."[152]

May 31, 1865 (Wednesday)

Unaware of the future awaiting the city, Brigadier General Edward Winslow captured the initial stages of a rising phoenix: "The citizens of this place [Atlanta] desire to hold a meeting for taking Union ground. I have advised delay. Are there any objections to mass meetings which are to be conducted on the basis of obedience to law, Constitution, and decidedly in favor of the Union? I deprecated the meeting, not wishing any excitement, and because there is at present so much uncertainty concerning the exact policy of the Government on the slavery and reconstruction issues."[153]

June 17, 1865 (Saturday)

President Andrew Johnson appointed "James Johnson, of Georgia, Provisional Governor of the State of Georgia, whose duty it shall be...to prescribe such rules and regulations as may be necessary and proper for convening a convention, composed of delegates to be chosen by that portion of the people of said State who are loyal to the United States, and no others, for the purpose of altering and amending the constitution..."[154]

---

150 Richards, *Civil War Diary*, 278.

151 *OR*, ser. II, vol. 8:579.

152 Andrews, *War-Time Journal of a Georgia Girl*, 275–76.

153 *OR*, ser. I, vol. 49, pt. 2:938–39.

154 "A Proclamation," *New York Times*, June 18, 1865, sec. 1, https://www.newspapers.com/image/20665119/.

June 27, 1865 (Tuesday)
The U.S. War Department created new military districts, each to encompass sections of the former Confederacy, such as "The Department of Georgia, Maj. Gen. James B. Steedman to command, to embrace the State of Georgia; headquarters at Augusta." This department resided in the Military District of Tennessee: "Maj. Gen. G. H. Thomas to command, to embrace the Department of the Tennessee, Department of Kentucky, Department of Georgia, and Department of Alabama; headquarters at Nashville."[155]

June 29, 1865 (Thursday)
Governor Joe Brown officially resigned.[156]

July 13, 1865 (Thursday)
Provisional Governor James Johnson issued a declaration to Georgia. "Whereas by the proclamation of Andrew Johnson…I have been appointed Provisional Governor…with instructions to prescribe, at the earliest period, such rules and regulations as may be necessary and proper for convening a convention of the people, composed of delegates to be chosen by that portion of the people who are loyal to the United States…."[157]

September 25, 1865 (Monday)
The U.S. Government completed the rebuilding of the Western & Atlantic Railroad and turned the line over to the state.[158]

October 11, 1865 (Wednesday) ◐
President Andrew Johnson released Alexander Stephens from jail on the condition that he agree "to appear at such time and place as the President may designate, to answer any charge that he may direct to be preferred against them…."[159]

October 25, 1865 (Wednesday)
The Georgia Constitution Convention started meeting in Milledgeville.[160]

October 26, 1865 (Thursday)
The Constitutional Convention delegates, meeting in Milledgeville, voted to repeal the Ordinance of Secession.

> We, the People of the State of Georgia in Convention, at our seat of Government, do declare and ordain, That an ordinance adopted by the same people, in convention, on the nineteenth day of January, A. D. eighteen hundred and sixty-one, entitled "An ordinance to dissolve the union between the State of Georgia and other States united with her under a compact of government entitled 'the constitution of the United States of America'"; also an ordinance, adopted by the same on the sixteenth day of March in the year last aforesaid, entitled "An ordinance to adopt and ratify the

---

[155] *OR*, ser. I, vol. 49, pt. 2:1040–41.

[156] Avery, *History of the State of Georgia*, 339.

[157] Candler, *Confederate Records of the State of Georgia*, 4:13.

[158] Avery, *History of the State of Georgia*, 348.

[159] "Alexander H. Stephens, Reagan and Others Paroled," *New York Times*, October 12, 1865, sec. 1, https://www.newspapers.com/image/20643470/.

[160] Candler, *Confederate Records of the State of Georgia*, 6:7.

> constitution of the Confederate States of America"; and also all ordinances and resolutions of the same, adopted between the sixteenth day of January and the twenty-fourth day of March, in the year aforesaid, subversive of, or antagonistic to the civil and military authority of the government of the United States of America, under the constitution thereof, be, and the same are hereby repealed.[161]

October 31, 1865 (Tuesday) (All Hallow'e'en)

The trial of Henry Wirz ended with a verdict of guilty.

> He claimed to be doing the work of the rebellion, and faithfully, in all his murderous cruelty and baseness, did he represent its spirit. It is by looking upon the cemeteries which have been filled from Libby, Belle isle [*sic*], Salisbury, Florence, and Andersonville, and other rebel prisons, and recalling the prolonged sufferings of the patriots who are sleeping there, that we can best understand the inner and real life of the rebellion, and the hellish criminality and brutality of the traitors who maintained it. For such crimes human power is absolutely impotent to enforce any adequate atonement.... It is recommended that the sentence be executed.

John Ransom, a former Andersonville prisoner noted of the indictment of Wirz, "It was a righteous judgment, still I think there are others who deserved hanging fully as much. He was but the willing tool of those higher in command. Those who put him there knew his brutal disposition, and should have suffered the same disposition made of him."[162]

November 7, 1865 (Tuesday)

Delegates ratified Georgia's new Constitution in Milledgeville.[163]

November 15, 1865 (Wednesday)

Georgians elected Charles J. Jenkins to serve as the new governor.[164]

December 9, 1865 (Saturday) ◗

Georgia ratified the 13th Amendment.[165]

December 14, 1865 (Thursday)

Georgians inaugurated Charles J. Jenkins as the state's new governor. During his address, Jenkins stated, "God is merciful! God is mighty! God in his abounding mercy and in the plenitude of his might so dispose our fortunes and theirs, that each class shall be to the other a blessing, not a curse."[166]

---

[161] *Journal of the Proceedings of the Convention of the People of Georgia*, October 26, 1865, 17–18.

[162] 40th Congress, 2d Session, "Trial of Henry Wirz," *Congressional Globe* Ex. Doc. 23 (1865): 814, https://www.loc.gov/rr/frd/Military_Law/pdf/Wirz-trial.pdf; Ransom, *Andersonville Diary*, 246–47.

[163] Hill, "Georgia Constitution."

[164] Shadgett, "James Johnson, Provisional Governor of Georgia," 18.

[165] Woolley, *Reconstruction of Georgia*, 15.

[166] Shadgett, "James Johnson, Provisional Governor of Georgia," 19; Avery, *History of the State of Georgia*, 353.

December 19, 1865 (Tuesday)
Governor Jenkins received a communication from President Andrew Johnson, via Secretary Steward.

> By direction of the President I have the honor herewith to transmit to you a copy of a communication which has been addressed to his Excellency, James Johnson, late Provisional Governor, whereby he has been relieved of the trust heretofore reposed in him, and directed to deliver into your possession the papers and property relating to the trust. I have the honor to tender you the cooperation of the Government of the United States, whenever it may be found necessary, in effecting the early restoration and the permanent prosperity of the state over which you have been called to preside.[167]

July 15, 1870 (Friday)
Georgia was readmitted to the Union.

[167] Avery, *History of the State of Georgia*, 354.

Appendix 1

Declaration of Secession[1]

The people of Georgia having dissolved their political connection with the Government of the United States of America, present to their confederates and the world the causes which have led to the separation. For the last ten years we have had numerous and serious causes of complaint against our non-slave-holding confederate States with reference to the subject of African slavery. They have endeavored to weaken our security, to disturb our domestic peace and tranquility, and persistently refused to comply with their express constitutional obligations to us in reference to that property, and by the use of their power in the Federal Government have striven to deprive us of an equal enjoyment of the common Territories of the Republic. This hostile policy of our confederates has been pursued with every circumstance of aggravation which could arouse the passions and excite the hatred of our people, and has placed the two sections of the Union for many years past in the condition of virtual civil war. Our people, still attached to the Union from habit and national traditions, and averse to change, hoped that time, reason, and argument would bring, if not redress, at least exemption from further insults, injuries, and dangers. Recent events have fully dissipated all such hopes and demonstrated the necessity of separation. Our Northern confederates, after a full and calm hearing of all the facts, after a fair warning of our purpose not to submit to the rule of the authors of all these wrongs and injuries, have by a large majority committed the Government of the United States into their hands. The people of Georgia, after an equally full and fair and deliberate hearing of the case, have declared with equal firmness that they shall not rule over them. A brief history of the rise, progress, and policy of anti-slavery and the political organization into whose hands the administration of the Federal Government has been committed will fully justify the pronounced verdict of the people of Georgia. The party of Lincoln, called the Republican party, under its present name and organization, is of recent origin. It is admitted to be an anti-slavery party. While it attracts to itself by its creed the scattered advocates of exploded political heresies, of condemned theories in political economy, the advocates of commercial restrictions, of protection, of special privileges, of waste and corruption in the administration of Government, anti-slavery is its mission and its purpose. By anti-slavery it is made a power in the state. The question of slavery was the great difficulty in the way of the formation of the Constitution. While the subordination and the political and social inequality of the African race was fully conceded by all, it was plainly apparent that slavery would soon disappear from what are now the non-slave-holding States of the original thirteen. The opposition to slavery was then, as now, general in those States and the Constitution was made with direct reference to that fact. But a distinct abolition party was not formed in the United States for

---

[1] "Confederate States of America–Georgia Secession," https://avalon.law.yale.edu/19th_century/csa_geosec.asp.

more than half a century after the Government went into operation. The main reason was that the North, even if united, could not control both branches of the Legislature during any portion of that time. Therefore such an organization must have resulted either in utter failure or in the total overthrow of the Government. The material prosperity of the North was greatly dependent on the Federal Government; that of the South not at all. In the first years of the Republic the navigating, commercial, and manufacturing interests of the North began to seek profit and aggrandizement at the expense of the agricultural interests. Even the owners of fishing smacks sought and obtained bounties for pursuing their own business (which yet continue), and $500,000 is now paid them annually out of the Treasury. The navigating interests begged for protection against foreign shipbuilders and against competition in the coasting trade. Congress granted both requests, and by prohibitory acts gave an absolute monopoly of this business to each of their interests, which they enjoy without diminution to this day. Not content with these great and unjust advantages, they have sought to throw the legitimate burden of their business as much as possible upon the public; they have succeeded in throwing the cost of light-houses, buoys, and the maintenance of their seamen upon the Treasury, and the Government now pays above $2,000,000 annually for the support of these objects. Theses interests, in connection with the commercial and manufacturing classes, have also succeeded, by means of subventions to mail steamers and the reduction in postage, in relieving their business from the payment of about $7,000,000 annually, throwing it upon the public Treasury under the name of postal deficiency. The manufacturing interests entered into the same struggle early, and has clamored steadily for Government bounties and special favors. This interest was confined mainly to the Eastern and Middle non-slave-holding States. Wielding these great States it held great power and influence, and its demands were in full proportion to its power. The manufacturers and miners wisely based their demands upon special facts and reasons rather than upon general principles, and thereby mollified much of the opposition of the opposing interest. They pleaded in their favor the infancy of their business in this country, the scarcity of labor and capital, the hostile legislation of other countries toward them, the great necessity of their fabrics in the time of war, and the necessity of high duties to pay the debt incurred in our war for independence. These reasons prevailed, and they received for many years enormous bounties by the general acquiescence of the whole country.

But when these reasons ceased they were no less clamorous for Government protection, but their clamors were less heeded—the country had put the principle of protection upon trial and condemned it. After having enjoyed protection to the extent of from 15 to 200 per cent. upon their entire business for above thirty years, the act of 1846 was passed. It avoided sudden change, but the principle was settled, and free trade, low duties, and economy in public expenditures was the verdict of the American people. The South and the Northwestern States sustained this policy. There was but small hope of its reversal; upon the direct issue, none at all.

All these classes saw this and felt it and cast about for new allies. The anti-slavery sentiment of the North offered the best chance for success. An anti-slavery party must necessarily look to the North alone for support, but a united North was now strong enough to control the Government in all of its departments, and a sectional party was therefore determined upon.

Time and issues upon slavery were necessary to its completion and final triumph. The feeling of anti-slavery, which it was well known was very general among the people of the North, had been long dormant or passive; it needed only a question to arouse it into aggressive activity. This question was before us. We had acquired a large territory by successful war with Mexico; Congress had to govern it; how, in relation to slavery, was the question then demanding solution. This state of facts gave form and shape to the anti-slavery sentiment throughout the North and the conflict began. Northern anti-slavery men of all parties asserted the right to exclude slavery from the territory by Congressional legislation and demanded the prompt and efficient exercise of this power to that end. This insulting and unconstitutional demand was met with great moderation and firmness by the South. We had shed our blood and paid our money for its acquisition; we demanded a division of it on the line of the Missouri restriction or an equal participation in the whole of it. These propositions were refused, the agitation became general, and the public danger was great. The case of the South was impregnable. The price of the acquisition was the blood and treasure of both sections—of all, and, therefore, it belonged to all upon the principles of equity and justice.

The Constitution delegated no power to Congress to excluded either party from its free enjoyment; therefore our right was good under the Constitution. Our rights were further fortified by the practice of the Government from the beginning. Slavery was forbidden in the country northwest of the Ohio River by what is called the ordinance of 1787. That ordinance was adopted under the old confederation and by the assent of Virginia, who owned and ceded the country, and therefore this case must stand on its own special circumstances. The Government of the United States claimed territory by virtue of the treaty of 1783 with Great Britain, acquired territory by cession from Georgia and North Carolina, by treaty from France, and by treaty from Spain. These acquisitions largely exceeded the original limits of the Republic. In all of these acquisitions the policy of the Government was uniform. It opened them to the settlement of all the citizens of all the States of the Union. They emigrated thither with their property of every kind (including slaves). All were equally protected by public authority in their persons and property until the inhabitants became sufficiently numerous and otherwise capable of bearing the burdens and performing the duties of self-government, when they were admitted into the Union upon equal terms with the other States, with whatever republican constitution they might adopt for themselves.

Under this equally just and beneficent policy law and order, stability and progress, peace and prosperity marked every step of the progress of these new communities until they entered as great and prosperous commonwealths into the sisterhood of American States. In 1820 the North endeavored to overturn this wise and successful policy and demanded that the State of Missouri should not be admitted into the Union unless she first prohibited slavery within her limits by her constitution. After a bitter and protracted struggle the North was defeated in her special object, but her policy and position led to the adoption of a section in the law for the admission of Missouri, prohibiting slavery in all that portion of the territory acquired from France lying North of 36 [degrees] 30 [minutes] north latitude and outside of Missouri. The venerable Madison at the time of its adoption declared it unconstitutional. Mr. Jefferson condemned the restriction and foresaw its consequences and predicted that it would result in the dissolution of the Union. His prediction is now history. The North demanded the application of the principle of prohibition of slavery to all of the territory acquired from Mexico and all other parts of the public domain then and in all future time. It was the announcement of her purpose to appropriate to herself all the public domain then owned and thereafter to be acquired by the United States. The claim itself was less arrogant and insulting than the reason with which she supported it. That reason was her fixed purpose to limit, restrain, and finally abolish slavery in the States where it exists. The South with great unanimity declared her purpose to resist the principle of prohibition to the last extremity. This particular question, in connection with a series of questions affecting the same subject, was finally disposed of by the defeat of prohibitory legislation.

The Presidential election of 1852 resulted in the total overthrow of the advocates of restriction and their party friends. Immediately after this result the anti-slavery portion of the defeated party resolved to unite all the elements in the North opposed to slavery and to stake their future political fortunes upon their hostility to slavery everywhere. This is the party to whom the people of the North have committed the Government. They raised their standard in 1856 and were barely defeated. They entered the Presidential contest again in 1860 and succeeded.

The prohibition of slavery in the Territories, hostility to it everywhere, the equality of the black and white races, disregard of all constitutional guarantees it its favor, were boldly proclaimed by its leaders and applauded by its followers.

With these principles on their banners and these utterances on their lips the majority of the people of the North demand that we shall receive them as our rulers.

The prohibition of slavery in the Territories is the cardinal principle of this organization.

For forty years this question has been considered and debated in the halls of Congress, before the people, by the press, and before the tribunals of justice. The majority of the people of the North in 1860 decided it in their own favor. We refuse to submit to that judgment, and in vindication of our refusal we offer the Constitution of our country and point to the total absence of any express power to exclude us. We offer the practice of our Government for the first thirty years of its existence in complete refutation of the position that any such power is either necessary or proper to the execution of any other power in relation to the Territories. We offer the judgment of a large minority of the people of the North, amounting to more than one-third, who united with the unanimous voice of the South against this usurpation; and, finally, we offer the judgment of the Supreme Court of the United States, the highest judicial tribunal of our country, in our favor. This evidence ought to be conclusive that we have never surrendered this right. The conduct of our adversaries admonishes us that if we had surrendered it, it is time to resume it.

The faithless conduct of our adversaries is not confined to such acts as might aggrandize themselves or their section of the Union. They are content if they can only injure us. The Constitution declares that persons charged with crimes in one State and fleeing to another shall be delivered up on the demand of the executive authority of the State from which they may flee, to be tried in the jurisdiction where the crime was committed. It would appear difficult to employ language freer from ambiguity, yet for above twenty years the non-slave-holding States generally have wholly refused to deliver up to us persons charged with crimes affecting slave property. Our confederates, with punic faith, shield and give sanctuary to all criminals who seek to deprive us of this property or who use it to destroy us. This clause of the Constitution has no other sanction than their good faith; that is withheld from us; we are remediless in the Union; out of it we are remitted to the laws of nations.

A similar provision of the Constitution requires them to surrender fugitives from labor. This provision and the one last referred to were our main inducements for confederating with the Northern States. Without them it is historically true that we would have rejected the Constitution. In the fourth year of the Republic Congress passed a law to give full vigor and efficiency to this important provision. This act depended to a considerable degree upon the local magistrates in the several States for its efficiency. The non-slave-holding States generally repealed all laws intended to aid the execution of that act, and imposed penalties upon those citizens whose loyalty to the Constitution and their oaths might induce them to discharge their duty. Congress then passed the act of 1850, providing for the complete execution of this duty by Federal officers. This law, which their own bad faith rendered absolutely indispensable for the protection of constitutional rights, was instantly met with ferocious revilings and all conceivable modes of hostility. The Supreme Court unanimously, and their own local courts with equal unanimity (with the single and temporary exception of the supreme court of Wisconsin), sustained its constitutionality in all of its provisions. Yet it stands to-day a dead letter for all practicable purposes in every non-slave-holding State in the Union. We have their convenants, we have their oaths to keep and observe it, but the unfortunate claimant, even accompanied by a Federal officer with the mandate of the highest judicial authority in his hands, is everywhere met with fraud, with force, and with legislative enactments to elude, to resist, and defeat him. Claimants are murdered with impunity; officers of the law are beaten by frantic mobs instigated by inflammatory appeals from persons holding the highest public employment in these States, and supported by legislation in conflict with the clearest provisions of the Constitution, and even the ordinary principles of humanity. In several of our confederate States a citizen cannot travel the highway with his servant who may voluntarily accompany him, without being declared by law a felon and being subjected to infamous punishments. It is difficult to perceive how we could suffer more by the hostility than by the fraternity of such brethren.

The public law of civilized nations requires every State to restrain its citizens or subjects from committing acts injurious to the peace and security of any other State and from attempting to excite insurrection, or to lessen the security, or to disturb the tranquillity of their neighbors, and our Constitution wisely gives Congress the power to punish all offenses against the laws of nations.

These are sound and just principles which have received the approbation of just men in all countries and all centuries; but they are wholly disregarded by the people of the Northern States, and the Federal Government is impotent to maintain them. For twenty years past the abolitionists and their allies in the Northern States have been engaged in constant efforts to subvert our institutions and to excite insurrection and servile war among us. They have sent emissaries among us for the accomplishment of these purposes. Some of these efforts have received the public sanction of a majority of the leading men of the Republican party in the national councils, the same men who are now proposed as our rulers. These efforts have in one instance led to the actual invasion of one of the slave-holding States, and those of the murderers and incendiaries who escaped public justice by flight have found fraternal protection among our Northern confederates.

These are the same men who say the Union shall be preserved.

Such are the opinions and such are the practices of the Republican party, who have been called by their own votes to administer the Federal Government under the Constitution of the United States. We know their treachery; we know the shallow pretenses under which they daily disregard its plainest obligations. If we submit to them it will be our fault and not theirs. The people of Georgia have ever been willing to stand by this bargain, this contract; they have never sought to evade any of its obligations; they have never hitherto sought to establish any new government; they have struggled to maintain the ancient right of themselves and the human race through and by that Constitution. But they know the value of parchment rights in treacherous hands, and therefore they refuse to commit their own to the rulers whom the North offers us. Why? Because by their declared principles and policy they have outlawed $3,000,000,000 of our property in the common territories of the Union; put it under the ban of the Republic in the States where it exists and out of the protection of Federal law everywhere; because they give sanctuary to thieves and incendiaries who assail it to the whole extent of their power, in spite of their most solemn obligations and covenants; because their avowed purpose is to subvert our society and subject us not only to the loss of our property but the destruction of ourselves, our wives, and our children, and the desolation of our homes, our altars, and our firesides. To avoid these evils we resume the powers which our fathers delegated to the Government of the United States, and henceforth will seek new safeguards for our liberty, equality, security, and tranquillity.

Approved, Tuesday, January 29, 1861

Appendix 2

Alexander Stephens Cornerstone Speech[1]

March 21, 1861

At half past seven o'clock on Thursday evening, the largest audience ever assembled at the Athenaeum was in the house, waiting most impatiently for the appearance of the orator of the evening, Hon. A. H. Stephens, vice president of the Confederate States of America. The committee, with invited guests, were seated on the stage, when, at the appointed hour, the Hon. C. C. Jones, Mayor, and the speaker, entered, and were greeted by the immense assemblage with deafening rounds of applause.

The Mayor then, in a few pertinent remarks, introduced Mr. Stephens, stating that at the request of a number of the members of the convention, and citizens of Savannah and the State, now here, he had consented to address them upon the present state of public affairs.

Mr. Stephens rose and spoke as follows:

Mr. Mayor, and Gentlemen of the Committee, and Fellow-Citizens:— For this reception you will please accept my most profound and sincere thanks. The compliment is doubtless intended as much, or more, perhaps, in honor of the occasion, and my public position, in connection with the great events now crowding upon us, than to me personally and individually. It is however none the less appreciated by me on that account. We are in the midst of one of the greatest epochs in our history. The last ninety days will mark one of the most memorable eras in the history of modern civilization.

[There was a general call from the outside of the building for the speaker to go out, that there were more outside than in.]

The Mayor rose and requested silence at the doors, that Mr. Stephens' health would not permit him to speak in the open air.

Mr. Stephens said he would leave it to the audience whether he should proceed indoors or out. There was a general cry indoors, as the ladies, a large number of whom were present, could not hear outside.

Mr. Stephens said that the accommodation of the ladies would determine the question, and he would proceed where he was.

[At this point the uproar and clamor outside was greater still for the speaker to go out on the steps. This was quieted by Col. Lawton, Col. Freeman, Judge Jackson, and Mr. J. W. Owens going out and stating the facts of the case to the dense mass of men, women, and children who were outside, and entertaining them in brief speeches— Mr. Stephens all this while quietly sitting down until the furor subsided.]

Mr. Stephens rose and said: When perfect quiet is restored, I shall proceed. I cannot speak so long as there is any noise or confusion. I shall take my time—I feel quite prepared

---

[1] Cleveland, *Alexander H. Stephens, in Public and Private*, 717–29.

to spend the night with you if necessary. [Loud applause.] I very much regret that every one who desires cannot hear what I have to say. Not that I have any display to make, or any thing very entertaining to present, but such views as I have to give, I wish all, not only in this city, but in this State, and throughout our Confederate Republic, could hear, who have a desire to hear them.

I was remarking, that we are passing through one of the greatest revolutions in the annals of the world. Seven States have within the last three months thrown off an old government and formed a new. This revolution has been signally marked, up to this time, by the fact of its having been accomplished without the loss of a single drop of blood. [Applause.]

This new constitution, or form of government, constitutes the subject to which your attention will be partly invited. In reference to it, I make this first general remark. It amply secures all our ancient rights, franchises, and liberties. All the great principles of Magna Charta are retained in it. No citizen is deprived of life, liberty, or property, but by the judgment of his peers under the laws of the land. The great principle of religious liberty, which was the honor and pride of the old constitution, is still maintained and secured. All the essentials of the old constitution, which have endeared it to the hearts of the American people, have been preserved and perpetuated. [Applause.] Some changes have been made. Of these I shall speak presently. Some of these I should have preferred not to have seen made; but these, perhaps, meet the cordial approbation of a majority of this audience, if not an overwhelming majority of the people of the Confederacy. Of them, therefore, I will not speak. But other important changes do meet my cordial approbation. They form great improvements upon the old constitution. So, taking the whole new constitution, I have no hesitancy in giving it as my judgment that it is decidedly better than the old. [Applause.]

Allow me briefly to allude to some of these improvements. The question of building up class interests, or fostering one branch of industry to the prejudice of another under the exercise of the revenue power, which gave us so much trouble under the old constitution, is put at rest forever under the new. We allow the imposition of no duty with a view of giving advantage to one class of persons, in any trade or business, over those of another. All, under our system, stand upon the same broad principles of perfect equality. Honest labor and enterprise are left free and unrestricted in whatever pursuit they may be engaged. This subject came well nigh causing a rupture of the old Union, under the lead of the gallant Palmetto State, which lies on our border, in 1833. This old thorn of the tariff, which was the cause of so much irritation in the old body politic, is removed forever from the new. [Applause.]

Again, the subject of internal improvements, under the power of Congress to regulate commerce, is put at rest under our system. The power claimed by construction under the old constitution, was at least a doubtful one—it rested solely upon construction. We of the South, generally apart from considerations of constitutional principles, opposed its exercise upon grounds of its inexpediency and injustice. Notwithstanding this opposition, millions of money, from the common treasury had been drawn for such purposes. Our opposition sprang from no hostility to commerce, or all necessary aids for facilitating it. With us it was simply a question, upon whom the burden should fall. In Georgia, for instance, we have done as much for the cause of internal improvements as any other portion of the country according to population and means. We have stretched out lines of railroads from the seaboard to the mountains; dug down the hills, and filled up the valleys at a cost of not less than twenty-five millions of dollars. All this was done to open an outlet for our products of the interior, and those to the west of us, to reach the marts of the world. No State was in greater need of such facilities than Georgia, but we did not ask that these works should be made by appropriations out of the common treasury. The cost of the grading, the superstructure, and equipments of our roads, was borne by those who entered on the enterprise. Nay, more—not only the cost of the iron, no small item in the aggregate cost, was borne in the same way—but we were compelled to pay into the common treasury several millions of dollars for the privilege of importing the iron, after the price was paid for it abroad. What justice was there in taking this money, which our people paid into the common treasury on the importation of our iron, and applying it to the improvement of rivers and harbors elsewhere?

The true principle is to subject the commerce of every locality, to whatever burdens may be necessary to facilitate it. If Charleston harbor needs improvement, let the commerce of Charleston bear the burden. If the mouth of the Savannah river has to be cleared out, let the sea-going navigation which is benefitted by it, bear the burden. So with the mouths of the Alabama and Mississippi river. Just as the products of the interior, our cotton, wheat, corn, and other articles, have to bear the necessary rates of freight over our railroads to reach the seas. This is again the broad principle of perfect equality and justice. [Applause.] And it is especially set forth and established in our new constitution.

Another feature to which I will allude, is that the new constitution provides that cabinet ministers and heads of departments may have the privilege of seats upon the floor of the Senate and House of Representatives—may have the right to participate in the debates and discussions upon the various subjects of administration. I should have preferred that this provision should have gone further, and required the President to select his constitutional advisers from the Senate and House of Representatives. That would have conformed entirely to the practice in the British Parliament, which, in my judgment, is one of the wisest provisions in the British constitution. It is the only feature that saves that government. It is that which gives it stability in its facility to change its administration. Ours, as it is, is a great approximation to the right principle.

Under the old constitution, a secretary of the treasury for instance, had no opportunity, save by his annual reports, of presenting any scheme or plan of finance or other matter. He had no opportunity of explaining, expounding, inforcing, or defending his views of policy; his only resort was through the medium of an organ. In the British parliament, the premier brings in his budget and stands before the nation responsible for its every item. If it is indefensible, he falls before the attacks upon it, as he ought to. This will now be the case to a limited extent under our system. In the new constitution, provision has been made by which our heads of departments can speak for themselves and the administration, in behalf of its entire policy, without resorting to the indirect and highly objectionable medium of a newspaper. It is to be greatly hoped that under our system we shall never have what is known as a government organ. [Rapturous applause.]

[A noise again arose from the clamor of the crowd outside, who wished to hear Mr. Stephens, and for some moments interrupted him. The mayor rose and called on the police to preserve order. Quiet being restored, Mr. S. proceeded.]

Another change in the constitution relates to the length of the tenure of the presidential office. In the new constitution it is six years instead of four, and the President rendered ineligible for a re-election. This is certainly a decidedly conservative change. It will remove from the incumbent all temptation to use his office or exert the powers confided to him for any objects of personal ambition. The only incentive to that higher ambition which should move and actuate one holding such high trusts in his hands, will be the good of the people, the advancement, prosperity, happiness, safety, honor, and true glory of the confederacy. [Applause.]

But not to be tedious in enumerating the numerous changes for the better, allow me to allude to one other—though last, not least. The new constitution has put at rest, forever, all the agitating questions relating to our peculiar institution—African slavery as it exists amongst us—the proper status of the negro in our form of civilization. This was the immediate cause of the late rupture and present revolution. Jefferson in his forecast, had anticipated this, as the "rock upon which the old Union would split." He was right. What was conjecture with him, is now a realized fact. But whether he fully comprehended the great truth upon which that rock stood and stands, may be doubted. The prevailing ideas entertained by him and most of the leading statesmen at the time of the formation of the old constitution, were that the enslavement of the African was in violation of the laws of nature; that it was wrong in principle, socially, morally, and politically. It was an evil they knew not well how to deal with, but the general opinion of the men of that day was that, somehow or other in the order of Providence, the institution would be evanescent and pass away. This idea, though not incorporated in the constitution, was the prevailing idea at that time. The constitution, it is true, secured every essential guarantee to the institution while it should last, and hence no argument can be justly urged against the constitutional guarantees thus secured, because of the common sentiment of the day. Those ideas, however, were fundamentally wrong. They rested upon the assumption of the equality of races. This was an error. It was a sandy foundation, and the government built upon it fell when the "storm came and the wind blew."

Our new government is founded upon exactly the opposite idea; its foundations are laid, its corner-stone rests upon the great truth, that the negro is not equal to the white man; that slavery—subordination to the superior race—is his natural and normal condition. [Applause.]

This, our new government, is the first, in the history of the world, based upon this great physical, philosophical, and moral truth. This truth has been slow in the process of its development, like all other truths in the various departments of science. It has been so even amongst us. Many who hear me, perhaps, can recollect well, that this truth was not generally admitted, even within their day. The errors of the past generation still clung to many as late as twenty years ago. Those at the North, who still cling to these errors, with a zeal above knowledge, we justly denominate fanatics. All fanaticism springs from an aberration of the mind—from a defect in reasoning. It is a species of insanity. One of the most striking characteristics of insanity, in many instances, is forming correct conclusions from fancied or erroneous premises; so with the anti-slavery fanatics; their conclusions are right if their premises were. They assume that the negro is equal, and hence conclude that he is entitled to equal privileges and rights with the white man. If their premises were correct, their conclusions would be logical and just—but their premise being wrong, their whole argument fails. I recollect once of having heard a gentleman from one of the northern States, of great power and ability, announce in the House of Representatives, with imposing effect, that we of the South would be compelled, ultimately, to yield upon this subject of slavery, that it was as impossible to war successfully against a principle in politics, as it was in physics or mechanics. That the principle would ultimately prevail. That we, in maintaining slavery as it exists with us, were warring against a principle, a principle founded in nature, the principle of the equality of men. The reply I made to him was, that upon his own grounds, we should, ultimately, succeed, and that he and his associates, in this crusade against our institutions, would ultimately fail. The truth announced, that it was as impossible to war successfully against a principle in politics as it was in physics and mechanics, I admitted; but told him that it was he, and those acting with him, who were warring against a principle. They were attempting to make things equal which the Creator had made unequal.

In the conflict thus far, success has been on our side, complete throughout the length and breadth of the Confederate States. It is upon this, as I have stated, our social fabric is firmly planted; and I cannot permit myself to doubt the ultimate success of a full recognition of this principle throughout the civilized and enlightened world.

As I have stated, the truth of this principle may be slow in development, as all truths are and ever have been, in the various branches of science. It was so with the principles announced by Galileo—it was so with Adam Smith and his principles of political economy. It was so with Harvey, and his theory of the circulation of the blood. It is stated that not a single one of the medical profession, living at the time of the announcement of the truths made by him, admitted them. Now, they are universally acknowledged. May we not, therefore, look with confidence to the ultimate universal acknowledgment of the truths upon which our system rests? It is the first government ever instituted upon the principles in strict conformity to nature, and the ordination of Providence, in furnishing the materials of human society. Many governments have been founded upon the principle of the subordination and serfdom of certain classes of the same race; such were and are in violation of the laws of nature. Our system commits no such violation of nature's laws. With us, all of the white race, however high or low, rich or poor, are equal in the eye of the law. Not so with the negro. Subordination is his place. He, by nature, or by the curse against Canaan, is fitted for that condition which he occupies in our system. The architect, in the construction of buildings, lays the foundation with the proper material—the granite; then comes the brick or the marble. The substratum of our society is made of the material fitted by nature for it, and by experience we know that it is best, not only for the superior, but for the inferior race, that it should be so. It is, indeed, in conformity with the ordinance of the Creator. It is not for us to inquire into the wisdom of his ordinances, or to question them. For his own purposes, he has made one race to differ from another, as he has made "one star to differ from another star in glory."

The great objects of humanity are best attained when there is conformity to his laws and decrees, in the formation of governments as well as in all things else. Our confederacy is founded upon principles in strict conformity with these laws. This stone which was rejected by the first builders "is become the chief of the corner"—the real "corner-stone"—in our new edifice. [Applause.]

I have been asked, what of the future? It has been apprehended by some that we would have arrayed against us the civilized world. I care not who or how many they may be against us, when we stand upon the eternal principles of truth, if we are true to ourselves and the principles for which we contend, we are obliged to, and must triumph. [Immense applause.]

Thousands of people who begin to understand these truths are not yet completely out of the shell; they do not see them in their length and breadth. We hear much of the civilization and christianization of the barbarous tribes of Africa. In my judgment, those ends will never be attained, but by first teaching them the lesson taught to Adam, that "in the sweat of his brow he should eat his bread," [applause,] and teaching them to work, and feed, and clothe themselves.

But to pass on: Some have propounded the inquiry whether it is practicable for us to go on with the confederacy without further accessions? Have we the means and ability to maintain nationality among the powers of the earth? On this point I would barely say, that as anxiously as we all have been, and are, for the border States, with institutions similar to ours, to join us, still we are abundantly able to maintain our position, even if they should ultimately make up their minds not to cast their destiny with us. That they ultimately will join us—be compelled to do it—is my confident belief; but we can get on very well without them, even if they should not.

We have all the essential elements of a high national career. The idea has been given out at the North, and even in the border States, that we are too small and too weak to maintain a separate nationality. This is a great mistake. In extent of territory we embrace five hundred and sixty-four thousand square miles and upward. This is upward of two hundred thousand square miles more than was included within the limits of the original thirteen States. It is an area of country more than double the territory of France or the Austrian empire. France, in round numbers, has but two hundred and twelve thousand square miles. Austria, in round numbers, has two hundred and forty-eight thousand square miles. Ours is greater than both combined.

It is greater than all France, Spain, Portugal, and Great Britain, including England, Ireland, and Scotland, together. In population we have upward of five millions, according to the census of 1860; this includes white and black. The entire population, including white and black, of the original thirteen States, was less than four millions in 1790, and still less in '76, when the independence of our fathers was achieved. If they, with a less population, dared maintain their independence against the greatest power on earth, shall we have any apprehension of maintaining ours now?

In point of material wealth and resources, we are greatly in advance of them. The taxable property of the Confederate States cannot be less than twenty-two hundred millions of dollars! This, I think I venture but little in saying, may be considered as five times more than the colonies possessed at the time they achieved their independence. Georgia, alone, possessed last year, according to the report of our comptroller-general, six hundred and seventy-two millions of taxable property. The debts of the seven confederate States sum up in the aggregate less than eighteen millions, while the existing debts of the other of the late United States sum up in the aggregate the enormous amount of one hundred and seventy-four millions of dollars. This is without taking into the account the heavy city debts, corporation debts, and railroad debts, which press, and will continue to press, as a heavy incubus upon the resources of those States. These debts, added to others, make a sum total not much under five hundred millions of dollars. With such an area of territory as we have—with such an amount of population—with a climate and soil unsurpassed by any on the face of the earth—with such resources already at our command—with productions which control the commerce of the world—who can entertain any apprehensions as to our ability to succeed, whether others join us or not?

It is true, I believe I state but the common sentiment, when I declare my earnest desire that the border States should join us. The differences of opinion that existed among us anterior to secession, related more to the policy in securing that result by co-operation than from any difference upon the ultimate security we all looked to in common.

These differences of opinion were more in reference to policy than principle, and as Mr. Jefferson said in his inaugural, in 1801, after the heated contest preceding his election, there might be differences of opinion without differences on principle, and that all, to some extent, had been federalists and all republicans; so it may now be said of us, that whatever differences of opinion as to the best policy in having a cooperation with our border sister slave States, if the worst came to the worst, that as we were all co-operationists, we are now all for independence, whether they come or not. [Continued applause.]

In this connection I take this occasion to state, that I was not without grave and serious apprehensions, that if the worst came to the worst, and cutting loose from the old government should be the only remedy for our safety and security, it would be attended with much more serious ills than it has been as yet. Thus far we have seen none of those incidents which usually attend revolutions. No such material as such convulsions usually throw up has been seen. Wisdom, prudence, and patriotism, have marked every step of our progress thus far. This augurs well for the future, and it is a matter of sincere gratification to me, that I am enabled to make the declaration. Of the men I met in the Congress at Montgomery, I may be pardoned for saying this, an abler, wiser, a more conservative, deliberate, determined, resolute, and patriotic body of men, I never met in my life. [Great applause.] Their works speak for them; the provisional government speaks for them; the constitution of the permanent government will be a lasting monument of their worth, merit, and statesmanship. [Applause.]

But to return to the question of the future. What is to be the result of this revolution?

Will every thing, commenced so well, continue as it has begun? In reply to this anxious inquiry, I can only say it all depends upon ourselves. A young man starting out in life on his majority, with health, talent, and ability, under a favoring Providence, may be said to be the architect of his own fortunes. His destinies are in his own hands. He may make for himself a name, of honor or dishonor, according to his own acts. If he plants himself upon truth, integrity, honor and uprightness, with industry, patience and energy, he cannot fail of success. So it is with us. We are a young republic, just entering upon the arena of nations; we will be the architects of our own fortunes. Our destiny, under Providence, is in our own hands. With wisdom, prudence, and statesmanship on the part of our public men, and intelligence, virtue and patriotism on the part of the people, success, to the full measures of our most sanguine hopes, may be looked for. But if unwise counsels prevail—if we become divided—if schisms arise—if dissensions spring up—if factions are engendered—if party spirit, nourished by unholy personal ambition shall rear its hydra head, I have no good to prophesy for you. Without intelligence, virtue, integrity, and patriotism on the part of the people, no republic or representative government can be durable or stable.

We have intelligence, and virtue, and patriotism. All that is required is to cultivate and perpetuate these. Intelligence will not do without virtue. France was a nation of philosophers. These philosophers become Jacobins. They lacked that virtue, that devotion to moral principle, and that patriotism which is essential to good government. Organized upon principles of perfect justice and right—seeking amity and friendship with all other powers—I see no obstacle in the way of our upward and onward progress. Our growth, by accessions from other States, will depend greatly upon whether we present to the world, as I trust we shall, a better government than that to which neighboring States belong. If we do this, North Carolina, Tennessee, and Arkansas cannot hesitate long; neither can Virginia, Kentucky, and Missouri. They will necessarily gravitate to us by an imperious law. We made ample provision in our constitution for the admission of other States; it is more guarded, and wisely so, I think, than the old constitution on the same subject, but not too guarded to receive them as fast as it may be proper. Looking to the distant future, and, perhaps, not very far distant either, it is not beyond the range of possibility, and even probability, that all the great States of the north-west will gravitate this way, as well as Tennessee, Kentucky, Missouri, Arkansas, etc. Should they do so, our doors are wide enough to receive them, but not until they are ready to assimilate with us in principle.

The process of disintegration in the old Union may be expected to go on with almost absolute certainty if we pursue the right course. We are now the nucleus of a growing power which, if we are true to ourselves, our destiny, and high mission, will become the controlling power on this continent. To what extent accessions will go on in the process of time, or where it will end, the future will determine. So far as it concerns States of the old Union, this process will be upon no such principles of reconstruction as now spoken of, but upon reorganization and new assimilation. [Loud applause.] Such are some of the glimpses of the future as I catch them.

But at first we must necessarily meet with the inconveniences and difficulties and embarrassments incident to all changes of government. These will be felt in our postal affairs and changes in the channel of trade. These inconveniences, it is to be hoped, will be but temporary, and must be borne with patience and forbearance.

As to whether we shall have war with our late confederates, or whether all matters of differences between us shall be amicably settled, I can only say that the prospect for a peaceful adjustment is better, so far as I am informed, than it has been.

The prospect of war is, at least, not so threatening as it has been. The idea of coercion, shadowed forth in President Lincoln's inaugural, seems not to be followed up thus far so vigorously as was expected. Fort Sumter, it is believed, will soon be evacuated. What course will be pursued toward Fort Pickens, and the other forts on the gulf, is not so well understood. It is to be greatly desired that all of them should be surrendered. Our object is peace, not only with the North, but with the world. All matters relating to the public property, public liabilities of the Union when we were members of it, we are ready and willing to adjust and settle upon the principles of right, equity, and good faith. War can be of no more benefit to the North than to us. Whether the intention of evacuating Fort Sumter is to be received as an evidence of a desire for a peaceful solution of our difficulties with the United States, or the result of necessity, I will not undertake to say. I would fain hope the former. Rumors are afloat, however, that it is the result of necessity. All I can say to you, therefore, on that point is, keep your armor bright and your powder dry. [Enthusiastic cheering.]

The surest way to secure peace, is to show your ability to maintain your rights. The principles and position of the present administration of the United States—the republican party—present some puzzling questions. While it is a fixed principle with them never to allow the increase of a foot of slave territory, they seem to be equally determined not to part with an inch "of the accursed soil." Notwithstanding their clamor against the institution, they seemed to be equally opposed to getting more, or letting go what they have got. They were ready to fight on the accession of Texas, and are equally ready to fight now on her secession. Why is this? How can this strange paradox be accounted for? There seems to be but one rational solution—and that is, notwithstanding their professions of humanity, they are disinclined to give up the benefits they derive from slave labor. Their philanthropy yields to their interest. The idea of enforcing the laws, has but one object, and that is a collection of the taxes, raised by slave labor to swell the fund, necessary to meet their heavy appropriations. The spoils is what they are after—though they come from the labor of the slave. [Continued applause.]

Mr. Stephens reviewed at some length, the extravagance and profligacy of appropriations by the Congress of the United States for several years past, and in this connection took occasion to allude to another one of the great improvements in our new constitution, which is a clause prohibiting Congress from appropriating any money from the treasury, except by a two-third vote, unless it be for some object which the executive may say is necessary to carry on the government.

When it is thus asked for, and estimated for, he continued, the majority may appropriate. This was a new feature.

Our fathers had guarded the assessment of taxes by insisting that representation and taxation should go together. This was inherited from the mother country, England. It was one of the principles upon which the revolution had been fought. Our fathers also provided in the old constitution, that all appropriation bills should originate in the representative branch of Congress, but our new constitution went a step further, and guarded not only the pockets of the people, but also the public money, after it was taken from their pockets.

He alluded to the difficulties and embarrassments which seemed to surround the question of a peaceful solution of the controversy with the old government. How can it be done? is perplexing many minds. The President seems to think that he cannot recognize our independence, nor can he, with and by the advice of the Senate, do so. The constitution makes no such provision. A general convention of all the States has been suggested by some.

Without proposing to solve the difficulty, he barely made the following suggestion:

"That as the admission of States by Congress under the constitution was an act of legislation, and in the nature of a contract or compact between the States admitted and the others admitting, why should not this contract or compact be regarded as of like character with all other civil contracts—liable to be rescinded by mutual agreement of both parties? The seceding States have rescinded it on their part, they have resumed their sovereignty. Why cannot the whole question be settled, if the north desire peace, simply by the Congress, in both branches, with the concurrence of the President, giving their consent to the separation, and a recognition of our independence?" This he merely offered as a suggestion, as one of the ways in which it might be done with much less violence by constructions to the constitution than many other acts of that government. [Applause.] The difficulty has to be solved in some way or other—this may be regarded as a fixed fact.

Several other points were alluded to by Mr. Stephens, particularly as to the policy of the new government toward foreign nations, and our commercial relations with them. Free trade, as far as practicable, would be the policy of this government. No higher duties would be imposed on foreign importations than would be necessary to support the government upon the strictest economy.

In olden times the olive branch was considered the emblem of peace; we will send to the nations of the earth another and far more potential emblem of the same, the cotton plant. The present duties were levied with a view of meeting the present necessities and exigencies, in preparation for war, if need be; but if we have peace, and he hoped we might, and trade should resume its proper course, a duty of ten per cent, upon foreign importations it was thought might be sufficient to meet the expenditures of the government. If some articles should be left on the free list, as they now are, such as breadstuffs, etc., then, of course, duties upon others would have to be higher—but in no event to an extent to embarrass trade and commerce. He concluded in an earnest appeal for union and harmony, on part of all the people in support of the common cause, in which we were all enlisted, and upon the issues of which such great consequences depend.

If, said he, we are true to ourselves, true to our cause, true to our destiny, true to our high mission, in presenting to the world the highest type of civilization ever exhibited by man—there will be found in our lexicon no such word as fail.

Mr. Stephens took his seat, amid a burst of enthusiasm and applause, such as the Athenaeum has never had displayed within its walls, within "the recollection of the oldest inhabitant."

[Reporter's Note.—Your reporter begs to state that the above is not a perfect report, but only such a sketch of the address of Mr. Stephens as embraces, in his judgment, the most important points presented by the orator.—G.]

Appendix 3

The Constitution of the State of Georgia[1]

ARTICLE I.

Declaration Of Fundamental Principles.

1. The fundamental principles of Free Government cannot be too well understood, nor too often recurred to.

2. God has ordained that men shall live under government; but as the forms and administration of civil government are in human, and therefore, fallible hands, they may be altered, or modified whenever the safety or happiness of the governed requires it. No government should be changed for light or transient causes; nor unless upon reasonable assurance that a better will be established.

3. Protection to person and property is the duty of Government; and a Government which knowingly and persistently denies, or withholds from the governed such protection, when within its power, releases them from the obligation of obedience.

4. No citizen shall be deprived of life, liberty or property, except by due process of law; and of life or liberty, only by the judgment of his peers.

5. The writ of "Habeas Corpus" shall not be suspended, unless in case of rebellion or invasion, the public safety way require it.

6. The right of the people to keep and bear arms shall not be infringed.

7. No religious test shall be required for the tenure of any office; and no religion shall be established by law; and no citizen shall be deprived of any right or privilege by reason of his religious belief.

8. Freedom of thought and opinion, freedom of speech, and freedom of the press, are inherent elements of political liberty. But while every citizen may freely speak, write and print, on any subject, he shall be responsible for the abuse of the liberty.

9. The right of the people to appeal to the courts; to petition Government on all matters of legitimate cognizance; and peaceably to assemble for the consideration of any matter of public concern--shall never be impaired.

10. For every right, there should be provided a remedy; and every citizen ought to obtain justice without purchase, without denial, and without delay--conformably to the laws of the land.

11. Every person charged with an offence against the laws of the State shall have the privilege and benefit of counsel:

Shall be furnished, on demand, with a copy of the accusation, and with a list of the witnesses against him:

Shall have compulsory process to obtain the attendance of his own witnesses:

---

[1] "The Constitution of the State of Georgia, 1861," https://vault.georgiaarchives.org/digital/collection/adhoc/id/374/.

Shall be confronted with the witnesses testifying against him; and
Shall have a public and speedy trial by an impartial jury.
12. No person shall be put in jeopardy of life or liberty more than once for the same offence.
13. No conviction shall work corruption of blood, or general forfeiture of estate.
14. Excessive bail shall not be required; nor excessive fines imposed; nor cruel and unusual punishments inflicted.
15. The power of the courts to punish for contempt shall be limited by Legislative Acts.
16. A faithful execution of the laws is essential to good order; and good order in society is essential to liberty.
17. Legislative Acts in violation of the fundamental law are void; and the Judiciary shall so declare them.
18. Ex post facto laws, and laws impairing the obligation of contracts, and retro-active legislation injuriously affecting the right of the citizen, are prohibited.
19. Laws should have a general operation; and no general law shall be varied in a particular case by special Legislation; except with consent of all persons to be affected thereby.
20. The right of taxation can be granted only by the people; and shall be exercised only to raise revenue for the support of Government, to pay the public debt; to provide for the common defence, and for such other purposes as are specified in the grant of powers.
21. In cases of necessity, private ways may be granted upon just compensation being first paid; and with this exception, private property shall not be taken except for public use; and then, only upon just compensation; such compensation except in cases of pressing necessity, to be first provided and paid.
22. The right of the people to be secure in their persons, houses, papers and effects, against unreasonable searches and seizures, shall not be violated; and no warrant shall issue but upon probable cause, supported by oath or affirmation, and particularly describing the place or places to be searched, and the persons and things to be seized.
23. Martial law shall not be declared, except in cases of extreme necessity.
24. Large standing armies, in time of peace, are dangerous to liberty.
25. No soldier shall, in time of peace, be quartered in any house without the consent of the owner; nor in time of war, but in a manner prescribed by law.
26. The person of a debtor shall not be detained in prison after delivering bona fide all his estate for the use of his creditors.
27. The enumeration of rights herein contained shall not be construed to deny to the people any inherent rights which they have hitherto enjoyed.
28. This declaration is a part of this Constitution, and shall never be violated on any pretence whatever.

ARTICLE II.

SECTION 1.

The Legislative, Executive and Judicial departments, shall be distinct; and each department shall be confided to a separate body of magistracy. No person or collection of persons, being of one department shall exercise any power properly attached to either of the others; except in cases herein expressly provided.

2. The Legislative power shall be vested in a General Assembly, which shall consist of a

Senate and House of Representatives.

3. The meeting of the General Assembly shall be annual, and on the first Wednesday in November, until such day of meeting shall be altered by law. A majority of each House shall constitute a quorum to transact business; but a smaller number may adjourn from day to day, and compel the attendance of their members in such manner as each House shall prescribe. No session of the General Assembly shall continue for more than forty days, unless the same shall be done by a vote of two-thirds of each branch thereof.

4. The compensation of the members and officers of the General Assembly shall be fixed by law, at the first session, subsequent to the adoption of this Constitution: and the same shall not be increased so as to affect the compensation of the members or officers of the Assembly by which the increase is adopted.

5. No person holding any military commission or other appointment, having any emolument or compensation annexed thereto, under this State or the Confederate States, or either of them, (except Justices of the Inferior Court, Justices of the Peace and officers of the militia), nor any defaulter for public money, or for legal taxes required of him, shall have a seat in either branch of the General Assembly; nor shall any Senator or Representative, after his qualification as such, be elected to any office or appointment by the General Assembly having any emoluments or compensation annexed thereto, during the time for which he shall have been elected.

6. No person convicted of any felony before any Court of this State, or of the Confederate States, shall be eligible to any office or appointment of honor, profit or trust, within this State.

7. No person who is a collector or holder of public money, shall be eligible to any office in this State, until the same is accounted for and paid into the Treasury.

SECTION 2.

1. The Senate shall consist of forty-four members, one to be chosen from each senatorial district, which district shall be composed of three contiguous counties. If a new county is established, it shall be added to a district which it adjoins until there shall be another arrangement of the senatorial districts. The senatorial districts shall not be changed except when a new census shall have been taken.

2. No person shall be a Senator who shall not have attained to the age of twenty-five years, and be a citizen of the Confederate States, and have been for three years an inhabitant of this State, and for one year a resident of the district from which he is chosen.

3. The presiding officer shall be styled the President of the Senate, and shall be elected viva voce from their own body.

4. The Senate shall have the sole power to try all impeachments. When sitting for that purpose, they shall be on oath or affirmation; and no person shall be convicted without the concurrence of two-thirds of the members present. Judgment, in cases of impeachment, shall not extend further than removal from office and disqualification to hold and enjoy any office of honor, profit or trust within this State; but the party convicted shall, nevertheless, be liable and subject to indictment, trial, judgment and punishment according to law.

SECTION 3.

1. The House of Representatives shall be composed as follows: The thirty-seven counties having the largest representative population shall have two Representatives each. Every other county shall have one Representative. The designation of the counties having two Representatives shall be made by the General Assembly immediately after the taking of each census.

2. No person shall be a Representative who shall not have attained to the age of twenty-one years, and be a citizen of the Confederate States, and have been for three years an inhabitant of this State, and for one year a resident of the county which he represents

3. The presiding officer of the House of Representatives shall be styled the Speaker, and shall be elected viva voce from their own body.

4. They shall have the sole power to impeach all persons who have been or may be in office.

5. All bills for raising revenue, or appropriating money, shall originate in the House of Representatives; but the Senate may propose or concur in amendments, as in other bills.

SECTION 4.

1. Each House shall be the judge of the election, returns, and qualifications of its own members; and shall have power to punish them for disorderly behavior or mis-conduct, by censure, fine, imprisonment or expulsion; but no member shall be expelled except by a vote of two-thirds of the House from which he is expelled.

2. Each House may punish, by imprisonment not extending beyond the session, any person not a member, who shall be guilty of a contempt, by any disorderly behavior in its presence; or who, during the session, shall threaten injury to the person or estate of any member, for anything said or done in either House; or who shall assault any member therefor; or who shall assault or arrest any witness going to or returning therefrom; or who shall rescue, or attempt to rescue, any person arrested by order of either House.

3. The members of both Houses shall be free from arrest, during their attendance on the General Assembly, and in going to and returning therefrom, except for treason, felony, or breach of the peace. And no member shall be liable to answer, in any other place, for anything spoken in debate in either House.

4. Each House shall keep a journal of its proceedings, and publish them immediately after its adjournment. The yeas and nays of the members on any question, shall, at the desire of one-fifth of the members present, be entered on the journals. The original journals shall be preserved (after publication) in the office of the Secretary of State; but there shall be no other record thereof.

5. Every bill, before it shall pass, shall be read three times and on three separate and distinct days in each House, unless in cases of actual invasion or insurrection. Nor shall any law or ordinance pass which refers to more than one subject matter, or contains matter different from what is expressed in the title thereof.

6. All Acts shall be signed by the President of the Senate and the Speaker of the House of Representatives; and no bill, ordinance, or resolution intended to have the effect of law, which shall have been rejected by either House, shall be again proposed under the same or any other title, without the consent of two-thirds of the House by which the same was rejected.

7. Neither House shall adjourn for more than three days, nor to any other place, without the consent of the other; and in case of disagreement between the two Houses, on a question of adjournment, the Governor may adjourn them.
8. Every Senator and Representative, before taking his seat, shall take an oath or affirmation to support the Constitution of the Confederate States and of this State; and also, that he hath not practiced any unlawful means, either directly or indirectly, to procure his election. And every person convicted of having given or offered a bribe, shall be disqualified from serving as a member of either House for the term for which he was elected.
9. Whenever this Constitution requires an Act to be passed by two-thirds of both Houses, the yeas and nays on the passage thereof shall be entered on the journals of each.

SECTION 5.

1. The General Assembly shall have power to make all laws and ordinances, consistent with this Constitution and not repugnant to the Constitution of the Confederate States, which they shall deem necessary and proper for the welfare of the State.
2. They may alter the boundaries of counties, and lay off and establish new counties; but every bill to establish a new county shall be passed by at least two-thirds of the members present, in each branch of the General Assembly.
3. They shall provide for the taking of a census or enumeration of the people of this State, at regular decades of years, commencing at such times as they may prescribe.
4. The General Assembly shall have power to appropriate money for the promotion of learning and science, and to provide for the education of the people.
5. The General Assembly shall have power by a vote of two-thirds of each branch, to grant pardons in cases of final conviction for treason, and to pardon or commute in cases of final conviction for murder.

SECTION 6.

1. The General Assembly shall have no power to grant corporate powers and privileges to private companies, except to banking, insurance, railroad, canal, plank road, navigation, mining, express, lumber, and telegraph companies; nor to make or change election precincts; nor to establish bridges and ferries; nor to change names, or legitimate children; but shall by law prescribe the manner in which such power shall be exercised by the Courts. But no bank charter shall be granted or extended, and no Act passed authorizing the suspension of specie payment by any chartered bank, except by a vote of two-thirds of each branch of the General Assembly.
2. No money shall be drawn from the Treasury of this State, except by appropriation made by law; and a regular statement and account of the receipt and expenditure of all public money shall be published from time to time.
3. No vote, resolution, law or order shall pass, granting a donation or gratuity in favor of any person, except by the concurrence of two-thirds of the General Assembly.
4. No law, shall be passed by which a citizen shall be compelled, directly or indirectly, to become a stockholder in, or contribute to a rail road or other work of internal improvement, without his consent; except the inhabitants of a corporate town or city. This provision shall not be construed to deny the power of taxation for the purpose of making levees

or dams to prevent the overflow of rivers.

SECTION 7.

1. The importation or introduction of negroes from any foreign country, other than the slave-holding States or Territories of the United States of America, is forever prohibited.
2. The General Assembly may prohibit the introduction of negroes from any State; but they shall have no power to prevent immigrants from bringing their slaves with them.
3. The General Assembly shall have no power to pass laws for the emancipation of slaves.
4. Any person who shall maliciously kill or maim a slave, shall suffer such punishment as would be inflicted in case the like offence had been committed on a free white person.

ARTICLE III.

SECTION 1.

1. The executive power shall be vested in a Governor, who shall hold his office during the term of two years, and until such time as a successor shall be chosen and qualified. He shall have a competent salary fixed by law, which shall not be increased or diminished during the period for which he shall have been elected; neither shall he receive, within that period, any other emolument from the Confederate States, or either of them, or from any foreign power.
2. The Governor shall be elected by the persons qualified to vote for members of the General Assembly, on the first Wednesday in October, in the year of our Lord 1861; and on the first Wednesday in October in every second year thereafter, until such time be altered by law; which election shall be held at the places of holding general elections, in the several counties of this State, in the manner prescribed for the election of members of the General Assembly. The returns for every election of Governor shall be sealed up by the managers, separately from other returns, and directed to the President of the Senate and Speaker of the House of Representatives; and transmitted to the Governor, or the person exercising the duties of Governor for the time being; who shall, without opening the said returns, cause the same to be laid before the Senate, on the day after the two houses shall have been organized; and they shall be transmitted by the Senate to the House of Representatives. The members of each branch of the General Assembly shall convene in the Representative chamber, and the President of the Senate, and the Speaker of the House of Representatives, shall open and publish the returns in presence of the General Assembly; and the person having the majority of the whole number of votes given in, shall be declared duly elected Governor of this State; but if no person have such majority, then from the two persons having the highest number of votes, who shall be in life, and shall not decline an election at the time appointed the Legislature to elect, the General Assembly shall immediately elect a Governor viva voce; and in all cases of election of a Governor by the General Assembly, a majority of the votes of the members present shall be necessary for a choice. Contested elections shall be determined by both Houses of the General Assembly, in such manner as shall be prescribed by law.
3. No person shall be eligible to the office of Governor who shall not have been a citizen of the Confederate States twelve years, and an inhabitant of this State six years, and who hath not attained the age of thirty years.
4. In case of the death, resignation, or disability of the Governor, the President of the Senate

shall exercise the executive powers of the government until such disability be removed, or a successor is elected and qualified. And in case of the death, resignation, or disability of the President of the Senate, the Speaker of the House of Representatives shall exercise the executive power of the government until the removal of the disability or the election and qualification of a Governor.

5. The Governor shall, before he enters on the duties of his office, take the following oath or affirmation: "I do solemnly swear or affirm (as the case may be,) that I will faithfully execute the office of Governor of the State of Georgia; and will, to the best of my abilities, preserve, protect and defend the constitution thereof."

SECTION 2.

1. The Governor shall be Commander-in-Chief of the army and navy of this State, and of the militia thereof.

2. He shall have power to grant reprieves for offences against the State, except in cases of impeachment, and to grant pardons, or to remit any part of a sentence, in all cases after conviction, except for treason or murder, in which cases he may respite the execution, and make report thereof to the next General Assembly.

3. He shall issue writs of elections to fill vacancies that happen in the Senate or House of Representatives, and shall have power to convene the General Assembly on extraordinary occasions; and shall give them, from time to time, information of the state of the republic, and recommend to their consideration such measures as he may deem necessary and expedient.

4. When any office shall become vacant by death, resignation, or otherwise, the Governor shall have power to fill such vacancy unless otherwise provided for by law; and persons so appointed shall continue in office until a successor is appointed agreeably to the mode pointed out by this Constitution, or by law in pursuance thereof.

5. A person once rejected by the Senate shall not be re-appointed by the Governor to the same office during the same session or the recess thereafter.

6. The Governor shall have the revision of all bills passed by both Houses, before the same shall become laws, but two-thirds of each House may pass a law notwithstanding his dissent; and if any bill should not be returned by the Governor within five days (Sundays excepted) after it has been presented to him, the same shall be a law, unless the General Assembly, by their adjournment, shall prevent its return. He may approve any appropriation and disapprove any other appropriation in the same bill, and the latter shall not be effectual unless passed by two-thirds of each House.

7. Every vote, resolution, or order, to which the concurrence of both Houses may be necessary, except on a question of election or adjournment, shall be presented to the Governor; and before it shall take effect, be approved by him, or being disapproved, shall be re-passed by two-thirds of each House, according to the rules and limitations prescribed in case of a bill.

8. There shall be a Secretary of State, a Comptroller General, a Treasurer, and Surveyor-General, elected by the General Assembly, and they shall hold their offices for the like period as the Governor, and shall have a competent salary, which shall not be increased or diminished during the period for which they shall have been elected. The General Assembly

may at any time consolidate any two of these offices, and require all the duties to be discharged by one officer.
9. The great seal of the State shall be deposited in the office of the Secretary of State, and shall not be affixed to any instrument of writing, but by order of the Governor or General Assembly; and the General Assembly shall, at their first session, after the rising of this convention, by law cause the great seal to be altered.
10. The Governor shall have power to appoint his own Secretaries, not exceeding two in number.

ARTICLE IV.

SECTION 1.

1. The Judicial powers of this State shall be vested in a Supreme Court for the correction of errors, a Superior, Inferior, Ordinary and Justices' Courts, and in such other courts as have been or may be established by law.
2. The Supreme Court shall consist of three Judges, who shall be appointed by the Governor with the advice and consent of two-thirds of the Senate, for such term of years as shall be prescribed by law, and shall continue in office until their successors shall be appointed and qualified, removable by the Governor on the address of two-thirds of each branch of the General Assembly, or by impeachment and conviction thereon.
3. The said Court shall have no original jurisdiction, but shall be a court alone for the trial and correction of errors in law and equity from the Superior Courts of the several circuits, and shall sit at least once a year, at a time prescribed by law, in each of one or more judicial districts, designated by the General Assembly for that purpose, at such point in each district as shall by the General Assembly be ordained, for the trial and determination of writs of error from the several Superior Courts included in such judicial districts.
4. The said Court shall dispose of and finally determine every case on the docket of such Court at the first or second term after such writ of error brought; and in case the plaintiff in error shall not be prepared at the first term of such Court after error brought, to prosecute the case, unless precluded by some providential cause from such prosecution, it shall be stricken from the docket, and the judgment below shall stand affirmed.

SECTION 2.

1. The Judges of the Superior Courts shall be appointed in the same manner as Judges of the Supreme Court from the circuits in which they are to serve, for the term of four years, and shall continue in office until their successors shall be appointed and qualified, removable by the Governor on the address of two-thirds of each branch of the General Assembly, or by impeachment and conviction thereon.
2. The Superior Court shall have exclusive jurisdiction in all cases of divorce, both total and partial; but no total divorce shall be granted, except on the concurrent verdicts of two special juries. In each divorce case, the Court shall regulate the rights and disabilities of the parties.
3. The Superior Court shall also have exclusive jurisdiction in all criminal cases, except as relates to people of color, fines for neglect of duty, contempts of Court; violations of road laws, and obstructions of water courses, jurisdiction of which shall be vested in such judicature or tribunal as shall be or may have been pointed out by law; and except in all other

minor offences committed by free white persons, and which do not subject the offender or offenders to loss of life, limb or member, or to confinement in the penitentiary; in all such cases, Corporation Courts, such as now exist, or may hereafter be constituted, in any incorporated city, or town, may be vested with jurisdiction, under such rules and regulations as the Legislature may hereafter by law direct.
4. All criminal cases shall be tried in the county where the crime was committed, except in cases where a jury cannot be obtained.
5. The Superior Court shall have exclusive jurisdiction in all cases respecting titles to land, which shall be tried in the county where the land lies. And also in all equity causes which shall be tried in the county where one or more of the defendants reside, against whom substantial relief is prayed.
6. It shall have appellate jurisdiction in all such cases as may be provided by law.
7. It shall have power to correct errors in inferior judicatories by writ of certiorari, and to grant new trials in the Superior Court on proper and legal grounds.
8. It shall have power to issue writs of mandamus, prohibition, scire facias, and all other writs which may be necessary for carrying its powers fully into effect.
9. The Superior and Inferior Courts shall have concurrent jurisdiction in all other civil causes; which shall be tried in the county where the defendant resides.
10. In cases of joint obligors, or joint promissors or copartners, or joint trespassers residing in different counties, the suit may be brought in either county.
11. In case of a maker and indorser or indorsers of promissory notes residing in different counties in this State, the same may be sued in the county where the maker resides.
12. The Superior and Inferior Courts shall sit in each county twice in every year, at such stated times as have been or may be appointed by the General Assembly.

SECTION 3.

1. The judges shall have salaries adequate to their services fixed by law, which shall not be diminished during their continuance in office; but shall not receive any other perquisites or emoluments whatever, from parties or others, on account of any duty required of them.
2. There shall be a State's Attorney and Solicitors appointed in the same manner as the Judges of the Supreme Court and commissioned by the Governor; who shall hold their offices for the term of four years, or until their successors shall be appointed and qualified, unless removed by sentence on impeachment, or by the Governor, on the address of two-thirds of each branch of the General Assembly. They shall have salaries adequate to their services fixed by law, which shall not be diminished during their continuance in office.
3. The Justices of the Inferior Courts shall be elected in each county by the persons entitled to vote for members of the General Assembly.
4. The Justices of the Peace shall be elected in each district by the persons us entitled to vote for members of the General Assembly.
5. The powers of a Court of Ordinary and of Probate, shall be vested in an Ordinary for each county, from whose decisions there may be an appeal to the Superior Court, under regulations prescribed by law. The ordinary shall be ex officio clerk of said Court, and may appoint a deputy-clerk. The ordinary, as clerk, or his deputy, may issue citations and grant temporary letters of administration, to hold until permanent letters are granted; and said

ordinary, as clerk, or his deputy, may grant marriage licenses. The ordinaries in and for the respective counties shall be elected, as other county officers are, on the first Wednesday in January, 1864, and every fourth year thereafter, and shall be commissioned by the Governor for the term of four years. In case of any vacancy of said office of ordinary, from any cause, the same shall be filled by election, as is provided in relation to other county officers, and until the same is filled, the clerk of the Superior Court for the time being shall act as clerk of said Court of Ordinary.

ARTICLE V.

1. The electors of Members of the General Assembly shall be free white male citizens of this State; and shall have attained the age of twenty-one years; and have paid all taxes which may have been required of them, and which they have had an opportunity of paying, agreeably to law, for the year preceding the election; and shall have resided six months within the district or county.

2. All elections, by the General Assembly, shall be viva voce and when the Senate and House of Representatives unite for the purpose of electing, they shall meet in the Representative chamber, and the President of the Senate shall in such cases preside, and declare the person or persons elected.

3. In all elections by the people, the electors shall vote by ballot, until the General Assembly shall otherwise direct.

4. All civil officers shall continue in the exercise of the duties of their several offices, during the periods for which they were appointed, or until they shall be superseded by appointments made in conformity with this Constitution; and all laws now in force shall continue to operate, so far as they are compatible with this Constitution, until they shall expire, be altered or repealed; and it shall be the duty of the General Assembly to pass all necessary laws and regulations for carrying this Constitution into full effect.

5. All militia and county officers shall be elected by the people in such manner as the General Assembly may by law direct.

6. This Constitution shall be amended only by a Convention of the people called for that purpose.

7. This Constitution shall not take effect until the same is ratified by the people. And to this end, there shall be an election held at all the places of public election in this State, on the first Tuesday in July, 1861, when all the citizens of this State entitled to vote for Governor, shall cast their ballots either for "Ratification" or "No Ratification." The election shall be conducted in the same manner as general elections, and the returns shall be made to the Governor. If a majority of the votes cast shall be for Ratification, the Governor shall by proclamation, declare this Constitution adopted by the people. But if for No Ratification, that fact shall be proclaimed by the Governor, and this Constitution shall have no effect whatever.

Done in Convention of the Delegates of the people of the State of Georgia, at Savannah, on the 23rd day of March, in the year of our Lord eighteen hundred and sixty-one.

Appendix 4

A Proclamation by

Joseph E. Brown, Governor of Georgia[1]

Whereas, by the oppressive and wicked conduct of the Government and people of that part of the late United States of America known as the anti-slavery States, war actually exists between them and the people of the Southern States, and whereas the President of the United States has issued his proclamation declaring his determination to blockade the ports of the Southern States, and is now collecting federal troops upon southern soil for the purpose of subjugating and enslaving us;

And Whereas, property belonging to the citizens of the State of Georgia, whenever found within the anti-slavery States, is seized and forcibly taken from its owners;

And Whereas, all contracts made with the enemy during the existence of hostilities are, by the law of nations, illegal and void, and all remedies for the enforcement of contracts in our courts between citizens of this State and citizens of the States now making war upon us, which were made prior to the commencement of hostilities are suspended till the termination of the war;

And Whereas, in the language of the law of nations "the purchase of bills on the enemy's country of the remission and deposit of funds there is a dangerous and illegal act, because it may be cherishing the .resources and relieving the wants of the enemy, and the remission of funds in money or bills to subjects of the enemy is unlawful," and whereas, sound policy, as well as inter- national law, absolutely forbids that any citizen of this State shall, under any pretext whatever, assist the enemy by remitting, paying or furnishing any money or other thing of value during the continuance of hostilities to the government or people of the States which have waged and are maintaining a most unnatural and wicked war against us;

And Whereas, justice requires that all sums due from citizens of this State to individuals in such hostile States who do not uphold and sustain the savage and cruel warfare inaugurated by their government should be promptly paid so soon as hostilities have ceased, and the independence of the Confederate States is recognized by the government of the United States.

Therefore, in view of these considerations, I, Joseph E. Brown, Governor and Commander-in-Chief of the Army and Navy of the State of Georgia, do issue this, my proclamation, commanding and enjoining upon each citizen or inhabitant of this State, that he abstain absolutely from all violations of the law above recited, that he do not, under any pretext whatever, remit, transfer, or pay to the government of the United States, or any one of the States composing said government, which is known as a free soil State, including

---

[1] Candler, *Confederate Records of the State of Georgia*, 2:33–37.

among others the States of Massachusetts, Rhode Island, Connecticut, New York, New Jersey, Pennsylvania, and Ohio, or to any citizen or inhabitant of any such State, any money, bills, draft, or other things of value, either in payment of any debt due or hereafter to become due, or for, or on account of, any other cause whatever, until the termination of hostilities. And I hereby invite each citizen or inhabitant of this State who is indebted to said government, or either of said States, or any citizen or inhabitant thereof, to pay the amount of such indebtedness, whenever due, into the Treasury of Georgia in any funds bankable in Augusta or Savannah, or to deposit the same subject to the order of the Treasurer of this State, in any one of the solvent banks of either of said cities, or in any legally authorized 'agency of either of said banks; and upon the making of any such deposit at the Treasury, or upon presentation of any such certificate of deposit, the Treasurer of this State is hereby directed and required to deliver to such person a certificate specifying the sum so deposited, which I hereby declare the faith and credit of this State will be pledged to repay to such depositor in funds bankable in Augusta and Savannah, with seven per cent. interest from the date of the deposit, so soon as hostilities shall have ceased, and it shall again be lawful for debtors to pay the same to creditors in the hostile States above mentioned. This will not only afford to such of our citizens as owe money to northern creditors, which international law and public policy forbid them at present to pay, a safe investment and the highest security for its return to them at the end of the war, but it will enable them, in the meantime, to perform a patriotic duty and to assist the State, and through her the Confederate States, in raising the funds necessary to the successful defence of our homes, our firesides and our altars.

And I do further command and strictly enjoin upon all and every chartered bank in this State which may be in possession of any note, bill, draft, or other paper binding any citizen of this State, to pay money to any one of said hostile States, or any inhabitant or corporation thereof, or belonging to any such State or person, to abstain from protesting any such draft, bill, or note, or other paper; provided, the person liable on such draft, note, bill, or other paper, will exhibit to such bank, or any of its agencies, having such paper in possession, a certificate showing that he has deposited the amount due on such paper in the Treasury of this State, or in any one of the banks above mentioned, to the credit of the Treasurer, or will at the time such paper becomes due, make such deposit. And I further command and require all Notarys Public in this State to abstain absolutely from the performance of any official act for the protest of any paper of the character above mentioned under such circumstances as are herein before specified.

Given under my hand and the Great Seal of this at the Capitol in Milledgeville, this twenty-sixth day of April in the year of our Lord eighteen hundred and sixty-one, and of the independence of the Confederate States of America the first.

Appendix 5

General Joseph E. Johnston's General Orders No. 5[1]

Headquarters Army of Tennessee, Dalton, Ga., January 8, 1864.

I. The following regulations are published for the government of the troops in this army in camp. They are to be read at the head of each company at least once every week. Copies are to be furnished all field, staff, and company officers:

1. The hours of service and roll-call as follows: Reveille at daylight; police immediately after reveille; surgeon's call fifteen minutes after reveille; stable call fifteen minutes after reveille; first sergeant's call half hour after reveille; breakfast at sunrise; adjutant's call at 9 a, m.; drill from 10 to 11.30 a. m.; officers' drill from 11 a. m. to 12 m.; dinner at 12.30 p. m.; drill from 2.30 to 4 p. m.; guard mounting at 4 p. m.; stable call at 4 p. m.; camp and company police at 4.30 p. m.; dress parade at sunset; supper immediately after parade; tattoo at 8 p. m.; taps one hour after tattoo.

Men are not to be excused from duty of any kind, except for disability, by their medical officers and for meritorious conduct by their regimental commanders or officers of higher rank. Company commanders and their subalterns are specially prohibited from assuming this power in any case whatever.

2. The roll of the enlisted men of each company is to be called by the first sergeant at reveille, at morning and afternoon drill, at dress parade, and at tattoo.

3. The artillery of each division, though it may be camped separately, is to report to division headquarters, and division commanders are responsible for the due observance of all orders therein. In the artillery, all company officers are to attend the stable call. In the quartermaster's department, division commanders are to enforce the same rules in respect to the care of animals as in the artillery, requiring all quartermasters to attend the stable calls for the animals of their trains; and in that department, as also in commissary, ordnance, and medical departments, they are to require roll-calls and reports of absentees at reveille and tattoo and the due performance of police and other necessary duties.

4. On Sundays there are no drills. Inspection is to be at 10 a. m., under the personal supervision of the brigade commanders, and the commanders of divisions are to supervise these inspections, being present with one of their brigades each Sunday.

Once a week the commander of each division, accompanied by all his brigade commanders, will visit and thoroughly inspect the camp. of each brigade, including stores and field transportation.

Whenever practicable, religious services are to be held in camp on Sundays, when the utmost decorum is to be observed. Religious services at night are not to extend beyond taps.

5. At reveille and tattoo the men are to be in ranks when the drum stops beating. A

---

[1] *OR*, ser. I, vol. 47, pt. 2:60–62.

preparatory signal is to be beaten five minutes before all other calls, at which the men assemble on their company grounds. Ranks are formed at the second beating of the drum. When it stops the companies are called to attention, and those who fall in after this are to be reported as "late."

First sergeants are to commit their rolls to memory, call them promptly, and immediately report to the company officers of highest rank present. Where there are more than one of the same surname numbers are to be used.

At reveille and tattoo all company officers are to be present, and at least one is to be present at all other roll-calls. First sergeants enter first in order for fatigue details, all absentees late and men whose arms or accouterments are in bad condition or who are neglectful of cleanliness in their persons, clothing, or tents.

The company officer to whom absentees are reported at any roll-call immediately reports them to the adjutant of the regiment, and the adjutant reports to the regimental commander the company officers improperly absent from such roll-call, and the regimental commander reports to the commander of the brigade.

The officers to whom absentees are reported are to take prompt measures for arresting and bringing them to punishment.

6. At surgeon's call the sick in camp assemble on their respective company grounds and are marched to the hospital by a non-commissioned officer, one of whom is detailed daily for that duty. None are to present themselves for treatment except in this manner without special permission. The non-commissioned officer takes with him the company sick-book, and returns it to the first sergeant after the surgeon has made the proper entries therein.

Company, regimental, and brigade commanders are required at all times to know how their sick are situated and are responsible for the prevention of neglect and ill treatment within the limits of their respective commands. It is likewise made their duty to see that the dead are decently interred and the places of burial suitably inclosed.

7. At the call for guard mounting the several guard details assemble on their respective regimental color lines, are carefully inspected, and then marched to the general parade ground by the first sergeant. Guards are to be mounted strictly in accordance with the Army Regulations, under the personal supervision of a brigade staff officer, and the several regimental adjutants are-to alternate in mounting the guard. The guard-house of each brigade is to be 60 yards in front of the color-line and near the center of the brigade when the ground will admit of it. All calls are to be sounded at the brigade guard-house and promptly repeated at the several regimental headquarters.

8. The old guard, upon the next day after being relieved, is to be the general fatigue party for that day. Its duties are to clean thoroughly all the encampments, except the company grounds, and to perform such other labor as may be necessary.

A non-commissioned officer and a sufficient number of privates of each company are to be detailed daily as company police, and are to thoroughly clean their company grounds immediately after breakfast and again at 4.30 p. m. The commanding officer of each company inspects his company grounds immediately after the times above prescribed.

At these inspections the quarters are to be in perfect order, knapsacks properly packed, and bedding neatly folded, the occupants of each tent or hut remaining in front of the same during its inspection.

The brigade officer of the day is responsible for the due performance of all police and fatigue duty within or near his lines. He is specially charged with seeing that the sinks of regiments and offal pits of companies are properly placed and arranged and fresh earth thrown into them daily; that slaughter pens are kept at least half a mile from the camps and not near any thoroughfare, the offal there buried daily and the hides removed; that the wagon yards and other places of keeping animals are regularly and well policed, and that nothing offensive to decency or detrimental to health be anywhere visible.

9. At the signal for parade each company is formed on its own company grounds, under arms, and is thoroughly inspected by its officers. When the music begins playing the companies are marched in their proper order to the general parade, which is the color-line of each regiment.

10. At taps all lights except those of commissioned officers, noncommissioned staff, and first sergeants are to be extinguished, and there is to be perfect quiet in the encampment; one officer of each company remaining on duty in his company grounds for half an hour after taps, enforcing obedience to these requirements, and then reporting to the adjutant of the regiment. All lights, except those of the field and staff, are extinguished at 11 p. m.

11. Brigade, regimental, and company commanders are required to give close and constant attention to the quality and quantity of rations issued to their men and the preparation of the same as food. The various medical officers are to make frequent inspections of the issues of food and the cooking utensils, and offer such suggestions from time to time as may seem likely to promote the health of the command.

12. In each brigade a brigade guard is detailed every day, consisting of the proper number of commissioned and non-commissioned officers and men, enough for a chain of sentinels entirely surrounding the brigade encampment, including the sinks, and, if practicable, the water.

Between daylight and dark officers wearing their side-arms are to pass the chain of sentinels of the brigade guard at will, and in this period enlisted men without arms and accouterments, having the written permission of the brigade commander, are allowed to pass the same chain of sentinels. But this does not authorize them to absent themselves from any duty whatever, nor to go more than 500 yards from their camps, unless they are general officers, brigade or regimental commanders, their staff officers, orderlies, or couriers, when on duty. Between dark and daylight the brigade guard challenges all persons attempting to pass the lines.

At all hours, whether by day or night, the brigade guard arrests all disorderly or suspicious persons. All citizens attempting to come within the lines will be sent to brigade headquarters. There is also a patrol in each brigade, moving day and night through the encampment, arresting suspicious persons, preventing nuisances, and suppressing all disorder.

13. From the divisions there is detailed daily, or at longer intervals as circumstances require, a picket guard, consisting of the proper number of commissioned and non-

commissioned officers and men, enough to cover all approaches to the camp and keep up by day and night an efficient patrol between the several picket stations. It receives special instructions from time to time.

Each brigade officer of the day has immediate control over the pickets detailed from his brigade and is responsible for their due performance of duty.

14. Every detachment maintains such guards as will effectually preserve order and prevent surprise.

The smaller the body the greater the necessity for vigilance. While one relief of a guard is on post another sleeps. The other relief is at the guard-house awake and ready for any emergency. Officers and men detailed for guard duty are to take with them their blankets and cooked rations, and are not on any pretense to revisit their quarters until relieved, unless in the proper and necessary discharge of duty.

15. One of the commanding officers of each guard is required to visit all the sentinels of each relief, assuring himself that they know and correctly perform all their duties.

Brigade officers of the day are to visit their guards at least once before dark and once during the night, after 12 p. m., ascertaining that both officers and men are properly instructed and duly vigilant.

All the guards, patrols, fatigue, and police parties of the command are under the general supervision and control of the division officer of the day, and he is responsible for their due performance of duty. He requires those under him to make written reports as soon as relieved, and forwards the same to division headquarters with such comments and suggestions as he may think expedient. He reports to the division commander in person when relieved, accompanied by the new division officer of the day.

16. A sentinel should always be ready to fire. He must, however, be sure of the presence of an enemy before firing; once satisfied of that he must fire at all hazards, as the safety of the command may depend upon it. Sentinels fire on all persons, deserting to the enemy or breaking through the lines and failing to stop when ordered, and upon all persons whom it is their duty to arrest and who cannot otherwise be secured.

At the approach of officers or rounds of the guards a sentinel challenges as prescribed by the Army Regulations. In other cases he orders, "Halt! About face!" and calls the corporal of the guard, with the number of the post. Persons on horseback are to dismount when approaching sentinels.

Officers of guards are required so to regulate the movements of the sentinels that they shall habitually turn on their posts at the same time, and all turn and move in the same direction.

Due honors are to be paid by guards and sentinels facing outward to salute, and acknowledged by the officers so complimented.

Proper salutations are always to be exchanged at meeting between officers, and between officers and privates.

17. All orders affecting the troops are to be read at the head of each company, that all may distinctly hear them.

The Rules and Articles of War of the Confederate States are to be read to each company immediately before or after each muster for pay. It is earnestly hoped that little or no cause will be given for enforcing the penalties therein pronounced against offenders; but all are distinctly notified and solemnly cautioned that serious violations of the same will be dealt with as therein provided, and no pardons granted.

18. A spirit of courtesy is to be cultivated, and harmony, devotion to the cause, obedience to superiors, and patient endurance of all hardships sought to be made the distinguishing characteristics of both officers and men. Language or conduct calculated to cause discontent among the troops is not to be tolerated, and in every instance the offender is to be put in arrest and brought to trial. This is made the duty of all officers of the command.

The habit of entering private houses uninvited, begging food from private families, and otherwise lessening the comforts and increasing the burdens of the women and children of the country, is un-soldierly in the extreme. The practice of committing depredations upon private property is detestable. Officers of all grades are to be held strictly accountable for the conduct of their men in these respects, and all damages suffered by citizens are to be deducted from the offenders' pay.

Officers are reminded that assiduous attention to every duty is the sacred obligation resting on them; and that the censure of their own consciences and of their countrymen everywhere will assuredly follow them up during the war, and to the end of life, if they prove remiss in any respect. The test of their fidelity is in the condition of the troops which, they command. Men well disciplined, well instructed, and well cared for point out the honest officer and true patriot. The reverse shows an officer unworthy of his position, and faithless to the cause.

By command of General Johnston: George WM. Brent, Assistant Adjutant-General.

Appendix 6

Special Field Orders, No. 15

January 16, 1865, Savannah[1]

I. The islands from Charleston south, the abandoned rice-fields along the rivers for thirty miles back from the sea, and the country bordering the Saint John's River, Fla., are reserved and set apart for the settlement of the negroes now made free by the acts of war and the proclamation of the President of the United States.

II. At Beaufort, Hilton Head, Savannah, Fernandina, Saint Augustine, and Jacksonville the blacks may remain in their chosen or accustomed vocations; but on the islands, and in the settlements hereafter to be established, no white person whatever, unless military officers and soldiers detailed for duty, will be permitted to reside; and the sole and exclusive management of affairs will be left to the freed people themselves, subject only to the United States military authority and the acts of Congress. By the laws of war and orders of the President of the United States the negro is free, and must be dealt with as such. He cannot be subjected to conscription or forced military service, save by the written orders of the highest military authority of the Department, under such regulations as the President or Congress may prescribe; domestic servants, blacksmiths, carpenters, and other mechanics will be free to select their own work and residence, but the young and able-bodied negroes must be encouraged to enlist as soldiers in the service of the United States, to contribute their share toward maintaining their own freedom and securing their rights as citizens of the United States. Negroes so enlisted will be organized into companies, battalions, and regiments, under the orders of the United States military authorities, and will be paid, fed, and clothed according to law. The bounties paid on enlistment may, with the consent of the recruit, go to assist his family and settlement in procuring agricultural implements, seed, tools, boats, clothing, and other articles necessary for their livelihood.

III. Whenever three respectable negroes, heads of families, shall desire to settle on land, and shall have selected for that purpose an island, or a locality clearly defined within the limits above designated, the inspector of settlements and plantations will himself, or by such subordinate officer as he may appoint, give them a license to settle such island or district, and afford them such assistance as he can to enable them to establish a peaceable agricultural settlement. The three parties named will subdivide the land, under the supervision of the inspector, among themselves and such others as may choose to settle near them, so that each family shall have a plot of not more than forty acres of tillable ground, and when it borders on some water channel with not more than 800 feet water front, in the possession of which land the military authorities will afford them protection until such time as they can protect themselves or until Congress shall regulate their title. The quartermaster may, on the requisition of the inspector of settlements and plantations, place at the disposal of the inspector one or more of the captured steamers to ply between the settlements and one

---

[1] *OR*, ser. I, vol. 47, pt. 2:60–62.

or more of the commercial points, heretofore named in orders, to afford the settlers the opportunity to supply their necessary wants and to sell the products of their land and labor.

IV. Whenever a negro has enlisted in the military service of the United States he may locate his family in any one of the settlements at pleasure and acquire a homestead and all other rights and privileges of a settler as though present in person. In like manner negroes may settle their families and engage on board the gun-boats, or in fishing, or in the navigation of the inland waters, without losing any claim to land or other advantages derived from this system. But no one, unless an actual settler as above defined, or unless absent on Government service, will be entitled to claim any right to land or property in any settlement by virtue of these orders.

V. In order to carry out this system of settlement a general officer will be detailed as inspector of settlements and plantations, whose duty it shall be to visit the settlements, to regulate their police and general management, and who will furnish personally to each head of a family, subject to the approval of the President of the United States, a possessory title in writing, giving as near as possible the description of boundaries, and who shall adjust all claims or conflicts that may arise under the same, subject to the like approval, treating such titles altogether as possessory. The same general officer will also be charged with the enlistment and organization of the negro recruits and protecting their interests while absent from their settlements, and will be governed by the rules and regulations prescribed by the War Department for such purpose.

VI. Brig. Gen. R. Saxton is hereby appointed inspector of settlements and plantations and will at once enter on the performance of his duties. No change is intended or desired in the settlement now on Beaufort Island, nor will any rights to property heretofore acquired be affected thereby.

By order of Maj. Gen. W. T. Sherman

Bibliography

Electronic Sources

Acts of the General Assembly of the State of Georgia, Passed in Milledgeville, at an Annual Session November and December 1861. Accessed July 2, 2021. https://archive.org/details/actsofgeneralass00georr.

Acts of the General Assembly of the State of Georgia: Passed in Milledgeville at an Annual Session in November and December, 1863; Also Extra Session of 1864. Documenting the American South. University Library, University of North Carolina at Chapel Hill. Accessed July 2, 2021. https://docsouth.unc.edu/imls/gagenas/georgia.html.

Acts of the General Assembly of the State of Georgia: Passed in Milledgeville, at an Annual Session in November, 1864; Also Extra Session of 1865, at Macon. Milledgeville: Boughton, Nisbet, Barnes & Moore, 1865. Accessed July 2, 2021. https://archive.org/details/actsofgeneralas00geor/page/46/mode/2up.

American Battlefield Trust. "Chickamauga." Accessed September 24, 2020. https://www.battlefields.org/learn/civil-war/battles/chickamauga.

———. "New Hope Church." Accessed August 15, 2020. https://www.battlefields.org/learn/civil-war/battles/new-hope-church.

"Eliza Bayard Clinch Anderson." Find a Grave. Accessed July 2, 2021.

"Approaches to Savannah." *Harper's Weekly* 6/277 (April 19, 1862): 247. Accessed June 1, 2021. https://archive.org/details/harpersweeklyv6bonn/page/247/mode/1up.

"William R. Boggs." The Generals of the American Civil War. Accessed July 2, 2020. http://www.generalsandbrevets.com/sgb/boggs.htm.

Brown, Joseph E. *Joseph E. Brown Papers.* 1859–1889. Digital Collections, David M. Rubenstein Rare Book & Manuscript Library, Duke University Libraries. Accessed July 26, 2021. https://idn.duke.edu/ark:/87924/r43j3d56r.

Bryan, William Jennings, ed. *The World's Famous Orations.* New York: Funk and Wagnalls, 1906; New York: Bartleby.com, 2003. Accessed July 3, 2021. https://www.bartleby.com/268/9/21.html#note268.35.

Civil War Philatelic Society. "Basic Rates." Accessed June 9, 2021. https://www.civilwarphilatelicsociety.org/?s=basic+rates.

Confederate Congress. "CHAP. LI.—An Act authorizing the suspension of the writ of habeas corpus" (October 13, 1862). In "The Statutes at Large of the Confederate States of America, Passed at the Second Session of the First Congress; 1862. Carefully Collated with the Originals at Richmond. Public Laws of the Confederate States of America, Passed at the Second Session of the First Congress; 1862. Private Laws of the Confederate States of America, Passed at the Second Session of the First Congress; 1862." Edited by James M. Matthews. Documenting the American South. Accessed July 2, 2021. https://docsouth.unc.edu/imls/csstat62/csstat62.html.

"Confederate States of America–Georgia Secession." The Avalon Project, Yale Law School. Accessed July 2, 2021.

https://avalon.law.yale.edu/19th_century/csa_geosec.asp.

———. "Provisional Congress of the Confederate States, First Session, February 4, 1861, to March 16, 1861." In volume 1 of *Journal of the Congress of the Confederate States of America, 1861–1865*. 7 vols. American Memory, Library of Congress. Accessed July 2, 2021. https://memory.loc.gov/ammem/amlaw/lwcc.html.

"The Constitution of the State of Georgia, 1861." Enrolled Acts and Resolutions, House and Senate, Legislature, RG 37-1-15, Georgia Archives. Accessed September 14, 2021. https://vault.georgiaarchives.org/digital/collection/adhoc/id/374/

Copeland, Susan. "Henry Rootes Jackson (1820–1898)." New Georgia Encyclopedia. Accessed June 9, 2021. https://www.georgiaencyclopedia.org/articles/government-politics/henry-rootes-jackson-1820-1898.

"Dates at Andersonville." Andersonville National Historic Site. National Park Service. April 14, 2015. Accessed June 1, 2021. https://www.nps.gov/ande/learn/historyculture/feb24.htm.

Elliott, Rev. Stephen. "Ezra's Dilemna [*sic*]: A Sermon Preached in Christ Church, Savannah, on Friday, August 21st, 1863, Being the Day of Humiliation, Fasting and Prayer, Appointed by the President of the Confederate States." Documenting the American South. University Library, University of North Carolina at Chapel Hill. Accessed July 3, 2021. https://docsouth.unc.edu/imls/elliottezra/elliott.html.

"February in Georgia History." 1850–1899. 1863. New Georgia Encyclopedia. Accessed July 2, 2021. https://www.georgiaencyclopedia.org/articles/history-archaeology/february-georgia-history#1850-1899.

"The First Confiscation Act." Freedmen and Southern Society Project, University of Maryland. Accessed July 2, 2021. http://www.freedmen.umd.edu/conact1.htm.

Fisher, Julia Johnson. *Diary, 1864*. Documenting the American South. University Library, University of North Carolina at Chapel Hill. Accessed July 2, 2021. https://docsouth.unc.edu/imls/fisherjulia/fisher.html.

Friedman, Morgan. Inflation Calculator. Accessed July 2, 2021. https://westegg.com/inflation/infl.cgi?money=350829&first=1863&final=2019.

Garrard, Kenner. "Sketch of the Roads &c near the Position of This Div. on the Left of the Army: North of Marietta, Georgia. 1864." Library of Congress Geography and Map Division. Accessed August 21, 2020. https://www.loc.gov/item/2006635272/.

GeorgiaInfo. "Georgia Seal." Accessed October 19, 2020. https://georgiainfo.galileo.usg.edu/images/uploads/gallery/GeorgiaSeal1799-1861.jpg. Site has been taken down.

"A Guide to the Samuel Hollingsworth Stout Papers, 1837 (1860–1865) 1902." Briscoe Center for American History, University of Texas at Austin. Accessed July 1, 2020. https://legacy.lib.utexas.edu/taro/utcah/00042/cah-00042.html.

Hill, Laverne W. "Georgia Constitution." New Georgia Encyclopedia. Accessed July 2, 2021. https://www.georgiaencyclopedia.org/articles/government-politics/georgia-constitution#The-Constitution-of-1865.

Huxford, Folks, comp. and ed. *History of Clinch County, Georgia*. Macon: J. W. Burke Company, 1916. Accessed July 2, 2021.

https://archive.org/details/historyofclinchc00huxf.

Johnston, Joseph E. "Some War Letters of General Joseph E. Johnston." *Journal of the Military Service Institution of the United States* 50 (1912): 318–28. Accessed July 2, 2021. https://hdl.handle.net/2027/uiug.30112071913427.

Journal of the Proceedings of the Convention of the People of Georgia: Held in Milledgeville in October and November, 1865: Together with the ordinances and resolutions adopted. Milledgeville: R. M. Orme & Son, printers for the Convention. October 26, 1865. Accessed July 2, 2021. https://babel.hathitrust.org/cgi/pt?id=mdp.35112104841426&view=1up&seq=38&q1=%22October%2026%22.

Journal of the Public and Secret Proceedings of the Convention of the People of Georgia, Held in Milledgeville and Savannah in 1861, Together with the Ordinances Adopted. Milledgeville: Boughton, Nisbet & Barnes, State Printers, 1863. Documenting the American South. University Library, University of North Carolina at Chapel Hill. Accessed July 6, 2021. https://docsouth.unc.edu/imls/georgia/georgia.html.

Journal of the Senate at an Extra Session of the General Assembly of the State of Georgia, Convened under the Proclamation of the Governor, March 25th, 1863. Milledgeville: Boughton, Nisbet & Barnes, State Printers, 1863. Documenting the American South. University Library, University of North Carolina at Chapel Hill. Accessed June 9, 2021. https://docsouth.unc.edu/imls/gaextr63/georgia.html.

Journal of the Senate of the Extra Session of the General Assembly, of the State of Georgia, Convened by Proclamation of the Governor, at Macon, February 15th, 1865. Milledgeville: Boughton, Nisbet, Barnes & Moore, State Printers, 1862. Documenting the American South. University Library, University of North Carolina at Chapel Hill. Accessed June 9, 2021. https://docsouth.unc.edu/imls/gaextr65/gaextr65.html.

Journal of the Senate of the State of Georgia, at the Annual Session of the General Assembly, Begun and Held in Milledgeville, the Seat of Government, in 1863. Milledgeville: Boughton, Nisbet, Barnes & Moore, State Printers, 1863. Documenting the American South. University Library, University of North Carolina at Chapel Hill. Accessed June 9, 2021. https://docsouth.unc.edu/imls/gasen63/gasen63.html.

Journal of the Senate of the State of Georgia, at the Annual Session of the General Assembly, Begun and Held in Milledgeville, the Seat of Government, in 1862. Milledgeville: Boughton, Nisbet, Barnes & Moore, State Printers, 1862. Documenting the American South. University Library, University of North Carolina at Chapel Hill. Accessed June 9, 2021. https://docsouth.unc.edu/imls/gasen62/gasen62.html.

King, William. *Diary of William King; Cobb County, Georgia, 1864.* Documenting the American South. University Library, University of North Carolina at Chapel Hill. Accessed August 31, 2020. https://docsouth.unc.edu/imls/kingwilliam/king.html.

Lee, Susanna Michele. "Twenty-Slave Law." Encyclopedia Virginia, Virginia Humanities. Accessed July 2, 2021. https://www.encyclopediavirginia.org/twenty-slave_law#start_entry.

"Letter—John Compton, 24 September 1863 [to his sister Margaret]." Pamplin Historical Park & the National Museum of the Civil War Soldier. Digital Archives.

Petersburg, VA. Accessed July 23, 2021. https://phparchives.wordpress.com/2020/09/14/letter-john-compton-24-september-1863/.

Lincoln, Abraham. *Abraham Lincoln Papers*: Series 1. General Correspondence. 1833 to 1916: Daniel E. Sickles to Abraham Lincoln. Telegram reporting progress of Sherman's campaign in Georgia. 1864. Manuscript/Mixed Material. Accessed September 14, 2021. https://www.loc.gov/item/mal3313100/.

———. "The Proclamation of Amnesty and Reconstruction." Freedmen and Southern Society Project, University of Maryland. Accessed July 2, 2021. http://www.freedmen.umd.edu/procamn.htm.

Matthew, Norman. "Confederate States Armory at Macon, Georgia." Macon Armory Pages. Accessed July 2, 2021. http://www.csarmory.org.

Mercer, George Anderson. *George Anderson Mercer Diary, 1851–1889*. Collection 00503. Southern Historical Collection, Wilson Library, University of North Carolina at Chapel Hill. Accessed July 2, 2021. https://findingaids.lib.unc.edu/00503/#folder_3a#1.

National Park Service. "Allatoona." The Civil War. Accessed July 2, 2021. https://www.nps.gov/civilwar/search-battles-detail.htm?battleCode=GA023.

———. "Confederate Georgia Troops: 46th Regiment, Georgia Infantry." The Civil War. Accessed July 2, 2021. https://www.nps.gov/civilwar/search-battle-units-detail.htm?battleUnitCode=CGA0046RI.

———. "Dallas." The Civil War. Accessed August 17, 2020. https://www.nps.gov/civilwar/search-battles-detail.htm?battleCode=GA011.

———. "Griswoldville." The Civil War. Accessed October 24, 2020. https://www.nps.gov/civilwar/search-battles-detail.htm?battleCode=GA025.

———. "Kennesaw Mountain." The Civil War. Accessed August 29, 2020. https://www.nps.gov/civilwar/search-battles-detail.htm?battleCode=GA015.

———. "Pickett's Mill." The Civil War. Accessed August 17, 2020. https://www.nps.gov/civilwar/search-battles-detail.htm?battleCode=GA012.

———. "Resaca." The Civil War. Accessed August 10, 2020. https://www.nps.gov/civilwar/search-battles-detail.htm?battleCode=GA008.

———. "Ringgold Gap." The Civil War. Accessed October 27, 2020. https://www.nps.gov/civilwar/search-battles-detail.htm?battleCode=GA005.

———. "Utoy Creek." The Civil War. Accessed September 10, 2020. https://www.nps.gov/civilwar/search-battles-detail.htm?battleCode=GA019.

Pierre. "Dahlonega, 'Gold Rush' US Mint Branch (1830–1861)." *Numismag*. May 31, 2017. Accessed July 2, 2021. https://numismag.com/en/2017/05/31/the-monetary-workshop-of-dahlonega-us-mint-1830-1861/.

Platter, Cornelius C. *Cornelius C. Platter Civil War Diary, 1864–1865*. Digital Library of Georgia. Accessed July 2, 2021. https://dlg.usg.edu/record/dlg_zlpd_ccp001#text.

Ruddy, Michael Palmer, ed. "The Letters of Henry Albert Potter, 4th Michigan Cavalry." Accessed September 12, 2020. http://freepages.rootsweb.com/%7Emruddy/genealogy/letters5.htm.

"The Second Confiscation Act." Freedmen and Southern Society Project, University of

Maryland. Accessed July 2, 2021. http://www.freedmen.umd.edu/conact2.htm.

Shaffer, Michael K. "History of Camp McDonald Park." Friends of Camp McDonald Park, 2018. Accessed July 2, 2021. http://www.campmcdonaldpark.org/history.html.

Smithsonian National Postal Museum. "The Confederate Postal System." Accessed October 27, 2020. https://postalmuseum.si.edu/exhibition/a-nation-divided/the-confederate-postal-system.

Statutes at Large of the Confederate States of America, Passed at the Third Session of the First Congress; 1863. Carefully Collated with the Originals at Richmond Public Laws of the Confederate States of America, Passed at the Third Session of the First Congress; 1863. Private Laws of the Confederate States of America, Passed at the Third Session of the First Congress; 1863" (May 1, 1863). Edited by James Muscoe Matthews. Documenting the American South. University Library, University of North Carolina at Chapel Hill. Accessed June 9, 2021. https://docsouth.unc.edu/imls/22conf/1863stat.html.

"Thomson, Mortimer (1832–1875)." The Vault at Pfaff's: An Archive of Art and Literature by the Bohemians of Antebellum New York. Lehigh University. Accessed July 2, 2021. https://pfaffs.web.lehigh.edu/node/54158.

Truman, W. L. "Memoirs of the Civil War." Accessed July 2, 2021. http://www.cedarcroft.com/cw/memoir/index.html.

Tucker, Henry H. "God in the War. A Sermon Delivered before the Legislature of Georgia, in the Capitol at Milledgeville, on Friday, November 15, 1861." Milledgeville: Boughton, Nisbet & Barnes, State Printers, 1861. Documenting the American South. University Library, University of North Carolina at Chapel Hill. Accessed June 9, 2021. https://docsouth.unc.edu/imls/tuckerh/tuckerh.html.

Winkler, Frederick C. *Letters of Frederick C. Winkler, 1862–1865*. N.p., 1963. Accessed July 3, 2021. https://catalog.hathitrust.org/Record/009628680.

Wooley, Edwin C. *Reconstruction of Georgia.* (*Studies in History, Economics and Public Law* 13/3 [1901]). New York: Columbia University Press, 1901. Accessed July 25, 2021. https://www.gutenberg.org/files/35559/35559-h/35559-h.htm#fna25_25.

Wyatt, Rick. *Georgia Flags Prior to 1879 (U.S.). Flags of the World*, 2013. Accessed July 3, 2021. https://www.crwflags.com/fotw/flags/us-ga1.html.

Primary Sources

Andrews, Eliza Frances. *The War-Time Journal of a Georgia Girl.* Atlanta: Cherokee Publishing Company, 1976.

Ashmore, Thomas P. *Grier's Almanac*. Delhi, India: Facsimile Publisher, 2019.

Basler, Roy P., ed. *The Collected Works of Abraham Lincoln.* 9 vols. New Brunswick, NJ: Rutgers University Press, 1953.

Baumgartner, Richard A., and Larry M. Strayer. *Yankee Tigers II: Civil War Correspondence from the Tiger Regiment of Ohio*. Huntington, WV: Blue Acorn Press, 2004.

Berry, Carrie. *A Confederate Girl: The Diary of Carrie Berry, 1864*. Edited by Kerry Graves. Mankato, MN: Blue Earth Books, 2000.

Bird, Edgeworth, and Sallie Bird. *The Granite Farm Letters: The Civil War Correspondence of Edgeworth & Sallie Bird*. Edited by John Rozier. Athens: University of Georgia Press, 1988.

Boyle, John Richards. *Soldiers True: The Story of the One Hundred Eleventh Regiment Pennsylvania Veteran Volunteers and of Its Campaigns in the War for the Union, 1861–1865*. Lavergne, TN: ICG Testing, 2020.

Brobst, John F. *Well Mary: Civil War Letters of a Wisconsin Volunteer*. Edited by Margaret Brobst Roth. Madison: University of Wisconsin Press, 1960.

Bull, Rice C. *Soldiering: The Civil War Diary of Rice C. Bull, 123rd New York Volunteer Infantry*. Edited by K. Jack Bauer. Novato, CA: Presidio Press, 1995.

Burge, Dolly Lunt. *The Diary of Dolly Lunt Burge 1848–1879*. Edited by Christine Jacobson Carter. Athens: University of Georgia Press, 2006.

Burney, Samuel A. *A Southern Soldier's Letters Home: The Civil War Letters of Samuel A. Burney, Cobb's Georgia Legion, Army of Northern Virginia*. Edited by Nat S. Turner III. Macon: Mercer University Press, 2002.

Candler, Allen Daniel. *The Confederate Records of the State of Georgia*. 1st ed. 6 vols. Atlanta: C. P. Byrd, State Printer, 1909.

Cannon, J. P. *Bloody Banners and Barefoot Boys: A History of the 27th Regiment Alabama Infantry CSA: The Civil War Memoirs and Diary Entries of J.P. Cannon, M.D*. Edited by Noel Crowson and John V. Brogden. Shippensburg, PA: Burd Street Press, 1997.

Cathey, M. Todd. *Captain A.T. Fielder's Civil War Diary, Company B 12th Tennessee Infantry*. Nashville: Tennessee Historical Society, 2012.

Cleveland, Henry, ed. *Alexander H. Stephens, in Public and Private: With Letters and Speeches, before, during, and since the War*. Philadelphia: National Publishing Company, 1866.

Collins, R. M. *Chapters from the Unwritten History of the War Between the States: Or, the Incidents in the Life of a Confederate Soldier in Camp, on the March, in the Great Battles, and in Prison*. London, England: Forgotten Books, 2015.

Connelly, T. W. *History of the Seventieth Ohio Regiment: From Its Organization to Its Mustering Out*. Delhi, India: Facsimile Publisher, 2017.

Connolly, James Austin. *Three Years in the Army of the Cumberland: The Letters and Diary of Major James A. Connolly*. Edited by Paul M. Angle. Civil War Centennial Series. Bloomington: Indiana University Press, 1987.

Conyngham, Capt. David P. *Sherman's March through the South*. 1865. Lexington, KY: Old South Books, 2014.

Cox, Jacob. *Atlanta*. Campaigns of the Civil War—IX. Leesburg, VA: Weider History Group, 2009.

Cumming, Kate. *Kate: The Journal of a Confederate Nurse*. Edited by Richard Barksdale Harwell. Baton Rouge: Louisiana State University Press, 1998.

Daniels, John. *Marching through Georgia: The Diary of John Daniels 13th Michigan Infantry, Co. C 3 Sept 1864 to 20 June 1865*. Privately Published, n.d.

Davis, Jefferson. *The Papers of Jefferson Davis*. 14 vols. Edited by Lynda Lasswell Crist, Mary Seaton Dix, Kenneth H. Williams, et al. Baton Rouge: Louisiana State University Press, 1991–2015.

Dixon, William Daniel. *The Blues in Gray: The Civil War Journal of William Daniel Dixon and the Republican Blues Daybook*. The Voices of the Civil War Series. Edited by Roger S. Durham. Knoxville: University of Tennessee Press, 2000.

Dougherty, Dave. *Making Georgia Howl! The 5th Ohio Volunteer Cavalry in Kilpatrick's Campaign and the Diary of Sgt. William H. Harding*. Point Pleasant, NJ: Winged Hussar Publishing, LLC, 2016.

Downing, Alexander G. *Downing's Civil War Diary*. 1916. Edited by Olynthus B. Clark. Memphis, TN: Old South Books, 2014.

Du Pont, Samuel Francis. *Samuel Francis Du Pont: A Selection from His Civil War Letters*. 3 vols. Edited by John D. Hayes. Ithaca, NY: Cornell University Press, 1969.

Ely, Marcus Bethune, and Martha Frances Ely. *A Just and Holy Cause? The Civil War Letters of Marcus Bethune and Martha Frances Ely, 1862–1865*. Edited by Linda S. McCardle. Macon: Mercer University Press, 2016.

Fielder, Herbert, ed. *A Sketch of the Life and Times and Speeches of Joseph E. Brown*. Lavergne, TN: ICG Testing, 2020.

Fletcher, Louisa Warren. *The Journal of a Landlady: The Fletcher/Kennesaw House Diary*. Edited by Henry Higgins and Connie Cox. Chapel Hill: Professional Press, 1995.

Flotow, Mark, ed. *In Their Letters, in Their Words: Illinois Civil War Soldiers Write Home*. Carbondale: Southern Illinois University Press, 2019.

Foster, Samuel T. *One of Cleburne's Command: The Civil War Reminiscences and Diary of Capt. Samuel T. Foster, Granbury's Texas Brigade, CSA*. Edited by Norman D. Brown. Austin: University of Texas Press, 1980.

French, Samuel Gibbs. *Two Wars: An Autobiography of Gen. Samuel G. French*. Huntington, WV: Blue Acorn Press, 1999.

Hewett, Janet, ed. *Supplement to the Official Records of the Union and Confederate Armies*. Wilmington, NC: Broadfoot Publishing, 1995.

Hitchcock, Henry. *Marching with Sherman*. Edited by M. A. De Wolfe Howe. Lincoln: University of Nebraska Press, 1995.

Holmes, James Taylor. *52d O. V. I. Then and Now*. Columbus, OH: Berlin Printing Company, 1898.

Jackman, John S. *Diary of a Confederate Soldier*. Edited by William C. Davis. Columbia: University of South Carolina Press, 1990.

Johnson, James. Image. Georgia Capitol Museum and the Richard B. Russell Library for Political Research and Studies. University of Georgia, Athens.

Jones, J. B. *A Rebel War Clerk's Diary: At the Confederate States Capital*. 2 vols. Modern War Studies. Edited by James I. Robertson. Lawrence: University Press of Kansas, 2015.

Joslyn, Mauriel Phillips, comp. and ed. *Charlotte's Boys: Civil War Letters of the Branch Family of Savannah*. Gretna, LA: Pelican Pub. Co., 2010.

Key, Thomas J., and Robert J. Campbell. *Two Soldiers: The Campaign Diaries of Thomas J. Key, and Robert J. Campbell*. Edited by Wirt Armistead Cate. Lavergne, TN: ICG Testing, 2016.

Lane, Mills, ed. *Dear Mother: Don't Grieve about Me. If I Get Killed, I'll Only Be Dead.*

Letters from Georgia Soldiers in the Civil War. Savannah: Library of Georgia, Beehive Foundation, 1990.

Lea, George S., and Ron Skellie. *May Angels Guard Thee: The Letters and Life of Private George S. Lea, Company C, 7th Regiment Mississippi Infantry, 1861–1864*. Birmingham, AL: Banner, 2012.

Lee, Robert E. *Lee's Dispatches: Unpublished Letters of General Robert E. Lee, C.S.A., to Jefferson Davis*. Edited by Douglas Southall Freeman. Baton Rouge: Louisiana State University Press, 1994.

———. *The Wartime Papers of Robert E. Lee*. Edited by Clifford Dowdey and Louis H. Manarin. New York: Da Capo Press, 1987.

Longstreet, James. *From Manassas to Appomattox: Memoirs of the Civil War in America*. New York: Barnes & Noble Books, 2004.

Loop, Myron B. *The Long Road Home: Ten Thousand Miles through the Confederacy with the 68th Ohio*. Edited by Richard A Baumgartner. Huntington, WV: Blue Acorn Press, 2006.

Mabrey, Benjamin Benn. *Yankee Soldier*. San Bernardino, CA: Crown Printers, 2012.

McAdams, Francis Marion. *Every-Day Soldier Life: Or a History of the One Hundred and Thirteenth Ohio Volunteer Infantry*. Lavergne, TN: ICG Testing, 2017.

McCurdy, Margaret Mahan, ed. *"Yours Truly Husband until Death…": Letters Home from War by Benjamin Franklin Chapman to His Wife, Sarah A. Busbin Chapman*. Kennesaw: United Daughters of the Confederacy, Georgia Division, Kennesaw Chapter 241, 2007.

Mottelay, Paul F., ed., and T. Campbell-Copeland, comp. *The Soldier in Our Civil War: A Pictorial History of the Conflict, 1861–1865, Illustrating the Valor of the Soldier as Displayed on the Battle-field. From sketches drawn by Forbes, Waud, Taylor, Beard, Becker, Lovie, Schell, Crane and … other eye-witnesses*. New York: Stanley Bradley Publishing Company, 1890.

Myers, Robert Manson, ed. *The Children of Pride*. New Haven, CT: Yale Univ. Press, 1973.

Nichols, George Ward. *The Story of the Great March*. New York: Harper and Brothers, 1865.

Nugent, William L., and Eleanor Smith Nugent. *My Dear Nellie: The Civil War Letters of William L. Nugent to Eleanor Smith Nugent*. Jackson: University Press of Mississippi, 1977.

Oake, William Royal. *On the Skirmish Line behind a Friendly Tree: The Civil War Memoirs of William Royal Oake, 26th Iowa Volunteers*. Edited by Stacy Dale Allen. Helena, MT: Farcountry Press, 2006.

Opdycke, Emerson. *To Battle for God and the Right: The Civil War Letterbooks of Emerson Opdycke*. Edited by Glenn Longacre and John E Haas. Urbana: University of Illinois Press, 2003.

Patrick, Robert. *Reluctant Rebel*. Edited by F. Jay Taylor. Baton Rouge: Louisiana State University Press, 1996.

Peddy, George W. *Saddle Bag and Spinning Wheel: Being the Civil War Letters of George*

W. Peddy, MD, Surgeon, 56th Georgia Volunteer Regiment, CSA. Edited by George Peddy Cuttino. Macon: Mercer University Press, 2008.

Public Laws of Georgia, Passed by the General Assembly, at Its Session Held in November and December, 1863. Edited by H. H. Waters. Lavergne, TN: ICG Testing, 2020.

Ransom, John L. *John Ransom's Andersonville Diary.* New York: Berkley Books, 1994.

Richards, Samuel P. *Sam Richards's Civil War Diary.* Edited by Wendy Hamand Venet. Athens: University of Georgia Press, 2009.

Richardson, James D., ed. *A Compilation of the Messages and Papers of the Confederacy.* Harrisburg, PA: Archive Society, 1996.

Shaw, Robert Gould, and Russell Duncan. *Blue-Eyed Child of Fortune: The Civil War Letters of Colonel Robert Gould Shaw.* Athens: University of Georgia Press, 1999.

Sherman, William T. *Home Letters of General Sherman.* Lexington, KY: Filiquarian Publishing, 2014.

———. *Marching through Georgia.* Edited by Mills Lane. New York: Arno Press, 1978.

———. *Memoirs of General W. T. Sherman.* New York: The Library of America, 1990.

———. *Sherman's Civil War: Selected Correspondence of William T. Sherman 1860–1865.* Edited by Brooks D. Simpson and Jean V. Berlin. Chapel Hill: University of North Carolina Press, 1999.

Stephenson, Philip Daingerfield. *The Civil War Memoir of Philip Daingerfield Stephenson, D.D: Private, Company K, 13th Arkansas Volunteer Infantry and Loader, Piece No. 4, 5th Company, Washington Artillery, Army of Tennessee, CSA.* Edited by Nathaniel Cheairs Hughes. Baton Rouge: Louisiana State University Press, 1998.

Taylor, Grant. *This Cruel War: The Civil War Letters of Grant and Malinda Taylor, 1862–1865.* Edited by Ann K. Blomquist and Robert A. Taylor. Macon: Mercer University Press, 2000.

Taylor, Paul, ed. *My Dear Nelly: The Selected Civil War Letters of General Orlando M. Poe to His Wife Eleanor.* Kent: Kent State University Press, 2020.

Taylor, Thomas Thomson. *Tom Taylor's Civil War.* Edited by Albert E. Castel. Lawrence: University Press of Kansas, 2000.

Thomas, Ella Gertrude Clanton. *The Secret Eye: The Journal of Ella Gertrude Clanton Thomas, 1848–1889.* Edited by Virginia Ingraham Burr. Chapel Hill: University of North Carolina Press, 1990.

Toalson, Jeff, ed. *No Soap, No Pay, Diarrhea, Dysentery & Desertion: A Composite Diary of the Last 16 Months of the Confederacy from 1864 to 1865 as Seen by the Soldiers, Farmers, Clerks, Nurses, Sailors, Farm Girls, Merchants, Nuns, Surgeons, Chaplains and Wives.* Lincoln, NE: iUniverse, 2006.

Toombs, Robert Augustus, Alexander Hamilton Stephens, and Howell Cobb. *The Correspondence of Robert Toombs, Alexander H. Stephens, and Howell Cobb.* Primary Source. Lavergne, TN: ICG Testing, 2015.

Tourgée, Albion W., and Peter C. Luebke. *The Story of a Thousand: Being a History of the Service of the 105th Ohio Volunteer Infantry in the War for the Union, from August 21, 1862, to June 6, 1865.* Civil War in the North. Kent: Kent State University Press, 2011.

U.S. Naval History Division. *Civil War Naval Chronology, 1861–1865.* 6 vols. Washington, DC: Navy Department, 1960–1966. Accessed July 23, 2021. https://catalog.hathitrust.org/Record/000408854.

United States Naval War Records Office, and United States Office of Naval Records and Library. *Official Records of the Union and Confederate Navies in the War of the Rebellion.* 30 vols. Washington, DC: US Government Printing Office, 1894–1922.

United States War Department. *The War of the Rebellion: A Compilation of the Official Records of the Union and Confederate Armies.* 70 vols. in 128. Washington, DC: US Government Printing Office, 1880–1901.

Upson, Theodore F. *With Sherman to the Sea: The Civil War Letters Diaries & Reminiscences of Theodore F. Upson.* Edited by Oscar Osburn Winther. Bloomington: Indiana University Press, 1958.

Vale, Joseph G. *Minty and the Cavalry: A History of Cavalry Campaigns in the Western Armies.* London, England: Forgotten Books, 2015.

Virginia State Convention. *Proceedings of the Virginia State Convention of 1861.* Richmond: Virginia State Library, 1965.

Walker, C. Irvine. *Great Things Are Expected of Us: The Letters of Colonel C. Irvine Walker, 10th South Carolina Infantry, C.S.A.* Edited by William Lee White and Charles Denny Runion. Knoxville: University of Tennessee Press, 2009.

Watkins, Samuel R. *Company Aytch or a Side Show of the Big Show: A Memoir of the Civil War.* Edited by Ruth Hill Fulton McAllister. Nashville: Turner, 2011.

Widney, Lyman S. *Campaigning with "Uncle Billy": The Civil War Memoirs of Sgt. Lyman S. Widney, 34th Illinois Volunteer Infantry.* Edited by Robert I. Girardi. Victoria, BC, Canada: Trafford, 2008.

Williams, Hiram Smith. *This War So Horrible: The Civil War Diary of Hiram Smith Williams.* Edited by Lewis N. Wynne and Robert A. Taylor. Tuscaloosa: University of Alabama Press, 1993.

Wills, Charles W. *Army Life of an Illinois Soldier.* Compiled by Mary E. Kellogg. Carbondale: Southern Illinois University Press, 1996.

Secondary Sources

Avery, I. W. *The History of the State of Georgia from 1850 to 1881.* New York: Brown & Derby, 1881.

Baumgartner, Richard A., and Larry M. Strayer. *Kennesaw Mountain, June 1864: Bitter Standoff at the Gibraltar of Georgia.* Huntington, WV: Blue Acorn Press, 2004.

Bonds, Russell S. *Stealing the General: The Great Locomotive Chase and the First Medal of Honor.* Yardley, PA: Westholme, 2007.

Bowman, Samuel M. *Sherman and His Campaigns: A Military Biography.* New York: Charles B. Richardson, 1865.

Bragg, William Harris. *Griswoldville.* Macon: Mercer University Press, 2009.

Bryan, Thomas Conn. *Confederate Georgia.* Athens: University of Georgia Press, 2009.

Calcutt, Rebecca Barbour. *Richmond's Wartime Hospitals.* Gretna, LA: Pelican, 2005.

Castel, Albert E. *Decision in the West: The Atlanta Campaign of 1864.* Lawrence:

University Press of Kansas, 1995.
Coleman, Kenneth, ed. *A History of Georgia*. Athens: University of Georgia Press, 1991.
Davis, Stephen. *Texas Brigadier to the Fall of Atlanta: John Bell Hood*. Macon: Mercer University Press, 2019.
Eicher, John H., and David J. Eicher. *Civil War High Commands*. Stanford: Stanford University Press, 2001.
Evans, David. *Sherman's Horsemen: Union Cavalry Operations in the Atlanta Campaign*. Bloomington: Indiana University Press, 1999.
Freehling, William W., and Craig M. Simpson, eds. *Secession Debated: Georgia's Showdown in 1860*. New York: Oxford University Press, 1992.
Garrett, Franklin M., and Harold H. Martin. *Atlanta and Environs: A Chronicle of Its People and Events*. 1954. Athens: University of Georgia Press, 2011.
Guss, John Walker. *Fort Pulaski*. Charleston, SC: Arcadia Publishing, 2015.
Hannings, Bud. *Every Day of the Civil War*. Jefferson, NC: McFarland, 2010.
Harper, F. Mikell, ed. *The Second Georgia Infantry Regiment, 1861–1865*. Macon: Indigo Custom Pub., 2005.
Hoehling, A. A. *Last Train from Atlanta*. Mechanicsburg, PA: Stackpole Books, 2017.
Inscoe, John C., ed. *The Civil War in Georgia: A New Georgia Encyclopedia Companion*. Athens: University of Georgia Press, 2011.
Irvine, Dallas. *Military Operations of the Civil War: A Guide-Index to the Official Records of the Union and Confederate Armies, 1861–1865*. 5 vols. Washington, DC: National Archives and Records Service, 1980. Accessed July 2, 2021. https://babel.hathitrust.org/cgi/pt?id=mdp.39015019763930&view=1up&seq=3.
King, Spencer B., Jr. *Darien: The Death and Rebirth of a Southern Town*. Macon: Mercer University Press, 1981.
Krakow, Kenneth K. *Georgia Place-Names: Their History and Origins*. Macon: Winship Press, 1994.
Luvaas, Jay, and Harold W. Nelson, eds. *Guide to the Atlanta Campaign: Rocky Face Ridge to Kennesaw Mountain*. Lawrence: University Press of Kansas, 2008.
McMurry, Richard M. *The Road Past Kennesaw: The Atlanta Campaign of 1864*. Honolulu: University Press of the Pacific, 2005.
Mosocco, Ronald A. *The Chronological Tracking of the American Civil War*. Williamsburg, VA: James River Publications, 1995.
Owens, Richard A. *An Index to the Illustrations of Harpers Weekly During the Civil War Years 1861–1865*. Fairfax, VA: Richard A. Owens, 2000.
Phillips, Ulrich Bonnell. *The Life of Robert Toombs*. New York: Macmillan, 1913.
Powell, David A. *The Chickamauga Campaign—A Mad Irregular Battle: From the Crossing of the Tennessee River through the Second Day. August 22–September 19, 1863*. El Dorado Hills, CA: Savas Beatie, 2016.
Ray, Janisse. *Drifting into Darien: A Personal and Natural History of the Altamaha River*. Athens: University of Georgia Press, 2011.
Reed, Wallace P., ed. *History of Atlanta, Georgia: With Illustrations and Biographical Sketches of Some of Its Prominent Men and Pioneers*. Syracuse, NY: D. Mason & Co.,

1889.

Sholes, A. E., comp. *Chronological History of Savannah*. Savannah: Kennickell Printing Co., 1975.

Sibley, F. Ray, Jr., ed. *Confederate Artillery Organizations: An Alphabetical Listing of the Officers and Batteries of the Confederacy, 1861–1865*. El Dorado Hills, CA: Savas Publishing, 2014.

Sifakis, Stewart. *Compendium of the Confederate Armies: South Carolina and Georgia*. Westminster, MD: Willow Bend Books, 2007.

Smedlund, William S. *Camp Fires of Georgia's Troops, 1861–1865*. Lithonia: Kennesaw Mountain Press, 1994.

Strayer, Larry M., and Richard A. Baumgartner. *Echoes of Battle*. Huntington, WV: Blue Acorn Press, 2004.

Warner, Ezra J. *Generals in Gray*. Baton Rouge: Louisiana State University Press, 1997.

Wills, Brian Steel. *George Henry Thomas: As True as Steel*. Lawrence: University Press of Kansas, 2012.

Journals

Bass, James Horace. "The Georgia Gubernatorial Elections of 1861 and 1863." *Georgia Historical Quarterly* 17/3 (September 1933): 167–88. Accessed July 3, 2021. www.jstor.org/stable/40576265.

Black, Robert C. "The Railroads of Georgia in the Confederate War Effort." *Journal of Southern History* 13/4 (November 1947): 511–34. Accessed July 3, 2021. https://doi.org/10.2307/2198325.

Davis, Robert S. "White and Black in Blue: The Recruitment of Federal Units on Civil War North Georgia." *Georgia Historical Quarterly* 85/3 (Fall 2001): 347–74. Accessed July 3, 2021. https://www.jstor.org/stable/40584443.

———, and Bill Kinsland. "Forgotten Union Guerrillas of the North Georgia Mountains." *North Georgia Journal* 5/2 (1988): 30–40.

Harrison, Lowell H. "The Diary of an 'Average' Confederate Soldier." *Tennessee Historical Quarterly* 29/3 (Fall 1970): 256–71. Accessed July 2, 2021. http://www.jstor.com/stable/42623731.

McInvale, Morton R. "'All That Devils Could Wish For:' The Griswoldville Campaign, November 1864." *Georgia Historical Quarterly* 60/2 (1976): 117–30. Accessed July 2, 2021. http://www.jstor.org/stable/40580270.

Neblett, Thomas R. "Major Edward C. Anderson and the C.S.S. *Fingal*." *Georgia Historical Quarterly* 52/2 (1968): 132–58. Accessed July 2, 2021. https://www.jstor.org/stable/40578823.

Shadgett, Olive Hall. "James Johnson, Provisional Governor of Georgia." *Georgia Historical Quarterly* 36/1 (1952): 1–21. Accessed July 2, 2021. http://www.jstor.org/stable/40577322.

Magazines

Holman, Tyler. "A Most Criminal and Remarkable Incident." *Georgia Backroads* 19/3 (Autumn 2020): 49.

Jordan, Michael L. "Recovery of CSS *Georgia*." *Civil War Navy* 8/1 (Summer 2020).

Shoup, Francis A. "Dalton Campaign—Works at Chattahoochee River—Interesting History." In *Confederate Veteran* 3 (September 1895): 262–65. Wilmington, NC: Broadfoot Publishing, 1988.

Index

About the Author

Michael K. Shaffer is Civil War historian, instructor, lecturer, newspaper columnist, and author. He is a member of the Society of Civil War Historians, Historians of the Civil War Western Theater, and the Georgia Association of Historians. Shaffer teaches Civil War Courses at Kennesaw State University's College of Graduate and Professional Education and at Emory University, and frequently speaks to various groups across the country.